PROMINENT SCIENTISTS

PROMINENT
SCIENTISTS
PROMINENT
SCIENTISTS

PROMINENT SCIENTISTS

AN INDEX TO COLLECTIVE BIOGRAPHIES

SECOND EDITION

Edited by PAUL A. PELLETIER

NEAL-SCHUMAN PUBLISHERS, INC.

Published by Neal-Schuman Publishers, Inc.
23 Cornelia St.
New York, NY 10014

Printed and bound in the United States of America.

Library of Congress Cataloging in Publication Data

Pelletier, Paul A., 1944–
    Prominent scientists.

    Includes index.
        1. Scientists—Biography—Indexes. I. Title.
Q141.P398   1985   509'.2'2 [B]   85-3079
ISBN 0-918212-78-2

Dedicated
in loving memory
to my wife

MARILYN

May 1950–December 1983

and for our daughters

ANN-MARIE and JENNIFER

Contents

Introduction

This is an index to the biographies of scientists which appear in books. The books that were chosen are collected biographies of scientists; collected biographies that included scientists; science histories; or works that included biographical sketches. The primary emphasis is on books published from 1960 through 1983, since *Index to Scientists*, by Norma Ireland (Westwood, Mass.: Faxon, 1962) covers the period from the 1930s to 1960. With the exception of *Pioneers of Canadian Science*, which has some biographies in English and some in French, only English-language works are represented. No individual biography is included.

There are 12,211 scientists listed in this edition, and they represent the contents of 262 works, containing 31,551 biographies. "Scientist" is broadly defined as those people in what is sometimes referred to as natural science (biology, chemistry, geology, physics, zoology, etc.) and includes those engaged in technology. Fields generally referred to as social sciences (economics, sociology, etc.) are not included, though individuals who are known for their work in social science sometimes appear because of their work in other areas that may be classified as natural science or technology. For example, only biographies that include the scientific works of Benjamin Franklin are included.

Works of collected biography, such as *Current Biography*, have been indexed only for biographees who are scientists. Similarly, in the indexing of *Biographical Memoirs of the Fellows of the Royal Society*, such nonscientist members of the Society as prime ministers or members of Parliament were omitted.

Works of a "Who's Who" nature, for example, *American Men and Women of Science*, were not indexed because of the abbreviated entries they contain and because entries change with each edition. They are also the obvious place to look for brief information on a living scientist.

How to Use This Book

There are two main sections to this book. The first is an alphabetical listing of scientists by their surnames. The second is a listing by the fields with which the scientists are connected.

The first section, Index to Scientists by Surname, is the actual index to the biographies of scientists in collected works. The scientists are listed alphabetically by their surnames, which appear in capital letters. Each name is followed by birth and death dates; the field(s) with which the scientist is associated; and symbols for the collected works in which his or her biography appears. A typical entry follows:

BORLAUG, Norman E. (1914–   ) Bot.; Genet.
     CB71   WAMB

Lower-case prefixes to names are disregarded in alphabetizing; that is, ibn al-Baytar is filed as if spelled Baytar. The same practice applies to names beginning with d', von, etc. Whenever a name *is* filed by D' or Von, etc., a cross-reference is entered under the alternate location for the name (e.g., ALLEN, James van SEE VAN ALLEN, James).

Some standardization of spelling for several names had to be established. The first choice for a main entry was the spelling used most often in the sources indexed. Cross-references are again used to refer from the various forms to the main entry. No attempt was made to Anglicize spellings, the more natural spelling being preferred for main entries (e.g., MENDELEEF rather than MENDELEYEV).

The citations to the biographies most often take the form of a four-letter symbol based on the title of the work represented (e.g., MNCS, *Mid-Nineteenth Century Scientists*). In some cases the last letter of the symbol stands for the author's name, (e.g., FOIF, *Fathers of Industries*, by Leonard Fanning). For multivolume works, one or more letters are replaced by a number that represents the volume or supplement number of the book in which the individual's biography appears (e.g., DAB1, the first supplement to *Dictionary of American Biography*). This method is intended to make the entries mnemonic while still being brief.

The second section, List of Scientists by Field, is intended to help the user locate people in particular areas of science. The fields are in alphabetical order, as are the scientists listed under them. This section should not be used as an index to all scientists in the Index to Scientists by Surname, since the versions of names that appear in approximately three hundred cross-references there are not included in the list by fields.

A Key to Books Indexed, a Key to Fields Listed and Their Abbreviations, and a Key to Other Abbreviations follows this section.

Key to Books Indexed

ABES   Asimov's Biographical Encyclopedia of Science and
               Technology
            Isaac Asimov
            New York: Doubleday, 1972 (rev. ed.)

ABET   Asimov's Biographical Encyclopedia of Science and
               Technology
            Isaac Asimov
            New York: Doubleday, 1982 (2nd rev. ed.)

ABFC   The American Biologist Through Four Centuries
            Arthur W. Hughes
            Springfield, Ill.: Charles C. Thomas, 1982

ACCE   American Chemists and Chemical Engineers
            Wyndham D. Miles
            Washington, D.C.: American Chemical Society, 1976

AMEM   American Entomologists
            Arnold Mallis
            New Brunswick, N.J.: Rutgers University, 1971

AMIH   American Inventors
            C.J. Hylander
            New York: Macmillan, 1934

AMJB   American Jewish Biographies
            New York: Facts on File, 1982

AMST   Ancient and Medieval Science
            Rene Taton
            New York: Basic, 1963

ANHD   The Art of Natural History
            S. Peter Dance
            New York: Overlook, 1978

AO80   The Annual Obituary 1980
            Roland Turner
            New York: St. Martin's, 1981

AO81   The Annual Obituary 1981
            New York: St. Martin's, 1982

AROW   Astronomers at the Royal Observatory, Cape of Good
               Hope
            Brian Warner
            Cape Town, South Africa: University of Cape Town,
               1979

ASIW   American Science and Invention
            Mitchell Wilson
            New York: Simon & Schuster, 1954

ASJD   American Science in the Age of Jackson
            George H. Daniels
            New York: Columbia University, 1968

ASTR   The Astronomers
            Colin Ronan
            New York: Hill and Wang, 1964

BBRS   Broca's Brain
            Carl Sagan
            New York: Random House, 1979

BCST   Black Contributors to Science and Energy Technology
            Washington, D.C.: U.S. Department of Energy, 1979

BDOS   A Biographical Dictionary of Scientists
            New York: Wiley, 1974 (2nd ed.)

BEOS   Biographical Encyclopedia of Scientists
            New York: Facts on File, 1981   2 vols.

BHMT   Biographical History of Medicine
            John H. Talbot
            New York: Grune & Stratton, 1970

BIOD   Biographical Dictionary of American Science
            Clark A. Elliott
            Westport, Conn.: Greenwood, 1979

BISC   Blacks in Science
            Hattie Carwell
            Hicksville, N.Y.: Exposition, 1977

BM–1   Biographical Memoirs
thru   Washington, D.C.: National Academy of Sciences,
BM53   1877–1982

BMST   Beginnings of Modern Science
            Rene Taton
            New York: Basic, 1964

BNBR   Biographies of Nevada Botanists, 1844–1958
            Olga Reifschneider
            Reno, Nev.: University of Nevada, 1964

BPSH   Black Pioneers of Science & Invention
            Louis Haber
            New York: Harcourt, Brace & World, 1970

BSIL   Benjamin Silliman and His Circle
Leonard G. Wilson
New York: Neale Watson, 1979

BWCL   The Birdwatcher's Companion: An Encyclopedic
            Handbook of North American Birdlife
Christopher Leahy
New York: Hill and Wang, 1982

CAVL   The Cavendish Laboratory, 1874–1974
New York: Science History Publications, 1974

CB40
thru   Current Biography
CB83   New York: H.W. Wilson, 1940–1983

CCSW   Catholic Churchmen in Science
James J. Walsh
Freeport, N.Y.: Books for Libraries, 1966

CDZZ   Concise Dictionary of Scientific Biography
American Council of Learned Societies
New York: Scribner, 1981

CHUB   Challengers of the Unknown
Fred Brewer
New York: Four Winds, 1965

COAC   Cavalcade of America
Carl Carner
New York: Crown, 1956

COBC   Contemporary British Chemists
W.A. Campbell
London: Taylor & Francis, 1971

CONS   The Conservationists
Douglas H. Strong
Reading, Mass.: Addison-Wesley, 1971

CSCJ   Crucibles: The Story of Chemistry
Bernard Jaffe
New York: Dover, 1976

CWSE   Contributions of Women: Science
Diane Emberlin
Minneapolis: Dillon Press, 1977

CWSN   Contemporary Women Scientists of America
Iris Noble
New York: Messner, 1979

DAB   Dictionary of American Biography
American Council of Learned Societies
New York: Scribner, 1928–1936

DAB1   Dictionary of American Biography Supplements
thru   American Council of Learned Societies
DAB5   New York: Scribner, 1944–1977

DANB   Dictionary of American Negro Biography
           New York: Norton, 1982

DARR   The Darwinian Revolution
           Michael Ruse
           Chicago: University of Chicago, 1979

DCPW   Descriptive College Physics
           Harvey E. White
           New York: Van Nostrand Reinhold, 1971

DGMT   Discovery: Great Moments in the Lives of Outstanding
               Naturalists
           John K. Terres
           New York: Lippincott, 1961

DMXE   Darwin and the Mysterious Mr. X
           Loren Eiseley
           New York: Dutton, 1979

DNB   The Dictionary of National Biography
           London: Oxford University Press, 1959–1960.   21 vols

DNB1   The Dictionary of National Biography Supplements
thru   London: Oxford University Press, 1901–
DNB7

DNFH   Doctors on the New Frontier
           William Hoffman
           New York: Macmillan, 1981

DODR   A Dozen Doctors: Autobiographical Sketches
           Chicago: University of Chicago, 1963

DSLP   Doctors Who Saved Lives
           Lynn and Gray Poole
           New York: Dodd, Mead, 1966

EAFC   Encyclopedia of American Forest and Conservation
               History
           New York: Macmillan, 1983   2 vols

EBAH   Eight Black American Inventors
           Robert C. Hayden
           Boston: Addison-Wesley, 1972

EDCJ   The Eighth Day of Creation: Makers of the Revolution in
               Biology
           Horace F. Judson
           New York: Simon & Schuster, 1979

EETD   Electrical and Electronic Technologies: A Chronology of
                   Events and Inventors to 1900
             Henry B. Davis
             Metuchen, N.J.: Scarecrow, 1981

EGSF   Einstein and the Generations of Science
             Lewis S. Feuer
             New York: Basic, 1974

ELEC   Electrochemistry: History and Theory
             William Ostwald
             Washington, D.C.: Smithsonian Institution, 1980

ENCE   Early Nineteenth Century European Scientists
             New York: Pergamon, 1967

EOMH   Explorers of Man
             H.R. Hays
             New York: Crowell, 1971

EPHG   Essays & Papers in the History of Modern Science
             Henry Guerlac
             Baltimore: Johns Hopkins, 1977

EQSA   Eternal Quest: Story of Great Naturalists
             Alexander Adams
             New York: Putnam, 1969

ESCS   Early Seventeenth Century Scientists
             New York: Pergamon, 1965

ESEH   Electricity in the 17th & 18th Centuries
             J.L. Heilbron
             Berkeley, Calif.: University of California, 1979

EXDC   Explorers of the Deep
             Donald W. Cox
             Maplewood, N.J.: Hammond, 1968

EXSB   Experiencing Science
             Jeremy Bernstein
             New York: Basic, 1978

EXSG   Explorers of the Sea: Famous Oceanographic
                   Expeditions
             New York: Ronald Press, 1964

FASP   Famous Astronomers
             James S. Pickering
             New York: Dodd, Mead, 1968

FBMV   Famous Biologists
             A.L. Mann and A.C. Vivian
             London: Museum Press, 1963

FBSC   Founders of British Science
            J.C. Crowther
            London: Cresset, 1960

FFIB   The Fungus Fighters
            Richard S. Baldwin
            Ithaca, N.Y.: Cornell University, 1981

FHUA   The Fossil Hunters
            Henry N. Andrews
            Ithaca, N.Y.: Cornell University, 1980

FIFE   First in the Field
            Robert Elam
            New York: Mason/Charter, 1977

FMAS   Famous Mathematicians
            Frances B. Stonaker
            New York: Lippincott, 1966

FMBB   Famous Men of Modern Biology
            Melvin Berger
            New York: Crowell, 1968

FNEC   Famous Names in Engineering
            James Carvill
            Woburn, Mass.: Butterworths, 1981

FOIF   Fathers of Industries
            Leonard Fanning
            New York: Lippincott, 1962

FPHM   Famous Physicists
            Alfred L. Mann
            New York: Day, 1963

FPSN   Famous Pioneers in Space
            Clarke Newlon
            New York: Dodd, Mead, 1963

GANC   Great American Naturalists
            Ruth A. Coates
            Minneapolis: Lerner Publishing, 1974

GASJ   The Golden Age of Science
            Bessie Z. Jones
            New York: Simon & Schuster, 1966

GASW   Great Adventures in Science
            Helen Wright and Samuel Rapport
            New York: Harper, 1956

GBAR   Great Black Americans
            Ben Richardson
            New York: Crowell, 1976

GDSP   Great Discoveries in Modern Science
        Patrick Pringle
        London: Harrap, 1955.

GENT   Gentlemen of Science
        Jack Morrell and Arnold Thackery
        London: Clarendon Press, 1981

GEXB   Great Experimenters
        William Bixby
        New York: McKay, 1964

GISA   Great Ideas of Science
        Isaac Asimov
        Boston: Houghton Mifflin, 1969

GJPS   German-Jewish Pioneers in Science 1900–1933
        David Nachmansohn
        New York: Springer-Verlag, 1979

GKGP   Grove Karl Gilbert
        Stephen J. Pyne
        Austin, Tex.: University of Texas, 1980

GMOP   Great Men of Physics
        Los Angeles: Tinnon-Brown, 1969

GNPA   Great Negroes Past and Present
        Russell Adams
        Chicago: Afro-Am Publishing, 1969

GOED   Giants of Electricity
        Percy Dunsheath
        New York: Crowell, 1967

GOTH   Guardians of Tomorrow
        S. Carl Hirsch
        New York: Viking, 1971

GRBW   Great Biologists
        John H. Williams
        New York: Bell, 1961

GRCH   Great Chemists
        New York: Interscience, 1961

GRTH   The Greatest Thinkers
        Edward de Bono
        New York: Putnam, 1976

GSAL   Greek Science After Aristotle
        G.E.R. Lloyd
        New York: Norton, 1973

HAOA   The History of American Ornithology Before Audubon
            Elsa G. Allen
            New York: Russell & Russell, 1969

HCEF   History of Chemical Engineering
            William Furter
            Washington, D.C.: American Chemical Society, 1980

HCOK   The Hidden Contributors
            Aaron E. Klein
            New York: Doubleday, 1971

HEXS   The Heart Explorers
            Tony Simon
            New York: Basic, 1966

HFGA   The Hall of Fame of Great Americans at New York
                University
            New York: New York University, 1967

HIUE   Healers in Uniform
            Edward Edelson
            New York: Doubleday, 1971

HLSM   History of the Life Sciences
            Lois Magner
            New York: Dekker, 1979

HNHB   The Heyday of Natural History, 1820–1870
            Lynn Barber
            Garden City, N.Y.: Doubleday, 1980

HOCS   Heroes of Conservation
            C.B. Squire
            New York: Fleet, 1974

HOPL   History of Programming Languages
            Richard L. Wexelblat
            New York: Academic Press, 1981

HOSS   Heroes of Science
            Walter Shepherd
            New York: Fleet, 1970

HRST   History of Rocketry & Space Travel
            Wernher von Braun & Frederick Ordway III
            New York: Crowell, 1969

HSSO   The Human Side of Scientists
            Ralph E. Oesper
            Cincinnati: University of Cincinnati, 1975

LLWO   The Ladu Laureates: Women Who Have Won the
                Nobel Prize
            Olga S. Opfell
            Metuchen, N.J.: Scarecrow Press, 1978

LSCS   Late Seventeenth Century Scientists
            New York: Pergamon, 1969

LSHS   The Land of Stevin and Huygens
            Dirk J. Struik
            Dordrecht, Holland: Reidel, 1981

MABH   Makers of North American Botany
            Harry B. Humphrey
            New York: Ronald Press, 1961

MADC   Men and Dinosaurs
            Edwin H. Colbert
            New York: Dutton, 1968

MAKS   Makers of Science: Mathematics, Physics, Astronomy
            Ivor B. Hart
            Freeport, N.Y.: Books for Libraries, 1968

MAMR   Microbes and Men
            Robert Reid
            New York: Saturday Review Press, 1975

MASW   Mathematics: The Alphabet of Science
            Margaret Willerding and Ruth Hayward
            New York: Wiley, 1972

MASY   Modern Americans in Science and Technology
            Edna Yost
            New York: Dodd, Mead, 1941

MATT   Mathematics Today
            New York: Springer-Verlag, 1978

MCCW   Men Who Created Cold
            Willis R. Woolrich
            New York: Exposition, 1967

MELW   Mathematics: An Everyday Language
            Ruric and Ed Wheeler
            New York: Wiley, 1979

MEQP   Math Equals
            Teri Perl
            Reading, Mass.: Addison-Wesley, 1978

MFIR   The Miracle Finders
            Donald Robinson
            New York: McKay, 1976

MGAH   Man's Great Achievements
            Edgar A. Haine
            New York: Vantage, 1976

MHM1   McGraw-Hill Modern Men of Science, Vol 1
            New York: McGraw-Hill, 1966

MHM2   McGraw-Hill Modern Men of Science, Vol 2
            New York: McGraw-Hill, 1968

MHSE   McGraw-Hill Modern Scientists & Engineers
            New York: McGraw-Hill, 1980   3 vols

MISU   Mathematics: An Introduction to Its Spirit and Use
            Scientific American
            San Francisco: W.H. Freeman, 1979

MMMA   Magic, Myth and Medicine
            Donald T. Atkinson
            New York: World, 1956

MMSB   Master Minds of Modern Science
            T.C. Bridges
            Freeport, N.Y.: Books for Libraries, 1969

MNCS   Mid-Nineteenth Century Scientists
            New York: Pergamon, 1969

MOS1   Men of Space. Vols 1–8
thru   Shirley Thomas
MOS8   New York: Chilton, 1960–1968

MPIP   Men Who Pioneered Inventions
            Lynn and Gray Poole
            New York: Dodd, Mead, 1969

MSAJ   Men of Science in America
            Bernard Jaffe
            New York: Simon & Schuster, 1958

MSCH   The Mind of the Scientist
            Michael Hoskin
            London: BBC, 1971

MSFB   Mad Scientists in Fact and Fiction
            Melvin Berger
            New York: Franklin Watts, 1980

MWBR   Men and Women Behind the Atom
            Sarah R. Riedman
            New York: Abelard-Schuman, 1958

NATJ   The Naturalists
            Alan C. Jenkins
            New York: Mayflower, 1978

NAW   Notable American Women 1607–1950:
                  A Biographical Dictionary
            Cambridge, Mass.: Belknap Press, 1971   3 vols

NAWM   Notable American Women, The Modern Period
            Cambridge, Mass.: Belknap Press, 1980

NBPS   The Nuclear Barons
            Peter Pringle and James Spigelman
            New York: Holt, Rinehart & Winston, 1981

NC-1   National Cyclopedia of American Biography.
thru   Vols 1–61
NC61   New York: James T. White, 1891–1982

NCSA   National Cyclopedia of American Biography.
thru   Supplements A through M
NCSM   New York: James T. White, 1924–1978

NEXB   Naturalist-Explorers
            Wyatt Blassingame
            New York: Watts, 1964

NHAH   Natural History in America
            Wayne Hanley
            New York: Quadrangle, 1977

NPWC   Nobel Prize Winners in Chemistry
            Eduard Farber
            New York: Henry Schuman, 1953

NTBM   New Trail Blazers of Technology
            Harland Manchester
            New York: Scribner, 1976

OGIV   100 Great Indians Through the Ages
            H.N. Verma
            New Delhi: Great Indian Publishers, 1975

OGML   100 Great Modern Lives
            New York: Hawthorne, 1965

OMNM   Of Men and Numbers
            Jane Muir
            New York: Dodd, Mead, 1961

ORNS   Ornithology from Aristotle to the Present
            Erwin Stresemann
            Cambridge, Mass.: Harvard University, 1975

PALF   Pioneers of Alcohol Fuels
            Neil Burns et al.
            Washington, D.C.: Citizen's Energy Project, 1981

PAMB   Pursuit of the Ancient Maya
        Robert L. Brunhouse
        Albuquerque: University of New Mexico, 1975

PAW1   The People's Almanac
        David Wallechinsky and Irving Wallace
        New York: Doubleday, 1975

PAW2   The People's Almanac #2
        David Wallechinsky and Irving Wallace
        New York: Bantam, 1978

PAW3   The People's Almanac #3
        David Wallechinsky and Irving Wallace
        New York: Bantam, 1981

PBTS   Picture Book of Todays Scientists
        Walter Gourlay
        New York: Sterling, 1962

PCWA   Pioneer Conservationists of Western America
        Peter Wild
        Missoula, Mont.: Mountain Press, 1979

PFEL   Physics for Everyone
        Lev D. Landau
        Moscow, U.S.S.R.: Mir Publishers, 1978

PGFS   Pioneer Germ Fighters
        Navin Sullivan
        New York: Atheneum, 1962

PGRM   Polish Greats
        Arnold Madison
        New York: McKay, 1980

PHLS   Encyclopedia of Pre-Historic Life
        Rodney Steel and Anthony Harvey
        New York: McGraw-Hill, 1979

PHYS   The Physicists
        C.P. Snow
        Boston: Little, Brown, 1981

PMAS   Project Mercury Astronauts
        Washington, D.C.: National Aeronautics and Space
            Administration, 1961

POAA   Pioneers of American Anthropology
        Seattle: University of Washington, 1966

POCS   Pioneers of Canadian Science
        Royal Society of Canada
        Toronto: University of Toronto, 1966

POEC   Philosophers of the Earth
            Anne Chisholm
            New York: Dutton, 1972

POPF   Pioneers of Psychology
            Raymond E. Fancher
            New York: Norton, 1979

PORS   Pioneers of Rocketry
            Michael Stoiko
            New York: Hawthorn Books, 1974

POSW   Pioneers of Science: Nobel Prize Winners in Physics
            Robert L. Weber
            London: Institute of Physics, 1980

PPEY   Political Profiles: The Eisenhower Years
            New York: Facts on File, 1977

PPJY   Political Profiles: The Johnson Years
            New York: Facts on File, 1976

PPKY   Political Profiles: The Kennedy Years
            New York: Facts on File, 1976

PPNF   Political Profiles: The Nixon/Ford Years
            New York: Facts on File, 1979

PPTY   Political Profiles: The Truman Years
            New York: Facts on File, 1978

PUNT   Pioneers of the Unseen
            Paul Tabori
            New York: Taplinger, 1972

QPAS   Quantum Physics in America, 1920–1935
            Katherine R. Sopka
            New York: Arno Press, 1980

ROPW   Rocket Pioneers
            Beryl Williams and Samuel Epstein
            New York: Messner, 1958

RPTC   Rutherford and Physics at the Turn of the Century
            New York: Dawson, 1979

RS-1   Biographical Memoirs of the Fellows of the Royal
thru   Society   Vols 1–28
RS28   London: Royal Society, 1955–1982

RTJG   The Road to Jaramillo: Critical Years of the
                 Revolution in Earth Science
            William Glen
            Stanford, Calif.: Stanford University Press, 1982

SGNF   Six Great Naturalists
        Richard S. Fitter
        London: Hamish Hamilton, 1959

SGSC   Six Great Scientists
        James G. Crowther
        London: Hamish Hamilton, 1955

SIRC   Scientists of the Industrial Revolution
        J.G. Crowther
        London: Cresset, 1962

SIWG   Scientists in Whitehall
        Philip Gummett
        Manchester, England: Manchester University, 1980

SLOR   The Star Lovers
        Robert Richardson
        New York: Macmillan, 1967

SMIL   Science Milestones
        Chicago: Windsor, 1954

SMST   Soviet Men of Science
        John Turkevich
        New York: Van Nostrand, 1963

SNAR   Science in Nineteenth Century America
        Nathan Reingold
        New York: Hill and Wang, 1964

SNCB   Some Nineteenth Century British Scientists
        New York: Pergamon, 1969

SOAC   The Society of Arcueil: A View of French Science at
              the Time of Napoleon I
        Maurice Crosland
        Cambridge, Mass.: Harvard University, 1967

SOEK   A Species of Eternity
        Joseph Kastner
        New York: Knopf, 1977

SOSC   Statesmen of Science
        J.G. Crowther
        London: Cresset, 1965

SOTT   Science of the Times, 1
        New York: Times, 1978

SOT2   Science of the Times, 2
        New York: Arno Press, 1979

SOT3   Science of the Times, 3
        New York: Arno Press, 1980

TGNH   They Gave Their Names to Science
            D.S. Halacy
            New York: Putnam, 1967

THOG   Toward a History of Geology
            Cambridge, Mass.: MIT Press, 1969

TINA   Those Inventive Americans
            Washington, D.C.: National Geographic Society,
                1971

TLLW   They Loved the Land
            Champaign, Ill.: Garrad, 1974

TMAL   The Telescope Makers
            Barbara Land
            New York: Crowell, 1968

TMSB   Triumphs of Modern Science
            Harry Sootin
            New York: Vanguard, 1960

TOWS   A Treasury of World Science
            New York: Philosophical Library, 1962

TPAE   Turning Points in American Electrical History
            James Brittain
            New York: IEEE Press, 1977

TPOS   12 Pioneers of Science
            Harry Sootin
            New York: Vanguard, 1960

VACE   The Virus That Ate Cannibals
            Carol Eron
            New York: Macmillan, 1981

VISC   Victorian Science
            New York: Doubleday, 1970

VTHB   Volts to Hertz: The Rise of Electricity
            Sanford Bordeau
            New York: Burgess, 1982

WAGW   Wild Animals, Gentle Women
            Margery Facklam
            New York: Harcourt Brace Jovanovich, 1978

WAMB   Webster's American Biographies
            Springfield, Mass.: G&C Merriam, 1974

WASM   Women and Science
            Valijean McLenighan
            Chicago: Raintree, 1979

Key to Fields Listed and Their Abbreviations

Field	Abbr.	Field	Abbr.
Aeronautics	Aero.	Computers	Comp.
Agriculture	Agr.	Conchology	Conch.
Alchemy	Alch.	Conservation	Cons.
Anatomy	Anat.	Cosmology	Cosmol.
Anthropology	Anthro.	Crystallography	Crystal.
Antiquarianism	Antiq.	Dairy Science	Dairy Sci.
Arboriculture	Arbori.	Dentistry	Dent.
Archaeology	Archaeol.	Ecology	Ecol.
Architecture	Archit.	Electrical Engineering	Elec. Engr.
Astrology	Astrol.	Electrical Science	Elec. Sci.
Astronautics	Astronaut.	Electrochemistry	Electrochem.
Astronomy	Astron.	Embryology	Embryol.
Astrophysics	Astrophys.	Engineering	Engr.
Bacteriology	Bact.	Entomology	Entom.
Biochemistry	Biochem.	Ethology	Ethol.
Biology	Biol.	Evolution	Evol.
Biophysics	Biophys.	Exploring	Exp.
Botany	Bot.	Forensic Science	Forens. Sci.
Chemical Engineering	Chem. Engr.	Forestry	Forest.
Chemistry	Chem.	Genetics	Genet.
Chronology	Chron.	Geography	Geog.
Climatology	Climat.	Geology	Geol.

Geomorphology	Geomorph.	Paleontology	Paleon.
Geophysics	Geophys.	Parapsychology	Parapsych.
Glaciology	Glaciol.	Parasitology	Parasit.
Herpetology	Herp.	Pathology	Path.
Horticulture	Hort.	Pharmacology	Pharm.
Hydrology	Hydrol.	Philology	Philol.
Ichthyology	Ichth.	Philosophy	Philos.
Immunology	Immunol.	Philosophy of Science	Philos. of Sci.
Instrumentation	Instr.	Photography	Photo.
Inventing	Invent.	Phrenology	Phren.
Limnology	Limn.	Physics	Phys.
Marine Biology	Mar. Biol.	Physiology	Physiol.
Mathematics	Math.	Polymathy	Polym.
Medicine	Med.	Psychiatry	Psychiat.
Metallurgy	Metal.	Psychology	Psych.
Meteorology	Meteor.	Rocketry	Rocket.
Microbiology	Microbiol.	Science Education	Sci. Ed.
Microscopy	Micros.	Science History	Sci. Hist.
Mineralogy	Mineral.	Science Illustration	Sci. Illus.
Mining	Mng.	Science Writing	Sci. Writ.
Natural History	Nat. Hist.	Seismology	Seism.
Natural Philosophy	Nat. Philos.	Soil Science	Soil Sci.
Navigation	Nav.	Space Law	Space Law
Oceanography	Ocean.	Spectroscopy	Spect.
Optics	Opt.	Speleology	Spel.
Ornithology	Ornith.	Surveying	Surv.

Textiles	Text.	Veterinary Medicine	Vet. Med.
Toxicology	Toxicol.	Virology	Virol.
Translation of Science Literature	Trans. Sci. Lit.	Volcanology	Volcan.
Tree Surgery	Tree Surg.	Zoology	Zool.

Key to Other Abbreviations

Born	b.
*Circa	c.
Died	d.
**Flourished	fl.

*Circa indicates that the date is approximate.

**Flourished indicates that the time period listed is when the individual performed his or her major works.

Index to Scientists
by Surname

A

AALL, Christian H. (1913-) Metal.; Electrochem. NCSL

ABAILARD, Pierre (1079-1142) Philos. CDZZ ZZ-1

ABANO, Pietro d' (1257-1315) Med.; Nat. Hist. BEOS BHMT CDZZ ZZ-1

ABBE, Cleveland (1838-1916) Meteor. ABES ABET BEOS BM-8 CDZZ DAB NC-8 WAMB ZZ-1

ABBE, Ernst (1840-1905) Phys. BEOS CDZZ HLSM ZZ-1

ABBOT, Charles (d. 1817) Bot. DNB

ABBOT, Charles G. (1872-1973) Astron. NCSA

ABBOT, Henry L. (1831-1927) Engr. BM13

ABBOTT, Charles C. (1843-1919) Nat. Hist. DAB NC10

ABBOTT, Horace E. (1896-1974) Agr. NC58

ABBOTT, John (1751-c.1840) Entom.; Ornith. AMEM ANHD BIOD HACA

ABBOTT, Maude (1869-1940) Med. IDWB

ABBOTT, Robert D. (1892-1954) Chem. NC43

ABBOTT, William L. (1860-1936) Nat. Hist. NC27

ABEGG, Richard W. (1869-1910) Chem. ABES ABET BDOS BEOS

ABEL, Clarke (1780-1826) Bot. DNB

ABEL, Frederick A. (1827-1902) Chem. ABES ABET BDOS BEOS

ABEL, John J. (1857-1938) Biochem. ABET ACCE BEOS BM24 CDZZ DAB2 DSLP ZZ-1

ABEL, Niels H. (1802-1829) Math. ABES ABET BDOS BEOS CDZZ ZZ-1

ABEL, Othenio (1875-1946) Paleon. CDZZ ZZ-1

ABELARD, Peter SEE ABAILARD, Pierre

ABELSON, Philip H. (1913-) Chem. ABES ABET BEOS CB65 MHM2 MHSE MOS6

ABERCROMBIE, John (1726-1806) Hort. DNB

ABERCROMBIE, Michael (1912-1979) Zool. RS26

ABERNETHY, John (1764-1831) Med. BHMT DNB

ABERT, James W. (1820-1897) Ornith. WFBG

ABERT, John J. (1786-1863) Geog. BIOD

ABETTI, Antonio (1846-1928) Astron. CDZZ ZZ-1

ABICH, Otto H. (1806-1886) Geol. CDZZ ZZ-1

ABNEY, William W. (1843-1920) Photo.; Astron. ABET CDZZ ZZ-1

ABRAHAM, Edward P. (1913-) Biochem. MHSE

ABRAHAM, Max (1875-1922) Phys. CDZZ ZZ-1

ABRAHAM BAR HIYYA HA-NASI (fl. before 1136) Math.; Astron. CDZZ ZZ-1

ABRAMS, Albert (1863-1923) Med. MSFB

ABREU, Aleixo de (1568-1630) Med. CDZZ ZZ-1

ABU HAMID, al-Gharnati (1080-1169) Geog. CDZZ ZZ-1

ABU KAMIL, Shuja ibn Aslam (c.850-c.930) Math. CDZZ ZZ-1

ABU MA SHAR, al-Balkhi (787-886) Astrol. CDZZ ZZ-1

ABUL-BARAKAT, al-Baghdadi (c.1080-1165) Phys.; Philos. CDZZ ZZ-1

ABUL-FIDA, Isma il ibn Ali (1273-1331) Geog. CDZZ ZZ-1

ABUL-WAFA al-BUZJANI, Muhammad (940-c.998) Math.; Astron. CDZZ ZZ-1

ACCUM, Friedrich C. (1769-1838) Chem. CDZZ DNB ZZ-1

ACHARD, Franz K. (1753-1821) Chem. CDZZ ZZ-1

ACHARIUS, Erik (1757-1819) Bot. CDZZ ZZ-1

ACHESON, Edward G. (1858-1931) Chem. ABES
ABET ACCE BDOS DAB1 IHMV

ACHILLINI, Alessandro (1463-1512) Anat. CDZZ
ZZ-1

ACKERET, Jakob (1898-) Aero. ICFW

ACONCIO, Jacopo (c.1520-1566) Engr. GE-1

ACOSTA, Cristobal (c.1525-c.1594) Nat. Hist.; Med.
CDZZ ZZ-1

ACOSTA, Jose de (1539-1600) Geog. CDZZ SBCS
ZZ-1

ACYUTA PISARATI (c.1550-1621) Astron. CDZZ
ZZ-1

ADAIR, Gilbert S. (1896-1979) Biophys. RS27

ADAM OF BODENSTEIN (1528-1577) Alch.; Med.
CDZZ ZZ-1

ADAM, Neil K. (1891-1973) Chem. RS20

ADAMS, Ansel (1902-1984) Photo.; Cons. LACC

ADAMS, Arthur (1820-1878) Conch. ANHD

ADAMS, Charles B. (1814-1853) Geol. BIOD DAB

ADAMS, Charles C. (1873-1955) Ecol. LACC NC46

ADAMS, Charles F. (1877-1960) Entom. NC50

ADAMS, Comfort A. (1868-1958) Elec. Engr. BM38
NCSA

ADAMS, Daniel (1773-1864) Math. NC20

ADAMS, Edward (1824-1855) Ornith. BWCL WFBG

ADAMS, Edwin P. (1878-1955) Phys. QPAS

ADAMS, Frank D. (1859-1942) Geol. CDZZ ZZ-1

ADAMS, Isaac Jr. (1836-1911) Chem. Engr. ACCE

ADAMS, John C. (1819-1892) Astron.; Math. ABES
ABET BDOS BEOS CDZZ DNB1 IEAS MGAH
TPOS ZZ-1

ADAMS, John E. (1899-1970) Geol. NC55

ADAMS, Leason H. (1887-1969) Geophys. BM52
MHM1 MHSE

ADAMS, Robert (1791-1875) Med. BHMT DNB

ADAMS, Roger (1889-1971) Chem. ACCE BEOS
BM53 CB47 CDZZ MHM1 MHSE NC57 NCSG
WAMB ZZXV

ADAMS, Walter S. (1876-1956) Astron. ABES ABET
BEOS BM31 CDZZ IEAS NCSE RS-2 WAMB
ZZ-1

ADAMS, William B. (1797-1872) Invent. DNB

ADAMSON, George P. (1864-1933) Chem. NC26

ADAMSON, Joy (1910-1980) Ethol. AO80 CB72
IDWB

ADANSON, Michel (1727-1806) Nat. Hist. ANHD
CDZZ ZZ-1

ADDAMS, Jane (1860-1935) Med. WIWM

ADDISON, Thomas (1793-1860) Med. ABES ABET
BDOS BEOS BHMT CDZZ DNB DSLP MMMA

ADELAIDE, Baron of SEE FLOREY, Howard W.

ADELARD OF BATH (fl. 1116-1142) Math.; Astron.
ABES ABET AMST CDZZ ZZ-1

ADER, Clement (1841-1925) Aero.; Invent. PAW3

ADET, Pierre A. (1763-1834) Chem. CDZZ ZZ-1

ADHEMAR, Alphones J. (1797-1862) Math. BEOS

ADKINS, Homer B. (1892-1949) Chem. ACCE BM27
DAB4

ADLER, Alfred (1870-1937) Psych. ABES ABET
BDOS PAW3

ADLER, Charles J. (1899-1980) Invent. AO80

ADRIAN, Edgar D. (1889-1977) Physiol. ABET BEOS
RS25

ADRIAN, Robert (1775-1843) Math. BIOD CDZZ
DAB DNB ZZ-1

AEPINUS, Franz U. (1724-1802) Phys. CDZZ EETD
ZZ-1

AETIUS OF AMIDA (fl. c.540) Med. DDZZ ZZ-1

AFANASYEV, Georgii D. (1906-) Geol. SMST

AGARDH, Carl A. (1785-1859) Bot.; Math. CDZZ
ZZ-1

AGARDH, Jacob G. (1813-1901) Bot. CDZZ ZZ-1

AGASSIZ, Alexander (1835-1910) Zool.; Ocean.
BM-7 CDZZ DAB EXDC EXSG NC-3 WAMB
ZZ-1

AGASSIZ, Elizabeth C. (1822-1907) Nat. Hist. IDWB

AGASSIZ, George R. (1862-1951) Zool.; Astron.
NC37

AGASSIZ, Jean L. R. SEE AGASSIZ, Louis J. R.

AGASSIZ, Louis J. R. (1807-1873) Nat. Hist. ABES
ABET ASIW BDOS BEOS BIOD BM-2 CDZZ
DAB EQSA FIFE HFGA HNHB LISD MSAJ
NC-2 NHAH PHLS SFNB SSAH WAMB YSMS

AGATHINUS, Claudius (fl. c.50) Med. CDZZ ZZ-1

AGEEV, Nikolai V. (1903-) Metal. SMST

AGNESI, Maria G. (1718-1799) Math. CDZZ IDWB
MEQP WIMO ZZ-1

AGNEW, Harold M. (1921-) Phys. MHM2 MHSE

AGNODICE (fl. c.300 B.C.) Med. IDWB

AGOSHKOV, Mikhail I. (1905-) Mng. SMST

AGRICOLA, Georgius (1494-1555) Med.; Engr. ABES
ABET BDOS BEOS CDZZ GE-1 GRCH HOSS
LISD SAIF TOWS ZZ-1

AGRIPPA, Heinrich C. (1486-1535) Med. MMMA
ZZ-1

AGRIPPA, Marcus V. (63 B.C.-12 B.C.) Engr. GE-1

AGUILON, Francois d' (1546-1617) Phys.; Math.
CDZZ ZZ-1

AHERN, George P. (1859-1942) Forest. LACC

AHMAD ibn YUSUF (d. 912) Math. CDZZ ZZ-1

AHMOSE (fl. c.1650 B.C.) Math. ABES ABET

AIDA YASUAKI (1747-1817) Math. CDZZ ZZ-1

AIGRAIN, Pierre R. (1924-) Phys. MHM2 MHSE

AIKEN, Howard H. (1900-1973) Math.; Engr. CB47
NC60

AIKIN, Arthur (1773-1854) Chem. DNB

AIKIN, Charles R. (1775-1847) Chem. DNB

AILLY, Pierre d' (1350-1420) Astrol. BEOS CDZZ
ZZ-1

AINSLIE, Charles N. (1856-1939) Entom. AMEM

AINSWORTH, William F. (1807-1896) Geol. DNB1

AINSWORTH, William L. (1892-1956) Geol. NC54

AIRY, George B. (1801-1892) Astron.; Math. ABES
ABET BEOS CDZZ DNB1 IEAS STYC ZZ-1

AITKEN, Alexander C. (1895-1967) Math. RS14

AITKEN, John (1839-1919) Phys.; Meteor. BM32

AITKEN, Robert G. (1864-1951) Astron. BEOS
BM32 CDZZ DAB5 IEAS NC42 ZZ-1

AITKEN, William (1825-1892) Path. DNB1

AITON, William (1731-1793) Bot. CDZZ DNB ZZ-1

AITON, William T. (1766-1849) Hort. CDZZ ZZ-1

AJIMA NAONOBU (1732-1798) Math. CDZZ ZZ-1

AKELEY, Carl E. (1864-1926) Nat. Hist. DAB
WAMB

AKERS, Alan W. SEE AKERS, Wallace A.

AKERS, Wallace A. (1888-1954) Chem. BDOS BEOS
DNB7

al- For names beginning with al- See last element of
name.

ALAIN DE LILLE (d. 1203) Philos. ZZ-1

ALBAN, Ernst (1791-1856) Engr. GE-1

ALBATEGNIUS SEE al-BATTANI, Abu abd Allah

ALBERT I OF MONACO (1848-1922) Ocean. CDZZ
ZZ-1

ALBERT OF SAXONY (1316-1390) Phys.; Math.
CDZZ ZZ-1

ALBERT, Abraham A. (1905-1972) Math. BM51
MHM1 MHSE

ALBERTI, Friedrich A. von (1795-1878) Geol. CDZZ
ZZ-1

ALBERTI, Leone B. (1404-1472) Math.; Nat. Hist.
ABES ABET BDOS CDZZ GE-1 ZZ-1

ALBERTI, Salomon (1540-1600) Med. CDZZ ZZ-1

ALBERTSON, Frederick W. (1892-1961) Ecol. NC53

ALBERTUS MAGNUS (1206-1280) Polym. ABES
ABET ANHD BDOS BEOS CDZZ NATJ ORNS
ZZ-1

ALBIN, Eleazar (fl. 1713-1759) Ornith. DNB HAOA

ALBINUS, Bernard (1653-1721) Med. CDZZ ZZXV

ALBINUS, Bernhard S. (1697-1770) Anat.; Med.
BDOS BEOS BHMT CDZZ ZZXV

ALBINUS, Christian B. (1698/9-1752) Anat. ZZXV

ALBINUS, Frederick B. (1715-1778) Anat.; Med.
ZZXV

ALBRECHT, Carl T. (1843-1915) Astron. CDZZ ZZ-1

ALBRIGHT, Arthur (1811-1900) Chem. BDOS BEOS

ALBRIGHT, Fuller (1900-1969) Med. BM48

ALBRIGHT, Horace M. (1890-) Cons. EAFC LACC
NCSH

ALBUMASAR SEE ABU MA SHAR, al-Balkhi

ALBUTT, Thomas C. SEE ALLBUTT, Thomas C.

ALBUZJANI SEE ABUL-WAFA al-BUZJANI, Muhammad

ALCABITIUS SEE al-QABISI, Sbu al-Saqr

ALCMAEON OF CROTONA (b. c.535 B.C.) Anat.;
Med. ABES ABET BEOS CDZZ HLSM ZZ-1

ALCOCK, Norman Z. (1918-) Phys. CB63

ALCUIN (735-804) Math. ABES ABET CDZZ ZZ-1

ALDEN, Harold L. (1890-1964) Astron. NC52

ALDER, Joshua (1792-1867) Zool. DNB

ALDER, Kurt (1902-1958) Chem. ABES ABET BDOS
BEOS CDZZ MHM1 MHSE NPWC ZZ-1

ALDEROTTI, Taddeo (1215-1295) Med. ABET CDZZ
TALS ZZ-1

ALDINI, Giovanni (1762-1834) Phys. CDZZ ZZ-1

ALDRICH, John M. (1866-1934) Entom. AMEM
NC46

ALDRIN, Edwin E. (1930-) Astronaut. IEAS

ALDROVANDI, Ulisse (1522-1605) Biol.; Nat. Hist.
ANHD BDOS BEOS BMST CDZZ HAOA ORNS
ZZ-1

ALEKIN, Oleg A. (1908-) Chem. SMST

ALEKSANDROV, Anatolii P. (1903-) Phys. SMST

ALEKSANDROV, Boris K. (1889-) Engr. SMST

ALEKSEEV, Aleksandr E. (1891-) Elec. Engr. SMST

ALEKSEEVSKII, Nikolai E. (1912-) Phys. SMST

ALEMBERT, Jean le Rond d' (1717-1783) Astron.;
Math. ABES ABET BDOS BEOS FNEC ZZ-1

ALEXANDER OF APHRODISIAS (fl. c.200) Philos.
CDZZ ZZ-1

ALEXANDER OF MYNDOS (fl. c.25-50) Biol. ZZ-1

ALEXANDER OF TRALLES (fl. 500s) Med. CDZZ
ZZ-1

ALEXANDER, Annie M. (1867-1950) Bot. BNBR

ALEXANDER, Archie A. (1887-1958) Engr. BCST
BISC SBPY

ALEXANDER, Jerome (1876-1959) Chem. NC52

ALEXANDER, John H. (1812-1867) Geol.; Engr.
BIOD BM-1 DAB NC-9

ALEXANDER, Stephen (1806-1883) Astron. BIOD
BM-2 DAB NC11

ALEXANDERSON, Ernst F. (1878-1975) Engr.
CB55 EETD TPAE WAMB

ALEXANDROFF, Pavel S. (1896-) Math. SMST

ALEXANDROV, Aleksandr D. (1912-) Math. SMST

ALEXIS OF PIEDMONT SEE RUSCELLI, Girolamo

ALEXOPOULOS, Constantine J. (1907-) Bot. MHSE

ALEY, Robert J. (1863-1935) Math. NC15

ALFONSO EL SABIO (1221-1284) Astron. CDZZ ZZ-1

ALFORD, William J. Jr. (1923-) Aero. ICFW

ALFRAGANUS SEE al-FARGHANI, Abul Abbas Ahmad

ALFVEN, Hannes O. (1908-) Phys. ABET BEOS IEAS MHSE POSW

ALGER, Cyrus (1781-1856) Invent. WAMB

ALGER, Francis (1807-1863) Mineral. BIOD

ALHAZEN SEE ibn al-HAYTHAM, Abu Ali al-Hasan

ALIBERT, Jean L. (1768-1837) Med. BHMT

ALIKHANOV, Abram I. (1904-1970) Phys. SMST

ALIKHANYAN, Artemii I. (1908-) Phys. SMST

ALIMARIN, Ivan P. (1903-) Chem. SMST

ALKINDUS SEE al-KINDI, Abu Yusuf

ALLAN, Thomas (1777-1833) Mineral. DNB

ALLBUTT, Thomas C. (1836-1925) Med. ABES ABET BEOS BHMT

ALLEE, Warden C. (1885-1955) Biol.; Zool. BM30 NC42

ALLEN, Arthur A. (1885-1964) Nat. Hist.; Ornith. CB61 DGMT LACC

ALLEN, Charles A. (1841-1930) Ornith. BWCL WFBG

ALLEN, Charles E. (1872-1954) Bot. BM29 NC42

ALLEN, Durward L. (1910-) Biol.; Cons. DGMT LACC

ALLEN, Edgar (1892-1943) Anat. BEOS CDZZ DAB3 ZZ-1

ALLEN, Edward T. (1875-1942) Forest. LACC

ALLEN, Eugene T. (1864-1964) Chem.; Geophys. BM40

ALLEN, Glover M. (1879-1942) Zool. DAB3 NC31

ALLEN, H. Julian (1910-1977) Astronaut. ICFW

ALLEN, Harrison (1841-1897) Anat. BIOD

ALLEN, Herbert S. (1873-1954) Nat. Philos. RS-1

ALLEN, James Van SEE VAN ALLEN, James

ALLEN, Joel A. (1838-1921) Zool. BM11 BWCL DAB NC-3

ALLEN, Norman P. (1903-1972) Metal. RS19

ALLEN, Oscar D. (1836-1913) Chem. BIOD

ALLEN, Peter (1905-) Chem. COBC

ALLEN, Robert P. (1905-1963) Ornith. BWCL DGMT LACC

ALLEN, Shirley W. (1883-1968) Forest. LACC

ALLEN, Thomas (1542-1632) Math. DNB

ALLEN, Timothy F. (1837-1902) Bot. BIOD DAB MABH

ALLEN, William H . (1856-1929) Chem. NC22

ALLEN, Zachariah (1795-1882) Invent. DAB NC-8

ALLER, Lawrence H. (1913-) Astron. MHM2 MHSE

ALLIS, Edward P. (1851-1947) Anat. NC39

ALLMAN, George J. (1812-1898) Biol. DNB1 VISC

ALLMAN, George J. (1824-1904) Math. DNB2

ALLMAN, William (1776-1846) Bot. DNB

ALPHARABIUS SEE al-FARABI, Abu Nasr Muhammad

ALPHER, Ralph A. (1921-) Phys. BEOS

ALPINI, Prospero (1553-1617) Bot.; Med. ABES ABET BDOS BEOS CDZZ ZZ-1

ALSBERG, Carl L. (1877-1940) Biochem. ACCE NC30

ALSOP, William K. (1872-1936) Chem. NC26

ALSTED, Johann H. (1588-1638) Nat. Philos. CDZZ ZZ-1

ALSTON, Edward R. (1845-1887) Zool. DNB

ALTER, David (1807-1881) Phys. BDOS BEOS BIOD DAB WAMB

ALTUM, Bernard (1824-1900) Ornith. ORNS

ALVAREZ, Luis W. (1911-) Phys. ABES ABET BEOS CB47 DCPW MHM1 MHSE POSW WAMB

ALZATE Y RAMIREZ, Jose A. (1738-1799) Nat. Hist. CDZZ ZZ-1

ALZHEIMER, Alois (1864-1915) Med. BHMT

AMAGAT, Emile H. (1841-1915) Phys. ABES ABET BEOS CDZZ ZZ-1

AMBARTSUMIAN, Viktor A. (1908-) Astrophys. ABES ABET BEOS IEAS MHM1 MHSE SMST

AMDAHL, Gene M. (1922-) Elec. Engr.; Comp. CB82

AMEGHINO, Florentino (1854-1911) Paleon.; Geol. CDZZ PHLS ZZ-1

AMES, Bruce N. (1928-) Biochem.; Genet. MHSE

AMES, Joseph S. (1864-1943) Phys. BM23 CDZZ DAB3 NCSA QPAS ZZ-1

AMES, Lawrence M. (1900-1966) Microbiol. NC52

AMES, Nathaniel (1708-1764) Math. NC-8

AMES, Oakes (1874-1950) Bot. DAB4 NC53

AMES, William (1576-1633) Nat. Philos. ZZ-1

AMICI, Giovanni B. (1786-1868) Opt.; Micros. ABET BDOS BEOS CDZZ ZZ-1

al-AMILI, Baha al-Din (1546-1621) Math.; Alchem. SCIN

AMIRASLANOV, Ali A. (1900-1962) Engr. SMST

AMMANN, Othmar H. (1879-1965) Engr. CB63 MHM1 MHSE

AMONTONS, Guillaume (1663-1705) Phys. ABES ABET BEOS CDZZ ZZ-1

AMOS, Harold (1919-) Virol. SBPY

AMPERE, Andre M. (1775-1836) Math.; Phys. ABES ABET BDOS BEOS CDZZ DCPW EETD FNEC GE-1 GOED HOSS HSSO MAKS SAIF TOWS VTHB ZZ-1

AMSLER-LAFFON, Jakob (1823-1912) Math. CDZZ ZZ-1

AMUNDSEN, Roald E. (1872-1928) Exp. ABES ABET BDOS MGAH

ANARITIUS SEE al-NAYRIZI, Abul Abbas al-Fadi

ANATOLIUS OF ALEXANDRIA (fl. c.269) Math. CDZZ ZZ-1

ANAXAGORAS (c.500 B.C.-428 B.C.) Math. ABES ABET AMST BDOS BEOS CDZZ HLSM IEAS ZZ-1

ANAXIMANDER OF MILITOS (c.611 B.C.-c.547 B.C.) Math.; Astron. ABES ABET AMST BDOS BEOS CDZZ HLSM IEAS ZZ-1

ANAXIMENES (c.570 B.C.-c.500 B.C.) Nat. Philos. ABES ABET AMST BEOS CDZZ HLSM ZZ-1

ANCEL, Paul A. (1873-1961) Biol. CDZZ ZZ-1

ANDERNACH, Gunther SEE GUINTER, Joannes

ANDERS, Edward (1926-) Chem. MHSE

ANDERS, William A. (1933-) Astronaut. CB69

ANDERSON, Alexander (1582-c.1619) Math. DNB

ANDERSON, Alexander P. (1862-1943) Bot.; Chem. NCSF

ANDERSON, Alfred L. (1900-1964) Geol. NC51

ANDERSON, Carl D. (1905-) Phys. ABES ABET BEOS CB51 DCPW NCSF PAW2 POSW WAMB

ANDERSON, Charles A. (1902-) Geol. MHM2 MHSE

ANDERSON, Charles L. (1827-1910) Nat. Hist. BNBR

ANDERSON, Edgar S. (1897-1969) Bot. BM49 MHM1 MHSE

ANDERSON, Elda E. (1899-1961) Phys. NAWM NC50

ANDERSON, Elizabeth G. (1836-1917) Med. WIWM

ANDERSON, Ernest M. (1877-1960) Geol. CDZZ ZZ-1

ANDERSON, James C. (1792-1861) Invent. DNB

ANDERSON, John (1833-1900) Nat. Hist. DNB1

ANDERSON, John A. (1876-1959) Astron. BM36

ANDERSON, John F. (1873-1958) Bact. NC47

ANDERSON, John S. (1908-) Chem. COBC

ANDERSON, John V. (1882-1958) Chem. RS-4

ANDERSON, Oskar J. (1887-1960) Math. CDZZ ZZ-1

ANDERSON, Philip W. (1923-) Phys. ABET BEOS MHM1 MHSE POSW SOTT

ANDERSON, Robert (fl. 1668-1696) Math. DNB

ANDERSON, Rudolph J. (1879-1961) Biochem. BM36

ANDERSON, Sterling R. (1916-1975) Elec. Engr. NC59

ANDERSON, Thomas (1819-1874) Chem. BDOS BEOS CDZZ ZZ-1

ANDERSON, Thomas (1832-1870) Bot. DNB

ANDERSON, William (d. 1778) Nat. Hist. DNB

ANDERSON, William (1766-1846) Hort. DNB

ANDOYER, Henri (1862-1929) Astron.; Math. CDZZ ZZ-1

ANDRADE, Edward N. (1887-1971) Phys. BEOS MHM2 MHSE RS18

ANDRAL, Gabriel (1797-1876) Med. BHMT

ANDRE, Charles L. (1842-1912) Astron.; Math. CDZZ ZZ-1

ANDREAE, Johann V. (1586-1654) Philos. CDZZ ZZ-1

ANDREE, Salomon A. (1854-1897) Aero. PAW2

ANDREEV, Nikolai N. (1881-) Phys. SMST

ANDREWES, Christopher H. (1896-) Virol. MHM2 MHSE VACE

ANDREWES, Frederick W. (1859-1932) Bact. DNB5

ANDREWS, Christopher C. (1829-1922) Forest. LACC

ANDREWS, Horace J. (1892-1951) Forest. LACC

ANDREWS, Launcelot W. (1856-1938) Chem. ACCE NC46

ANDREWS, Roy C. (1884-1960) Nat. Hist. ABES ABET BEOS CB41 CB53 NC44 WAMB

ANDREWS, Thomas (1813-1885) Chem.; Phys. ABES ABET BDOS BEOS CDZZ MCCW ZZ-1

ANDREWS, Thomas (1847-1907) Metal. DNB2

ANDREWS, William (fl. 1656-1683) Astrol. DNB

ANDREWS, William (1802-1880) Nat. Hist. DNB

ANDRIANOV, Kuzma A. (1904-) Chem. SMST

ANDRUSOV, Nikolai I. (1861-1924) Geol.; Paleon. CDZZ ZZ-1

ANFINSEN, Christian B. (1916-) Biochem. ABET BEOS MHM2 MHSE WAMB

ANGELI, Stefano D. (1623-1697) Math.; Phys. CDZZ ZZ-1

ANGELL, James R. (1869-1949) Psych. BM26 CB40

ANGELUS, Johannes (1453-1512) Astron. CDZZ ZZ-1

ANGSTROM, Anders, J. (1814-1874) Phys. ABES ABET BDOS BEOS CDZZ ZZ-1

ANGUILLARA, Luigi (1512-1570) Bot. CDZZ ZZ-1

ANICHKOV, Nikolai N. (1885-1964) Path. SMST

ANNAND, Percy N. (1898-1950) Entom. AMEM NC40

ANREP, Gleb (1891-1955) Physiol. RS-2

ANSCHUTZ, Richard (1852-1937) Chem. CDZZ ZZ-1

ANSTED, David T. (1814-1880) Geol. DNB

ANTHELME, Voituret (1618-1683) Astron. CDZZ ZZ-1

ANTHEMIUS OF TRALLES (fl. 500) Math. CDZZ GE-1 ZZ-1

ANTHONY, John G. (1804-1877) Conch. BIOD DAB

ANTHONY, William A. (1835-1908) Phys. DAB! NC11

ANTIPHON (c.450 B.C.-c.400 B.C.) Math. CDZZ
ZZ-1

ANTISELL, Thomas (1817-1893) Geol. ACCE NC19

ANTONIADE, Eugene M. (1870-1944) Astron. BEOS
CDZZ IEAS ZZ-1

ANUCHIN, Dmitrii N. (1843-1923) Geog.; Anthro.
CDZZ ZZ-1

ANVILLE, Jean B. d' (1697-1782) Geog. CDZZ ZZ-1

APATHY, Stephan (1863-1922) Med.; Zool. CDZZ
ZZ-1

APELT, Ernst F. (1812-1859) Philos. CDZZ ZZ-1

APIAN, Peter (1495-1552) Astron.; Geog. ABET
CDZZ ZZ-1

APKER, LeRoy (1915-) Phys. BEOS MHM1 MHSE

APOLLODORUS (fl. 98-117) Engr. GE-1

APOLONIUS OF PERGA (261 B.C.-190 B.C.) Math.
ABES ABET BDOS BEOS CDZZ IEAS ZZ-1

APPELL, Paul E. (1855-1930) Math.; Phys. CDZZ
ZZ-1

APPERT, Nicolas F. (c.1750-1841) Invent. ABES
ABET BDOS BEOS SAIF

APPLEGATH, Augustus (1788-1871) Invent. GE-1

APPLETON, Edward V. (1892-1965) Phys. ABES
ABET BDOS BEOS CB45 CDZZ GDSP MHM1
MHSE POSW RS12 ZZ-1

APPLETON, John H. (1844-1930) Chem. ACCE

AQUINAS, Thomas (c.1225-1274) Nat. Philos. ABES
ABET CDZZ GRTH ZZ-1

ARAGO, Dominique F. (1786-1853) Phys.; Astron.
ABES ABET BDOS BEOS CDZZ EETD SOAC
ZZ-1

ARANZIO, Guilio C. (1529-1589) Anat.; Med. CDZZ
ZZ-1

ARATUS OF SOLI (c.310 B.C.-c.240 B.C.) Astron.
CDZZ ZZ-1

ARBER, Agnes R. (1879-1960) Bot. CDZZ DNB7
IDWB RS-6 ZZ-1

ARBER, E. A. Newell (1870-1918) Paleon. FHUA

ARBER, Werner (1929-) Genet.; Biochem. ABET
BEOS MHSE SOT2

ARBOGAST, Louis F. (1759-1803) Math. VDZZ ZZ-1

ARBOS, Philippe (1882-1956) Geog. CDZZ ZZ-1

ARBUCKLE, Howard B. (1870-1945) Chem. ACCE

ARBUTHNOT, John (1667-1735) Med. BHMT CDZZ
ZZ-1

ARBUZOV, Aleksandr E. (1877-1968) Chem. SMST

ARCHBOLD, Richard (1907-1976) Zool. NC59

ARCHER, Frederick S. (1813-1857) Photo.; Invent.
ABET DNB

ARCHER, William A. (1894-) Bot. BNBR

ARCHIAC, Etienne J. d' (1802-1868) Geol. CDZZ
ZZ-1

ARCHIBALD, Raymond E. (1875-1955) Math. NC46

ARCHIGENES (fl. 98-117) Med. CDZZ ZZ-1

ARCHIMEDES (287 B.C.-212 B.C.) Math.; Phys.
ABES ABET AMST BDOS BEOS CDZZ DCPW
FMAS FNEC FPHM GE-1 GISA HOSS LISD
MAKS OMNM PAW1 PFEL SAIF SMIL TOWS
WTCM ZZ-1

ARCHYTAS OF TARENTUM (fl. c.375 B.C.) Math.
ABET CEZZ GE-1 ZZ-1

ARDERNE, John (1306/7-1380/9) Med. BHMT

ARDERON, William (1703-1767) Nat. Hist. DNB

ARDREY, Robert (1908-1980) Anthro. AO80

ARDUINI, Giovanni (1714-1795) Geol. CDZZ ZZ-1

ARETAEUS THE CAPPADICIAN (fl. 50) Med. CDZZ
ZZ-1

ARFVEDSON, Johann A. (1792-1841) Chem. CDZZ
ZZXV

ARGAND, Emile (1879-1940) Geol. CDZZ ZZ-1

ARGAND, Jean R. (1768-1822) Math. CDZZ ZZ-1

ARGELANDER, Friedrich W. (1799-1875) Astron. ABES ABET BEOS CDZZ IEAS ZZ-1

ARGENVILLE, Antoine J. d' (1680-1765) Nat. Hist. CDZZ ZZ-1

ARGOLI, Andrea (1570-1657) Astron.; Astrol. CDZZ ZZ-1

ARGYRIS, John H. (1913-) Engr. MHSE

ARISTAEUS (fl. c.350 B.C.-330 B.C.) Math. CDZZ ZZ-1

ARISTARCHUS OF SAMOS (310 B.C.-250 B.C.) Astron.; Math. ABES ABET AMST ASTR BDOS BEOS IEAS ZZ-1

ARISTOTLE (384 B.C.-322B.C.) Nat. Philos. ABES ABET AMST BDOS BEOS CDZZ EETD FASP FBMV GRBW GRCH GRTH IEAS LISD MAKS NATJ ORNS SAIF ZZ-1

ARISTOXENUS (fl. c.330 B.C.) Phys. CDZZ ZZ-1

ARISTYLLUS (fl. c.270 B.C.) Astron. ZZ-1

ARKADIEV, Vladimir K. (1884-1953) Phys. CDZZ EETD ZZ-1

ARKELL, William J. (1904-1958) Paleon.; Geol. CDZZ DNB7 RS-4 ZZ-1

ARKWRIGHT, Joseph A. (1864-1944) Bact. DNB6

ARKWRIGHT, Richard (1732-1792) Invent. ABES ABET BDOS BEOS DNB FOIF GE-1 SAIF

ARMSBY, Henry P. (1853-1921) Agr. BM19

ARMSTRONG, Edward A. (1900-) Ornith. DGMT

ARMSTRONG, Edward F. (1878-1945) Chem. CDZZ ZZ-1

ARMSTRONG, Edwin H. (1890-1954) Elec. Engr. ABES ABET CDZZ DAB5 NTBM TPAE WAMB ZZ-1

ARMSTRONG, Harry G. (1899-) Med.; Aero. HIUE

ARMSTRONG, Henry E. (1848-1937) Chem. BDOS BEOS CDZZ DNB5 GRCH ZZ-1

ARMSTRONG, J. Tarbottom (1848-1933) Chem. NC24

ARMSTRONG, Jack (1911-) Phys.; Astronaut. MOS4

ARMSTRONG, Neil A. (1930-) Astronaut. ABES ABET CB69 IEAS PPNF WAMB

ARMSTRONG, William G. (1810-1900) Engr. FNEC

ARNALD OF VILLANOVA (c.1240-1311) Med. ABET CDZZ BEOS ZZ-1

ARNAULD, Antoine (1612-1694) Math. CDZZ ZZ-1

ARNETT, Edward M. (1922-) Chem. MHSE

ARNETT, Eugene (1875-1938) Agr. NC29

ARNOLD, Charles E. (1876-1947) Chem. NC50

ARNOLD, Chester A. (1901-1977) Paleon. FHUA

ARNOLD, Harold de Forest (1883-1933) Phys. DAB1 CDZZ ZZ-1

ARNOLD, Joseph (1782-1818) Nat. Hist. DNB

ARNOLD, Lloyd (1888-1963) Bact. NC51

ARNOLD, Richard K. (1913-) Forest. LACC

ARNON, Daniel I. (1910-) Biochem. MHM2 MHSE

ARNOTT, George (1799-1868) Bot. DNB

ARNSTEIN, Karl (1887-1975) Aero. ICFW

AROMATARI, Giuseppe D. (1587-1660) Embryo. CDZZ ZZ-1

ARONHOLD, Siegfried H. (1819-1884) Math. CDZZ ZZ-1

AROUET, Francois SEE VOLTAIRE, Francois M. A. de

ARREST, Heinrich L. d' (1822-1875) Astron. ABET CDZZ ZZ-1

ARRHENIUS, Svante A. (1859-1927) Chem.; Phys. ABES ABET BDOS BEOS CDZZ CSCJ GASJ GRCH HSSO NPWC SAIF ZZ-1

ARROW, Kenneth J. (1921-) Math. IMMO

ARSONVAL, Arsene d' (1851-1940) Phys. CDZZ ZZ-1

ARTACHAIES (fl. 500 B.C.) Engr. GE-1

ARTEDI, Peter (1705-1735) Biol. CDZZ ZZ-1

ARTHUR, Joseph C. (1850-1942) Bot. DAB3 MABH NC12

ARTIN, Emil (1898-1962) Math. CDZZ ZZ-1

ARTOBOLEVSKII, Ivan I. (1905-) Engr. SMST

ARTSIMOVICH, Lev A. (1909-1973) Phys. ABET CDZZ SMST ZZ-1

ARYABHATA I (b.476) Math.; Astron. CDZZ FMAS ZZ-1

ARYABHATA II (fl. c.950-1000) Astron.; Math. ZZ-1

ARZACHEL SEE al-ZARQALI, Abu Ishaq Ibrahim

ASADA GORYU (1734-1799) Astron. CDZZ GE-1 ZZ-1

ASCHAN, Ossian (1860-1939) Chem. GRCH

ASCHOFF, Karl SEE ASCHOFF, Ludwig

ASCHOFF, Ludwig (1866-1942) Med. BDOS BEOS BHMT

ASCLEPIADES (c.130 B.C.-c.40 B.C.) Med. CDZZ ZZ-1

ASELLI, Gaspare (1581-1625) Anat. BDOS BEOS BHMT CDZZ ZZ-1

ASHBURNER, Charles A. (1854-1880) Geol. BIOD WAMB

ASHE, Willian W. (1872-1932) Forest. LACC

ASHFORD, Bailey K. (1873-1934) Med. DAB1 HIUE

ASHMEAD, William H. (1855-1908) Entom. AMEM DAB NC20

ASHMOLE, Elias (1617-1692) Nat. Philos. CDZZ ZZ-1

ASHTON, Thomas (fl. 1466) Alchem. DNB

ASIMOV, Isaac (1920-) Biochem.; Sci. Writ. ABES ABET AMJB CB68 WAMB

ASPDIN, Joseph (1779-1855) Invent. GE-1

ASPLUNDH, Carl H. (1903-1967) Forest. NC55

ASRATYAN, Ezras A. (1903-) Physiol. SMST

ASSALTI, Pietro (1680-1728) Med. CDZZ ZZ-1

ASTAUROV, Boris L. (1904-) Biol. SMST

ASTBURY, William T. (1898-1961) Crystal. ABET BDOS BEOS CDZZ RS-9 ZZ-1

ASTIN, Allen V. (1904-1984) Phys. CB56

ASTON, Francis W. (1877-1945) Chem.; Phys. ABES ABET BDOS BEOS CDZZ DCPW DNB6 GRCH HOSS MWBR NPWC ZZ-1

ASTRUC, Jean (1684-1766) Med. CDZZ ZZ-1

ASTWOOD, Edwin B. (1909-1976) Med. MHM2 MHSE

ATHENAEUS OF ATTALIA (fl. c.50) Med. CDZZ ZZ-1

ATIYAH, Michael F. (1929-) Math. MHSE

ATKINS, William R. (1884-1959) Chem. RS-5

ATKINSON, George F. (1854-1918) Bot.; Zool. BM29 DAB MABH NC13

ATKINSON, Henry (1781-1829) Math. DNB

ATKINSON, William B. (1919-1962) Anat. NC50

ATWATER, Caleb (1778-1867) Nat. Hist. BIOD

ATWATER, Wilbur O. (1844-1907) Agr. CDZZ WAMB ZZ-1

ATWOOD, George (1745-1807) Math.; Phys. CDZZ DNB ZZ-1

ATWOOD, Luther (1826-1868) Chem. NC13

ATWOOD, Wallace (1872-1949) Geol.; Geog. DAB4

ATWOOD, William (1830-1884) Chem. NC13

AUBERT, Alexander (1730-1805) Astron. DNB

AUBUISSON DE VOISINS, Jean F. d' (1769-1841) Geol. CDZZ ZZ-1

AUDEBERT, Jean B. (1759-1800) Nat. Hist. ANHD

AUDOUIN, Jean V. (1797-1841) Zool. CDZZ ZZ-1

AUDUBON, John J. (1785-1851) Ornith. ABES ABET ABFC ANHD ASIW BDOS BEOS BIOD BWCL CDZZ COAC DAB EQSA FIFE GANC HFGA

HNHB LACC LISD NATJ NC-6 NHAH ORNS SGNF TLLW WAMB WFBG ZZ-1

AUENBRUGGER, Joseph L. (1722-1809) Med. BEOS BHMT CDZZ ZZ-1

AUER, Karl von Welsbach (1858-1929) Chem. ABES ABET BEOS

AUERBACH, Charlotte (1899-) Genet. IDWB MHSE

AUERBACH, Isaac L. (1921-) Comp. NCSM

AUERBACH, Leopold (1828-1897) Med. BHMT

AUGER, Pierre V. (1899-) Phys. BEOS MHM2 MHSE

AUGUSTINE OF HIPPO, Saint (354-430) Philos. CDZZ ZZ-1

AUGUSTUS FREDERICUS SECUNDUS SEE FREDE-RICK II, HOHENSTAUFEN

AUSTEN, Peter T. (1852-1907) Chem. ACCE DAB NC13

AUSTEN, Ralph SEE GODWIN-AUSTEN, Robert

AUSTIN, Louis W. (1867-1932) Phys. CDZZ NC24 ZZ-1

AUSTIN, Mary H. (1868-1934) Cons. PCWA SFNB

AUTOLYCUS OF PITANE (fl. c.300 B.C.) Astron.; Math. CDZZ ZZ-1

AUVERGNE, William SEE WILLIAM OF AUVERGNE

AUWERS, Arthur J. von (1838-1915) Astron. CDZZ ZZ-1

AUWERS, Karl F. von (1863-1939) Chem. CDZZ ZZ-1

AUZOUT, Adrien (1622-1691) Astron.; Math. CDZZ ZZ-1

AVAKYAN, Artavazd A. (1907-1966) Biol. SMST

AVEBURY, Lord SEE LUBBOCK, John

AVENPACE SEE ibn EZRA, Abraham ben Meir

AVERROES SEE ibn RUSHD, Abul-Walid Muhammad

AVERY, Carlos (1868-1930) Cons. LACC

AVERY, Oswald T. (1887-1955) Biol. ABES ABET BEOS BM32 CDZZ HLSM MHM2 MHSE NC44 RS-2 ZZ-1

AVICENNA (980-1037) Med. ABES ABET BDOS BEOS BHMT CDZZ GRCH LISD SCIN THOG ZZXV

AVOGADRO, Amedeo (1776-1856) Phys.; Chem. ABES ABET BDOS BEOS CDZZ CSCJ HOSS ZZ-1

AVSYUK, Grigorii A. (1906-) Glaciol. SMST

ibn al-AWWAM ABU ZAKARIFYYA YAHYA (fl. c.1150-1175) Agr. CDZZ ZZ-1

AXELROD, Julius (1912-) Pharm. ABET BEOS MHSE

AYALA, Francisco J. (1934-) Biol. BEOS

AYERS, Joseph W. (1904-) Chem. NCSF

AYERZA, Abel (1861-1918) Med. BHMT

AYLWARD, David A. (1882-1970) Cons. LACC

AYRES, William L. (1905-1976) Math. NC60

AYRES, William O. (1817-1887) Zool.; Ichth. BIOD

AYRTON, Hertha (1854-1923) Phys. IDWB

AYRTON, William E. (1847-1908) Elec. Engr. BDOS BEOS DNB2

AZARA, Felix de (1742-1821) Math.; Nat. Hist. CDZZ ZZ-1

B

BAADE, Wilhelm H. (1893-1960) Astron. ABES ABET BEOS CDZZ IEAS MHM1 MHSE SLOR WAMB ZZ-1

BABBAGE, Charles (1792-1871) Math.; Comp. ABES ABET BDOS BEOS CDZZ DARR DNB EETD GE-1 MELW MNCS MPIP SAIF SOSC STYC ZZ-1

BABBITT, Milton (1916-) Math. CB62

BABCOCK, Earle J. (1865-1925) Mng. ACCE

BABCOCK, Ernest B. (1877-1954) Nat. Hist. BM32 NCSD

BABCOCK, Harold D. (1882-1968) Astron. BEOS BM45 IEAS

BABCOCK, Horace W. (1912-) Astron. BEOS MHM2 MHSE

BABCOCK, Stephen M. (1843-1931) Chem. ACCE BDOS BEOS CDZZ DAB1 GRCH HSSO WAMB ZZ-1

BABINET, Jacques (1794-1972) Phys.; Meteor. ABES ABET BEOS CDZZ ZZ-1

BABINGTON, Charles C. (1808-1895) Bot. CDZZ DNB1 ZZ-1

BABINGTON, William (1756-1833) Geol.; Mineral. CDZZ DNB ZZ-1

BABINSKI, Joseph (1857-1932) Med. BHMT

BABO, Clemens V. von (1818-1899) Chem. BDOS BEOS

BACCELLI, Guido (1830-1916) Med. CDZZ ZZ-1

BACH, Aleksei N. (1857-1946) Biochem. CDZZ ZZ-1

BACHE, Alexander D. (1806-1867) Geophys. ASJD BEOS BIOD BM-1 CDZZ DAB GASJ NC-3 WAMB ZZ-1

BACHE, Franklin (1792-1864) Chem. ACCE BIOD DAB NC-5

BACHELARD, Gaston (1884-1962) Philos. CDZZ ZZ-1

BACHELIER, Louis (1870-1946) Math. CDZZ ZZ-1

BACHER, Robert F. (1905-) Phys. CB47

BACHET DE MEZIRIAC, Claude G. (1581-1638) Math. CDZZ ZZ-1

BACHMAN, John (1790-1874) Zool. ASJD BIOD BWCL DAB NHAH WFBG

BACHMANN, Augustus Q. (1652-1723) Bot. CDZZ ZZ-1

BACHMANN, Paul G. (1837-1920) Math. CDZZ ZZ-1

BACHMANN, Werner E. (1901-1951) Chem. ACCE BM34 DAB5

BACHUONE, Arnaldus (1235-1313) Chem. GRCH

BACK, Ernest A. (1880-1959) Entom. AMEM NC47

BACK, Ernest E. (1881-1959) Phys. CDZZ ZZ-1

BACKLUND, Jons O. (1846-1916) Astron. CDZZ ZZ-1

BACKUS, John W. (1925-) Math.; Comp. HOPL MASW

BACON, Francis (1561-1626) Philos. ABES ABET BDOS BEOS CDZZ DNB ESCS GRTH LISD SMIL ZZ-1

BACON, John M. (1846-1904) Aero. DNB2

BACON, Roger (c.1220-1292) Nat. Philos.; Opt. ABES ABET BDOS BEOS BHMT CCSW CDZZ DNB FPHM GE-1 GRCH LISD MAKS TOWS ZZ-1

BADDILEY, James (1918-) Chem. COBC

BADGER, Richard M. (1896-1974) Chem. MHM2 MHSE

BADGER, Walter L. (1886-1958) Chem. ACCE NC47

BADHAM, Charles D. (1806-1857) Nat. Hist. DNB

BADI-al-ZAMAN al-JAZARI SEE al-JAZARI, Badi al-Zaman

BAEKELAND, Leo H. (1863-1944) Chem. ABES ABET ACCE ASIW BDOS BEOS BM24 CDZZ DAB3 GRCH HSSO MASY NC15 NC32 SAIF WAMB ZZ-1

BAER, Karl E. von (1792-1876) Biol.; Anthro. ABES ABET BDOS BEOS BHMT CDZZ HLSM WFBG ZZ-1

BAEYER, Adolph J. von (1835-1918) Chem. ABES ABET BDOS BEOS CDZZ GRCH HSSO NPWC TOWS ZZ-1

BAFFIN, William (1584-1622) Exp. ABES ABET

al-BAGHDADI, Abu Mansur (d. 1037) Math. CDZZ ZZXV

BAGLIVI, Georgius (1668-1707) Biol. CDZZ ZZ-1

BAGNALL, Kenneth W. (1925-) Chem. COBC

BAGNOLD, Ralph A. (1896-) Phys. MHSE

BAIER, Johann J. (1677-1735) Med.; Geol. CDZZ ZZ-1

BAIKIE, William B. (1825-1864) Nat. Hist. DNB

BAILAK al-QABAJAQI SEE BAYLAK al-QIBJAQI

BAILAR, John C. (1904-) Chem. BEOS MHM1 MHSE

BAILEY, Alfred M. (1894-) Nat. Hist. DGMT

BAILEY, Charles P. (1910-) Med. HEXS

BAILEY, Edgar H. (1848-1933) Chem. ACCE

BAILEY, Edward B. (1881-1965) Geol. CDZZ RS11 ZZ-1

BAILEY, Florence A. (1863-1948) Ornith. DAB4 NAW NC13 NCSA SFNB

BAILEY, Irving W. (1884-1967) Bot. BM45

BAILEY, Jacob W. (1811-1857) Chem. ASJD BIOD DAB MABH

BAILEY, John (1750-1819) Agr. DNB

BAILEY, John W. (1895-1967) Biol. NC52

BAILEY, Kenneth (1909-1963) Biochem. RS10

BAILEY, Liberty H. Jr. (1858-1954) Bot.; Hort. CB48 CDZZ DAB5 MABH NC43 WAMB ZZ-1

BAILEY, Loring W. (1839-1925) Geol. CDZZ ZZ-1

BAILEY, Richard W. (1885-1957) Engr. RS-4

BAILEY, Solon I. (1854-1931) Astron.; Meteor. BM15 CDZZ DAB1 NC28 ZZ-1

BAILEY, William W. (1843-1914) Bot. NC29

BAILLIE, Matthew (1761-1823) Anat.; Med. BDOS BEOS BHMT CDZZ DNB ZZ-1

BAILLOU, Guillaume de (1538-1616) Med. BHMT CDZZ ZZ-1

BAILLY, Jean S. (1736-1793) Astron. CDZZ ZZ-1

BAILY, Francis (1774-1844) Astron. ABES ABET BEOS CDZZ DNB IEAS ZZ-1

BAIN, Alexander (1818-1903) Psych. CDZZ ZZ-1

BAIN, Edgar C. (1891-1971) Metal. BM49

BAINBRIDGE, John (1582-1643) Astron. DNB

BAINES, John (1787-1838) Math. DNB

BAIRD, John L. (1888-1946) Invent. BDOS BEOS EETD GDSP HOSS MMSB MPIP SAIF

BAIRD, Spencer F. (1823-1887) Zool. BDOS BEOS BIOD BM-3 BWCL CDZZ DAB LACC NC-3 WAMB WFBG ZZ-1

BAIRE, Rene L. (1874-1932) Math. CDZZ ZZ-1

BAIRSTOW, Leonard (1880-1963) Engr. RS11

al-BAIRUNI SEE al-BIRUNI, Abu Rayhan Muhammad

ibn al-BAITAR SEE ibn al-BAYTAR al-MALAQI, Duja al-Din

ibn BAJJA, Abu Bakr Muhammad (d. 1139) Philos. CDZZ ZZ-1

BAKER, Alan (1939-) Math. MHSE

BAKER, Charles F. (1872-1927) Entom. AMEM

BAKER, Charles L. (1939-) Comp. HOPL

BAKER, Edwin M. (1893-1943) Chem. ACCE

BAKER, George (1722-1809) Med. BHMT

BAKER, Henry (1698-1774) Micros. ABET CDZZ DNB ZZ-1

BAKER, Henry F. (1866-1956) Math. DNB7 RS-2

BAKER, Herbert B. (1862-1935) Chem. DNB5

BAKER, Hugh P. (1878-1950) Forest. LACC

BAKER, John C. (1884-1967) Chem. NC55

BAKER, John F. (1901-) Engr. MHSE

BAKER, John G. (1834-1920) Bot. CDZZ ZZ-1

BAKER, John H. (1894-) Cons. CB49 LACC

BAKER, Marcus (1849-1903) Geog.; Math. BIOD

BAKER, Thomas (c.1625-1689) Math. DNB

BAKER, Thomas R. (1837-1930) Nat. Hist.; Chem. NC22

BAKER, William M. (1839-1896) Med. BHMT

BAKER, William O. (1915-) Chem. MHM2 MHSE

BAKER, Wilson (1900-) Chem. COBC

BAKEWELL, Robert (1725-1795) Agr. BDOS BEOS

BAKEWELL, Robert (1768-1843) Geol. CDZZ DNB ZZ-1

BAKH, Aleksei SEE BACH, Aleksei N.

al-BAKRI, Abu Ubayd Abdallah (c.1010-1094) Geog. CDZZ ZZ-1

BAKULEV, Aleksandr N. (1890-) Med. SMST

BALAM, Richard (fl. 1653) Math. DNB

BALANDIN, Aleksey A. (1898-1967) Chem. CDZZ SMST ZZ-1

BALARD, Antoine J. (1802-1876) Chem. ABES ABET BDOS BEOS CDZZ ZZ-1

BALAVIGNUS (fl. c.1300) Med. MMMA

BALBIANI, Edouard G. (1823-1899) Biol. CDZZ ZZ-1

BALBUS (fl. c.100) Math.; Surv. CDZZ ZZ-1

BALDES, Edward J. (1898-1975) Biophys. NC59

BALDI, Bernardino (1553-1617) Phys. CDZZ ZZ-1

BALDWIN, Herbert B. (1864-1939) Chem. NC29

BALDWIN, Laommi (1745-1807) Engr. WAMB YSMS

BALDWIN, Laommi Jr. (1780-1838) Engr. WAMB YSMS

BALDWIN, Matthias W. (1795-1866) Invent. GE-1

BALDWIN, S. Prentiss (1868-1938) Ornith. NC45

BALDWIN, William (1779-1819) Bot. BIOD DAB MABH

BALFOUR, Andrew (1630-1694) Bot. DNB

BALFOUR, Francis M. (1851-1882) Zool. ABET BEOS CDZZ DNB

BALFOUR, Isaac B. (1853-1922) Bot. CDZZ DNB4 ZZ-1

BALFOUR, John H. (1808-1884) Bot. CDZZ ZZ-1

BALIANI, Giovanni B. (1582-1666) Phys. CDZZ ZZ-1

BALKE, Clarence W. (1880-1948) Chem. NC37

al-BALKHI SEE ABU MA SHAR, al-Balkhi

BALL, Charles J. (1846-1901) Invent. MCCW

BALL, Elmer D. (1870-1943) Entom. AMEM NC18

BALL, Eric G. (1904-) Biochem. MHM2 MHSE

BALL, Max W. (1885-1954) Geol. NC44

BALL, Robert S. (1840-1913) Astron. DNB3

BALL, William (d. 1690) Astron. DNB

BALLANTINE, Alexander T. (1836-1901) Invent. MCCW

BALLE, William SEE BALL, William

BALLONIUS SEE BAILLOU, Guillaume de

BALLS, Arnold K. (1891-1966) Biochem. BM41

BALLS, William L. (1882-1960) Bot. RS-7

BALMER, Johann J. (1825-1898) Math.; Phys. ABES ABET BDOS BEOS CDZZ ZZ-1

BALSAMO, Giuseppe (1743-1795) Alch. MSFB

BALTIMORE, David (1938-) Virol. ABET BEOS CB83 DNFH MHSE VACE

BAMBERGER, Eugen (1857-1932) Chem. BEOS CDZZ ZZ-1

BAMFORD, Clement H. (1912-) Chem. COBC

BANACH, Stefan (1892-1945) Math. CDZZ ZZ-1

BANACHIEWICZ, Thaddeus (1882-1954) Astron. CDZZ ZZ-1

BANCROFT, Edward (1744-1921) Chem. ACCE

BANCROFT, Wilder D. (1867-1953) Chem. ACCE CDZZ DAB5 GRCH HSSO NC14 ZZ-1

BANG, Bernhard (1848-1932) Med. BHMT

BANISTER, John (1650-1692) Bot.; Entom. BIOD
   CDZZ DAB MABH ZZ-1

BANKER, Howard J. (1866-1940) Biol. NC30

BANKS, Joseph (1743-1820) Bot. ABES ABET ANHD
   BDOS BEOS CDZZ NATJ NEXB ZZ-1

BANKS, Nathan (1868-1953) Entom. AMEM NC40

BANKS, Theodore R. (1903-1976) Chem. NC60

BANKSIDE, Baron of SEE HINTON, Christopher

ibn al-BANNA al-MARRAKUSHI (1256-1321) Math.
   CDZZ ZZ-1

BANNEKER, Benjamin (1731-1806) Astron.; Math.
   BIOD BPSH DANB HCOK NC-5 SABL SBAH
   SBPY WAMB

BANNERMAN, David (1886-1979) Ornith. DGMT

BANTA, Arthur M. (1877-1946) Zool. NC35

BANTI, Guido (1852-1925) Path. CDZZ ZZ-1

BANTING, Frederick G. (1891-1941) Med. ABES
   ABET BDOS BEOS BHMT CDZZ DNB6 DSLP
   FMBB GDSP ZZ-1

BANU MUSA, Ahmad (fl. 830-870) Math.; Astron.
   CDZZ ZZ-1

BANU MUSA, al-Hasan (fl. 830-870) Math.; Astron.
   CDZZ ZZ-1

BANU MUSA, Muhammad (fl. 830-870) Math.;
   Astron. CDZZ ZZ-1

BARANSKII, Nikolai N. (1881-1963) Geog. SMST

BARANY, Robert (1876-1936) Med. ABET BDOS
   BEOS BHMT CDZZ PAW2 ZZ-1

BARANZANO, Giovanni A. (1590-1622) Astron.
   CDZZ ZZ-1

BARBA, Alvaro A. (1569-c.1640) Metal. CDZZ ZZ-1

BARBER, George W. (1890-1948) Entom. AMEM

BARBER, Harry G. (1871-1960) Entom. AMEM

BARBER, Herbert S. (1882-1950) Entom. AMEM

BARBER, Horace N. (1914-1971) Bot. RS18

BARBIER, Joseph E. (1839-1889) Math.; Astron.
   CDZZ ZZ-1

BARBOUR, Henry G. (1885-1943) Physiol. CDZZ
   ZZ-1

BARBOUR, Thomas (1884-1946) Zool. BM27 DAB4

BARCHUSEN, Johann C. (1666-1723) Chem. CDZZ
   ZZ-1

BARCLAY, John (1758-1826) Anat. CDZZ ZZ-1

BARCROFT, Joseph (1872-1947) Physiol. BDOS
   BEOS BHMT CDZZ DNB6 ZZ-1

BARD, Philip (1898-) Physiol. NCSM

BARD, Samuel (1742-1821) Med. ACCE BHMT

BARDEEN, John (1908-) Phys. ABES ABET BEOS
   CB57 MHM1 MHSE POSW TINA TPAE WAMB

BARGER, George (1878-1939) Chem. BDOS BEOS
   CDZZ DNB5 ZZXV

BARGHOORN, Elso S. (1915-1984) Paleon. ABET

BARHAM, Henry (c.1670-1726) Nat. Hist. DNB

BARKENBUS, Charles (1894-1959) Chem. NC50

BARKER, Franklin D. (1877-1936) Zool. NC27

BARKER, George F. (1835-1910) Chem. ACCE DAB
   NC-4

BARKER, Horace A. (1907-) Biochem. MHM2 MHSE

BARKER, John (1901-1970) Bot. RS18

BARKER, Thomas (1722-1809) Sci. Writ. DNB

BARKHAISEN, Johann SEE BARCHUSEN, Johann C.

BARKHAUSEN, Heinrich G. (1881-1956) Elec.Engr.
   ABES ABET BEOD CDZZ ZZ-1

BARKLA, Charles G. (1877-1944) Phys. ABES ABET
   BDOS BEOS CDZZ DNB6 POSW ZZ-1

BARLOW, Edward (1639-1719) Invent. DNB

BARLOW, Francis (1626-1702) Nat. Hist. ANHD

BARLOW, Peter (1776-1862) Math.; Phys. CDZZ DNB GE-1 ZZ-1

BARLOW, William (1845-1934) Crystal. CDZZ ZZ-1

BARNARD, Christiaan N. (1922-) Med. ABES ABET BEOS CB68 MFIR SAIF

BARNARD, Daniel P. IV (1898-1976) Engr. NC58

BARNARD, Edward E. (1857-1923) Astron. ABES ABET BEOS CDZZ DAB IEAS NC-7 SLOR WAMB ZZ-1

BARNARD, Frederick A. (1809-1889) Math.; Astron. BIOD BM20

BARNARD, John G. (1815-1882) Engr.; Phys. BIOD BM-5

BARNARD, Joseph E. (1870-1949) Opt.; Micros. BDOS BEOS

BARNARD, William S. (1849-1887) Nat. Hist. NC12

BARNES, Arthur H. (1904-1957) Phys. NC47

BARNES, Charles R. (1858-1910) Bot. DAB MABH NC13

BARNES, Robert P. (1898-) Chem. SBPY

BARNES, Will C. (1858-1936) Cons. LACC

BARNES, William (1860-1930) Entom. AMEM

BARNES, Willis L. (1840-1922) Astron. NC20

BARNETT, Harold M. (1903-1956) Chem. NC45

BARNHART, John H. (1871-1949) Bot. NC38

BAROCIUS, Franciscus (1537-1604) Math.; Astron. CDZZ ZZ-1

BAROZZI, Franciscus SEE BAROCIUS, Franciscus

BARR, Lloyd S. (1899-1970) Nat. Hist. NC56

BARR, Murray L. (1908-) Anat. MHM1 MHSE

BARRABAND, Jacques (1768-1809) Nat. Hist. ANHD

BARRANDE, Joachim (1799-1883) Paleon. CDZZ PHLS ZZ-1

BARRE DE ST. VENANT SEE SAINT-VENANT, Adhemar J. de

BARRELL, Joseph (1869-1919) Geol. BM12 CDZZ ZZ-1

BARRER, Richard M. (1910-) Chem. COBC

BARRESWIL, Charles L. (1817-1870) Chem. CDZZ ZZ-1

BARRETT, Jack W. (1912-) Chem. COBC

BARRETT, Storrs B. (1864-1937) Astron. NC28

BARRINGER, Daniel M. (1860-1929) Geol. ABES ABET BEOS

BARRINGER, Emily D. (1876-1961) Med. WIWM

BARROIS, Charles (1851-1939) Geol.; Paleon. CDZZ ZZ-1

BARROW, Isaac (1630-1677) Math.; Opt. BDOS BEOS CDZZ ZZ-1

BARROW, John (1764-1848) Exp. WFBG

BARRY, David (1780-1835) Med. DNB

BARRY, Edward H. (1894-1976) Engr. NC59

BARRY, James SEE STUART, Miranda

BARRY, Martin (1802-1855) Embryol. CDZZ ZZ-1

BARSCHALL, Henry H. (1915-) Phys. MHSE

BARSKI, Georges (1909-) Biol. MHSE

BARTELL, Floyd E. (1883-1961) Chem. NC49

BARTELMEZ, George W. (1885-1967) Anat. BM43

BARTELS, Julius (1899-1964) Geophys. CDZZ MHM1 MHSE ZZ-1

BARTHEL, Oliver E. (1877-1969) Engr. NC55

BARTHEZ, Paul J. (1734-1806) Physiol. CDZZ ZZ-1

BARTHOLIN, Caspar (1585-1629) Anat. BHMT CDZZ ZZ-1

BARTHOLIN, Erasmus (1625-1698) Math.; Phys. ABES ABET BDOS BEOS CDZZ ZZ-1

BARTHOLIN, Thomas (1616-1680) Anat. BHMT
CDZZ ZZ-1

BARTHOLOMEW, Elam (1852-1934) Bot. MABH

BARTLETT, Frederic C. (1886-1969) Psych. MHM2
MHSE RS16

BARTLETT, Neil (1932-) Chem. ABES ABET BEOS
MHM2 MHSE

BARTLETT, Paul D. (1907-) Chem. BEOS MHM1
MHSE

BARTLETT, William H. (1804-1893) Math. BIOD
BM-7 DAB1

BARTLEY, Arthur M. (1891-) Cons. NCSJ

BARTOLI, Daniello (1608-1685) Phys. CDZZ ZZ-1

BARTOLOMEO DA VARIGNANA (c.1260-1321) Med.
TALS

BARTOLOTTI, Gian G. (c.1470-1530) Med. CDZZ
ZZ-1

BARTON, Benjamin S. (1766-1815) Bot.; Zool. BIOD
CDZZ DAB NC-8 MABH ZZ-1

BARTON, Derek H. (1918-) Chem. ABET BEOS
COBC MHM1 MHSE

BARTON, Donald C. (1889-1939) Geol. NC40

BARTON, William P. (1786-1856) Bot.; Med. BIOD
DAB NC13

BARTOW, Edward (1870-1958) Chem. ACCE NC48

BARTRAM, John (1699-1777) Bot. BIOD CDZZ DAB
EAFC FIFE GANC IPNW LHES MABH NC-7
NHAH PAW1 SBCS WAMB ZZ-1

BARTRAM, William (1739-1823) Bot.; Ornith.
BIOD BWCL CDZZ DAB EAFC FIFE GANC
HAOA LHES NC-7 NEXB NHAH WAMB WFBG
ZZ-1

BARUS, Carl (1856-1935) Phys. BM22 CDZZ DAB1
NC26 QPAS ZZ-1

BARY, Heinrichde SEE DE BARY, (Heinrich) Anton

BASCOM, Florence (1862-1945) Geol. DAB3 NAW

BASCOM, Willard (1916-) Mng.; Ocean. EXDC
EXSG PBTS

BASEDOW, Karl A. von (1799-1854) Med. BHMT

BASHKIROV, Andrei N. (1903-) Chem. SMST

BASIL VALENTINE SEE VALENTINE, Basil

BASKERVILLE, Charles (1870-1922) Chem. Engr.
ACCE DAB

BASOLO, Fred (1920-) Chem. MHSE

BASOV, Nicolai G. (1922-) Phys. ABES ABET BEOS
MHM1 MHSE POSW SMST

BASSANI, Francesco (1853-1916) Paleon. CDZZ
ZZ-1

BASSI, Agostino (1773-1856) Agr. BDOS BEOS
CDZZ ZZ-1

BASSI, Laura (1711-1778) Phys. IDWB

BASSINI, Edoardo (1844-1924) Med.; Anat. BHMT

BASSLER, Raymond S. (1878-1961) Geol.; Paleon.
CDZZ NC49 ZZ-1

BASSO, Sebastian (fl. c.1575) Nat. Philos. CDZZ
ZZ-1

BASTIAN, Adolf (1825-1905) Anthro. EOMH

BASTIAN, Henry C. (1837-1915) Bact. CDZZ ZZ-1

BATAILLON, Jean E. (1864-1953) Biol.; Zool. CDZZ
ZZ-1

BATCHELOR, George K. (1920-) Math. MHM2
MHSE

BATE, Henry SEE HENRY BATE OF MALINES

BATEMAN, Harry (1882-1946) Math. BM25 CDZZ
DAB4 ZZ-1

BATEMAN, Thomas (1778-1821) Med. BHMT

BATES, Carlos G. (1885-1949) Forest. LACC

BATES, David R. (1916-) Phys. MHSE

BATES, Henry W. (1825-1892) Nat. Hist. ABET BDOS
BEOS CDZZ DNB1 NATJ ZZ-1

BATES, Leslie F. (1897-1978) Phys. BEOS MHM2
MHSE

BATES, Marston (1906-) Zool. CB56

BATES, Roger G. (1912-) Chem. MHSE

BATES, William H. (1860-1926) Med. PAW1

BATESON, Gregory (1904-1980) Anthro. AO80

BATESON, William (1861-1926) Genet. ABES ABET BDOS BEOS CDZZ DNB4 HLSM ZZ-1

BATHER, Francis A. (1863-1934) Paleon. CDZZ ZZ-1

al-BATTANI, Abu abd Allah Muhammad (fl. 877-901) Astron.; Math. ABET BEOS CDZZ IEAS ZZ-1

BATTERSBY, Alan R. (1925-) Chem. COBC MHSE

BATTLEY, Richard (1770-1856) Chem. DNB

ibn BATTUTA (1304-1368/69) Exp. CDZZ ZZ-1

BAUDRIMONT, Alexandre E. (1806-1880) Chem.; Physiol. CDZZ ZZ-1

BAUER, Alfred F. (1906-1974) Engr. NC59

BAUER, Edmond (1880-1963) Phys.; Chem. CDZZ ZZ-1

BAUER, Franz A. (1758-1840) Micros. CDZZ ZZ-1

BAUER, Georg SEE AGRICOLA, Georgius

BAUER, Louis A. (1865-1932) Geophys. CDZZ DAB1 ZZ-1

BAUER, Norman (1915-1960) Chem. NC48

BAUER, Paul S. (1904-1977) Geol.; Ocean. NC59

BAUERMAN, Hilary (1835-1909) Mineral.; Geol. DNB2

BAUHIN, Gaspard (1560-1624) Anat.; Bot. CDZZ ZZ-1

BAUHIN, Jean (1541-1613) Bot. CDZZ ZZ-1

BAUMANN, Eugen (1846-1896) Chem. ABES ABET

BAUME, Antoine (1728-1804) Chem. CDZZ ZZ-1

BAUMHAUER, Edouard H. von (1820-1885) Chem. CDZZ ZZ-1

BAUMHAUER, Heinrich A. (1848-1926) Chem.; Mineral. CDZZ ZZ-1

BAWDEN, Frederick C. (1908-1972) Bot. ABES ABET BEOS RS19

BAWN, Cecil E. (1908-) Chem. COBC

BAXENDELL, Joseph (1815-1887) Meteor.; Astron. DNB1

BAXTER, Dow V. (1898-1965) Forest. NC53

BAXTER, Florus R. (1857-1944) Chem. NC34

BAXTER, Gregory P. (1876-1953) Chem. NC52

BAXTER, William (c.1787-1871) Bot. DNB

BAYEN, Pierre (1725-1798) Chem. CDZZ ZZ-1

BAYER, Johann (1572-1625) Astron. ABES ABET BEOS CDZZ IEAS ZZ-1

BAYES, Thomas (1702-1761) Math. CDZZ ZZ-1

BAYLAK al-QIBJAQI (fl. c.1250) Mineral. CDZZ ZZ-1

BAYLE, Gaspard L. (1744-1816) Med. BHMT

BAYLEY, Richard (1745-1801) Med. BHMT

BAYLIS, Edward (1791-1861) Math. DNB

BAYLISS, Leonard E. (1900-1964) Physiol. CDZZ ZZ-1

BAYLISS, William M. (1860-1924) Physiol. ABES ABET BDOS BEOS CDZZ DNB4 ZZ-1

BAYLY, William (1737-1810) Astron. DNB

BAYMA, Joseph (1816-1892) Math.; Phys. BIOD DAB NC17

BAYNE-JONES, Stanhope (1888-1970) Bact. NC55 NCSD

ibn al-BAYTAR al-MALAQI, Duja al-Din (c.1190-1248) Pharm.; Bot. CDZZ ZZ-1

BAZALGETTE, Joseph W. (1819-1891) Engr. BDOS

BEACH, Frank A. (1911-) Psych. MHM1 MHSE

BEADLE, George W. (1903-) Genet. ABES ABET BEOS CB56 MHM1 MHSE PAW2 PBTS WAMB

BEAL, George D. (1887-) Chem. NCSG

BEAL, William J. (1833-1924) Bot. DAB MABH NC11

BEALE, Lionel S. (1828-1906) Micros. CDZZ ZZ-1

BEALS, Carlyle S. (1899-1979) Astron. RS27

BEALS, Edward A. (1855-1931) Meteor. NC24

BEAMER, Raymond H. (1889-1957) Entom. AMEM

BEAMS, Jesse W. (1898-1977) Phys. MHM2 MHSE NCSI

BEAN, Alan L. (1932-) Astronaut. IEAS

BEAN, Ernest F. (1882-1961) Geol. NC49

BEAN, Tarleton H. (1846-1916) Ichth. DAB NC24

BEAR, Firman E. (1884-1968) Cons. LACC

BEARD, Andrew (1849-1921) Invent. SABL

BEATH, John M. (1825-1916) Engr. MCCW

BEAUFORT, Francis (1774-1857) Hydrol. BEOS

BEAUFOY, Mark (1764-1827) Astron.; Phys. DNB

BEAUGRAND, Jean (c.1595-c.1640) Math. CDZZ ZZ-1

BEAUMONT, Elie de SEE ELIE DE BEAUMONT, Jean B.

BEAUMONT, William (1785-1853) Physiol. ABES ABET BDOS BEOS BHMT BIOD CDZZ HIUE LISD MMMA TOWS ZZ-1

BECCARI, Nello (1883-1957) Anat. CDZZ ZZ-1

BECCARIA, Giambatista (1716-1781) Phts. CDZZ ZZ-1

BECHAMP, Pierre J. (1816-1908) Chem.; Biochem. CDZZ ZZXV

BECHE, Henry de la SEE DE LA BECHE, Henry T.

BECHER, Johann J. (1635-1683) Chem. ABES ABET BDOS BEOS CDZZ CSCJ HLSM HSSO ZZ-1

BECHEREAU, Louis (1880-1970) Aero. ICFW

BECK, Louis C. (1798-1853) Med.; Chem. ACCE ASJD BIOD DAB

BECKE, Friedrich J. (1855-1931) Mineral. CDZZ ZZ-1

BECKER, George F. (1847-1919) Geol. CDZZ DAB GKGP WAMB ZZ-1

BECKER, John V. (1913-) Aero. ICFW

BECKER, Victor H. (1852-1912) Engr. MCCW

BECKET, Frederick M. (1875-1942) Electrochem.; Metal. ACCE

BECKMANN, Ernst O. (1853-1923) Chem. BDOS BEOS CDZZ HSSO ZZ-1

BECKMANN, Johann (1739-1811) Nat. Hist.; Mng. CDZZ ZZ-1

BECKWITH, Edward P. (1877-1966) Chem.; Engr. NC52

BECQUEREL, Alexandre E. (1820-1891) Phys. ABET CDZZ ZZ-1

BECQUEREL, Antoine C. (1788-1878) Electrochem. CDZZ ZZ-1

BECQUEREL, (Antoine) Henri (1852-1908) Phys. ABES ABET BDOS BEOS CDZZ DCPW EETD GASJ HOSS POSW SAIF TPOS ZZ-1

BECQUEREL, Paul (1879-1955) Biol. CDZZ ZZ-1

BEDDOE, John (1826-1911) Anthro. CDZZ ZZ-1

BEDDOES, Thomas (1760-1808) Med.; Chem. BDOS BEOS CDZZ ZZ-1

BEDE (673-735) Philos. ABES ABET CDZZ DNB ZZ-1

BEDELL, Frederick (1868-1958) Phys. NC51

BEDFORD, Clayton W. (1885-1922) Chem. ACCE

BEDSON, Samuel P. (1886-1969) Bact. RS16

BEEBE, B. Warren (1913-) Geol. NCSL

BEEBE, Charles W. (1877-1962) Zool.; Ocean. ABES ABET BDOS BEOS CB41 EXDC NC47 NCSA SFNB WAMB

BEECHER, Charles E. (1856-1904) Paleon. BIOD BM-6 DAB NC13

BEECHING, Richard (1913-) Phys. CB63

BEECKMAN, Isaac (1588-1637) Phys. CDZZ ZZ-1

BEER, Gavin de SEE DE BEER, Gavin R.

BEER, Wilhelm (1797-1850) Astron. ABES ABET BEOS CDZZ ZZ-1

BEEVOR, Charles E. (1854-1908) Med. CDZZ ZZ-1

BEGHIN, Henri (1876-1969) Phys. CDZZ ZZ-1

BEGUIN, Jean (c.1550-c.1620) Chem. CDZZ GRCH ZZ-1

BEGUYER DE CHANCOURTOIS, Alexandre E. (1820-1886) Geol. ABES ABET

BEHAIM, Martin (1459-1507) Geog. CDZZ ZZ-1

BEHR, Hans H. (1818-1904) Entom. AMEM BIOD

BEHREND, Anton F. (1856-1926) Chem. CDZZ ZZXV

BEHREND, Bernard A. (1875-1932) Elec. Engr. NC35 TPAE

BEHRING, Emil A. von (1854-1917) Med. ABES ABET BDOS BEOS BHMT CDZZ MAMR PAW2 ZZ-1

BEIJERINCK, Martinus W. (1851-1931) Microbiol. ABES ABET BHMT CDZZ TMSB ZZXV

BEILBY, George T. (1850-1924) Chem. BDOS BEOS DNB4

BEILSTEIN, Friedrich K. (1838-1906) Chem. ABES ABET BDOS BEOS CDZZ ZZ-1

BEKESY, Georg von (1889-1972) Phys. ABES ABET BEOS BM48 CB62 MHM1 MHSE WAMB

BEKETOV, Nikolai N. (1827-1911) Chem. CDZZ ZZ-1

BEKHTEREV, Vladimir M. (1857-1927) Psych. CDZZ ZZ-1

BEL, Joseph A. SEE LE BEL, Joseph A.

BELAIEW, Nicholas SEE BELIAEV, Nikolai

BELCHER, Ronald (1909-) Chem. COBC

BELDING, David L. (1884-1970) Biol. LACC

BELEHRADEK, Jan (1896-1980) Biol. AO80

BELIAEV, Nikolai (1878-1955) Metal. CDZZ ZZ-1

BELIDOR, Bernard F. de (1693-1761) Phys. BDOS CDZZ GE-1 ZZ-1

BELL, Alexander G. (1847-1922) Invent. ABES ABET AMIH ASIW BDOS BEOS BM23 CDZZ COAC DNB4 EETD FOIF HFGA HOSS IHMV INYG SAIF SMIL TECH TINA TPAE WAMB ZZ-1

BELL, Charles (1774-1842) Anat. BDOS BEOS BHMT CDZZ MMMA ZZ-1

BELL, Eric T. (1883-1960) Math. CDZZ NC54 ZZ-1

BELL, Ernest L. (1876-1964) Entom. AMEM

BELL, Henry (1766-1830) Invent. GE-1

BELL, Isaac L. (1816-1904) Metal. DNB2

BELL, James (1824-1908) Chem. DNB2

BELL, (Susan) Jocelyn B. (1943-) Astron. BEOS

BELL, John (1763-1820) Anat. BHMT

BELL, John G. (1812-1889) Nat. Hist. WFBG

BELL, Louis (1864-1923) Phys.; Engr. DAB

BELL, Patrick (1799-1969) Invent. BDOS DNB

BELL, Robert (1841-1917) Geol. CDZZ ZZ-1

BELL, Ronald P. (1907-) Chem. COBC

BELL, Thomas (1792-1880) Nat. Hist. ANHD DNB

BELLANCA, Giuseppe M. (1886-1960) Aero. NC52

BELLANI, Angelo (1776-1852) Phys.; Chem. CDZZ ZZ-1

BELLARDI, Luigi (1818-1889) Paleon.; Entom. CDZZ ZZ-1

BELLARMINE, Robert (1542-1621) Philos. CDZZ ZZ-1

BELLAVITIS, Giusto (1803-1880) Math. CDZZ ZZ-1

BELLEVAL, Pierre R. de (c.1564-1632) Med. CDZZ ZZ-1

BELLINGSHAUSEN, Fabian SEE BELLINSGAUZEN, Faddei F.

BELLINI, Lorenzo (1643-1704) Physiol. CDZZ ZZ-1

BELLINSGAUZEN, Faddei F. (1779-1852) Ocean. ABET CDZZ ZZ-1

BELLMAN, Richard (1920-) Math. MHSE

BELON, Pierre (1517-1564) Zool.; Bot. ABES ABET ANHD BDOS BEOS BMST CDZZ HAOA NATJ ORNS ZZ-1

BELOPOLSKY, Aristarkh A. (1854-1934) Astrophys. CDZZ ZZ-1

BELOUSOV, Vladimir V. (1907-) Geol. BEOS SMST

BELOV, Nikolai V. (1891-) Crystal. SMST

BELOZERSKY, Andrei N. (1905-1973) Biochem. MHM2 MHSE SMST

BELT, Thomas (1832-1878) Geol. DNB

BELTRAMI, Eugenio (1835-1900) Math. CDZZ ZZ-1

BELYAYEV, Anatoli I. (1906-1967) Metal. SMST

BELYAYEV, Pavel (1925-1970) Astronaut. CB65 IEAS

BENACERRAF, Baruj (1920-) Immunol. ABET AMJB BEOS MHSE

BENCHLEY, Belle J. (1882-) Vet. Med. CB40 WAGW

BENDER, Karl SEE BENDIRE, Charles E.

BENDER, Lauretta (1897-) Med.; Psychiat. MFIR

BENDIRE, Charles E. (1836-1897) Ornith. BWCL WFBG

BENDIX, Vincent (1882-1945) Invent. WAMB

BENEDEN, Edouard van (1846-1910) Zool. ABES ABET BDOS BEOS CDZZ ZZ-1

BENEDEN, Pierre J. van (1809-1894) Zool. CDZZ ZZ-1

BENEDETTI, Alessandro (c.1450-1512) Anat. CDZZ ZZ-1

BENEDETTI, Giovanni B. (1530-1590) Math.; Phys. BMST CDZZ ZZ-1

BENEDETTI-PICHLER, Anton A. (1894-1964) Chem. ACCE

BENEDICKS, Carl A. (1875-1958) Metal. CDZZ ZZ-1

BENEDICT, Francis G. (1870-1957) Chem. ACCE BM32 CDZZ ZZ-1

BENEDICT, Manson (1907-) Engr. MHM1 MHSE

BENEDICT, Ruth F. (1887-1948) Anthro. CB41 DAB4 NAW NC36 WAMB

BENEDICT, Stanley R. (1884-1936) Biochem. ACCE BM27 DAB2

BENEDICT, Wayne L. (1906-1971) Chem. NC56

BENIOFF, Victor Hugo (1899-1968) Seism. BM43 MHM1 MHSE NC54

BENIVIENI, Antonio (1443-1502) Anat. CDZZ ZZ-1

BENJAMIN, Foster H. (1895-1936) Entom. AMEM

BENNET, Abraham (1750-1799) Elec. Sci. BDOS BEOS

BENNET-CLARK, Thomas A. (1903-1975) Biol.; Bot. RS23

BENNETT, Alfred W. (1833-1902) Bot. DNB2

BENNETT, Edward T. (1797-1836) Zool. DNB

BENNETT, George M. (1892-1959) Chem. DNB7 RS-5

BENNETT, H. Stanley (1910-) Biol.; Med. CB66

BENNETT, Hugh H. (1881-1960) Cons. LACC

BENNETT, John H. (1812-1875) Med. BHMT DNB

BENNETT, John J. (1801-1876) Bot. DNB

BENNETT, Logan J. (1907-1957) Biol.; Cons. LACC NC47

BENOIT, Justin M. (1844-1922) Phys. CDZZ ZZ-1

BENSLEY, Robert R. (1867-1956) Anat. CDZZ ZZ-1

BENSON, Arthur R. (1896-) Cons. LACC

BENSON, William N. (1885-1957) Geol. RS-4

BENT, Arthur C. (1866-1954) Ornith. BWCL

BENT, Silas (1820-1887) Ocean. BIOD ZZ-1

BENTHAM, George (1800-1884) Bot. BDOS BEOS CDZZ DNB ZZ-1

BENTLEY, Robert (1821-1893) Bot. DNB1

BENTLEY, WILSON A. (1865-1931) Meteor. DAB1 NC23

BENTON, Linn B. (1844-1932) Invent. NCSA

BENZ, Karl (1844-1929) Engr. BDOS BEOS ICFW MPIP SAIF

BENZENBERG, Johann F. (1777-1846) Astron.; Phys. CDZZ ZZ-1

BENZER, Seymour (1921-) Biol. BEOS MHM2 MHSE

BERANEK, Leo L. (1914-) Phys. CB63 MHSE NCSM

BERARD, Jacques E. (1789-1869) Chem. CDZZ SOAC ZZ-1

BERARD, Joseph F. (1789-1828) Med. CDZZ ZZ-1

BERBERIAN, Dicran A. (1903-) Bact. NCSJ

BERENGARIO DA CARPI, Giacomo (c.1460-1530) Med. CDZZ ZZ-1

BERG, Aksel I. (1893-) Engr. SMST

BERG, Clifford O. (1912-) Biol. CHUB

BERG, Ernst J. (1871-1941) Phys. NC35

BERG, Lev S. (1876-1950) Geog.; Ichth. CDZZ ZZ-1

BERG, Paul (1926-) Biochem. ABET AMJB BEOS MHM2 MHSE

BERGEL, Franz (1900-) Chem. COBC

BERGER, Hans (1873-1941) Psychiat. ABES ABET BDOS BEOS CDZZ ZZ-2

BERGER, Johann G. (1659-1736) Physiol. CDZZ ZZ-2

BERGERON, Tor H. (1891-) Meteor. BEOS

BERGEY, David H. (1860-1937) Bact. NC28

BERGIUS, Friedrich K. (1884-1949) Chem. ABES ABET BDOS BEOS CDZZ NPWC ZZ-2

BERGMAN, Torbern O. (1735-1784) Chem.; Phys. ABES ABET BDOS BEOS CDZZ THOG ZZ-2

BERGMANN, Max (1886-1944) Biochem. ACCE BEOS CDZZ DAB3 ZZXV

BERGMANN, Werner (1904-1959) Chem. NC48

BERGSON, Henri L. (1859-1941) Philos. CDZZ ZZ-2

BERGSTROM, Sune (1916-) Biochem. BEOS

BERIGARD, Claude G. de (c.1578-1664) Med.; Phys. CDZZ ZZ-2

BERING, Vitus (1681-1741) Geog. ABET CDZZ ZZ-2

BERINGER, Johann B. (c.1667-1740) Med.; Nat. Hist. BEOS CDZZ PHLS ZZ-2

BERKELEY, George (1685-1753) Philos. of Sci. CDZZ ZZ-2

BERKELEY, Miles J. (1803-1889) Bot.; Zool. CDZZ ZZ-2

BERKELEY, Randal M. (1865-1942) Chem. DNB6

BERKEY, Charles P. (1867-1955) Geol. BM30 NC46

BERKMAN, Boris (1893-) Med. NCSG

BERKNER, Lloyd V. (1905-1967) Phys.; Engr. CB49 MHM2 MHSE

BERLINER, Emile (1851-1929) Invent. ABES ABET AMIH WAMB

BERNAL, John D. (1901-1971) Phys. BEOS CDZZ MHM2 MHSE RS26 ZZXV

BERNARD OF CHARTRES (d. c.1130) Philos. CDZZ ZZ-2

BERNARD OF LE TREILLE (c.1240-1292) Astron.; Philos. CDZZ ZZ-2

BERNARD OF TREVISAN (fl. c.1378) Alch. CDZZ ZZ-2

BERNARD OF VERDUN (fl. c.1275) Astron. CDZZ ZZ-1

BERNARD, Claude (1813-1878) Physiol. ABES ABET BDOS BEOS BHMT CDZZ HLSM ZZ-2

BERNARD, Noel (1874-1911) Bot. CDZZ ZZ-2

BERNARD SILVESTRE (fl. 1150) Philos. ZZ-2

BERNAYS, Albert J. (1823-1892) Chem. DNB1

BERNER, Robert A. (1935-) Geol.; Ocean. MHSE

BERNHEIM, Hippolyte (1840-1919) Psych. CDZZ ZZ-2

BERNOULLI, Daniel (1700-1792) Math.; Phys. ABES ABET BDOS BEOS CDZZ DCPW FNEC GE-1 ICFW SMIL ZZ-2

BERNOULLI, Jacques (1654-1705) Math.; Astron. BDOS BEOS CDZZ ZZ-2

BERNOULLI, Jacques II (1759-1789) Math. CDZZ ZZ-2

BERNOULLI, Jean (1667-1748) Math. BDOS BEOS CDZZ ZZ-2

BERNOULLI, Nikolaus I (1687-1759) Math. CDZZ ZZ-2

BERNOULLI, Nikolaus II (1695-1726) Math. CDZZ ZZ-2

BERNSHTEYN, Sergei SEE BERNSTEIN, Sergey N.

BERNSTEIN, Benjamin A. (1881-1964) Math. NC51

BERNSTEIN, Felix (1878-1956) Math. CDZZ ZZ-2

BERNSTEIN, Julius (1839-1917) Physiol. CDZZ ZZXV

BERNSTEIN, Sergey N. (1880-1968) Math. CDZZ SMST ZZXV

BERNTHSEN, Heinrich A. (1855-1931) Chem. CDZZ HSSO ZZ-2

BERRY, Charles A. (1923-) Med. CB69

BERRY, Edward R. (1879-1934) Chem.; Elec. Engr. NC26

BERRY, Edward W. (1875-1945) Paleon. BM45 DAB3 FHUA NC33

BERRY, Leonidas H. (1902-) Med. BISC

BERS, Lipman (1914-) Math. MHM1 MHSE

BERSON, Jerome A. (1924-) Chem. MHSE

BERT, Paul (1833-1886) Physiol.; Nat. Hist. ABES ABET BDOS BEOS BHMT ZZ-2

BERTHELOT, Pierre E. (1827-1907) Chem. ABES ABET BDOS BEOS CDZZ GASJ GRCH HSSO ZZ-2

BERTHIER, Pierre (1782-1861) Mineral. CDZZ ZZ-2

BERTHOLD, Arnold A. (1803-1861) Physiol. CDZZ ZZ-2

BERTHOLLET, Amedee B. (1780-1810) Chem. SOAC

BERTHOLLET, Claude L. (1748-1822) Chem. ABES ABET BDOS BEOS CDZZ GRCH SOAC ZZ-2

BERTHOLON, Pierre (1741-1800) Phys. CDZZ ZZ-2

BERTHOUD, Ferdinand (1727-1807) Instr. BDOS

BERTI, Gasparo (c.1600-1643) Phys.; Astron. CDZZ ZZ-2

BERTILLON, Alphonse (1853-1914) Forens. Sci. SAIF

BERTIN, Louis E. (1840-1924) Engr. CDZZ ZZ-2

BERTINI, Eugenio (1846-1933) Math. CDZZ ZZ-2

BERTRAND, Charles E. (1851-1917) Bot. CDZZ FHUA ZZ-2

BERTRAND, Gabriel (1867-1962) Biochem. CDZZ ZZ-2

BERTRAND, Joseph L. (1822-1900) Math. CDZZ ZZ-2

BERTRAND, Marcel A. (1847-1907) Geol. CDZZ ZZ-2

BERTRAND, Paul (1879-1944) Bot. FHUA

BERWICK, William E. (1888-1944) Math. CDZZ ZZ-2

BERZELIUS, Jons J. (1779-1848) Chem. ABES ABET BDOS BEOS BHMT CDZZ CSCJ EETD ENCE GRCH HOSS HSSO TOWS ZZ-2

BESICOVITCH, Abram S. (1891-1970) Math. BEOS MHM1 MHSE RS17

BESLEY, Fred W. (1872-1960) Forest. LACC

BESSEL, Friedrich W. (1784-1846) Astron. ABES ABET BDOS BEOS CDZZ IEAS ZZ-2

BESSEMER, Henry (1813-1898) Invent. ABES ABET BDOS BEOS CDZZ DNB1 FNEC FOIF INYG OGML SAIF ZZXV

BESSEY, Charles E. (1845-1915) Bot. DAB MABH NC-8 CDZZ ZZ-2

BESSON, Jacques (c.1530-c.1573) Math.; Engr. GE-1

BEST, Charles H. (1899-1978) Physiol. ABES ABET BEOS CB57 MHM1 MHSE RS28

BETANCOURT Y MOLINA, Augustin de (1758-1824) Phys.; Engr. CDZZ ZZ-2

BETHE, Hans A. (1906-) Phys. ABES ABET BEOS CB40 CB50 DCPW GJPS IEAS MHM1 MHSE NCSI POSW PPEY PPTY WAMB

BETHUNE, Charles J. (1838-1932) Entom. AMEM

BETTI, Enrico (1823-1892) Math. CDZZ ZZ-2

BEUDANT, Francois S. (1787-1850) Mineral.; Geol. CDZZ ZZ-2

BEVAN, Edward J. (1856-1921) Chem. BDOS BEOS

BEVANS, John (1693-1771) Astron. DNB

BEVIER, George M. (1888-1972) Geol. NC58

BEVILACQUA, Edward M. (1920-1968) Chem. ACCE

BEVIS, John SEE BEVANS, John

BEWICK, Thomas (1753-1828) Nat. Hist. ANHD WFBG

BEXON, Gabriel L. (1747-1784) Biol. CDZZ ZZ-2

BEYER, Samuel W. (1865-1931) Geol. NC40

BEYRICH, Heinrich E. (1815-1896) Geol.; Paleon. CDZZ ZZ-2

BEZOLD, Albert von (1836-1868) Physiol. CDZZ ZZ-2

BEZOUT, Etienne (1739-1783) Math. CDZZ ZZ-2

BHABHA, Homi J. (1909-1966) Phys. BDOS CB56 CDZZ NBPS RS13 ZZXV

BHASKARA I (fl. 629) Astron. CDZZ ZZ-2

BHASKARA II (b. 1115) Astron.; Math. CDZZ OGIV ZZ-2

BHATNAGAR, Shanti S. (1894-1955) Chem. RS-8

BIAGGIO PELICANI SEE BLASIUS OF PARMA

BIALOBRZESKI, Czeslaw (1878-1953) Phys. CDZZ ZZ-2

BIANCHI, Luigi (1856-1928) Math. CDZZ ZZ-2

BICHAT, M. F. Xavier (1771-1802) Med.; Anat. ABES ABET BDOS BEOS BHMT CDZZ HLSM ZZ-2

BICHKOWSKY, F. Russell (1889-1951) Chem. NC39

BICKERTON, Alexander W. (1842-1929) Cosmol. CDZZ ZZ-2

BICKFORD, William (1774-1834) Invent. BDOS

BICKLEY, Everett H. (1888-1972) Invent. NC60

BICKMORE, Albert S. (1839-1914) Nat. Hist. NC-8

BIDDER, Friedrich H. (1810-1894) Anat.; Physiol. CDZZ ZZ-2

BIDDER, George P. (1863-1953) Mar. Biol. DNB7

BIDDLE, Owen (1737-1799) Astron. BIOD

BIDLOO, Govard (1649-1713) Anat.; Biol. CDZZ ZZXV

BIELA, Wilhelm von (1784-1856) Astron. ABES ABET BEOS CDZZ ZZ-2

BIENAYME, Irenee J. (1796-1878) Math. CDZZ ZZXV

BIENEWITZ, Peter SEE APIAN, Peter

BIERMANN, Ludwig F. (1907-) Astrophys. MHSE

BIESTERFIELD, J.H. SEE BISTERFELD, Johann

BIFFEN, Rowland H. (1894-1949) Genet. BDOS BEOS
DNB6

BIGELEISEN, Jacob (1919-) Chem. MHM1 MHSE

BIGELOW, Edward F. (1860-1938) Nat. Hist. NC29

BIGELOW, Erastus B. (1814-1879) Invent. BDOS
WAMB

BIGELOW, Frank H. (1851-1924) Astron. DAB NC10

BIGELOW, Henry B. (1879-1967) Zool. BM48

BIGELOW, Henry J. (1818-1890) Med. BHMT

BIGELOW, Jacob (1786-1879) Bot.; Med. BIOD DAB
MABH WAMB

BIGELOW, Maurice A. (1872-1955) Biol. NC15 NC44

BIGELOW, Willard D. (1866-1939) Chem. NC38

BIGOURDAN, Camille G. (1851-1932) Astron.; Sci.
Hist. CDZZ ZZ-2

BIGSBY, John J. (1792-1881) Geol. DNB

BILHARZ, Theodor (1825-1862) Anat.; Zool. CDZZ
ZZ-2

BILLINGS, Elkanah (1820-1876) Paleon. CDZZ ZZ-2

BILLINGS, John S. (1838-1913) Med. BHMT BM-8
HIUE

BILLINGS, William D. (1910-) Bot. BNBR

BILLROTH, Christian A. (1829-1894) Anat. BEOS
BHMT CDZZ ZZ-2

BILLY, Jacques de (1602-1679) Math.; Astron. CDZZ
ZZ-2

BILSING, Sherman W. (1885-1954) Entom. AMEM

BINET, Alfred (1857-1911) Psych. ABES ABET BDOS
CDZZ RPTC ZZ-2

BINGHAM, Eugene C. (1878-1945) Chem.; Cons.
ACCE

BINNEY, Amos (1803-1847) Zool. BIOD DAB

BINNEY, Edward W. (1812-1881) Geol. DNB

BINNEY, William G. (1833-1909) Conch. BIOD

BION, Nicolas (c.1652-1733) Instr. CDZZ ZZ-2

BIOT, Jean B. (1774-1862) Phys. ABES ABET BDOS
BEOS CDZZ SOAC ZZ-2

BIOT, Maurice A. (1905-) Phys. MHSE

BIRCH, Arthur J. (1915-) Chem. MHSE

BIRCH, Francis (1903-) Geophys. MHSE

BIRD, Golding (1814-1854) Med. BHMT

BIRD, John (1709-1776) Math.; Opt. CDZZ DNB
ZZ-2

BIRD, Robert B. (1924-) Chem Engr. MHSE

BIRGE, Edward A. (1861-1950) Zool.; Limn. CDZZ
LACC NC12 ZZ-2

BIRGE, Raymond T. (1887-) Phys. CB40 QPAS

BIRINGUCCIO, Vannoccio (1480-1538/9) Metal.
BDOS CDZZ GE-1 ZZ-2

BIRKELAND, Kristian O. (1867-1917) Phys. BDOS
BEOS

BIRKHOFF, George D. (1884-1944) Math. BEOS
CDZZ DAB3 NCSF WAMB ZZ-2

BIRKIGT, Marc (1878-1952) Engr. ICFW

BIRMINGHAM, John (c.1816-1884) Astron. CDZZ
DNB ZZ-2

BIRNIE, James H. (1909-) Med. SBPY

BIRT, William R. (1804-1881) Astron. CDZZ ZZ-2

al-BIRUNI, Abu Rayhan Muhammad (973-c.1050)
Astron.; Math. CDZZ SCIN THOG ZZ-2

BISAT, William S. (1886-1973) Engr. RS20

BISCHOF, Carl G. (1792-1870) Chem.; Geol. CDZZ
ZZ-2

BISCHOFF, Ernst (1884-1935) Chem. NC39

BISCHOFF, Gottlieb W. (1797-1854) Bot. CDZZ
ZZ-2

BISCHOFF, Theodor L. (1807-1882) Anat.; Physiol.
CDZZ ZZ-2

BISHOP, George (1785-1861) Astron. DNB

BISHOP, Howard B. (1878-1961) Chem. NCSE

BISHOP, Oakley M. (1887-1931) Chem. NC24

BISHOPP, Fred C. (1884-1970) Entom. NC55

BISTERFELD, Johann H. (c.1605-1655) Philos.
CDZZ ZZ-2

al-BITRUJI al-ISHBILI, Abu Ishaq (fl. C.1190)
Astron. CDZZ ZZXV

BITTNER, John J. (1904-1961) Biol. ABES ABET
BEOS

BIZZOZERO, Giulio C. (1846-1901) Med. CDZZ ZZ-2

BJERKNES, Carl A. (1825-1903) Math.; Phys. CDZZ
ZZ-2

BJERKNES, Jacob A. (1897-1975) Meteor. ABES
ABET BEOS MHM1 MHSE

BJERKNES, Vilhelm F. (1862-1951) Phys.; Geophys.
BEOS CDZZ SAIF ZZ-2

BJERRUM, Niels J. (1879-1958) Chem.; Phys. BEOS
CDZZ GRCH ZZ-2

BJORNSON, Bjorn (1898-1969) Engr. NC55

BLACK, Davidson (1884-1934) Anat.; Anthro. ABET
CDZZ ZZ-2

BLACK, Greene V. (1836-1915) Chem. ACCE

BLACK, Harold S. (1898-1984) Elec. Engr. MHM1
MHSE TPAE

BLACK, James (c.1787-1867) Med.; Geol. CDZZ
ZZ-2

BLACK, Joseph (1728-1799) Chem.; Phys. ABES
ABET BDOS BEOS BHMT CDZZ DNB EPHG
GRCH HLSM HSSO MCCW SIRC ZZ-2

BLACKETT, Patrick M. (1897-1974) Phys. ABES
ABET BEOS CB49 MHM1 MHSE POSW RS21
SIWG

BLACKMAN, Frederick F. (1866-1947) Bot. BEOS
CDZZ DNB6 ZZ-2

BLACKMAN, Geoffrey E. (1903-1980) Agr. RS27

BLACKMAN, Maulsby W. (1876-1943) Entom. AMEM
NC32

BLACKMAN, Vernon H. (1872-1967) Bot. RS14

BLACKWALL, John (1790-1881) Zool. DNB

BLACKWELL, David (1919-) Math. SBPY

BLACKWELL, Eliot (1880-1969) Geol. BM48

BLACKWELL, Elizabeth (1821-1910) Med. BHMT
COAC DNB2 NAW WIWM

BLACKWELL, Otto B. (1884-1970) Elec. Engr. TPAE

BLAEU, Willem J. (1571-1638) Geog. BEOS CDZZ
ZZ-2

BLAGDEN, Charles (1748-1820) Chem. BDOS BEOS
BHMT CDZZ ZZ-2

BLAGONRAVOV, Anatoli A. (1894-1975) Rocket.
CB58 PBTS

BLAGRAVE, John (d. 1611) Math. DNB

BLAGRAVE, Joseph (1610-1682) Astrol. DNB

BLAINVILLE, Henri M. de (1777-1850) Anat.; Zool.
CDZZ ZZ-2

BLAIR, Andrew A. (1848-1932) Chem. NC25

BLAIR, Patrick (d. 1728) Bot.; Med. CDZZ DNB
ZZ-2

BLAIR, Robert (d. 1828) Opt. DNB

BLAIR, William R. (1874-1962) Phys. NC53

BLAISDELL, Frank E. (1862-1947) Entom. AMEM

BLAISE SEE BLASIUS OF PARMA

BLAKE, Eli W. (1795-1886) Invent. DAB NC-9

BLAKE, Francis (1850-1913) Astron. DAB NC13
NC22

BLAKE, Francis G. (1887-1952) Med. BM28

BLAKE, James (1815-1893) Chem.; Phys. ACCE

BLAKE, John B. (1745-1773) Nat. Hist. DNB

BLAKE, R. Kingsley (1914-1975) Chem. NC59

BLAKER, Ernest (1870-1947) Chem.; Phys. NC36

BLAKESLEE, Albert F. (1874-1954) Bot.; Genet.
   ABES ABET BDOS BEOS BM33 CB41 MABH

BLAKESLEE, Howard W. (1880-1952) Sci. Writ.
   DAB5

BLAKISTON, Thomas W. (1832-1891) Ornith. DNB1

BLALOCK, Alfred (1899-1964) Med. BM53 MHM1
   MHSE

BLANC, Alberto C. (1906-1960) Anthro. CDZZ ZZ-2

BLANCHARD, Jean P. (1753-1809) Aero. ABES
   ABET COAC PAW2

BLANCHARD, Raoul (1877-1965) Geog. CDZZ ZZ-2

BLANCHARD, Thomas (1788-1864) Invent. GE-1
   WAMB YSMS

BLANCK, Frederick C. (1881-1965) Chem. NC51

BLAND, Miles (1786-1867) Math. DNB

BLAND, Thomas (1809-1885) Nat. Hist. BIOD DAB

BLANE, Gilbert (1749-1834) Med. BDOS BEOS

BLANFORD, Henry F. (1834-1893) Meteor.; Geol.
   DNB1

BLANFORD, William T. (1832-1905) Geol.; Zool.
   DNB2

BLASCHKE, Wilhelm J. (1885-1962) Math. CDZZ
   ZZ-2

BLASIUS OF PARMA (c.1345-1416) Nat. Philos.
   CDZZ ZZ-2

BLATCHLEY, Willis S. (1859-1940) Entom. AMEM

BLATHERWICK, Norman R. (1887-1961) Chem.
   NC46

BLAUW, Willem SEE BLAEU, Willem J.

BLAZHKO, Sergei N. (1870-1956) Astron. CDZZ
   ZZ-2

BLEANEY, Brebis (1915-) Phys. MHM2 MHSE

BLEININGER, Albert V. (1872-1946) Chem.; Geol.
   ACCE

BLERIOT, Louis (1872-1936) Aero. PAW2

BLICHFELDT, Hans F. (1873-1945) Math. BM26
   CDZZ DAB3 ZZ-2

BLINKS, Lawrence R. (1900-) Bot. MHM2 MHSE

BLINOVA, Ekaterina N. (1906-) Meteor. SMST

BLISS, Donald E. (1903-1951) Bot. NC40

BLISS, Gilbert A. (1876-1961) Math. BM31 CDZZ
   DAB5 NCSA ZZ-2

BLISS, Nathaniel (1700-1764) Astron. DNB

BLISS, William J. (1867-1941) Math. NCSA

BLIZARD, Everitt P. (1916-1966) Phys. NC56

BLOCH, Felix (1905-1983) Phys. ABES ABET BEOS
   CB54 MHM1 MHSE NCSI POSW WAMB

BLOCH, Herman S. (1912-) Chem. MHSE

BLOCH, Konrad E. (1912-) Biochem. ABES ABET
   BEOS MHM1 MHSE WAMB

BLOCK, D. Julian (1874-1939) Chem. NCSC

BLOCK, Edward (1902-1961) Chem. Engr. NC51

BLODGET, Lorin (1823-1901) Climat. BIOD

BLODGETT, Katherine B. (1898-1979) Phys.; Chem.
   CB40 CB52

BLOEDE, Victor G. (1849-1937) Chem. NC27

BLOEMBERGEN, Nicolaas (1920-) Phys. ABES
   ABET BEOS MHM1 MHSE

BLOKHINTSEV, Dmitri I. (1908-1979) Phys. SMST
   SOVL

BLOM, Frans (1893-1962) Archaeol. PAMB

BLOMEFIELD, Leonard (1800-1893) Nat. Hist. DNB1

BLOMEFIELD, Miles (1525-c.1574) Alchem. DNB

BLOMQUIST, Hugo L. (1888-1964) Bot. NC52

BLOMSTRAND, Christian W. (1826-1897) Chem.;
Mineral. CDZZ ZZ-2

BLONDEL, Andre E. (1863-1938) Phys. CDZZ ZZ-2

BLONDEL, Nicolas F. (1618-1686) Engr. CDZZ GE-1
ZZ-2

BLONDLOT, Rene P. (1849-1930) Phys. CDZZ ZZ-2

BLOOM, William (1899-1972) Anat. NC57

BLOXAM, Andrew (1801-1878) Nat. Hist. DNB

BLUMBERG, Baruch S. (1925-) Med. ABET AMJB
BEOS CB77 MHSE PAW2

BLUMBERG, Randolph (1926-1977) Engr.; Ocean.
NC60

BLUMENBACH, Johann F. (1752-1840) Nat. Hist.;
Anthro. ABET BEOS CDZZ ZZ-2

BLUMENSTOCK, David I. (1913-1963) Geog.;
Climat. NC50

BLUNDELL, James (1790-1877) Physiol.; Med.
BHMT

BLYTH, Edward (1810-1873) Nat. Hist. CDZZ
DMXE DNB ZZ-2

BOARTS, Robert M. (1904-1960) Chem. Engr. NC48

BOAS, Franz (1858-1942) Anthro. BM24 CB40 CDZZ
DAB3 NC12 POAA WAMB ZZ-2

BOASE, Henry S. (1799-1883) Geol. DNB

BOBART, Jacob (1599-1680) Bot. DNB

BOBART, Jacob (1641-1719) Bot. DNB

BOBILLIER, Etienne (1798-1840) Math. CDZZ ZZ-2

BOCAGE, Andre (1892-1953) Med. BHMT

BOCHART DE SARON, Jean B. (1730-1794) Astron.
CDZZ ZZ-2

BOCHER, Maxime (1867-1918) Math. CDZZ DAB
NC18 ZZ-2

BOCHNER, Salomon (1899-1982) Math. MHM1 MHSE

BOCHVAR, Andrei A. (1902-) Metal. SMST

BOCK, Jerome (1498-1554) Bot. CDZZ ZZ-2

BODE, Hendrik W. (1905-) Engr. TPAE

BODE, Johann E. (1747-1826) Astron. ABES ABET
BDOS BEOS CDZZ IEAS ZZ-2

BODEGA Y QUADRA, Juan F. de la (1743-1794) Exp.
SSNW

BODENHEIMER, Fritz S. (1897-1959) Entom.; Zool.
CDZZ ZZ-2

BODENSTEIN, Adam SEE ADAM OF BODENSTEIN

BODENSTEIN, Max (1871-1942) Chem. ABET BEOS
CDZZ HSSO ZZXV

BODINE, Joseph H. (1894-1954) Zool. NC46

BODINGTON, George (1799-1882) Med. BHMT

BODLEY, Rachel L. (1831-1888) Chem. ACCE
BIOD IDWB NAW

BODMER, Johann G. (1786-1864) Engr. GE-1

BOE, Franz de la SEE SYLVIUS, Franciscus

BOECK, Caesar P. (1845-1917) Med. BHMT

BOEHME, Jacob (1575-1624) Philos. CDZZ ZZ-2

BOERHAAVE, Hermann (1688-1738) Chem.; Med.
ABES ABET BDOS BEOS BHMT CDZZ GRCH
HLSM ZZ-2

BOERMA, Addeke H. (1912-) Agr. CB74

BOETHIUS, Anicius M. (c.480-524) Math.; Philos.
ABET BEOS CDZZ ZZ-2

BOETIUS DE BOODT, Anselmus SEE BOODT,
Anselm B. de

BOGDANOV, Aleksandr A. (1873-1928) Philos.; Med.
CDZZ ZZ-2

BOGERT, Marston T. (1868-1954) Chem. ACCE
BM45 NC14

BOGOLYUBOV, Nikolai N. (1900-) Math. BEOS
MHSE SMST

BOGOROV, Vyeniamin G. (1904-) Ocean. SMST

BOGUSLAVSKY, Palm H. von (1789-1851) Astron. CDZZ ZZ-2

BOHEIM, Martin SEE BEHAIM, Martin

BOHL, Piers (1865-1921) Math. CDZZ ZZ-2

BOHLER, John (1797-1872) Bot. DNB

BOHN, Henry G. (1796-1884) Nat. Hist. ANHD

BOHN, Johannes (1640-1718) Med. CDZZ ZZ-2

BOHN, Rene (1862-1922) Chem. BEOS

BOHR, Aage N. (1922-) Phys. ABET BEOS MHM2 MHSE PAW2 POSW

BOHR, Harald (1887-1951) Math. CDZZ ZZ-2

BOHR, Niels H. (1885-1962) Phys. ABES ABET BDOS BEOS CB45 CDZZ CSCJ DCPW EGSF GMOP HSSO IFBS MHM1 MHSE MWBR PAW2 PHYS POSW RS-9 SAIF TOWS ZZ-2

BOISBAUDRAN, Paul E. de (1838-1912) Chem. ABES ABET BEOS CDZZ ZZ-2

BOISLAURENT, Francois B. SEE BUDAN DE BOIS-LAURENT, Ferdinand

BOK, Bart J. (1906-1983) Astron. ABET BEOS

BOKII, Georgii B. (1909-) Crystal. SMST

BOL, Hans (1534-1593) Nat. Hist. ANHD

BOLK, Lodewijk (1866-1930) Anat. CDZZ ZZ-2

BOLL, Jacob (1828-1880) Nat. Hist.; Geol. BIOD DAB

BOLLARD, Nicholas (fl. c.1500) Nat. Hist. DNB

BOLLES, Frank (1856-1893) Nat. Hist. SFNB

BOLLEY, Henry L. (1865-1956) Bot. NC43

BOLLSTADT, Albrecht von SEE ALBERTUS MAGNUS

BOLOS OF MENDES (fl. c.200 B.C.) Biol. CDZZ ZZ-2

BOLOTOV, Andrei T. (1738-1833) Biol.; Agr. CDZZ ZZ-2

BOLSHAKOV, Kirill A. (1906-) Chem. SMST

BOLT, Richard H. (1911-) Phys. CB54

BOLTER, Andrew (1820-1901) Entom. NC24

BOLTON, Elmer K. (1886-1968) Chem. ACCE MHM1 MHSE

BOLTON, Henry C. (1843-1903) Chem. ACCE BIOD DAB NC10

BOLTWOOD, Bertram B. (1870-1927) Chem. ABES ABET BDOS BEOS BM14 CDZZ DAB NC15 ZZ-2

BOLTZMANN, Ludwig E. (1844-1906) Phys. ABES ABET BDOS BEOS CDZZ TOWS ZZ-2

BOLYAI, Farkas (1775-1856) Math. CDZZ ZZ-2

BOLYAI, Janos (1802-1860) Math. ABES ABET BDOS BEOS CDZZ ZZ-2

BOLZA, Oskar (1857-1942) Math. CDZZ DAB3 ZZ-2

BOLZANO, Bernard (1781-1848) Philos.; Math. CDZZ ZZ-2

BOMBELLI, Rafael (1526-1572) Math. CDZZ SXWS ZZ-2

BOMBIERI, Enrico (1940-) Math. MHSE

BONANNI, Filippo SEE BUONANNI, Filippo

BONAPARTE, Charles Lucien (1803-1857) Ornith.; Zool. ASJD BIOD BWCL CDZZ ORNS WFBG ZZ-2

BONAVENTURA, Federigo (1555-1602) Meteor. CDZZ ZZ-2

BONCOMPAGNI, Baldassarre (1821-1894) Sci. Hist. CDZZ ZZ-2

BOND, George F. (1915-) Med. EXDC

BOND, George P. (1825-1865) Astron. ABES ABET BEOS BIOD CDZZ DAB NC-5 WAMB ZZ-2

BOND, William C. (1789-1859) Astron. ABES ABET BEOS BIOD CDZZ DAB IEAS NC-8 WAMB ZZ-2

BONDI, Hermann (1919-) Math. ABET BEOS IEAS SIWG

BONE, William A. (1871-1938) Chem. DNB5

BONET, Theophile (1620-1689) Med. BHMT

BONNER, James F. (1910-) Biol. BEOS MHM1 MHSE

BONNER, Tom W. (1910-1961) Phys. BM38

BONNET, Charles (1720-1793) Nat. Hist.; Biol. ABES ABET BDOS BEOS CDZZ HLSM ZZ-2

BONNET, Pierre O. (1819-1892) Math. CDZZ ZZ-2

BONNEY, Thomas G. (1833-1923) Geol. CDZZ DNB4 ZZ-2

BONNIER, Gaston (1853-1922) Bot. CDZZ ZZ-2

BONOMO, Giovan C. (1666-1696) Med. CDZZ ZZ-2

BONVICINO, Costanzo B. (1739-1812) Chem. CDZZ ZZ-2

BOODT, Ansel B. de (c.1550-1632) Mineral. CDZZ ZZ-2

BOOKER, Walter M. (1907-) Pharm. SBPY

BOOLE, George (1815-1864) Math. ABES ABET BDOS BEOS CDZZ DNB MASW WTGM ZZ-2

BOOTH, Edward SEE BARLOW, Edward

BOOTH, Harold S. (1891-1950) Chem. ACCE

BOOTH, James C. (1810-1888) Chem. ACCE BIOD DAB NC13

BOOTH, Samuel C. (1812-1895) Mineral. NC15

BORCH, Oluf SEE BORRICHIUS, Olaus

BORCHARDT, Carl W. (1817-1880) Math. CDZZ ZZ-2

BORDA, Jean C. de (1733-1791) Phys.; Math. BDOS BEOS CDZZ ZZ-2

BORDEN, Gail (1801-1871) Invent. ABES ABET FOIF MCCW WAMB

BORDET, Jules J. (1870-1961) Bact.; Immunol. ABES ABET BDOS BEOS CDZZ RS-8 ZZ-2

BORDEU, Theophile de (1722-1776) Med. CDZZ ZZ-2

BOREL, Emile (1871-1956) Math. CDZZ ZZ-2

BOREL, Pierre (c.1620-1671) Med.; Chem. CDZZ ZZ-2

BORELLI, Giovanni A. (1608-1679) Math.; Physiol. ABES ABET BDOS BEOS BHMT CDZZ TOWS ZZ-2

BORESKOV, Georgii K. (1907-) Chem. SMST

BORGOGNONI OF LUCCA (c.1205-1298) Med. CDZZ ZZ-2

BORING, Edwin G. (1886-1968) Psych. BM43 CB62

BORLAUG, Norman E. (1914-) Bot.; Genet. BEOS CB71 WAMB

BORMAN, Frank (1928-) Astronaut. CB69 IEAS PPNF

BORN, Ignaz E. von (1742-1791) Mineral.; Conch. ANHD CDZZ GE-1 ZZ-2

BORN, Max (1882-1970) Phys. ABES ABET BDOS BEOS CB55 CDZZ GLPS MHM1 MHSE PAW2 POSW RS17 ZZXV

BORODIN, Aleksandr P. (1833-1887) Chem. CDZZ ZZ-2

BORREL, Jean SEE BUTEO, Johannes

BORRER, William (1781-1862) Bot. DNB

BORRICHIUS, Olaus (1626-1690) Chem. CDZZ ZZ-2

BORRIES, Bodo von (1905-1956) Micros. CDZZ ZZ-2

BORRO, Girolamo (1512-1592) Nat. Philos. CDZZ ZZXV

BORROWMAN, George (1880-1946) Chem. NCSC

BORST, Lyle B. (1912-) Phys. CB54

BORTHWICK, Harry A. (1898-1974) Bot. BM48 SWWP

BORTKIEWICZ, Ladislaus J. (1868-1931) Math. CDZZ ZZ-2

BORTOLOTTI, Ettore (1866-1947) Math. CDZZ ZZ-2

BORY DE SAINT VINCENT, Jean (1778-1846) Biol. CDZZ ZZ-2

BOSC, Louis A. (1759-1828) Nat. Hist. CDZZ ZZ-2

BOSCH, Carl (1874-1940) Chem. ABES ABET BDOS
BEOS CDZZ GRCH HSSO NPWC ZZ-2

BOSE, Georg M. (1710-1761) Phys. CDZZ ESEH
ZZ-2

BOSE, Jagadischandra (1858-1937) Phys.; Bot. ABET
BEOS CDZZ MMSB ZZ-2 ZZXV

BOSE, Satyendranath (1894-1974) Phys. ABET BEOS
CDZZ RS21 ZZ-2

BOSKOVIC, Rudjer J. (1711-1787) Nat. Philos. CDZZ
ZZ-2

BOSS, Lewis (1846-1912) Astron. BEOS BM-9 CDZZ
DAB IEAS NC13 ZZ-2

BOSSART, Karel J. (1904-1975) Rocket. ICFW

BOSSE, Abraham (1602-1676) Sci. Illus. CDZZ ZZ-2

BOSSUT, Charles (1730-1814) Math. CDZZ ZZ-2

BOSTOCK, John (1773-1846) Med. BHMT CDZZ
ZZ-2

BOSWELL, Percy G. (1886-1960) Geol. RS-7

BOTALLO, Leonardo (c.1519-1587/8) Med. CDZZ
ZZ-2

BOTHE, Walther W. (1891-1957) Phys. ABES ABET
BEOS CB55 CDZZ MHM1 MHSE POSW ZZ-2

BOTTAZZI, Filippo (1867-1941) Physiol. CDZZ ZZ-2

BOTTERI, Mateo (1808-1877) Nat. Hist. WFBG

BOTTGER, Rudolph C. (1806-1881) Chem. CDZZ
ZZ-2

BOUCHER DE CREVECOEUR DE PERTHES, Jacques
(1788-1868) Paleon. ABES ABET BEOS CDZZ
ZZXV

BOUDART, Michel (1924-) Chem. MHSE

BOUE, Ami (1794-1881) Geol. CDZZ ZZ-2

BOUELLES, Charles de SEE BOUVELLES, Charles

BOUGAINVILLE, Louis A. de (1729-1811) Geog.; Math.
ABET CDZZ ZZ-2

BOUGUER, Pierre (1698-1758) Phys. ABES ABET
BEOS CDZZ ZZ-2

BOUILLARD, Jean B. (1796-1881) Med. BHMT

BOUIN, Pol A. (1870-1962) Biol. CDZZ ZZ-2

BOULE, Marcellin (1861-1942) Paleon.; Geol. CDZZ
ZZ-2

BOULLANGER, Nicolas A. (1722-1759) Geol. CDZZ
ZZ-2

BOULLIAU, Ismael (1605-1694) Math.; Astron. CDZZ
ZZ-2

BOULTON, Matthew (1728-1809) Invent. BDOS BEOS
DNB

BOUQUET, Jean C. (1819-1895) Math. CDZZ ZZ-2

BOUR, Edmond (1832-1866) Math. CDZZ ZZ-2

BOURBAKI, Nicolas (Collective pseudonym, 1930-)
Math. BEOS CDZZ ZZ-2

BOURDELIN, Claude (c.1621-1699) Chem. CDZZ
ZZ-2

BOURDELOT, Pierre M. (1610-1685) Med. CDZZ
ZZ-2

BOURDON, Eugene (1808-1884) Instr. CDZZ FNEC
ZZ-2

BOURGEOIS, Louyse (1563-1636) Med. WIWM

BOURGUET, Louis (1678-1742) Geol.; Phys. CDZZ
ZZXV

BOURNE, Edward J. (1922-) Chem. COBC

BOURNE, Gilbert C. (1861-1933) Zool. DNB5

BOURNON, Jacques L. de (1751-1825) Mineral.
CDZZ ZZ-2

BOURSIER DE COUDRAY SEE DU COUDRAY,
Anhelique M.

BOUSSINESQ, Joseph V. (1842-1929) Phys. CDZZ
ZZ-2

BOUSSINGAULT, Jean B. (1802-1887) Agr. ABES
ABET BDOS BEOS CDZZ ZZ-2

BOUTON, Charles L. (1869-1922) Math. NC30

BOUTROUX, Pierre L. (1880-1922) Math. CDZZ ZZ-2

BOUTWELL, John M. (1874-1968) Geol. NC54

BOUVARD, Alexis (1767-1843) Astron. ABET CDZZ ZZ-2

BOUVELLES, Charles (c.1470-c.1553) Philos.; Math. CDZZ ZZ-2

BOVELL, James (1817-1880) Med. POCS

BOVERI, Theodor H. (1862-1915) Biol. ABET BDOS BEOS CDZZ ZZ-2

BOVET, Daniel (1907-) Pharm. ABES ABET BEOS MHM1 MHSE

BOVIE, William T. (1882-1958) Biophys. NC44

BOVING, Adam G. (1869-1957) Entom. AMEM

BOWDEN, Frank P. (1903-1968) Chem. RS15

BOWDITCH, Henry P. (1840-1911) Physiol. BHMT CDZZ ZZ-2

BOWDITCH, Nathaniel (1773-1838) Math.; Astron. ASIW BIOD CDZZ COAC DAB LISD NC-6 SNAR WAMB YSMS ZZ-2

BOWDOIN, James (1726-1790) Phys.; Chem. BIOD NC-2

BOWEN, Edmund J. (1898-1980) Chem. AO80 BEOS COBC MHM1 MHSE RS27

BOWEN, George T. (1803-1828) Chem.; Med. NC12 TPAE

BOWEN, Ira S. (1898-1973) Astrophys. BEOS BM53 CB51 MHM1 MHSE

BOWEN, Norman L. (1887-1956) Geol. BM52 CDZZ MHM2 MHSE RS-3 WAMB ZZ-2

BOWER, Frederick O. (1855-1948) Bot. BDOS CDZZ DNB6 ZZ-2

BOWER, Gordon H. (1932-) Math. IMMO

BOWER, Henry (1833-1896) Chem. ACCE

BOWERBANK, James S. (1797-1877) Geol. DNB

BOWERS, Edward A. (1857-1924) Forest. LACC

BOWIE, William (1872-1940) Geol. BM26 CDZZ ZZ-2

BOWKER, Albert H. (1919-) Math. CB66

BOWLES, William (1705-1780) Nat. Hist. DNB

BOWMAN, Isaiah (1878-1950) Geog. BM33 CDZZ ZZ-2

BOWMAN, John E. (1785-1841) Nat. Hist. DNB

BOWMAN, John E. (1819-1954) Chem. DNB

BOWMAN, John R. (1910-1962) Chem. NC55

BOWMAN, William (1816-1892) Med. BDOS BEOS BHMT CDZZ ZZ-2

BOWSER, Edward A. (1837-1910) Math. BIOD NC19

BOYCE, John S. (1889-1971) Forest. NC57

BOYCOTT, Arthur E. (1877-1938) Nat. Hist. DNB5

BOYD, John S. (1891-1981) Med. RS28

BOYD, Louise A. (1887-) Geog. CB60

BOYD, William C. (1903-) Biochem.; Immunol. ABES ABET BEOS MHM1 MHSE

BOYD ORR, John (1880-1971) Agr. RS18

BOYDEN, Seth (1788-1870) Invent. GE-1 WAMB

BOYDEN, Uriah A. (1804-1879) Engr.; Invent. WAMB

BOYE, Martin H. (1812-1909) Chem.; Geol. ACCE DAB

BOYER, Herbert W. (1936-) Biochem. BEOS

BOYER, Marion H. (1901-1982) Chem. Engr. CB51

BOYKIN, Otis (1920-) Invent. BCST

BOYLE, Albert J. (1910-1967) Chem. NC54

BOYLE, Robert (1627-1691) Phys.; Chem. ABES ABET BDOS BEOS BHMT CDZZ DNB EETD FBSC FNEC GRCH IFBS LISD LSCS MAKS MCCW SAIF SMIL TOWS ZZ-2

BOYLSTON, Zabdiel (1680-1766) Med. BIOD SBCS

BOYS, Charles V. (1855-1944) Phys. BDOS CDZZ DNB6 ZZXV

BOYS, Samuel F. (1911-1972) Phys. RS19

BRACE, DeWitt B. (1859-1905) Opt. BIOD CDZZ DAB ZZ-2

BRACHET, Albert (1869-1930) Embryol. CDZZ ZZ-2

BRACHET, Jean L. (1909-) Biol. BEOS MHM2 MHSE

BRACKENRIDGE, William D. (1810-1893) Bot. BIOD DAB

BRACONNOT, Henri (1781-1855) Chem. ABET BEOS CDZZ ZZ-2

BRADBURY, Frank R. (1911-) Chem. COBC

BRADBURY, Norris E. (1909-) Phys. CB49

BRADBURY, Ora C. (1890-1969) Biol. NC57

BRADFORD, John R. (1863-1935) Physiol. DNB5

BRADFORD, Joshua T. (1818-1871) Med. CDZZ ZZ-2

BRADLEY, Albert J. (1899-1972) Crystal. RS19

BRADLEY, Charles E. (1874-1960) Chem. NC50

BRADLEY, Frank H. (1838-1879) Geol. BIOD

BRADLEY, Harold C. (1878-) Cons. LACC

BRADLEY, Humphrey (c.1584-c.1625) Engr. BDOS

BRADLEY, James (1693-1762) Astron. ABES ABET BDOS BEOS CDZZ DNB IEAS TOWS ZZ-2

BRADLEY, John H. (1898-1962) Geol. NC50

BRADLEY, John N. (1931-) Chem. COBC

BRADLEY, Preston (1888-) Cons. LACC

BRADLEY, Richard (d. 1732) Bot. CDZZ DNB ZZ-2

BRADWARDINE, Thomas (c.1290-1349) Math. CDZZ ZZ-2

BRADY, Henry B. (1835-1891) Nat. Hist. DMB1

BRADY, St. Elmo (1884-1966) Chem. SBPY

BRAGG, William H. (1862-1942) Phys. ABES ABET BDOS BEOS CDZZ DNB6 POSW ZZ-2

BRAGG, William L. (1890-1971) Phys. ABES ABET BDOS BEOS CAVL CDZZ MHM1 MHSE POSW RS25

BRAHE, Tycho (1546-1601) Astron. ABES ABET ASTR BDOS BEOS BMST CDZZ DCPW FASP LISD IEAS PAW2 SGAC SLOR STSW SXWS TOWS WOSM ZZ-2

BRAHMADEVA (fl. c.1092) Astron. CDZZ ZZ-2

BRAHMAGUPTA (598-668) Astron. ABES ABET BEOS CDZZ OGIV ZZ-2

BRAID, James (1795-1860) Med. ABES ABET BEOS DNB

BRAIKENRIDGE, William (c.1700-1762) Math. CDZZ ZZ-2

BRAILLE, Louis (1809-1852) Invent. SAIF

BRAIN, Walter R. (1895-1966) Med. RS14

BRAINERD, Ezra (1844-1924) Bot.; Geol. DAB MABH

BRAINERD, George W. (1909-1956) Anthro. NC46

BRAINERD, John G. (1904-) Elec. Engr. TPAE

BRAMAH, Joseph (1748-1814) Engr. BDOS BEOS DNB FNEC GE-1

BRAMBELL, Francis W. (1901-1970) Zool. BEOS MHM1 MHSE RS19

BRAMER, Benjamin (c.1588-1652) Math. CDZZ ZZ-2

BRAMLETTE, Milton N. (1896-1977) Geol. BM52

BRAMSON, M. L. (1896-1981) Invent.; Med. AO81

BRANCKER, Thomas (1633-1676) Math. DNB

BRAND, Albert R. (1889-1940) Ornith. NC35 ORNS

BRAND, Hennig (b. 1630) Chem. ABES ABET BDOS BEOS

BRANDBORG, Stewart M. (1925-) Cons. LACC

BRANDE, William T. (1788-1866) Chem. CDZZ DNB ZZ-2

BRANDEGEE, Mary K. (1844-1920) Bot. BIOD NAW

BRANDEGEE, Townshend (1843-1925) Bot. BIOD DAB MABH

BRANDES, Heinrich W. (1777-1834) Astron.; Phys. CDZZ ZZ-2

BRANDIS, Dietrich (1824-1907) Bot. DNB2

BRANDRETH, Thomas S. (1788-1873) Math. DNB

BRANDT, Georg (1694-1768) Chem. ABES ABET BEOS CDZZ ZZ-2

BRANDT, Herbert (1884-1955) Ornith. NC45

BRANDT, Johann F. (1802-1879) Zool. CDZZ WFBG ZZ-2

BRANS, Carl H. (1935-) Phys. BEOS

BRANSON, Herman R. (1914-) Biophys. BISC SBPY

BRASHEAR, John A. (1840-1920) Instr. CDZZ DAB ZZ-2

BRASHMAN, Nikolai D. (1796-1866) Math. CDZZ ZZ-2

BRATTAIN, Walter H. (1902-) Phys. ABES ABET BEOS CB57 MHM1 MHSE NCSI POSW TINA TPAE WAMB

BRATTLE, Thomas (1658-1713) Astron. BIOD

BRAUER, Richard D. (1901-1977) Math. MHSE NC60 NCSJ

BRAUMAN, John I. (1937-) Chem. MHSE

BRAUN, Alexander C. (1805-1877) Bot.; Philos. CDZZ ZZ-2

BRAUN, Armin C. (1911-) Biol. MHM1 MHSE

BRAUN, Emma L. (1889-1971) Bot. NAWM

BRAUN, (Karl) Ferdinand (1850-1918) Phys. ABES ABET BEOS CDZZ POSW ZZ-2

BRAUN, (J.) Werner (1914-1972) Bact. CB57

BRAUN, Wernher von SEE VON BRAUN, Wernher

BRAUNER, Bohuslav (1855-1935) Chem. CDZZ ZZ-2

BRAUNMUHL, Anton von (1853-1908) Math. CDZZ ZZ-2

BRAUNSTEIN, Aleksandr E. (1902-) Biochem. MHM2 MHSE SMST

BRAVAIS, Auguste (1811-1863) Phys.; Crystal. CDZZ ZZ-2

BRAY, William C. (1879-1946) Chem. BM26 NC35

BRAYLEY, Edward W. (1802-1870) Sci. Writ. DNB

BREASTED, James H. (1865-1935) Archaeol. BM18 WAMB

BRECKINRIDGE, Mary (1881-1965) Med. NAWM

BRECKMAN, Jack N. (1922-1973) Invent.; Engr. NC58

BREDIKHIN, Fedor A. (1831-1904) Astron. CDZZ ZZ-2

BREDON, Simon (c.1300-c.1372) Math.; Astron. CDZZ ZZ-2

BREDT, Konrad J. (1855-1937) Chem. BEOS

BREEN, James (1826-1866) Astron. DNB

BREFELD, Julius O. (1839-1925) Bot. CDZZ ZZ-2

BREGUET, Louis (1880-1955) Aero. ICFW

BREGUET, Louis F. (1804-1883) Instr. CDZZ ZZ-2

BREHM, Alfred E. (1829-1884) Nat. Hist. ANHD

BREHM, Christian L. (1787-1864) Ornith. ORNS

BREISLAK, Scipione (1750-1826) Geol.; Nat. Hist. CDZZ ZZ-2

BREIT, Gregory (1899-) Phys. BEOS MHSE QPAS

BREITHAUPT, Johann F. (1791-1873) Mineral. CDZZ ZZ-2

BREITHUT, Frederick E. (1880-1962) Chem. ACCE

BREKHOVSKIKH, Leonid M. (1917-) Phys. SMST

BREMER, Frederic (1892-) Physiol. MHM2 MHSE

BREMIKER, Carl (1804-1877) Math.; Astron. CDZZ ZZ-2

BRENDEL, Otto R. (1862-1939) Astron. CDZZ ZZ-2

BRENNER, Sydney (1927-) Biol. BEOS

BRESCHET, Gilbert (1783-1845) Anat. CDZZ ZZ-2

BRESLOW, Ronald (1931-) Chem. MHSE

BRET, Jean J. (1781-1819) Math. CDZZ ZZ-2

BRETEUIL, Emelie de SEE CHATELET, Emelie de

BRETONNEAU, Pierre F. (1778-1862) Med. ABET
BEOS BHMT CDZZ ZZ-2

BREUER, Josef (1842-1925) Med.; Physiol. ABET
CDZZ ZZ-2

BREUIL, (Abbe) Henri E. (1877-1961) Anthro. CCSW
CDZZ ZZ-2

BREWER, George E. (1899-1968) Cons. LACC

BREWER, Leo (1919-) Chem. MHM1 MHSE

BREWER, Thomas M. (1814-1880) Ornith. BIOD
BWCL DAB NC22 WFBG

BREWER, William H. (1828-1910) Agr. BM12 DAB
LACC NC13

BREWSTER, David (1781-1868) Phys. ABES ABET
BDOS BEOS CDZZ DNB ZZ-2

BREWSTER, Jonathan (1593-1659) Alch. ACCE

BREWSTER, William (1851-1919) Ornith. BWCL DAB
LACC NC12 NC22 NHAH SFNB

BREYER, Frank G. (1886-1966) Chem. Engr. NC53

BRIAN, Percy W. (1910-1979) Bot. RS27

BRIANCHON, Charles J. (1783-1864) Math. CDZZ
ZZ-2

BRIDFERTH SEE BYRHTFERTH

BRIDGE, Thomas W. (1848-1909) Zool. DNB2

BRIDGES, Calvin B. (1889-1938) Genet. BM22 CDZZ
DAB2 NC30 ZZ-2

BRIDGES, Robert (1806-1882) Bot.; Chem. ACCE
BIOD DAB NC-5

BRIDGMAN, Percy W. (1882-1961) Phys. ABES ABET
BDOS BEOS BM41 CB55 CDZZ MHM1 MHSE
NC48 POSW RS-8 WAMB ZZ-2

BRIERLEY, John R. (1886-1961) Chem. NC49

BRIGGS, Henry (1561-1630) Math. ABES ABET
BDOS BEOS CDZZ DNB ZZ-2

BRIGGS, John J. (1819-1876) Nat. Hist. DNB

BRIGGS, Lyman J. (1874-1963) Phys. NC53

BRIGHAM, William T. (1841-1926) Geol.; Bot. NC16

BRIGHT, Harry A. (1890-1961) Chem. NC49

BRIGHT, J. Russell (1908-1973) Chem. NC57

BRIGHT, Richard (1789-1858) Med. ABET BDOS
BEOS BHMT CDZZ MMMA ZZ-2

BRIGHTWEN, Elija (1830-1906) Nat. Hist. DNB2

BRILL, Alexander W. von (1842-1935) Math. CDZZ
ZZ-2

BRILL, Harvey D. (1881-1972) Chem. NC57

BRILL, John L. (1902-1971) Chem. NC57

BRILL, Robert H. (1929-) Chem. CHUB

BRILLOUIN, Marcel L. (1854-1948) Math.; Phys.
CDZZ ZZ-2

BRINDLEY, James (1716-1772) Engr. BDOS GE-1

BRINELL, Johann A. (1849-1925) Metal. BDOS
CDZZ ZZ-2

BRING, Erland S. (1736-1798) Math. CDZZ ZZ-2

BRINK, Royal A. (1897-) Genet. MHM2 MHSE

BRINKLEY, John (1763-1835) Astron.; Math. CDZZ
ZZ-2

BRINSMADE, James B. (1884-1936) Phys. NC28
QPAS

BRIOSCHI, Francesco (1824-1897) Math. CDZZ ZZ-2

BRIOT, Charles A. (1817-1882) Math.; Phys. CDZZ
ZZ-2

BRISBANE, Thomas M. (1773-1860) Astron. CDZZ DNB ZZ-2

BRISSON, Barnabe (1777-1828) Engr.; Math. CDZZ ZZ-2

BRISSON, Mathurin J. (1723-1806) Phys.; Nat. Hist. ANHD CDZZ HAOA ZZ-2

BRISTOL, Charles L. (1859-1931) Biol. NC25

BRISTOW, Henry W. (1817-1889) Geol. DNB1

BRITTAIN, Thomas (1806-1884) Nat. Hist. DNB

BRITTEN, James (1846-1924) Bot. CDZZ ZZ-2

BRITTON, Edgar C. (1891-1962) Chem. ACCE CB52 NC52

BRITTON, Elizabeth G. (1858-1934) Bot. CWSE MABH NAW NC25

BRITTON, Nathaniel L. (1859-1934) Bot. BM19 CDZZ DAB1 MABH NC12 NC25 ZZ-2

BRITTON, Wilton E. (1868-1939) Entom. AMEM NCSA

BROADBENT, William H. (1835-1907) Med. BHMT

BROCA, Pierre Paul (1824-1880) Anthro.; Med. ABES ABET BBRS BDOS BEOS BHMT CDZZ ZZ-2

BROCARD, Pierre R. (1845-1922) Math.; Meteor. CDZZ ZZ-2

BROCCHI, Giovanni B. (1772-1826) Geol. CDZZ ZZ-2

BROCHANT DE VILLIERS, Andre J. (1772-1840) Geol.; Mineral. CDZZ ZZ-2

BROCKLESBY, John (1811-1889) Meteor.; Micros. BIOD

BRODE, Robert B. (1900-) Phys. MHM2 MHSE

BRODE, Wallace R. (1900-1974) Chem.; Spect. CB58 MHM2 MHSE

BRODEL, Max (1870-1941) Anat. CDZZ ZZXV

BRODETSKY, Selig (1888-1954) Math. DNB7

BRODIE, Benjamin C. (1783-1862) Physiol.; Med. BEOS CDZZ ZZ-2

BRODIE, Benjamin C. Jr. (1817-1880) Chem. CDZZ ZZ-2

BRODIE, Bernard B. (1909-) Pharm. BEOS CB69

BROGGER, Waldemar C. (1851-1940) Geol. CDZZ ZZ-2

BROGLIE, Louis C.V.M. de (1875-1960) Phys. CDZZ RS-7 ZZ-2

BROGLIE, Louis V. de (1892-) Phys. ABES ABET ASIW BEOS CB55 EGSF MHM2 MHSE POSW SAIF

BROGLIE, Maurice SEE BROGLIE, Louis C.V.M. de

BROILI, Ferdinand (1874-1946) Paleon.; Geol. CDZZ ZZ-2

BROMELL, Magnus von (1679-1731) Geol. CDZZ ZZ-2

BROMFIELD, Louis (1896-1956) Cons. LACC

BROMFIELD, William A. (1801-1851) Bot. DNB

BROMLEY, Stanley W. (1899-1954) Entom. NC44

BROMWICH, Thomas J. (1875-1929) Math. CDZZ ZZ-2

BRONGNIART, Adolphe T. (1801-1876) Paleon. CDZZ FHUA PHLS ZZ-2

BRONGNIART, Alexandre (1770-1847) Geol. BDOS BEOS CDZZ ZZ-2

BRONK, Detlev W. (1897-1975) Physiol.; Biophys. BEOS BM50 CB49 MHM2 MHSE RS22

BRONN, Heinrich G. (1800-1862) Paleon.; Zool. CDZZ ZZ-2

BRONNER, Augusta F. (1881-1966) Psych. NAWM

BRONOWSKI, Jacob (1908-) Math.; Sci. Writ. CB58

BRONSTED, Johannes N. (1879-1947) Chem. ABES ABET BDOS BEOS CDZZ GRCH ZZ-2

BROOKE, John M. (1826-1906) Astron.; Phys. BIOD DAB NC22

BROOKER, Leslie G. (1902-1971) Chem.; Photo. ACCE

BROOKES, Joshua (1761-1833) Anat. DNB

BROOKOVER, Charles (1870-1922) Anat. NC20

BROOKS, Alfred H. (1871-1924) Geol. CDZZ ZZ-2

BROOKS, Benjamin T. (1885-1962) Chem. ACCE
NCSE

BROOKS, Charles F. (1891-1958) Meteor. NCSH

BROOKS, William K. (1848-1908) Zool. BM-7 CDZZ
DAB NC23 ZZ-2

BROOKS, William R. (1844-1921) Astron. CDZZ DAB
NC-5 ZZ-2

BROOM, Robert (1866-1951) Paleon. ABET BEOS
CDZZ DNB7 MADC PHLS ZZ-2

BROOME, Harvey (1902-1968) Cons. LACC

BROQUIST, Harry P. (1919-) Chem. MHSE

BROSCIUS, Joannes SEE BROZEK, Jan

BROUGHAM, Henry (1778-1868) Math. SOSC

BROUN, John A. (1817-1879) Meteor. DNB

BROUNCKER, William (1620-1685) Math. ABET
BDOS BEOS CDZZ ZZ-2

BROUSSAIS, Francois J. (1772-1838) Med. BHMT
CDZZ ZZ-2

BROUSSONET, Pierre A. (1761-1807) Zool.; Bot.
CDZZ ZZ-2

BROUWER, Dirk (1902-1966) Astron. ABET BEOS
BM41 CB51 CDZZ MHM1 MHSE ZZ-2

BROUWER, Luitzen E. (1881-1966) Math. BDOS
BEOS CDZZ RS15 ZZ-2

BROWER, David R. (1912-) Cons. CB73 EAFC
HOCS LACC PCWA PPNF

BROWER, Egmont G. (1885-1918) Invent. NC24

BROWN, Alexander C. (1838-1922) Chem. BDOS
BEOS CDZZ ZZ-2

BROWN, Barnum (1873-1963) Paleon. MADC NC51

BROWN, Carl B. (1910-1963) Geol.; Cons. LACC

BROWN, Charles L. (1873-1960) Biol. BNBR

BROWN, Claudeus J. (1904-) Biol. LACC

BROWN, Donald D. (1931-) Biol. MHSE

BROWN, Ernest W. (1866-1938) Math. BM21 DAB2
DNB5 NC15 ZZ-2

BROWN, George G. (1896-1957) Chem. Engr. ACCE

BROWN, George H. (1908-) Elec. Engr. ACCE
MHSE

BROWN, George L. (1903-1971) Physiol. RS20

BROWN, Harold (1927-) Phys. CB61 CB77

BROWN, Harrison S. (1917-) Geol. CB55 MHM2
MHSE

BROWN, Herbert C. (1912-) Chem. ABET BEOS
MHM1 MHSE SOT3

BROWN, James G. (1880-1954) Bot. NC44

BROWN, John (1735-1788) Med. BHMT

BROWN, John (1810-1882) Med. BHMT

BROWN, John W. (1836-1863) Bot. DNB

BROWN, Joseph (1733-1785) Phys.; Astron. BIOD

BROWN, Kenneth R. (1895-1958) Chem. NC46

BROWN, Leslie H. (1918-1980) Agr.; Ornith. DGMT

BROWN, Mortimer J. (1882-1945) Chem. NC34

BROWN, Morton (1931-) Math. MHSE

BROWN, Rachel F. (1898-1980) Biochem. AO80
FFIB IDWB WPSH

BROWN, Robert (1773-1858) Bot. ABES ABET BEOS
CDZZ DCPW DNB ZZ-2

BROWN, Robert H. (1916-) Astron. BEOS

BROWN, Roland W. (1893-1961) Paleon. FHUA

BROWN, Russell W. (1905-) Microbiol. SBPY

BROWN, Samuel (1776-1852) Engr. DNB

BROWN, Samuel (1817-1856) Chem. DNB

BROWN, Walter J. (1900-1972) Engr.; Invent. NC57

BROWN-SEQUARD, Charles E. (1817-1894) Physiol. BDOS BEOS BHMT BM-4 CDZZ DNB1 ZZ-2

BROWNE, Arthur L. (1867-1933) Chem. ACCE NC25

BROWNE, Charles A. (1870-1947) Chem. ACCE DAB4 NC35

BROWNE, Daniel J. (1804-1867) Agr. BIOD

BROWNE, Ralph C. (1880-1960) Invent. NC46

BROWNE, Thomas (1605-1682) Nat. Hist. BHMT CDZZ ZZ-2

BROWNE, William (1628-1678) Bot. DNB

BROWNING, Bryce E. (1894-) Cons. LACC

BROWNING, George M. (1908-) Agr. LACC

BROWNING, John M. (1855-1925) Invent. WAMB

BROWNING, Philip E. (1866-1937) Chem. NC28

BROWNRIGG, William (1711-1800) Chem. CDZZ DNB ZZ-2

BROZEK, Jan (1585-1652) Math. CDZZ ZZ-2

BRUCE, Archibald (1777-1818) Mineral. BIOD

BRUCE, David (1855-1931) Microbiol. BDOS BEOS CDZZ ZZ-2

BRUCE, Donald (1884-1966) Forest. LACC

BRUCE, James (1730-1794) Exp. CDZZ ZZ-2

BRUCE, William S. (1867-1921) Ocean. DNB3

BRUCKE, Ernst W. von (1819-1892) Physiol. CDZZ ZZ-2

BRUECKNER, Keith A. (1924-) Phys. MHSE

BRUES, Charles T. II (1879-1955) Entom. AMEM

BRUHL, John M. von (1736-1809) Astron. DNB

BRUHNS, Karl C. (1830-1881) Astron. CDZZ ZZ-2

BRUMPT, Emile (1877-1951) Parasit. CDZZ ZZ-2

BRUN, Edmond A. (1898-) Phys. MHM2 MHSE

BRUNDAGE, Perry S. (1887-1971) Chem. NC58

BRUNEL, Isambard K. (1806-1859) Engr. BDOS SAIF SGEC

BRUNEL, Marc I. (1769-1849) Engr. BDOS GE-1

BRUNELLESCHI, Filippo (1377-1446) Engr. CDZZ GE-1 ZZ-2

BRUNER, Henry L. (1861-1945) Zool. NC34

BRUNER, Lawrence (1856-1937) Entom. AMEM NC13

BRUNFELS, Otto (1489-1534) Bot. CDZZ ZZ-2

BRUNHES, Jean (1869-1930) Geog. BDOS CDZZ ZZ-2

BRUNNER, John T. (1842-1919) Chem. BDOS

BRUNNOW, Franz F. (1821-1891) Astron. BIOD NC13

BRUNO, Giordano (1548-1600) Philos. ABES ABET BEOS BMST CDZZ IEAS ZZ-2

BRUNSCHVICG, Leon (1869-1944) Philos. CDZZ ZZ-2

BRUNSCHWIG, Hieronymus (c.1450-c.1512) Med. CDZZ ZZ-2

BRUNT, David (1886-1965) Meteor. RS11

BRUNTON, Thomas Lauder (1844-1916) Physiol. BHMT CDZZ ZZ-2

BRUNTON, William (1777-1851) Engr. DNB GE-1

BRUSH, Charles F. (1849-1929) Invent. DAB1 NC20

BRYAN, Frank (1890-1960) Geol. NC48

BRYAN, George H. (1864-1928) Aero. ICFW

BRYAN, Kirk (1888-1950) Geol. CDZZ ZZ-2

BRYCE, James (1806-1877) Geol. DNB

BRYSON OF HERACLEA (fl. c.400 B.C.) Math. CDZZ ZZ-2

BRYTTE, Walter (fl. c.1370) Astron. CDZZ ZZ-2

BUACHE, Philippe (1700-1773) Geog. CDZZ ZZ-2

BUBB, Frank W. (1892-1961) Math. NC50

BUBRISKI, Stanley W. (1921-1965) Chem. NC52

BUCH, Christian L. von SEE VON BUCH, Christian

BUCH, Leopold von (1774-1853) Geol. CDZZ GASJ
ZZ-2

BUCHANAN, John Y. (1844-1925) Ocean.; Chem.
CDZZ ZZ-2

BUCHEISTER, Carl W. (1901-) Nat. Hist. LACC

BUCHER, Walter H. (1889-1965) Geol. BM40 CDZZ
MHM1 MHSE ZZ-2

BUCHERER, Alfred H. (1863-1927) Phys. CDZZ
ZZ-2

BUCHI, George H. (1921-) Chem. MHSE

BUCHNER, Eduard (1860-1917) Chem.; Biochem.
ABES ABET BDOS BEOS CDZZ NPWC TOWS
ZZ-2

BUCHNER, Friedrich K. (1824-1899) Med.; Sci. Hist.
CDZZ ZZ-2

BUCHNER, Hans E. (1850-1902) Bact. ABES ABET
BEOS

BUCHOLZ, Christian F. (1770-1818) Chem. CDZZ
ZZ-2

BUCKINGHAM, Amyand D. (1930-) Chem. COBC

BUCKINGHAM, Earle (1887-1978) Engr. NC61

BUCKINGHAM, Edgar (1867-1940) Phys. CDZZ
NC29 ZZ-2

BUCKLAND, Francis T. (1826-1880) Nat. Hist. BEOS
DNB HNHB

BUCKLAND, William (1784-1856) Geol.; Paleon.
CDZZ DARR DNB MADC PHLS ZZ-2

BUCKLER, William (1814-1884) Entom. DNB

BUCKLEY, Edmund S. (1904-) Astronaut. ICFW

BUCKLEY, Oliver E. (1887-1959) Phys. BM37

BUCKLEY, Samuel B. (1809-1884) Bot.; Nat. Hist.
BIOD DAB NC-5

BUCKMAN, James (1816-1884) Geol. DNB

BUCKTON, George B. (1818-1905) Entom. DNB2

BUCQUET, Jean B. (1746-1780) Chem. CDZZ ZZ-2

BUDAN DE BOISLAURENT, Ferdinand (fl. 1800-1853)
Math. CDZZ ZZ-2

BUDD, William (1811-1880) Med. ABET BEOS BHMT
CDZZ ZZ-2

BUDDINGTON, Arthur F. (1890-) Geol. MHM1 MHSE

BUDDLE, Adam (d. 1715) Bot. DNB

BUDDLE, John (1773-1843) Mng. DNB

BUDKER, Gersh I. (1918-) Phys. SMST

BUDNIKOV, Pyotr P. (1885-1968) Chem. SMST

BUECHNER, Helmut K. (1918-1975) Zool.; Ecol.
NC59

BUERGER, Martin J. (1903-) Crystal. MHM2 MHSE

BUFFON, Georges L. Compte de SEE LECLERC,
Georges L.

BUGAEV, Nicolay V. (1837-1903) Math. CDZZ ZZXV

BUHLER, Charlotte B. (1893-1974) Psych. NAWM

BUISSIERE, Paul (d. 1739) Anta. DNB

BULKELEY, Gershom (1636-1713) Alch.; Chem.
ACCE

BULLARD, Edward C. (1907-1980) Geophys. AO80
BEOS CB54 MHM1 MHSE

BULLARD, Ralph H. (1895-1961) Chem. NC49

BULLEN, Keith E. (1906-1976) Math. BEOS MHM1
MHSE RS23

BULLER, Arthur H. (1874-1944) Bot. CDZZ DNB6
MABH ZZ-2

BULLER, Walter L. (1838-1906) Ornith. DNB2

BULLERWELL, William (1916-1977) Geophys. RS24

BULLITT, James B. Jr. (1906-1957) Chem. NC49

BULLOCH, William (1868-1941) Bact. CDZZ DNB6 ZZ-2

BULLOCK, William (fl. 1827) Nat. Hist. DNB

BULMAN, Oliver M. (1902-1974) Paleon. RS21

BUMPUS, Hermon C. (1862-1942) Zool. NC32

BUMSTEAD, Henry A. (1870-1920) Phys. BM13 DAB NC21

BUNBURY, Charles J. (1809-1886) Paleon. FHUA

BUNGE, Gustav von (1844-1920) Physiol. CDZZ ZZ-2

BUNSEN, Robert W. (1811-1899) Chem. ABES ABET BDOS BEOS CDZZ GASJ GRCH HOSS HSSO TOWS ZZ-2

BUNTING, Mary I. (1910-) Bact. CB67

BUNYAKOVSKY, Viktor Y. (1804-1889) Math. CDZZ ZZXV

BUONAMICI, Francesco (d. 1603) Med. CDZZ ZZ-2

BUONANNI, Filippo (1638-1725) Nat. Hist. CDZZ ZZ-2

BUONO, Paolo del (1625-1659) Phys. CDZZ ZZ-2

BUOT, Jacques (d. c.1675) Astron. CDZZ ZZ-2

BURALI-FORTI, Cesare (1861-1931) Math. CDZZ ZZ-2

BURBANK, Luther (1849-1926) Hort. ABES ABET BEOS COAC GANC MMSB TLLW WAMB

BURBIDGE, Eleanor M. (1922-) Astron. BEOS IEAS

BURBIDGE, Frederick W. (1847-1905) Bot. DNB2

BURBIDGE, Geoffrey (1925-) Astrophys. BEOS IEAS

BURBIDGE, Margaret (1920-) Astron. IDWB

BURBURY, Samuel H. (1831-1911) Math. DNB2

BURCH, Cecil R. (1901-) Phys. MHM1 MHSE

BURCHELL, William J. (c.1782-1863) Nat. Hist. DNB

BURDACH, Karl F. (1776-1847) Physiol. CDZZ ZZ-2

BURDEN, W. Douglas (1898-1978) Nat. Hist. NCSF

BURDENKO, Nicolai N. (1876-1964) Med. CDZZ ZZ-2

BURDON-SANDERSON, John S. (1828-1905) Physiol. BHMT CDZZ VISC ZZ-2

BURG, Anton B. (1904-) Chem. MHSE

BURG, Johann T. (1766-1834) Astron. CDZZ ZZ-2

BURGENI, Alfred A. (1903-1970) Chem. NC55

BURGER, Herman C. (1893-1965) Phys. CDZZ ZZ-2

BURGERSDIJK, Frank (1590-1635) Nat. Philos. CDZZ ZZ-2

BURGESS, Albert F. (1873-1953) Entom. AMEM NC43

BURGESS, Charles F. (1873-1945) Chem. Engr. ACCE

BURGESS, Edward (1848-1891) Entom. BIOD DAB

BURGI, Joost (1552-1632) Math.;Astron. CDZZ ZZ-2

BURHOP, Eric H. (1911-1980) Phys. AO80 RS27

BURIDAN, Jean (c.1295-c.1358) Philos.; Phys. ABET BEOS CDZZ ZZ-2

BURKE, Harry E. (1878-1963) Entom. AMEM

BURKE, Oliver W. (1910-1975) Invent. NC60

BURKHOLDER, Paul R. (1903-1972) Mar. Biol. BM47

BURKITT, Denis P. (1911-) Med. MFIR MHSE

BURLEY, Walter (c.1275-c.1345) Nat. Philos. CDZZ ZZ-2

BURN, Caspar G. (1897-1976) Bact.; Path. NC59

BURN, Joshua H. (1892-) Pharm. MHM2 MHSE

BURNELL, Jocelyn SEE BELL, (Susan) Jocelyn

BURNET, (Frank) Macfarlane (1899-) Immunol.; Med. ABES ABET BEOS CB54 MHM1 MHSE PAW2

BURNET, Thomas (c.1635-1715) Geol. BEOS CDZZ ZZ-2

BURNETT, George M. (1921-1980) Chem. AO80

BURNETT, Gilbert T. (1800-1835) Bot. DNB

BURNETT, Waldo I. (1827-1854) Biol. BIOD

BURNHAM, John B. (1869-1939) Cons. LACC

BURNHAM, Sherburne W. (1838-1921) Astron. CDZZ DAB NC11 ZZ-2

BURNSIDE, William (1852-1927) Math. CDZZ DNB4 ZZ-2

BURPEE, David (1893-1980) Hort. AO80 SWWP

BURR, Theodore (1771-1822) Engr.; Invent. GE-1 INYG

BURRAU, Carl J. (1867-1944) Astron.; Math. CDZZ ZZ-2

BURRELL, George A. (1882-1957) Chem. Engr. NC46

BURRESS, Walter M. (1893-1950) Geol. NC40

BURRILL, Thomas J. (1839-1916) Bot. DAB DNB NC12 NC18

BURRITT, Elijah H. (1794-1838) Astron. BIOD

BURROUGHS, John (1837-1921) Nat. Hist. FIFE GANC LACC SFNB WAMB

BURROUGHS, William S. (1855-1898) Invent. WAMB

BURROW, Reuben (1747-1792) Math. DNB

BURROWS, Edwin G. (1891-1958) Anthro. NC47

BURT, Cyril L. (1883-1971) Psych. ABET

BURT, William A. (1792-1858) Invent. WAMB

BURT, William I. (1893-1965) Chem. Engr. ACCE

BURTON, Alan C. (1904-) Biophys.; Physiol. CB56

BURTON, Charles E. (1846-1882) Astron. DNB

BURTON, Robert (1577-1640) Sci. Writ. BDOS

BURTON, William M. (1865-1954) Chem. ACCE NC41

BURWELL, Charles S. (1893-1967) Med. MHM2 MHSE

BURWELL, Robert L. Jr. (1912-) Chem. MHSE

BURY, Edward (1794-1858) Engr. DNB

BUSCH, August L. (1804-1855) Astron. CDZZ ZZ-2

BUSCH, Daryle H. (1928-) Chem. MHSE

BUSCK, August (1870-1944) Entom. AMEM

BUSEMANN, Adolf (1901-) Aero. ICFW

BUSH, Vannevar (1890-1974) Elec. Engr. ABES ABET CB40 CB47 MHM2 MHSE PPEY PPTY WAMB WMSW

BUSHNELL, David (1742-1824) Invent. GE-1 WAMB YSMS

BUSIGNIES, Henri G. (1905-1981) Engr. AO81 MHM1 MHSE

BUSK, George (1807-1886) Med.; Nat. Hist. CDZZ DNB1 ZZ-2

BUSS, Robert R. (1913-) Elec. Engr. TPAE

BUSSIERE, Paul SEE BUISSIERE, Paul

BUTENANDT, Adolf F. (1903-) Chem. ABES ABET BEOS HSSO MHM2 MHSE NPWC

BUTEO, Johannes (c.1492-c.1568) Math. CDZZ ZZ-2

ibn BUTLAN, Abul Hasan al-Mukhtar (c.100-1068) Med. CDZZ ZZ-2

BUTLER, Amos W. (1860-1937) Zool. NC28

BUTLER, Bert S. (1877-1960) Geol. NC49

BUTLER, John A. (1899-1977) Biochem. COBC RS25

BUTLER, Ovid M. (1880-1960) Forest. EAFC LACC

BUTLER, Stuart T. (1926-) Phys. MHSE

BUTLEROV, Aleksandr M. (1828-1886) Chem. ABES ABET BDOS BEOS CDZZ GRCH ZZ-2

BUTSCHLI, Otto (1848-1920) Zool.; Mineral. CDZZ ZZ-2

BUXTON, Patrick A. (1892-1955) Entom. DNB7 RS-2

BUXTON, Richard (1786-1865) Bot. DNB

BUYS BALLOT, Christoph H. (1817-1890) Meteor.;
   Chem. BEOS CDZZ ZZ-2

BUYUKMIHCI, Hope S. (c.1930-) Cons. WAGW

BYERLY, Perry (1897-) Geophys. MHM2 MHSE

BYERLY, William E. (1849-1935) Math. DAB1 NC27

BYERS, Horace G. (1872-1956) Chem. ACCE NCSA

BYERS, Horace R. (1906-) Meteor. MHM2 MHSE

BYKHOVSKII, Boris E. (1908-) Zool. SMST

BYKOVSKY, Valery F. (1934-) Astronaut. CB65
   IEAS

BYRD, Richard E. (1888-1957) Exp. ABES ABET
   BEOS CB42 NC46 WAMB

BYRHFERTH (fl. 1000) Math. DNB

C

CABANIS, Pierre J. (1757-1808) Med.; Philos. CDZZ
   ZZ-3

CABEO, Niccolo (1586-1650) Math.; Meteor. CDZZ
   EETD ESEH ZZ-3

CABOT, Samuel Jr. (1815-1885) Ornith. BIOD

CABOT, Samuel (1850-1906) Chem. NC23

CABRERA, Blas (1878-1945) Phys. CDZZ ZZ-3

CADET, Louis C. (1731-1799) Chem. CDZZ ZZ-3

CADET DE GASSICOURT, Charles L. (1769-1821)
   Chem. CDZZ ZZ-3

CADET DE VAUX, Antoine A. (1743-1828) Chem.;
   Agr. CDZZ ZZ-3

CADOGAN, John I. (1930-) Chem. COBC

CADOGAN, William (1711-1797) Med. BHMT

CADWALLADER, Thomas (1703-1779) Med. BHMT

CADY, George H. (1906-) Chem. MHSE

CADY, Hamilton P. (1874-1943) Chem. ACCE NC32

CADY, William H. (1877-1969) Chem. NC55

CAGLIOSTRO, Count SEE BALSAMO, Guiseppe

CAGNIARD DE LA TOUR, Charles (1777-1859) Phys.
   BEOS CDZZ ZZ-3

CAHALANE, Victor H. (1901-) Biol. DGMT LACC

CAHOURS, Auguste A. (1813-1891) Chem. BEOS
   CDZZ ZZ-3

CAILLETET, Louis P. (1832-1913) Phys. ABES
   ABET BDOS BEOS CDZZ ZZ-3

CAIN, Stanley A. (1902-) Bot.; Cons. LACC

CAIN, William (1847-1930) Math. DAB1

CAIRNS, William D. (1871-1955) Math. NC47

CAIUS, Johannes (1510-1573) Med. BHMT CDZZ
   ZZ-3

CAJAL, Santiago R. SEE RAMON Y CAJAL, Santiago

CAJORI, Florian (1859-1930) Math. NC27

CALANDRELLI, Giuseppe (1749-1827) Astron. CDZZ
   ZZ-3

CALANDRELLI, Ignazio (1792-1866) Astron.; Math.
   CDZZ ZZ-3

CALCAGNINI, Celio (1479-1541) Astron. BMST

CALDANI, Leopoldo M. (1725-1813) Anat. CDZZ
   ZZ-3

CALDAS, Francisco J. de (1768-1816) Bot.; Astron.
   CDZZ ZZ-3

CALDECOTT, John (1800-1849) Astron.; Meteor.
   DNB

CALDIS, Panos D. (1896-1974) Bot. NC58

CALDWELL, Frank W. (1889-1974) Aero. ICFW

CALDWELL, George C. (1834-1907) Chem. ACCE
   NC-4 NC26

CALDWELL, Joseph (1773-1835) Math. DAB

CALDWELL, Mary L. (1890-1972) Chem. ACCE

CALDWELL, Peter C. (1927-1979) Zool. RS27

CALKINS, Gary N. (1869-1943) Zool. CDZZ DAB3
NC33 ZZ-3

CALLAN, Nicholas (1799-1864) Elec. Sci. CDZZ
ZZ-3

CALLANDREAU, Pierre J. (1852-1904) Astron.
CDZZ ZZ-3

CALLENDAR, Hugh L. (1863-1930) Phys.; Engr.
CDZZ DNB4 FNEC ZZ-3

CALLINICOS OF HELIOPOLIS (fl. C.673) Chem.
ABET BEOS CDZZ ZZ-3

CALLIPPUS (c.370 B.C.-c.300 B.C.) Astron.; Math.
ABET BEOS CDZZ ZZ-3

CALLISON, Charles H. (1913-) Cons. LACC

CALLOWAY, Nathaniel (1907-) Chem. SBPY

CALMAN, William T. (1871-1952) Zool. DNB7

CALMETTE, Albert (1863-1933) Bact. CDZZ ZZ-3

CALVERT, Frederick C. (1819-1873) Chem. DNB

CALVERT, Philip P. (1871-1961) Entom. AMEM
NC12

CALVIN, Melvin (1911-) Chem. ABES ABET
BEOS CB62 FMBB MHM1 MHSE MOS6 NCSI
PALF WAMB

CAMERARIUS, Rudolph J. (1665-1721) Bot. BDOS
BEOS CDZZ ZZXV

CAMERON, (Gordon) Roy (1899-1966) Path. BEOS
MHM1 MHSE RS14

CAMERON, Thomas W. (1894-) Parasit. MHM1
MHSE

CAMM, Sydney (1893-1966) Aero. ICFW

CAMPANELLA, Tommaso (1568-1639) Nat. Philos.
CDZZ ZZXV

CAMPANI, Giuseppe (1635-1715) Astron.; Micros.
CDZZ GE-1 ZZ-3

CAMPANUS OF NOVARA (c.1220-1296) Math.;
Astron. CDZZ ZZ-3

CAMPBELL, Clyde H. (1883-1946) Chem. NC42

CAMPBELL, Douglas H. (1859-1953) Bot. BM29
CDZZ DAB5 MABH NCSA ZZ-3

CAMPBELL, Edward D. (1863-1925) Chem. ACCE
NC28

CAMPBELL, George A. (1870-1954) Engr.; Math.
NC45 TPAE

CAMPBELL, Norman R. (1880-1949) Phys. CDZZ
ZZ-3

CAMPBELL, Sullivan G. (1922-1972) Math. NC57

CAMPBELL, Thomas M. (1883-1956) Agr. DANB

CAMPBELL, William W. (1862-1938) Astron. CDZZ
ZZ-3

CAMPER, Peter (1722-1789) Med. BHMT CDZZ
ZZ-3

CAMUS, Charles E. (1699-1768) Math.; Astron. CDZZ
ZZ-3

CANANO, Giovan B. (1515-1579) Anat. CDZZ ZZ-3

CANCRIN, Franz L. von (1738-1812) Metal. CDZZ
ZZ-3

CANDOLLE, Alphonse de (1806-1893) Bot. CDZZ
ZZ-3

CANDOLLE, Augustin P. de (1778-1841) Bot. ABES
ABET BDOS BEOS CDZZ SOAC ZZ-3

CANJAR, Lawrence N. (1923-1972) Chem. Engr.
NC57

CANNAN, R. Keith (1894-1971) Biochem. NC56

CANNIZZARO, Stanislao (1826-1910) Chem. ABES
ABET BDOS BEOS CDZZ GRCH ZZ-3

CANNON, Annie J. (1863-1941) Astron. ABET BEOS
CDZZ CWSE CWSN DAB3 IDWB IEAS NAW
NCSB WAMB WASM ZZ-3

CANNON, Herbert G. (1897-1963) Zool. RS-9

CANNON, Lillian E. (1897-) Biochem. NCSM

CANNON, Walter B. (1871-1945) Physiol. ABES
ABET BEOS BHMT CDZZ ZZXV

CANTON, John (1718-1772) Phys. ABET BEOS
CDZZ DNB EETD ESEH ZZ-3

CANTOR, Georg F. (1845-1918) Math. ABES ABET
BDOS BEOS CDZZ OMNM WTGM ZZ-3

CANTOR, Moritz B. (1829-1920) Math. CDZZ ZZ-3

CAPPER, James (1743-1825) Meteor. DNB

CAPRA, Baldassar (c.1580-1626) Astron. CDZZ ZZ-3

CAPRIO, Amerigo F. (1895-1976) Chem. NC59

CAPSTAFF, John G. (1879-1960) Invent. NC49

CARAMUEL Y LOBKOWITZ, Juan (1606-1682) Math.
CDZZ ZZ-3

CARANGEOT, Arnould (1742-1806) Crystal.; Entom.
CDZZ ZZ-3

CARAS, Roger A. (1928-) Nat. Hist.; Cons. AMJB

CARATHEODORY, Constantin (1873-1950) Math.
CDZZ ZZ-3

CARBUTT, John (1832-1905) Chem. NC22

CARCAVI, Pierre de (c.1600-1684) Math. CDZZ ZZ-3

CARDANO, Girolamo (1501-1576) Math. ABES
ABET BDOS BEOS CDZZ EETD GE-1 MASW
MELW MISU OMNM SXWS TBSG ZZ-3

CARDOZO, William W. (1905-1962) Med. DANB

CAREY, Eban J. (1889-1947) Anat. NCSF

CAREY, Henry A. (1890-1965) Anthro.; Archaeol.
NC52

CARHART, Arthur H. (1892-) Cons. LACC

CARHART, Henry S. (1844-1920) Chem. ACCE

CARLANDER, Kenneth D. (1915-) Biol. LACC

CARLISLE, Anthony (1768-1840) Med. CDZZ ZZ-3

CARLL, John F. (1828-1904) Geol. BIOD

CARLSON, Antin J. (1875-1956) Physiol. BM35 CDZZ
NC45 ZZ-3

CARLSON, Chester (1906-1968) Invent. NTBM SAIF
WAMB

CARLSON, J. Gordon (1908-) Zool. NCSK

CARLSON, Norman K. (1912-) Forest. BMBR

CARMICHAEL, Leonard (1898-1973) Psych. BM51
MHM2 MHSE

CARNALL, Rudolf von (1804-1874) Geol. CDZZ
ZZ-3

CARNAP, Rudolf (1891-1970) Philos. BEOS

CARNE, Joseph (1728-1858) Geol. DNB

CARNOT, Lazare N. (1753-1823) Phys.; Math. CDZZ
GE-1 ZZ-3

CARNOT, Nicholas S. (1796-1832) Phys. ABES ABET
BDOS BEOS CDZZ FNEC GE-1 HOSS MCCW
TGNH ZZ-3

CARNOT, Sadi SEE CARNOT, Nicholas S.

CARO, Heinrich (1834-1910) Chem. ABET BEOS
CDZZ ZZ-3

CAROTHERS, Wallace H. (1896-1937) Chem. ABES
ABET ACCE ASIW BDOS BEOS BM20 CDZZ
DAB2 GRCH NC38 SAIF WAMB ZZ-3

CARPENTER, Frederic W. (1876-1925) Zool. NC20

CARPENTER, George W. (1802-1860) Mineral.; Chem.
BIOD

CARPENTER, Henry C. (1875-1940) Metal. CDZZ
DNB5 ZZ-3

CARPENTER, Malcolm S. (1925-) Astronaut. CB62
EXDC FPSN IEAS PMAS WESE

CARPENTER, Philip H. (1852-1891) Paleon.; Zool.
DNB1

CARPENTER, Philip P. (1819-1877) Conch. DNB

CARPENTER, William B. (1813-1885) Med.; Nat. Hist.
ANHD CDZZ DNB VISC ZZ-3

CARPI, Berengario SEE BERENGARIO DA CARPI,
Giacomo

CARPUE, Joseph C. (1764-1846) Anat. DNB

CARR, Emma P. (1880-1972) Chem. ACCE CB59
NAWM NCSF

CARR, Ezra S. (1819-1894) Chem.; Geol. ACCE

CARR, Herbert W. (1857-1931) Philos. CDZZ ZZ-3

CARR, William H. (1902-) Cons. LACC

CARRE, Edmund (1822-1890) Engr. MCCW

CARREL, Alexis (1873-1944) Med. ABES ABET BDOS BEOS CB40 CDZZ DAB3 DSLP PAW2 ZZ-3

CARRIER, Willis H. (1876-1950) Invent. FOIF MASY

CARRINGTON, Alan (1934-) Chem. COBC

CARRINGTON, Hereward (1880-1958) Phys. PUNT

CARRINGTON, Richard C. (1826-1875) Astron. ABES ABET BDOS BEOS CDZZ DNB ZZ-3

CARROLL, James (1854-1907) Bact. ABET CDZZ ZZ-3

CARRUTHERS, George R. (1931-) Astrophys. BISC SBPY

CARRUTHERS, William (1830-1922) Bot. FHUA

CARSON, James (1772-1843) Med. BHMT

CARSON, Rachel L. (1907-1964) Biol. CB51 CWSN EAFC EXDC GANC GOTH HOCS IDWB LACC LISD NAWM NC51 NCSI NHAH SFNB TLLW WAMB WASM

CARSWELL, Robert (1793-1857) Path. DNB

CARTAN, Elie J. (1869-1951) Math. BEOS CDZZ ZZ-3

CARTER, Edna (1872-1963) Phys. NC52

CARTER, Herbert E. (1910-) Biochem. MHM1 MHSE

CARTER, T. Donald (1893-) Zool.; Nat. Hist. DGMT

CARTWRIGHT, Edmund (1743-1823) Invent. BDOS BEOS DNB GE-1

CARTY, John J. (1861-1932) Elec. Engr. BEOS BM18 WAMB

CARUS, Julius V. (1823-1903) Zool. CDZZ ZZXV

CARUS, Paul (1852-1919) Philos. of Sci. CDZZ ZZXV

CARVER, George W. (1860-1943) Chem. ABES ABET ACCE BEOS BISC BPSH CB40 DAB3 DANB GANC GBAR GNPA HCOK MASY SABL SBAH SBPY SSAH

CARVER, Jonathan (1710-1780) Nat. Hist. IPNW

CARVETH, Hector R. (1873-1942) Electrochem. ACCE

CARY, Austin F. (1865-1936) Forest. EAFC LACC

CASAL JULIAN, Gaspar R. (1680-1759) Med.; Nat. Hist. CDZZ ZZ-3

CASAMAJOR, Paul (1831-1887) Chem. ACCE

CASE, Theodore W. (1888-1944) Phys.; Chem. NC59 NCSD

CASE, Willard E. (1857-1918) Electrochem. NC19

CASERIO, Marjorie (1929-) Chem. MHSE

CASEY, John (1820-1891) Math. DNB1

CASEY, Thomas L. (1831-1896) Engr. BM-4

CASEY, Thomas L. (1857-1925) Entom. AMEM

CASEY, William H. (1918-1976) Engr. NC60

CASIMIR, Hendrik B. (1909-) Phys. BEOS

CASPERSSON, Torljorn O. (1910-) Chem. BEOS

CASSEGRAIN, N. (fl. 1672) Phys. BDOS CDZZ ZZ-3

CASSELMAN, Elbridge J. (1893-1965) Chem. NC52

CASSERI, Giulio (c.1552-1616) Anat. CDZZ ZZ-3

CASSIN, John (1813-1869) Ornith. BIOD BWCL DAB NC22 WFBG

CASSINI, Giovanni D. (1625-1712) Astron. ABES ABET BDOS BEOS CDZZ HSSO IEAS TOWS ZZ-3

CASSINI, Jacques (1677-1756) Astron. CDZZ ZZ-3

CASSINI, Jean D. (1748-1845) Astron. CDZZ ZZ-3

CASSINI DE THURY, Cesar F. (1714-1784) Astron. CDZZ ZZ-3

CASSIODORUS SENATOR, Flavius M. (c.480-c.575) Sci. Ed. CDZZ ZZ-3

CASSIRER, Ernst A. (1874-1945) Philos. CDZZ ZZ-3

CASTAING, Raymond (1921-) Phys. MHSE

CASTALDI, Luigi (1890-1945) Anat. CDZZ ZZ-3

CASTEL, Louis B. (1688-1757) Phys.; Math. CDZZ ZZ-3

CASTELLI, Benedetto (1578-1643) Astron.; Opt. CDZZ ZZ-3

CASTELNUOVO, Guido (1865-1952) Math. CDZZ ZZ-3

CASTIGLIANO, Alberto (1847-1884) Engr. CDZZ FNEC ZZ-3

CASTILLO, Juan D. del (1744-1793) Bot. SSNW

CASTILLON, Johann (1704-1791) Math. CDZZ ZZ-3

CASTLE, William E. (1867-1962) Biol. BM38 CDZZ NC16 ZZ-3

CASTNER, Hamilton Y. (1858-1898) Chem. ACCE BDOS BEOS

CASWELL, Alexis (1799-1877) Astron. BIOD BM-6 DAB

CATALAN, Miguel A. (1894-1957) Spect. CDZZ ZZ-3

CATALDI, Pietro A. (1552-1626) Math. CDZZ ZZ-3

CATESBY, Mark (1683-1749) Nat. Hist.; Bot. ANHD BIOD BWCL CDZZ DAB DNB FIFE HAOA IPNW LHES NHAH ZZ-3

CATHCART, Edward P. (1877-1954) Physiol. DNB7

CATTELL, James M. (1860-1944) Psych. BM25 CDZZ DAB3 ZZ-3

CATTON, Thomas (1760-1838) Astron. DNB

CAUCHY, Augustin L. (1789-1857) Math. ABES ABET BDOS BEOS CDZZ ZZ-3

CAUDELL, Andrew N. (1872-1936) Entom. AMEM

CAULLERY, Maurice J. (1868-1958) Biol. CDZZ RS-6 ZZ-3

CAUS, Salomon de (1576-1626) Engr. GE-1

CAVALIERI, Bonaventure (1598-1647) Math. ABET BDOS BEOS CDZZ ZZ-3

CAVALLI-SFORZA, Luigi L. (1922-) Genet. BEOS

CAVALLO, Tiberius (1749-1809) Phys. CDZZ MCCW ZZ-3

CAVANAUGH, George W. (1870-1938) Chem. NC30

CAVANILLES, Antonio J. (1745-1804) Bot. CDZZ ZZ-3

CAVE, Henry (1874-1963) Engr.; Invent. NC54

CAVENDISH, Charles (1591-1654) Math. DNB1

CAVENDISH, Henry (1731-1810) Chem.; Phys. ABES ABET BDOS BEOS CDZZ CSCJ EETD ESEH GASW GRCH HLSM HOSS HSSO LECE LISD SAIF SIRC TOWS ZZ-3

CAVENDISH, William (1808-1891) Sci. Ed. SOSC

CAVENTOU, Joseph B. (1795-1877) Chem. ABET BDOS BEOS CDZZ ZZ-3

CAVETT, Jesse W. (1900-1963) Chem. NC50

CAWLEY, Aloysius (1884-1956) Med. NC47

CAYEUX, Lucien (1864-1944) Geol. CDZZ ZZ-3

CAYLEY, Arthur (1821-1895) Math. ABET BDOS BEOS CDZZ DNB1 MASW SNCB ZZ-3

CAYLEY, George (1773-1857) Aero. BEOS GE-1 ICFW

CAZENAVE, Alphee (1795-1877) Med. BHMT

CECH, Eduard (1893-1960) Math. CDZZ ZZ-3

CELAYA, Juan de (c.1490-1558) Nat. Philos. CDZZ ZZ-3

CELL, John W. (1907-1967) Math. NC54

CELS, Jacques P. (1740-1806) Bot. CDZZ ZZ-3

CELSIUS, Anders (1701-1744) Astron. ABES ABET BDOS BEOS CDZZ FNEC ZZ-3

CELSUS, Aulus C. (30 B.C.-A.D. 50) Sci. Writ. ABET BDOS BHMT LISD ZZ-3

CENSORINUS (fl. c.225) Sci. Writ. CDZZ ZZ-3

CENTNERSZWER, Mieczyslaw (1871-1944) Chem. CDZZ ZZ-3

CERASKY, Vitold SEE TSERASKY, Vitold K.

CERENKOV, Pavel A. SEE CHERENKOV, Pavel A.

CERNAN, Eugene A. (1934-) Astronaut. CB73 IEAS

CERVANTES, Vicente (1755-1829) Pharm.; Bot. CDZZ SSNW ZZ-3

CESALPINO, Andrea (1519-1603) Bot.; Med. BDOS BEOS CDZZ HLSM ZZXV

CESARO, Ernesto (1859-1906) Math. CDZZ ZZ-3

CESI, Federico (1585-1630) Bot. CDZZ ZZ-3

CESTONI, Giacinto (1637-1718) Nat. Hist. CDZZ ZZ-3

CETTI, Francois (1726-1780) Nat. Hist. WFBG

CEULEN, Ludolph van (1540-1610) Math. CDZZ ZZ-3

CEVA, Giovanni (1647/8-1734) Math. CDZZ ZZ-3

CEVA, Tomasso (1648-1737) Math. CDZZ ZZ-3

CHABRY, Laurent (1855-1893) Physiol.; Embryol. CDZZ ZZ-3

CHADWICK, Edwin (1800-1890) Med. BHMT

CHADWICK, James (1891-1974) Phys. ABES ABET BEOS CB45 DCPW MHM1 MHSE MWBR POSW RS22 SAIF

CHADWICK, Roy (1893-1947) Aero. DNB6

CHADWICK, Wallace L. (1897-) Engr. MHM1 MHSE

CHAGAS, Carlos R. (1879-1934) Med. CDZZ ZZ-3

CHAIN, Ernst B. (1906-1979) Biochem. ABES ABET BEOS DSLP GJPS MHM1 MHSE

CHALLIS, James (1803-1882) Astron. ABET CDZZ DNB ZZ-3

CHALMERS, Lionel (1715-1777) Med.; Meteor. BIOD

CHAMBERLAIN, Charles J. (1863-1943) Bot. CDZZ DAB3 ZZ-3

CHAMBERLAIN, Clark W. (1870-1948) Phys. NC37

CHAMBERLAIN, Owen (1920-) Phys. ABES ABET BEOS CB60 MHM1 MHSE POSW WAMB

CHAMBERLAND, Charles E. (1851-1908) Bact. ABET CDZZ ZZ-3

CHAMBERLIN, Rollin T. (1881-1948) Geol. BM41

CHAMBERLIN, Thomas C. (1843-1928) Geol.; Cosmol. ABES ABET BEOS BM15 CDZZ GKGP RPTC TOWS ZZ-3

CHAMBERS, Arthur D. (1870-1961) Chem. Engr. ACCE

CHAMBERS, Robert (1802-1871) Biol.; Geol. CDZZ DARR ZZ-3

CHAMBERS, Robert (1880-1957) Biol. NC46

CHAMISSO, Adelbert von (1781-1838) Bot. BEOS CDZZ ZZXV

CHAMOT, Emile M. (1868-1950) Chem.; Micros. ACCE

CHAMPION, John G. (1815-1854) Bot. DNB

CHANCE, Alexander M. (1844-1917) Chem. BDOS BEOS

CHANCE, Britton (1913-) Biophys. ABES ABET BEOS MHM1 MHSE

CHANCEL, Gustav C. (1822-1890) Chem. CDZZ ZZ-3

CHANDLER, Charles F. (1836-1925) Chem. BM14 DAB NC13 NC23 WAMB

CHANDLER, Seth C. (1846-1913) Astron. BEOS CDZZ DAB NC-9 ZZ-3

CHANDLER, William H. (1841-1906) Chem. ACCE

CHANDRASEKHAR, Subrahmanyan (1910-) Astron. ABES ABET BEOS IEAS MHM1 MHSE PBTS

CHANEY, Lucian W. (1857-1935) Biol. NC27

CHANEY, Newcomb K. (1883-1966) Chem. NCSA

CHANEY, Ralph W. (1890-1971) Paleon. MHM1 MHSE

CHANG, Min Chueh (1908-) Biol. BEOS

CHANG HENG (78-142) Astron.; Math. BEOS GE-1

CHANG JUNG (fl. 1 B.C.) Engr. GE-1

CHANG JUNG (fl. 1220) Engr. GE-1

CHANG SSU-HSUN (fl. 975) Engr. GE-1

CHANG YONGSIL (fl. 1432) Engr. GE-1

CHANUTE, Octave (1832-1910) Aero. DAB ICFW
WAMB

CHAPIN, James P. (1899-) Zool.; Ornith. DGMT

CHAPLINE, William R. (1891-) Cons. LACC

CHAPLYGIN, Sergei A. (1869-1942) Phys.; Math.
CDZZ ZZ-3

CHAPMAN, Alvan W. (1809-1899) Bot. CDZZ MABH
ZZ-3

CHAPMAN, David L. (1869-1958) Chem. CDZZ
DNB7 RS-4 ZZ-3

CHAPMAN, Edward J. (1821-1904) Mineral. DNB2

CHAPMAN, Frank M. (1864-1945) Ornith. BM25
BWCL DAB3 LACC NC-9 NC36 ORNS SFNB
WAMB

CHAPMAN, Henry C. (1845-1909) Biol. DAB

CHAPMAN, Herman H. (1874-1963) Forest. EAFC
LACC

CHAPMAN, James C. (1889-1925) Phys. NC20

CHAPMAN, John (1774-1845) Cons. DAB GANC
HOCS

CHAPMAN, John (1822-1894) Med. BHMT

CHAPMAN, Nathaniel (1780-1853) Med. BHMT

CHAPMAN, Norman B. (1916-) Chem. COBC

CHAPMAN, Royal N. (1889-1939) Ecol. NC29

CHAPMAN, Sydney (1888-1970) Math.; Phys. BEOS
CB57 MHM1 MHSE RS17

CHAPPE, Claude (1763-1805) Invent. BDOS BEOS
GE-1

CHAPPE D'AUTEROCHE, Jean B. (1728-1769) Astron.
CDZZ ZZ-3

CHAPTAL, Jean A. (1756-1832) Chem. ABES ABET
BDOS BEOS CDZZ SOAC ZZ-3

CHARAKA (fl. c.100 B.C.) Med. OGIV

CHARCH, William H. (1898-1958) Chem. ACCE

CHARCOT, Jean B. (1867-1936) Med.; Ocean. CDZZ
ZZ-3

CHARCOT, Jean M. (1825-1893) Med. ABET BDOS
BEOS BHMT CDZZ ZZ-3

CHARDENON, Jean P. (1714-1769) Chem.; Med.
CDZZ ZZ-3

CHARDONNET, Louis M. (1839-1924) Chem. ABES
ABET BEOS CDZZ ZZ-3

CHARGAFF, Erwin (1905-) Biochem. ABES ABET
BEOS HLSM MHM2 MHSE

CHARLES, Jacques A. (1746-1823) Phys. ABES
ABET BDOS BEOS CDZZ FNEC ICFW MCCW
ZZ-3

CHARLES, Wyville T. SEE THOMSON, Charles W.

CHARLETON, Walter (1620)-1707) Ornith. CDZZ
ORNS ZZ-3

CHARLEVOIX, Pierre F. (1682-1761) Nat. Hist. HAOA

CHARNEY, Jule G. (1917-1981) Meteor. AO81 MHM1
MHSE

CHARNLEY, John (1911-1982) Med. MFIR

CHARPENTIER, Jean de (1786-1885) Mng.; Glaciol.
ABET BEOS CDZZ ZZ-3

CHARPY, Augustin G. (1865-1945) Metal.; Chem.
CDZZ ZZ-3

CHARY, Chintamanny R. (d. 1880) Astron. DNB

CHARYK, Joseph V. (1920-) Aero. CB70 MOS7

CHASE, Agnes M. (1869-1963) Bot. NAWM

CHASE, March F. (1876-1935) Chem. NCSA

CHASE, Pline E. (1820-1886) Astron. BIOD DAB
NC-6

CHASLES, Michel (1793-1880) Math. CDZZ ZZ-3

CHATELET, Gabrielle E. du (1706-1749) Sci. Writ. CDZZ MEQP ZZ-3

CHATELIER, Henri L. SEE LE CHARTELIER, Henri L.

CHATT, Joseph (1914-) Chem. COBC MHSE

CHAULIAC, Guy de (1920-1367) Med. CDZZ ZZ-3

CHAUVEAU, Jean B. (1827-1917) Physiol.; Vet. Med. CDZZ ZZ-3

CHAUVENET, William (1820-1870) Math.; Astron. BIOD BM-1 DAB NC11

CHAZY, Jean F. (1882-1955) Phys. CDZZ ZZ-3

CHEADLE, Vernon I. (1910-) Bot. MHM2 MHSE

CHEBOTARYOV, Nikolai G. (1894-1947) Math. CDZZ ZZ-3

CHEBYSHEV, Pafnuty L. (1821-1894) Math. CDZZ ZZ-3

CHEN TENG (fl. 190) Engr. GE-1

CHEN YAO-TSO (fl. 1000) Engr. GE-1

CHENEVIX, Richard (1774-1830) Chem.; Mineral. CDZZ DNB SOAC ZZ-3

CHENG KUO (fl. 246 B.C.) Engr. GE-1

CHENG TANG SHIH (fl. 130 B.C.) Engr. GE-1

CHEPIL, William S. (1904-1963) Soil Sci. LACC

CHERENKOV, Pavel A. (1904-) Phys. ABES ABET BEOS MHM1 MHSE PAW2 POSW

CHERN, Shiing-shen (1911-) Math. MHM1 MHSE

CHERNOV, Dmitri K. (1839-1921) Metal. CDZZ ZZ-3

CHERNYAEV, Ilya I. (1893-1966) Chem. CDZZ SMST ZZ-3

CHERNYSHEV, Feodosii N. (1856-1914) Geol.; Paleon. CDZZ ZZ-3

CHERONIS, Nicholas D. (1896-1962) Chem. ACCE NC49

CHERRIE, George K. (1865-1948) Nat. Hist. NC36

CHERRY, Thomas M. (1898-1966) Math. RS14

CHERSIPHRON OF KNOSSOS (fl. 550 B.C.) Engr. GE-1

CHERWELL, Lord SEE LINDEMANN, Frederick

CHESEBROUGH, Robert A. (1837-1933) Chem. ACCE

CHESELDEN, William (1688-1752) Anat.; Physiol. BHMT DNB

CHESNEY, Cummings C. (1863-1947) Elec. Engr. TPAE

CHESNUT, Victor K. (1867-1938) Bot. NC13

CHESTER, Robert (fl. 1182) Astron. DNB

CHESTNUT, Harold (1917-) Engr. TPAE

CHEVALLIER, Jean B. (1793-1879) Chem. CDZZ ZZ-3

CHEVALLIER, Temple (1794-1873) Astron. CDZZ DNB ZZ-3

CHEVENARD, Pierre A. (1888-1960) Metal. CDZZ ZZ-3

CHEVREUL, Michel E. (1786-1889) Chem. ABES ABET BDOS BEOS CDZZ GRCH ZZ-3

CHEVROLET, Louis J. (1878-1941) Invent. NC53

CHEW, Geoffrey F. (1924-) Phys. DCPW MHM2 MHSE

CHEYNE, George (1671-1743) Med.; Math. BHMT CDZZ ZZ-3

CHEYNE, John (1777-1836) Med. BHMT

CHEYNE, (William) Watson (1852-1932) Bact. DNB5

CHIA JANG (fl. 6 B.C.) Engr. GE-1

CHIA KU SHAN SHOU (fl. 1315) Engr. GE-1

CHIARUGI, Giulio (1859-1944) Anat. CDZZ ZZ-3

CHICHIBABIN, Alexai Y. (1871-1945) Chem. CDZZ ZZ-3

CHILD, Charles M. (1869-1954) Zool. BM30 CDZZ DAB5 ZZ-3

CHILDREN, George (1742-1818) Elec. Sci. DNB

CHILDREY, Joshua (1623-1670) Meteor.; Nat. Hist. CDZZ ZZ-3

CHILDS, George H. (1890-1963) Nat. Hist. NC52

CHILTON, Thomas H. (1899-) Chem. Engr. NCSL

CHIN CHIU-SHAO (c.1202-c.1261) Math. CDZZ ZZ-3

CHINAKAL, Nikolai A. (1888-) Mng. SMST

CHIRNSIDE, R.C. (1904-) Chem. COBC

CHISHOLM, Alec H. (1890-) Nat. Hist. DGMT

CHITTENDEN, Russell H. (1856-1943) Chem. BDOS BEOS BM24 CDZZ DAB3 ZZ-3

CHITTENDON, Frank H. (1858-1929) Entom. AMEM NC24

CHIZHIKOV, David M. (1895-) Metal. SMST

CHLADNI, Ernst F. (1756-1827) Phys. ABES ABET BEOS CDZZ ZZ-3

CHMUTOV, Konstantin V. (1902-) Chem. SMST

CHODAT, Robert (1865-1934) Bot. CDZZ ZZ-3

CHOU KUNG (fl. c.1100 B.C.) Math. BEOS

CHRISTENSEN, Jonas J. (1892-1964) Bot. NC52

CHRISTIANSEN, Christian (1843-1917) Phys. CDZZ ZZXV

CHRISTIE, Samuel H. (1784-1865) Phys. CDZZ DNB ZZ-3

CHRISTIE, William H. (1845-1922) Astron. BEOS CDZZ DNB4 IEAS ZZ-3

CHRISTMANN, Jacob (1554-1613) Math.; Astron. CDZZ ZZ-3

CHRISTOFFEL, Elwin B. (1829-1900) Math. CDZZ ZZ-3

CHRISTOFILOS, Nicholas C. (1916-1972) Phys. CB65

CHRISTOL, Jules de (1802-1861) Paleon. CDZZ ZZ-3

CHRISTOPHERS, S. Richard (1873-1978) Med. MHM2 MHSE RS25

CHRISTY, David (1802-1868) Geol. BIOD

CHRISTY, Henry (1810-1865) Anthro. DNB

CHRYSTAL, George (1851-1911) Math.; Phys. CDZZ ZZ-3

CHU SHIH-CHIEH (fl. 1280-1303) Math. BEOS CDZZ ZZ-3

CHUANG, Hsiung-Pi (fl. 120 B.C.) Engr. GE-1

CHUBB, Lewis W. (1882-1952) Engr. CB47

CHUFAROV, Grigorii I. (1900-) Chem. SMST

CHUGAEV, Lev A. (1873-1922) Chem. CDZZ ZZ-3

CHUKHANOV, Zinovii F. (1912-) Engr. SMST

CHUKHROV, Fyodor V. (1908-) Geol. SMST

CHUQUET, Nicolas (fl. c.1450-1500) Math. CDZZ ZZ-3

CHURCHILL, Edward D. (1895-) Med. CB63

CHURCHMAN, John (1753-1805) Surv. NC-9

CHWISTEK, Leon (1884-1944) Philos. CDZZ ZZ-3

CIAMICIAN, Giacomo L. (1857-1922) Chem. CDZZ GRCH ZZ-3

CIERCA Y CODORNICE, Juan de la (1886-1936) Aero. ICFW

CIRUELO, Pedro (1470-1554) Math. CDZZ ZZ-3

CIST, Jacob (1782-1825) Geol. BIOD DAB

CLAFF, C. Lloyd (1895-1974) Zool.; Invent. NC61

CLAIRAUT, Alexis C. (1713-1765) Math. ABES ABET BEOS CDZZ ZZ-3

CLAISEN, Ludwig (1851-1930) Chem. BDOS BEOS CDZZ ZZ-3

CLANNY, William R. (1776-1850) Invent. DNB

CLAP, Thomas (1703-1767) Astron. BIOD

CLAPEYRON, Benoit P. (1799-1864) Engr. ABET
CDZZ FNEC GE-1 ZZ-3

CLAPP, Cornelia M. (1849-1934) Zool. NAW

CLAPP, Earle H. (1877-1970) Forest. EAFC LACC

CLAPPEL, Louis S. (1916-) Cons. LACC

CLARK, Alvan (1804-1887) Astron. BIOD CDZZ
DAB IEAS ZZ-3

CLARK, Alvan G. (1832-1897) Astron. ABES ABET
BEOS BIOD CDZZ DAB NC-5 WAMB ZZ-3

CLARK, Austin H. (1880-1954) Entom. AMEM

CLARK, Bruce L. (1880-1945) Paleon. NC35

CLARK, Charles E. (1910-1965) Math. NC52

CLARK, Charles R. (1912-1960) Chem. NC47

CLARK, Eliot R. (1881-1963) Anat. NC53

CLARK, Eugenie (1922-) Ichth. CB53 CWSE
WAGW WAWL

CLARK, George B. (1827-1891) Astron. CDZZ ZZ-3

CLARK, Henry J. (1826-1873) Zool.; Bot. BIOD
BM-1 DAB

CLARK, James L. (1883-1969) Nat. Hist. NC55

CLARK, John G. (1907-) Archaeol. MHSE

CLARK, Josiah L. (1822-1898) Engr. CDZZ DNB1
ZZ-3

CLARK, Thomas (1801-1867) Chem. CDZZ DNB
ZZ-3

CLARK, Thomas E. (1869-1962) Invent. NC53

CLARK, Victor M. (1925-) Chem. COBC

CLARK, Virginius (1886-1948) Aero. ICFW

CLARK, Wilfrid SEE LE GROS CLARK, Wilfrid E.

CLARK, William (1788-1869) Anat. DNB

CLARK, William (1821-1880) Engr. DNB

CLARK, William B. (1860-1917) Geol. BM-9

CLARK, William M. (1884-1964) Chem. ACCE BM39
CDZZ MHM1 MHSE NC52 NCSF ZZ-3

CLARK, William S. (1826-1886) Bot. ACCE DAB

CLARK, William T. (1783-1852) Engr. DNB

CLARK, Wilson F. (1921-) Cons. LACC

CLARKE, Arthur C. (1917-) Sci. Writ. CB66 EXSB
ICFW MOS8

CLARKE, Cyril A. (1907-) Med. BEOS

CLARKE, Edith (1883-1959) Engr. NAWM

CLARKE, Edward D. (1769-1822) Mineral.; Geol.
CDZZ ZZ-3

CLARKE, Frank W. (1847-1931) Geol. ACCE BM15
CDZZ ZZ-3

CLARKE, Hans T. (1887-1972) Chem. BM46 NC57

CLARKE, Henry (1743-1818) Math. DNB

CLARKE, Jacob A. (1817-1880) Anat. DNB

CLARKE, John M. (1857-1925) Paleon. BM12 DAB

CLARKE, Nancy T. (1825-1901) Med. WIWM

CLARKE, Samuel (1675-1729) Math.; Phys. CDZZ
ZZ-3

CLARKE, William B. (1798-1878) Geol. CDZZ
ZZ-3

CLARKSON, Ralph P. (1886-1964) Engr.; Invent.
NC53

CLASSEN, Alexander (1843-1934) Chem. CDZZ
ZZXV

CLAUDE, Albert (1898-) Biol. ABET BEOS
MHSE

CLAUDE, Francois A. (1858-1938) Astron. CDZZ
ZZ-3

CLAUDE, Georges (1870-1960) Chem. ABES ABET
BDOS BEOS CDZZ ZZ-3

CLAUDIUD PTOLEMY SEE PTOLEMY, Claudius

CLAUS, Adolf C. (1838-1900) Chem. CDZZ ZZ-3

CLAUS, Carl E. (1796-1864) Chem.; Pharm. ABET CDZZ ZZ-3

CLAUSEN, Jens C. (1891-1969) Biol. MHM1 MHSE

CLAUSEN, Roy E. (1891-1956) Genet. BM39 NC43

CLAUSEN, Thomas (1801-1885) Math.; Astron. CDZZ ZZ-3

CLAUSIUS, Rudolf J. (1822-1888) Phys. ABES ABET BDOS BEOS CDZZ FNEC MCCW PFEL ZZ-3

CLAVASIO SEE DOMINICUS DE CLAVASIO

CLAVIUS, Christoph (1537-1612) Math.; Astron. ABET BMST CDZZ ZZ-3

CLAWSON, Marion (1905-) Agr. LACC

CLAY, Jacob (1882-1955) Phys. CDZZ ZZ-3

CLAYPOLE, Edward W. (1835-1901) Geol. BIOD NC13

CLAYTON, John (fl. 1671-1694) Ornith. HAOA

CLAYTON, John (1693-1773) Bot. BIOD DAB DNB NC19 SBCS

CLEAVELAND, Parker (1780-1858) Mineral. ACCE BIOD CDZZ DAB ZZ-3

CLEBSCH, Rudolf F. (1833-1872) Math. CDZZ ZZ-3

CLEGG, Samuel (1781-1861) Invent. DNB GE-1

CLELAND, Ralph E. (1892-1971) Bot. BM53 MHM1 MHSE NC57

CLEMENCE, Gerald M. (1908-1974) Astron. BEOS MHM1 MHSE

CLEMENT, Joseph (1779-1844) Engr. GE-1

CLEMENT, Nicholas (1778-1841) Chem. CDZZ ZZ-3

CLEMENT, Roland C. (1912-) Ornith. LACC

CLEMENTS, Frederic E. (1874-1945) Bot.; Ecol. CDZZ DAB3 LACC MABH NC34 ZZ-3

CLEMO, George R. (1889-) Chem. COBC

CLEMSON, Thomas G. (1807-1888) Chem.; Agr. ACCE BIOD

CLEOMEDES (fl. before 100) Astron. CDZZ ZZ-3

CLEPPER, Henry E. (1901-) Forest. LACC

CLERCK, Carl A. (1709-1765) Entom. CDZZ ZZ-3

CLERSELIER, Claude (1614-1684) Sci. Writ. CDZZ ZZ-3

CLEVE, Per Teodor (1840-1905) Chem.; Geol. ABES ABET BEOS CDZZ ZZ-3

CLEVELAND, Lemuel R. (1892-1969) Entom. BM51

CLIFF, Edward P. (1909-) Forest. EAFC LACC SWWP

CLIFFORD, William K. (1845-1879) Math. CDZZ DNB ZZ-3

CLIFT, William (1775-1849) Anat.; Paleon. CDZZ DNB ZZ-3

CLIFTON, Charles E. (1904-1976) Bact. NC59

CLINE, Isaac M. (1861-1955) Meteor. NC42

CLINE, Lewis M. (1909-1971) Geol. NC57

CLINTON, George P. (1867-1937) Bot.; Agr. BM20

CLOKEY, Ira W. (1878-1950) Bot. BNBR

CLOOS, Ernst (1898-1974) Geol. BM52 NC58

CLOOS, Hans (1886-1951) Geol. CDZZ MHM1 MHSE ZZ-3

CLOSE, Maxwell H. (1822-1903) Geol. DNB2

CLOUD, Preston (1912-) Geol. MHSE

CLOUET, Jean F. (1751-1801) Chem.; Metal. CDZZ ZZ-3

CLOW, Archie (1909-) Sci. Writ. COBC

CLOWES, George H. (1877-1958) Chem. NC48

CLUSIUS, Carolus SEE L'ECLUSE, Charles de

CLYMER, George (1754-1834) Invent.; Engr. GE-1

COAN, Titus (1801-1882) Geol. BIOD

COANDA, Henri (1885-1972) Aero. ICFW

COATES, Charles E. (1866-1939) Chem. NC36

COATES, Christopher (1899-) Ichth. CHUB

COBB, Nathan A. (1859-1932) Biol.; Agr. DAB1
NC23

COBB, Ralph W. (1887-1968) Metal. NC55

COBB, W. Montague (1904-) Anat. NCSJ SBPY

COBB, William B. (1891-1933) Geol. NC30

COBBOLD, Thomas S. (1828-1886) Parasit. DNB

COBLENTZ, William W. (1873-1962) Spect. ABES
ABET BEOS BM39 CB54 CDZZ NC52 NCSE
ZZ-3

COCCHI, Igino (1827-1913) Geol. CDZZ ZZ-3

COCHON DE LAPPARENT SEE LAPPARENT,
Albert A. de

COCHRAN, William (1922-) Phys. MHM2 MHSE

COCHRANE, Alexander (1802-1865) Chem. ACCE

COCHRANE, Archibald SEE DUNDONALD, Archibald C.

COCHRANE, Edward L. (1892-1959) Engr. BM35

COCKCROFT, John D. (1897-1967) Phys. ABES
ABET BDOS BEOS CB48 CDZZ DCPW MHM1
MHSE PAW2 POSW RS14 SAIF ZZ-3

COCKE, Elton C. (1901-1975) Biol. NC61

COCKER, Edward (1631-1675) Math. BDOS BEOS

COCKERELL, Christopher (1910-) Engr. NTBM
SAIF

COCKERELL, Theodore A. (1866-1948) Entom. AMEM
DAB4

COCKERILL, John (1790-1840) Engr. GE-1

COCKERILL, William (1759-1832) Text. BDOS GE-1

CODAZZI, Delfino (1824-1873) Math. CDZZ ZZ-3

CODDINGTON, Henry (d. 1845) Math. DNB

COE, Wesley, R. (1869-1960) Biol. NC47

COEHN, Alfred (1863-1938) Chem. HSSO

COFFIN, James H. (1806-1873) Meteor. BIOD BM-1
DAB NC-8

COFFIN, John H. (1815-1890) Math. BIOD BM-8
NC-5

COFFMAN, John D. (1882-) Forest. LACC

COGGESHALL, Arthur S. (1873-1958) Paleon. NC47

COGGESHALL, George W. (1867-1944) Chem. NC33

COGGESHALL, Henry (1623-1690) Math. DNB

COGHILL, George E. (1872-1941) Embryol.; Anat.
BM22 CDZZ DAB3 ZZ-3

COGROSSI, Carlo F. (1682-1769) Med. CDZZ
ZZ-3

COHEN, Abraham (1870-1951) Math. NC40

COHEN, Barnett (1891-1952) Bact. NC42

COHEN, Bernard (1924-) Phys. AMJB

COHEN, Diana (Contemporary) Nat. Hist. WAWL

COHEN, Ernst J. (1869-1944) Chem. CDZZ ZZ-3

COHEN, Jacob de Silva (1838-1927) Med.; Phys.
DAB

COHEN, Morris R. (1880-1947) Philos. of Sci. CDZZ
ZZ-3

COHEN, Paul J. (1934-) Math. MHSE

COHEN, Seymour S. (1917-) Biochem. BEOS MHM2
MHSE

COHN, Edwin J. (1892-1953) Biochem. BM35 CDZZ
DAB5 WAMB ZZ-3

COHN, Essie W. (1902-1963) Chem. NC51

COHN, Ferdinand J. (1828-1898) Bot.; Bact. ABES
ABET BDOS BEOS BHMT CDZZ ZZ-3

COHN, Lassar (1858-1922) Chem. CDZZ ZZ-3

COHN, Nathan (1907-) Engr. MHSE

COHN, Waldo E. (1910-) Biochem. MHM2 MHSE

COHNHEIM, Julius (1839-1884) Path. BDOS BEOS BHMT

COHOE, Wallace P. (1875-1966) Chem. ACCE

COITER, Volcher (1534-1576) Anat.; Ornith. CDZZ HAOA ZZ-3

COKE, Thomas W. (1752-1842) Agr. BDOS

COKER, William C. (1872-1953) Bot. NC42

COLBERT, Edwin H. (1905-) Paleon. CB65 NCSH

COLBETH, I. Milton (1894-) Chem. NCSH

COLBURN, Zarah (1804-1839) Math. DAB

COLBY, William E. (1875-1964) Cons. EAFC LACC

COLDEN, Cadwallader (1688-1776) Bot.; Med. BHMT BIOD CDZZ DNB SBCS WAMB ZZ-3

COLDEN, Jane (1724-1766) Bot. BIOD CWSE DAB MABH NAW

COLDING, Ludvig A. (1815-1888) Engr.; Phys. CDZZ ZZXV

COLE, Francis J. (1872-1959) Zool. RS-5

COLE, Frank N. (1861-1926) Math. CDZZ DAB NC13 ZZ-3

COLE, Humfray (c.1520-1591) Instr. GE-1

COLE, Kenneth S. (1900-1984) Biophys. MHM2 MHSE

COLE, Rufus (1872-1966) Med. BM50

COLEBROOK, Leonard (1883-1967) Bact. RS17

COLEMAN, David A. (1892-1938) Chem. NC29

COLEMAN, Ernest (1942-) Phys. BCST

COLEMAN, Joseph J. (1838-1888) Phys. MCCW

COLEMAN, William H. (d. 1863) Bot. DNB

COLEY, Henry (1633-c.1695) Math. DNB

COLLES, Abraham (1773-1843) Med. BHMT

COLLET-DESCOTILS, Hippolyte (1773-1815) Chem. CDZZ SOAC ZZ-3

COLLETT, Armand R. (1895-1973) Chem. NC57

COLLETT, John (1828-1899) Geol. BIOD

COLLIE, John N. (1859-1942) Chem. CDZZ DNB6 ZZ-3

COLLIER, Peter (1835-1896) Chem. ACCE BIOD

COLLINGNON, Charles (1725-1785) Anat. DNB

COLLINGWOOD, Cuthbert (1826-1908) Nat. Hist. DNB2

COLLINGWOOD, Edward F. (1900-1970) Math. RS17

COLLINGWOOD, George H. (1890-1958) Forest. LACC

COLLINS, Frank S. (1848-1920) Bot. DAB MABH

COLLINS, Guy N. (1872-1938) Genet. DAB2

COLLINS, John (1625-1683) Math. CDZZ DNB ZZ-3

COLLINS, Michael (1930-) Astronaut. CB75 IEAS

COLLINS, Samuel (1618-1710) Anat. DNB

COLLINS, Samuel C. (1898-) Engr. MHM1 MHSE

COLLINSON, Peter (1694-1768) Nat. Hist. CDZZ DNB ZZ-3

COLLIP, James B. (1892-1965) Med. CDZZ RS19 ZZ-3

COLMAN, Benjamin (1673-1747) Med.; Nat. Hist. BIOD

COLOMBO, Matteo R. (c.1516-1559) Anat.; Physiol. ABET BDOS BEOS CDZZ ZZ-3

COLPITTS, Edwin H. (1872-1949) Elec. Engr. TPAE

COLT, Samuel (1814-1862) Invent. BDOS INYG WAMB

COMAS SOLA, Jose (1868-1937) Astron. CDZZ ZZ-3

COMBE, Andrew (1797-1847) Physiol. DNB

COMBES, Charles P. (1801-1872) Mng. CDZZ ZZ-3

COMBES, Raoul (1883-1964) Bot. CDZZ ZZ-3

COMENIUS, John A. (1592-1670) Nat. Philos. CDZZ ZZ-3

COMFORT, Alex (1920-) Med. CB74

COMMANDINO, Federigo (1509-1575) Math. BMST CDZZ ZZ-3

COMMERSON, Philbert (1727-1773) Nat. Hist. CDZZ ZZ-3

COMMON, Andrew A. (1841-1903) Astron. CDZZ DNB2 ZZ-3

COMMONER, Barry (1917-) Cons. AMJB CB70 HOCS POEC SOTT

COMPTON, Arthur H. (1892-1962) Phys. ABES ABET ASIW BDOS BEOS BM38 CB40 CB58 CDZZ MWBR NCSG PAW2 POSW QPAS WAMB ZZ-3

COMPTON, Karl T. (1887-1954) Phys. CB41 CDZZ DAB5 NC42 QPAS ZZ-3

COMRIE, Leslie J. (1893-1950) Astron.; Comp. CDZZ DNB6 ZZ-3

COMSTOCK, Anna B. (1854-1930) Entom. AMEM CWSE NAW NC22

COMSTOCK, Cyrus B. (1831-1910) Engr. BM-7

COMSTOCK, Daniel F. (1883-1970) Phys. NC55 NCSD

COMSTOCK, Frank M. (1855-1929) Nat. Hist. NC26

COMSTOCK, George C. (1855-1934) Astron. BM20 CDZZ DAB1 NC12 ZZ-3

COMSTOCK, John H. (1848-1931) Entom. AMEM DAB1 NC22

COMSTOCK, William P. (1880-1956) Entom. AMEM

COMTE, Isidore A. (1798-1857) Philos.; Math. CDZZ ZZ-3

CONANT, James B. (1893-1978) Chem. BEOS PPEY PPTY RS25

CONDAMINE, Charles SEE LA CONDAMINE, Charles M. de

CONDILLAC, Etienne B. de (1714-1780) Philos.; Psych. CDZZ ZZ-3

CONDON, Edward U. (1902-1974) Phys. BM48 CB46 MHM2 MHSE NCSH PPTY QPAS WAMB

CONDORCET, Marie J. de (1743-1794) Math. CDZZ ZZ-3

CONDRA, George E. (1869-1958) Cons. LACC

CONGREVE, William (1772-1828) Rocket. CDZZ DNB GE-1 ICFW IEAS PORS ROPW ZZ-3

CONKLIN, Edwin G. (1863-1952) Biol. BM31 CDZZ DAB5 NC12 ZZ-3

CONKLIN, William A. (1837-1913) Nat. Hist. NC-2

CONNAUGHTON, Charles A. (1908-) Forest. LACC

CONON OF SAMOS (fl. 245 B.C.) Math.; Astron. ABET BEOS CDZZ ZZ-3

CONRAD, Charles Jr. (1930-) Astronaut. CB65 IEAS

CONRAD, G. Miles (1911-1964) Biol. NC52

CONRAD, Timothy A. (1803-1877) Paleon. ASJD BIOD CDZZ NC-8 ZZ-3

CONSTANCE, Lincoln (1909-) Bot. MHM2 MHSE

CONSTANT, Hayne (1904-1968) Engr. RS19

CONSTANTINE THE AFRICAN (fl. 1065-1085) Med. CDZZ ZZ-3

CONWAY, Edward J. (1894-1968) Biochem. RS15

CONYBEARE, William D. (1787-1857) Geol. BEOS CDZZ DNB ZZ-3

COOK, Albert J. (1842-1916) Entom. AMEM

COOK, Arthur H. (1911-) Chem. COBC

COOK, George H. (1818-1889) Chem.; Geol. ACCE BIOD BM-4 NC-6

COOK, James (1728-1778) Exp. ABES ABET BDOS BEOS BHMT CDZZ DNB WFBG ZZ-3

COOK, James W. (1900-) Chem. COBC

COOK, Melville T. (1869-1953) Bot. NC40

COOK, Melvin A. (1911-) Chem. MHSE

COOK, Orator F. (1867-1949) Biol. NC38

COOKE, C. Montague (1874-1948) Zool. NC36

COOKE, C. Wythe (1887-) Geol.; Paleon. NCSK

COOKE, Josiah P. (1827-1894) Chem. ACCE BIOD
BM-4 CDZZ DAB NC-6 ZZ-3

COOKE, Lloyd M. (1916-) Chem. SBPY

COOKE, Thomas (1807-1868) Opt. DNB IEAS

COOKE, William F. (1806-1879) Elec. Engr. BDOS
BEOS DNB

COOKSON, Richard C. (1922-) Chem. COBC

COOLEY, Denton A. (1920-) Med. CB76 MFIR

COOLEY, Robert A. (1873-1968) Entom. NC54

COOLIDGE, Albert S. (1894-1977) Chem. NC60

COOLIDGE, Dane (1873-1940) Nat. Hist. NC35

COOLIDGE, Harold J. (1904-) Zool. LACC

COOLIDGE, Julian L. (1873-1954) Math. CDZZ
DAB5 NC46 ZZ-3

COOLIDGE, William D. (1873-1975) Chem. ABET
BM53 TPAE

COON, Carleton S. (1904-1981) Anthro. AO81
MHM1 MHSE NCSI

COONS, Albert H. (1912-1978) Med. MHM1 MHSE

COOPER, Ashley P. (1768-1841) Med. BHMT

COOPER, Daniel (c.1817-1842) Nat. Hist. DNB

COOPER, Edward J. (1798-1863) Astron. DNB

COOPER, Franklin S. (1908-) Phys. MHSE

COOPER, Gustav A. (1902-) Paleon. MHM2 MHSE

COOPER, Irving S. (1922-) Med. CB74 DNFH
LGIH MFIR

COOPER, James G. (1830-1902) Zool.; Bot. BIOD
DAB

COOPER, Kenneth (1931-) Med. DNFH

COOPER, Leon N. (1930-) Phys. ABET BEOS
MHSE POSW WAMB

COOPER, Leroy G. Jr. (1927-) Astronaut. CB63
IEAS PMAS WESE

COOPER, Peter (1791-1883) Invent. GE-1 INYG

COOPER, Thomas (1759-1839) Chem.; Geol. ACCE
BIOD CDZZ DAB DNB MSAJ NC11 WAMB
WFBG

COOPER, William (1798-1864) Ornith.; Nat. Hist.
BIOD BWCL WFBG

COOPER, William S. (1884-) Bot. LACC

COPAUX, Hippolyte E. (1872-1934) Chem. CDZZ
ZZ-3

COPE, Arthur C. (1909-1966) Chem. ACCE NC53

COPE, Edward D. (1840-1897) Paleon. ABES ABET
ABFC BEOS BIOD BM13 CDZZ DAB MADC
NC-7 NHAH PHLS SNAR ZZXV

COPELAND, Ralph (1837-1905) Astron. DNB2

COPERNICUS, Nicolaus (1473-1543) Astron. ABES
ABET ASTR BDOS BEOS BMST CDZZ FASP
GRTH HOSS IEAS LISD MAKS PAW2 PGRM
SAIF SGSC SMIL STSW SXWS TOWS WOSM
ZZ-3

COPLAND, James (1791-1870) Med. BHMT

COQUILLET, Daniel W. (1856-1911) Entom. AMEM
DAB

CORDIER, Pierre L. (1777-1861) Geol.; Mineral.
CDZZ ZZ-3

CORDUS, Euricus (1486-1535) Med.; Bot. CDZZ
ZZ-3

CORDUS, Valerius (1515-1544) Bot.; Pharm. CDZZ
ZZ-3

COREY, Elias J. (1928-) Chem. BEOS

CORI, Carl F. (1896-1984) Biochem. ABES ABET
BEOS CB47 MHM1 MHSE NCSH WAMB

CORI, Gerty T. (1896-1957) Biochem. ABES ABET ACCE BEOS CB47 CDZZ CWSN IDWB LLWO MHM1 MHSE NAWM NCSH NC48 ZZ-3

CORIOLIS, Gustave G. de (1792-1843) Phys. ABES ABET BEOS CDZZ FNEC TGNH ZZ-3

CORLISS, George H. (1817-1888) Invent. BDOS WAMB

CORMACK, Allan M. (1924-) Phys. ABET BEOS SOT3

CORNELIUS, David W. (1885-1942) Phys. NC35

CORNELIUS, Yngve R. (1905-1966) Engr.; Invent. NC53

CORNELL, Edward S. Jr. (1892-1972) Engr.; Invent. NC57

CORNELY, Paul B. (1906-) Med. SBPY

CORNER, Edred J. (1906-) Bot. BEOS

CORNER, George W. (1889-1981) Med. AO81 MHM1 MHSE

CORNETS DE GROOT SEE DE GROOT, Jan C.

CORNETTE, Claude M. (1744-1794) Chem.; Med. CDZZ ZZ-3

CORNFORTH, John W. (1917-) Chem. ABET BEOS COBC MHSE PAW2

CORNIL, Andre V. (1837-1908) Med. BHMT

CORNISH, Charles J. (1858-1906) Nat. Hist. DNB2

CORNU, Marie Alfred (1841-1902) Opt. CDZZ ZZ-3

CORONEL, Luis N. (d. 1531) Nat. Philos. CDZZ ZZ-3

CORONELLI, Vincenzo M. (1650-1718) Geog. CDZZ ZZ-3

CORRENS, Erich (1896-1981) Chem. AO81

CORRENS, Karl E. (1864-1933) Bot.; Genet. ABES ABET BEOS CDZZ HLSM ZZ-3

CORRIGAN, Dominic J. (1802-1880) Med. BHMT

CORT, Henry (1740-1800) Invent. BDOS BEOS GE-1

CORTES DE ALBACAR, Martin (d. 1582) Cosmol. CDZZ ZZ-3

CORTI, Alfonso G. (1822-1876) Anat. CDZZ ZZ-3

CORTI, Bonaventura (1729-1813) Phys.; Bot. CDZZ ZZ-3

CORVI, Guglielmo de SEE GUGLIELMO DE CORVI

CORVISART, Jean N. (1755-1821) Med. BEOS BHMT CDZZ ZZ-3

CORY, Charles B. (1857-1921) Ornith. BIOD DAB NC13 WFBG

CORYELL, Charles D. (1912-1971) Chem. ACCE NC56

COSBY, Stanley W. (1890-1961) Soil Sci. NC49

COSSERAT, Eugene M. (1866-1931) Math.; Astron. CDZZ ZZ-3

COSTA, Emanuel M. da (1717-1791) Nat. Hist. DNB

COSTA, Joseph L. (1897-1969) Chem. Engr. NC55

COSTA IBN LUCA SEE QUSTA ibn LUQA al-BALA-BAKKI

COSTANTIN, Julien N. (1857-1936) Bot. CDZZ ZZ-3

COSTER, Dirk (1889-1950) Phys. ABES ABET BEOS CDZZ ZZ-3

COTES, Roger (1682-1716) Math.; Astron. CDZZ DNB ZZ-3

COTTA, Carl B. von (1808-1879) Geol. CDZZ ZZ-3

COTTAM, Clarence (1899-1974) Biol.; Cons. DGMT LACC NC58

COTTE, Louis (1740-1815) Meteor. CDZZ ZZ-3

COTTING, John R. (1778-1867) Chem.; Geol. BIOD NC-5

COTTON, Donald (1939-) Chem. BCST

COTTON, Frank A. (1930-) Chem. MHM2 MHSE

COTTON, William (1786-1866) Engr. BDOS

COTTRELL, Alan H. (1919-) Metal.; Phys. BEOS MHM2 MHSE

COTTRELL, Frederick G. (1877-1948) Chem. ACCE BM27 CDZZ DAB4 MASY NC38 NTBM ZZ-3

COTTRELL, T.L. (1923-) Chem. COBC

COTUGNO, Domenico F. (1736-1822) Med. BHMT CDZZ ZZ-3

COTZIAS, George C. (1918-) Med. MFIR

COUCH, John N. (1896-) Bot. MHM2 MHSE

COUCH, Jonathan (1789-1870) Nat. Hist. DNB

COUCH, Richard Q. (1816-1863) Nat. Hist. DNB

COUES, Elliott (1842-1899) Ornith. BIOD BM-6 BWCL CDZZ DAB NC-5 NHAH SFNB WFBG ZZ-3

COULOMB, Charles A. de (1736-1806) Phys. ABES ABET BDOS BEOS BMST CDZZ DCPW EETD ESEH FNEC GE-1 HOSS VTHB ZZ-3

COULSON, Charles A. (1910-1974) Math. BEOS COBC MHM2 MHSE RS20

COULSON, E. Jack (1904-1971) Biochem. NC56

COULTER, John M. (1851-1928) Bot. BM14 DAB MABH

COULTER, Stanley (1853-1943) Biol. NC33

COUNCILMAN, William T. (1854-1933) Path. BM18 CDZZ ZZ-3

COUPER, Archibald S. (1831-1892) Chem. ABES ABET BDOS BEOS CDZZ GRCH ZZ-3

COUPER, James H. (1794-1866) Nat. Hist. BIOD

COURANT, Richard (1888-1972) Math. CB66 MHM2 MHSE NC58

COURNAND, Andre F. (1895-) Med. ABET BEOS CB57 MFIR MHM1 MHSE

COURNOT, Antoine A. (1801-1877) Math. CDZZ ZZ-3

COURRIER, Robert (1895-) Med. MHM2 MHSE

COURTEN, William (1642-1702) Nat. Hist. DNB

COURTENAY, Edward H. (1803-1853) Math. BIOD

COURTIVRON, Gaspard de (1715-1785) Phys. CDZZ ZZ-3

COURTOIS, Bernard (1777-1838) Chem. ABES ABET BEOS CDZZ HSSO ZZ-3

COURVOISIER, Ludwig (1843-1918) Med. BHMT

COUSTEAU, Jacques Y. (1910-) Ocean. ABES ABET BEOS CB53 CB76 EXDC HOCS SAIF

COUTURAT, Louis (1868-1914) Math. CDZZ ZZ-3

COVERT, Lloyd W. (1906-1966) Chem. NC52

COVILLE, Frederick V. (1867-1937) Bot. LACC MABH NC12 NC27

COVINA, Simon de (fl. c.1300s) Med. MMMA

COWAN, Clyde L. Jr. (1919-1974) Phys. ABET NC58

COWAN, George A. (1920-) Chem. MHM1 MHSE

COWDRY, Edmund V. (1888-1975) Anat. CB48 NC61

COWELL, Philip H. (1870-1949) Astron. CDZZ ZZ-1

COWLES, Alfred H. (1858-1929) Metal. ACCE

COWLES, Henry C. (1869-1939) Bot.; Ecol. DAB2 MAHB NC39 WAMB

COWLES, Rheinart P. (1872-1948) Zool. NC37

COWPER, Edward (1790-1852) Invent. DNB

COX, Allan (1926-) Geol. MHSE

COX, Gordon (1906-) Chem. COBC

COX, Harold R. (1907-) Virol. CB61

COX, Leslie R. (1897-1965) Geol.; Paleon. RS12

COX, William T. (1878-1961) Forest. LACC

COXE, John R. (1773-1864) Pharm. ACCE BHMT

COXWELL, Henry T. (1819-1900) Aero. DNB1

COYTE, William B. (c.1741-1810) Bot. DNB

CRABTREE, William (1610-c.1644) Astron. CDZZ DNB ZZ-3

CRAFTS, Edward C. (1910-) Forest. LACC

CRAFTS, James M. (1839-1917) Chem. ABES ABET ACCE BDOS BEOS BM-9 DAB NC13

CRAIG, David (1905-1964) Chem. Engr. ACCE NC52

CRAIG, James B. (1912-) Cons. LACC

CRAIG, John (d. 1731) Math. CDZZ DNB ZZ-3

CRAIG, Lyman C. (1906-1974) Biochem. ABES ABET BEOS BM49 CB64 MHM2 MHSE

CRAIG, Thomas (1855-1900) Math. BIOD DAB

CRAIGIE, James (1899-1978) Virol. RS25

CRAM, Donald J. (1919-) Chem. BEOS MHM2 MHSE

CRAMER, Gabriel (1704-1752) Math. CDZZ ZZ-3

CRAMER, Harald (1893-) Math. MHM2 MHSE

CRAMER, Johann A. (1710-1777) Chem. CDZZ ZZXV

CRAMER, Pieter (d. 1777) Nat. Hist. ANHD

CRAMPTON, Guy C. (1881-1951) Entom. AMEM

CRAMPTON, Henry C. (1875-1956) Zool. NC42

CRANDALL, Irving B. (1890-1927) Phys. NC22

CRANDALL, Willard R. (1894-1960) Chem. NC47

CRANE, Evan J. (1889-1966) Chem. ACCE

CRANE, Horace R. (1907-) Phys. MHSE

CRAPONNE, Adam de (1526-1575) Engr. GE-1

CRATHORNE, Arthur R. (1873-1946) Chem. NC35

CRAVERI, Federico (1815-1890) Meteor.; Nat. Hist. WFBG

CRAWFORD, Adair (1748-1795) Phys.; Chem. CDZZ DNB ZZXV

CRAWFORD, Charles W. (1888-1957) Chem. NC47

CRAWFORD, James C. (1880-1950) Entom. AMEM

CRAWFORD, Russell T. (1876-1958) Astron. NC44

CRAWLEY, Edwin S. (1862-1933) Math. NC24

CREASER, Charles W. (1897-1965) Biol. NC51

CREDE, Carl S. (1819-1892) Med. BHMT MMMA

CREDNER, (Karl) Hermann G. (1841-1913) Geol. CDZZ ZZ-3

CREEVEY, Caroline A. (1843-1920) Bot. NC30

CREIGHTON, Charles (1847-1927) Med. CDZZ ZZ-3

CREIGHTON, H. Jermain (1886-) Chem. NCSE

CRELL, Lorenz F. von (1745-1816) Chem. CDZZ ZZ-3

CRELLE, August L. (1780-1855) Math.; Engr. CDZZ ZZ-3

CREMONA, Antonio L. (1830-1903) Math. CDZZ ZZ-3

CRESCAS, Hasdai (c.1340-1412) Philos. CDZZ ZZ-3

CRESSON, Ezra T. (1838-1926) Entom. AMEM DAB NC23

CRESSWELL, Daniel (1776-1844) Math. DNB

CREW, Francis A. (1886-1973) Genet. RS20

CREW, Henry (1859-1953) Phys. BM37 NC15

CREWE, Albert V. (1927-) Phys. CB64

CRICK, Francis H. (1916-) Biochem. ABES ABET BEOS CB83 EDCJ FMBB MHM1 HLSM MHSE SAIF

CRIPPS, Richard S. (1889-1942) Chem. RS-1

CRISTOL, Stanley J. (1916-) Chem. MHSE

CRITTENDEN, Eugene C. (1880-1956) Phys. NC53

CROCCO, Gaetano A. (1877-1968) Rocket. ICFW

CROCKER, Lucretia (1829-1886) Sci. Ed. BIOD

CROCKER, William (1874-1950) Bot. DAB4 NCSD

CROLL, James (1821-1890) Geol. BEOS CDZZ DNB1 ZZ-3

CROLLIUS, Oswald (c.1560-1609) Med. CDZZ ZZ-3

CROMMELIN, Andrew C. (1865-1939) Astron. CDZZ ZZ-3

CROMPTON, Rookes E. (1845-1940) Elec. Engr. BDOS

CROMPTON, Samuel (1753-1827) Invent. BDOS DNB GE-1

CRONIN, James W. (1931-) Phys. ABET BEOS

CRONSTEDT, Axel F. (1722-1765) Mineral. ABES ABET BDOS BEOS CDZZ ZZ-3

CROOKES, William (1832-1919) Phys. ABES ABET BDOS BEOS CDZZ DCPW EETD SAIF ZZ-3

CROONE, William (1633-1684) Physiol. CDZZ ZZ-3

CROSBY, Cyrus R. (1879-1937) Entom. AMEM

CROSFIELD, George (1785-1847) Bot. DNB

CROSS, Charles F. (1855-1935) Chem. BEOS DNB5

CROSS, Charles W. (1854-1949) Geol. ABES ABET BM32 CDZZ DAB4 ZZ-3

CROSS, L.C. (1918-) Chem. COBC

CROSS, Walter M. (1878-1931) Chem. NC28

CROSS, Walter M. (1904-1954) Chem. NC44

CROSSE, Andrew (1784-1855) Elec. Sci. DNB

CROSSFIELD, A. Scott (1921-) Aero.; Engr. CB69 NOS2

CROSSLEY, Moses L. (1884-1971) Chem. ACCE

CROSTHWAIT, David N. Jr. (1892-1976) Engr. BCST BISC SBPY

CROUSAZ, Jean P. de (1663-1750) Philos.; Math. CDZZ ZZ-3

CRUIKSHANK, William C. (1745-1800) Anat. BHMT CDZZ DNB ZZ-3

CRUM, Walter (1796-1867) Chem. CDZZ ZZ-3

CRUM BROWN, Alexander SEE BROWN, Alexander C.

CRUVEILHIER, Jean (1791-1874) Anat. BHMT CDZZ ZZ-3

CRUZ, Oswaldo G. (1872-1917) Med. CDZZ ZZXV

CTESIBIUS OF ALEXANDRIA (fl. 270 B.C.) Invent. ABES ABET BDOS BEOS CDZZ GE-1 ZZ-3

CUDWORTH, Ralph (1617-1688) Philos. CDZZ ZZ-3

CUENOT, Lucien (1866-1951) Zool.; Biol. CDZZ ZZ-3

CUGNOT, Nicolas J. (1725-1804) Engr. BDOS BEOS GE-1

CULLEN, William (1710-1790) Med.; Chem. BHMT CDZZ SIRC ZZ-3

CULLEN, William (1867-1948) Chem. DNB6

CULMANN, Karl (1821-1881) Engr. CDZZ ZZ-3

CULPEPER, Nicholas (1616-1654) Med. BDOS BEOS BHMT DNB

CULVER, Harold E. (1883-1970) Geol. NC59

CUMING, Hugh (1791-1865) Nat. Hist. DNB

CUMMING, James (1777-1861) Phys. CDZZ ZZ-3

CUMMING, Joseph G. (1812-1868) Geol. DNB

CUMMING, William (c.1822-1855) Ophth. DNB

CUMMINGS, Byron (1880-1954) Archaeol. NC44

CUNHA, Jose A. da (1744-1787) Math. CDZZ ZZXV

CUNITZ, Marie (c.1600-1664) Astron. IDWB

CUNNINGHAM, Allan (1791-1839) Bot. DNB

CUNNINGHAM, Bert (1883-1943) Zool. NC34

CUNNINGHAM, Burris B. (1912-1971) Chem. NC57

CUNNINGHAM, Gordon H. (1892-1921) Math. RS10

CUNNINGHAM, James (d. c.1709) Bot. DNB

CUNNINGHAM, Susan J. (1842-1921) Math. NC-6

CURIE, Marie S. (1867-1934) Chem. ABES ABET BDOS BEOS BHMT CDZZ CSCJ DCPW GASW GRCH HOSS HSSO IDWB IFBS LISD LLWO MGAH MMSB MWBR NPWC OGML PAW2 PGRM POSW SAIF SGSC SMIL SSDH TOWS WIWM ZZ-3

CURIE, Pierre (1859-1906) Chem. ABES ABET BDOS BEOS CDZZ DCPW LISD MMSB MWBR OGML POSW SSDH TOWS ZZ-3

CURL, Gilbert (1911-1968) Phys. NC54

CURLEY, James (1796-1889) Phys. BIOD

CURLING, Thomas B. (1811-1888) Med. BHMT

CURME, George O. (1888-1976) Chem. BM52 NC60 NCSD

CURTIS, Carlton C. (1864-1945) Bot. NC36

CURTIS, Charles G. (1860-1953) Engr. FNEC

CURTIS, Francis J. (1894-1960) Chem. ACCE

CURTIS, Harry A. (1884-1963) Chem. Engr. NC50

CURTIS, Heber D. (1872-1942) Astron. ABET BEOS BM22 CDZZ DAB3 ZZ-3

CURTIS, John (1791-1862) Entom. DNB1

CURTIS, Moses A. (1808-1872) Bot. BIOD DAB MABH

CURTIS, Otis F. (1888-1949) Bot. MABH

CURTIS, William (1746-1799) Bot. BDOS DNB

CURTIS, William C. (1911-) Phys. SBPY

CURTIS, William E. (1889-1969) Phys. RS16

CURTISS, Glenn H. (1878-1930) Aero.; Invent. DAB1 ICFW WAMB

CURTISS, Ralph H. (1880-1929) Astron. CDZZ ZZ-3

CURTIUS, Theodor (1857-1928) Chem. BEOS CDZZ NC43 ZZ-3

CURTMAN, Louis J. (1878-1958) Chem. NC43

CURTZE, E.L. Maximilian (1837-1903) Math. CDZZ ZZ-3

CUSA, Nicholas SEE NICHOLAS OF CUSA

CUSHING, Harvey W. (1869-1939) Med. BDOS BEOS BHMT BM22 COAC CDZZ TBSG ZZ-3

CUSHING, Jonathan P. (1793-1835) Chem. ACCE

CUSHMAN, Allerton S. (1867-1930) Chem. NC26

CUSHMAN, Joseph A. (1881-1949) Paleon. CDZZ DAB4 PHLS ZZ-3

CUSHMAN, Robert A. (1880-1957) Entom. AMEM

CUSHNY, Arthur R. (1866-1926) Pharm. CDZZ ZZXV

CUSICK, James T. (1882-) Chem. NCSE

CUTBUSH, Edward (1772-1843) Chem. ACCE

CUTBUSH, James (1788-1823) Bot. ACCE BIOD DAB

CUTLER, Manasseh (1742-1823) Bot. BIOD DAB WAMB

CUTTING, C. Suydam (1889-1972) Nat. Hist. NC57 NCSJ

CUTTING, Hiram A. (1832-1892) Nat. Hist.; Geol. BIOD NC10

CUTTS, Henry E. (1867-1946) Chem. NC35

CUVIER, Frederic (1773-1838) Zool. CDZZ ZZ-3

CUVIER, Georges L. (1769-1832) Zool.; Paleon. ABES ABET ANHD BDOS BEOS CDZZ EQSA GASJ HLSM LISD PHLS SAIF THOG TOWS ZZ-3

CYRIAQUE DE MANGIN, Clement SEE HENRION, Didier

CYSAT, Johann B. (1586-1657) Astron. ABET CDZZ ZZ-3

CZAPEK, Emil (1891-1959) Chem. NC51

CZEKANOWSKI, Aleksander P. (1833-1876) Geol.; Exp. CDZZ ZZ-3

CZERMAK, Johann N. (1828-1873) Physiol. CDZZ ZZ-3

CZERSKI, Jan (1845-1892) Geol.; Zool. CDZZ ZZ-3

D

D'ABANO, Pietro SEE ABANO, Pietro d'

DABNEY, Charles W. (1859-1945) Chem. ACCE
DAB3

DABOLL, Nathan (1750-1818) Math. BIOD NC23

DA COSTA, Jacob (1833-1900) Med. BHMT

D'ACOSTA, Jose SEE ACOSTA, Jose d'

DADOURIAN, Haroutune M. (1878-1974) Phys. NC58

DAGGETT, Frank S. (1855-1920) Ornith. NC38

DAGUERRE, Louis J. (1789-1851) Invent.; Photo.
ABES ABET BDOS BEOS ENCE GE-1 LISD
MPIP SAIF

DAHL, Anders (1751-1789) Bot. BDOS

DAHL, Ole J. (1931-) Comp. HOPL

DAILEY, Ulysses G. (1885-1961) Med. GNPA

D'AILLY, Pierre SEE AILLY, Pierre d'

DAIMLER, Gottlieb W. (1834-1900) Invent. ABES
ABET BDOS BEOS ICFW MPIP OGML SAIF

DAINELLI, Giotto (1878-1968) Geol.; Geog. CDZZ
ZZ-3

DAINTON, Frederick S. (1914-) Chem. BEOS COBC
MHSE

DAINTREE, Richard (1831-1878) Geol. DNB

DAKIN, Henry D. (1880-1952) Biochem. ACCE DAB5
DNB7

DALBY, Isaac (1744-1824) Math. DNB

DALE, Henry H. (1875-1968) Pharm.; Physiol. ABES
ABET BDOS BEOS BHMT CDZZ DODR MHM2
MHSE RS16 ZZXV

DALECHAMPS, Jacques (1513-1588) Bot.; Med. CDZZ
ZZ-3

D'ALEMBERT, Jean le Rond SEE ALEMBERT, Jean le
Rond

DALEN, Nils G. (1869-1937) Engr.; Invent. BEOS
POSW

DALENCE, Joachim (c.1640-1707) Astron.; Phys.
CDZZ ZZ-3

DALGARNO, Alexandre (1928-) Phys. MHSE

DALIBARD, Thomas F. (1703-1779) Nat. Hist. CDZZ
ZZ-3

DALITZ, Richard H. (1925-) Phys. MHM2 MHSE

DALL, William H. (1845-1927) Paleon.; Nat. Hist.
BM31 CDZZ DAB NC10 NC27 ZZ-3

DALLDORF, Gilbert (1900-) Med. MHM2 MHSE

DALLERY, Thomas C. (1754-1835) Invent. GE-1

DALRYMPLE, John (1803-1852) Ophth. DNB

DALTON, John (1766-1844) Chem. ABES ABET
BDOS BEOS CDZZ CSCJ DNB GRCH HOSS
HSSO IFBS LISD MCCW SAIF ZZ-3

DALTON, John C. (1825-1889) Physiol. BHMT BIOD
BM-3 CDZZ ZZXV

DALY, Ivan de Burg (1893-1974) Physiol. RS21

DALY, Reginald A. (1871-1957) Geol. BM34 CDZZ
ZZ-3

DALYELL, John G. (1775-1851) Nat. Hist. DNB

DALZELL, Nicol A. (1817-1878) Bot. DNB

DAM, (Carl P.) Henrick (1895-1976) Biochem. ABES
ABET BEOS CB49 MHM1 MHSE NCSG PAW2

al-DAMIRI, Muhammad ibn Musa (1341-1405) Nat.
Hist. CDZZ ZZ-3

DAMON, William E. (1838-1911) Nat. Hist. NC15

DAMPF, Alfonso (1884-1948) Entom. AMEM

DAMTOFT, Walter J. (1890-) Forest. LACC

DANA, Edward S. (1849-1935) Mineral.; Crystal.
BM18

DANA, James D. (1813-1895) Nat. Hist.; Geol. ASJD
BEOS BIOD BM-9 BSIL CDZZ DAB MSAJ
THOG WAMB YSMS ZZ-3

DANA, James F. (1793-1827) Chem.; Geol. ACCE
ASJD BIOD DAB NC10 TPAE

DANA, Samuel L. (1795-1868) Chem. BIOD DAB
NC-8

DANA, Samuel T. (1883-1978) Forest. LACC

DANCER, Thomas (c.1755-1811) Bot. DNB

DANCKWERTS, Peter V. (1916-) Chem. Engr.
MHM2 MHSE

DANDELIN, Germinal P. (1794-1847) Math.; Engr.
CDZZ ZZ-3

DANE, Carle H. (1900-1968) Geol. NC54

DANFORTH, Charles H. (1883-1969) Anat.; Genet.
BM44 CDZZ ZZ-3

DANFORTH, Richard S. (1885-1962) Invent. NC51

DANFORTH, Samuel (1696-1777) Alch. ACCE

DANFORTH, Samuel Jr. (1740-1827) Med.; Chem.
ACCE

DANIELL, John F. (1790-1845) Chem.; Meteor.
ABES ABET BDOS BEOS CDZZ DNB EETD
ZZ-3

DANIELL, William F. (1818-1865) Bot. DNB

DANIELS, Farrington (1889-1972) Chem. ACCE
BEOS CB65 MHM1 MHSE NC58 NCSH

DANILOV, Stepan N. (1889-) Chem. SMST

DANJON, Andre L. (1890-1967) Astron. MHM2 MHSE

DANSGAARD, Willi (1922-) Meteor. BEOS

DANTI, Egnatio (1536-1583) Cosmol.; Math. CDZZ
ZZ-3

DANTZIG, George B. (1914-) Math. IMMO MHSE

DA ORTA, Garcia SEE ORTA, Garcia da

DARBOUX, Jean G. (1842-1917) Math. CDZZ ZZ-3

DARBY, Abraham (1678-1717) Engr. BDOS BEOS
GE-1 SAIF

D'ARCAMBAL, Alexander H. (1890-1968) Metal.
NC58

D'ARCET, Jean (1725-1801) Chem. CDZZ ZZ-3

DARCY, Henri P. (1805-1858) Engr. FNEC

D'ARCY, Patrick (1725-1779) Math.; Astron. CDZZ
ZZ-3

DARITY, William A. (1924-) Med. SBPY

DARLING, Frank Fraser (1903-1979) Cons. DGMT
LACC POEC

DARLING, Jay N. (1876-1962) Cons. EAFC

DARLING, William (1802-1884) Anat. DNB

DARLINGTON, Cyril D. (1903-1981) Biol. AO81
BEOS MHM1 MHSE

DARLINGTON, Henry T. (1875-1964) Bot. NC51

DARLINGTON, William (1782-1863) Bot. BIOD
CDZZ DAB MABH ZZ-3

DARNELL, James E. Jr. (1930-) Med.; Biol. MHSE

DART, Raymond A. (1893-) Anat. ABES ABET
BEOS CB66 MHM1 MHSE PHLS

DARWIN, Charles G. (1887-1962) Phys. CDZZ MHM2
MHSE RS-9 ZZ-3

DARWIN, Charles R. (1809-1882) Nat. Hist.; Evol.;
Geol. ABES ABET ABFC BDOS BEOS CDZZ
DARR DNB EQSA FBMV FMBB GASJ GISA
GRBW GRTH HLSM HNHB LISD MGAH MNSC
MSCH NATJ NEXB OGML PHLS SAIF SGSC
SMIL SNAR SSDH TOWS TPOS ZZ-3

DARWIN, Erasmus (1731-1802) Bot.; Med. ABES
ABET BDOS BEOS CDZZ DNB HLSM NATJ
SIRC ZZ-3

DARWIN, Francis (1848-1925) Bot. CDZZ DNB4
ZZ-3

DARWIN, George H. (1845-1912) Astron.; Math.
ABES ABET BEOS CDZZ DNB3 ZZ-3

DASMANN, Raymond F. (1919-) Cons. LACC

DASYPODIUS, Cunrodus (c.1530-1600) Math.;
Astron. CDZZ ZZ-3

DAUBENTON, Louis J. (1716-1800) Med.; Nat. Hist.
CDZZ ZZXV

DAUBENY, Charles G. (1795-1867) Chem.; Geol.
CDZZ DNB VISC ZZ-3

DAUBREE, Gabriel A. (1814-1896) Geol. ABES ABET
BEOS CDZZ ZZ-3

DAUSSET, Jean (1916-) Biol.; Med. ABET BEOS
CB81 MHSE

DAVAINE, Casimir J. (1812-1882) Med.; Biol. BDOS
BEOS CDZZ ZZ-3

DAVENPORT, Charles B. (1866-1944) Zool.; Genet.
BEOS BM25 CDZZ DAB3 NC15 ZZ-3

DAVENPORT, Harold (1907-1969) Math. RS17

DAVENPORT, Thomas (1802-1851) Invent. EETD
TBTM WAMB

DAVEY, John (1846-1923) Tree Surg. DAB NC22

DAVID, Edward E. (1925-) Elec. Engr. CB74

DAVID, Tannatt W. (1858-1934) Geol.; Exp. CDZZ
MMSB ZZ-3

DAVIDOV, August Y. (1823-1885) Phys.; Math. CDZZ
ZZ-3

DAVIDSON, Anstruther (1880-1932) Bot.; Entom.
NC14

DAVIDSON, Charles R. (1875-1970) Astron. RS17

DAVIDSON, Donald M. (1902-1960) Geol. NC53

DAVIDSON, George (1825-1911) Geog.; Astron.
BM18 DAB NC-7

DAVIDSON, James N. (1911-1972) Biochem. RS19

DAVIDSON, Norman (1916-) Chem. MHSE

DAVIDSON, Thomas (1817-1885) Paleon. DNB

DAVIDSON, William L. (1915-) Phys. CB52

DAVIE, Thomas B. (1895-1955) Path. DNB7

DAVIES, Charles (1798-1876) Math. NC-3

DAVIES, David C. (1827-1885) Geol.; Mng. DNB

DAVIES, Hugh (c.1739-1821) Bot. DNB

DAVIES, John D. (1929-) Engr. SIWG

DAVIES, Thomas (1837-1891) Mineral. DNB1

DAVIES, Thomas S. (1795-1851) Math. DNB

DAVIES, William (1814-1891) Paleon. DNB1

DA VINCI, Leonardo SEE LEONARDO DA VINCI

DAVIS, Bergen (1869-1958) Phys. BM34

DAVIS, Bradley M. (1871-1957) Bot. NC46

DAVIS, Carroll C. (1888-1957) Chem. ACCE NC44

DAVIS, Charles H. (1807-1877) Astron.; Ocean.
BIOD BM-4 YSMS

DAVIS, Dean W. (1894-1963) Cons. LACC

DAVIS, George E. (1850-1907) Chem. Engr. HCEF

DAVIS, Hallowell (1896-) Physiol. MHSE

DAVIS, Harvey N. (1881-1952) Engr. CB47 DAB5
NC40

DAVIS, Herbert S. (1875-1958) Ichth. LACC

DAVIS, John J. (1885-1965) Entom. AMEM NC52

DAVIS, Kenneth P. (1906-) Forest. LACC

DAVIS, Martin D. (1928-) Math.; Comp. MHSE

DAVIS, Nathan S. (1817-1904) Med. BHMT

DAVIS, Robert H. (1870-1965) Invent. GDSP

DAVIS, Tenney L. (1890-1949) Chem. ACCE

DAVIS, Walter S. (1899-1958) Soil Sci. LACC

DAVIS, William (1771-1807) Math. DNB

DAVIS, William M. (1850-1934) Geog.; Geomorph.
BEOS BM23 CDZZ GKGP TOWS WAMB ZZ-3

DAVIS, William T. (1862-1945) Entom. AMEM

DAVISON, Alvin (1868-1915) Biol. NC18

DAVISON, John M. (1840-1915) Chem. NC17

DAVISON, William (1593-c.1669) Med.; Chem. CDZZ
DNB ZZ-3

DAVISSON, Clinton J. (1881-1958) Phys. ABES ABET BEOS BM36 CDZZ NCSC POSW WAMB ZZ-3

DAVY, Edmund (1785-1857) Chem. DNB

DAVY, Edward (1806-1885) Invent. DNB

DAVY, Humphry (1778-1829) Chem. ABES ABET BDOS BEOS CDZZ DNB EETD ENCE GOED GRCH HOSS HSSO IFBS MAKS SAIF TPOS ZZ-3

DAVY, John (1790-1868) Physiol.; Chem. CDZZ DNB ZZ-3

DAWES, Chester L. (1886-1977) Elec. Engr. NC60

DAWES, William R. (1799-1868) Astron. BEOS CDZZ DNB ZZ-3

DAWKINS, Richard (1941-) Ethol. BEOS

DAWKINS, William B. (1837-1929) Geol.; Paleon. DNB4

DAWLEY, Robert W. (1897-1949) Chem. NC40

DAWSON, Alden B. (1892-1968) Zool. NC54

DAWSON, Charles (1864-1916) Paleon. CDZZ ZZ-3

DAWSON, George M. (1849-1901) Paleon. DNB2 MADC

DAWSON, John (1734-1820) Math. DNB

DAWSON, John W. (1820-1899) Geol. CDZZ DNB1 FHUA POCS ZZ-3

DAY, Albert M. (1897-) Biol. CB48 LACC

DAY, Arthur L. (1869-1960) Phys. BM47 NC16 NCSA

DAY, David T. (1859-1925) Chem.; Mng. ACCE BDOS BEOS CDZZ DAB ZZ-3

DAY, Edward C. (1884-1962) Biol.; Astron. NC52

DAY, Francis (1829-1889) Ichth. DNB1

DAY, William C. (1857-1905) Chem. BIOD

ibn al-DAYA SEE AHMAD ibn YUSUF

DAYTON, William A. (1885-1958) Forest. LACC

DEACON, George E. (1906-) Ocean. MHM1 MHSE

DEACON, Henry (1822-1876) Chem. BDOS BEOS

DEAN, Bashford (1867-1928) Ichth. CDZZ DAB ZZ-3

DEAN, Ernest W. (1888-1959) Chem. Engr. NC50

DEAN, George A. (1873-1956) Entom. AMEM

DEANE, James (1801-1858) Geol. BIOD

DE BAKEY, Michael E. (1908-) Med. CB64 HEXS MFIR MHM2 MHSE

DE BARY, (Heinrich) Anton (1831-1888) Bot. BEOS CDZZ ZZ-3

DEBEAUNE, Florimond (1601-1652) Math. CDZZ ZZ-3

DE BEER, Gavin R. (1899-1972) Biol. BEOS MHM1 MHSE RS19

DEBENHAM, Frank (1883-1965) Exp.; Geog. CDZZ ZZ-3

DEBIERNE, Andre L. (1874-1949) Chem. ABET BEOS

DE BRAHM, William G. (1717-1799) Surv.; Engr. BIOD DAB

DEBRAY, Henri J. (1827-1888) Chem. CDZZ ZZ-3

DE BROGLIE, Louis SEE BROGLIE, Louis C.V.M. and Louis V. de

DEBUS, Kurt H. (1908-1983) Engr. CB73

DEBYE, Peter J. (1884-1966) Chem.; Phys. ABES ABET ACCE BDOS BEOS BM46 CB63 CDZZ MHM1 MHSE NPWC PAW2 RS16 ZZ-3

DECHALES, Claude F. (1621-1678) Math. CDZZ ZZ-3

DE CHALMOT, Guillaume L. (d. 1898) Electrochem.; Metal. ACCE

DE CHAULIAC, GUY (c.1300-1368) Med. BHMT

DECHELETTE, Joseph (1862-1914) Archaeol. ZZ-3

DECHEN, Heinrich von (1800-1889) Mng. CDZZ ZZ-3

DECKER, Charles E. (1868-1958) Paleon. NC50

DEDEKIND, Julius W. (1831-1916) Math. ABES ABET BEOS CDZZ ZZ-4

DE DUVE, Christian R. (1917-) Biochem.; Biol. ABET BEOS MHSE

DEE, John (1527-1608) Math. CDZZ ZZ-4

DEERE, John (1804-1886) Invent. INYG WAMB

DEERING, George C. (c.1695-1749) Bot. DNB

DE FOREST, Erastus L. (1834-1888) Math. BIOD DAB

DE FOREST, Lee (1873-1961) Elec. Engr. ABES ABET AMIH ASIW BEOS CDZZ EETD FOIF NC58 NCSA TBTM TINA TPAE WAMB ZZ-4

DE GEER, Charles SEE GEER, Charles de

DE GEER, Gerard SEE GEER, Gerard J. de

DEGERING, Edward F. (1894-1967) Chem. NC53

DE GOLYER, Everette L. (1886-1956) Geophys. BM33 CDZZ NC43 ZZ-4

DE GRAAFF-HUNTER, James (1881-1967) Surv. RS13

DE GROOT, Jan C. (1554-1640) Phys. CDZZ ZZ-4

DE HAAS, Wander SEE HAAS, Wander J. de

DE HAVILLAND, Geoffrey (1882-1965) Aero. ICFW

DEHMELT, Hans (1922-) Phys. MHSE

DEHN, Max (1878-1952) Math. CDZZ ZZ-4

DEISS, Charles F. (1903-1959) Geol. NC44

DEJERINE, Joseph J. (1849-1917) Med. BHMT

DEKAY, James E. (1792-1851) Zool. ASJD BIOD DAB

DE KRUIF, Paul (1890-1971) Microbiol. CB42 CB63

DE LA BECHE, Henry T. (1796-1855) Geol. BDOS BEOS CDZZ DNB ZZ-4

DE LA BOE, Franz SEE SYLVIUS, Franciscus

DE LA CONDAMINE, Charles SEE LA CONDAMINE, Charles M. de

DELACOUR, Jean (1890-) Ornith. DGMT

DELAFIELD, Joseph (1790-1875) Geol. BIOD

DELAFOSSE, Gabriel (1796-1878) Mineral.; Crystal. CDZZ ZZXV

DELAGE, Yves (1854-1920) Biol. CDZZ ZZ-4

DELAMAIN, Richard (fl. c.1530) Math. CDZZ ZZ-4

DELAMBRE, Jean B. (1749-1822) Astron.; Geophys. ABET BDOS BEOS CDZZ ZZ-4

DELANEY, Martin R. (1812-1885) Anthro. GNPA

DELAROCHE, Francois (c.1775-1813) Nat. Hist. SOAC

DE LA RUE, Warren (1815-1889) Astron.; Chem. ABES ABET BDOS BEOS CDZZ DNB ZZ-4

DE LA SABLIERE, Marguerite (1630-1693) Astron. IDWB

DE LA TORRE-BUENO SEE TORRE-BUENO, Jose R. de la

DELAUNAY, CHARLES E. (1816-1872) Astrophys. CDZZ ZZ-4

DE LAVAL, Carl G. (1845-1913) Invent. BDOS FNEC

DELAVAL, Edward H. (1729-1814) Chem. DNB

DELBRUCK, Max (1906-1981) Biol. ABET AO81 BEOS MHM1 MHSE RS28 WAMB

DELEPINE, Stephane M. (1871-1965) Chem. CDZZ ZZ-4

DE LESSEPS, Ferdinand M. (1805-1894) Engr. BDOS MGAH SGEC

DELGADO, Jose (1915-) Med. CB76

D'ELHUYAR, Don F. (1755-1833) Mineral. ABES ABET

DELIGNE, Pierre (1944-) Math. MHSE

DELILE, Alire (1778-1850) Bot. CDZZ ZZ-4

DELISLE, Guillaume (1675-1726) Geog. CDZZ ZZ-4

DELISLE, Joseph N. (1688-1768) Astron.; Geog. ABET CDZZ ZZ-4

DELLA PORTA, Giambattista SEE PORTA, Giambattista D.

DELLA TORRE, Giovanni M. (1713-1782) Sci. Writ. CDZZ ZZ-4

DELLINGER, John H. (1886-1962) Phys. NC53

DELONE, Boris N. (1890-) Math. SMST

DELORIA, Ella C. (1888-1971) Anthro. NAWM

DELPORTA, Eugene J. (1882-1955) Astron. CDZZ ZZ-4

DEL RIO, Andres M. (1764-1849) Mineral. ABES ABET BEOS

DELUC, Jean A. (1727-1817) Geol.; Phys. BEOS CDZZ DNB ZZ-4

DE LUCA, Luigi M. (1941-) Biochem. MHSE

DEMARCAY, Eugene A. (1852-1904) Chem. ABES ABET BEOS

DE MARGERIE, Emmanuel M. (1862-1953) Geol. RS-1

DEMBOWSKI, Ercole (1812-1881) Astron. CDZZ ZZ-4

DEMEREC, Milislav (1895-1966) Genet. BEOS BM42 MHM1 MHSE

DEMIDOV, Anatole N. (1812-1870) Exp. ANHD

DEMIKHOV, Vladimir P. (1916-) Med. CB60

DE MILT, Clara M. (1891-1953) Chem. ACCE

DEMOCRITUS (c.470-c.380 B.C.) Phys.; Math. ABES ABET BEOS CDZZ EETD GISA HLSM IFBS SAIF ZZ-4

DEMOIVRE, Abraham SEE MOIVRE, Abraham de

DE MONDEVILLE, Henri (c.1260-1320) Med. BHMT

DE MORGAN, Augustus (1806-1871) Math. ABET CDZZ DNB ZZ-4

DE MORGUES, James SEE LE MOYNE, Jacques

DEMPSTER, Arthur J. (1886-1950) Phys. ABES ABET BEOS BM27 NC38

DENIS, Jean B. (c.1640-1704) Med. ABET CDZZ ZZ-4

DENISSE, Jean F. (1915-) Astron. MHM2 MHSE

DENNIS, David W. (1849-1916) Biol. NC38

DENNIS, Louis M. (1863-1936) Chem. NC15 NC27

DENNIS, Martin (1851-1916) Chem. ACCE

DENNISON, David M. (1900-1976) Phys. BM52 QPAS

DENNY, Henry (1803-1871) Entom. DNB

DENSEN-GERBER, Judianne (1934-) Psychiat. CB83

DENSMORE, Frances T. (1867-1957) Anthro. NAWM POAA

DENSON, COSTEL D. (1934-) Chem. Engr. SBPY

DENT, Charles E. (1911-1976) Chem.; Med. MHM2 MHSE RS24

DENT, Frederick J. (1905-1973) Engr. RS20

DENTON, Sherman F. (1856-1937) Nat. Hist. NC27

DENYS, Nicolas (1598-1688) Nat. Hist. HAOA

DEPARCIEUX, Antoine (1703-1768) Math. CDZZ ZZ-4

DEPERET, Charles (1854-1929) Paleon. CDZZ ZZ-4

DE POURTALES, Louis SEE POURTALES, Louis F. de

DEPREZ, Marcel (1843-1918) Engr. CDZZ ZZ-4

DERBY, Ira H. (1873-1950) Chem. NC37

DERHAM, William (1657-1735) Nat. Hist. CDZZ ZZ-4

DEROSNE, (Louis) Charles (1780-1846) Chem.; Invent. CDZZ ZZ-4

DERYAGIN, Boris V. (1902-) Chem. SMST

DERYUGIN, Konstantin M. (1878-1938) Ocean.; Zool. CDZZ ZZ-4

DESAGULIERS, John T. (1683-1744) Nat. Philos.
ABES ABET CDZZ BEOS ESEH ZZ-4

DESARGUES, Girard (1591-1661) Math. BDOS BEOS
CDZZ ZZ-4

DESCARTES, Rene (1596-1650) Math. ABES ABET
BDOS BEOS BHMT CDZZ EETD ESCS FMAS
FNEC GRTH HLSM HOSS HSSO IFBS LISD
LSHS MAKS MASW MELW MISU OMNM POPF
TOWS ZZ-4

DESCH, Cyril H. (1874-1958) Metal. BDOS BEOS

DES CLOIZEAUX, Alfred L. (1817-1897) Mineral.;
Crystal. CDZZ ZZ-4

DESCOTILS, Hippolyte SEE COLLET-DESCOTILS,
Hippolyte

DESCOURTILZ, Jean T. (d. 1855) Nat. Hist. ANHD

DESCOURTILZ, Michel E. (1775-1836) Med.; Nat.
Hist. CDZZ ZZ-4

DESHAYES, Gerard P. (1797-1875) Paleon. CDZZ
PHLS ZZ-4

DESLANDERS, Henri (1853-1948) Astron.; Phys.
CDZZ ZZ-4

DESMAREST, Nicolas (1725-1815) Geol. ABES ABET
BEOS CDZZ THOG ZZ-4

DESMIER DE SAINT SIMEON SEE ARCHIAC, Etienne
J. d'

DESOR, Pierre J. (1811-1882) Glacial.; Paleon.
CDZZ ZZ-4

DESORMES, Charles B. (1777-1862) Chem. BDOS
BEOS CDZZ ZZ-4

DESPAGNET, Jean (fl. c.1620) Alch. CDZZ ZZ-4

DESSAIGNES, Victor (1800-1885) Chem. CDZZ ZZ-4

DETHIER, Vincent G. (1915-) Biol. MHM2 MHSE

DETRE, Laszlo (1874-1939) Bact. NC30

DETWEILER, Albert H. (1906-1970) Archaeol. NC55

DETWILER, Samuel R. (1890-1957) Anat. BM35

DEUTSCH, Martin (1917-) Phys. MHM2 MHSE

DEVAUX, Henri (1862-1956) Bot.; Phys. CDZZ ZZ-4

DE VIGNI, Antoine SEE SAUGRAIN, Antoine F.

DE VILLANOVA SEE BACHUONE, Arnaldus

DEVILLE, Henri E. (1818-1881) Chem. BDOS BEOS
CDZZ HSSO ZZ-4

DEVONSHIRE, Duke of SEE CAVENDISH, William

DE VOTO, Bernard (1897-1955) Cons. CB43 EAFC
SFNB

DE VRIES, Hugo SEE VRIES, Hugo de

DEVYATKOV, Nikolai D. (1907-) Elec. Engr. SMST

DEWAR, James (1842-1923) Chem.; Phys. ABES
ABET BDOS BEOS CDZZ DCPW HOSS STYC
ZZ-4

DEWAR, Michael J. (1918-) Chem. BEOS

DEWEY, Chester (1784-1867) Chem.; Bot. ACCE
ASJD BIOD DAB MABH NC-6

DEWEY, John (1859-1952) Philos. BM30

DE WITT, Lydia M. (1859-1928) Path. NAW

DEXTER, Aaron (1750-1829) Chem. ACCE

DEZALLIER D'ARGENVILLE SEE ARGENVILLE,
Antoine J. d'

DICEARCHUS OF MESSINA (fl. 310 B.C.) Sci. Writ.
ABET BEOS CDZZ ZZ-4

DICK, Gladys R. (1881-1963) Path. NAWM

DICK, Robert (1811-1866) Geol.; Bot. DNB

DICKE, Robert H. (1916-) Phys. ABET BEOS
IEAS MHM2 MHSE

DICKINSON, Roscoe G. (1894-1945) Chem.; Crystal.
CDZZ ZZ-4

DICKSON, Alexander (1836-1887) Bot. DNB

DICKSON, James (c.1737-1822) Bot. DNB

DICKSON, Leonard E. (1874-1954) Math. CDZZ
DAB5 NC18 ZZ-4

DICKSTEIN, Samuel (1851-1939) Math. CDZZ ZZ-4

DIDEROT, Denis (1713-1784) Sci. Writ. ABES ABET BDOS CDZZ ZZ-4

DIEBOLD, John (1926-) Comp. CB67

DIELS, Otto P. (1876-1954) Chem. ABES ABET BDOS BEOS CDZZ MHM1 MHSE NPWC ZZ-4

DIESEL, Rudolf C. (1858-1913) Invent. ABES ABET BDOS BEOS FNEC FOIF SAIF SGEC SMIL TBTM

DIETRICH, Barod de SEE HOLBACH, Paul H. d'

DIETRICH VON FREIBERG (c.1250-c.1310) Opt.; Nat. Philos. CDZZ ZZ-4

DIETZ, Harry F. (1890-1954) Entom. AMEM

DIETZ, Robert S. (1914-) Geol. MHSE

DIEUDONNE, Jean (1906-) Math. MHSE

DIGBY, Kenelm (1603-1665) Nat. Philos. CDZZ ZZ-4

DIGGES, Leonard (c.1520-1559) Math. CDZZ DNB GE-1 ZZ-4

DIGGES, Thomas (1546-1595) Math. CDZZ DNB GE-1 ZZ-4

DILG, Will H. (1867-1927) Cons. LACC

DILLENIUS, Johann J. (1687-1747) Bot. CDZZ ZZ-4

DILLER, Joseph S. (1850-1928) Geol. DAB1

DILLON, Jacques V. (1760-1807) Engr. GE-1

DILLON, John H. (1905-) Phys. NCSK

DILLWYN, Lewis W. (1778-1855) Nat. Hist. DNB

DIMMOCK, George (1852-1930) Zool. NC26

DINAKARA (b. c.1550) Astron. CDZZ ZZ-4

DINES, William H. (1855-1927) Meteor. DNB4

DINGLER, Hugo A. (1881-1954) Philos. CDZZ ZZ-4

DINI, Ulisse (1845-1918) Math. CDZZ ZZ-4

DINO DEL GARBO (fl. 1297-1327) Med. TALS

DINOSTRATUS (fl. 300 B.C.) Math. CDZZ ZZ-4

DINSMORE, Sanford C. (1879-1944) Chem. BNBR

DIOCLES (fl. c.190 B.C.) Math.; Phys. CDZZ ZZXV

DIOCLES OF CARYSTUS (fl. c.300 B.C.) Med. ABET CDZZ ZZ-4

DIONIS DU SEJOUR, Achille P. (1734-1794) Astron.; Math. CDZZ ZZ-4

DIONYSODORUS (fl. 200 B.C.) Math. CDZZ ZZ-4

DIOPHANTUS OF ALEXANDRIA (c.210-c.290) Math. ABES ABET BDOS BEOS CDZZ ZZXV

DIOSCORIDES, Pedanius (fl. 50-70) Med. ABES ABET BDOS BEOS BHMT CDZZ LISD ZZ-4

DIRAC, Paul A. (1902-1984) Phys.; Math. ABES ABET BEOS DCPW MHM1 MHSE POSW

DIRICHLET, Gustav P. (1805-1859) Math. BEOS CDZZ ZZ-4

DITCHBURN, Robert W. (1903-) Phys. MHM2 MHSE

DITMARS, Raymond L. (1876-1942) Zool. CB40 DAB3 NC10

DITTMAR, William (1833-1892) Chem. CDZZ ZZ-4

DIVINI, Eustachio (1610-1685) Instr. CDZZ ZZ-4

DIVIS, Prokop (1698-1765) Elec. Sci. CDZZ ZZ-4

DIX, Dorothea L. (1802-1887) Med. WIWM

DIXON, Arthur L. (1867-1955) Math. RS-1

DIXON, Harold B. (1852-1930) Chem. CDZZ ZZ-4

DIXON, Henry H. (1869-1953) Bot. CDZZ DNB7 ZZ-4

DIXON, Jeremiah (1733-1779) Astron. CDZZ WAMB ZZ-4

DIXON, Joseph S. (1884-1952) Zool. LACC

DIXON, Roland B. (1875-1934) Anthro. DAB1

DIXON, Samuel G. (1851-1918) Bact. NC35

DIXON, Thomas F. (c.1881-1949) Rocket. MOS2

DJERASSI, Carl (1923-) Chem. MHM2 MHSE

DJERASSI, Isaac (1925-) Med. AMJB MFIR

DMCHOWSKI, Leon (1909-1981) Med. MFIR

DOBBIN, Carroll E. (1892-1967) Geol. NC54 NCSH

DOBELL, Cecil C. (1886-1949) Zool. CDZZ ZZ-4

DOBEREINER, Johann W. (1780-1849) Chem. ABES ABET BDOS BEOS CDZZ HSSO ZZ-4

DOBSON, George E. (1848-1895) Zool. DNB1

DOBSON, Gordon M. (1889-1976) Phys. RS23

DOBSON, Matthew (c.1735-1784) Med. BHMT

DOBZHANSKY, Theodosius G. (1900-1975) Biol.; Genet. ABET BEOS CB62 MHM1 MHSE RS23

DOCHEZ, Alphonse R. (1882-1964) Med. BM42

DOCK, Lavinia L. (1858-1956) Med. NAWM

DOD, Daniel (1788-1823) Engr. GE-1

DODART, Denis (1634-1707) Bot.; Physiol. CDZZ ZZ-4

DODDS, Edward C. (1899-1973) Biochem. RS21

DODGE, Barnett F. (1895-1972) Chem. Engr. ACCE

DODGE, Bernard O. (1872-1960) Bot. BM36

DODGE, Francis D. (1868-1942) Chem. ACCE

DODGE, Homer L. (1887-) Phys. NCSG

DODGE, Marcellus H. (1881-1963) Cons. LACC

DODGE, Raymond (1871-1942) Psych. BM29

DODGSON, Charles L. (1832-1898) Math. CDZZ DNB1 ZZ-4

DODOENS, Rembert (1516-1585) Med.; Bot. CDZZ ZZ-4

DOELL, Richard R. (1923-) Geophys. MHSE

DOELTER, Cornelio A. (1850-1930) Mineral. CDZZ ZZ-4

DOGEL, Valentin A. (1882-1955) Zool. CDZZ ZZ-4

DOHME, Alfred R. (1867-1952) Chem. NC41

DOHRN, Felix A. (1840-1909) Zool. CDZZ ZZXV

DOISY, Edward A. (1893-) Biochem. ABES ABET BEOS CB49 MHM1 MHSE NCSH PAW2 WAMB

DOKUCHAEV, Vasily V. (1846-1903) Soil Sci.; Geog. BEOS CDZZ ZZ-4

DOLBEAR, Amos E. (1837-1910) Phys.; Astron. EETD NC-9

DOLGOPLOSK, Boris A. (1905-) Chem. SMST

DOLLFUS, Audouin C. (1924-) Astron. BEOS IEAS

DOLLINGER, Ignaz C. von (1770-1841) Physiol.; Embryol. BEOS CDZZ ZZ-4

DOLLO, Louis A. (1857-1931) Paleon. CDZZ MADC ZZ-4

DOLLOND, John (1706-1761) Opt. ABES ABET BDOS BEOS CDZZ IEAS ZZ-4

DOLOMIEU, Dieudonne (1750-1801) Geol. ABET CDZZ ZZ-4

DOMAGK, Gerhard (1895-1964) Biochem. ABES ABET BDOS BEOS CB58 CDZZ HLSM MHM2 MHSE RS10 ZZ-4

DOMBEY, Joseph (1742-1794) Med.; Bot. CDZZ ZZ-4

DOMINGO DE SOTO SEE SOTO, Domingo de

DOMINICUS DE CLAVASIO (fl. c.1350) Math.; Astrol. CDZZ ZZ-4

DOMINIS, Marko A. (1560-1626) Phys. CDZZ ZZ-4

DOMINUS OF LARISSA (fl. 400) Math. CDZZ ZZ-4

DON, George (1798-1856) Bot. DNB

DONALDSON, Henry H. (1857-1938) Med. BM20 CDZZ NC11 ZZ-4

DONATI, Giovanni B. (1826-1873) Astron. ABES ABET BEOS CDZZ ZZ-4

DONCHIAN, Paul S. (1895-1967) Invent. NC53

DONDERS, Franciscus C. (1818-1889) Physiol. ABET CDZZ ZZ-4

DONDI, Giovanni de (1318-1389) Astron. BDOS BEOS CDZZ GE-1 ZZ-4

DONKIN, Bryan (1768-1855) Invent. BDOS GE-1

DONKIN, William F. (1814-1869) Astron. DNB

DONN, Benjamin (1729-1798) Math. DNB

DONNAN, Frederick G. (1870-1956) Chem. BDOS BEOS CDZZ DNB7 RS-3 ZZ-4

DONNAY, Joseph D. (1902-) Crystal.; Mineral. MHSE

DONNELL, Lloyd H. (1895-) Engr. MHSE

DONOVAN, Edward (1768-1837) Nat. Hist. ANHD DNB

DOOB, Joseph L. (1910-) Math. MHM1 MHSE

DOODSON, Arthur T. (1890-1968) Math.; Geophys. BEOS RS14

DOODY, Samuel (1656-1706) Bot. DNB

DOOLITTLE, Charles L. (1843-1919) Astron. DAB NC20

DOOLITTLE, Eris (1869-1920) Astron. DAB NC19

DOOLITTLE, James H. (1896-) Aero. ICFW MOS3 WAMB

DOPPELMAYR, Johann G. (1671-1750) Astron.; Phys. CDZZ ZZ-4

DOPPLER, Christian J. (1803-1853) Phys.; Astron. ABES ABET BDOS BEOS CDZZ HOSS SAIF TGNH ZZ-4

DORAN, James M. (1885-1942) Chem. NC31

DOREMUS, Robert O. (1824-1906) Chem.; Phys. DAB NC28

DOREMUS, Thomas E. (1874-1962) Cons. LACC

DOREY, Stanley F. (1891-1972) Engr. RS19

DORFFEL, Georg S. (1643-1688) Astron. CDZZ ZZ-4

DORN, Friedrich E. (1848-1916) Phys. ABES ABET BEOS

DORN, Gerard (fl. 1566-1584) Med.; Alch. CDZZ ZZ-4

DORNBERGER, Walter R. (1895-1980) Rocket. AO80 CB65 MOS2

DORNIER, Claudius (1884-1969) Aero. ICFW

DORNO, Carl W. (1865-1942) Meteor. CDZZ ZZ-4

DORODNITSYN, Anatolii A. (1910-) Meteor. SMST

DORR, John V. (1872-1962) Chem. Engr. ACCE

DORSET, Marion (1872-1935) Biochem. DAB1 NC26

DORSEY, George A. (1868-1931) Anthro. DAB1

DORST, Jean P. (1924-) Zool.; Ecol. POEC

DOSITHEUS (fl. c.230 B.C.) Math.; Astron. CDZZ ZZ-4

DOTEN, Samuel B. (1875-1955) Entom. BNBR

DOUBLEDAY, Edward (1811-1849) Entom. DNB

DOUBLEDAY, Henry (1808-1875) Nat. Hist. DNB

DOUBLEDAY, Neltje de Graff (1865-1918) Nat. Hist. DAB

DOUGHERTY, Dora (1921-) Aero. CB63

DOUGLAS, Alexander E. (1916-1981) Phys. RS28

DOUGLAS, Claude G. (1882-1963) Physiol. RS10

DOUGLAS, David (1798-1834) Nat. Hist. DNB NATJ

DOUGLAS, Donald W. (1892-1981) Aero. AO81 BEOS MHM1 MHSE

DOUGLAS, James (1675-1742) Nat. Hist. CDZZ ZZ-4

DOUGLAS, James (1837-1918) Chem.; Metal. ACCE

DOUGLAS, Jesse (1897-1965) Math. CDZZ ZZ-4

DOUGLAS, Philip A. (1917-) Cons. LACC

DOUGLAS, Robert J. (1920-) Geol. MHM2 MHSE

DOUGLAS, Silas H. (1816-1890) Chem.; Geol. ACCE BIOD

DOUGLASS, Andrew E. (1867-1962) Astron. ABES ABET BEOS NC16 NCSD

DOUGLASS, Earl (1862-1931) Paleon. MADC NC26

DOUGLASS, William (1691-1753) Med.; Nat. Hist. BIOD DAB NC-3 SBCS

DOVE, Heinrich W. (1803-1879) Meteor.; Phys. CDZZ ZZ-4

DOVER, Thomas (1662-1742) Med. BHMT

DOWNING, Arthur M. (1850-1917) Astron. CDZZ ZZ-4

DOWNING, Elliot R. (1868-1944) Biol. NC37

DOWNS, J. Cloyd (1885-1957) Chem. NC46

DOYLE, Arthur C. (1859-1930) Med. BHMT

DRACH, Jules J. (1871-1941) Math. CDZZ ZZ-4

DRAGSTEDT, Lester R. (1893-1975) Med.; Physiol. BM51 MHM2 MHSE

DRAKE, Carl J. (1885-1965) Entom. AMEM

DRAKE, Charles F. (1846-1874) Nat. Hist. DNB

DRAKE, Daniel (1785-1852) Med.; Nat. Hist. ASJD BHMT BIOD DAB

DRAKE, Edwin L. (1819-1880) Engr. ABET BDOS FOIF

DRAKE, Frank D. (1930-) Astron. ABET BEOS CB63 IEAS MOS6

DRAKE, George L. (1889-) Forest. LACC

DRAKE, Noah F. (1864-1945) Geol. NC49

DRAPARNAUD, Jacques P. (1772-1804) Zool.; Bot. CDZZ ZZ-4

DRAPER, Charles S. (1901-) Aero.; Rocket. CB65 ICFW MHM1 MHSE NOS3

DRAPER, Henry (1837-1882) Astron.; Chem. ABET ACCE BEOS BIOD BM-3 CDZZ DAB IEAS NC-6 SNAR WAMB ZZ-4

DRAPER, John C. (1835-1885) Chem.; Anat. ACCE

DRAPER, John W. (1811-1882) Chem. ABES ABET ACCE BEOS BIOD BM-2 CDZZ DNB NC-3 SNAR TPAE WAMB ZZ-4

DREBBEL, Cornelius (1572-1633) Invent. CDZZ GE-1 MPIP ZZ-4

DRESSELHAUS, Mildred (1930-) Phys. CWSN

DREW, Charles R. (1904-1950) Med. BPSH CB44 DANB GBAR GNPA HCOK SABL SHAH SBPY

DREW, Frederick (1836-1891) Geol. DNB1

DREW, John (1809-1857) Astron. DNB

DREYER, Johann L. (1852-1926) Astron. BEOS CDZZ DNB4 IEAS ZZ-4

DRICKAMER, Harry G. (1918-) Chem. BEOS MHM2 MHSE

DRIESCH, Hans A. (1867-1941) Biol. BDOS BEOS CDZZ HLSM ZZ-4

DROWN, Thomas M. (1842-1904) Chem.; Metal. ACCE BIOD DAB

DROWNE, Solomon (1753-1834) Med.; Bot. NC-8

DRUCE, George C. (1850-1932) Bot. DNB5

DRUCKER, Daniel C. (1918-) Engr. MHSE

DRUDE, Paul K. (1863-1906) Phys. CDZZ ZZ-4

DRUMMOND, Jack E. (1891-1952) Biochem. DNB7

DRUMMOND, James L. (1783-1853) Anat. DNB

DRUMMOND, Thomas (1797-1840) Invent. BDOS DNB GE-1

DRURY, Alan N. (1889-1980) Path. RS27

DRURY, Dru (1725-1803) Entom. DNB

DRURY, Newton B. (1889-) Cons. LACC

DRYDEN, Hugh L. (1898-1965) Phys.; Engr. BM40 CB59 MHM2 MHSE MOS2 ICFW NC52 PPEY PPKY

DRYGALSKI, Erich von (1865-1949) Geog. CDZZ ZZ-4

DUANE, William (1872-1935) Phys. BM18 CDZZ DAB1 NCSA QPAS ZZ-4

DUBBS, Jesse A. (1855-1918) Med. CDZZ ZZ-4

DUBINI, Angelo (1813-1902) Med. CDZZ ZZ-4

DUBININ, Mikhail M. (1901-) Chem. MHM2 MHSE
SMST

DUBININ, Nikolai P. (1907-) Biol. SMST

DU BOIS, Eugene F. (1882-1959) Med.; Paleon.
BHMT BM36 PHLS TPOS

DUBOIS, Jacques (1479-1555) Med. BHMT CDZZ
ZZ-4

DUBOIS, Marie Eugene (1858-1940) Paleon. ABES
ABET BEOS

DU BOIS-REYMOND, Emil H. (1818-1896) Physiol.
ABES ABET BDOS BEOS BHMT CDZZ ZZ-4

DU BOIS-REYMOND, Paul D. (1831-1889) Math.
CDZZ ZZ-4

DUBOS, Rene J. (1901-1982) Microbiol. ABES ABET
BEOS CB52 CB73 MHM1 MHSE NCSJ POEC
WAMB

DUBOSCQ, Octave (1868-1943) Zool. CDZZ ZZ-4

DU BRIDGE, Lee A. (1901-) Phys. CB48

DU BUAT, Pierre L. (1734-1809) Phys. CDZZ ZZ-4

DUCATEL, Julius T. (1796-1849) Chem. NC-4

DU CHAILLU, Paul B. (c.1831-1903) Nat. Hist.
NATJ

DU CHATELET, Emilie (1706-1749) Math.; Phys.
IDWB WIMO

DUCHENNE, Guillaume (1806-1875) Med. BHMT

DUCHESNE, Joseph (c.1544-1609) Chem. CDZZ
ZZ-4

DUCKWORTH, Henry E. (1915-) Phys. MHM2 MHSE

DUCKWORTH, Wynfrid L. (1870-1956) Anat. DNB7

DUCLAUX, Emile (1840-1904) Biochem. CDZZ
ZZ-4

DU COUDRAY, Angelique M. (1712-1789) Med.
WIWM

DUDITH, Andreas (1533-1589) Astron.; Math. CDZZ
ZZ-4

DUDLEY, Charles B. (1842-1909) Chem. ACCE DAB
NC12

DUDLEY, Dud (1599-1684) Invent. GE-1

DUDLEY, Paul (1675-1751) Nat. Hist. BIOD SBCS

DUDLEY, Robert (1573-1649) Nav. CDZZ ZZ-4

DUDLEY, Sheldon F. (1884-1956) Med. RS-2

DUDLEY, William R. (1849-1911) Bot. DAB MABH
NC22

DUELL, Prentice (1894-1960) Archaeol. NC44

DU FAY, Charles F. (1698-1739) Phys. ABES ABET
BDOS BEOS CDZZ EETD ESEH ZZ-4

DUFFIELD, Samuel P. (1833-1916) Chem.; Med.
ACCE

DUFOUR, Guillaume H. (1787-1875) Engr. CDZZ
ZZ-4

DUFRENOY, Ours P. (1792-1857) Geol.; Mineral.
CDZZ ZZ-4

DUGAN, Raymond S. (1878-1940) Astron. CDZZ
NC36 ZZ-4

DUGGAR, Benjamin M. (1872-1956) Bot. ABES
ABET BEOS BM32 CB52 CDZZ MABH NC46
ZZ-4

DUHAMEL, Henri L. (1700-1782) Chem.; Bot. BDOS
BEOS CDZZ GRCH ZZ-4

DU HAMEL, Jean B. (1623-1706) Anat. CDZZ ZZ-4

DUHAMEL, Jean M. (1797-1872) Math.; Phys. CDZZ
ZZ-4

DUHEM, Pierre M. (1861-1916) Phys.; Chem. CDZZ
ZZ-4

DUISBERG, Carl (1861-1935) Chem. HSSO

DUJARDIN, Felix (1801-1860) Zool. ABET BDOS
BEOS CDZZ ZZ-4

DUKE, Charles (1935-) Astronaut. SBPY

DUKE, Peggy E. (Contemporary) Cons. WAWL

DUKE-ELDER, William S. (1898-1978) Med. RS26

DULBECCO, Renato (1914-) Virol. ABET BEOS
MHSE

DULEY, Frank L. (1888-) Agr. LACC

DULLAERT OF GHENT (c.1470-1523) Philos. CDZZ ZZ-4

DULONG, Pierre L. (1785-1838) Chem. ABES ABET BDOS BEOS CDZZ SOAC ZZ-4

DUMANSKII, Anton V. (1880-1967) Chem. SMST

DUMAS, Jean B. (1800-1884) Chem. ABES ABET BDOS BEOS CDZZ GRCH HSSO ZZ-4

DUMBLETON SEE JOHN OF DUMBLETON

DUMEE, Jeanne (fl. 1680) Astron. IDWB

DUMERIL, Andre M. (1774-1860) Zool. CDZZ ZZXV

DU MONCEAU, Duhamel SEE DUHAMEL, Henri L.

DU MONCEL, Theodore A. (1821-1884) Elec. Sci. CDZZ ZZ-4

DUMOND, Jesse W. (1892-1976) Phys. BM52 NC59

DUNBAR, Carl O. (1891-) Geol. MHM1 MHSE

DUNBAR, Helen F. (1902-1959) Psych. NAWM

DUNBAR, Paul B. (1882-1968) Chem. CB49 NC54

DUNBAR, William (1749-1810) Math.; Astron. BIOD DAB

DUNCAN, Albert B. (1903-1972) Chem. NC57

DUNCAN, Catherine G. (1908-1968) Path. NC54

DUNCAN, John C. (1882-1967) Astron. CDZZ NC54 ZZ-4

DUNCAN, Peter M. (1821-1891) Geol. DNB1

DUNCAN, Robert K. (1868-1914) Chem. DAB

DUNCAN, William J. (1894-1960) Engr. RS-7

DUNDONALD, Archibald C. (1749-1831) Chem. CDZZ ZZ-4

DUNER, Nils C. (1839-1914) Astron. CDZZ ZZ-4

DUNGLISON, Robley (1788-1869) Physiol.; Med. BIOD CDZZ ZZ-4

DUNHAM, Charles L. (1906-) Med. CB66

DUNHAM, Edward K. (1860-1922) Bact. NC30

DUNHAM, Ethel C. (1883-1969) Med. NAWM

DUNHAM, Kingsley C. (1910-) Geol. MHSE

DUNLAP, Matthew E. (1891-1971) Invent. NC56

DUNLOP, James (1795-1848) Astron. DNB

DUNLOP, John B. (1840-1921) Invent. BDOS DNB3 SAIF

DUNN, Emmett R. (1894-1956) Zool. NC43

DUNN, Gano S. (1870-1953) Engr. BM28

DUNN, Gordon E. (1905-) Metal. CB66

DUNN, Leslie C. (1893-1974) Genet. BM49 MHM2 MHSE NCSJ

DUNN, Louis G. (1908-) Rocket. MOS3

DUNN, Paul M. (1898-) Forest. LACC

DUNN, Samuel (d. 1794) Math. DNB

DUNNE, John W. (1875-1949) Aero. ICFW

DUNNING, Emily SEE BARRINGER, Emily D.

DUNNING, John R. (1907-1975) Phys. ABES ABET BEOS CB48

DUNNINGTON, Francis P. (1851-1944) Chem. NC34

DU NOUY, Pierre SEE LECOMTE DU NOUY, Pierre

DUNOYER DE SEGONZAC, Louis D. (1880-1963) Phys. CDZZ ZZ-4

DUNS SCOTUS, John (1266-1308) Philos. CDZZ DNB ZZ-4

DUNSTAN, Wyndham R. (1861-1949) Chem. DNB6

DUNTHORNE, Richard (1711-1775) Astron. DNB

DUPERREY, Louis I. (1786-1865) Nav. CDZZ ZZ-4

DUPIN, Pierre C. (1784-1873) Math. CDZZ GE-1 ZZ-4

DUPLAIX, Nicole (Contemporary) Zool. WAWL

DU PONT, Eleuthere I. (1771-1834) Chem. ACCE COAC

DU PONT, Francis G. (1850-1905) Chem. NC23

DU PONT, Francis I. (1873-1942) Chem. DAB3

DUPRE, Athanase L. (1808-1869) Phys.; Math. CDZZ ZZ-4

DUPRE, August (1835-1907) Chem. DNB2

DUPUYTREN, Guillaume (1777-1835) Med. BHMT

DURAN REYNALS, Francisco (1899-1958) Biol. NC46

DURAND, Elias (1794-1873) Bot. BIOD MABH

DURAND, William F. (1859-1958) Engr. BM48

DURANT, Charles F. (1805-1873) Aero. DAB

DURER, Albrecht (1471-1528) Math. ABET ANHD BDOS BMST CDZZ ZZ-4

DURKEE, Frank W. (1861-1939) Chem. NC29

DUROZIER, Paul L. (1826-1897) Med. BHMT

DURR, Ludwig (1878-1956) Aero. ICFW

DURY, Charles (1847-1931) Entom. NC24

DURYEA, Charles E. (1861-1938) Invent. DAB2 NCSD WAMB

DUSHMAN, Saul (1883-1954) Phys.; Chem. ACCE

DU SIMITIERE, Pierre E. (c.1736-1784) Nat. Hist. DAB

DUSSAUCE, Hyppolite E. (1829-1869) Geol. CDZZ ZZ-4

DUTCHER, William (1846-1920) Cons. LACC

DU TOIT, Alexander L. (1878-1949) Geol. BEOS CDZZ ZZ-4

DU TOIT, Petrus J. (1888-1967) Vet. Med. RS15

DUTROCHET, Rene J. (1776-1847) Physiol. BDOS BEOS CDZZ ZZ-4

DUTTON, Clarence E. (1841-1912) Geol.; Phys. ABES ABET BEOS BM32 ZZ-4

DUTTON, Joseph E. (1874-1905) Biol. DNB2

DUTTON, Walt L. (1889-) Forest. LACC

DUVAL, Mathias M. (1844-1907) Physiol.; Anat. CDZZ ZZ-4

DUVE, Christian R. de SEE DE DUVE, Christian R.

DUVERNEY, Joseph G. (1648-1730) Anat. CDZZ ZZ-4

DU VIGNEAUD, Vincent (1901-1978) Biochem. ABES ABET BEOS CB56 MHM1 MHSE NCSI WAMB

DYADKOVSKY, Iustin E. (1784-1841) Med. CDZZ ZZXV

DYAR, Harrison G. (1866-1934) Entom. AMEM DAB NC14

DYCK, Walther F. (1856-1934) Math. CDZZ ZZ-4

DYER, Joseph C. (1780-1871) Invent. DNB

DYER, Rolla E. (1886-1971) Med. MHM1 MHSE

DYKE, Edwin (1917-1978) Elec. Engr. NC61

DYSON, Frank W. (1868-1939) Astron. BDOS CDZZ DNB5 IEAS MMSB ZZ-4

DYSON, Freeman J. (1923-) Phys. ABET BEOS CB80 MHM2 MHSE

DZHELEPOV, Boris S. (1910-) Phys. SMST

E

EABORN, Colin (1923-) Chem. COBC

EADS, James B. (1820-1887) Engr. BDOS BM-3 COAC HFGA INYG TECH WAMB

EAGLE, Harry (1905-) Med. MHSE

EARLY, James J. (1875-1961) Invent. NC50

EASLEY, Annie (1932-) Comp. BCST

EAST, Edward M. (1879-1938) Genet. BM23 CDZZ DAB2 NC47 NCSD ZZ-4

EASTMAN, Albert S. (1882-1946) Chem. NC37

EASTMAN, George (1854-1932) Invent. ABES ABET BEOS DAB1 SAIF TECH WAMB

EASTMAN, John R. (1836-1913) Astron.; Math. DAB NC13

EASTON, Cornelis (1864-1929) Astron.; Climat. CDZZ ZZ-4

EASTWOOD, Alice (1859-1953) Bot. BNBR NAWM

EATON, Amos (1776-1842) Chem.; Geol. ACCE ASJD BIOD CDZZ DAB NC-5 ZZ-4

EATON, Daniel C. (1834-1895) Bot. BIOD DAB MABH NC11

EATON, Elon H. (1866-1934) Ornith. NC28

EATON, Melvin C. (1891-1966) Chem. NC52

EAVENSON, Alban (1869-1958) Chem. NC49

EBASHI, Setsuro (1922-) Biochem. BEOS

EBEL, Johann G. (1764-1830) Anat.; Bact. CDZZ ZZ-4

EBEL, William K. (1899-1972) Aero. NC57

EBERTH, Carl J. (1835-1926) Anat. CDZZ ZZ-4

ECCLES, John C. (1903-) Physiol. ABES ABET BEOS CB72 MHM1 MHSE

ECCLES, William H. (1875-1966) Phys. RS17

ECKARSLEY, Thomas L. (1886-1959) Phys. DNB7

ECKART, Carl H. (1902-1973) Phys. BM48 MHM2 MHSE QPAS

ECKERD, James W. (1916-1972) Chem. Engr. NC58

ECKERSLEY, Thomas L. (1886-1959) Phys. RS-5

ECKERT, John P. (1919-) Engr. ABET MHM2 MHSE

ECKERT, Wallace J. (1902-1971) Astrophys. CDZZ NC58 ZZXV

ECKLEBERRY, Don (1921-) Ornith. DGMT

ECKSTORM, Fannie H. (1865-1946) Ornith. DAB4

EDDINGTON, Arthur S. (1882-1944) Astron.; Phys. ABES ABET BDOS BEOS CB41 CDZZ DNB6 IEAS SGAC ZZ-4

EDDY, Henry T. (1844-1921) Math. DAB NC15

EDDY, Samuel (1897-) Zool. LACC

EDELMAN, Gerald M. (1929-) Biochem. ABET BEOS MHSE PAW2 WAMB

EDER, Josef M. (1855-1944) Chem. CDZZ ZZ-4

EDGE, Mabel R. (1877-1962) Cons. EAFC LACC

EDGERTON, Harold E. (1903-) Elec. Engr. CB66 MHSE

EDGEWORTH, Michael P. (1812-1881) Bot. DNB

EDGEWORTH, Richard L. (1744-1817) Invent. BDOS

EDINGER, Tilly (1897-1967) Paleon. NAWM

EDISON, Thomas A. (1847-1931) Invent. ABES ABET ACCE AMIH ASIW BDOS BEOS BM15 CDZZ COAC DAB1 EETD FOIF GASW GEXB HFGA HOSS IHMV INYG MGAH MPIP OGML SAIF SMIL TECH TINA TOWS TPAE WAMB ZZ-4

EDLEN, Bengt (1906-) Phys. ABET BEOS

EDLUND, Milton C. (1924-) Phys. MHM1 MHSE

EDMAN, Pehr V. (1916-1977) Chem. RS25

EDMINSTER, Frank C. (1903-) Cons. LACC

EDMONDS, Richard (1801-1886) Sci. Writ. DNB

EDMONDSTON, Laurence (1795-1879) Nat. Hist. DNB

EDMONDSTON, Thomas (1825-1846) Nat. Hist. DNB

EDSALL, John T. (1902-) Biochem. BEOS MHM1 MHSE

EDSON, Dwight J. (1896-1976) Geol. NC59

EDWARDES, David (1502-c.1542) Med. CDZZ ZZ-4

EDWARDS, Charles A. (1882-1960) Metal. RS-6

EDWARDS, Edward (1803-1879) Zool. DNB

EDWARDS, George (1694-1773) Nat. Hist. ANHD
DNB HAOA

EDWARDS, George (1908-) Engr. MHSE

EDWARDS, Henry (1830-1891) Entom. AMEM

EDWARDS, Martin A. (1905-) Elec. Engr. TPAE

EDWARDS, Wilfred N. (1890-1956) Paleon. FHUA

EDWARDS, William (1719-1789) Engr. GE-1

EDWARDS, William F. (1776-1842) Physiol. CDZZ
ZZ-4

EDWARDS, William H. (1822-1909) Entom. AMEM
DAB ZZ-4

EGAS MONIZ, Antonio C. (1874-1955) Med. ABES
ABET BDOS BEOS BHMT CDZZ MHM1 MHSE
ZZ-4

EGERTON, Alfred C. (1886-1959) Chem. RS-6

EGERTON, Philip de Malpas (1806-1881) Paleon.
DNB

EGLESTON, Nathaniel H. (1822-1912) Forest. EAFC

EGLOFF, Gustav (1886-1955) Chem. ACCE CB40

EGOROV, Dimitrii F. (1869-1931) Math. CDZZ ZZ-4

EHRENBERG, Christian G. (1795-1876) Biol.; Paleon.
ABET ANHD BDOS BEOS CDZZ PHLS ZZ-4

EHRENFEST, Paul (1880-1933) Phys. CDZZ ZZ-4

EHRENSTEIN, Maximilian (1899-1968) Biochem.
NC54

EHRET, Georg D. (1708-1770) Bot. CDZZ ZZ-4

EHRICKE, Krafft (1917-) Engr. CB58 FPSN MOS1

EHRLICH, Paul (1854-1915) Bact. ABES ABET
BDOS BEOS BHMT CDZZ DSLP FMBB GRCH
HLSM HSSO MAMR PAW2 PGFS SAIF SMIL
TMSB ZZ-4

EHRLICH, Paul R. (1932-) Biol. AMJB CB70 POEC

EICHELBERGER, William S. (1865-1947) Astron.
NCSC

EICHENWALD, Aleksandr A. (1864-1944) Phys.
CDZZ ZZ-4

EICHLER, August W. (1839-1887) Bot. BEOS CDZZ
ZZ-4

EICHWALD, Karl E. (1795-1876) Geol.; Paleon. CDZZ
ZZ-4

EIFFEL, Alexandre G. (1832-1923) Engr. ICFW

EIGEN, Manfred (1927-) Chem. ABES ABET BEOS
MHM2 MHSE

EIGENMANN, Carl H. (1863-1927) Ichth. BM18
CDZZ DAB NC13 ZZ-4

EIGENMANN, Rosa S. (1858-1947) Ichth. BIOD NAW

EIGHTS, James (1778-1882) Nat. Hist.; Geol. BIOD

EIJKMAN, Christian (1858-1930) Med. ABES ABET
BDOS BEOS CDZZ ZZ-4

EIMBECK, William (1841-1909) Math. BIOD

EINARSEN, Arthur S. (1897-1965) Biol. NC53

EINSTEIN, Albert (1879-1955) Phys. ABES ABET
ASTR BBRS BDOS BEOS BM51 CB41 CB53
CDZZ DAB5 DCPW EGSF GASW GDSP GMOP
GRTH HOSS HSSO IEAS IFBC LISD MGAH
MMSB MWBR NCSF OGML PHYS POSW PPEY
PPTY RPTC RS-1 SAIF SGSC SLOR SMIL
TOWS WAMB ZZ-4

EINTHOVEN, Willem (1860-1927) Physiol. ABES
ABET BDOS BEOS BHMT CDZZ SAIF ZZ-4

EISELEY, Loren C. (1907-1977) Anthro. CB60 NCSJ
WAMB

EISEN, Gustavus A. (1847-1940) Hort.; Archaeol.
NCSB

EISENHART, Luther P. (1876-1965) Math. BM40
CDZZ NC53 ZZ-4

EISENMANN, Eugene (1906-1981) Ornith. BWCL

EISENSCHIML, Otto (1880-1963) Chem. ACCE CB63

EISENSTEIN, Ferdinand G. (1823-1852) Math. CDZZ
ZZ-4

EKEBERG, Anders G. (1767-1813) Chem. ABES
ABET BEOS CDZZ ZZ-4

EKLUND, A. Sigvard (1911-) Phys. CB62

EKLUND, Carl R. (1909-1962) Nat. Hist. NC48

EKMAN, Vagn W. (1874-1954) Ocean. BEOS CDZZ
ZZ-4

ELDER, Albert L. (1901-) Chem. CB60

ELDER, Clarence L. (1935-) Invent. BCST

ELDERHORST, William (1828-1861) Chem. ACCE

ELDREDGE, Inman F. (1883-1963) Forest. LACC

ELDRIDGE, Charles H. (1886-1952) Chem.; Metal.
ACCE

ELEY, Daniel D. (1914-) Biochem. COBC

ELHUYAR, Fausto d' (1755-1833) Chem.; Mineral.
BEOS CDZZ ZZ-4

ELHUYAR, Juan J. d' (1754-1796) Chem.; Mineral.
CDZZ ZZ-4

ELIE DE BEAUMONT, Jean B. (1798-1874) Geol.
BEOS CDZZ ZZ-4

ELION, Edward (1900-1961) Chem. NC50

ELIOT, Charles W. (1834-1926) Chem. ACCE

ELIOT, John (1839-1908) Meteor. DNB2

ELKIN, William L. (1855-1933) Astron. BM18 CDZZ
DAB1 NC12 NC24 ZZ-4

ELKIND, Mortimer M. (1922-) Biophys. MHSE

ELKINGTON, George R. (1801-1865) Invent. BDOS

ELLER VON BROCKHAUSEN, Johann T. (1689-1760)
Med.; Chem. CDZZ ZZ-4

ELLERY, Robert L. (1827-1908) Astron. DNB2

ELLET, Charles (1810-1862) Engr. BDOS BEOS
WAMB

ELLET, William H. (1806-1859) Chem. NC11

ELLICOTT, Andrew (1754-1820) Math.; Surv. BIOD
DAB

ELLICOTT, John (c.1706-1772) Phys. DNB

ELLINGSON, Herman E. (1903-1970) Phys.; Math.
NC56

ELLIOT, Daniel G. (1835-1915) Zool. ANHD DAB
NC-5 NC16

ELLIOT SMITH, Grafton (1871-1937) Anat. CDZZ
ZZ-4

ELLIOTT, Edwin B. (1851-1937) Math. DNB5

ELLIOTT, Ezekiel B. (1823-1888) Math.; Invent.
BIOD

ELLIOTT, Stephen (1771-1830) Bot. BIOD DAB
NC-4

ELLIOTT, Thomas R. (1877-1961) Med. BEOS RS-7

ELLIS, Alexander J. (1814-1890) Math. DNB1

ELLIS, Carleton (1876-1941) Chem. ACCE DAB3
NC32

ELLIS, Charles D. (1895-1980) Phys. AO80 RS27

ELLIS, Francis C. (1890-1957) Invent. NC48

ELLIS, Havelock (1859-1939) Psych. LISD

ELLIS, Job B. (1829-1905) Bot. DAB MABH

ELLIS, John (1705-1776) Nat. Hist. ANHD DNB

ELLIS, William (1828-1916) Meteor.; Astron. CDZZ
ZZ-4

ELLMS, Joseph W. (1867-1950) Chem. NC39

ELLSWORTH, Lincoln (1880-1951) Engr.; Exp. WAMB

ELLWOOD, Walter B. (1902-1965) Phys. NC52

ELSASSER, Walter M. (1904-) Geophys. ABES ABET
BEOS MHM1 MHSE

ELSTER, Johann P. (1854-1920) Phys. ABET CDZZ
ZZ-4

ELTON, Charles S. (1900-) Ecol. BEOS POEC

ELVEHJEM, Conrad A. (1901-1962) Biochem. ABES
ABET ACCE BEOS CB48 CDZZ MHM1 MHSE
ZZ-4

ELWES, Henry J. (1846-1922) Bot.; Entom. DNB4

ELYUTIN, Vyacheslav P. (1907-) Metal. SMST

EMANUEL, Nikolai M. (1915-) Chem. SMST

EMANUELLI, Pio (1888-1946) Astron. CDZZ ZZ-4

EMBDEN, Gustav G. (1874-1933) Physiol. BEOS
    CDZZ GJPS ZZ-4

EMBODY, George C. (1876-1939) Ichth. LACC

EMDEN, Robert (1862-1940) Astrophys. CDZZ ZZ-4

EMELEUS, Harry J. (1903-) Chem. BEOS COBC
    MHM1 MHSE

EMELYANOV, Vasilii S. (1901-) Metal. SMST

EMERSON, Alfred E. (1896-1976) Zool. BM53

EMERSON, Benjamin K. (1843-1932) Geol. CDZZ
    DAB1 ZZ-4

EMERSON, George B. (1797-1881) Bot. BIOD

EMERSON, Gladys A. (1903-) Biochem. CWSE
    IDWB WPSH

EMERSON, Robert (1903-1959) Bot. BIOD CDZZ
    ZZ-4

EMERSON, Rollins A. (1873-1947) Genet. BM25
    DAB4 NC39

EMERSON, William (1701-1782) Math. DNB

EMERTON, James H. (1847-1931) Entom. AMEM
    NC22

EMICH, Friedrich (1860-1940) Chem. HSSO

EMILIANI, Cesare (1922-) Geol. BEOS

EMMET, John P. (1796-1842) Chem. ASJD BIOD

EMMET, William L. (1859-1941) Engr. BM22

EMMETT, Paul H. (1900-) Chem. MHM2 MHSE

EMMONS, Ebenezer (1799-1863) Geol. BIOD CDZZ
    ZZ-4

EMMONS, Howard W. (1912-) Engr. MHSE

EMMONS, Samuel F. (1841-1911) Geol.; Mng. BM-7
    CDZZ ZZ-4

EMORY, William H. (1811-1887) Engr. BIOD

EMPEDOCLES (c.495 B.C.-c.435 B.C.) Nat. Philos.
    ABES ABET AMST BEOS CDZZ EETD HLSM
    SAIF ZZ-4

ENCKE, Johann F. (1791-1865) Astron. ABES ABET
    BEOS CDZZ IEAS SLOR ZZ-4

ENDERS, John F. (1897-) Bact. ABES ABET BEOS
    CB55 MFIR MHM1 MHSE PAW2 PGFS WAMB

ENGEL, Friedrich (1861-1941) Math. CDZZ ZZ-4

ENGELBRECHT, Mildred A. (1899-1973) Bact. NC58

ENGELHARD, Charles P. (1867-1950) Chem. Engr.
    ACCE

ENGELHARDT, Francis E. (1835-1927) Chem.; Pharm.
    ACCE

ENGELHARDT, George P. (1871-1942) Entom. AMEM

ENGELHARDT, Wladimir A. (1894-) Biochem. MHM2
    MHSE SMST

ENGELMANN, George (1809-1884) Bot.; Meteor.
    BEOS BIOD BM-4 BNBR CDZZ DAB MABH
    NC-6 ZZXV

ENGELMANN, Henry (1831-1899) Geol. BIOD

ENGELMANN, Theodor W. (1843-1909) Physiol.
    BDOS BEOS CDZZ ZZ-4

ENGELS, Friedrich (1820-1895) Philos. CDZZ ZZXV

ENGLE, Earl T. (1896-1957) Anat. NC48

ENGLER, Heinrich G. (1844-1930) Bot. BDOS BEOS
    CDZZ ZZXV

ENRIQUES, Federigo (1871-1946) Math. CDZZ
    ZZ-4

ENSKOG, David (1884-1947) Phys. CDZZ ZZ-4

ENT, George (1604-1689) Med. CDZZ ZZ-4

EOTVOS, Roland von (1848-1919) Phys. ABET BDOS
    BEOS CDZZ ZZ-4

EPHRUSSI, Boris (1901-) Genet.; Biol. EDCJ

EPICURUS (341 B.C.-270 B.C.) Nat. Philos. ABES
    ABET BDOS EETD ZZ-4

EPPLEY, Marion (1883-1960) Chem. NC49

EPSTEIN, Paul S. (1883-1966) Phys. BM45

ERASISTRATUS (c.310 B.C.-250 B.C.) Med. ABES
ABET AMST BDOS BEOS CDZZ HLSM ZZ-4

ERASMUS, Disiderius (1466-1536) Med. BHMT

ERASTUS, Thomas (1523-1583) Philos. CDZZ ZZ-4

ERATOSTHENES OF CYRENE (c.276 B.C.-195 B.C.)
Astron. ABES ABET ASTR BDOS BEOS CDZZ
FASP HOSS IEAS SMIL ZZ-4

ERB, Wilhelm H. (1840-1921) Med. BHMT

ERCKER, Lazarus (c.1530-c.1594) Chem.; Metal.
BDOS BEOS CDZZ GE-1 GRCH ZZ-4

ERDELYI, Arthur (1908-1977) Math. RS25

ERDMANN, Otto L. (1804-1869) Chem. CDZZ ZZ-4

ERICSSON, John (1803-1889) Invent. ABES ABET
AMIH ASIW BDOS FNEC WAMB

ERIKSON, Erik H. (1902-) Psych. CB71 MFIR

ERIKSON, Henry A. (1869-1957) Phys. NC46

ERIUGENA, Johannes S. (800/25-875/900) Philos.
CDZZ ZZ-4

ERLANGER, Joseph (1874-1965) Physiol. ABET
BDOS BEOS BM41 CDZZ MHM1 MHSE NC51
ZZ-4

ERLENMEYER, Richard A. (1825-1909) Chem.
ABET BEOS CDZZ ZZ-4

ERMAN, Georg A. (1806-1877) Phys.; Meteor. CDZZ
ZZ-4

ERNI, Henri (1822-1885) Chem. ACCE

ERNST, Charles A. (1872-1939) Chem. NC42

ERNST, Wallace G. (1931-) Geol. MHSE

ERRERA, Leo A. (1858-1905) Bot.; Biol. CDZZ
ZZ-4

ERRINGTON, Paul L. (1902-1962) Zool. DGMT
LACC

ESAKI, Leo (1925-) Phys. ABES ABET BEOS
MHM1 MHSE POSW

ESAU, Katherine (1898-) Bot. IDWB MHM1 MHSE

ESCHENMOSER, Albert (1925-) Chem. BEOS

ESCHER VON DER LINTH, Hans C. (1767-1823) Geol.
CDZZ ZZ-4

ESCHERICH, Theodor (1857-1911) Med. CDZZ ZZ-4

ESCHMEYER, Reuben W. (1905-1955) Ichth. LACC

ESCHOLT, Mikkel P. (c.1610-1669) Geol. CDZZ
ZZ-4

ESCHSCHOLTZ, Johann F. (1793-1831) Med.; Zool.
ANHD CDZZ ZZ-4

ESCLANGON, Ernest B. (1876-1954) Astron.; Phys.
CDZZ ZZ-4

ESCLUSE, Charles de l' SEE L'ECLUSE, Charles de

ESHELBY, John D. (1916-) Phys. MHSE

ESKOLA, Pentti E. (1883-1964) Mineral.; Geol. CDZZ
ZZ-4

ESMARCH, J. Friedrich von (1823-1908) Med. BHMT

ESNAULT-PELTERIE, Robert (1881-1957) Astronaut.
HRST ICFW MOS8 PORS

ESPENSCHIED, Lloyd (1889-) Elec. Engr. TPAE

ESPY, James P. (1785-1860) Meteor. BEOS BIOD
CDZZ DAB WAMB ZZ-4

ESSELEN, Gustavus J. (1888-1952) Chem. Engr. ACCE

ESSEN, Louis (1908-) Phys. MHM2 MHSE

ESSIG, Edward O. (1884-1964) Entom. AMEM NC51

ESSON, William (1839-1916) Chem. CDZZ ZZ-4

ESTERMANN, Immanuel (1900-1973) Phys. NC57

ESTES, William K. (1919-) Psych. MHM2

ESTIENNE, Charles (c.1505-1564) Anat.; Nat. Hist.
CDZZ ZZ-4

ETARD, Alexandre L. (1852-1919) Chem. BDOS

ETHERIDGE, Robert (1819-1903) Paleon. DNB2

EUCKEN, Arnold T. (1884-1950) Chem. CDZZ HSSO ZZ-4

EUCLID, (fl. c.300 B.C.) Math. ABES ABET AMST BDOS BEOS CDZZ FMAS GRTH HOSS IFBS LISD MAKS MELW OMNM TOWS ZZ-4

EUCTEMON (fl. 400s B.C.) Astron. CDZZ ZZ-4

EUDEMUS OF RHODES (fl. 350 B.C.-300 B.C.) Philos. CDZZ ZZ-4

EUDOXUS OF CNIDUS (c.400 B.C.-c.350 B.C.) Astron.; Math. ABES ABET BDOS BEOS CDZZ IEAS ZZ-4

EUGSTER, Hans P. (1925-) Geol. MHSE

EULER, Leonhard (1707-1783) Math.; Phys. ABES ABET BDOS BEOS CDZZ FNEC GE-1 MASW MATT MELW OMNM ZZ-4

EULER, Ulf S. von (1905-) Phys. BEOS MHSE

EULER-CHELPIN, Hans K. von (1873-1964) Biochem. ABET BEOS CDZZ NPWC ZZ-4

EUPALINUS (fl. 500 B.C.) Engr. ABES

EUSTACHIO, Bartolommeo (1524-1574) Anat. ABES ABET BDOS BEOS BHMT CDZZ ZZ-4

EUSTIS, Henry L. (1819-1885) Engr. BIOD

EUTOCIUS OF ASCALON (b. c.480) Math. CDZZ ZZ-4

EVANS, Alexander W. (1868-1959) Bot. CDZZ NC50 ZZXV

EVANS, Alice C. (1881-1975) Bact. NAWM

EVANS, Caleb (1831-1886) Geol. DNB

EVANS, Charles A. (1884-1968) Physiol. RS16

EVANS, Charles F. (1885-1963) Cons. LACC

EVANS, Clifford (1920-) Anthro. SWWP

EVANS, Frederick J. (1815-1885) Ocean. CDZZ ZZ-4

EVANS, Griffith C. (1887-1973) Math. MHM1 MHSE

EVANS, Herbert M. (1882-1971) Anat.; Physiol. BM45 CB59 MSAJ RS18

EVANS, John (1812-1861) Geol. BIOD

EVANS, Lewis (1700-1756) Geog.; Geol. CDZZ ZZ-4

EVANS, Lewis (1755-1827) Math. DNB

EVANS, Meredith G. (1904-1952) Chem. DNB7

EVANS, Oliver (1755-1819) Invent. AMIH ASIW BDOS GE-1 INYG MCCW TINA WAMB

EVANS, Robley D. (1907-) Phys. BEOS

EVANS, Thomas S. (1777-1818) Math. DNB

EVANS, Ulick R. (1889-1980) Metal. RS27

EVANS, Ward V. (1880-1957) Chem. ACCE

EVANS, William H. (1876-1956) Entom. CDZZ ZZ-4

EVE, Joseph (1760-1835) Invent. DAB GE-1

EVELYN, John (1620-1706) Arbori. CDZZ ZZ-4

EVENDEN, Frederick G. (1921-) Cons. LACC

EVEREST, George (1790-1866) Geog. GE-1

EVERETT, Douglas H. (1916-) Chem. COBC

EVERHART, Benjamin M. (1818-1904) Bot. NC10

EVERMANN, Barton W. (1853-1932) Ichth. DAB1 LACC NC13

EVERSHED, John (1864-1956) Phys. CDZZ DNB7 RS-3 ZZ-4

EWART, Alfred J. (1872-1937) Bot. DNB5

EWBANK, Thomas (1792-1870) Engr.; Sci. Writ. NC-7

EWELL, Ervin E. (1867-1904) Chem. BIOD

EWING, Dwight T. (1888-1954) Chem. NC44

EWING, Henry E. (1883-1951) Entom. AMEM NC41

EWING, James (1866-1943) Path. BHMT BM26 CDZZ ZZ-4

EWING, James A. (1855-1935) Phys. BEOS CDZZ ZZ-4

EWING, (William) Maurice (1906-1974) Geol.; Ocean. ABES ABET BEOS BM51 CB63 CHUB EXDC MHM1 MHSE PBTS RS21

EWINS, Arthur J. (1882-1957) Chem. BDOS BEOS DNB7 RS-4

EXLEY, Thomas (1775-1855) Math. DNB

EYDE, Samuel (1866-1940) Electrochem. BDOS BEOS

EYKHFELD, Iogan G. (1893-) Chem. CB61

EYRING, Henry (1901-) Chem. BEOS CB61 MHM1 MHSE

EYSENCK, Hans J. (1916-) Psych. CB72

EYTELWEIN, Johann A. (1764-1848) Engr. CDZZ GE-1 ZZ-4

EYTON, Thomas C. (1809-1880) Nat. Hist. DNB

ibn EZRA, Abraham ben Meir (c.1090-c.1164) Math.; Astron. CDZZ ZZ-4

F

FABBRONI, Giovanni V. (1752-1822) Phys. CDZZ ZZ-4

FABIAN, Harold P. (1885-1975) Cons. NC58

FABRE, Jean Henri (1823-1915) Entom.; Nat. Hist. BEOS CDZZ FBMV NATJ SGNF SSDH ZZ-4

FABRICIUS, Johann C. (1745-1808) Entom. CDZZ ZZ-4

FABRICIUS ab AQUEPENDENTE, Hieronymus (1537-1619) Med. ABES ABET BDOS BEOS BHMT CDZZ DSLP HLSM ZZ-4

FABRY, Charles (1867-1945) Phys. ABES ABET CDZZ ZZ-4

FABRY, Louis (1862-1939) Astron. CDZZ ZZ-4

FABRY, Wilhelm (1560-1624) Med. BHMT

FABYAN, George (1867-1936) Phys. NC26

FACCIO, Nicolas (1664-1753) Math. DNB

FADDEEV, Ludwig D. (1934-) Math. MHSE

al-FADL ibn HATIM al-NAYRIZI SEE al-NAYRIZI, Abul Abbas al-Fadl

FAGE, Arthur (1890-1977) Engr. RS24

FAGET, Maxime A. (1921-) Engr. MHSE

FAGNANO DEI TOSCHI, Giovanni C. (1682-1766) Math. CDZZ ZZ-4

FAHLBERG, Constantin (1850-1910) Chem. ACCE

FAHRENHEIT, Daniel Gabriel (1686-1736) Phys. ABES ABET BDOS BEOS CDZZ FNEC HOSS MCCW ZZ-4

FAIRBAIRN, Peter (1799-1861) Engr. DNB

FAIRBAIRN, William (1789-1874) Engr. BDOS DNB GE-1 VISC

FAIRCHILD, David G. (1869-1954) Bot. CB53 DAB5 NCSC WAMB

FAIRCHILD, Sherman M. (1896-1971) Invent. NC58

FAIREY, Charles R. (1887-1956) Aero. ICFW

FAIRHALL, Lawrence T. (1888-1957) Phys. NC46

FAIRLEY, Neil H. (1891-1966) Med. RS12

FAJANS, Kasimir (1887-) Chem. BEOS HSSO

FALCONER, Hugh (1808-1865) Paleon.; Bot. CDZZ ZZ-2

FALES, Elisha N. (1887-1970) Aero. NC57

FALK, K. George (1880-1953) Chem. NC42

FALL, Henry C. (1862-1939) Entom. AMEM

FALLOPIUS, Gabriel (1523-1562) Anat. ABES ABET BDOS BEOS BHMT CDZZ ZZ-4

FALLOT, Arthur (1850-1911) Med. BHMT

FALLOWS, Fearon (1789-1831) Astron. AROW DNB

FANKUCHEN, Isidor (1905-1964) Crystal. CDZZ ZZ-4

FANNING, John T. (1837-1911) Engr. FNEC

FANO, Gino (1871-1952) Math. CDZZ ZZ-4

FANO, Robert M. (1917-) Elec. Engr. TPAE

al-FARABI, Abu Nasr Muhammad (c.870-950) Philos. CDZZ SCIN ZZ-4

FARADAY, Michael (1791-1867) Philos. ABES ABET BDOS BEOS CDZZ DCPW DNB EETD ELEC FNEC FPHM GASJ GASW GE-1 GEXB GISA GMOP GOED GRCH HOSS HSSO IFBS LISD MAKS MCCW MGAH OGML PAW1 SAIF SMIL SSDH TOWS VTHB ZZ-4

FARB, Peter (1929-1980) Nat. Hist.; Anthro. AO80

FARBER, Eduard (1892-1969) Chem. ACCE

FARBER, Sidney (1903-1973) Med. CB67 MFIR MHSE

FARCOT, Marie J. (1798-1875) Engr. GE-1

FAREY, John (1766-1826) Geol. CDZZ DNB ZZ-4

al-FARGHANI, Abul Abbas Ahmad (d. c.861) Astron. CDZZ ZZ-4

FARINACCI, Nicholas T. (1903-1966) Chem. NC51

FARKAS, Laszlo (1904-1948) Chem. CDZZ ZZ-4

FARLOW, William G. (1844-1919) Bot. DAB MABH NC12 NC22

FARMAN, Henri (1874-1958) Aero. ICFW

FARMAN, Maurice (1877-1964) Aero. ICFW

FARMER, Chester J. (1886-1969) Biochem. NC54

FARMER, John B. (1865-1944) Bot. CDZZ DNB6 ZZ-4

FARMER, Moses G. (1820-1893) Invent. NC-7 TPAE

FARNSWORTH, Philo T. (1906-1971) Engr.; Invent. WAMB

FARQUHAR, Francis P. (1887-) Cons. LACC

FARR, William (1807-1883) Med. BHMT

FARRAR, John (1779-1853) Math.; Phys. BIOD CDZZ DAB ZZ-4

FARREN, William S. (1892-1970) Engr. RS17

FARRIS, Edmond J. (1907-1961) Anat. NC50

FASTING, George F. (1891-1958) Bact. NC47

FATOU, Pierre J. (1878-1929) Math. CDZZ ZZ-4

FAUJAS DE SAINT-FOND, Barthelmy (1741-1819) Geol. CDZZ ZZ-4

FAULHABER, Johann (1580-1635) Math. CDZZ ZZ-4

FAURE FREMIET, Emmanuel (1883-1971) Biol. RS18

FAUVEL, Sulpice A. (1813-1884) Med. BHMT

FAVORSKY, Alexei Y. (1860-1945) Chem. CDZZ ZZ-4

FAVRE, Pierre A. (1813-1880) Chem. CDZZ ZZ-4

FAWCETT, Sherwood L. (1919-) Phys. CB72

FAY, Arthur C. (1896-1964) Bact. NC51

FAYE, Herve (1814-1902) Astron.; Geophys. CDZZ ZZ-4

al-FAZARI, Muhammad ibn Ibrahim (fl. c.760-800) Astron. CDZZ ZZ-4

FEARNSIDES, William G. (1879-1968) Geol. RS15

FEATHER, Norman (1904-1978) Phys. RS27

FEATHERSTONHAUGH, George W. (1780-1866) Geol. CDZZ ZZXV

FECHNER, Gustav T. (1801-1887) Psych.; Phys. ABES ABET BEOS CDZZ ELEC ZZ-4

FEDDERSEN, Berend W. (1832-1918) Phys. CDZZ ZZ-4

FEDEROV, Sergei F. (1896-) Geol. SMST

FEDEROV, Yevgenii K. (1910-) Geophys. SMST

FEE, Antoine L. (1789-1874) Bot. CDZZ ZZ-4

FEFFERMAN, Charles L. (1949-) Math. MHSE

FEHLING, Hermann C. (1812-1885) Chem. BEOS

FEIGE, Fritz (1891-1971) Chem. HSSO

FEIGL, Georg (1890-1945) Math. CDZZ ZZ-4

FEIT, Walter (1930-) Math. MHSE

FEJER, Lipot (1880-1959) Math. CDZZ ZZ-4

FEJOS, Paul (1897-1963) Anthro. NC49

FELD, Bernard T. (1919-) Phys. AMJB

FELIX, Arthur (1887-1956) Bact. RS-3

FELL, George B. (1916-) Cons. LACC

FELL, Honore B. (1900-) Biol. IDWB MHM2 MHSE

FELLER, William (1906-1970) Math. MHM1 MHSE

FELLERS, Carl R. (1893-1960) Bact. NC49

FELT, Ephraim P. (1868-1943) Entom. AMEM NC12

FELTON, Lloyd D. (1885-1953) Bact. NC40

FENGER, Christian (1840-1902) Med. BHMT

FENN, Wallace O. (1893-1971) Physiol. BM50 MHM2 MHSE

FENNEMAN, Nevin M. (1865-1945) Geol. CDZZ NCSD ZZ-4

FENNER, Clarence N. (1870-1949) Volcan. CDZZ NCSD ZZ-4

FEOKTISTOV, Konstantin (1926-) Astronaut. CB67

FERDMAN, David L. (1903-1970) Biochem. SMST

FERGUSON, Alfred L. (1884-1972) Chem. NC57

FERGUSON, James (1710-1776) Astron. CDZZ DNB ZZ-4

FERGUSON, Lloyd N. (1918-) Chem. SBPY

FERGUSON, Margaret C. (1863-1951) Bot. NAWM

FERGUSON, Meade (1869-1942) Nact. NC31

FERGUSON, Thomas B. (1841-1922) Invent. DAB

FERGUSON, William (1820-1887) Bot.; Entom. DNB

FERGUSON, William C. (1861-1930) Chem. NC23

FERGUSSON, William (1808-1877) Med. BHMT

FERMAT, Pierre de (1601-1665) Math. ABES ABET BDOS BEOS CDZZ MASW MELW ZZ-4

FERMI, Enrico (1901-1954) Phys. ABES ABET BDOS BEOS BM30 CB45 CDZZ DAB5 DCPW GEXB HOSS MASY MHM1 MHSE MSAJ MWBR NC40 PAW2 PHYS POSW PPTY RS-1 SAIF TECH WAMB ZZ-4

FERMOR, Lewis L. (1880-1954) Geol. DNB7 RS-2

FERNALD, Charles H. (1838-1921) Entom. AMEM DAB

FERNALD, Henry T. (1866-1952) Entom. AMEM NC18

FERNALD, Merritt L. (1873-1950) Bot. BM28 CDZZ DAB4 MABH NC38 ZZ-4

FERNANDEZ-MORAN, Humberto (1924-) Med. MHSE

FERNEL, Jean F. (1497-1558) Med. ABES ABET BDOS BEOS BHMT CDZZ SXWS ZZ-4

FERNOW, Bernhard E. (1851-1923) Forest. EAFC LACC WAMB

FERRANTI, Sebastian Z. de (1864-1930) Elec. Engr. BDOS DNB4

FERRARI, Ludovico (1522-1565) Math. CDZZ ZZ-4

FERRARIS, Galileo (1847-1897) Phys.; Elec. Engr. CDZZ ZZ-4

FERREIN, Antoine (1693-1769) Anat. CDZZ ZZ-4

FERREL, William (1817-1891) Meteor.; Geophys. BEOS BIOD BM-3 CDZZ DAB ZZ-4

FERRIER, David (1843-1928) Med. ABET BDOS BEOS CDZZ DSLP ZZ-4

FERRIS, Gordon F. (1893-1958) Entom. AMEM NC47

FERRO, Scipione (1465-1526) Math. CDZZ ZZ-4

FERRY, John D. (1912-) Chem. MHSE

FERSMAN, Aleksandr E. (1883-1945) Mineral.; Geol. CDZZ ZZ-4

FESENKOV, Vasili G. (1889-) Astrophys. SMST

FESHBACH, Herman (1917-) Phys. MHSE

FESSARD, ALFRED E. (1900-) Physiol. MHM2 MHSE

FESSENDEN, Reginald A. (1866-1932) Phys.; Invent.
ABES ABET BEOS CDZZ WAMB ZZ-4

FEUERBACH, Karl W. (1800-1934) Math. CDZZ
ZZ-4

FEUILLE, Louis (1660-1732) Astron.; Bot. CDZZ
ZZ-4

FEULGEN, Robert J. (1884-1955) Biochem. CDZZ
ZZ-4

FEWKES, Jesse W. (1850-1930) Archaeol.; Anthro.
BM15 WAMB

FEYNMAN, Richard P. (1918-) Phys. ABES ABET
BEOS CB55 DCPW MHM1 MHSE POSW WAMB

FFIRTH, Stubbins H. (1784-1820) Med. BHMT

FIBIGER, Johannes A. (1867-1928) Med. BDOS BEOS

FIBONACCI, Leonardo (1170-1230) Math. ABES
ABET BEOS CDZZ MELW ZZ-4

FICHOT, Lazare E. (1867-1939) Hydrol. CDZZ ZZ-4

FICK, Adolf E. (1829-1901) Physiol. BHMT CDZZ
ZZ-4

FIELD, Frederick (1826-1885) Chem. DNB

FIELD, George (c.1777-1854) Chem. DNB

FIELD, Herbert H. (1868-1921) Zool. DAB

FIELD, Joshua (1787-1863) Invent.; Engr. GE-1

FIELD, Richard M. (1885-1961) Geol. NC50

FIELDING, Gabriel (1916-) Med. CB62

FIELDING, Henry B. (d. 1851) Bot. DNB

FIELDS, John C. (1863-1932) Math. CDZZ ZZ-4

FIELDS, Paul R. (1919-) Chem. MHSE

FIESER, Louis F. (1899-1977) Chem. MHM2 MHSE

FIESSINGER, Noel (1881-1946) Med.; Biol. CDZZ
ZZ-4

FIFE, Harvey R. (1899-1959) Chem. NC47

FILDES, Paul G. (1882-1971) Bact. RS19

FILON, Louis N. (1875-1937) Math. DNB5

FINCH, George I. (1888-1970) Chem. BEOS COBC
RS18

FINE, Henry B. (1858-1928) Math. CDZZ DAB ZZ-4

FINE, Oronce (1494-1555) Astron.; Math. CDZZ
ZZXV

FINK, Colin G. (1881-1953) Electrochem. ACCE
NCSE

FINK, Frank W. (1905-1974) Aero. NC58

FINK, Thomas (1561-1656) Math.; Astron. CDZZ
ZZ-4

FINKELNBURG, Wolfgang (1905-) Phys. NBPS

FINLAY, Carlos J. (1833-1915) Med. BDOS BEOS
BHMT CDZZ ZZ-4

FINLEY, Harold E. (1905-) Zool. SBPY

FINLEY, James (1762-1828) Engr. GE-1

FINSCH, Otto (1839-1917) Ornith. ORNS

FINSEN, Niels R. (1860-1904) Med. ABES ABET
BEOS CDZZ ZZ-4

FIRMICUS MATERNUS (fl. 330-354) Astrol. CDZZ
ZZ-4

FISCHER, Charles A. (1884-1922) Math. NC20

FISCHER, Emil H. (1852-1919) Chem.; Biochem.
ABES ABET BDOS BEOS BHMT CDZZ GRCH
HSSO NPWC PAW2 ZZ-5

FISCHER, Ernst O. (1918-) Chem. ABET BEOS
MHSE

FISCHER, Franz (1877-1947) Chem. GRCH HSSO

FISCHER, Hans (1881-1945) Chem. ABES BDOS
BEOS CDZZ GRCH HSSO NPWC ZZXV

FISCHER, Hermann O. (1888-1960) Biochem. BM40
CDZZ HSSO ZZ-5

FISCHER, Johann G. (1771-1853) Nat. Hist. WFBG

FISCHER, Nicolaus W. (1782-1850) Chem. CDZZ
ZZ-5

FISCHER, Otto P. (1852-1932) Chem. BEOS

FISCHER, Richard (1869-1955) Pharm. ACCE

FISCHER VON WALDHEIM, Gotthelf (1771-1853) Paleon. PHLS

FISH, Marie P. (1902-) Ichth. CB41

FISHER, Albert K. (1856-1948) Ornith. NC37

FISHER, Alexander M. (1794-1822) Math. NC19

FISHER, Chester G. (1881-1965) Chem.; Instr. ACCE

FISHER, Clarence S. (1876-1941) Archaeol. NC40

FISHER, Elizabeth F. (1873-1941) Geol. NCSC

FISHER, George (1794-1873) Astron. DNB

FISHER, Herry L. (1885-1961) Chem. ACCE CB54

FISHER, Joseph L. (1914-) Cons. LACC

FISHER, Ronald A. (1890-1962) Genet. ABET BDOS BEOS CDZZ MHM1 MHSE RS-9 ZZ-5

FISK, James B. (1910-1981) Phys. CB59

FISKE, Augustus H. (1880-1945) Chem. NC33

FISKE, Thomas S. (1865-1944) Math. NC12

FITCH, Asa (1809-1879) Entom. AMEM BIOD CDZZ DAB WAMB ZZ-5

FITCH, John (1743-1798) Invent. ABES ABET AMIH GE-1 INYG TINA WAMB

FITCH, Val L. (1923-) Phys. ABET BEOS MHM1 MHSE

FITTIG, Rudolph (1835-1910) Chem. BDOS BEOS CDZZ ZZ-5

FITTON, William H. (1780-1861) Geol. CDZZ DNB ZZ-5

FITZ, Henry (1808-1863) Opt.; Instr. BIOD

FITZ, Reginald H. (1843-1913) Med. BHMT

FITZ GERALD, Francis A. (1870-1929) Electrochem. ACCE

FITZGERALD, George F. (1851-1901) Phys. ABES ABET BDOS BEOS CDZZ DCPW ZZ-5

FITZGERALD, William P. (1880-1942) Chem. NC31

FITZ-JAMES, Philip C. (1920-) Microbiol. MHM2 MHSE

FITZ-RANDOLPH, Raymond B. (1872-1922) Bact. NC-6

FITZROY, Robert (1805-1865) Meteor. ABET BEOS CDZZ DNB ZZ-5

FIXMAN, Marshall (1930-) Chem. MHSE

FIZEAU, Armand H. (1819-1896) Phys. ABES ABET BDOS BEOS CDZZ DCPW ZZ-5

FLAGG, Thomas W. (1805-1884) Nat. Hist. DAB

FLAMEL, Nicolas (1330-1418) Alch. MSFB

FLAMMARION, Nicolas C. (1842-1925) Astron. ABES ABET BEOS CDZZ ZZ-5

FLAMSTEED, John (1646-1719) Astron. ABES ABET BDOS BEOS CDZZ DNB HOSS IEAS ZZ-5

FLECHSIG, Paul E. (1847-1929) Med. CDZZ ZZ-5

FLECK, Alexander (1889-1968) Chem. RS17

FLEISCHER, Johannes (1539-1593) Opt. CDZZ ZZ-5

FLEMING, Alexander (1881-1955) Bact. ABES ABET BDOS BEOS CB44 CDZZ DNB7 DSLP FMBB GDSP HLSM MAMR MHM1 MHSE OGML PGFS RS-2 SAIF SMIL TMSB ZZ-5

FLEMING, Charles E. (1889-) Agr. BNBR

FLEMING, John (1785-1857) Zool.; Geol. CDZZ DNB ZZ-5

FLEMING, John A. (1849-1945) Engr. ABES ABET BDOS BEOS CDZZ DNB6 HOSS ZZ-5

FLEMING, John A. (1877-1956) Geophys. BM39 CB40 NC42

FLEMING, Williamina P. (1857-1911) Astron. BEOS CDZZ DAB IDWB NAW ZZ-5

FLEMMING, Walther (1843-1905) Anat. ABES ABET BDOS BEOS CDZZ ZZ-5

FLEMYNG, Malcolm (d. 1784) Physiol. DNB

FLEROV, Georgii N. (1913-) Phys. ABES ABET
    BEOS SMST

FLETCHER, Abraham (1714-1793) Math. DNB

FLETCHER, Alice (1838-1923) Anthro. POAA

FLETCHER, Harvey (1884-1981) Phys. AO81 NCSF

FLETCHER, James (1852-1908) Entom. AMEM DNB2

FLETCHER, James (1919-) Phys. CB72 PPNF

FLETCHER, Walter M. (1873-1933) Physiol. CDZZ
    STYC ZZ-5

FLETT, John S. (1869-1947) Geol. CDZZ DNB6
    ZZ-5

FLETTNER, Anton (1885-1961) Aero. ICFW

FLEURE, Herbert J. (1877-1969) Geol. RS16

FLEXNER, Simon (1863-1946) Bact.; Path. CDZZ
    NC52 ZZ-5

FLICKINGER, Don D. (1907-) Med. MOS3

FLINT, Albert S. (1853-1923) Astron. DAB NC10
    NC35

FLINT, Austin (1812-1886) Med. BHMT

FLINT, Joseph M. (1872-1944) Anat. NC33

FLINT, Wesley P. (1883-1943) Entom. AMEM

FLOOD, Valentine (d. 1847) Anat. DNB

FLORENSOV, Nikolai A. (1909-) Geol. SMST

FLOREY, Howard W., Baron of Adelaide (1898-1968)
    Path. ABES ABET BDOS BEOS CB44 CDZZ
    DSLP MHM1 MHSE RS17 ZZ-5

FLORIN, Rudolf (1894-1965) Bot. FHUA

FLORY, Paul J. (1910-) Chem. ABET BEOS CB75
    MHSE PAW2

FLOURENS, Jean P. (1794-1867) Physiol. BEOS
    CDZZ ZZ-5

FLOWER, William H. (1831-1899) Zool. CDZZ ZZ-5

FLOWERS, Brian (1924-) Phys. SIWG

FLOYER, John (1649-1734) Med. BEOS

FLUDD, Robert (1574-1637) Alch. CDZZ ZZ-5

FLUGGE-LOTZ, Irmgard (1903-1974) Engr. NAWM

FLUKE, Charles L. (1891-1959) Entom. AMEM

FOCHE, Heinrich (1890-1979) Aero. ICFW

FOCK, Vladimir A. (1898-) Phys. BEOS SMST
    SOVL

FOERSTE, August F. (1862-1936) Paleon. CDZZ
    NC29 ZZ-5

FOKKER, Anthony (1890-1939) Aero. ICFW

FOL, Hermann (1845-1892) Biol. CDZZ ZZ-5

FOLEY, Arthur L. (1867-1945) Phys. NC43

FOLGER, Walter (1765-1849) Math.; Astron. BIOD
    DAB YSMS

FOLIN, Otto K. (1867-1934) Biochem. BHMT BM27
    CDZZ DAB1 NC25 ZZ-5

FOLKERS, Karl A. (1906-) Chem. ABES ABET
    BEOS CB62 MFIR MHM1 MHSE

FOLKES, Martin (1690-1754) Antiq. CDZZ ZZ-5

FOLLEY, Sydney J. (1906-1970) Physiol. RS18

FOLSOM, Justus W. (1871-1936) Entom. AMEM

FONTAINE (DES BERTINS), Alexis (1704-1771) Math.
    CDZZ ZZ-5

FONTANA, Domenico (1543-1607) Engr. GE-1

FONTANA, Felice (1730-1805) Biol. CDZZ ZZ-5

FONTENELLE, Bernard de (1657-1757) Sci. Ed.
    ABET BDOS CDZZ ZZ-5

FOOTE, Paul D. (1888-1971) Phys. BM50 NC56

FOPPL, August (1854-1924) Engr.; Phys. CDZZ ZZ-5

FORBES, Alexander (1882-1965) Physiol. BM40
    CDZZ ZZ-5

FORBES, David (1828-1876) Geol. DNB

FORBES, Edward (1815-1854) Zool.; Paleon. ABES ABET ANHD BEOS CDZZ DNB ZZ-5

FORBES, George (1849-1936) Phys. TPAE

FORBES, James D. (1809-1868) Glaciol.; Geol. CDZZ DNB GENT ZZ-5

FORBES, Reginald D. (1891-1977) Forest. NC60

FORBES, Stephen A. (1844-1930) Zool.; Entom. AMEM BM15 CDZZ DAB LACC NC13 NC22 ZZ-5

FORBES, William A. (1855-1883) Zool. DNB

FORBES, William T. (1885-1968) Entom. NC54

FORBUSH, Edward H. (1858-1929) Ornith. DAB LACC SFNB

FORBUSH, Scott E. (1904-1984) Geophys. MHM2 MHSE

FORCHAMMER, Johan G. (1794-1865) Geol.; Ocean. CDZZ ZZ-5

FORD, Edmund B. (1901-) Genet. BEOS MHM1 MHSE

FORD, Walter B. (1874-1971) Math. NC55

FORD, William W. (1871-1941) Bact. NC30

FORDOS, Mathurin J. (1816-1878) Chem. CDZZ ZZ-5

FOREGGER, Richard V. (1872-1960) Chem. CDZZ ZZ-5

FOREL, Auguste H. (1848-1931) Med.; Entom. CDZZ ZZ-5

FOREL, Francois A. (1841-1912) Zool.; Limn. CDZZ ZZXV

FOREMAN, James K. (1928-1980) Chem. AO80

FORESTER, Frank SEE HERBERT, Henry W.

FORFAIT, Pierre A. (1752-1807) Engr. GE-1

FORRESTER, Jay W. (1918-) Elec. Engr. MHM1 MHSE

FORSSKAL, Peter (1732-1763) Bot. CDZZ ZZ-5

FORSSMANN, Werner T. (1904-1979) Med. ABET BEOS CB57 MFIR MHM1 MHSE

FORSTER, Benjamin M. (1764-1829) Sci. Writ. DNB

FORSTER, Edward (1765-1849) Bot. DNB

FORSTER, Johann G. (1754-1794) Geog. CDZZ DNB ZZ-5

FORSTER, Johann R. (1729-1798) Nat. Hist.; Ornith. BWCL CDZZ HAOA WFBG ZZ-5

FORSTER, Martin O. (1872-1945) Chem. DNB6

FORSTER, Thomas F. (1761-1825) Bot. DNB

FORSTER, Thomas I. (1789-1960) Nat. Hist. DNB

FORSYTH, Alexander J. (1769-1843) Invent. DNB

FORSYTH, Andrew R. (1858-1942) Math. CDZZ DNB6 ZZ-5

FORTIN, Jean N. (1750-1831) Instr. BDOS CDZZ ZZ-5

FORTUNE, Robert (1813-1880) Bot. DNB

FOSDICK, Leonard S. (1903-1969) Chem. NC54

FOSHAG, William F. (1894-1956) Geol. NC44

FOSSEY, Diane (1933-) Ethol. WAGW

FOSTER, Henry (1797-1831) Geophys. CDZZ ZZ-5

FOSTER, John S. (1890-1964) Phys. RS12

FOSTER, John S. Jr. (1922-) Phys. CB71 MHM1 MHSE

FOSTER, John W. (1815-1873) Geol. BIOD

FOSTER, Laurence S. (1901-1973) Chem. NC57

FOSTER, Michael (1836-1907) Physiol. BEOS BHMT CDZZ DNB2 ZZ-5

FOSTER, Samuel (d. 1652) Math. DNB

FOSTER, Walter (fl. 1627-1650) Math. DNB

FOSTER, William (1869-1937) Chem. NC39

FOTHERGILL, John (1712-1780) Med. BHMT

FOTIADI, Epaminond E. (1907-) Geophys. SMST

FOUCAULT, Jean B. (1819-1868) Phys. ABES ABET BDOS BEOS CDZZ HOSS SAIF ZZ-5

FOUCHY, Jean P. de (1707-1788) Astron. CDZZ ZZ-5

FOUQUE, Ferdinand A. (1828-1904) Geol.; Mineral. CDZZ ZZ-5

FOURCROY, Antoine F. de (1755-1809) Chem. ABES ABET BDOS BEOS CDZZ ZZ-5

FOURIER, Jean B. (1768-1830) Math.; Phys. ABES ABET BDOS BEOS CDZZ FNEC TOWS ZZ-5

FOURNEAU, Ernest F. (1872-1949) Chem. BEOS CDZZ ZZ-5

FOURNEYRON, Benoit (1802-1867) Engr. BDOS BEOS CDZZ FNEC ZZ-5

FOWLER, Alfred (1868-1940) Astrophys. BEOS CDZZ DNB5 ZZ-5

FOWLER, John (1817-1898) Engr. BDOS

FOWLER, John (1826-1864) Invent. DNB

FOWLER, Lorenzo N. (1811-1896) Phren. BIOD

FOWLER, Lydia F. (1822-1879) Med. WIWM

FOWLER, Orson S. (1809-1887) Phren. BIOD

FOWLER, Ralph H. (1889-1944) Phys. CDZZ DNB6 ZZ-5

FOWLER, William A. (1911-) Phys. BEOS CB74 MHSE

FOWLER-BILLINGS, Katharine (1902-) Geol. CB40

FOWNES, George (1815-1849) Chem. CDZZ DNB ZZ-5

FOX, Adrian C. (1905-) Cons. LACC

FOX, Charles (1797-1878) Sci. Writ. DNB

FOX, Charles (1810-1874) Engr. DNB

FOX, Errol L. (1892-1931) Chem. NC23

FOX, Harold M. (1889-1967) Zool. BEOS RS14

FOX, Michael W. (1937-) Vet. Med. CB77

FOX, Philip (1878-1944) Astron. NC14 NCSC

FOX, Robert W. (1789-1877) Sci. Writ. DNB

FOX, Sidney W. (1912-) Biochem. ABES ABET BEOS MOS6 NCSJ

FOX, Thomas G. (1921-1977) Chem. NC60

FOX TALBOT SEE TALBOT, William H.

FOYN, Svend (1809-1894) Invent. BDOS

FRACASTORIUS, Hieronymus SEE FRACASTORO, Girolamo

FRACASTORO, Girolamo (c.1478-1553) Med. BDOS BEOS BHMT CDZZ DSLP ZZ-5

FRAENKEL, Adolf A. (1891-1965) Math. CDZZ ZZ-5

FRAENKEL-CONRAT, Heinz L. (1910-) Biochem. ABES ABET BEOS MHM1 MHSE

FRAIPONT, Julien (1857-1910) Zool.; Paleon. CDZZ ZZ-5

FRALICH, Charles E. (1902-1964) Geol. NC51

FRANCAIS, Francois (1768-1810) Math. CDZZ ZZ-5

FRANCAIS, Jacques F. (1775-1833) Math. CDZZ ZZ-5

FRANCESCA, Piero della (c.1415-1492) Math. CDZZ ZZ-5

FRANCIS OF MARCHIA (fl. c.1310-1340) Philos. CDZZ ZZ-5

FRANCIS OF MEYRONNES (c.1285-c.1330) Philos. CDZZ ZZ-5

FRANCIS, James B. (1815-1892) Engr. FNEC TECH

FRANCIS, John M. (1867-1924) Chem. NC20

FRANCIS, Thomas Jr. (1900-1969) Med. BEOS BM44 MHM1 MHSE

FRANCK, James (1882-1964) Phys. ABES ABET BDOS BEOS CB57 CDZZ GJPS HSSO MHM2 MHSE POSW RS11 ZZ-5

FRANCK, Sebastian (1499-1542) Philos. CDZZ ZZ-5

FRANDSEN, Peter (1876-) Zool. BNBR

FRANK, Bernard (1902-1964) Cons. LACC

FRANK, Glev M. (1904-) Biophys. SMST

FRANK, Ilya M. (1908-) Phys. ABES ABET BEOS MHM1 MHSE PAW2 POSW SMST

FRANK, Johann P. (1745-1821) Med. BHMT

FRANK, Philipp (1884-1966) Phys.; Math. CDZZ ZZ-5

FRANKLAND, Edward (1825-1899) Chem. ABES ABET BDOS BEOS CDZZ ZZ-5

FRANKLAND, Percy F. (1858-1946) Chem.; Bact. CDZZ DNB6 ZZ-5

FRANKLIN, Benjamin (1706-1790) Phys.; Ocean.; Meteor. ABES ABET AMIH ASIW BDOS BEOS BIOD BMST CDZZ COAC DAB DCPW ESEH EXDC EETD FPHM GE-1 GOED HFGA HOSS LISD MSAJ NC-1 SAIF SBCS SMIL SSAH TOWS TPAE WAMB ZZ-5

FRANKLIN, Edward C. (1862-1937) Chem. ACCE DAB2 HSSO NC30

FRANKLIN, Fabian (1853-1939) Math. DAB2

FRANKLIN, Henry J. (1883-1958) Entom. AMEM NC46

FRANKLIN, John (1786-1847) Exp. DNB

FRANKLIN, Kenneth J. (1897-1966) Physiol. RS14

FRANKLIN, Kenneth L. (1923-) Astron. ABET

FRANKLIN, Rosalind E. (1920-1958) Chem.; Biol. ABET BEOS CDZZ EDCJ EXSB IDWB ZZ-5

FRANKLIN, William S. (1863-1930) Phys. NC22

FRANTZ, Virginia K. (1896-1967) Path. NAWM

FRARY, Francis C. (1884-1970) Chem.; Metal. ACCE

FRARY, Hobart D. (1887-1920) Math. NC23

FRASCH, Herman (1851-1914) Chem. ABET ACCE BDOS BEOS GRCH NC19

FRASER, Francis C. (1903-1978) Zool. RS25

FRASER, John (1750-1811) Bot. DNB

FRASER, Louis (fl. 1840-1860) Nat. Hist. DNB

FRAUNHOFER, Joseph von (1787-1826) Phys.; Opt. ABES ABET BDOS BEOS CDZZ HOSS IEAS TMAL TOWS ZZ-5

FRAZER, James G. (1854-1941) Anthro. CDZZ ZZ-5

FRAZER, John F. (1812-1872) Geophys.; Chem. ACCE BIOD BM-1 DAB

FRAZER, Joseph C. (1875-1944) Chem. NC34

FRAZER, Persifor (1844-1909) Geol.; Chem. DAB NC-4

FRAZER, Robert A. (1891-1959) Math.; Phys. RS-7

FREAR, William (1860-1922) Chem. ACCE

FREAS, Thomas B. (1868-1928) Chem. DAB NC22

FRED, Edwin B. (1887-) Bact. CB50 NCSF

FREDERICK II OF HOHENSTAUFEN (1194-1250) Ornith. CDZZ NATJ ORNS ZZ-5

FREDERICK, Francis H. (1907-1968) Geol. NC54

FREDERICK, Lafayette (1923-) Bot. SBPY

FREDERICK, William G. (1909-1976) Chem. NC59

FREDERICQ, Leon (1851-1935) Physiol. CDZZ ZZ-5

FREDHOLM, Erik Ivar (1866-1927) Math. BDOS BEOS CDZZ ZZ-5

FREDINE, Clarence G. (1909-) Cons. LACC

FREED, Karl F. (1942-) Chem. MHSE

FREEMAN, Benjamin W. (1890-1963) Invent. NC50

FREEMAN, Edward M. (1875-1954) Bot. NC40

FREEMAN, Joan M. (1918-) Phys. MHSE

FREEMAN, John R. (1855-1932) Engr. BM17

FREEMAN, Thomas (d. 1821) Engr.; Astron. BIOD DAB

FREER, Paul C. (1862-1912) Chem.; Med. ACCE NC19

FREETH, Francis A. (1884-1970) Chem. RS22

FREGE, (Friedrich) Gottlob (1848-1925) Math. ABES
ABET BEOS CDZZ ZZ-5

FREIDLINA, Rakhil K. (1906-) Chem. SMST

FREIESLEBEN, Johann K. (1774-1846) Geol.; Mineral.
CDZZ ZZ-5

FREIND, John (1675-1728) Chem.; Med. CDZZ ZZ-5

FREIS, Edward R. (1912-) Med. MFIR

FREISER, Henry (1920-) Chem. MHSE

FREITAG, Robert F. (1920-) Astronaut. MOS7

FREKE, John (1688-1756) Med. BHMT

FREMIET, Emmanuel SEE FAURE FREMIET, Emmanuel

FREMY, Edmond (1814-1894) Chem. ABET CDZZ
ZZ-5

FRENCH, Charles S. (1907-) Bot. MHM2 MHSE

FRENCH, Dudley K. (1881-1960) Chem. NC49

FRENET, Jean F. (1816-1900) Math. CDZZ ZZ-5

FRENICLE DE BESSY, Bernard (c.1605-1675) Math.;
Phys. CDZZ ZZ-5

FRENKEL, Yakov I. (1894-1954) Phys. CDZZ ZZ-5

FRENKEL-BRUNSWIK, Else (1908-1958) Psych.
NAWM

FRENZEL, Friedrich A. (1842-1902) Mineral. CDZZ
ZZ-5

FRERE, John (1740-1807) Archaeol. ABET CDZZ
ZZ-5

FRERICHS, Fridrich T. von (1819-1885) Med. BHMT

FRESENIUS, Carl R. (1818-1897) Chem. CDZZ
HSSO ZZ-5

FRESNEL, Augustin J. (1788-1827) Opt. ABES
ABET BDOS BEOS CDZZ GE-1 ZZ-5

FREUD, Anna (1895-1982) Psych. CB79 IDWB MFIR

FREUD, Benjamin B. (1884-1955) Chem. Engr. ACCE

FREUD, Sigmund (1856-1939) Psych. ABET BDOS
BEOS BHMT CDZZ GRTH LISD OGML PAW3
POPF RPTC SMIL TMSB ZZ-5

FREUDENBERG, Karl J. (1886-) Chem. MHM2
MHSE

FREUNDLICH, Erwin F. (1885-1964) Astron. CDZZ
ZZ-5

FREUNDLICH, Herbert M. (1880-1941) Chem. BDOS
BEOS CDZZ ZZXV

FREY, Charles N. (1885-1972) Biochem. NC56

FREY, Henry M. (1929-) Chem. COBC

FREY, Maximilian R. von (1852-1932) Physiol. CDZZ
ZZ-5

FREY-WYSSLING, Albert F. (1900-) Bot. BEOS
MHM2 MHSE

FRIBERGIUS, Kalbius SEE RULEIN VON CALW,
Ulrich

FRIEDEL, Charles (1832-1899) Chem. ABES ABET
BDOS BEOS

FRIEDEL, Georges (1865-1933) Crystal. CDZZ ZZ-5

FRIEDLANDER, Gerhart (1916-) Chem. MHM2
MHSE

FRIEDLANDER, Paul (1857-1923) Chem. BEOS

FRIEDMAN, Herbert (1916-) Astrophys. ABET
BEOS CB63 MHM1 MHSE TMAL

FRIEDMANN, Aleksandr A. (1888-1925) Math.; Phys.
ABET BEOS CDZZ ZZ-5

FRIEDMANN, Herbert (1900-) Zool. ABES BEOS
MHM2 MHSE

FRIEDRICH, Hans R. (1911-1958) Engr. NC46

FRIEDRICHS, Kurt O. (1901-) Math. MHSE

FRIEND, Charlotte (1921-) Microbiol. CWSN

FRIEND, Clarence L. (1878-1958) Astron. NC48

FRIEND, John A. (1881-1966) Chem. CDZZ ZZ-5

FRIEND, Roger B. (1896-1962) Entom. AMEM

FRIES, Elias M. (1794-1878) Bot. BDOS BEOS
CDZZ ZZ-5

FRIES, Jakob F. (1773-1843) Phys.; Math. CDZZ
ZZ-5

FRIESE-GREENE, William (1855-1921) Invent. BDOS

FRISCH, Karl von (1886-1974) Zool. ABES ABET
BEOS CB74 MHM1 MHSE

FRISCH, Otto R. (1904-1979) Phys. ABES ABET
BEOS RS27

FRISH, Sergei E. (1899-) Phys. SMST

FRISI, Paolo (1728-1784) Math.; Phys. CDZZ ZZ-5

FRISON, Theodore H. (1895-1945) Entom. AMEM

FRITSCH, Felix E. (1879-1954) Bot. BEOS DNB7

FRITSCH, Gustav T. (1838-1927) Anat.; Zool. BDOS
BEOS CDZZ ZZ-5

FRITZ, Emanuel (1886-) Forest. LACC

FRITZSCHE, Carl J. (1808-1871) Chem. CDZZ ZZ-5

FROBENIUS, Georg F. (1849-1917) Math. CDZZ
ZZ-5

FROEHLICH, Jack E. (1921-) Engr. CB59

FROLICH, Alfred (1871-1953) Med. BHMT

FROLICH, Per K. (1899-1977) Chem. Engr. NC60

FROME, Michael (1920-) Cons. LACC

FROMM-REICHMANN, Frieda (1889-1957) Psych.
NAWM

FRONTINUS, Sextus J. (c.35-c.104) Engr. ABET
BEOS GE-1

FROST, Edwin B. (1866-1935) Astron. BM19 CDZZ
DAB1 NC-9 NC25 ZZ-5

FROST, Percival (1817-1898) Math. DNB1

FROST, William D. (1867-1957) Bact. NC46

FROUDE, William (1810-1879) Engr. CDZZ DNB
FNEC ZZ-5

FRUMKIN, Aleksandr N. (1895-) Chem. SMST

FRUTON, Joseph A. (1912-) Biochem. MHM2 MHSE

FRY, H. Shipley (1876-1949) Chem. NC38

FRY, Joshua (c.1700-1754) Surv.; Math. BIOD

FRY, William J. (1918-1968) Biophys. NC54

FRYER, John (1839-1928) Trans. Sci. Lit. ACCE

FUBINI, Eugene G. (1913-) Engr. TPAE

FUBINI, Guido (1879-1943) Math. CDZZ ZZ-5

FUBINI, Sergio P. (1928-) Phys. MHSE

FUCHS, Immanuel L. (1833-1902) Math. CDZZ ZZ-5

FUCHS, Johann N. von (1774-1856) Chem.; Mineral.
CDZZ ZZ-5

FUCHS, Leonhard (1501-1566) Bot. ABES ABET
BDOS BEOS CDZZ LISD ZZXV

FUCHS, Nathaniel (1898-1956) Chem. NC44

FUCHS, Vivien E. (1908-) Geol. BEOS

FUCHSEL, Georg C. (1722-1773) Geol. CDZZ ZZ-5

FUERTES, Louis A. (1874-1927) Sci. Illus. BWCL

FUETER, Karl R. (1880-1950) Math. CDZZ ZZ-5

FUHLROTH, Johann K. (1804-1877) Nat. Hist.;
Paleon. CDZZ ZZ-5

FULCHER, Gordon S. (1884-) Phys. NCSA

FULLAM, Frank L. (1870-1951) Chem. DAB5

FULLAWAY, David T. (1880-1964) Entom. NC58

FULLER, Dudley D. (1913-) Engr. MHSE

FULLER, Henry C. (1879-1942) Chem. NC42

FULLER, Henry S. (1917-1964) Entom. AMEM

FULLER, Henry W. (1831-1929) Chem. NC16

FULLER, John L. (1910-) Biol. CB59

FULLER, R. Buckminster (1895-1983) Invent.; Engr.
CB60 CB76 WAMB

FULTON, Bentley B. (1889-1960) Entom. AMEM

FULTON, John F. (1899-1960) Physiol. CDZZ ZZ-5

FULTON, Robert (1765-1815) Invent. ABES ABET AMIH ASIW BDOS GE-1 HFGA INYG SAIF SMIL TINA WAMB

FUNK, Casimir (1884-1967) Biochem. ABES ABET ACCE BEOS BHMT CB45 CDZZ ZZ-5

FUNKHOUSER, William D. (1881-1948) Entom. NC40

FUOSS, Raymond M. (1905-) Chem. MHM2 MHSE

FURBISH, Kate (1834-1931) Bot. BIOD IDWB

FURMAN, Nathaniel H. (1892-1965) Chem. ACCE CB51

FURRY, Wendell H. (1907-) Phys. QPAS

FURUKAWA, Junji (1912-) Chem. MHSE

FUSON, Reynold C. (1895-) Chem. MHM2 MHSE

FUSORIS, Jean (1365-1436) Astron. CDZZ ZZXV

FUSS, Nicolaus (1755-1826) Math.; Astron. CDZZ ZZ-5

FYFE, Andrew (1754-1824) Anat. DNB

FYODOROV, Evgraf S. (1853-1919) Crystal.; Geol. CDZZ ZZ-5

G

GABB, William M. (1839-1878) Geol.; Paleon. BIOD BM-6 CDZZ DAB NC-4 ZZ-5

GABOR, Dennis (1900-1979) Elec. Engr.; Invent. ABET BEOS CB72 MHSE POSW RS26

GABRIEL, Siegmund (1851-1924) Chem. BDOS BEOS CDZZ ZZ-5

GABRIELSON, Ira N. (1889-1977) Biol.; Cons. DGMT LACC

GADBURY, John (1627-1704) Astrol. DNB

GADDUM, John H. (1900-1965) Physiol. RS13

GADOLIN, Johan (1760-1852) Chem. ABES ABET BDOS BEOS CDZZ ZZ-5

GAERTNER, Joseph (1732-1791) Bot. CDZZ ZZ-5

GAERTNER, Karl F. von (1772-1850) Bot. CDZZ HLSM ZZ-5

GAFFKY, Georg T. (1850-1918) Bact. ABES ABET BEOS CDZZ ZZ-5

GAGARIN, Yuri A. (1934-1968) Astronaut. ABES ABET CB61 FPSN IEAS MOS3 OGML

GAGE, Simon H. (1851-1944) Embryol. NC36

GAGER, Charles S. (1872-1943) Bot. MABH NC38

GAGER, Frank M. (1904-1977) Elec. Engr. NC60

GAGLIARDI, Domenico (1660-c.1725) Anat. CDZZ ZZ-5

GAGNEBIN, Elie (1891-1949) Geol. CDZZ ZZ-5

GAHAN, Arthur B. (1880-1960) Entom. AMEM

GAHN, Johann G. (1745-1818) Mineral.; Chem. ABES ABET BEOS CDZZ ZZ-5

GAILLOT, Aimable J. (1834-1921) Astron.; Astrophys. CDZZ ZZ-5

GAIMARD, Joseph P. (1796-1858) Nat. Hist. ANHD CDZZ ZZ-5

GAINES, Walter L. (1881-1950) Dairy Sci. CDZZ ZZ-5

GAJDUSEK, D. Carleton (1923-) Virol. ABET BEOS CB81 MHSE PAW2 VACE

GALAMBOS, Robert (1914-) Psych. MHM2 MHSE

GALDIKAS, Birute (Contemporary) Ethol. WAGW

GALE, George (c.1797-1850) Aero. DNB

GALE, Henry G. (1874-1942) Phys. DAB3

GALEAZZI, Domenico G. (1686-1775) Anat.; Biochem. CDZZ ZZ-5

GALEN OF PERGAMUM (c.130-200) Med. ABES ABET AMST BDOS BEOS BHMT CDZZ GSAL HEXS HLSM LISD MMMA TOWS ZZ-5

GALERKIN, Boris G. (1871-1945) Math.; Phys.
CDZZ ZZXV

GALILEI, Galileo (1564-1642) Astron.; Phys. ABES
ABET ASTR BDOS BEOS CDZZ DCPW ESCS
FASP FPHM GASW GISA GMOP HOSS IEAS
IFBS LISD MAKS MCCW MGAH MPIP MSCH
PAW2 PFEL SAIF SGSC SMIL STSW TMAL
TOWS WOSM ZZ-5

GALILEO SEE GALILEI, Galileo

GALIN, Lev A. (1912-) Engr. SMST

GALL, Franz J. (1758-1828) Med. ABES ABET
BEOS CDZZ ZZ-5

GALLE, Johann G. (1812-1910) Astron. ABES
ABET BEOS CDZZ IEAS ZZ-5

GALLOIS, Jean (1632-1707) Sci. Hist. CDZZ ZZ-5

GALLOWAY, Beverly T. (1863-1938) Bot. DAB2
NC12

GALLOWAY, Thomas (1796-1851) Math. DNB

GALLOWAY, Thomas W. (1866-1929) Biol. NC22

GALLY, Merritt (1838-1916) Invent. DAB NC-4

GALOIS, Evariste (1811-1832) Math. ABET BEOS
CDZZ FMAS MATT OMNM ZZ-5

GALSTON, Arthur W. (1925-) Bot. MHSE

GALTON, Francis (1822-1911) Anthro. ABES ABET
BDOS BEOS BHMT CDZZ HLSM POPF SNCB
TOWS ZZ-5

GALVANI, Luigi (1737-1798) Anat.; Phys. ABES
ABET BDOS BEOS BHMT CDZZ EETD ELEC
FNEC FPHM GOED IFBS SMIL TOWS ZZ-5

GALWAY, Desma H. (1917-) Bot. BMBR

GALY-CAZALAT, Antoine (1796-1869) Engr. GE-1

GAMALEYA, Nikolay F. (1859-1949) Microbiol.
CDZZ ZZ-5

GAMBEL, William (c.1819-1849) Ornith. BIOD
WFBG

GAMBEY, Henri P. (1787-1847) Instr. BDOS CDZZ
ZZ-5

GAMBLE, James L. (1883-1959) Med. BM36

GAMBLE, Josias C. (1776-1848) Chem. BDOS

GAMGEE, Arthur (1841-1909) Physiol. DNB2

GAMOW, George (1904-1959) Phys.; Sci. Writ. ABES
ABET BEOS CB51 CDZZ IEAS MHM1 MHSE
WAMB ZZ-5

GANESA (b. 1507) Astron. CDZZ ZZ-5

GANNETT, Henry (1846-1914) Geog. LACC

GANONG, William F. (1864-1941) Bot. MABH NC14

GANT, James Q. (1906-) Med. NCSK

GANTT, William H. (1892-1980) Psych. AO80

GARBO, Dino del SEE DINO DEL GARBO

GARDEN, Alexander (1730-1791) Bot.; Nat. Hist.
BIOD DAB SBSC WAMB

GARDINER, Edward G. (1854-1907) Biol. NC14

GARDINER, James T. (1842-1912) Engr. BIOD

GARDINER, William C. (1904-) Chem. Engr. NCSJ

GARDNER, George (1812-1849) Bot. DNB

GARDNER, Irvine C. (1889-1972) Phys. NC58

GARDNER, Julia A. (1882-1960) Paleon. NAWM

GARDNER, Nathaniel L. (1864-1937) Bot. MABH

GARDNER, Willard (1883-1964) Phys. NC53

GAREY, John C. (1911-1956) Bact. NC43

GARGRAVE, George (1710-1785) Astron. DNB

GARMAN, Harrison (1856-1944) Nat. Hist. NC14
NC33

GARMAN, Samuel (1843-1927) Zool. DAB NC10

GARNER, William E. (1879-1960) Chem. DNB7
RS-7

GARNETT, Thomas (1766-1802) Med. CDZZ ZZ-5

GARNJOBST, Laura F. (1895-1977) Biol. NC61

GARNOT, Prosper (1794-1838) Med.; Zool. CDZZ ZZ-5

GARRATT, George A. (1898-) Forest. LACC

GARREAU, Lazare (1812-1892) Bot. CDZZ ZZ-5

GARRETT, Elizabeth SEE ANDERSON, Elizabeth G.

GARROD, Alfred B. (1819-1909) Med. BHMT

GARROD, Alfred H. (1846-1879) Zool. DNB

GARROD, Archibald E. (1857-1936) Med.; Biochem. BEOS DNB5 HLSM

GARTH, Samuel (1661-1718) Med. BHMT

GASCHE, Fred (1903-1966) Engr. NC53

GASCOIGNE, William (c.1612-1644) Opt.; Astron. ABET CDZZ DNB ZZ-5

GASKELL, Walter H. (1847-1914) Physiol. BDOS BEOS CDZZ DNB3 ZZ-5

GASSENDI, Pierre (1592-1655) Philos.; Astron. ABES ABET BDOS BEOS CDZZ ZZ-5

GASSER, Herbert S. (1888-1963) Physiol. ABES ABET BDOS BEOS CB45 CDZZ MHM1 MHSE NC61 NCSE RS10 ZZ-5

GASSICOURT SEE CADET DE GASSICOURT, Louis C.

GASSIOT, John P. (1797-1877) Elec. Sci. CDZZ DNB ZZ-5

GATENBY, James B. (1892-1960) Zool. DNB7

GATES, David M. (1921-) Ecol. POEC

GATES, Reginald R. (1882-1962) Genet. CDZZ RS10 ZZ-5

GATES, Sidney B. (1893-1973) Aero. RS20

GATES, William E. (1863-1940) Archaeol. PAMB

GATLING, Richard J. (1818-1903) Invent. ABET BDOS INYG WAMB

GATTERMANN, Ludwig (1860-1920) Chem. BDOS BEOS

GATTINGER, Augustin (1825-1903) Bot. BIOD

GAUDIN, Antoine M. (1900-1974) Mineral. MHM2 MHSE NC58

GAUDIN, Marc A. (1804-1880) Chem. CDZZ ZZ-5

GAUDRY, Albert J. (1827-1908) Paleon. CDZZ ZZ-5

GAUGER, Alfred W. (1892-1963) Chem. Engr. NC50

GAULTIER DE CLAUBRY, Henri F. (1792-1878) Chem. CDZZ ZZ-5

GAUSS, Karl F. (1777-1855) Math. ABES ABET BDOS BEOS CDZZ EETD FMAS FNEC GE-1 GOED IEAS MASW MATT HELW OMNM TOWS VTHB WTGM ZZ-5

GAUTHEY, Emiland M. (1732-1806) Engr. GE-1

GAUTIER, Armand E. (1837-1920) Chem. CDZZ ZZ-5

GAUTIER, Hubert (1660-1737) Engr. GE-1

GAUTIER, Paul F. (1842-1909) Instr. CDZZ ZZ-5

GAY, Frederick P. (1874-1939) Bact. BM28 CDZZ DAB2 NCSB ZZ-5

GAYANT, Louis (b. 1673) Anat. CDZZ ZZ-5

GAYDON, Alfred G. (1911-) Phys. MHM1 MHSE

GAY-LUSSAC, Joseph L. (1778-1850) Chem.; Phys. ABES ABET BDOS BEOS BHMT CDZZ GASJ GRCH HOSS HSSO MCCW SOAC ZZ-5

GEBER SEE JABIR ibn HAYYAN

GEDDES, Patrick (1854-1932) Biol. DNB5

GEE, Geoffrey (1910-) Chem. COBC

GEE, Haldane (1901-1962) Bact. NC50

GEE, N. Gist (1876-1937) Biol. NC28

GEER, Charles de (1720-1778) Entom. ANHD BDOS BEOS CDZZ ZZ-5

GEER, Gerard J. de (1858-1943) Geol. BDOS BEOS CDZZ ZZ-5

GEER, William C. (1876-1964) Chem. NC50

GEGENBAUER, Karl (1826-1903) Anat. ABES ABET BEOS CDZZ ZZXV

GEHLEN, Adolf F. (1775-1815) Chem. CDZZ ZZXV

GEIGER, Ernest (1896-1959) Biochem. NC47

GEIGER, Hans W. (1882-1945) Phys. ABES ABET
BDOS BEOS CDZZ TGNH ZZ-5

GEIJER, Per (1886-1976) Geol. MHM2 MHSE

GEIKIE, Archibald (1835-1924) Geol. BDOS BEOS
CDZZ DNB4 VISC ZZ-5

GEIKIE, James (1839-1915) Geol. CDZZ ZZ-5

GEIRINGER, Hilda (1893-1973) Math. NAWM

GEISER, Karl F. (1843-1934) Math. CDZZ ZZ-5

GEISSLER, Heinrich (1814-1879) Invent. ABES ABET
DCPW ZZ-5

GEITEL, F.K. Hans (1855-1923) Phys. CDZZ ZZ-5

GELFAND, Izrail M. (1913-) Math. BEOS MHM2
MHSE SMST

GELFOND, Alexander O. (1906-1968) Math. CDZZ
SMST ZZ-5

GELLIBRAND, Henry (1597-1636) Math.; Astron.
ABES ABET BEOS CDZZ DNB ZZ-5

GELL-MANN, Murray (1929-) Phys. ABES ABET
AMJB BEOS CB66 DCPW MHM1 MHSE POSW
SCLB WAMB

GELMO, Paul J. (1879-1961) Chem. CDZZ ZZ-5

GEMINUS (fl. c.70 B.C.) Astron.; Math. CDZZ ZZ-5

GEMINUS, Thomas (c.1510-1562) Med. CDZZ ZZ-5

GEMMA, Frisius R. (1508-1555) Geog.; Math. ABET
CDZZ ZZ-5

GENTH, Frederick A. (1820-1893) Chem.; Mineral.
ACCE BIOD BM-4 CDZZ DAB NC-7 ZZ-5

GENTZEN, Gerhard (1909-1945) Math. CDZZ ZZ-5

GEOFFROY, Claude J. (1685-1752) Chem.; Bot.
CDZZ ZZ-5

GEOFFROY, Etienne F. (1672-1731) Chem.; Med.
CDZZ ZZ-5

GEOFFROY, Etienne L. (1725-1810) Zool.; Med.
CDZZ ZZ-5

GEOFFROY ST. HILAIRE, Etienne (1772-1884) Zool.
CDZZ HLSM THOG ZZ-5

GEOFFROY ST. HILAIRE, Isidore (1805-1861) Zool.
CDZZ ZZ-5

GERARD OF BRUSSELS (fl. c.1210-1250) Math. CDZZ
ZZ-5

GERARD OF CREMONA (c.1114-1187) Sci. Ed.
CDZZ ZZXV

GERARD OF SILTEO (fl. 1200s) Astron. CDZZ ZZ-5

GERARD, John (1545-1613) Bot.; Hort. BDOS BEOS
CDZZ ZZ-5

GERARD, Ralph W. (1900-1974) Physiol. BM53 CB65
MHM2 MHSE

GERASIMOVICH, Boris P. (1889-1937) Astrophys.
CDZZ ZZ-5

GERBERT D'AURILLAC, Pope Sylvester II (c.945-
1003) Math. ABET CDZZ ZZ-5

GERBEZIUS, Marcus (1658-1718) Med. CDZZ ZZ-5

GERGONNE, Joseph D. (1771-1859) Math. CDZZ
ZZ-5

GERHARD, William W. (1809-1872) Med. BHMT

GERHARDT, Charles F. (1816-1856) Chem. BDOS
BEOS CDZZ HSSO ZZ-5

GERMAIN, Sophie (1776-1831) Math. ABET CDZZ
IDWB MEQP WIMO ZZ-5

GERMANUS, Henricus M. (fl. 1480-1496) Geog. CDZZ
ZZ-5

GERSHON-COHEN, Jacob (1899-1971) Med. NC57

GESELL, Arnold L. (1880-1961) Psych. ABES ABET
BM37 CDZZ ZZ-5

GESNER, Konrad von (1516-1565) Nat. Hist. ABES
ABET BDOS BEOS CDZZ HAOA LISD NATJ
ORNS ZZ-5

GESS, German SEE HESS, Germain H.

GESSNER, Johannes (1709-1790) Bot.; Geol. CDZZ
ZZ-5

GETMAN, Frederick H. (1877-1941) Chem. NC30

GEUTHER, Anton (1833-1889) Chem. CDZZ ZZ-5

al-GHAZZALI, Abu Hamid (1058-1111) Philos. SCIN

GHERARDI, Bancroft (1873-1941) Engr. BM30 TPAE

GHERING, Leonard G. (1909-1967) Chem. NC54

GHETALDI, Marino (1566/8-1626) Math. CDZZ ZZ-5

GHINI, Luca (c.1490-1556) Bot. CDZZ ZZ-5

GHIORSO, Albert (1915-) Phys. MHSE

GHISI, Martino (1715-1794) Med. CDZZ ZZ-5

GIAEVER, Ivar (1929-) Phys. ABET BEOS MHM1
MHSE POSW

GIAMBELLI, Federigo (c.1530-c.1590) Engr. GE-1

GIARD, Alfred (1846-1908) Biol. CDZZ ZZ-5

GIAUQUE, William F. (1895-1982) Chem. ABES
ABET BEOS CB50 MHM1 MHSE NPWC PAW2
WAMB

GIBB, Claude D. (1898-1959) Engr. RS-5

GIBBES, Lewis R. (1810-1894) Nat. Hist.; Chem.
ACCE BIOD

GIBBON, John H. Jr. (1903-1973) Med. BM53 HEXS
MFIR MHSE

GIBBONS, William (1781-1845) Entom. NC13

GIBBS, George (1776-1833) Mineral. BIOD

GIBBS, George (1815-1873) Anthro. SASH

GIBBS, George (1861-1940) Engr. BSIL

GIBBS, Josiah W. (1839-1903) Phys. ABES ABET
ACCE ASIW ASJD BDOS BEOS BIOD BM-6
CDZZ DAB GRCH HFGA HSSO LISD MSAJ
NC-4 SNAR WAMB ZZ-5

GIBBS, Oliver W. (1822-1908) Chem. ACCE BM-7
CDZZ DAB NC10 WAMB ZZ-5

GIBBS, William F. (1886-1967) Engr. BEOS BM42
MHM1 MHSE

GIBBS, Wolcott SEE GIBBS, Oliver W.

GIBSON, Alexander (1800-1867) Bot. DNB

GIBSON, Robert B. (1882-1959) Biochem. NC50

GIBSON, William H. (1850-1896) Nat. Hist. DAB

GIDLEY, James W. (1866-1931) Paleon. DAB1 NC24

GIES, William J. (1872-1956) Biochem. ACCE

GIESEL, Friedrich O. (1852-1927) Chem. CDZZ
ZZ-5

GIFFARD, Henri (1825-1882) Aero. BDOS

GIFFORD, John C. (1870-1949) Forest. LACC

GILBERT, Charles H. (1859-1928) Zool. DAB NC28

GILBERT, Grove K. (1843-1918) Geol.; Geog. CDZZ
GKGP WAMB ZZ-5

GILBERT, Harvey N. (1889-1971) Chem. ACCE

GILBERT, Joseph H. (1817-1901) Chem. DNB2

GILBERT, Walter (1932-) Biol. ABET BEOS

GILBERT, William (1544-1603) Med.; Phys. ABES
ABET BDOS BEOS BHMT CDZZ DCPW EETD
ESCS ESEH HOSS LISD MAKS SMIL SXWS
TOWS VTHB ZZ-5

GILBERTUS (Anglicus) (c.1180-1250) Med. BHMT
MMMA

GILBRETH, Lillian E. (1878-1972) Engr. CWSE
NAWM

GILCHRIST, Percy C. (1851-1935) Chem. Engr. BDOS
BEOS

GILES OF LESSINES (c.1235-c.1304) Astron. CDZZ
ZZ-5

GILES OF ROME (1247-1316) Phys.; Astron. CDZZ
ZZ-5

GILL, David (1843-1914) Astron. ABES ABET AROW
BEOS CDZZ DNB3 GASJ ZZ-5

GILL, Theodore N. (1837-1914) Ichth. BM-8 CDZZ
DAB NC12 WAMB ZZ-5

GILL, Thomas H. (1891-) Forest. LACC

GILLAIN, Marie A. (1773-1847) Med. WIWM

GILLESPIE, Louis J. (1886-1941) Biochem. NC30

GILLETT, Charles A. (1904-) Forest. LACC

GILLETTE, Clarence P. (1859-1941) Entom. AMEM NC13

GILLIARD, E. Thomas (1912-) Ornith. DGMT

GILLILAND, Edwin R. (1909-1973) Chem. Engr. BM49 HCEF NC57

GILLIS, James M. (1811-1865) Astron. BIOD BM-1 DAB NC-9 WAMB

GILLMANN, Henry (1833-1915) Paleon. DAB

GILLULY, James (1896-1980) Geol. AO80 MHM1 MHSE

GILMAN, Henry (1893-) Chem. BEOS

GILMORE, Charles W. (1874-1945) Paleon. MADC NC34 PHLS

GILRUTH, Robert R. (1913-) Aero. CB63 MHSE MOS4 ICFW

GINZBURG, Vitalii L. (1916-) Phys. SMST

GINZTON, Edward L. (1915-) Engr. MHM2 MHSE

GIORDANI, Francesco (1896-) Chem. CB57

GIORGI, Giovanni (1871-1950) Elec. Engr. CDZZ ZZ-5

GIRARD, Albert (1595-1632) Math. CDZZ ZZ-5

GIRARD, Charles F. (1822-1895) Zool. BIOD DAB

GIRARD, Philippe H. de (1775-1845) Engr. GE-1

GIRARD, Pierre S. (1765-1836) Engr. CDZZ ZZ-5

GIRAUD, Herbert J. (1817-1888) Chem.; Bot. DNB

GIRAULT, Alexandre A. (1884-1941) Entom. AMEM

GIRTANNER, Christoph (1760-1800) Med.; Chem. CDZZ ZZ-5

GIST, Lewis A. (1921-) Chem. SBPY

GLADDING, Thomas S. (1853-1939) Chem. NC34

GLADSTONE, John H. (1827-1902) Chem. CDZZ DNB2 ZZ-5

GLAISHER, James (1809-1903) Meteor. CDZZ DNB2 ZZ-5

GLAISHER, James W. (1848-1928) Math.; Astron. CDZZ DNB4 ZZ-5

GLANVILL, Joseph (1636-1680) Philos. CDZZ ZZ-5

GLANVILLE, William H. (1900-1976) Engr. RS23

GLASCOCK, Hardin R. (1921-) Forest. LACC

GLASER, Christopher (c.1615-1672) Pharm.; Chem. CDZZ ZZ-5

GLASER, Donald A. (1926-) Phys. ABES ABET BEOS CB61 MHM1 MHSE POSW WAMB

GLASER, Johann H. (1629-1679) Anat.; Bot. CDZZ ZZ-5

GLASHOW, Sheldon L. (1932-) Phys. ABET BEOS POSW SOT3

GLASS, H. Bentley (1906-) Biol. CB66

GLAUBER, Johann R. (1604-1668) Chem. ABES ABET BDOS BEOS CDZZ GRCH ZZ-5

GLAURET, Hermann (1892-1934) Aero. ICFW

GLAZEBROOK, Richard T. (1854-1935) Phys. BEOS CDZZ DNB5 ZZ-5

GLEICHEN-RUSSWORM, Wilhelm F. von (1717-1783) Micros. CDZZ ZZ-5

GLENIE, James (1750-1817) Math. DNB

GLENN, John H. Jr. (1921-) Astronaut. CB62 FPSN IEAS MOS5 OGML PMAS PPKY WAMB WESE

GLENNY, Alexander T. (1882-1965) Bact. RS12

GLICK, Philip M. (1905-) Cons. LACC

GLISSON, Francis (1597-1677) Med. BDOS BEOS BHMT CDZZ HLSM ZZ-5

GLOCKER, George (1890-1969) Chem. NC55

GLOVER, Towend (1813-1883) Entom. AMEM BIOD DAB NC23

GLUECK, Nelson (1900-1971) Archaeol. CB69

GLUECKAUF, Eugen (1906-1981) Chem. AO81

GMELIN, Johann G. (1709-1755) Bot.; Nat. Hist. ABET CDZZ ZZ-5

GMELIN, Leopold (1788-1853) Chem. ABET BDOS BEOS CDZZ GRCH ZZ-5

GOBLEY, Nicolas T. (1811-1876) Chem. CDZZ ZZ-5

GODDARD, Maurice K. (1912-) Cons. LACC

GODDARD, Robert H. (1882-1945) Phys.; Rocket. ABES ABET BBRS BEOS CDZZ DAB3 FPSN HRST ICFW IEAS MASY MOS1 NC35 PAW3 PORS ROPW SAIF SMIL TECH WAMB ZZ-5

GODEL, Kurt (1906-1978) Math. ABES ABET BEOS MHSE RS26

GODFREY, Ambrose (d. 1741) Chem. DNB

GODFREY, Thomas (1704-1749) Math.; Astron. BIOD CDZZ DAB WAMB ZZ-5

GODIN, Louis (1704-1760) Astron. CDZZ ZZ-5

GODLOVE, Isaac H. (1892-1954) Chem.; Phys. NC43

GODMAN, John D. (1794-1830) Anat.; Nat. Hist. ASJD BIOD DAB NC-7

GODWIN, Harry (1901-) Bot. BEOS MHM2 MHSE

GODWIN-AUSTEN, Henry H. (1834-1923) Geol. DNB4

GODWIN-AUSTEN,Robert A. (1808-1884) Geol. CDZZ ZZ-5

GOEBEL, Karl (1855-1932) Bot. CDZZ ZZ-5

GOEDAERT, Johannes (1617-1668) Entom. CDZZ ZZ-5

GOEPPERT, Heinrich R. (1800-1884) Bot.; Paleon. CDZZ FHUA ZZ-5

GOEPPERT-MAYER, Maria SEE MAYER, Maria G.

GOESSMANN, Charles A. (1827-1910) Chem. ACCE DAB

GOETHALS, George (1858-1928) Engr. MGAH

GOETHE, Johann W. von (1749-1832) Zool.; Geol. ABES ABET CDZZ ZZ-5

GOETT, Harry J. (Contemporary) Aero. MOS7

GOETTE, Alexander W. (1840-1922) Zool. CDZZ ZZ-5

GOGUEL, Jean M. (1908-) Geol. MHM2 MHSE

GOHORY, Jacques (1520-1576) Nat. Hist.; Alch. CDZZ ZZ-5

GOLD, Ernest (1881-1976) Meteor. RS23

GOLD, John S. (1898-1970) Math. NC56

GOLD, Thomas (1920-) Astron. ABES ABET BEOS CB66 IEAS

GOLDBACH, Christian (1690-1764) Math. ABET CDZZ ZZ-5

GOLDBERGER, Joseph (1874-1929) Med. ABES ABET BEOS CDZZ ZZ-5

GOLDBERGER, Marvin L. (1922-) Phys. MHM1 MHSE

GOLDHABER, Maurice (1911-) Phys. ABES ABET BEOS MHM2 MHSE

GOLDMAN, Hetty (1881-1972) Archaeol. NAWM NC56

GOLDMARK, Peter C. (1906-1977) Invent. ABET CB40 CB50 MHM2 MHSE NC60

GOLDRING, Winifred (1881-1971) Paleon. NAWM

GOLDSBROUGH, George R. (1881-1963) Math. RS10

GOLDSCHMIDT, Johann W. (1861-1923) Chem. ABES ABET BDOS BEOS

GOLDSCHMIDT, Richard B. (1878-1958) Zool.; Biol. BM39 CDZZ ZZ-5

GOLDSCHMIDT, Victor (1853-1933) Crystal. CDZZ ZZ-5

GOLDSCHMIDT, Victor M. (1888-1947) Chem. BEOS CDZZ ZZ-5

GOLDSMITH, Alfred N. (1888-1974) Engr. TPAE

GOLDSMITH, Edward (1833-1925) Mineral. NC20

GOLDSMITH, Julian R. (1918-) Geol. MHM2 MHSE

GOLDSMITH, Lester M. (1893-1975) Engr. NC59

GOLDSTEIN, Eugen (1850-1930) Phys. ABES ABET
BDOS BEOS CDZZ DCPW ZZ-5

GOLDSTEIN, Herbert (1922-) Phys. MHM2 MHSE

GOLDSTINE, Herman H. (1913-) Math. CB52

GOLGI, Camillo (1843-1926) Med. ABES ABET
BDOS BEOS BHMT CDZZ ZZ-5

GOLITSYN, Boris B. (1862-1916) Phys.; Seism.
CDZZ ZZ-5

GOLTZ, Friedrich L. (1834-1902) Physiol. CDZZ
ZZ-5

GOMBERG, Moses (1866-1947) Chem. ABES ABET
ACCE BEOS BM41 DAB4 CDZZ GRCH HSSO
NC16 ZZ-5

GOMER, Robert (1924-) Phys. MHSE

GOMPERTZ, Benjamin (1779-1865) Math. CDZZ
DNB ZZ-5

GOOCH, Frank A. (1852-1929) Chem. BM15 NC12

GOOCH, Robert (1784-1830) Med. BHMT

GOOD, Adolphus C. (1856-1894) Nat. Hist. BIOD
DAB NC23

GOOD, Robert A. (1922-) Med. BEOS CB72 MFIR
MHSE

GOODALE, George L. (1839-1923) Bot. DAB MABH

GOODALL, Jane (1934-) Ethol. CB67 IDWB WAGW

GOODDING, Leslie N. (1880-) Bot. BNBR

GOODE, George B. (1851-1896) Ichth. BIOD BM-4
DAB NC-3

GOODENOUGH, Florence L. (1886-1959) Psych.
NAWM

GOODEVE, Charles F. (1904-1980) Metal. RS27

GOODEY, Tom (1885-1953) Zool. DNB7

GOODPASTURE, Ernest W. (1886-1960) Path. BEOS
BM38 MHM1 MHSE PGFS

GOODRICH, Edwin S. (1868-1946) Anat.; Evol. BEOS
CDZZ DNB6 ZZ-5

GOODRICKE, John (1764-1786) Astron. ABES ABET
BEOS CDZZ DNB SLOR ZZ-5

GOODSIR, John (1814-1867) Anat.; Zool. CDZZ DNB
ZZ-5

GOODSPEED, Arthur W. (1860-1943) Phys. NC15
NC32

GOODWIN, Harry M. (1870-1949) Phys. NC38

GOODYEAR, Charles (1800-1860) Chem.; Invent.
ABES ABET ACCE AMIH ASIW BDOS COAC
FOIF IHMV INYG TBTM TINA WAMB

GOPEL, Adolph (1812-1847) MAth. CDZZ ZZ-5

GORDAN, Paul A. (1837-1912) Math. BDOS BEOS
CDZZ ZZ-5

GORDON, Cyrus H. (1908-) Archaeol. CB63

GORDON, Geoffrey A. (1948-) Comp. HOPL

GORDON, James E. (1852-1893) Elec. Engr. DNB1

GORDON, Mervyn H. (1872-1953) Bact. DNB7

GORDON, Neil (1886-1949) Chem. ACCE NCSC

GORDON, Seth E. (1890-) Cons. LACC

GORDON, Walter (1893-1940) Phys. CDZZ ZZ-5
BDOS

GORDON, William T. (1884-) Paleon. FHUA

GORE, George (1826-1908) Electrochem. CDZZ
DNB2 ZZ-5

GORE, John E. (1845-1910) Astron. DNB2

GORER, Peter A. (1907-1961) Med.; Immunol. BEOS
RS-7

GORGAS, William C. (1854-1920) Med. ABES ABET
BDOS BHMT HFGA MMMA

GORGEY, Arthur (1818-1916) Chem. CDZZ ZZ-5

GORHAM, Frederic P. (1871-1933) Bact. NC23

GORHAM, John (1783-1829) Chem. ACCE BIOD
DAB

GORINI, Luigi (1903-1976) Bact. BM52 NC59

GORRIE, John (1803-1855) Med. BHMT WAMB

GORSKI, Ivan I. (1893-) Phys. SMST

GORTER, Cornelis J. (1907-) Phys. MHM2 MHSE

GORTNER, Ross A. (1885-1942) Biochem. ACCE BM23 DAB3 NC33

GOSS, Charles M. (1899-) Anat. NCSK

GOSSAGE, William (1799-1877) Chem. BDOS BEOS

GOSSE, Philip H. (1810-1888) Nat. Hist. ANHD DNB HNHB MSFB NATJ

GOSSELET, Jules A. (1832-1916) Geol.; Paleon. CDZZ ZZ-5

GOTTLIEB, Melvin B. (1917-) Phys. CB74

GOTTSCHALK, John S. (1912-) Cons. LACC

GOUDSMIT, Samuel A. (1901-1978) Phys. ABES ABET BEOS CB54 DCPW MHM1 MHSE

GOUGH, Herbert J. (1890-1965) Engr. RS12

GOUGH, John (1757-1825) Sci. Writ. DNB

GOULD, Augustus A. (1805-1866) Conch. BIOD BM-5 CDZZ DAB ZZ-5

GOULD, Benjamin A. Jr. (1824-1896) Astron. BEOS BIOD CDZZ DAB IEAS NC-5

GOULD, John (1804-1881) Ornith. ANHD CDZZ DNB ZZ-5

GOULD, Lawrence M. (1896-) Geol.; Exp. CB78

GOULD, Stephen J. (1941-) Paleon. CB82

GOULIAN, Mehrain (1929-) Biochem. CB68

GOURDINE, Meredith (1929-) Phys. BCST BISC SBPY

GOURSAT, Edouard J. (1858-1936) Math. CDZZ ZZ-5

GOUY, Louis G. (1854-1926) Phys. CDZZ ZZ-5

GOWANS, James L. (1924-) Med. MHSE

GOWEN, John W. (1883-1967) Biol. NC56

GOWERS, William (1845-1915) Med. BHMT

GRAAF, Regnier de (1641-1673) Anat. ABES ABET BDOS BEOS CDZZ ZZ-5

GRAAF, Robert J. van de SEE VAN DE GRAAF, Robert J.

GRABAU, Amadeus W. (1870-1946) Geol.; Paleon. CDZZ ZZ-5

GRACE, John H. (1873-1958) Math. RS-4

GRAEBE, Karl J. (1841-1927) Chem. ABES ABET BDOS BEOS CDZZ ZZ-5

GRAFF, Kasimir R. (1878-1950) Astron. CDZZ ZZ-5

GRAFFE, Karl H. (1799-1873) Math. CDZZ ZZ-5

GRAHAM, Clarence H. (1906-1971) Physiol. BM46 MHM1 MHSE

GRAHAM, Edward H. (1902-1966) Cons. LACC

GRAHAM, Evarts A. (1883-1957) Med. BM48

GRAHAM, Frank V. (1887-1944) Chem. NC33

GRAHAM, George (c.1674-1751) Instr. CDZZ ZZ-5

GRAHAM, Helen T. (1890-1971) Biochem. NC56

GRAHAM, James D. (1790-1865) Engr.; Astron. BIOD

GRAHAM, Thomas (1805-1869) Chem.; Phys. ABES ABET BDOS BEOS CDZZ DNB GRCH TOWS ZZ-5

GRAHAM BROWN, Thomas (1882-1965) Physiol. RS12

GRAHAME, David C. (1912-1958) Chem. NC47

GRAINGER, Richard D. (1801-1865) Anat.; Physiol. DNB

GRAM, Hans C. (1853-1938) Bact. ABES ABET BDOS BEOS CDZZ ZZ-5

GRAMME, Zenobe T. (1826-1901) Invent. ABET CDZZ ZZ-5

GRAMONT, Antoine A. (1861-1923) Phys.; Mineral. CDZZ ZZ-5

GRANDEURY, Francois C. (1839-1917) Paleon. CDZZ
FHUA ZZ-5

GRANDI, Guido (1671-1742) Math. CDZZ ZZ-5

GRANGER, Christopher M. (1885-1967) Forest.
LACC

GRANGER, Walter W. (1872-1941) Paleon. CDZZ
DAB3 MADC NC35 ZZ-5

GRANIT, Ragnar A. (1900-) Physiol. ABES ABET
BEOS MHM2 MHSE

GRANT, David N. (1891-1964) Med. HIUE

GRANT, James W. (1788-1865) Astron. DNB

GRANT, Kenneth E. (1920-) Cons. LACC

GRANT, Madison (1865-1937) Nat. Hist. DAB2

GRANT, Robert (1814-1892) Astron. DNB1

GRANT, Robert E. (1793-1874) Anat. DNB

GRASHCHENKOV, Nikolai I. (1901-1965) Med.
SMST

GRASHOF, Franz (1826-1893) Phys. CDZZ ZZ-5

GRASSELLI, Caesar A. (1850-1927) Chem. ACCE
DAB

GRASSELLI, Eugene R. (1810-1882) Chem.; Instr.
ACCE

GRASSI, Giovanni B. (1854-1926) Entom.; Parasit.
BDOS BEOS CDZZ ZZ-5

GRASSMANN, Hermann G. (1809-1877) Math. ABET
CDZZ ZZXV

GRATIOLET, Louis P. (1815-1865) Anat.; Anthro.
CDZZ ZZ-5

GRATON, Caryl (1880-1970) Geol. NC55

GRAUNT, John (1620-1674) Math. ABET CDZZ
ZZ-5

GRAVE, Dmitry A. (1863-1939) Math. CDZZ ZZ-5

GRAVES, Alvin C. (1909-) Phys. CB52

GRAVES, Henry S. (1871-1951) Forest. EAFC LACC

GRAVES, John T. (1806-1870) Math. DNB

GRAVES, Robert J. (1796-1853) Med. BHMT MMMA

'sGRAVESANDE, Willem J. (1688-1742) Phys.; Math.
CDZZ ZZ-5

GRAWE, Oliver R. (1901-1965) Geol. NC56

GRAY, Asa (1810-1888) Bot. ABES ABET ADJD
BDOS BEOS BHMT BIOD BM-3 CDZZ DAB
GASJ HFGA LISD MABH NHAH SSAH WAMB
YSMS ZZ-5

GRAY, Elisha (1835-1901) Invent. EETD NC-4
WAMB

GRAY, George R. (1808-1872) Zool. DNB

GRAY, Harry B. (1935-) Chem. BEOS MHSE

GRAY, Henry (1825-1861) Anat.; Physiol. CDZZ
ZZ-5

GRAY, John A. (1848-1920) Math. NC19

GRAY, John E. (1800-1875) Nat. Hist. ANHD DNB

GRAY, Joseph A. (1884-1966) Phys. RS13

GRAY, Louis H. (1905-1965) Biol. RS12

GRAY, Robert (1825-1887) Ornith. DNB

GRAY, Samuel F. (fl. 1780-1836) Nat. Hist. DNB

GRAY, Stephen (1696-1736) Elec. Sci. ABES ABET
BDOS BEOS CDZZ DNB EETD ESEH ZZ-5

GRAY, Thomas T. (1881-1931) Chem. NC24

GREAVES, John (1602-1652) Math. DNB

GREAVES, Joseph E. (1880-1954) Bact. NC47

GREBE, John J. (1900-) Chem. CB55

GREELEY, Arthur W. (1912-) Forest. LACC

GREELEY, William B. (1897-1955) Forest. LACC

GREEN, Alexander H. (1832-1896) Geol. DNB1

GREEN, Charles (1785-1870) Aero. DNB

GREEN, David E. (1910-) Biochem. MHSE

GREEN, Francis M. (1835-1902) Astron. BIOD

GREEN, Gabriel M. (1891-1919) Math. DAB

GREEN, George (1793-1841) Math. CDZZ DNB
ZZXV

GREEN, George K. (1911-1977) Phys. NC60

GREEN, J. Wilbur (1873-1971) Phys. NC58

GREEN, Jacob (1790-1841) Chem.; Biol. ACCE
ASJD BIOD CDZZ DAB NC13 ZZ-5

GREEN, Samuel B. (1859-1910) Forest. LACC

GREEN, Traill (1813-1897) Chem. ACCE

GREEN, Warren K. (1891-1964) Astron. NC51

GREENAWAY, Franck (1917-) Chem. COBC

GREENE, Edward L. (1843-1915) Bot. BNBR DAB
MABH NC19

GREENE, William H. (1853-1918) Chem. ACCE

GREENMAN, Milton J. (1866-1937) Biol. NC32

GREENOUGH, George B. (1778-1855) Geol. CDZZ
DNB ZZ-5

GREENSTEIN, Jesse L. (1909-) Astron. ABES
ABET BEOS CB63 MHM1 MHSE

GREENSTEIN, Jesse P. (1902-1959) Biochem. NC45

GREENWOOD, Henry B. (1897-1961) Invent. NC49

GREENWOOD, Isaac (1702-1745) Math. BIOD CDZZ
DAB SBCS ZZ-5

GREENWOOD, Norman N. (1925-) Chem. COBC

GREGG, Willis R. (1880-1938) Meteor. DAB2 NC32

GREGOR, Harry P. (1916-) Chem. Engr. PALF

GREGOR, William (1761-1817) Mineral. ABES ABET
BDOS BEOS DNB

GREGORIUS, Joseph S. (1896-1974) Engr. NC58

GREGORY, David (1659-1708) Math.; Astron. ABES
ABET BDOS CDZZ DNB ZZ-5

GREGORY, Duncan F. (1813-1844) Math. CDZZ DNB
ZZ-5

GREGORY, Frederick G. (1893-1961) Bot. CDZZ
RS-9 ZZ-5

GREGORY, James (1638-1675) Math.; Astron. ABES
ABET BDOS BEOS CDZZ DNB ZZ-5

GREGORY, John W. (1864-1932) Geol. DNB5

GREGORY, Olinthus G. (1774-1841) Math. CDZZ
ZZ-5

GREGORY, William (1803-1858) Chem.; Biol. CDZZ
ZZ-5

GREGORY, William K. (1876-1970) Paleon. BM46
NCSA

GREN, Friedrich A. (1760-1798) Chem.; Phys. CDZZ
ZZ-5

GRESSLY, Amanz (1814-1865) Geol.; Paleon. CDZZ
ZZ-5

GREVILLE, Robert K. (1794-1866) Bot. DNB

GREW, Nehemiah (1641-1712) Bot.; Med. ABES
ABET BDOS CDZZ HLSM LISD ZZ-5

GREW, Theophilus (d. 1759) Math.; Astron. BIOD
DAB

GRIESS, Peter J. (1829-1888) Chem. BDOS BEOS
CDZZ HSSO ZZ-5

GRIFFIN, John J. (1802-1877) Chem. DNB

GRIFFIN, Lawrence E. (1874-1949) Zool. NC37

GRIFFIN, Roger C. (1883-1956) Chem. Engr. ACCE

GRIFFITH, Alan A. (1893-1963) Engr. ICFW RS10

GRIFFITH, Edward (1790-1858) Nat. Hist. DNB

GRIFFITH, Fred (1877-1941) Bact. BEOS HLSM

GRIFFITH, George A. (1901-) Cons. LACC

GRIFFITH, Richard J. (1784-1878) Geol. CDZZ
GE-1 ZZ-5

GRIFFITH, Robert E. (1798-1850) Bot.; Conch.
BIOD

GRIFFITH, Wendell H. (1895-1968) Biochem. NC54

GRIFFITH, William (1810-1845) Bot. CDZZ DNB ZZ-5

GRIFFITHS, David (1867-1935) Hort. MABH

GRIFFITHS, Ernest H. (1851-1932) Phys. DNB5

GRIFFITHS, Ezer (1888-1962) Phys. RS-8

GRIGNARD, Francois A. (1871-1935) Chem. ABES ABET BDOS BEOS CDZZ NPWC ZZ-5

GRIJNS, Gerrit (1865-1944) Physiol. CDZZ ZZ-5

GRIMALDI, Francesco M. (1618-1663) Astron. ABES ABET BDOS BEOS CDZZ ZZ-5

GRIMES, James S. (1807-1903) Phren. BIOD

GRINARD, Victor (1871-1935) Chem. GRCH

GRINBERG, Aleksandr A. (1898-1966) Chem. SMST

GRINNEL, Joseph (1877-1939) Zool. BWCL CDZZ ZZ-5

GRINNELL, George B. (1849-1938) Nat. Hist. DAB2 EAFC LACC WAMB

GRISCOM, John (1774-1852) Chem. ACCE BIOD DAB

GRISCOM, Ludlow (1890-1959) Ornith. BWCL NC61 NCSE

GRISEBACH, August H. (1814-1879) Bot. CDZZ ZZ-5

GRISOGONO, Federico (1772-1538) Cosmol.; Astrol. CDZZ ZZ-5

GRISSOM, Virgil I. (1926-1967) Astronaut. CB65 FPSN IEAS MOS7 PMAS WESE

GRISWOLD, Ralph E. (1934-) Comp. HOPL

GRODDECK, Albrecht von (1837-1887) Geol.; Mineral. CDZZ ZZ-5

GROSS, Evgenii F. (1897-) Phys. SMST

GROSS, Ludwick (1904-) Med. MHSE

GROSS, Paul M. (1895-) Chem. CB63

GROSS, Samuel D. (1805-1884) Med. BHMT

GROSSETESTE, Robert (c.1168-1253) Nat. Philos.; Opt. ABET BDOS CDZZ ZZ-5

GROSSMAN, Ernst A. (1863-1933) Astron. CDZZ ZZ-5

GROSSMANN, Marcel (1878-1936) Math. CDZZ ZZ-5

GROTE, Augustus R. (1841-1903) Entom. AMEM BIOD CDZZ DAB NC22 ZZ-5

GROTE, Irvine W. (1899-1972) Chem. NC57

GROTH, Paul H. von (1843-1927) Mineral.; Crystal. CDZZ ZZ-5

GROTTHUSS, Theodor von (1785-1822) Chem.; Phys. CDZZ ZZ-5

GROVE, William R. (1811-1896) Phys.; Electrochem. ABES ABET BEOS CDZZ DNB1 SOSC VISC ZZ-5

GRUBB, Howard (1844-1931) Opt. CDZZ ZZ-5

GRUBB, Thomas (1800-1878) Opt. CDZZ ZZ-5

GRUBENMANN, Johann U. (1850-1924) Mineral. CDZZ ZZ-5

GRUBER, Max von (1853-1927) Med. CDZZ ZZ-5

GRUBY, David (1810-1898) Microbiol. CDZZ ZZ-5

GRUENEWALD, Edward R. (1879-1938) Chem. NC28

GRZIMEK, Bernhard (1909-) Zool. CB73

GUA DE MALVES, Jean P. de (c.1712-1786) Math.; Mineral. CDZZ ZZ-5

GUCCIA, Giovanni B. (1855-1914) Math. CDZZ ZZ-5

GUDDEN, Johann B. von (1824-1886) Med. CDZZ ZZ-5

GUDERMANN, Christoph (1798-1852) Math. CDZZ ZZ-5

GUDERNATSCH, J. Frederick (1881-1962) Anat. NC52

GUDGER, Eugene (1866-1956) Ichth. NCSD

GUENTHER, Adam W. (1848-1923) Math. CDZZ ZZ-5

GUERICKE, Otto von (1602-1686) Phys. ABES ABET BDOS BEOS CDZZ EETD ESEH FPHM GE-1 HOSS ZZ-5

GUERTLER, William M. (1880-1959) Metal. CDZZ ZZ-5

GUETTARD, Jean E. (1715-1786) Geol.; Nat Hist. ABES ABET BEOS CDZZ ZZ-5

GUGGENHEIM, Edward A. (1888-1972) Chem. RS17

GUGLIELMO DE CORVI (1250-1326) Med. TALS

GUIBERT, Nicolas (c.1547-c.1620) Chem. CDZZ ZZ-5

GUIDI, Guido (1508-1569) Anat.; Med. CDZZ ZZ-5

GUIGNARD, Jean L. (1852-1928) Bot. CDZZ ZZ-5

GUILFORD, Joy P. (1897-) Psych. MHM2 MHSE

GUILLANDINUS SEE WIELAND, Melchoir

GUILLAUME, Charles E. (1861-1938) Phys. ABES ABET BDOS BEOS CDZZ POSW ZZ-5

GUILLEMIN, Ernest A. (1898-) Engr. MHM2 MHSE

GUILLEMIN, Roger (1924-) Med. ABET BEOS MHSE PAW2 SOTT

GUILLET, Leon A. (1873-1946) Metal. CDZZ ZZ-5

GUILLIERMOND, Marie A. (1876-1945) Bot. CDZZ ZZ-5

GUINAND, Pierre L. (c.1744-1824) Invent. BDOS

GUINTER, Joannes (c.1505-1574) Med. CDZZ ZZ-5

GUION, Connie M. (1882-) Med. CB62

GULDBERG, Cato M. (1836-1902) Chem. ABES ABET BDOS BEOS CDZZ ZZ-5

GULDIN, Paul (1577-1643) Math. CDZZ ZZ-5

GULL, William (1816-1899) Med. BHMT

GULLAND, John M. (1898-1947) Chem.; Biochem. CDZZ ZZ-5

GULLIVER, George (1804-1882) Anat.; Physiol. DNB

GULLSTRAND, Allvar (1862-1930) Med.; Opt. ABET BDOS BEOS CDZZ ZZ-5

GUMMERE, John (1784-1845) Math. BIOD DAB NC23

GUNDISSALINUS, Dominicus (fl. c.1170) Trans. Sci. Lit. CDZZ ZZ-5

GUNN, Robert C. (1808-1881) Nat. Hist. DNB

GUNN, Ross (1897-1966) Phys. NC52

GUNTER, Edmund (1581-1626) Math.; Nav. CDZZ DNB ZZ-5

GUNTER, Herman (1885-) Geol. NCSJ

GUNTHER, Albert C. (1830-1914) Nat. Hist. ANHD DNB3

GUNTHER, Robert W. (1869-1940) Zool. DNB5

GURNEE, Jeanne (c.1930-) Spel. WAWL

GURNEY, Goldsworthy (1793-1875) Invent. GE-1

GURVICH, Aleksandr G. (1874-1954) Biol. CDZZ ZZ-5

GUSTAFSON, John K. (1906-) Geol. NCSK

GUTBIER, Felix A. (1876-1926) Chem. CDZZ ZZ-5

GUTENBERG, Beno (1889-1960) Geol.; Seism. ABES ABET BEOS CDZZ ZZ-5

GUTENBERG, Johann (1398-1468) Invent. ABES ABET BDOS SAIF

GUTERMUTH, Clinton R. (1900-) Cons. LACC

GUTHE, Karl E. (1866-1915) Phys. DAB NC22

GUTHRIE, George J. (1785-1856) Med. BHMT

GUTHRIE, Samuel (1782-1848) Chem.; Med. ABES ABET ACCE BEOS BIOD DAB NC11

GUTOWSKY, Herbert S. (1919-) Chem. MHSE

GUY, Henry L. (1887-1956) Engr. RS-4

GUY DE CHAULIAC SEE CHAULIAC, Guy de

GUYE, Charles E. (1866-1942) Phys. CDZZ ZZ-5

GUYE, Philippe A. (1862-1922) Chem. GRCH

GUYER, Michael F. (1874-1959) Zool. CDZZ NCSA ZZ-5

GUYONNEAU DE PAMBOUR SEE PAMBOUR, Francois M.

GUYOT, Arnold H. (1807-1884) Geog.; Glaciol. ABET BEOS BIOD BM-2 CDZZ ZZ-5

GUYTON DE MORVEAU, Louis B. (1737-1816) Chem. ABES ABET BEOS CDZZ ZZ-5

GWYNNE-VAUGHAN, David T. (1871-1915) Bot. CDZZ ZZ-5

GYLLENHAAL, Leonhard (1752-1840) Entom. CDZZ ZZ-5

GYORGY, Paul (1893-1976) Biochem.; Med. MHSE

H

HAAGEN-SMIT, Arie J. (1900-1977) Biochem. CB66 NC59

HAAK, Theodore (1605-1690) Trans. Sci. Lit. CDZZ ZZ-5

HAAR, Alfred (1885-1933) Math. CDZZ ZZ-5

HAAS, Arthur E. (1884-1941) Phys. CDZZ ZZ-5

HAAS, Wander J. de (1878-1960) Phys. CDZZ ZZ-5

HAASIS, Frank A. (1908-1965) Bot. NC52

HAAST, Johann F. von (1822-1887) Geol. CDZZ DNB ZZ-5

HABASH al-HASIB, Ahmad ibn Abdallah (d.864/74) Math.; Astron. CDZZ ZZ-5

HABER, Fritz (1868-1934) Chem. ABES ABET BDOS BEOS CDZZ GJPS GRCH HSSO NPWC SAIF ZZ-5

HABER, Heinz (1913-) Phys. CB52

HABERLANDT, Gottlieb (1854-1945) Bot. CDZZ ZZ-5

HACHETTE, Jean N. (1769-1834) Math.; Phys. CDZZ ZZ-6

HACHMUTH, Karl H. (1904-1966) Chem. Engr. NC53

HADAC, Emil (1913-) Bot. POEC

HADAMARD, Jacques (1865-1963) Math. CDZZ RS11 ZZ-6

HADDOW, Alexander (1907-1976) Med. MHM2 MHDE RS23

HADDOW, Alexander J. (1912-1978) Entom. RS26

HADEN, Russell L. (1888-1952) Med. NC45

HADFIELD, Robert A. (1858-1940) Metal. ABES ABET BDOS BEOS CDZZ ZZ-6

HADLEY, George (1685-1768) Meteor. BEOS DNB

HADLEY, John (1682-1744) Instr. BDOS BEOS CDZZ DNB ZZ-6

HAECKEL, Ernst H. (1834-1919) Zool. ABES ABET ANHD BDOS BEOS BHMT CDZZ ZZ-6

HAENKE, Tadeo (c.1761-1817) Bot. SSNW

HAENSEL, Vladimir (1914-) Chem. MHSE

HAFENRICHTER, Atlee L. (1897-) Cons. LACC

HAFFKINE, Waldemar M. (1860-1930) Bact. ABET CDZZ ZZ-6

HAFSTAD, Lawrence R. (1904-) Phys. CB56 MHM1 MHSE

HAGEN, Hermann A. (1817-1893) Entom. AMEM BIOD DAB NC-5

HAGEN, John P. (1908-) Phys. CB57 MASY

HAGENBECK, Carl (1844-1913) Nat. Hist. NATJ

HAGENSTEIN, William D. (1915-) Forest. LACC

HAGER, Albert D. (1817-1893) Geol. BIOD

HAGIHARA, Yusuke (1897-) Astrophys. MHM1 MHSE

HAGSTRUM, Homer D. (1915-) Phys. MHSE

HAGUE, Arnold (1840-1917) Geol. BM-9 CDZZ ZZ-6

HAHN, Dorothy (1876-1950) Chem. NAW

HAHN, Erwin L. (1921-) Phys. MHSE

HAHN, Otto (1879-1968) Chem. ABES ABET BDOS
BEOS CB51 CDZZ GJPS HSSO MHM1 MHSE
NPWC RS16 SAIF ZZ-6

HAHNEMANN, Christian F. (1755-1843) Med. CDZZ
MSFB ZZ-6

HAIDINGER, Wilhelm K. (1795-1871) Mineral.; Geol.
CDZZ ZZ-6

HAILSTONE, John (1759-1847) Geol. DNB

HAILSTONE, Samuel (1768-1851) Bot. DNB

HAKLUYT, Richard (1552-1616) Geog. CDZZ ZZ-6

HALBOUTY, Michel T. (1909-) Geol. MHSE

HALDANE, John B. (1892-1964) Genet.; Biochem.
ABES ABET BDOS CB40 GASW MHM1 MHSE
MMSB RS12 ZZ-6

HALDANE, John S. (1860-1936) Physiol. BDOS BEOS
BHMT CDZZ ZZ-6

HALDANE, Richard B. (1856-1928) Philos. CDZZ
SOSC ZZ-6

HALDEMAN, Samuel S. (1812-1880) Zool. AMEM
ASJD BIOD BM-2 DAB NC-9

HALE, George E. (1868-1938) Astrophys. ABES ABET
ASIW BDOS BEOS BM21 CDZZ DAB2 IEAS
NC11 NC38 TMAL WAMB ZZ-6

HALE, William (1797-1870) Rocket. CDZZ ZZ-6

HALE, William J. (1876-1955) Chem. ACCE NC44

HALE-WHITE, William (1857-1949) Med. BHMT

HALES, Stephen (1677-1761) Bot.; Chem. ABES
ABET BDOS BEOS BHMT CDZZ DNB EPHG
HLSM LISD ZZ-6

HALEY, Andrew G. (1904-) Space Law MOS7

HALFORD, Henry (1766-1844) Med. BHMT

HALL, Arthur L. (1872-1955) Geol. RS-2

HALL, Asaph (1829-1907) Astron. ABES ABET BEOS
BM-6 CDZZ DAB IEAS NC11 NC22 SLOR
WAMB ZZ-6

HALL, B. Vincent (1907-1975) Zool. NC59

HALL, Charles M. (1863-1914) Chem. ABES ABET
BDOS BEOS CDZZ DAB FOIF HSSO SAIF
SMIL WAMB ZZ-6

HALL, Chester M. (1703-1771) Invent. DNB

HALL, Edwin H. (1855-1938) Phys. BM21 CDZZ
DAB2 NC39 ZZ-6

HALL, Granville S. (1846-1924) Psych. ABES ABET
CDZZ ZZ-6

HALL, James (1761-1832) Geol.; Chem. ABES
ABET BEOS CDZZ DNB TOWS ZZ-6

HALL, James Jr. (1811-1898) Paleon.; Geol. BDOS
BEOS BIOD CDZZ DAB NC-3 PHLS WAMB
ZZ-6

HALL, John H. (1781-1841) Invent. INYG

HALL, Lloyd A. (1894-1971) Chem. ACCE BPSH
SBPY

HALL, Lyman B. (1852-1935) Chem. ACCE

HALL, Marshall (1790-1857) Med. ABES ABET BDOS
BEOS BHMT CDZZ DNB ZZ-6

HALL, Maurice C. (1881-1938) Parasit.; Zool. NC29

HALL, Philip (1904-) Math. MHM1 MHSE

HALL, Robert A. (1880-1944) Chem. NC33

HALL, Robert W. (1872-1963) Biol. NC51

HALL, William L. (1873-1960) Forest. LACC

HALL, William S. (1861-1948) Math. NC37

HALL, William T. (1874-1957) Sci. Writ.; Trans. Sci.
Lit. ACCE

HALLE, Thore G. (1884-1964) Paleon. FHUA

HALLER, Albrecht von (1708-1777) Physiol.; Anat.
ABES ABET BDOS BEOS BHMT CDZZ HLSM
ZZ-6

HALLEY, Edmond (1656-1742) Astron.; Geophys.
ABES ABET ASTR BDOS BEOS BHMT CDZZ
EETD HOSS IEAS MELW SGAC SLOR SMIL
STSW TOWS ZZ-6

HALLIBURTON, William D. (1860-1931) Physiol.;
Biochem. CNB5

HALLIER, Ernst H. (1831-1904) Bot.; Parasit. CDZZ ZZ-6

HALLOCK, Charles (1834-1917) Cons. DAB

HALLOPEAU, Henri (1842-1919) Med. BHMT

HALLOWELL, Alfred I. (1892-1974) Anthro. BM51 NCSH

HALLOWELL, Edward (1808-1860) Herp. BIOD

HALLWACHS, Wilhelm L. (1859-1922) Phys. CDZZ HSSO ZZ-6

HALM, Jacob K. (1866-1944) Astron. CDZZ ZZ-6

HALPHEN, Georges H. (1844-1889) Math. CDZZ ZZ-6

HALSTED, George B. (1853-1922) Math. CDZZ DAB ZZ-6

HALSTED, William S. (1852-1922) Med. ABES ABET BEOS BHMT BM17 CDZZ ZZ-6

HALTON, Immaneul (1628-1699) Astron. DNB

HAMBERG, Axel (1863-1933) Geog.; Geol. CDZZ ZZ-6

HAMBURGER, Viktor (1900-) Embryol. MHM2 MHSE

al-HAMDANI, Abu Muhammad al-Hasan (c.893-c.951) Geog. CDZZ ZZ-6

HAMILTON, Alice (1869-1970) Med. CWSN NAWM WIWM WPSH WASM

HAMILTON, David J. (1849-1909) Path. DNB2

HAMILTON, James A. (1747-1815) Astron. DNB

HAMILTON, William (1730-1803) Geol.; Archaeol. CDZZ ZZ-6

HAMILTON, William (1755-1797) Nat. Hist. DNB

HAMILTON, William (1788-1856) Philos. CDZZ ZZ-6

HAMILTON, William D. (1936-) Biol. BEOS

HAMILTON, William J. (1902-) Zool. LACC

HAMILTON, William R. (1805-1865) Math.; Opt. ABES ABET BDOS BEOS CDZZ DNB ZZ-6

HAMMERLING, Joachim A. (1901-1980) Biol. BEOS RS28

HAMMETT, Frederick S. (1885-1953) Biol. NC42

HAMMETT, Louis P. (1894-) Chem. MHM1

HAMMICK, Dalziel L. (1887-1966) Chem. RS13

HAMMON, William M. (1904-) Microbiol. CB57

HAMMOND, Edward C. (1912-) Med. CB57 MFIR

HAMMOND, Edward S. (1921-) Chem. MHM2

HAMMOND, George S. (1921-) Chem. BEOS MHM2 MHSE

HAMMOND, John H. Jr. (1888-1965) Invent. CB62 RS11

HAMMOND, William A. (1828-1900) Med.; Ornith. BHMT BIOD WFBG

HAMOR, William A. (1887-1961) Chem. NCSF

HAMPSON, William (c.1854-1926) Chem. Engr. ABET CDZZ ZZ-6

HAMY, Maurice T. (1861-1936) Astrophys. CDZZ ZZ-6

HAN KUNG-LIEN (fl. 1090) Engr. GE-1

HAN TSEN (fl. 50) Engr. GE-1

HANBURY BROWN, Robert (1916-) Astron. MHM2 MHSE

HANCE, Henry F. (1827-1886) Bot. DNB

HANCOCK, Albany (1806-1873) Zool. DNB

HANCOCK, Thomas (1786-1865) Invent. BDOS

HANCOCK, Walter (1799-1852) Engr. DNB

HANDLER, Philip (1917-1981) Biochem. CB64 MHSE

HANDYSIDE, William (1793-1850) Engr. DNB

HANFORD, William E. (1908-) Chem. MHSE

HANKEL, Hermann (1839-1873) Math. CDZZ ZZ-6

HANKEL, Wilhelm G. (1814-1899) Phys.; Chem. CDZZ ZZ-6

HANKS, Henry G. (1826-1907) Geol.; Chem. BIOD

HANLEY, John B. (1913-1975) Geol. NC59

HANMER, Hiram R. (1896-) Chem. NCSJ

HANN, James (1799-1856) Math. CDZZ ZZ-6

HANN, Julius F. von (1839-1921) Meteor.; Climat.
CDZZ ZZ-6

HANS, Edmund (1886-1959) Invent. NC49

HANSEN, Emil C. (1842-1909) Bot.; Physiol. CDZZ
ZZ-6

HANSEN, Gerhard H. (1841-1912) Bact. BEOS BHMT
CDZZ ZZ-6

HANSEN, Hazel D. (1899-1962) Archaeol. NC49

HANSEN, Peter A. (1795-1874) Astron. CDZZ ZZ-6

HANSEN, William W. (1909-1949) Phys. BM27 CDZZ
DAB4 ZZ-6

HANSKY, Aleksey P. (1870-1908) Astron. CDZZ
ZZ-6

HANSON, Emmeline J. (1919-1973) Zool.; Biophys.
RS21

HANSON, Herman R. (1876-1972) Chem. NC57

HANSTEEN, Christopher (1784-1873) Phys.; Astron.
CDZZ ZZ-6

HANTZSCH, Arthur R. (1857-1935) Chem. BDOS
BEOS CDZZ GRCH ZZ-6

HARBERS, Henry C. (1911-1976) Engr. NC59

HARCOURT, A.G. Vernon (1834-1919) Chem. CDZZ
DNB3 ZZ-6

HARCOURT, William V. (1789-1871) Chem. BDOS
BEOS VISC

HARDEN, Arthur (1865-1940) Biochem. ABES ABET
BDOS BEOS CDZZ DNB5 NPWC ZZ-6

HARDIN, Garrett (1915-) Ecol. CB74 PCWA

HARDING, Arthur M. (1884-1947) Math. NCSF

HARDING, Carl L. (1765-1834) Astron. CDZZ ZZ-6

HARDING, Ferdinand R. (1902-1968) Photo. NC55

HARDMAN, Edward T. (1845-1887) Geol. DNB

HARDTNER, Henry E. (1870-1935) Forest. LACC

HARDY, Alister (1896-) Mar. Biol. EXSG

HARDY, Arthur C. (1895-) Phys. NCSE

HARDY, Arthur S. (1847-1930) Math. DAB

HARDY, Claude (c.1598-1678) Math. CDZZ ZZ-6

HARDY, Godfrey H. (1877-1947) Math. BEOS CDZZ
DNB6 ZZ-6

HARDY, William B. (1864-1934) Physiol. BEOS
CDZZ DNB5 ZZXV

HARE, Robert (1781-1858) Chem. ABET ACCE
BDOS BEOS BIOD CDZZ DAB GE-1 GRCH
TPAE ZZ-6

HARES, Charles J. (1881-1970) Geol. NC56

HARGRAVE, Lawrence (1850-1915) Aero. ICFW

HARGREAVES, James (1720-1778) Text. BDOS
BEOS DNB GE-1 SAIF

HARIDATTA I (fl. 683) Astron. CDZZ ZZ-6

HARIDATTA II (fl. 1638) Astron. CDZZ ZZ-6

HARINGTON, Charles R. (1897-1972) Biochem. RS18

HARIOT, Thomas SEE HARRIOT, Thomas

HARKER, Alfred (1859-1939) Geol. CDZZ ZZ-6

HARKINS, William D. (1873-1951) Chem. ABET
ACCE BEOS BM47 CDZZ DAB5 NC42 ZZ-6

HARKNESS, Ruth (1900-) Exp. WAGW

HARKNESS, William (1837-1903) Astron. BIOD
CDZZ DAB NC-8 ZZ-6

HARLAN, Richard (1796-1843) Anat.; Zool. ASJD
BIOD CDZZ DAB WFBG ZZ-6

HARLEY, George (1829-1899) Med. BHMT

HARLOW, Harry F. (1905-) Psych. MHM1 MHSE

HARNED, Herbert S. (1888-1969) Chem. BM51

HARNWELL, Gaylord P. (1903-1982) Phys. CB56

HARPER, Henry W. (1859-1943) Chem. NCSE

HARPER, Robert A. (1862-1946) Bot. BM25 CDZZ
MABH NCSA ZZ-6

HARPER, Roland M. (1878-1966) Bot.; Geog. CDZZ
ZZ-6

HARPER, Verne L. (1902-) Forest. LACC

HARPESTRAENG, Henrik (d. 1244) Med. CDZZ ZZ-6

HARRAR, Jacob G. (1906-) Biol.;Bot. CB64 MHM2
MHSE

HARRIES, Carl (1866-1923) Chem. HSSO

HARRIMAN, John (1760-1831) Bot. DNB

HARRINGTON, Mark W. (1848-1926) Astron.; Meteor.
BIOD DAB NC10

HARRIOT, Thomas (1560-1621) Math.; Phys. BDOS
BEOS CDZZ DNB MSAJ ZZ-6

HARRIS, Charles M. (1868-1923) Nat. Hist. NC17

HARRIS, Cyril M. (1917-) Phys. CB77 MHSE

HARRIS, Geoffrey W. (1913-1971) Anat. BEOS
MHM2 MHSE RS18

HARRIS, Gilbert D. (1864-1952) Geol.; Paleon. NC41

HARRIS, Isaac F. (1879-1953) Chem. NC42

HARRIS, James A. (1880-1930) Bot. DAB MABH

HARRIS, James A. (1932-) Chem. BCST BISC
SBPY

HARRIS, John (1667-1719) Nat. Philos. BDOS CDZZ
DNB ZZ-6

HARRIS, John E. (1910-1968) Zool. RS15

HARRIS, Moses (1730-1788) Nat. Hist. ANHD DNB

HARRIS, Rollin A. (1863-1918) Ocean. DAB NC22

HARRIS, Thaddeus W. (1795-1856) Entom. ABES
BIOD DAB

HARRIS, Walter (1647-1732) Med. BHMT

HARRISON, George R. (1898-1979) Phys. MHM1
MHSE

HARRISON, James M. (1915-) Geol. MHM2 MHSE

HARRISON, John (1693-1776) Instr. ABES ABET
BDOS CDZZ GE-1 ZZ-6

HARRISON, John (1773-1833) Chem. ACCE BIOD
NC13

HARRISON, John W. (1881-1967) Bot. RS14

HARRISON, Robert (1715-1802) Math. DNB

HARRISON, Ross G. (1870-1959) Biol.; Embryol.
BDOS BEOS BM35 CDZZ RS-7 WAMB ZZ-6

HARRISON, Thomas S. (1881-1964) Geol. NC52

HARROW, Benjamin (1888-1970) Biochem. ACCE

HARSHBERGER, John W. (1869-1929) Bot. DAB
MABH NC13

HARSHMAN, Walter S. (1858-1924) Astron. NC27

HART, Edward (1854-1931) Chem. ACCE DAB1

HART, Edwin B. (1874-1953) Biochem. ACCE BM28
CDZZ DAB5 NC43 ZZ-6

HARTERT, Ernst (1859-1933) Ornith. ORNS

HARTIG, Theodor (1805-1880) Forest.; Entom. CDZZ
ZZ-6

HARTING, Pieter (1812-1885) Micros.; Zool. CDZZ
ZZ-6

HARTLEY, David (1705-1757) Psych. CDZZ ZZ-6

HARTLEY, Harold B. (1878-1972) Chem. RS19
COBC

HARTLEY, Percival (1881-1957) Biol. RS-3

HARTLIB, Samuel (d. 1662) Sci. Ed. CDZZ ZZ-6

HARTLINE, Haldan K. (1903-1983) Biophys. ABES
ABET BEOS MHM2 MHSE

HARTMAN, Frank A. (1883-) Med. DODR

HARTMAN, Frank E. (1890-1952) Chem. NC39

HARTMANN, Carl F. (1796-1863) Mineral.; Mng. CDZZ ZZ-6

HARTMANN, Georg (1489-1564) Instr. CDZZ ZZ-6

HARTMANN, Johannes (1568-1631) Chem.; Med. CDZZ ZZ-6

HARTMANN, Johannes F. (1865-1936) Astron. ABET BEOS CDZZ ZZ-6

HARTREE, Douglas R. (1897-1958) Math.; Phys. CDZZ DNB7 RS-4 ZZ-6

HARTRIDGE, Hamilton (1886-1976) Physiol. RS23

HARTSOEKER, Nicolaas (1656-1725) Phys. CDZZ ZZ-6

HARTT, Charles F. (1840-1878) Geol. BIOD

HARTWIG, (Carl) Ernst (1851-1923) Astron. CDZZ ZZ-6

HARTZELL, Frederick Z. (1879-1958) Entom. AMEM

HARTZOG, George B. (1920-) Cons. LACC

HARVEY, Edmund N. (1887-1959) Physiol. BM39 CB52 NC45

HARVEY, Edward M. (1888-1959) Bot. NC48

HARVEY, Ellery H. (1895-) Chem. NCSK

HARVEY, Ethel B. (1885-1965) Biol. NAWM

HARVEY, Fred A. (1882-1945) Phys. NC50

HARVEY, Hildebrand W. (1887-1970) Ocean. RS18

HARVEY, Rodney B. (1890-1945) Bot. NC44

HARVEY, William (1578-1657) Med. ABES ABET BDOS BEOS BHMT BMST CDZZ ESCS FBMV HEXS HLSM LISD MMMA SAIF SMIL TOWS ZZ-6

HARVEY, William H. (1811-1866) Bot. CDZZ DNB ZZ-6

al-HASAN ibn Muhammad al-Wazsen SEE LEO THE AFRICAN

HASCHE, R. Leonard (1896-1959) Chem. NC52

HASELDEN, Thomas (d. 1740) Math. DNB

HASEMAN, Leonard (1884-1969) Entom. NC58

HASENOHRL, Friedrich (1874-1915) Phys. CDZZ ZZ-6

HASKINS, Caryl P. (1908-) Chem. CB58 NCSE

HASLAM, Robert T. (1888-1961) Chem. Engr. NC55

HASLER, Maurice F. (1907-1968) Phys. NC54

HASLETT, Caroline H. (1895-1957) Elec. Engr. DNB7

HASS, Hans (1919-) Zool.; Ocean. CB55

HASS, Henry B. (1902-) Chem. CB56 MHSE

HASSEL, Odd (1897-1981) Chem. ABET AO81 BEOS MHSE

HASSENFRATZ, Jean H. (1755-1827) Chem. CDZZ ZZ-6

HASSID, William Z. (1897-1974) Biochem. BM50

HASSLER, Ferdinand R. (1770-1843) Math.; Geophys. BIOD CDZZ DAB NC-3 ZZ-6

HASTINGS, Albert B. (1895-) Biochem. MHM1 MHSE

HASTINGS, Charles S. (1848-1932) Phys. BM20 DAB1

HASZELDINE, Robert N. (1925-) Chem. COBC

HATCHER, John B. (1861-1904) Paleon. BIOD

HATCHETT, Charles (1765-1847) Chem. ABES ABET BEOS CDZZ ZZ-6

HATHAWAY, Jarret L. (1906-1973) Engr. NC58

HATSCHEK, Berthold (1854-1941) Zool. CDZZ ZZ-6

HATTON, Ronald G. (1886-1965) Hort. RS12

HAUG, Gustave E. (1861-1927) Geol.; Paleon. CDZZ ZZ-6

HAUGHTON, Samuel (1821-1897) Geol. DNB1

HAUGHWOUT, Frank G. (1877-1960) Zool. NC46

HAUKSBEE, Francis (c.1670-1713) Phys.; Instr. ABES
ABET BDOS BEOS CDZZ DNB EETD ESEH
GE-1 ZZ-6

HAUKSBEE, Francis (1688-1763) Phys.; Instr. CDZZ
ZZ-6

HAUROWITZ, Felix M. (1896-) Biochem. MHM2
MHSE

HAUSDORFF, Felix (1868-1942) Math. CDZZ ZZ-6

HAUSEN, Christian A. (1693-1743) Elec. Sci. ESEH

HAUSER, Charles R. (1900-1970) Chem. MHSE

HAUSER, Ernst A. (1896-1956) Chem. ACCE

HAUTEFEUILLE, Paul G. (1836-1902) Chem. CDZZ
ZZ-6

HAUY, Rene J. (1743-1822) Crystal.; Mineral. ABES
ABET BEOS BMST CDZZ GASJ ZZ-6

HAVELOCK, Thomas H. (1877-1968) Math. RS17

HAVERS, Clopton (1655-1702) Med. ABET CDZZ
ZZ-6

HAWES, Austin F. (1879-1962) Forest. LACC

HAWKES, Leonard (1891-1981) Geol. RS28

HAWKING, Stephen W. (1942-) Phys. ABET BEOS
MHSE

HAWKINS, Gerald S. (1928-) Astron. ABET BEOS

HAWKINS, Herbert L. (1887-1968) Geol. RS16

HAWKINS, Thomas (1810-1889) Geol. DNB

HAWKINS, Walter L. (1911-) Chem. SBPY

HAWLEY, Ralph C. (1880-1971) Forest. LACC

HAWORTH, Adrian H. (1768-1833) Bot.; Entom.
CDZZ DNB ZZ-6

HAWORTH, Leland J. (1904-1979) Phys. CB50 NCSH

HAWORTH, Robert D. (1898-) Chem. COBC

HAWORTH, Walter N. (1883-1950) Chem. ABES
ABET BDOS BEOS CDZZ DNB6 NPWC ZZ-6

IBN HAWQAL, Abul Qasim Muhammad (fl. c.950-1000)
Geog. CDZZ ZZ-6

HAWTHORNE, Edward W. (1921-) Physiol. SBPY

HAWTHORNE, William R. (1913-) Engr. MHM2
MHSE

HAY, Clarence L. (1884-1969) Archaeol. NC54

HAY, Donald L. (1893-1938) Phys. NC28

HAY, Oliver P. (1846-1930) Paleon. DAB

HAYDEN, Edward E. (1858-1932) Meteor. BIOD
NC-8

HAYDEN, Ferdinand V. (1829-1887) Geol. BIOD
BM-3 CDZZ WAMB ZZ-6

HAYDEN, George D. (1878-1962) Invent. NC51

HAYDEN, Horace H. (1769-1844) Geo.; Dent. BIOD

HAYES, Augustus A. (1806-1882) Chem. ASJD BIOD
DAB

HAYES, Charles (1678-1760) Math. DNB

HAYFORD, John F. (1868-1925) Geophys. ABET
BM16 CDZZ ZZ-6

HAYGARTH, John (1740-1827) Med. BHMT

HAYNES, Elwood (1857-1925) Chem.; Metal. ACCE

HAYNES, Henry W. (1831-1912) Archaeol. NC18

HAYNES, Williams (1886-1970) Sci. Writ. ACCE

HAYES, James D. (1933-) Geol. BEOS

ibn al-HAYTHAM, Abu Ali al-Hassan (965-1038) Opt.;
Astron. ABES ABET BEOS CDZZ SCIN ZZ-6

HAYWARD, Robert B. (1829-1903) Math. DNB2

HAZARD, Rowland (1829-1898) Text. ACCE

HAZEN, Elizabeth L. (1885-1975) Bact.; Biochem.
FFIB NAWM

HAZLEHURST, Thomas H. (1906-1949) Chem. NC39

HAZZARD, Albert S. (1901-) Biol. LACC

HEAD, Henry (1861-1940) Med. BHMT

HEADLEE, Thomas J. (1877-1946) Entom. AMEM NC40

HEADLEY, Frank B. (1878-) Agr. BNBR

HEALD, Frederick D. (1872-1954) Bot. NC44

HEALD, Weldon F. (1901-1967) Cons. LACC

HEARST, Walter R. (1900-1960) Chem. NC49

HEATH, Fred H. (1883-1952) Chem. ACCE

HEATH, Harold (1868-1951) Zool. NC40

HEATH, Robert (d. 1779) Math. DNB

HEATH, Thomas L. (1861-1940) Math. CDZZ ZZ-6

HEATHCOAT, John (1783-1861) Invent. BDOS

HEAVISIDE, Oliver (1850-1925) Phys.; Engr. ABES ABET BDOS BEOS CDZZ DNB4 EETD ZZ-6

HEBARD, Morgan (1887-1946) Entom. AMEM NC41

HEBB, Donald O. (1904-) Psych. MHM2 MHSE

HEBERDEN, William (1710-1801) Med. BHMT

HEBRA, Ferdinand von (1816-1880) Med. BHMT

HECATAEUS OF MILETUS (c.550 B.C.-c.476 B.C.) Geog. ABES ABET BEOS CDZZ ZZ-6

HECHT, Daniel F. (1777-1833) Math. CDZZ ZZ-6

HECHT, Selig (1892-1947) Physiol.; Biophys. BEOS DAB4

HECK, Nicholas H. (1882-1953) Seism. NC45

HECKE, Erich (1887-1947) Math. CDZZ ZZ-6

HECKMANN, Otto H. (1901-) Astron. MHM1 MHSE

HECTOR, James (1834-1907) Geol. DNB2

HEDBERG, Hollis D. (1903-) Geol. MHSE

HEDIN, Sven A. (1856-1952) Geog. CDZZ NC40 ZZ-6

HEDLEY, William (1779-1843) Engr. GE-1

HEDRICK, Earle R. (1876-1943) Math. NC32

HEDWIG, Johann (1730-1799) Bot. CDZZ ZZ-6

HEER, Oswald (1809-1883) Paleon.; Bot. CDZZ FHUA ZZ-6

HEERMANN, Adolphus L. (c.1827-1865) Nat. Hist. WFBG

HEEZEN, Bruce C. (1924-1977) Ocean.; Geol. ABES ABET BEOS MHSE NC60

HEFNER-ALTENECK, Friedrich von (1845-1904) Engr. CDZZ ZZ-6

HEGNER, Robert W. (1880-1942) Zool. NC36

HEIDELBERGER, Michael (1888-) Immunol. BEOS MHM2 MHSE

HEIDEMANN, Otto (1842-1916) Entom. AMEM

HEIDENHAIN, Martin (1864-1949) Anat.; Micros. CDZZ ZZ-6

HEIDENHAIN, Rudolf P. (1834-1897) Physiol. BHMT CDZZ ZZ-6

HEILBRON, Ian M. (1886-1959) Chem. BDOS DNB7

HEILBRONN, Hans A. (1908-1975) Math. RS22

HEILMAN, Fordyce R. (1905-1960) Bact. NC51

HEILPRIN, Angelo (1853-1907) Geol.; Paleon. DAB NC12

HEIM, Albert (1849-1937) Geol. CDZZ ZZ-6

HEIM, Albert A. (1882-1965) Geol.; Geog. CDZZ ZZ-6

HEIM, Roger J. (1900-) Nat. Hist. MHM2 MHSE

HEIN, Illo (1893-1948) Bot. NC34

HEINDI, Leopold A. (1916-1978) Geol. NC60

HEINE, Heinrich E. (1821-1881) Math. CDZZ ZZ-6

HEINEMANN, Edward H. (1908-) Aero. ICFW MHM1 MHSE

HEINRICH, Carl (1880-1955) Entom. AMEM

HEINROTH, Oskar (1871-1945) Ornith. ORNS

HEINTZLEMAN, B. Frank (1888-1965) Forest. LACC

HEISE, George W. (1888-) Chem. NCSH

HEISENBERG, Werner K. (1901-1976) Phys. ABES ABET BEOS CB57 DCPW EGSF HSSO POSW RS23 TOWS

HEISKANEN, Weikko A. (1895-1971) Geophys. MHM1 MHSE

HEISTER, Lorenz (1683-1758) Anat.; Med. BHMT CDZZ ZZ-6

HEITLER, Walter H. (1904-1981) Phys. AO81 RS28

HEKTOEN, Ludvig (1863-1951) Path.; Microbiol. BM28 CDZZ ZZ-6

HELBAEK, Hans (c.1900-1981) Paleon. AO81

HELL, Maximilian (1720-1792) Astron. CDZZ ZZ-6

HELLER, Amos A. (1867-1944) Bot. BNBR

HELLER, Edmund (1875-1939) Nat. Hist. NC35

HELLINGER, Ernst (1883-1950) Math. CDZZ ZZ-6

HELLINS, John (d. 1827) Math.; Astron. DNB

HELLOT, Jean (1685-1766) Chem. CDZZ ZZ-6

HELLRIEGEL, Hermann (1831-1895) Chem. ABET CDZZ ZZ-6

HELM, Jacob A. (1761-1831) Med. BHMT

HELMERSEN, Grigory P. (1803-1885) Geol. CDZZ ZZ-6

HELMERT, Friedrich R. (1843-1917) Astron. CDZZ ZZ-6

HELMHOLTZ, Hermann L. von (1821-1894) Phys.; Physiol. ABES ABET BDOS BEOS BHMT CDZZ EETD GASJ LISD MMMA PFEL POPF TOWS ZZ-6

HELMONT, Jan B. van SEE VAN HELMONT, Johann

HEMMING, George W. (1821-1905) Math. DNB2

HEMPEL, Walter (1851-1916) Chem. HSSO

HENBEST, Harold B. (1924-) Chem. COBC

HENCH, Philip S. (1896-1965) Med. ABES ABET BEOS MFIR MHM1 MHSE PAW2

HENCKEL, Johann F. (1678-1744) Chem.; Mineral. CDZZ ZZ-6

HENDERSON, Cornelius L. (1887-) Engr. SBPY

HENDERSON, David W. (1903-1968) Biol. RS16

HENDERSON, Everette L. (1896-1966) Chem. NC53

HENDERSON, George G. (1862-1942) Chem. DNB6

HENDERSON, James H. (1917-) Bot. SBPY

HENDERSON, Lawrence J. (1878-1942) Chem. ACCE BHMT BM23 CDZZ DAB3 ZZ-6

HENDERSON, Thomas (1798-1844) Astron. ABES ABET AROW BEOS CDZZ DNB ZZ-6

HENDERSON, William E. (1870-1962) Chem. ACCE

HENDERSON, William F. (1892-1962) Chem. ACCE

HENDERSON, Yandell (1873-1944) Physiol. CDZZ ZZ-6

HENDREY, Waldersee B. (1900-1962) Chem. ACCE

HENDRICK, Ellwood (1861-1930) Chem. ACCE DAB NC22

HENDRICKS, Sterling B. (1902-1981) Chem. AO81 MHM1 MHSE

HENDRIXSON, Walter S. (1859-1925) Chem. ACCE

HENFREY, Arthur (1819-1859) Bot. CDZZ DNB ZZ-6

HENG, Chang SEE CHANG HENG

HENIUS, Max (1859-1935) Chem. NC27

HENKING, Hermann (1858-1942) Zool. CDZZ ZZ-6

HENLE, Friedrich G. (1809-1885) Anat.; Path. ABES ABET BEOS BHMT CDZZ ZZ-6

HENLEY, William T. (c.1813-1882) Elec. Engr. DNB

HENNEDY, Roger (1809-1877) Bot. DNB

HENNESSY, Henry (1826-1901) Phys. DNB2

HENOCH, Eduard H. (1820-1910) Med. BHMT

HENRICHS, James R. (1910-) Bot. BNBR

HENRICHSEN, Sophus (1845-1928) Phys. CDZZ ZZ-6

HENRICI, Arthur T. (1889-1943) Bact.; Microbiol. DAB3

HENRION, Didier (c.1580-c.1632) Math. CDZZ ZZ-6

HENRY BATE OF MALINES (1246-c.1310) Astron. CDZZ ZZ-6

HENRY OF DENMARK SEE HARPESTRANG, Henrik

HENRY OF HESSE (1325-1397) Phys.; Astron. CDZZ ZZ-6

HENRY OF MONDEVILLE (c.1260-c.1320) Med. CDZZ ZZ-6

HENRY, James P. (1914-) Med. MOS7

HENRY, Joseph (1797-1878) Phys.; Invent. ABES ABET ASIW ASJD BDOS BEOS BIOD BM-5 CDZZ DAB EETD FNEC GASJ GE-1 GOED HFGA HOSS INYG MSAJ NC-3 SAIF SMIL SNAR TINA TPAE TPOS VTHB WAMB YSMS ZZ-6

HENRY, Joseph L. (1924-) Anat.; Dent. SBPY

HENRY, Paul P. (1848-1905) Astron.; Opt. CDZZ ZZ-6

HENRY, Prosper M. (1859-1903) Astron.; Opt. CDZZ ZZ-6

HENRY, Thomas (1734-1816) Chem. CDZZ ZZ-6

HENRY, Warren E. (1909-) Chem. SBPY

HENRY, William (1774-1836) Chem. BDOS BEOS CDZZ ZZ-6

HENSEL, Kurt (1861-1941) Math. CDZZ ZZ-6

HENSEN, Viktor (1835-1924) Physiol.; Mar. Biol. BDOS BEOS CDZZ ZZ-6

HENSHALL, James A. (1836-1925) Nat. Hist. DAB

HENSHAW, Henry W. (1850-1930) Ornith. DAB

HENSHAW, Samuel (1852-1941) Entom. AMEM

HENSHAW, Thomas (1618-1700) Sci. Writ. DNB

HENSLOW, John S. (1796-1861) Bot. CDZZ DARR DNB WFBG SBAH

HENSON, Matthew A. (1865-1955) Exp. GNPA SABL SBAH

HENSON, William (1812-1888) Aero. ICFW

HENTZ, Nicholas M. (1797-1856) Entom. AMEM ASJD BIOD NHAH

HENWOOD, William J. (1805-1875) Mineral. DNB

HEPTING, George H. (1907-) Forest. LACC

HERACLEIDES OF PONTICUS (388 B.C.-315 B.C.) Astron. ABES ABET BEOS CDZZ ZZXV

HERACLITOS OF EPHESOS (fl. c.500 B.C.) Philos. ABES ABET AMST BEOS CDZZ HLSM ZZ-6

HERAPATH, John (1790-1868) Phys. CDZZ DNB ZZ-6

HERAPATH, William B. (1820-1868) Med.; Chem. CDZZ DNB ZZ-6

HERB, Raymond G. (1908-) Phys. MHSE

HERBART, Johann F. (1776-1841) Philos.; Psych. CDZZ ZZ-6

HERBERT, Paul A. (1899-) Forest. LACC

HERBERT, William (1778-1847) Nat. Hist. CDZZ ZZ-6

HERBRAND, Jacques (1908-1931) Math. CDZZ ZZ-6

HERBST, Robert L. (1935-) Cons. LACC

HERDMAN, William A. (1858-1924) Mar. Biol. DNB4

HERELLE, Felix d' (1873-1949) Microbiol. ABET BEOS CDZZ ZZ-6

HERGET, Paul (1908-1981) Astron. AO81 MHM2 MHSE

HERIGONE, Pierre (d. c.1643) Math. CDZZ ZZ-6

HERING, Daniel W. (1850-1938) Phys. NC42

HERING, Heinrich E. Jr. (1866-1948) Med. BHMT

HERING, Karl E. (1834-1918) Physiol.; Psych. CDZZ ZZ-6

HERMANN THE LAME (1013-1054) Astron.; Math. CDZZ ZZ-6

HERMANN, Carl H. (1898-1961) Phys.; Crystal. CDZZ ZZ-6

HERMANN, Jakob (1678-1733) Math. CDZZ ZZ-6

HERMBSTAEDT, Sigismund F. (1760-1833) Chem. CDZZ ZZXV

HERMINIER, Felix SEE L'HERMINIER, Felix L.

HERMITE, Charles (1822-1901) Math. ABES ABET BEOS CDZZ ZZ-6

HERMS, William B. (1876-1949) Entom. AMEM NC36

HERNANDEZ, Francisco (1517-1587) Nat. Hist. CDZZ ZZ-6

HERO OF ALEXANDRIA (fl. 60) Engr.; Math. ABES ABET BDOS BEOS CDZZ FNEC GE-1 ZZ-6

HERODOTUS OF HALICARNASSUS (d. c.425 B.C.) Nat. Philos. CDZZ ZZ-6

HEROLD, Stanley C. (1883-1959) Geol. NC47

HERON, Sam D. (1891-1963) Engr. ICFW

HEROPHILOS (335 B.C.-280 B.C.) Anat. ABES ABET AMST BDOS BEOS CDZZ HLSM SMIL ZZ-6

HEROULT, Paul L. (1863-1914) Metal. ABES ABET BDOS BEOS CDZZ SMIL ZZ-6

HERR, Clarence S. (1901-) Forest. LACC

HERRE, Albert (1868-1962) Nat. Hist. BNBR NC52

HERRERA, Alfonso L. (1868-1942) Biol. CDZZ ZZ-6

HERRESHOFF, John B. (1850-1932) Chem. Engr. ACCE

HERRICK, Charles J. (1868-1960) Med. BM43 CDZZ DODR ZZ-6

HERRICK, Clarence L. (1858-1904) Med. CDZZ ZZ-6

HERRICK, Edward C. (1811-1862) Astron.; Entom. ASJD BIOD DAB NC11

HERRICK, Francis H. (1858-1940) Biol. NC-3 NC31

HERRICK, Glenn W. (1870-1965) Entom. AMEM NC18

HERRICK, James B. (1861-1954) Med. BHMT

HERRICK, Samuel (1911-1974) Astron. MOS4

HERRING, Augustus M. (1867-1926) Aero. DAB

HERRING, William C. (1914-) Phys. BEOS MHM1 MHSE

HERSCHEL, Alexander S. (1836-1907) Astron. DNB2

HERSCHEL, Caroline L. (1750-1848) Astron. ABES ABET BEOS CDZZ DNB IDWB IEAS SLOR TMAL WIMO ZZ-6

HERSCHEL, Friedrich W. SEE HERSCHEL, William

HERSCHEL, John F. (1792-1871) Astron. ABES ABET BDOS BEOS CDZZ DARR DNB IEAS TOWS VISC ZZ-6

HERSCHEL, William (1738-1822) Astron. ABES ABET ASTR BDOS BEOS CDZZ DNB FASP GASJ IEAS LECE MSCH SAIF SGAC SSDH STSW TMAL ZZ-6

HERSEY, Mayo D. (1886-) Phys. NCSA

HERSHEY, Alfred D. (1908-) Bact. ABET BEOS CB70 HLSM MHM2 MHSE WAMB

HERSKOVITS, Melville J. (1895-1963) Anthro. BM42 WAMB

HERSTEIN, Karl M. (1896-1961) Chem. Engr. ACCE

HERTER, Christian A. (1865-1910) Biochem. ACCE DAB

HERTWIG, Karl W. (1850-1937) Biol. CDZZ ZZ-6

HERTWIG, Wilhelm A. (1849-1922) Zool. CDZZ ZZ-6

HERTY, Charles H. (1867-1938) Chem. ACCE DAB2 NC18 NC41

HERTY, Charles H. Jr. (1896-1953) Chem. ACCE BM31

HERTZ, Gustav L. (1887-1975) Phys. ABES ABET GJPS POSW

HERTZ, Heinrich R. (1857-1894) Phys. ABES ABET BDOS BEOS CDZZ DCPW EETD FNEC HOSS SAIF TOWS TPOS VTHB ZZ-6

HERTZ, Roy (1919-) Med. MFIR

HERTZSPRUNG, Ejnar (1873-1967) Astron. ABES ABET BEOS CDZZ IEAS ZZ-6

HERZBERG, Gerhard (1904-) Phys. ABET BEOS CB73 MHM2 MHSE

HERZBERGER, Max (1899-) Phys. MHSE

HERZFELD, Karl F. (1892-1978) Phys. MHM2 MHSE

HESKETH, Edward (1854-1942) Engr. MCCW

HESS, Frederic O. (1901-1981) Engr. AO81

HESS, Germain H. (1802-1850) Chem. ABES ABET BDOS BEOS CDZZ ZZ-6

HESS, Harry H. (1906-1969) Geol. ABES ABET BEOS BM43 ZZ-6

HESS, Victor F. (1883-1964) Phys. ABES ABET BDOS BEOS CB63 CDZZ DCPW PAW2 POSW ZZ-6

HESS, Walter R. (1881-1973) Physiol. ABES BEOS DODR MHM1 MHSE

HESSE, Ludwig O. (1811-1874) Math. CDZZ ZZ-6

HESSEL, Johann F. (1796-1872) Mineral.; Crystal. CDZZ ZZ-6

HESSEL, Sidney A. (1907-1974) Entom. NC58

HESTER, Jackson B. (1904-1962) Soil Sci. NC49

HEURAET, Hendrik van (1633-1660) Math. CDZZ ZZ-6

HEURNE, Jan van (1543-1601) Med. CDZZ ZZ-6

HEVELIUS, Johannes (1611-1687) Astron. ABES ABET BEOS CDZZ IEAS ZZ-6

HEVESEY, George Von (1885-1966) Chem. ABES ABET BDOS BEOS CDZZ CB59 DODR HSSO MHM1 MHSE NPWC RS13 ZZ-6

HEWETT, Donnel F. (1881-1971) Geol. BM44 MHM1 MHSE

HEWETT, Edgar L. (1865-1946) Archaeol. NCSC

HEWISH, Antony (1924-) Astron. ABET BEOS IEAS MHSE POSW

HEWITSON, William C. (1806-1878) Nat. Hist. DNB

HEWITT, Charles G. (1885-1920) Entom. AMEM

HEWITT, John T. (1868-1954) Chem. RS-1

HEWITT, Oliver H. (1916-) Ornith. LACC

HEWITT, Peter C. (1861-1921) Invent. DAB

HEWSON, William (1739-1774) Med. BHMT CDZZ DNB ZZ-6

HEY, William (1736-1819) Med. BHMT

HEYERDAHL, Thor (1914-) Exp.; Anthro. CB47 CB72

HEYMANS, Corneille J. (1892-1968) Med. BHMT CB72

HEYN, Emil (1867-1922) Metal. CDZZ ZZ-6

HEYNITZ, Friedrich A. von (1725-1802) Mng. CDZZ ZZ-6

HEYROVSKY, Jaroslav (1890-1967) Electrochem. ABES ABET BDOS BEOS CB61 CDZZ MHM1 MHSE PAW2 RS13 ZZ-6

HEYTESBURY, William (fl. c.1335) Math. CDZZ ZZ-6

HIARNE, Urban (1641-1724) Med.; Chem. CDZZ ZZ-6

HIBBARD, Claude W. (1905-1973) Paleon. NC57

HIBBERT, Harold (1877-1945) Chem. BM32 NC33

HIBBS, Albert R. (1924-) Phys. MOS5

HICETAS OF SYRACUSE (fl. 400s B.C.) Astron. CDZZ ZZ-6

HICKEY, Joseph J. (1907-) Zool. LACC

HICKLING, Henry G. (1883-1954) Geol. RS-2

HICKS, Henry (1837-1899) Geol. DNB1

HICKS, John B. (1823-1897) Med. BHMT

HIGGINS, Bryan (1737-1818) Chem. CDZZ ZZ-6

HIGGINS, William (1763-1825) Chem. BDOS BEOS CDZZ DNB ZZ-6

HIGGINSON, Francis (1587-1630) Ornith. HAOA

HIGHMORE, Nathaniel (1613-1685) Anat.; Med. CDZZ ZZ-6

HIGINBOTHAM, William A. (1910-) Phys. CB47

HILBERT, David (1862-1943) Math. ABES ABET BEOS CDZZ HSSO ZZ-6

HILDEBRAND, Joel H. (1881-1983) Chem. BEOS CB55 MHM1 MHSE

HILDEBRANDT, Georg F. (1764-1816) Chem. CDZZ ZZ-6

HILDEGARD OF BINGEN (1098-1179) Cosmol.; Med. CDZZ WIWM ZZ-6

HILDITCH, Thomas P. (1886-1965) Chem. BDOS BEOS CDZZ RS12 ZZ-6

HILDRITH, Samuel P. (1783-1863) Nat. Hist. ASJD BIOD DAB NC-9

HILE, Ralph O. (1904-) Biol. LACC

HILGARD, Ernest R. (1904-) Psych. MHM1 MHSE

HILGARD, Eugene W. (1833-1916) Geol.; Agr. BM-9

HILGARD, Julius E. (1825-1890) Geophys. BIOD BM-3 NC10

HILL, Archibald V. (1886-1977) Physiol. ABES ABET BEOS

HILL, Arthur J. (1888-) Chem. NCSF

HILL, Carl M. (1908-) Chem. SBPY

HILL, Geoffrey T. (1895-1956) Aero. ICFW

HILL, George W. (1838-1914) Math.; Astron. BM-8 CDZZ DAB NC13 ZZ-6

HILL, Henry A. (1915-1979) Chem. SBPY

HILL, Henry B. (1849-1903) Chem. BIOD BM-5 DAB

HILL, Herbert M. (1856-1927) Chem. NC20

HILL, James P. (1873-1954) Zool. BEOS RS-1

HILL, John (1707-1775) Bot. CDZZ ZZ-6

HILL, Justina H. (1893-) Bact. CB41

HILL, Leonard E. (1866-1952) Physiol. DNB7

HILL, Lester S. (1890-1961) Math. CDZZ ZZ-6

HILL, Maurice N. (1919-1966) Ocean. RS13

HILL, Robert R. (1885-) Agr. LACC

HILL, Terrell L. (1917-) Chem.; Biophys. MHSE

HILL, Thomas (1818-1891) Math.; Astron. BIOD DAB

HILL, Walter N. (1846-1884) Chem. NC12

HILL, William L. (1899-1964) Chem. NC50

HILLARY, Edmund P. (1919-) Exp. ABES ABET

HILLARY, William (1700-1763) Med. BHMT

HILLE, Einar (1894-) Math. MHM1 MHSE

HILLEBRAND, William F. (1853-1925) Chem. ACCE BM12 DAB NC14

HILLEMAN, Maurice (1919-) Med. MFIR

HILLIER, James (1915-) Phys. ABES ABET BEOS MHM2 MHSE NCSK

HILLMANN, Fred H. (1863-1954) Bot.; Entom. BNBR

HILLS, Franklin G. (1868-1941) Chem. NC30

HILTON, Robert W. (1873-1923) Chem. NC28

HIMES, Charles F. (1838-1918) Photo. DAB

HINCKS, Thomas (1818-1899) Zool. DNB1

HIND, Henry Y. (1823-1908) Geol. DNB2

HIND, John (1796-1866) Math. DNB

HIND, John R. (1823-1895) Astron. CDZZ DNB1 ZZ-6

HINDENBURG, Carl F. (1741-1808) Math. CDZZ ZZ-6

HINDES, Earle P. (1888-1962) Geol. NC50

HINDLE, Edward (1886-1973) Zool. RS20

HINDS, John I. (1847-1921) Chem. NC26

HINDS, Warren E. (1876-1936) Entom. AMEM NC29

HINKS, Arthur R. (1873-1945) Astron. DNB6

HINSHELWOOD, Cyril N. (1897-1967) Chem. ABES
ABET BDOS BEOS CB57 CDZZ MHM1 MHSE
RS19 ZZ-6

HINTON, Christopher, Baron of Bankside (1901-)
Engr. ABES ABET MHM1 MHSE NBPS SGEC

HINTON, Howard E. (1912-1977) Entom. RS24

HINTON, Martin A. (1883-1961) Zool. RS-9

HINTON, Walter (1889-1981) Aero. AO81

HIPPARCHUS OF NICAEA (fl. 162 B.C.-127 B.C.)
Astron. ABES ABET AMST ASTR BDOS BEOS
CDZZ FASP IEAS ZZXV

HIPPIAS OF ELIS (fl. 400 B.C.) Philos.; Math. CDZZ
ZZ-6

HIPPOCRATES OF CHIOS (fl. c.450 B.C.-400 B.C.)
Math.; Astron. CDZZ ZZ-6

HIPPOCRATES OF COS (460 B.C.-370 B.C.) Med.
ABES ABET BDOS BEOS BHMT CDZZ GISA
LISD MMMA SAIF SMIL TOWS ZZ-6

HIRAYAMA, Kiyotsugu (1874-1943) Astrophys. CDZZ
ZZ-6

HIRN, Gustave A. (1815-1890) Phys. CDZZ ZZ-6

HIRONAKA, Heisuke (1931-) Math. MHSE

HIRSCH, Peter B. (1925-) Metal. BEOS

HIRSCHFELDER, Joseph O. (1911-) Chem.; Phys.
CB50 MHM2 MHSE

HIRSH, Leonard F. (1901-1962) Chem. Engr. NC50

HIRST, Edmund L. (1898-1975) Chem. BEOS MHM1
MHSE RS22

HIRST, Thomas A. (1830-1892) Math. DNB1

HIRST, William (fl. 1760s) Astron. DNB

HIRSZFELD, Ludwig (1884-1954) Bact. CDZZ ZZ-6

HIS, Wilhelm (1831-1904) Anat.; Med. BDOS BEOS
BHMT CDZZ ZZ-6

HIS, Wilhelm Jr. (1863-1934) Med. BHMT

HISAW, Frederick L. (1891-1972) Zool. MHM2 MHSE

HISINGER, Wilhelm (1766-1852) Chem.; Mineral.
ABES ABET BEOS CDZZ ZZ-6

HITCH, Emmet F. (1882-1956) Chem. NC42

HITCHCOCK, Albert S. (1865-1935) Bot. CDZZ
MABH NC26 ZZXV

HITCHCOCK, Edward (1793-1864) Geol. ASJD
BIOD BM-1 BSIL CDZZ DAB MADC YSMS
ZZ-6

HITCHCOCK, Edward (1828-1911) Physiol. DAB
NC13

HITCHCOCK, Ethan A. (1798-1870) Alch. ACCE

HITCHCOCK, Lauren B. (1900-1972) Chem. Engr.
ACCE

HITCHCOCK, Romyn (1851-1923) Chem.; Bot. NC19

HITCHENS, Arthur P. (1877-1949) Bact. NC36

HITCHINGS, Edson F. (1853-1937) Entom. NC30

HITCHINGS, George H. (1905-) Med. BEOS MFIR

HITCHINS, Malachy (1741-1908) Astron. DNB

HITTORF, Johann W. (1824-1914) Chem.; Phys. ABES
ABET BDOS BEOS CDZZ ZZ-6

HITZIG, Eduard (1838-1907) Psychiat. ABET BDOS
BEOS CDZZ ZZ-6

HJELM, Peter J. (1746-1813) Mineral. ABES ABET
BEOS

HJORT, Johan (1869-1948) Mar. Biol. CDZZ EXSG
ZZ-6

HOADLEY, Leigh (1895-1975) Embryol. NC58

HOADLY, Benjamin (1706-1757) Med. BHMT

HOAGLAND, Charles L. (1907-1946) Biochem. DAB4

HOAGLAND, Dennis R. (1884-1949) Bot. BM29
CDZZ DAB4 CDZZ MABH ZZ-6

HOAGLAND, Mahlon B. (1921-) Biochem. ABES ABET BEOS MHSE

HOAR, William S. (1913-) Zool. MHM1 MHSE

HOBBES, Thomas (1588-1679) Math.; Opt. CDZZ ZZ-6

HOBBS, Perry L. (1861-1912) Chem. NC16

HOBSON, Edward (1782-1830) Bot. DNB

HOBSON, Ernest W. (1856-1933) Math. CDZZ DNB5 ZZ-6

HOCHBAUM, H. Albert (1911-) Ornith. DGMT

HOCKENSMITH, Roy D. (1905-) Soil Sci. LACC

HODGE, William V. (1903-1975) Math. BEOS MHM1 MHSE RS22

HODGES, Nathaniel (1629-1688) Med. BHMT

HODGKIN, Alan L. (1914-) Biophys. ABES ABET BEOS MHM1 MHSE

HODGKIN, Dorothy C. (1910-) Chem. ABES ABET BEOS COBC IDWB LLWO MHM1 MHSE WPSH

HODGKIN, Thomas (1798-1866) Med. BEOS BHMT

HODGKINSON, Eaton (1789-1861) Math.; Engr. BDOS CDZZ GE-1 ZZ-6

HODGKINSON, George C. (1816-1880) Meteor. DNB

HODGSON, Joseph (1788-1869) Med. BHMT

HODIERNA, Gionbatista SEE ODIERNA, Gionbatista

HOE, Richard M. (1812-1886) Invent. BDOS WAMB

HOEK, Martinus (1834-1873) Astron. CDZZ ZZ-6

HOENE-WRONSKI, Jozef M. (1776-1853) Philos.; Math. CDZZ ZZXV

HOEVEN, Jan van der (1801-1868) Anat.; Nat. Hist. CDZZ ZZ-6

HOFF, Karl E. von (1771-1837) Geol.; Geog. CDZZ ZZ-6

HOFF, Nicholas J. (1906-) Aero. MHSE

HOFFMAN, Joseph G. (1909-) Biophys. CB58

HOFFMAN, Samuel K. (1902-) Rocket. MHM1 MHSE

HOFFMANN, Friedrich (1660-1742) Med.; Chem. BDOS BEOS CDZZ ZZ-6

HOFFMANN, Hans (1929-) Math. IMMO

HOFFMANN, Roald (1937-) Chem. BEOS MHSE

HOFMANN, August W. von (1818-1892) Chem. ABES ABET BDOS BEOS CDZZ GRCH HSSO ZZ-6

HOFMANN, Klaus H. (1911-) Biochem. CB61

HOFMEISTER, Wilhelm F. (1824-1877) Bot. ABET BDOS BEOS CDZZ ZZ-6

HOFSTADTER, Robert (1915-) Phys. ABES ABET AMJB BEOS CB62 MHM1 MHSE POSW WAMB

HOGARTH, William (1697-1764) Med. BHMT

HOGBEN, Lancelot T. (1895-1975) Biol.; Sci Writ. CB41 RS24

HOGG, John (1800-1869) Nat. Hist. DNB

HOHENHEIM, Paracelsus von SEE PARACELSUS

HOKE, Calm M. (1887-1952) Chem.; Mineral. ACCE

HOLADAY, William M. (1901-) Engr. CB58

HOLBACH, Paul H. d' (1723-1789) Philos. of Sci. CDZZ ZZ-6

HOLBORN, Ludwig C. (1860-1926) Phys. CDZZ ZZ-6

HOLBROOK, John E. (1794-1871) Zool. BIOD BM-5 CDZZ DAB NHAH ZZXV

HOLBROOK, Stewart H. (1893-1964) Cons. LACC

HOLCOMBE, Amasa (1787-1873) Instr. NC-3

HOLDEN, Edward S. (1846-1914) Astron. BM-8 CDZZ DAB NC-7 ZZ-6

HOLDEN, Moses (1777-1864) Astron. DNB

HOLDER, Charles F. (1851-1915) Nat. Hist. DAB

HOLDER, Douglas W. (1923-1977) Aero. RS24

HOLDER, Joseph B. (1824-1888) Zool. BIOD DAB

HOLDER, Otto L. (1859-1937) Math. CDZZ ZZ-6

HOLE, Winston L. (1910-1970) Phys. NC55

HOLGATE, Thomas F. (1859-1945) Math. NCSE

HOLL, Maximilian SEE HELL, Maximilian

HOLLAENDER, Alexander (1898-) Biophys. MHM2 MHSE

HOLLAND, James P. (1934-) Med. SBPY

HOLLAND, John P. (1840-1914) Invent. AMIH EXDC WAMB

HOLLAND, Ray P. (1884-1973) Cons. NC58

HOLLAND, Thomas H. (1868-1947) Geol. DNB6

HOLLAND, William J. (1848-1932) Entom. AMEM DAB1 NC13

HOLLANDER, Franklin (1899-1966) Physiol. NC51

HOLLERITH, Herman (1860-1929) Invent. TINA

HOLLEY, Robert W. (1922-) Biochem. ABES ABET BEOS CB67 MHM2 MHSE WAMB

HOLLICK, Charles A. (1857-1933) Geol.; Paleon. DAB1 NC24

HOLLINGSWORTH, Dorothy F. (1916-) Med. COBC

HOLLINGWORTH, Leta S. (1886-1939) Psych. IDWB WPSH

HOLLISTER, Ned (1876-1924) Zool. NC20

HOLLOMON, J. Herbert (1919-) Metal. CB64

HOLLOWAY, James K. (1900-1964) Entom. AMEM

HOLLY, William G. (1899-) Chem. SBPY

HOLM, Herman T. (1854-1932) Bot. MABH

HOLMBOE, Bernt M. (1795-1850) Math. CDZZ ZZ-6

HOLMES, Arthur (1890-1965) Geol.; Geophys. ABET BDOS BEOS CDZZ MHM1 MHSE RS12 ZZ-6

HOLMES, D. Brainerd (1921-) Engr. CB63

HOLMES, Francis S. (1815-1882) Geol.; Nat. Hist. BIOD

HOLMES, Gordon M. (1876-1965) Med. BHMT RS12

HOLMES, Harry N. (1879-1958) Chem. ACCE

HOLMES, Joseph A. (1859-1915) Forest. LACC

HOLMES, Oliver W. (1809-1894) Med. ABES ABET BDOS BEOS BHMT HSSO LISD

HOLMES, William H. (1846-1933) Anthro.; Geol. BM17 SASH

HOLMGREN, Arthur H. (1912-) Bot. BNBR

HOLMGREN, Frithiof (1831-1897) Physiol. CDZZ ZZ-6

HOLROYD, Ronald (1904-1973) Chem. RS20

HOLTEDAHL, Olaf (1885-1975) Geol. MHM2 MHSE RS22

HOLTFRETER, Johannes F. (1901-) Zool. MHM2 MHSE

HOLTON, Edward C. (1866-1934) Chem. NCSD

HOLWELL, John (1649-1686) Math. DNB

HOMBERG, Wilhelm (1652-1715) Chem. CDZZ ZZ-6

HOME, Everard (1756-1832) Med. CDZZ ZZ-6

HOME, Francis (1719-1813) Med. BHMT

HONDA, Kotaro (1870-1954) Phys. ABES ABET BEOS CDZZ ZZ-6

HONIGSCHMID, Otto (1878-1945) Chem. CDZZ HSSO ZZ-6

HOOD, J. Douglas (1889-) Entom. NCSD

HOOD, Thomas (fl. 1582-1598) Math. DNB

HOOKE, Robert (1635-1703) Phys. ABES ABET ANHD BDOS BEOS BHMT CDZZ DCPW FHUA FNEC GE-1 HLSM LISD LSCS PHLS TOWS ZZ-6

HOOKER, Elon H. (1869-1938) Engr.; Chem. ACCE

HOOKER, Davenport (1887-1965) Anat.; Embryol. NC58

HOOKER, Joseph D. (1817-1911) Bot. BDOS BEOS CDZZ DARR DNB2 GASJ ZZ-6

HOOKER, Samuel C. (1864-1935) Chem. ACCE
DAB1

HOOKER, William J. (1785-1865) Bot. BEOS CDZZ
ZZ-6

HOOKER, Worthington (1806-1867) Sci. Writ. ACCE

HOOTON, Earnest A. (1887-1954) Anthro. CB40
DAB5 NC40 WAMB

HOOVER, Charles R. (1885-1942) Chem. NC31

HOOVER, Herbert C. (1874-1964) Engr. BM39

HOPE, Frederick W. (1797-1862) Entom. DNB

HOPE, James (1801-1841) Med. BEOS BHMT

HOPE, Thomas C. (1766-1844) Chem. BDOS BEOS
CDZZ ZZ-6

HOPF, Heinz (1894-1971) Math. CDZZ ZZ-6

HOPFIELD, John J. (1933-) Phys.; Biol. MHSE

HOPKE, Theodore M. (1858-1940) Chem. NC30

HOPKINS, Albert (1807-1872) Astron. NC-6

HOPKINS, Andrew D. (1857-1948) Entom. AMEM
NC13 NC41

HOPKINS, B. Smith (1873-1952) Chem. ACCE

HOPKINS, Cyril G. (1868-1919) Chem. ACCE

HOPKINS, Frederick G. (1861-1947) Biochem. ABES
ABET BDOS BEOS BHMT CDZZ DNB6 GDSP
ZZ-6

HOPKINS, Lemuel (1750-1801) Med. BHMT

HOPKINS, William (1793-1866) Geol.; Math. CDZZ
DNB ZZ-6

HOPKINSON, Bertram (1874-1918) Phys. DNB3

HOPKINSON, John (1849-1898) Phys. CDZZ DNB1
ZZ-6

HOPPE-SEYLER, Felix I. (1825-1895) Biochem.
ABET BEOS CDZZ ZZ-6

HOPPER, Grace M. (1906-) Math.; Comp. HOPL
IDWB

HORBACZEWSKI, Jan (1854-1942) Biochem. CDZZ
ZZ-6

HORECKER, Bernard L. (1914-) Biochem. MHM2
MHSE

HORN, David W. (1877-1962) Chem. NC49

HORN, George H. (1840-1897) Entom. AMEM BIOD
CDZZ DAB NC-7 ZZ-6

HORN D'ARTURO, Guido (1879-1967) Astron. CDZZ
ZZ-6

HORNADAY, Fred E. (1900-) Forest. LACC

HORNADAY, William T. (1854-1937) Zool. DAB2
LACC

HORNBLOWER, Jonathan (1717-1780) Engr. DNB
GE-1

HORNE, Johannes van (1621-1670) Anat. CDZZ
ZZ-6

HORNE, William D. (1865-1960) Chem. Engr. ACCE

HORNEMANN, Jens W. (1770-1841) Bot. BWCL
WFBG

HORNER, Johan F. (1831-1886) Med. BHMT

HORNER, Leonard (1785-1864) Geol. CDZZ DNB
ZZ-6

HORNER, William E. (1793-1853) Anat. BHMT BIOD

HORNER, William G. (1786-1837) Math. CDZZ DNB
ZZ-6

HORNEY, Karen D. (1885-1952) Psych. NAWM

HORNIG, Donald F. (1920-) Chem. CB64 MHM2
MHSE

HORNSBY, Thomas (1733-1810) Astron. CDZZ DNB
ZZ-6

HORNUNG, John A. (1872-1930) Nat. Hist. NC23

HORREBOW, Christian (1718-1776) Astron. CDZZ
ZZ-6

HORREBOW, Peder N. (1679-1764) Astron. CDZZ
ZZ-6

HORROCKS, Jeremiah (1618-1641) Astron. ABES
ABET BEOS CDZZ DNB SLOR ZZ-6

HORSBURGH, James (1762-1836) Hydrol. DNB

HORSFALL, Frank L. (1906-1971) Med. BM50

HORSFALL, James G. (1905-) Bot. BEOS MHM2
MHSE

HORSFIELD, Thomas (1773-1859) Nat. Hist. BIOD
DAB DNB

HORSFORD, Eben N. (1818-1893) Chem. ACCE
BIOD CDZZ DAB ZZ-6

HORSLEY, Victor A. (1857-1916) Med. BHMT CDZZ
ZZ-6

HORSTADIUS, Sven O. (1898-) Zool. MHM2 MHSE

HORSTMANN, August F. (1842-1929) Chem. CDZZ
ZZ-6

HORTEN, Reimar (1913-) Aero. ICFW

HORTEN, Walter (1915-) Aero. ICFW

HORTENSIUS, Martinus (1605-1639) Astron. CDZZ
ZZ-6

HORTON, Frank (1878-1957) Phys. RS-4

HOSACK, David (1769-1835) Med.; Bot. BHMT
CDZZ ZZ-6

HOSEMANN SEE OSIANDER, Andreas

HOSKINS, Leandor M. (1860-1937) Math. NC28

HOSKINS, William (1862-1934) Chem. ACCE

HOSMER, Ralph S. (1874-1963) Forest. LACC

HOTCHKISS, Rollin D. (1911-) Biol. MHM2 MHSE

HOTTEL, Hoyt C. (1903-) Chem. Engr. HCEF

HOUEL, Guillaume J. (1823-1886) Math.; Astron.
CDZZ ZZ-6

HOUGH, Franklin B. (1822-1885) Forest.; Bot. BIOD
EAFC LACC

HOUGH, George W. (1836-1909) Astron. CDZZ DAB
NC-8 ZZ-6

HOUGH, Romeyn B. (1857-1924) Nat. Hist. NC20

HOUGH, Sydney S. (1870-1923) Astron. AROW

HOUGHTEN, Ferry C. (1888-1945) Phys. NC32

HOUGHTON, Douglass (1809-1845) Geol. ACCE
BIOD CDZZ ZZ-6

HOUNSFIELD, Godfrey N. (1919-) Elec. Engr.
BEOS CB80 SOT3

HOUSE, Herbert O. (1929-) Chem. MHSE

HOUSE, Royal E. (1814-1895) Invent. EETD WAMB

HOUSSAY, Bernardo A. (1887-1971) Physiol. ABES
ABET BEOS CB48 CDZZ MHM1 MHSE RS20
ZZXV

HOUSTON, Edwin J. (1847-1914) Engr. NC13 TPAE

HOUSTON, John (1802-1845) Anat. DNB

HOUSTON, William V. (1900-1968) Phys. BM44
MHM2 MHSE

HOVGAARD, William (1857-1950) Engr. BM36

HOWARD, Charles D. (1873-1944) Chem. NC34

HOWARD, Henry (1868-1951) Chem. Engr. DAB5

HOWARD, John (1726-1790) Med. BHMT

HOWARD, John (1753-1799) Math. DNB

HOWARD, Leland O. (1857-1950) Entom. AMEM
BM33 CDZZ DAB4 NC12 ZZ-6

HOWARD, Luke (1772-1864) Meteor. DNB

HOWARD, William G. (1887-1948) Forest. LACC

HOWE, Elias (1819-1867) Invent. ABES ABET AMIH
ASIW BDOS HFGA INYG MPIP SAIF WAMB

HOWE, Harrison E. (1881-1942) Chem. Engr. ACCE

HOWE, Herbert A. (1858-1926) Astron. DAB NC20

HOWE, James L. (1859-1955) Chem. ACCE CDZZ
NC-9 NC47 ZZ-6

HOWE, Marshall A. (1867-1936) Bot. BM19 MABH
NCSA

HOWE, Sidney (1928-) Cons. LACC

HOWE, William (1620-1656) Bot. DNB

HOWELL, John T. (1903-) Bot. BNBR

HOWELL, Thomas J. (1842-1912) Bot. DAB MABH

HOWELL, Wallace E. (1914-) Meteor. CB50

HOWELL, William H. (1860-1945) Physiol. BM26 CDZZ NCSF ZZ-6

HOWELLS, William W. (1908-) Anthro. MHM1 MHSE

HOWES, Edward (fl. 1650) Math. DNB

HOWES, Thomas G. (1853-1905) Zool. DNB2

HOWITT, Alfred W. (1830-1908) Anthro. DNB2

HOY, Philo R. (1816-1892) Entom. NC15

HOYLE, Fred (1915-) Astron. ABES ABET BEOS CB60 IEAS MHM2 MHSE PBTS

HOYT, Minerva L. (1866-1945) Cons. NC35

HOYT, William H. (1855-1929) Ornith. NC23

HRDLICKA, Ales (1869-1943) Anthro. BM23 CB41 CDZZ DAB3 WAMB ZZ-6

HSUN MAO (fl. 50) Engr. GE-1

HUBACHEK, Frank B. (1894-) Cons. LACC

HUBBARD, Bernard (1888-1962) Exp. CB43

HUBBARD, Henry G. (1850-1899) Entom. AMEM BIOD DAB

HUBBARD, John (1931-1980) Phys.; Math. AO80

HUBBARD, John C. (1879-1954) Phys. NC44

HUBBARD, Joseph S. (1823-1863) Astron. BIOD BM-1 DAB NC-9

HUBBARD, Oliver P. (1809-1900) Geol.; Mineral. BIOD NC-9

HUBBARD, Philip G. (1921-) Elec. Engr. SBPY

HUBBARD, Prevost (1881-1971) Invent. NC56

HUBBERT, Marion K. (1903-) Geol.; Geophys. MHM2 MHSE

HUBBLE, Edwin P. (1889-1953) Astron.; Cosmol. ABES ABET BDOS BEOS BM41 CDZZ DAB5 IEAS MSAJ NC42 WAMB ZZ-6

HUBBS, Carl L. (1894-1979) Biol. LACC MHM2 MHSE

HUBEL, David H. (1926-) Physiol. BEOS

HUBER, Gotthelf C. (1865-1934) Anat. DAB1

HUBER, Johann J. (1707-1778) Anat.; Bot. CDZZ ZZ-6

HUBER, Maksymilian T. (1872-1950) Engr. CDZZ ZZ-6

HUBODA, Michael (1913-) Cons. LACC

HUBRECHT, Ambrosius A. (1853-1915) Zool.; Embryol. CDZZ ZZ-6

HUCKEL, Erich (1896-1980) Phys. RS28

HUDDART, Joseph (1741-1816) Hydrol. DNB

HUDDE, Jan (1628-1704) Math. CDZZ ZZ-6

HUDLESTON, Wilfred (1828-1909) Geol. DNB2

HUDSON, Charles T. (1828-1903) Nat. Hist. DNB2

HUDSON, Claude S. (1881-1952) Chem. ACCE BM32 CDZZ DAB5 GRCH HSSO NC40 ZZ-6

HUDSON, John W. (1905-1972) Biol. NC57

HUDSON, Robert G. (1895-1965) Geol.; Mineral. RS12

HUDSON, William (1733-1793) Bot. CDZZ DNB ZZ-6

HUDSON, William (1896-1978) Engr. RS25

HUDSON, William H. (1841-1922) Nat. Hist. DNB4

HUEBNER, Robert J. (1914-) Med. CB68 MFIR

HUFNAGEL, Leon (1893-1933) Astron. CDZZ ZZ-6

HUGGETT, Arthur (1897-1968) Physiol. RS16

HUGGINS, Charles B. (1901-) Med. ABES ABET BEOS MHM1 MHSE PAW2

HUGGINS, L. Gale (1900-1971) Invent. NC56

HUGGINS, Lady SEE LINDSAY, Margaret

HUGGINS, William (1824-1910) Astrophys. ABES
ABET BDOS BEOS CDZZ DNB2 ZZ-6

HUGH OF ST. VICTOR (d. 1141) Math. CDZZ ZZ-6

HUGHES, Donald J. (1915-1960) Phys. NC45

HUGHES, Edward D. (1906-1963) Chem. RS10

HUGHES, John R. (1928-) Physiol. BEOS

HUGHES, Josiah (1884-1965) Biochem. NC53

HUGONIOT, Pierre H. (1851-1887) Phys. CDZZ ZZ-6

HUISGEN, Rolf (1920-) Chem. BEOS MHM2 MHSE

HUIZENGA, John R. (1921-) Chem. MHM2 MHSE

HULETT, George A. (1867-1955) Chem. BM34 NC44

HULL, Albert W. (1880-1966) Phys. BM41 CDZZ
EETD NC53 ZZ-6

HULL, Clark L. (1884-1952) Psych. BM33

HULST, George D. (1846-1900) Entom. AMEM

HULST, Hendrik van de SEE VAN DE HULST, Hendrik

HUMASON, Milton L. (1891-1972) Astron. ABES
ABET BEOS

HUMBERT, Marie G. (1859-1921) Math. CDZZ ZZ-6

HUMBERT, Pierre (1891-1953) Math. CDZZ ZZ-6

HUMBOLDT, Alexander von (1769-1859) Geol. ABES
ABET ABFC BDOS BEOS CDZZ EQSA LISD
NEXB SOAC THOG TOWS ZZ-6

HUME, David (1711-1776) Philos. BEOS CDZZ ZZ-6

HUME-ROTHERY, William (1899-1968) Metal.;
Chem. CDZZ RS15 ZZ-6

HUMPHREY, Harry B. (1873-1955) Bot. MABH

HUMPHREY, James E. (1861-1897) Bot. MABH

HUMPHREYS, Andrew A. (1810-1883) Engr. BIOD
BM-2 DAB

HUMPHREYS, William J. (1862-1949) Phys.; Meteor.
DAB4

HUMPHRY, George M. (1820-1896) Med. BHMT

HUNAYN ibn IGHAQ al-IBADI, Abu Zayd (808-873)
Med. SCIN CDZZ ZZXV

HUND, August (1887-1952) Engr.; Phys. NC41

HUNDT, Magnus (1449-1519) Anat. CDZZ ZZ-6

HUNGERFORD, Herbert B. (1885-1963) Entom.
AMEM NC50 NCSH

HUNSAKER, Jerome C. (1886-) Aero. BEOS ICFW
MHM1 MHSE WAMB

HUNT, Edward B. (1822-1863) Phys. BIOD BM-3

HUNT, Franklin L. (1883-) Phys. NCSA

HUNT, Frederick V. (1905-1972) Phys. MHM2 MHSE

HUNT, Harriot K. (1805-1875) Med. WIWM

HUNT, James (1833-1869) Anthro. CDZZ ZZ-6

HUNT, Mary H. (1831-1906) Chem. ACCE

HUNT, Reid (1870-1948) Physiol. BM26

HUNT, Robert (1807-1887) Sci. Writ. DNB

HUNT, Thomas S. (1826-1892) Chem.; Geol. ACCE
BIOD BM15 CDZZ DAB NC-3 ZZ-6

HUNTER, A. Stuart (1897-1958) Chem. NC46

HUNTER, Howard L. (1904-1975) Chem. NC61

HUNTER, John (1728-1793) Med. BDOS BEOS BHMT
CDZZ DNB MMMA SAIF ZZ-6

HUNTER, Matthew A. (1878-1961) Electrochem.
ACCE

HUNTER, Philip V. (1883-1956) Elec. Engr. DNB7

HUNTER, William (1718-1783) Anat. BEOS BHMT
CDZZ DNB ZZ-6

HUNTINGTON, Edward V. (1874-1952) Math. CDZZ
DAB5 ZZ-6

HUNTINGTON, George (1850-1916) Med. BHMT

HUNTINGTON, George S. (1861-1927) Med. BHMT BM18

HUNTRESS, Ernest H. (1898-1970) Chem. ACCE

HUNTSMAN, Archibald G. (1883-1973) Biol. MHM1 MHSE

HUNTSMAN, Benjamin (1704-1776) Invent. BDOS GE-1

HURSTON, Zora N. (1901-1960) Anthro. DANB

HURTER, Ferdinand (1844-1898) Chem. BDOS BEOS

HURWITZ, Adolf (1859-1919) Math. CDZZ ZZ-6

HURWITZ, Henry Jr. (1918-) Phys. MHM1 MHSE

HUSCHKE, Emil (1797-1858) Anat.; Embryol. CDZZ ZZ-6

HUSSEY, Obed (1792-1859) Invent. BDOS DAB INYG WAMB

HUSSEY, William J. (1862-1926) Astron. CDZZ DAB ZZ-6

HUTCHINS, Thomas (1730-1789) Geog. BIOD

HUTCHINSON, Arthur (1866-1937) Mineral. DNB5

HUTCHINSON, George E. (1903-) Zool. BEOS MHM2 MHSE

HUTCHINSON, John (1811-1861) Physiol. CDZZ ZZ-6

HUTCHINSON, John (1884-1972) Bot. BEOS MHM2 MHSE RS21

HUTCHINSON, John I. (1867-1935) Math. NC26

HUTCHINSON, Jonathan (1828-1913) Med. BHMT

HUTTEN, Ulrich von (1488-1523) Med. BHMT

HUTTON, Charles (1737-1823) Math. CDZZ DNB ZZ-6

HUTTON, Frederick W. (1836-1905) Geol. DNB2

HUTTON, James (1726-1797) Geol.; Agr. ABES ABET BDOS BEOS CDZZ DNB HLSM LISD SIRC THOG ZZ-6

HUTTON, Robert F. (1921-) Biol. LACC

HUTTON, William (1798-1860) Geol. DNB

HUXHAM, John (1692-1768) Med. BHMT

HUXLEY, Andrew F. (1917-) Physiol. ABES ABET BEOS MHM1 MHSE

HUXLEY, Hugh E. (1924-) Biol. BEOS MHM2 MHSE

HUXLEY, Julian S. (1887-1975) Biol. BEOS CB42 CB63 MHM2 MHSE RS22

HUXLEY, Thomas H. (1825-1895) Zool.; Evol. ABES ABET ABFC BDOS BEOS CDZZ DARR DNB1 EQSA GASJ HLSM HNHB SGNF STYC TOWS ZZ-6

HUYGENS, Christiaan (1629-1695) Phys.; Astron. ABES ABET BDOS BEOS CDZZ DCPW EETD GE-1 HOSS IEAS LISD LSCS LSHS SAIF SMIL ZZ-6

HYATT, Alpheus (1838-1902) Zool.; Paleon. BIOD BM-6 CDZZ DAB NC-3 NC23 PHLS WAMB ZZ-6

HYATT, John W. (1837-1920) Invent. ABES ABET BDOS GASW

HYDE, H. van Zile (1906-) Med. CB60

HYDE, Ida H. (1857-1945) Physiol. NAW

HYDE, Jesse E. (1884-1943) Zool. NC32

HYDE, Roscoe R. (1884-1943) Zool. NC32

HYER, Robert S. (1860-1929) Phys. DAB

HYLACOMYLUS SEE WALDSEEMULLER, Martin

HYLANDER, Clarence J. (1897-1964) Biol. NC53

HYLLERAAS, Egil A. (1898-1965) Phys. CDZZ ZZ-6

HYMAN, Libbie H. (1888-1969) Zool. BEOS NAWM

HYMERS, John (1803-1887) Math. DNB

HYNEK, Josef A. (1910-) Astrophys. CB68

HYPATIA (c.370-415) Math. ABET BEOS CDZZ IDWB MEQP WIMO ZZ-6

HYPSICLES OF ALEXANDRIA (fl. c.200 B.C.-150 B.C.) Math.; Astron. CDZZ ZZ-6

HYRTL, Joseph (1810-1894) Anat. BHMT CDZZ
ZZ-6

I

I HSING (682-727) Engr. GE-1 BEOS

IABLOTCHKOV, Pavel SEE JABLOCHKOFF, Pavel N.

IAMBLICHUS (c. 250-c.330) Philos. CDZZ ZZ-7

IBANEZ E IBANEZ DE IBERO, Carlos (1825-1891)
Geog. CDZZ ZZ-7

ibn For names beginning with ibn See last element of
name.

ibn al For names beginning with ibn al See last element
of name.

IBRAHIM ibn SINAN ibn THABIT (908-946) Math.;
Astron. CDZZ ZZ-7

IBRAHIM ibn YAQUB al-ISRAILI (fl. c.950-1000)
Geog. CDZZ ZZ-7

IDDINGS, Joseph P. (1857-1920) Geol. CDZZ NC15
ZZ-7

IDDLES, Harold A. (1896-1976) Chem. NC59

IDE, John J. (1890-1962) Aero. NC46

IDELSON, Naum I. (1885-1951) Astron. CDZZ ZZ-7

al-IDRISI, Abu abd Allah (1100-1166) Geog. CDZZ
ZZ-7

IERSALIMSKII, Nikolai D. (1901-) Microbiol. SMST

ILIFF, Neil A. (1916-) Chem. COBC

ILLICK, Joseph S. (1884-1967) Forest. LACC

ILLIGER, Carl (1775-1813) Ornith. ORNS

ILLING, Vincent C. (1890-1969) Geol. RS16

ILTIS, Hugo (1882-1952) Genet. NC42

IMAGE, Thomas (1772-1856) Geol. DNB

IMAMURA, Akitune (1870-1948) Seism. CDZZ ZZ-7

IMBRIE, John (1925-) Geol. BEOS

IMHOTEP (fl. 2980 B.C.-2950 B.C.) Engr.; Med.
ABES ABET

IMMS, Augustus D. (1880-1949) Entom. DNB6

IMOUTHES SEE IMHOTEP

IMSCHENETSKY, Alexander (1905-) Microbiol.
MHM2 MHSE SMST

INFELD, Leopold (1898-1968) Phys. CB41 CB63
CDZZ ZZ-7

ING, Harry R. (1899-1974) Chem. RS22

INGENHOUSZ, Jan (1730-1799) Med.; Phys. ABES
ABET BDOS BEOS CDZZ DNB ZZ-7

INGERSOLL, Ernest (1852-1946) Nat. Hist. NC-9

INGHAM, Albert E. (1900-1967) Math. RS14

INGLE, Dwight J. (1907-1978) Physiol. MHM2 MHSE

INGLIS, Claude C. (1883-1974) Engr. RS21

INGOLD, Christopher K. (1893-1970) Chem. BEOS
COBC MHM1 MHSE RS18

INGRAM, Vernon M. (1924-) Biochem. BEOS

INGRASSIA, Giovanni F. (c.1510-1580) Med. CDZZ
ZZ-7

INNES, John (1739-1777) Anat. DNB

INNES, Robert T. (1861-1933) Astron. ABET CDZZ
ZZ-7

INO, Tadataka (1745-1818) Astron. CDZZ ZZ-7

IOFFE, Abram F. (1880-1960) Phys. CDZZ ZZXV

IPATIEFF, Vladimir N. (1867-1952) Chem. ABES
ABET ACCE BDOS BEOS BM47 CDZZ GRCH
NCSE ZZ-7

IRINYI, Janos (1817-1895) Chem. CDZZ ZZ-7

IRVINE, Alexander (1793-1873) Bot. DNB

IRVINE, James C. (1877-1952) Chem. BDOS BEOS

IRVINE, William (1743-1789) Chem. DNB

IRVING, Harry M. (1905-) Chem. COBC

IRVING, Roland D. (1847-1888) Geol.; Mng. BIOD

ISAAC ISRAELI (fl. c.900) Med. CDZZ ZZ-7

ISAACA, Susan (1885-1948) Psych. IDWB

ISAACS, Alick (1921-1967) Virol. BDOS BEOS
RS13

ISAACS, Charles E. (1811-1860) Med. CDZZ ZZ-7

ISELIN, Columbus O. (1904-1971) Ocean. CB48
MHM2 MHSE

ISERMANN, Samuel (1878-1949) Chem. ACCE

ISHAQ ibn HUNAYN, Abu Yaqub (d. 910/1) Med.
CDZZ ZZ-7

ISHIWARA, Jun (1881-1947) Phys. CDZZ ZZ-7

ISHIZAKA, Kimishige (1925-) Immunol. MHSE

ISHLINSKII, Aleksandr Y. (1913-) Math.; Phys.
SMST

ISIDORE OF SEVILLE (c.560-636) Sci. Ed. ABES
BHMT CDZZ ZZ-7

ISIDOROS OF MILETOS (fl. c.500s) Math. CDZZ
GE-1 ZZ-7

ISSEL, Arturo (1842-1922) Geol. CDZZ ZZ-7

ITTNER, Martin H. (1870-1945) Chem. ACCE CB42

IVANOV, Ilya I. (1870-1932) Biol. ABET CDZZ ZZ-7

IVANOV, Leonid A. (1871-1962) Bot. SMST

IVANOV, Piotr P. (1878-1942) Embryol. CDZZ ZZ-7

IVANOVSKY, Dmitri I. (1864-1920) Bot.; Microbiol.
ABET BEOS CDZZ ZZ-7

IVERSON, Kenneth E. (1920-) Comp. HOPL

IVES, Herbert E. (1882-1953) Phys. BM29 CDZZ
NC41 ZZ-7

IVES, James E. (1865-1943) Phys. NC31 NCSA

IVLER, Daniel (1926-1976) Bact. NC59

IVORY, James (1765-1842) Math. CDZZ DNB ZZ-7

IVY, Andrew C. (1893-) Physiol. NCSE

IVY, John S. (1898-) Geol. NCSL

IWAHASHI, Zenbei (fl. 1790) Instr. GE-1

J

JABIR ibn AFLAH al-ISHBILI, Abu Muhammad (fl.
c.1130) Astron. CDZZ ZZ-7

JABIR ibn HAYYAN (fl. 790-810) Alch. ABES ABET
BDOS BEOS CDZZ GRCH SCIN ZZ-7

JABLOCHKOFF, Pavel N. (1847-1894) Invent. BDOS

JACCARD, Auguste (1833-1895) Geol.; Paleon. CDZZ
ZZ-7

JACK, Kenneth H. (1918-) Chem. COBC

JACKMAN, Alonzo (1808-1879) Math. NC16

JACKSON, Charles L. (1847-1935) Chem. BM37
NC11

JACKSON, Charles T. (1805-1880) Chem.; Geol.
ABES ABET ACCE ASJD BEOS BIOD CDZZ
DAB NC-3 TBSG WAMB ZZ-7

JACKSON, Dunham (1888-1946) Math. BM33 DAB4

JACKSON, Frederick G. (1881-1949) Chem. NC39

JACKSON, Frederick J. (1860-1929) Nat. Hist. DNB4

JACKSON, Herbert (1863-1936) Chem. DNB5

JACKSON, John (1887-1958) Chem. AROW RS-5

JACKSON, John B. (1806-1879) Anat. BIOD

JACKSON, John H. (1834-1911) Med. BEOS BHMT
CDZZ ZZ-7

JACKSON, Richard F. (1881-1943) Chem. NCSE

JACKSON, Robert T. (1861-1948) Paleon. NC42

JACKSON, Willis (1904-1970) Engr. RS17

JACOB, Edward (c.1710-1788) Nat. Hist. DNB

JACOB, Francois (1920-) Biol. ABES ABET BEOS CB66 EDCJ MHM1 MHSE

JACOB, William S. (1813-1862) Astron. DNB

JACOBI, Abraham (1830-1919) Med. BHMT

JACOBI, Karl G. (1804-1851) Math. ABET BDOS BEOS CDZZ ZZ-7

JACOBI, Mary P. (1842-1906) Med. IDWB WIWM

JACOBI, Moritz H. von (1801-1874) Phys. CDZZ ZZ-7

JACOBS, Eastman (1902-) Aero. ICFW

JACOBS, Elbridge (1873-1957) Geol. NC47

JACOBS, Michael (1808-1871) Meteor. BIOD

JACOBS, Morris B. (1905-1965) Chem. NC52

JACOBS, Walter A. (1883-1967) Biochem. ACCE BM51 CDZZ ZZXV

JACOBS, William S. (1772-1843) Chem. ACCE

JACOBSON, Leon O. (1911-) Med. CB62 MHM2 MHSE

JACOBSON, Nathan (1910-) Math. MHM2 MHSE

JACOBUS SYLVIUS SEE DUBOIS, Jacques

JACOBY, Harold (1865-1932) Astron. NC23

JACQUARD, Joseph M. (1752-1834) Invent. BDOS GE-1 SAIF

JACQUES, Harry E. (1880-1963) Entom. AMEM

JACQUET, Pierre A. (1906-1967) Chem. Engr. CDZZ ZZ-7

JACQUIN, Nikolaus J. (1727-1817) Bot.; Chem. CDZZ ZZ-7

JACQUINOT, Pierre (1910-) Phys. MHM2 MHSE

JADASSOHN, Joseph (1863-1936) Med. BHMT

JAEGER, Alphons O. (1886-1953) Chem. NC40

JAEGER, Edmund C. (1887-) Biol. BNBR

JAEGER, Ellsworth (1897-1962) Nat. Hist. NC52

JAEGER, Frans M. (1877-1945) Crystal.; Chem. CDZZ ZZ-7

JAEGER, Georg F. (1785-1866) Paleon.; Med. CDZZ ZZ-7

JAEGER, John C. (1907-1979) Geophys. RS28

JAEKEL, Otto (1863-1929) Paleon. CDZZ ZZ-7

JAFFE, Bernard (1896-) Sci. Writ. NCSF

JAGANNATHA (fl. c.1720-1740) Astron.; Math. CDZZ ZZ-7

JAGGAR, Thomas A. Jr. (1871-1953) Geol.; Volcan. CDZZ NCSC ZZ-7

al-JAHIZ, Abu Uthman (c.776-868/9) Nat. Hist. CDZZ ZZ-7

JAHN, Hans M. (1853-1906) Chem. CDZZ ZZ-7

JAI SINGH, Sawai (1686-1743) Instr. GE-1

JAMES OF VENICE (d. c.1148) Philos. CDZZ ZZ-7

JAMES, Charles (1880-1928) Chem. ACCE DAB NC26

JAMES, Edwin (1797-1861) Bot. BIOD DAB

JAMES, Harlean (1877-1969) Cons. LACC

JAMES, Joseph H. (1868-1948) Chem. NC36

JAMES, Reginald W. (1891-1964) Phys. RS11

JAMES, Thomas P. (1803-1882) Bot. BIOD DAB MABH

JAMES, William (1842-1910) Psych. ABES ABET CDZZ LISD PAW3 POPF ZZ-7

JAMES, William O. (1900-1978) Bot. RS25

JAMESON, James S. (1856-1888) Nat. Hist. DNB

JAMESON, Robert (1774-1854) Geol.; Nat. Hist. CDZZ DNB ZZ-7

JAMESON, William (1796-1873) Bot. DNB

JAMIESON, Walter A. (1890-1957) Biol. NCSD

JANISZEWSKI, Zygmunt (1888-1920) Math. CDZZ ZZ-7

JANOV, Arthur (1924-) Psych. CB80

JANSEN, Zacharias (1588-1631) Opt. BEOS CDZZ ZZ-7

JANSKY, C.M. (1895-1975) Engr. NC58

JANSKY, Karl G. (1905-1950) Elec. Engr. ABES ABET BEOS IEAS TPAE WAMB

JANSSEN, Pierre J. (1824-1907) Phys. ABES ABET BDOS BEOS CDZZ IEAS SLOR ZZ-7

JARDINE, James (1776-1858) Engr. DNB

JARDINE, James T. (1881-1954) Forest. LACC

JARS, Antoine G. (1732-1769) Mng.; Metal. CDZZ ZZ-7

JARVES, Deming (1790-1869) Chem. DAB

JASTROW, Robert (1925-) Phys. CB73

JAUREGG, Julius von SEE WAGNER VON JAUREGG, Julius

al-JAWHARI, al-Abbas ibn Said (fl. c.830) Math.; Astron. CDZZ ZZ-7

JAY, James M. (1927-) Bact. SBPY

JAYASIMHA (1686-1743) Astron. CDZZ ZZ-7

JAYNE, Harry W. (1857-1910) Chem. NC19

JAYNE, Horace F. (1859-1913) Zool.; Anat. DAB

JAYNES, Richard A. (1935-) Genet. CHUB

al-JAYYANI, Abu abd Allah Muhammad (c.989-c.1080) Math.; Astron. CDZZ ZZ-7

al-JAZARI, Badi al-Zaman (fl. 1206) Phys. CDZZ ZZXV

JEANS, James H. (1877-1946) Phys.; Astron. ABES ABET BDOS BEOS CB41 CDZZ DNB6 IEAS ZZ-7

JEAURAT, Edme S. (1724-1803) Astron. CDZZ ZZ-7

JEFFERIES, Richard (1848-1887) Nat. Hist. DNB

JEFFERSON, Geoffrey (1886-1961) Med. RS-7

JEFFERSON, Thomas (1743-1826) Agr.; Bot. ABES ABET BIOD CDZZ COAC DAB GOTH HFGA NC-3 TECH TINA ZZ-7

JEFFERY, George B. (1891-1957) Math. DNB7 RS-4

JEFFREY, Edward C. (1866-1952) Bot. CDZZ DAB5 FHUA NC39 ZZ-7

JEFFREY, Max L. (1887-1971) Invent. NC56

JEFFREYS, Harold (1891-) Astron.; Geophys. ABES ABET BEOS MHM1 MHSE

JEFFREYS, John G. (1809-1885) Mar. Biol. CDZZ DNB ZZ-7

JEFFRIES, John (1744-1819) Aero.; Meteor. BIOD DAB YSMS

JEFFRIES, Zay (1888-1965) Metal. CDZZ ZZ-7

JEMISON, George M. (1908-) Forest. LACC

JENCKS, William P. (1927-) Biochem. MHSE

JENKIN, Henry C. (1833-1885) Engr. CDZZ DNB ZZ-7

JENKINS, C. Francis (1867-1934) Invent. AMIH

JENKINS, Edward H. (1850-1931) Chem. ACCE

JENKINS, Glenn L. (1898-) Chem. NCSJ

JENKINS, Robert M. (1923-) Biol. LACC

JENKINSON, John W. (1871-1915) Embryol. CDZZ ZZ-7

JENKS, John W. (1819-1895) Zool. BIOD NC10

JENNER, Edward (1749-1823) Med. ABES ABET BDOS BEOS BHMT CDZZ DNB LISD MAMR MMMA PGFS SAIF SMIL TOWS ZZ-7

JENNER, Edward (1803-1872) Bot. DNB

JENNER, William (1815-1898) Med. BHMT

JENNINGS, Herbert S. (1868-1947) Zool. BM47 CDZZ DAB4 NC47 NCSA ZZ-7

JENNINGS, Otto E. (1877-1964) Bot. NC52

JENSEN, Carl O. (1864-1934) Vet. Med. CDZZ ZZ-7

JENSEN, J. Hans (1907-1973) Phys. ABES ABET BEOS MHM1 MHSE POSW

JENSEN, Johan L. (1859-1925) Math. CDZZ ZZ-7

JENYNS, Leonard SEE BLOMEFIELD, Leonard

JEPSON, Willis L. (1867-1946) Bot. CDZZ DAB4 MABH ZZ-7

JERRARD, George B. (1804-1863) Math. CDZZ ZZ-7

JESSOP, William (1745-1814) Engr. GE-1

JEVONS, William S. (1835-1882) Math. CDZZ ZZ-7

JEWETT, Frank B. (1879-1949) Elec. Engr. BM27 CB46 CDZZ TPAE ZZ-7

JEWETT, Frank F. (1844-1921) Chem. NC20

JEX-BLAKE, Sophia (1840-1912) Med. IDWB

JILLSON, Willard R. (1890-) Geol. NCSA

JOACHIM, Georg SEE RHETICUS, George J.

JOACHIMSTHAL, Ferdinand (1818-1861) Math. CDZZ ZZ-7

JOBLOT, Louis (1645-1723) Micros.; Phys. CDZZ ZZ-7

JOBS, Steven P. (1955-) Elec. Engr.; Comp. CB83

JODIDI, Samuel L. (1867-1944) Biochem. NC33

JOESTING, Henry R. (1903-1965) Geophys. NC52

JOHANNES LAURATIUS DE FUNDIS (fl. 1428-1473) Astrol. CDZZ ZZ-7

JOHANNES LEO SEE LEO THE AFRICAN

JOHANNSEN, Albert (1871-1962) Mineral. CDZZ ZZ-7

JOHANNSEN, Wilhelm L. (1857-1927) Biol. ABES ABET BEOS CDZZ ZZ-7

JOHN DANKO SEE JOHN OF SAXONY

JOHN OF DUMBLETON (d. c.1349) Nat. Philos. CDZZ ZZ-7

JOHN OF GMUNDEN (c.1382-1442) Astron.; Math. CDZZ ZZ-7

JOHN OF GODDESDEN (c.1280-1361) Med. BHMT

JOHN OF HALIFAX SEE SACROBOSCO, Johannes de

JOHN OF LIGNERES (fl. c.1300-1350) Astron.; Math. CDZZ ZZ-7

JOHN OF MURS (fl. c.1300-1350) Math.; Astron. CDZZ ZZ-7

JOHN OF PALERMO (fl. 1221-1240) Trans. Sci. Lit. CDZZ ZZ-7

JOHN OF SAXONY (fl. c.1300-1350) Astron. CDZZ ZZ-7

JOHN OF SICILY (fl. c.1250-1300) Astron. CDZZ ZZ-7

JOHN PHILOPONUS (fl. c.517-549) Philos. CDZZ ZZ-7

JOHN SIMONIS OF SELANDIA (fl. 1400s) Astron. CDZZ ZZ-7

JOHN, Fritz (1910-) Math. MHM2 MHSE

JOHNS, Carl O. (1870-1942) Biochem. NC30

JOHNSON, Alan W. (1917-) Chem. COBC

JOHNSON, Arnold B. (1834-1915) Phys. NC16

JOHNSON, Campbell (1921-) Engr. BISC

JOHNSON, Charles W. (1863-1932) Entom. AMEM

JOHNSON, Clarence L. (1910-) Aero. CB68 ICFW MHSE

JOHNSON, Douglas W. (1878-1944) Geophys. BM24 CDZZ ZZ-7

JOHNSON, Duncan S. (1867-1937) Bot. MABH NC32

JOHNSON, Francis S. (1918-) Astrophys. MHSE

JOHNSON, John B. (1887-1970) Phys. NC55

JOHNSON, Katherine (1918-) Phys. BCST

JOHNSON, Kelly SEE JOHNSON, Clarence L.

JOHNSON, Manuel J. (1805-1859) Astron. CDZZ DNB ZZ-7

JOHNSON, Marian A. (1901-1964) Bot. NC51

JOHNSON, Martin (1884-1937) Nat. Hist. NC28

JOHNSON, Martin W. (1893-) Biol. MHSE

JOHNSON, Nelson K. (1892-1954) Meteor. DNB7

JOHNSON, Otis C. (1839-1912) Chem. NC19

JOHNSON, Samuel W. (1830-1909) Chem. ACCE BM-7

JOHNSON, Thomas (c.1600-1644) Bot. CDZZ DNB ZZ-7

JOHNSON, Treat B. (1875-1947) Biochem. ACCE BM27 DAB4 NC35

JOHNSON, Virginia E. (1925-) Psych. CB76

JOHNSON, Walter R. (1794-1852) Phys.; Geol. ACCE ASJD BIOD

JOHNSON, Willard D. (1859-1917) Geophys. CDZZ ZZ-7

JOHNSON, William (c.1610-1665) Chem. CDZZ ZZ-7

JOHNSON, William W. (1841-1927) Math. DAB NC23

JOHNSTON, George (1797-1855) Nat. Hist. DNB

JOHNSTON, James F. (1796-1855) Chem. DNB

JOHNSTON, John (1806-1879) Chem.; Phys. BIOD

JOHNSTON, John (1881-1950) Chem. DAB4

JOHNSTONE, John (1603-1675) Nat. Hist. DNB

JOLIOT, (Jean) Frederic (1900-1958) Phys. ABES ABET BDOS BEOS CB46 CDZZ DCPW HSSO MWBR NPWC RS-6 SAIF ZZ-7

JOLIOT-CURIE, Frederic SEE JOLIOT, (Jean) Frederic

JOLIOT-CURIE, Irene (1897-1956) Phys. ABES ABET BDOS BEOS CB40 CDZZ DCPW IDWB LLWO MWBR NPWC SAIF ZZ-7

JOLLY, Philipp J. von (1809-1884) Phys. CDZZ ZZ-7

JOLY, Charles J. (1864-1906) Astron. DNB2

JOLY, John (1857-1933) Geol.; Mineral. BEOS CDZZ DNB5 ZZ-7

JONES, Anson (1798-1858) Med. BHMT

JONES, Bennett M. (1887-1975) Engr. ICFW RS23

JONES, Bernard M. (1882-1953) Chem. DNB7

JONES, Donald F. (1890-1963) Genet. BM46 NC49

JONES, Ewart R. (1911-) Chem. BEOS COBC

JONES, Frank M. (1869-1962) Nat. Hist. NC50

JONES, Frederick M. (1893-1961) Invent. BCST DANB EBAH SBPY

JONES, Frederic Wood (1879-1954) Anat.; Anthro. DNB7 RS-1

JONES, Grinnell (1884-1947) Chem. NC36

JONES, Harold S. (1890-1960) Astron. ABES ABET AROW BDOS BEOS CB55 CDZZ DNB7 IEAS MHM1 MHSE RS-7 ZZ12

JONES, Harry C. (1865-1916) Chem. CDZZ DAB ZZ-7

JONES, Hugh (c.1692-1760) Math. BIOD DAB

JONES, John (1729-1791) Med. BHMT

JONES, John K. (1912-1977) Chem. RS25

JONES, John V. (1856-1901) Phys. DNB2

JONES, Joseph (1833-1896) Med.; Chem. ACCE

JONES, Lewis R. (1864-1945) Bot. NC35

JONES, Owen T. (1878-1967) Geol. RS13

JONES, Richard U. (1877-1941) Chem. NC30

JONES, Robert T. (1910-) Aero. ICFW

JONES, Thomas P. (1773-1848) Chem. ACCE TECH

JONES, Thomas R. (1810-1880) Zool. DNB

JONES, Thomas R. (1819-1911) Geol.; Paleon. DNB2

JONES, Walter J. (1865-1935) Chem. BM20 NC43

JONES, Webster N. (1887-1962) Chem. Engr. ACCE

JONES, William (1675-1749) Math. CDZZ DNB ZZ-7

JONES, William L. (1827-1914) Chem.; Geol. BIOD NC-9

JONQUIERES, Ernest J. de (1820-1901) Math. CDZZ ZZ-7

JONSSON, J. Erik (1901-) Engr. MHSE

JONSTON, John (1603-1675) Nat. Hist.; Med. CDZZ ZZ-7

JORDAN, (Claude) Alexis (1814-1897) Bot. CDZZ ZZ-7

JORDAN, Camille (1838-1922) Math. BEOS CDZZ ZZ-7

JORDAN, David S. (1851-1931) Ichth. CDZZ DAB LACC NC-2 NC22 WAMB ZZ-7

JORDAN, Edward C. (1910-) Elec. Engr. TPAE

JORDAN, Edwin O. (1866-1936) Bact. BM20 CDZZ DAB2 ZZ-7

JORDAN, Ernst P. (1902-) Phys.; Math. BEOS

JORDAN, Frank C. (1865-1941) Astron. NC35

JORDAN, Karl H. (1861-1959) Entom. DNB7 RS-6

JORDAN, Sara C. (1884-1959) Med. NAWM

JORDAN, Stroud (1885-1947) Chem. NCSD

JORDANUS DE NEMORE (fl. c.1220) Phys.; Math. CDZZ GE-1 ZZ-7

JORDEN, Edward (1569-1632) Geol. THOG

JORGENSEN, Sophus M. (1837-1914) Chem. CDZZ ZZ-7

JOSEPHSON, Brian D. (1940-) Phys. ABET BEOS MHSE POSW

JOSLIN, Benjamin F. (1796-1861) Phys.; Meteor. BIOD

JOSSELYN, John (c.1608-1675) Nat. Hist. BIOD HAOA

JOUFFROY D'ABBANS, Claude de (c.1751-1832) Engr. GE-1

JOULE, James P. (1818-1889) Phys. ABES ABET BDOS BEOS CDZZ DNB EETD FNEC GISA HOSS HSSO IFBS MCCW MNCS SAIF TOWS ZZ-7

JOURDAIN, Francis C. (1865-1940) Ornith. DNB5

JOY, Alfred H. (1882-1973) Astron. BM47 MHM1 MHSE

JOY, Charles A. (1823-1891) Chem.; Mineral. ACCE

JOYCE, J. Wallace (1907-1970) Geophys. NC55

JUAN Y SANTACILLA, Jorge (1713-1773) Geophys. CDZZ ZZ-7

JUDAY, Chancey (1871-1944) Zool. CDZZ LACC NC42 ZZ-7

JUDD, Benjamin I. (1904-) Cons. LACC

JUDD, Deane B. (1900-1972) Phys. NC56

JUDD, Orange (1822-1892) Agr. BIOD

JUEL, Sophus C. (1855-1935) Math. CDZZ ZZ-7

JUKES, Joseph B. (1811-1869) Geol.; Geophys. CDZZ DNB ZZ-7

JULIAN, Percy L. (1899-1975) Chem. BM52 BPSH CB47 GNPA HCOK MHSE SABL WAMB

JULIEN, Alexis A. (1840-1919) Geol. NC18

JULIUS, Willem H. (1860-1925) Phys. CDZZ ZZ-7

ibn JULJUL, Sulayman ibn Hasan (944-c.994) Med. CDZZ ZZ-7

JULLIOT, Henri (1856-1923) Aero. ICFW

JUNCKER, Johann (1679-1759) Chem. CDZZ ZZ-7

JUNG, Carl G. (1875-1961) Psych. ABES ABET BDOS BEOS CDZZ PAW3 ZZ-7

JUNGIUS, Joachim (1587-1657) Math. CDZZ ZZ-7

JUNKERS, Hugo (1859-1935) Aero. ICFW

JUSSIEU, Adrien H. de (1797-1853) Bot. CDZZ ZZ-7

JUSSIEU, Antoine de (1616-1758) Bot.; Paleon. CDZZ ZZ-7

JUSSIEU, Antoine L. de (1748-1838) Bot. ABET BDOS BEOS CDZZ ZZ-7

JUSSIEU, Bernard de (1699-1777) Bot. CDZZ ZZ-7

JUSSIEU, Joseph de (1704-1779) Nat. Hist. CDZZ ZZ-7

JUST, Ernest E. (1883-1941) Zool. BISC BPSH DAB3 DANB GNPA HCOK SBAH SBPY WAMB

JUSTI, Johann H. von (1720-1771) Mng. CDZZ ZZ-7

JUVE, Arthur E. (1901-1965) Chem. Engr. ACCE

JUVE, Walter H. (1890-1944) Chem. NC35

K

KABAT, Elvin A. (1914-) Immunol.; Biochem. MHSE

KABLUKOV, Iván A. (1857-1942) Chem. CDZZ ZZ-7

KAC, Mark (1914-) Math. MHM2 MHSE

KAEMPFER, Engelbert (1651-1716) Geog.; Bot. CDZZ ZZ-7

KAESTNER, Abraham G. (1719-1800) Math. CDZZ ZZ-7

KAGAN, Benjamin F. (1869-1953) Math. CDZZ ZZ-7

KAHLENBERG, Louis A. (1870-1941) Chem. ACCE CDZZ HSSO ZZ-7

KAHN, Herman (1922-1983) Phys. CB62

KAISER, Frederik (1808-1872) Astron. CDZZ ZZ-7

KALBE, Ulrich SEE RULEIN VON CALW, Ulrich

KALBFLEISCH, Martin (1804-1873) Chem. ACCE NC15

KALM, Pehr (1716-1779) Nat. Hist. CDZZ HAOA ZZ-7

KALMAN, Rudolf E. (1930-) Math.; Engr. MHM2 MHSE

KALMBACH, Edwin R. (1884-) Biol. LACC

KALUZA, Theodor F. (1885-1954) Phys.; Math. CDZZ ZZ-7

KAMAL al-DIN, Abul Hasan (d. 1320) Opt.; Math. CDZZ ZZ-7

KAMALAKARA (b. c.1610) Astron. CDZZ ZZ-7

KAMEN, Martin D. (1913-) Biochem. ABES ABET BEOS MHSE

KAMERLINGH-ONNES, Heike (1853-1926) Phys. ABES ABET BDOS BEOS CDZZ DCPW PAW2 POSW ZZ-7

KAMM, Oliver (1888-1965) Biochem. ACCE

KAMMERER, Paul (1880-1926) Biol. BEOS PAW2

KAMP, Peter van SEE VAN DE KAMP, Peter

KANAKA (fl. c.775-820) Astron. CDZZ ZZ-7

KANDALL, Ezra O. (1818-1899) Astron.; Math. BIOD

KANE, Robert J. (1809-1890) Chem. BDOS BEOS CDZZ ZZ-7

KANT, Immanuel (1724-1804) Philos. ABES ABET BEOS CDZZ IEAS TOWS ZZ-7

KANTOROVICH, Leonid V. (1912-) Math. SMST

KANTROWITZ, Adrian (1918-) Med. CB67

KANTROWITZ, Arthur R. (1913-) Phys. CB66 ICFW MHM2 MHSE MOS3

KAO HSUAN (fl. 1130) Engr. GE-1

KAPITZA, Peter L. (1894-) Phys. ABES ABET BEOS CB55 MHSE PBTS POSW RUSP SMST SOT2 SOVL

KAPLAN, Henry S. (1918-) Med. MFIR

KAPLAN, Joseph (1902-) Phys. CB56

KAPLANSKY, Irving (1917-) Math. MHM2 MHSE

KAPOSI, Moriz (1837-1902) Med. BHMT

KAPP, Roland (1903-1965) Chem. NC53

KAPTEYN, Jacobus C. (1851-1922) Astron. ABES
ABET BEOS CDZZ IEAS ZZ-7

al-KARAJI, Abu Bakr (fl. c.990-1010) Math. CDZZ
ZZ-7

KARANDEEV, Konstantin B. (1907-) Elec. Engr.
SMST

KARAS, Stephen A. (1896-1973) Chem. NC58

KARAVAEV, Nikolai M. (1890-) Chem. SMST

KARGIN, Valentin A. (1907-1969) Chem. MHM2
MHSE SMST

KARIM, Sultan M. (1935-) Med. MFIR

KARLE, Isabella L. (1921-) Crystal. CWSN MHSE

KARLIN, Samuel (1924-) Math. MHSE

KARMAN, Harvey L. (1924-) Med. MFIR

KARMAN, Theodore von (1881-1963) Aero. ABET
BM38 CB55 CDZZ FNEC FPSN ICFW MHM2
MHSE MOS1 RS12 WAMB ZZ-7

KARPINSKI, Louis C. (1878-1956) Math. CDZZ ZZXV

KARPINSKY, Alexander P. (1847-1936) Geol. CDZZ
ZZ-7

KARRER, Paul (1889-1971) Chem. ABES ABET
BDOS BEOS CDZZ NPWC RS24 ZZXV

KARSTEN, Karl J. (1782-1853) Math.; Mng. CDZZ
ZZ-7

al-KASHI, Ghiyath al-Din (c.1429) Astron.; Math.
CDZZ ZZ-7

KASNER, Edward (1878-1955) Math. BM31 NC16
NC41

KASSNER, James L. (1894-1970) Chem. NC56

KASTLE, Joseph H. (1864-1916) Chem. ACCE NC15

KASTLER, Alfred (1902-1984) Phys. ABES ABET
BEOS CB67 MHM2 MHSE POSW

KATCHALSKI, Ephraim (1916-) Biol. MHM2

KATER, Henry (1777-1835) Geophys. CDZZ DNB
ZZ-7

KATZ, Alexander E. (1887-1957) Chem. Engr. ACCE

KATZ, Bernard (1911-) Physiol. ABET BEOS MHSE

KATZ, Donald (1907-) Engr. NCSK

KATZ, Joseph J. (1912-) Chem. MHM1 MHSE

KATZIR, Ephraim (1916-) Biophys. CB75 MHSE

KATZMAN, Morris (1904-1957) Chem. NC48

KAUFERT, Frank H. (1905-) Forest. LACC

KAUFFMAN, Calvin H. (1869-1931) Bot. DAB MABH

KAUFMAN, Joyce J. (1929-) Chem. MHSE

KAUFMANN, Albert R. (1911-1974) Metal. NC59

KAUFMANN, Herbert M. (1870-1950) Chem. NC55
NCSE

KAUFMANN, Nicolaus SEE MERCATOR, Nicolaus

KAUFMANN, Walter (1871-1947) Phys. CDZZ ZZ-7

KAVANAGH, Thomas C. (1912-1978) Engr. MHM2
MHSE

KAVRAYSKY, Vladimir V. (1884-1954) Astron.; Geophys. CDZZ ZZ-7

KAWIN, Charles C. (1877-1957) Chem. ACCE

KAY, George F. (1873-1943) Geol. CDZZ ZZ-7

KAY, Herbert D. (1893-1976) Dairy Sci. RS23

KAYSER, Heinrich J. (1853-1940) Phys. CDZZ RS-1
ZZ-7

KAZANSKII, Boris A. (1891-) Chem. SMST

KAZARNOVSKII, Isaak A. (1890-) Chem. SMST

KEARNEY, Thomas H. (1874-1956) Bot. NC45

KEATING, William H. (1799-1840) Mineral. ACCE
BIOD DAB

KEATS, John (1795-1821) Med. BHMT

KEBLER, Lyman F. (1863-1955) Chem. ACCE

KECKERMANN, Bartholomew (c.1572-1609) Astron.; Math. CDZZ ZZ-7

KEDZIE, Robert C. (1823-1902) Chem. ACCE BIOD DAB NC-8

KEEBLE, Frederick W. (1870-1952) Bot. DNB7

KEELER, James E. (1857-1900) Astron. ABES ABET BDOS BEOS BIOD BM-5 CDZZ DAB NC10 ZZ-7

KEEN, Bernard A. (1890-1981) Agr. RS28

KEEN, Frederick P. (1890-) Forest. LACC

KEEN, William W. (1837-1932) Med. BHMT

KEENAN, Philip C. (1908-) Astron. BEOS

KEESOM, Willem H. (1876-1956) Phys. ABET CDZZ ZZ-7

KEETON, William T. (1933-1980) Zool. AO80

KEILIN, David (1887-1963) Biochem. ABET BDOS BEOS CDZZ MHM2 MHSE RS10 ZZ-7

KEILL, James (1673-1719) Physiol.; Anat. CDZZ ZZ-7

KEILL, John (1671-1721) Math.; Phys. CDZZ DNB ZZ-7

KEIR, James (1735-1820) Chem. BDOS BEOS CDZZ DNB ZZ-7

KEITH, Arthur (1864-1944) Geol. DAB3

KEITH, Arthur (1866-1955) Anat.; Anthro. BDOS BEOS BHMT BM29 CDZZ NCSC RS-1 ZZ-7

KEITH, Percival C. (1900-1976) Chem. Engr. NC59

KEITH, Walter J. (1861-1934) Chem. NC26

KEKULE VON STRADONITZ, Friedrich A. (1829-1896) Chem. ABES ABET BDOS BEOS CDZZ HSSO SAIF ZZ-7

KELDSYSH, Mstislav V. (1911-1978) Math.; Phys. CB62 SMST

KELLAWAY, Charles H. (1889-1952) Path. DNB7

KELLER, Harry F. (1861-1924) Chem. ACCE

KELLERMAN, Karl F. (1879-1934) Bact. DAB1 MABH NC26

KELLERMAN, William A. (1850-1908) Bot. MABH NC26

KELLEY, Claude D. (1907-) Cons. LACC

KELLEY, Edward (1555-1595) Alch. DNB

KELLEY, Evan W. (1882-1966) Forest. LACC

KELLEY, Louise (1894-1961) Chem. ACCE

KELLEY, Walter P. (1878-1965) Soil. Sci. BM40

KELLICOTT, David S. (1842-1898) Zool. NC13

KELLNER, David (fl. c.1670-1700) Med.; Chem. CDZZ ZZ-7

KELLNER, Karl (1851-1905) Engr. BDOS BEOS

KELLOGG, Albert (1813-1887) Bot. BIOD CDZZ DAB MABH NC25

KELLOGG, Arthur R. (1892-1969) Zool.; Paleon. BM46 CB49 MHM2 MHSE NC54

KELLOGG, James L. (1866-1938) Biol. NC29

KELLOGG, Oliver D. (1873-1932) Math. NC23

KELLOGG, Vernon L. (1867-1937) Entom.; Zool. AMEM BM20 CDZZ NC15 NC28 ZZ-7

KELLY, Howard A. (1858-1943) Med. BHMT

KELLY, Junea W. (1886-1969) Ornith.; Cons. NC55

KELLY, Mervin J. (1894-1971) Phys. BM46 CB56 TPAE

KELLY, Patrick (1756-1842) Math.; Astron. DNB

KELLY, William (1811-1888) Invent. BDOS INYG WAMB

KELLY, William A. (1896-1968) Geol. NC54

KELSER, Raymond A. (1892-1952) Vet. Med.; Microbiol. BM28 CDZZ DAB5 ZZ-7

KELSEY, Frances O. (1914-) Med. CB65 DNFH

KELVIN, Lord SEE THOMSON, William

KEMBLE, Edwin C. (1889-) Phys. MHM2 MHSE QPAS

KEMENY, John G. (1926-) Math. CB71

KEMP, James F. (1859-1926) Geol. BM16

KEMP, Kenneth L. (1807-1843) Chem. MCCW

KEMP, Stanley W. (1882-1945) Zool.; Ocean. DNB6

KENDALL, Arthur I. (1877-1959) Bact. NC49

KENDALL, Edward C. (1886-1972) Biochem. ABES ABET BEOS BM47 CB50 CDZZ HSSO MFIR MHM1 MHSE PAW2 WAMB ZZXV

KENDALL, James P. (1889-1978) Chem. COBC RS26

KENDALL, William C. (1861-1939) Ichth. NC34

KENDREW, John C. (1917-) Biochem. ABES ABET BEOS CB63 COBC EDCJ MHM1 MHSE

KENDRICK, James (1771-1847) Bot. DNB

KENDRICK, Pearl (1890-1980) Microbiol. AO80

KENNAWAY, Ernest L. (1881-1958) Chem. DNB7 RS-4

KENNEDY, Alexander B. (1847-1928) Engr. CDZZ ZZ-7

KENNEDY, Alfred L. (1818-1896) Chem. ACCE

KENNEDY, Clarence H. (1879-1952) Entom. AMEM NCSE

KENNEDY, Eugene P. (1919-) Biochem. MHM2 MHSE

KENNEDY, George C. (1919-) Geol. MHM2 MHSE

KENNEDY, William Q. (1903-1979) Geol. RS26

KENNELLY, Arthur E. (1861-1939) Elec. Engr. ABES ABET BDOS BEOS BM22 CDZZ TPAE ZZ-7

KENNER, George W. (1922-1978) Chem. COBC RS21

KENNICOTT, Robert (1835-1866) Zool. BIOD DAB NC24

KENNY, Frederick (1894-1971) Chem. NC57

KENT, Robert H. (1886-1961) Phys. BM42

KENYON, David (1914-1970) Invent. NC55

KENYON, Joseph (1885-1961) Chem. RS-8

KEPLER, Johannes (1571-1630) Astron.; Phys. ABES ABET ASTR BDOS BEOS BMST CDZZ DCPW ESCS EXSB FASP HOSS IEAS LISD MAKS MGAH PAW2 SAIF SGAC STSW TMAL TOWS WOSM ZZ-7

KER, John B. (c.1765-1842) Bot. DNB

KEREKJARTO, Bela (1898-1946) Math. CDZZ ZZ-7

KERMACK, William O. (1898-1970) Biochem. RS17

KERR, Andrew A. (1877-1929) Anthro. NC28

KERR, John (1824-1907) Phys. BDOS BEOS CDZZ ZZ-7

KERR, John G. (1869-1957) Zool. CDZZ DNB7 RS-4 ZZ-7

KERR, Washington C. (1827-1885) Geol. BIOD

KERSEY, John (1616-1690) Math. DNB

KERSHNER, Richard B. (1913-) Phys. MOS5

KERST, Donald W. (1911-) Phys. ABES ABET BEOS CB50 DCPW

KERSTEN, Harold J. (1898-1955) Biophys. NC45

KESAVA (fl. 1496) Astron. CDZZ ZZ-7

KETTERING, Charles F. (1876-1958) Engr.; Invent. ABET BM34 CDZZ MASY NC48 NCSE WAMB ZZ-7

KETTLE, Edgar H. (1882-1936) Path. DNB5

KETTLEWELL, Henry B. (1907-1979) Genet.; Entom. BEOS

KETY, Seymour S. (1915-) Physiol. BEOS MHM2 MHSE

KEY, A. (1905-) Chem. COBC

KEYNES, John M. (1883-1946) Math. CDZZ ZZ-7

KEYS, David A. (1890-) Phys. CB58

KEYSERLING, Alexander A. (1815-1891) Geol.; Bot. CDZZ ZZ-7

KEYT, Alonzo T. (1827-1885) Physiol. BIOD

ibn KHALDUN, Abd al-Rahman (1332-1406) Sci. Writ. CDZZ SCIN ZZ-7

al-KHALILI, Shams al-Din Abu (fl. c.1365) Astron.; Math. CDZZ ZZXV

KHAN, Fazlur R. (1929-) Engr. MHSE

KHARASCH, Morris S. (1895-1957) Chem. ACCE BM34 CDZZ ZZ-7

KHARITON, Yulii B. (1904-) Phys. SMST

KHARKEVICH, Aleksandr A. (1904-1965) Phys. SMST

al-KHAYYAMI, Ghiyath al-Din Abul Fath (1048-1131) Math.; Astron. ABET BEOS CDZZ SCIN ZZ-7

al-KHAZIN, Abu Jafar Muhammad (d. 961/71) Astron.; Math. CDZZ ZZ-7

al-KHAZINI, Abul-Fath abd al-Rahman (fl. c.1115-1130) Astron. CDZZ ZZ-7

KHINCHIN, Aleksandr Y. (1894-1959) Math. CDZZ ZZ-7

KHITRIN, Lev N. (1907-1965) Phys. SMST

KHORANA, Har Gobind (1922-) Chem. ABES ABET BEOS CB70 MHSE WAMB

KHRUSHCHOV, Grigorii K. (1897-1962) Vet. Med. SMST

al-KHUJANDI, Abu Muhammad (d. 1000) Math.; Astron. CDZZ ZZ-7

KHUNRATH, Conrad (d. c.1614) Med.; Chem. CDZZ ZZ-7

KHUNRATH, Heinrich (c.1560-1605) Alch.; Med. CDZZ ZZ-7

ibn KHURRADADHBIH, Abul-Qasim (c.820-c.912) Geog. CDZZ ZZ-7

al-KHUWARIZMI, Abu abd Allah (fl. c.975) Sci. Ed. CDZZ ZZ-7

al-KHWARIZMI, Muhammad ibn Musa (780-850) Math.; Astron. ABES BEOS CDZZ FMAS SCIN ZZ-7

KIDD, Franklin (1890-1974) Chem. RS21

KIDD, John (1775-1851) Chem.; Anat. ABES ABET BEOS CDZZ ZZ-7

KIDD, William (1803-1867) Nat. Hist. DNB

KIDDER, Alfred V. (1885-1963) Archaeol. BM39

KIDDER, George W. (1902-) Biol.; Biochem. CB49

KIDDINU (fl. 379 B.C.) Astron. ABES ABET BEOS

KIDSTON, Robert (1852-1924) Paleon. FHUA

KIELMEYER, Carl F. (1765-1844) Physiol.; Anat. CDZZ ZZ-7

KIENLE, Roy H. (1896-1957) Chem. NC50

KIERAN, John (1892-) Sci. Writ. DGMT

KIESS, Carl C. (1887-1967) Chem. NC50

KIHARA, Hitoshi (1893-) Genet. MHM2 MHSE

KIKOIN, Isaak K. (1908-) Phys. SMST

KILIANI, Heinrich (1855-1945) Chem. HSSO

KILLEFFER, David H. (1895-1970) Chem.; Sci. Writ. ACCE

KILLIAN, James R. (1904-) Engr. PPEY

KILLIAN, John A. (1891-1957) Biochem. NCSD

KIMBALL, George E. (1906-1967) Chem. BM43

KIMBALL, James H. (1874-1943) Meteor. NC32

KIMBALL, Thomas L. (1918-) Cons. LACC

KIMBALL, George H. (1908-) Geog.; Meteor. CB52

KIMURA, Hisashi (1870-1943) Astron. CDZZ ZZ-7

KIMURA, Motoo (1924-) Genet. BEOS

KINAHAN, George H. (1829-1908) Geol. DNB2

KINDELBERGER, James H. (1895-1962) Aero. ICFW

al-KINDI, Abu Yusuf (c.801-c.866) Philos. CDZZ
GRCH SCIN ZZXV

KING, Charles B. (1868-1957) Invent. NC48

KING, Charles G. (1896-) Biochem. ABES ABET
BEOS CB67 MHM2 MHSE NCSI

KING, Clarence R. (1842-1901) Geol. BIOD BM-6
CDZZ GKGP SFNB WAMB ZZ-7

KING, Edward S. (1861-1931) Astron. DAB

KING, Frederick E. (1906-) Chem. COBC

KING, George (1840-1909) Bot. DNB2

KING, Harold (1887-1956) Chem. DNB7 RS-2

KING, Louis V. (1886-1956) Math.; Phys. RS-3

KING, Philip B. (1903-) Geol. MHM2 MHSE

KING, Ralph T. (1900-) Forest. LACC

KING, Ronald W. (1905-) Phys.; Elec. Engr. TPAE

KING, Samuel A. (1828-1914) Aero. DAB

KING, Starr (1824-1864) Nat. Hist. SFNB

KING, William (1809-1886) Geol. DNB

KING, William B. (1889-1963) Geol. RS-9

KING-HELE, Desmond G. (1927-) Astrophys. MHSE

KINGSBURY, Edwin F. (1886-) Phys. NCSC

KINGSLEY, Charles (1819-1875) Nat. Hist. ANHD

KINNEAR, Norman B. (1882-1957) Ornith. DNB7

KINNERSLEY, Ebenezer (1711-1778) Elec. Sci. BIOD
CDZZ ZZ-7

KINNEY, Abbot (1850-1920) Cons. EAFC

KINNICUTT, Leonard P. (1854-1911) Chem. ACCE
DAB NC25

KINSEY, Alfred C. (1894-1956) Zool. BEOS CB54
LISD MFIR NCSH WAMB

KINZEL, Augustus B. (1900-) Metal. MHM2 MHSE

KIPPING, Frederic S. (1863-1949) Chem. ABES
ABET BDOS BEOS CDZZ DNB6 GRCH ZZ-7

KIRBY, Harold (1900-1952) Zool. NC41

KIRBY, William (1759-1850) Entom. DNB

KIRCH, Gottfried (1639-1710) Astron. CDZZ ZZ-7

KIRCH, Maria M. (1670-1720) Astron. CDZZ ZZ-7
IDWB

KIRCHER, Athanasius (1601-1680) Polym. ABES
ABET ANHD BHMT BMST CDZZ EETD ESEH
ZZ-7

KIRCHOF, Konstantin S. (1764-1833) Chem. ABET
CDZZ ZZ-7

KIRCHOFF, Gustav R. (1824-1887) Phys. ABES
ABET BDOS BEOS CDZZ DCPW FNEC HOSS
HSSO SAIF TOWS ZZ-7

KIRILLIN, Vladimir A. (1913-) Phys. SMST

KIRK, Edwin (1884-1955) Paleon. NC45

KIRK, John (1832-1922) Nat. Hist. DNB4

KIRK, Paul L. (1902-1970) Biochem. NC56

KIRK, Raymond E. (1890-1957) Chem. ACCE NC47

KIRKALDY, David (1820-1897) Metal.; Engr. CDZZ
ZZ-7

KIRKES, William S. (1822-1864) Med. BHMT

KIRKMAN, Thomas P. (1806-1895) Math. CDZZ
ZZ-7

KIRKPATRICK, Sidney D. (1894-1973) Chem. Engr.;
Sci. Writ. ACCE

KIRKWOOD, Daniel (1814-1895) Astron. ABES ABET
BEOS BIOD CDZZ DAB NC-4 ZZ-7

KIRKWOOD, John G. (1907-1959) Chem. ACCE
CDZZ ZZ-7

KIRNER, Walter R. (1895-1972) Chem. NC57

KIRTLAND, Jared P. (1793-1877) Zool. BIOD BM-2
BWCL DAB WFBG

KIRWAN, Richard (1733-1812) Chem.; Geol. BDOS
BEOS CDZZ DNB ZZ-7

KISTIAKOWSKY, George B. (1900-1982) Chem.
BEOS CB60 MHSE PPEY

KITAIBEL, Pal (1757-1817) Bot.; Chem. CDZZ ZZ-7

KITASATO, Shibasaburo (1852-1931) Bact. ABES
ABET BDOS BEOS CDZZ ZZ-7

KITTEL, Charles (1916-) Phys. BEOS MHM1 MHSE

KITTLITZ, Friedrich H. (1799-1874) Nat. Hist. BWCL
WFBG

KJELDAHL, Johan G. (1849-1900) Chem. ABET
BDOS BEOS CDZZ ZZ-7

KLAPROTH, Martin H. (1743-1817) Chem. ABES
ABET BDOS BEOS CDZZ GRCH ZZ-7

KLASON, Johan P. (1848-1937) Chem. GRCH

KLAU, Christoph SEE CALVIUS, Christopher

KLEBS, Edwin (1834-1913) Med. BHMT

KLEBS, Georg A. (1857-1918) Bot. CDZZ ZZ-7

KLECZKOWSKI, Alfred A. (1908-1970) Biol. RS17

KLEEGMAN, Sophia J. (1901-1971) Med. NAWM

KLEIN, Christian F. (1849-1925) Math. ABET BDOS
BEOS CDZZ ZZ-7

KLEIN, Edmund (1921-) Med. MFIR

KLEIN, Hermann J. (1844-1914) Astron.; Meteor.
CDZZ ZZ-7

KLEIN, Jacob T. (1685-1759) Zool. CDZZ ZZ-7

KLEIN, Melanie (1882-1960) Psych. IDWB

KLEINENBERG, Nicolaus (1842-1897) Biol. CDZZ
ZZ-7

KLEIST, Ewald G. von (c.1700-1748) Phys. ABET
CDZZ EETD ESEH ZZ-7

KLEITMAN, Nathaniel (1895-) Physiol. CB57

KLEMIN, Alexander (1888-1950) Aero. ICFW

KLEMM, Wilhelm (1896-) Chem. HSSO

KLEON (fl. 258 B.C.-252 B.C.) Engr. GE-1

KLINE, John R. (1891-1955) Math. NC45

KLINE, Nathan S. (1916-) Med. AMJB CB65 DNFH
LGIH MFIR

KLINGENSTIERNA, Samuel (1698-1765) Phys. BDOS
BEOS CDZZ ZZ-7

KLOPSTEG, Paul E. (1889-) Elec. Engr. CB59

KLOTS, Alexander B. (1903-) Entom. DGMT

KLUCKHOHN, Clyde K. (1905-1960) Anthro. BM37
CB51 NCSH

KLUGEL, Georg S. (1739-1812) Math.; Phys. CDZZ
ZZ-7

KLUMPKE, Dorothea (fl. 1900s) Astron. IDWB

KLUYVER, Albert J. (1888-1956) Biochem. CDZZ
MHM2 MHSE RS-3 ZZ-7

KLYNE, William (1913-) Chem. COBC

KNAB, Frederick (1865-1918) Entom. AMEM DAB
NC24

KNAPP, John L. (1767-1845) Bot. DNB

KNEELAND, Samuel (1821-1888) Zool. BIOD DAB
NC26

KNEIPP, Leon F. (1880-1966) Forest. LACC

KNESER, Adolf (1862-1930) Math. CDZZ ZZ-7

KNIGHT, Burke H. (1891-) Chem. NCSE

KNIGHT, Charles M. (1848-1941) Chem. NC32

KNIGHT, Gowin (1713-1772) Invent. DNB

KNIGHT, Henry G. (1878-1942) Chem. ACCE NCSF

KNIGHT, Jonathan (1787-1858) Engr. GE-1

KNIGHT, Margaret (1838-1914) Invent. IDWB

KNIGHT, Thomas A. (1759-1838) Bot.; Hort. CDZZ
DNB ZZ-7

KNIGHT, Wilbur C. (1858-1903) Geol. BIOD

KNIGHT, William (1786-1844) Nat. Philos. DNB

KNIPLING, Edward F. (1909-) Entom. CB75 MHM2 MHSE

KNIPOVICH, Nikolai M. (1862-1939) Mar. Biol. CDZZ ZZ-7

KNISELY, Melvin H. (1904-1975) Anat. NC59

KNOPF, Adolph (1882-1966) Geol. BM41 NC53

KNOPF, Eleanora F. (1883-1974) Geol. NAWM

KNOPOFF, Leon (1925-) Geophys. MHM2 MHSE

KNOPP, Konrad (1882-1957) Math. CDZZ ZZ-7

KNORR, Georg W. (1705-1761) Paleon. CDZZ ZZ-7

KNOTT, Cargill G. (1856-1922) Nat. Philos.; Seism. CDZZ ZZ-7

KNOWLES, Chester L. (1894-1972) Chem. Engr. NC57

KNOWLES, Francis G. (1915-1974) Biol. RS21

KNOWLTON, Frank H. (1860-1926) Paleon.; Ornith. DAB FHUA NC10 NC47

KNOX, Robert (1793-1862) Anat. CDZZ DNB ZZ-7

KNUDSEN, Martin H. (1871-1949) Phys. CDZZ ZZ-7

KNUDSEN, Vern O. (1893-) Phys. NCSH

KNUNYANTS, Ivan L. (1906-) Chem. SMST

KNUTH, Paul E. (1854-1900) Bot. CDZZ ZZ-7

KOBEL, Jacob (1460/5-1533) Math. CDZZ ZZ-7

KOBZAREV, Yurii B. (1905-) Elec. Engr. SMST

KOCH, Fred C. (1876-1948) Biochem. ACCE DAB4 NC46

KOCH, Helge von (1870-1924) Math. CDZZ ZZ-7

KOCH, (Heinrich) Robert (1843-1910) Biochem. ABES ABET BDOS BEOS BHMT CDZZ FBMV FMBB HLSM LISD MAMR PAW2 PGFS SAIF ZZ-7

KOCHER, Emil T. (1841-1917) Med. BDOS BEOS BHMT DSLP

KOCHETKOV, Nikolai K. (1915-) Chem. SMST

KOCHIN, Nikolai Y. (1901-1944) Phys.; Math. CDZZ ZZ-7

KOCHINA, Pelageya Y. (1899-) Geophys. SMST

KOEBELE, Albert (1852-1924) Entom. AMEM

KOELLIKER, Rudolf A. von (1817-1905) Biol. ABES ABET BDOS BEOS BHMT CDZZ ZZ-7

KOELREUTER, Joseph G. (1733-1806) Bot. CDZZ LECE ZZ-7

KOENIG, Friedrich (1774-1833) Engr. GE-1

KOENIG, George A. (1844-1913) Chem.; Mineral. DAB NC17

KOENIG, Johann S. (1712-1757) Math.; Phys. CDZZ ZZ-7

KOENIG, Julius (1849-1914) Math. CDZZ ZZ-7

KOENIG, Karl R. (1832-1901) Phys. CDZZ ZZ-7

KOENIGS, Gabriel (1858-1931) Math. CDZZ ZZ-7

KOENIGSWALD, Gustav von (1902-) Paleon. PHLS

KOFOID, Charles A. (1865-1947) Zool. BM26 CDZZ DAB4 NCSA ZZ-7

KOHLER, August K. (1866-1948) Micros. CDZZ ZZ-7

KOHLER, Elmer P. (1865-1938) Chem. DAB2 BM27

KOHLER, Wolfgang (1887-1967) Psych. ABES ABET MHM1 MHSE NC55

KOHLRAUSCH, Friedrich W. (1840-1910) Chem.; Phys. BDOS CDZZ ZZ-7

KOHLRAUSCH, Rudolph H. (1809-1858) Phys. CDZZ ZZ-7

KOHN, Walter (1923-) Phys. BEOS MHM1 MHSE

KOHOUTEK, Lubos (1935-) Astron. CB74

KO HUNG (c.283-343) Alch. BEOS

KOKATNUR, Vanan R. (1886-1950) Chem. ACCE

KOLBE, Adolph W. (1818-1884) Chem. ABES ABET BDOS BEOS CDZZ ZZ-7

KOLFF, William J. (1912-) Med. MFIR

KOLLER, Carl (1857-1944) Med. ABES ABET BDOS BEOS

KOLMOGOROV, Andrei N. (1903-) Math. BEOS SMST

KOLOSOV, Gury V. (1867-1936) Phys.; Math. CDZZ ZZ-7

KOLOSOV, Nikolai G. (1897-) Med. SMST

KOLREUTER, Josef G. (1733-1806) Bot. HLSM

KOLTHAFF, Izaak M. (1894-) Chem. MHM1 MHSE

KOLTZOFF, Nikolai K. (1872-1940) Zool.; Genet. CDZZ ZZ-7

KOMAROV, Vladimir M. (1927-1967) Astronaut. IEAS

KOMP, William H. (1893-1955) Entom. AMEM

KOMPFNER, Rudolf (1909-1977) Phys.; Elec. Engr. TPAE

KONDAKOV, Ivan L. (1857-1931) Chem. CDZZ ZZ-7

KONDRATIEV, Victor N. (1902-) Chem. MHM2 MHSE SMST

KONIG, Arthur (1856-1901) Phys. CDZZ ZZ-7

KONIG, Emanuel (1658-1731) Nat. Hist.; Med. CDZZ ZZ-7

KONIG, Friedrich (1774-1833) Invent. SAIF

KONIGSBERGER, Leo (1837-1921) Math. CDZZ ZZ-7

KONINCK, Laurent G. de (1809-1887) Chem.; Paleon. CDZZ ZZ-7

KONKOLY THEGE, Miklos von (1842-1916) Astron.; Geophys. CDZZ ZZ-7

KONOBEEVSKII, Sergei T. (1890-) Phys. SMST

KONORSKI, Jerzy (1903-1973) Physiol. MHM2 MHSE

KONOVALOV, Dmitry P. (1856-1929) Chem. CDZZ ZZ-7

KONSTANTINOV, Boris P. (1910-1969) Phys. SMST

KOONTZ, Roscoe L. (1922-) Biophys. BISC

KOPAL, Zdenek (1914-) Astron. CB69

KOPP, Hermann F. (1817-1892) Chem. ABES ABET BDOS BEOS CDZZ GRCH ZZ-7

KOPPEN, Wladimir P. (1846-1940) Climat. BEOS

KOPROWSKI, Hilary (1916-) Virol. CB68

KORNBERG, Arthur (1918-) Biochem. ABES ABET BEOS CB68 MHM1 MHSE PAW2 PBTS WAMB

KOROLEV, Sergei P. (1907-1966) Engr.; Rocket. BDOS BEOS CDZZ ICFW IEAS ZZ-7

KOROTKOV, Aleksei A. (1910-1967) Chem. SMST

KORSAKOV, Sergei S. (1853-1900) Med. BHMT

KORSHAK, Vasili V. (1909-) Chem. SMST

KORTEWEG, Diederik J. (1848-1941) Math. CDZZ ZZ-7

KORZHINSKI, Dmitrii S. (1899-) Geol. MHM2 MHSE SMST

KOSSEL, (Karl) Albrecht (1853-1927) Chem. ABES ABET BDOS BEOS CDZZ GRCH ZZ-7

KOSSELL, Walther (1888-1956) Phys. CDZZ ZZ-7

KOSTANECKI, Stanislaw (1860-1910) Chem. CDZZ ZZ-7

KOSTENKO, Mikhail P. (1889-) Elec. Engr. SMST

KOSTERLITZ, Hans W. (1903-) Pharm. BEOS

KOSTINSKY, Sergey K. (1867-1936) Astron. CDZZ ZZ-7

KOSYGIN, Yurii A. (1911-) Geol. SMST

KOTCHER, Ezra (1903-) Aero. ICFW

KOTELNIKOV, Aleksandr P. (1865-1944) Math. CDZZ ZZ-7

KOTELNIKOV, Vladimir A. (1908-) Elec. Engr. SMST

KOTO, Bunjiro (1856-1935) Geol.; Seism. CDZZ ZZ-7

KOTON, Mikhail M. (1908-) Chem. SMST

KOUTS, Herbert J. (1919-) Phys. MHM1 MHSE

KOUWENHOVEN, William B. (1886-1975) Elec. Engr. BEOS MHM1 MHSE

KOVALENKOV, Valentin I. (1884-) Elec. Engr. SMST

KOVALEV, Nikolai N. (1908-) Elec. Engr. SMST

KOVALEVSKAYA, Sofya SEE KOVALEVSKY, Sonya

KOVALEVSKI, Alexander O. (1840-1901) Embryol. ABES ABET BDOS BEOS CDZZ ZZ-7

KOVALEVSKY, Sonya (1850-1891) Math. ABET BEOS CDZZ IDWB MEQP WIMO ZZ-7

KOVALEVSKY, Vladimir O. (1842-1883) Paleon. CDZZ ZZ-7

KOVALSKII, Aleksandr A. (1906-) Chem. SMST

KOVALSKY, Marian A. (1821-1884) Astron. CDZZ ZZ-7

KOVDA, Viktor A. (1904-) Soil Sci. SMST

KOYRE, Alexandre (1892-1964) Sci. Hist. CDZZ ZZ-7

KOZYREV, Nikolai A. (1908-1983) Astron. ABES ABET BEOS CB70

KRAEMER, Elmer O. (1898-1943) Chem. NC32

KRAEMER, Henry (1868-1924) Bot. DAB NC26

KRAEPELIN, Emil (1856-1926) Med. BHMT

KRAFFT-EBING, Richard (1840-1902) Med. ABES ABET

KRAFT, Christopher C. Jr. (1924-) Engr. CB66

KRAFT, Jens (1720-1765) Math.; Phys. CDZZ ZZ-7

KRAFT, Robert P. (1927-) Astron. BEOS

KRAMER, Benjamin (1888-1972) Biochem. NC57

KRAMER, Paul J. (1904-) Bot. BEOS MHM1 MHSE

KRAMERS, Hendrik A. (1894-1952) Phys. CDZZ ZZ-7

KRAMP, Chretien (1760-1826) Phys.; Astron. CDZZ ZZ-7

KRASHENINNIKOV, Stepan P. (1711-1755) Geog.; Anthro. CDZZ ZZ-7

KRASIK, Sidney (1911-1965) Phys. NC51

KRASILNIKOV, Nikolai A. (1896-) Microbiol. SMST

KRASNO, Louis R. (1914-) Med. MFIR

KRASNOV, Andrey N. (1862-1915) Geog.; Bot. CDZZ ZZ-7

KRASOVSKY, Theodosy N. (1878-1948) Geophys. CDZZ ZZ-7

KRATZER, Nicolas (1486-1550) Instr.; Astron. BDOS BEOS DNB

KRAUS, Charles A. (1875-1967) Chem. ACCE BEOS BM42 CDZZ NCSH ZZ-7

KRAUSE, Ernst L. (1839-1903) Sci. Ed. CDZZ ZZ-7

KRAUSEL, Richard (1890-1966) Bot.; Paleon. FHUA

KRAYBILL, Henry R. (1891-1956) Biochem. NC48

KRAYENHOFF, Cornelius R. (1758-1840) Geophys. CDZZ ZZ-7

KREBS, Hans A. (1900-1981) Biochem. ABES ABET AO81 BEOS CB54 GJPS MHM1 MHSE

KREHL, Ludolf von (1861-1937) Med. BHMT

KREMER, Gerhard SEE MERCATER, Gerhardus

KREPS, Evgenii M. (1899-) Physiol. SMST

KRETSCHMER, Ernst (1888-1964) Med. BHMT

KREWSON, Charles F. (1905-1968) Biochem. NC54

KRISHNAN, Kariamanikkam S. (1898-1961) Phys. RS13

KRICK, Irving P. (1906-) Meteor. CB50

KROEBER, Alfred L. (1876-1960) Anthro. BM36 WAMB

KROEGER, William J. (1906-1966) Invent. NC51

KROGH, Schack A. (1874-1949) Zool.; Physiol. ABET BDOS BEOS BHMT CDZZ ZZ-7

KROGMAN, Wilton M. (1903-) Anthro. MHM2 MHSE

KRONBERGER, Hans (1920-1970) Phys. RS18

KRONECKER, Hugo (1839-1914) Physiol. ABES BHMT CDZZ ZZ-7

KRONECKER, Leopold (1823-1891) Math. ABET BEOS CDZZ MELW ZZ-7

KRONIG, August K. (1822-1879) Phys. CDZZ ZZ-7

KROPA, Edward L. (1907-1965) Chem. NC51

KROPOTKIN, Petr A. (1892-1921) Geog.; Glaciol. CDZZ ZZ-7

KRSNA (fl. 1653) Astron. CDZZ ZZ-7

KRUBER, Aleksandr A. (1871-1941) Geog. CDZZ ZZ-7

KRUESI, Paul J. (1878-1965) Metal. ACCE

KRUPP, Alfred (1812-1887) Invent. BDOS

KRUTCH, Joseph W. (1893-1970) Nat. Hist. PCWA SFNB WAMB

KRUZHILIN, Georgii N. (1911-) Phys. SMST

KRYLOV, Alaksandr P. (1904-) Mng. SMST

KRYLOV, Aleksei N. (1863-1945) Math.; Engr. CDZZ ZZ-7

KRYLOV, Nikolai M. (1879-1955) Math. CDZZ ZZ-7

KUBLER-ROSS, Elisabeth (1926-) Psychiat. CB80

KUCHEMANN, Dietrich (1911-1976) Engr. RS26

KUCKRO, William E. (1877-1951) Chem. NC39

KUENEN, Donald (1912-) Zool.; Ecol. POEC

KUENEN, Johannes P. (1866-1922) Phys. CDZZ ZZ-7

KUENEN, Philip H. (1902-1976) Geol. MHM1 MHSE

KUFFLER, Stephen W. (1913-1980) Physiol. BEOS RS28

KUHLMANN, Charles F. (1803-1881) Chem. GRCH

KUHN, Adam (1741-1817) Bot.; Med. BIOD DAB NC-7

KUHN, Alfred (1885-1968) Zool. CDZZ ZZ-7

KUHN, Richard (1900-1967) Chem. ABES ABET BEOS CDZZ NPWC ZZ-7

KUHN, Roland (1912-) Med. MFIR

KUHN, Werner (1899-1963) Chem. CDZZ ZZ-7

KUHNE, Wilhelm F. (1837-1900) Physiol.; Chem. ABES ABET BDOS BEOS BHMT CDZZ ZZ-7

KUIPER, Gerard P. (1905-1973) Astron. ABES ABET BEOS CB59 IEAS

KULEBAKIN, Viktor S. (1891-1970) Elec. Engr. SMST

KUMM, Henry W. (1901-) Med. CB55

KUMMER, Ernst E. (1810-1893) Math. CDZZ ZZ-7

KUNCKEL, Johann (1630-1703) Chem. CDZZ ZZ-7

KUNDT, August A. (1839-1894) Phys. ABES ABET BEOS CDZZ ZZ-7

KUNGSHU, Pan (fl. 470 B.C.) Engr. GE-1

KUNKEL, Beverly W. (1881-1969) Biol. NC55

KUNKEL, Louis O. (1884-1960) Bot. BM38

KUNO, Hisashi (1910-1969) Geol. MHM2 MHSE

KUNTH, Carl S. (1788-1850) Bot. CDZZ ZZXV

KUNTZE, Carl E. (1843-1907) Bot. CDZZ ZZXV

KUNZE, Richard E. (1838-1919) Nat. Hist. DAB

KUO SHOU-CHING (fl. 1290) Engr.; Astron. GE-1

KUPREVICH, Vasilii F. (1897-1969) Bot. SMST

KURCHATOV, Igor V. (1903-1960) Phys. ABES ABET BEOS CB57 CDZZ ZZ-7

KURDYUMOV, Georgii V. (1902-) Metal. SMST

KURLBAUM, Ferdinand (1857-1927) Phys. CDZZ
ZZ-7

KURNAKOV, Nikolai S. (1860-1941) Chem. CDZZ
ZZ-7

KUROSAWA MOTOSHIGE (fl. 1690) Metal. GE-1

KURSANOV, Andrei L. (1902-) Biochem. MHM2
MHSE SMST

KURSANOV, Dmitri N. (1899-) Chem. SMST

KURSCHAK, Jozsef (1864-1933) Math. CDZZ ZZ-7

KURTI, Nicholas (1908-) Phys. BEOS MHSE

KURTZ, Thomas E. (1928-) Comp. HOPL

KUSCH, Ploykarp (1911-) Phys. BEOS CB56 MHM1
MHSE POSW WAMB

KUSHYAR ibn LABBAN ibn BASHAHRI, Abul-Hasan
(fl. c.1000) Math.; Astron. CDZZ ZZ-7

KUSSMAUL, Adolf (1822-1902) Med. BHMT

KUTTA, Martin W. (1867-1944) Aero. ICFW

KUTZING, Friedrich T. (1807-1893) Bot. CDZZ ZZ-7

KUZIN, Aleksandr M. (1906-) Biochem. SMST

KUZNETSOV, Sergei I. (1900-) Microbiol. SMST

KUZNETSOV, Valerii A. (1906-) Geol. SMST

KUZNETSOV, Vladimir D. (1887-1963) Phys. SMST

KYESER, Konrad (1366-1405) Engr. GE-1

KYLIN, Johann H. (1879-1949) Bot. CDZZ ZZ-1

L

LABAT, Jean B. (1663-1728) Nat. Hist. HAOA

LA BROSSE, Guy de (1586-1641) Bot.; Med. CDZZ
EPHG ZZ-7

LACAILLE, Nicolas L. de (1713-1762) Astron. ABES
ABET BDOS BEOS CDZZ IEAS ZZ-7

LACAZE-DUTHIERS, Felix J. de (1821-1901) Zool.
CDZZ ZZ-7

LACEPEDE, Bernard G. de (1756-1825) Zool. CDZZ
ZZ-7

LACEY, John F. (1841-1913) Cons. EAFC LACC

LACHAPELLE, Marie-Louise (1769-1821) Med. WIWM

LACHMANN, Gustav (1896-) Aero. ICFW

LACK, David L. (1910-1973) Ornith. BEOS DGMT
RS20

LA CONDAMINE, Charles M. de (1701-1774) Math.
ABES ABET BDOS BEOS CDZZ PAW3 ZZxv

LACROIX, Alfred (1863-1948) Mineral.; Geol. CDZZ
ZZ-7

LACROIX, Sylvestre F. (1765-1843) Math. CDZZ
ZZ-7

LADD, Edwin F. (1859-1925) Chem. DAB

LADD-FRANKLIN, Christine (1847-1930) Math.; Phys.
NC26

LADENBURG, Albert (1842-1911) Chem. CDZZ ZZ-7

LADENBURG, Rudolf W. (1882-1952) Phys. CDZZ
ZZ-7

LAENNEC, Rene Theophile (1781-1826) Med. ABET
BDOS BEOS BHMT CDZZ SMIL TOWS ZZ-7

LA FAILLE, Charles de (1597-1652) Math. CDZZ
ZZ-7

LA FARGE, Oliver (1901-1963) Anthro. NCSF

LA FORGE, Frederick B. (1882-1958) Chem. ACCE

LAGLER, Karl F. (1912-) Zool. LACC

LAGNY, Thomas F. de (1660-1734) Math. CDZZ ZZ-7

LAGRANGE, Joseph L. (1736-1813) Phys.; Astron.
ABES ABET BDOS BEOS CDZZ FMAS FNEC
IEAS MATT ZZ-7

LAGUERRE, Edmond N. (1834-1886) Math. CDZZ
ZZ-7

LA HIRE, Gabriel P. de (1677-1719) Astron.; Geophys. CDZZ ZZ-7

LA HIRE, Philippe de (1640-1718) Astron.; Math.
CDZZ GE-1 ZZ-7

LAHONTAN, Armand L. de (1667-1715) Nat. Hist.
HAOA

LAKE, Simon (1867-1945) Invent. DAB3 TBTM
WAMB

LALANDE, Joseph J. de (1732-1807) Astron. ABES
ABET BEOS CDZZ ZZ-7

LALLA (fl. 700s) Astron. CDZZ ZZ-7

LALLEMAND, Andre (1904-1978) Astron. MHM2
MHSE

LALOUVERE, Antoine de (1600-1664) Math. CDZZ
ZZ-7

LAMARCK, Jean B. (1744-1829) Bot.; Zool.; Evol.
ABES ABET BDOS BEOS CDZZ EQSA GRBW
HLSM LECE LISD PHLS TBSG TOWS ZZ-7

LAMB, Arthur B. (1880-1952) Chem. ACCE BM29
DAB5 NC46

LAMB, Daniel S. (1843-1929) Path.; Anat. NC27

LAMB, George B. (1896-1956) Geophys. NC45

LAMB, Horace (1849-1934) Math.; Geophys. CDZZ
DNB5 ZZ-7

LAMB, Hubert H. (1913-) Climat. BEOS

LAMB, Willis E. Jr. (1913-) Phys. BEOS CB56
MHM1 MHSE NCSJ POSW WAMB

LAMBERT, Aylmer B. (1761-1842) Bot. DNB

LAMBERT, Johann H. (1728-1777) Math.; Phys.
ABES ABET BEOS CDZZ HSSO TOWS ZZ-7

LAMBERT, Walter D. (1879-1968) Surv. BM43 NC54

LAMBO, Thomas A. (1923-) Med. MFIR

LAME, Gabriel (1795-1870) Math. CDZZ FNEC ZZ-7

LA MER, Victor K. (1895-1966) Chem. ACCE BM45
NC52

LAMETHERIE, Jean C. de (1743-1817) Sci. Writ.;
Mineral. CDZZ ZZ-7

LA METTRIE, Julien O. de (1709-1751) Med.; Psych.
CDZZ ZZ-7

LAMME, Benjamin G. (1864-1924) Engr. NC28 TPAE

LAMONT, Johann von (1805-1879) Astron.; Phys.
ABES ABET BEOS CDZZ DNB ZZ-7

LA MOUNTAIN, John (1830-1878) Aero. DAB

LAMOUROUX, Jean V. (1776-1825) Nat. Hist. CDZZ
ZZ-7

LAMSON-SCRIBNER, Frank (1851-1938) Bot. NC40

LAMY, Bernard (1640-1715) Math. CDZZ ZZ-7

LAMY, Guillaume (fl. c.1668-1678) Med. CDZZ
ZZ-7

LANCEFIELD, Rebecca C. (1895-1981) Bact. AO81

LANCHESTER, Frederick W. (1868-1946) Engr. BDOS
CDZZ ICFW ZZ-7

LANCISI, Giovanni M. (1654-1720) Med. BDOS BEOS
CDZZ ZZ-7

LANCRET, Michel A. (1774-1807) Math. CDZZ ZZ-7

LAND, Edwin H. (1909-) Invent.; Photo. ABES
ABET CB53 CB81 MHM1 MHSE NCSH NTBM
WAMB

LANDAU, Edmund (1877-1938) Math. CDZZ ZZ-7

LANDAU, Lev D. (1908-1968) Phys. ABES ABET
BEOS CB63 CDZZ MHM1 MHSE PAW2 POSW
RS15 SMST SOVL ZZ-7

LANDEE, Franc A. (1911-1968) Chem. NC54

LANDEN, John (1719-1790) Math. CDZZ DNB ZZ-7

LANDIS, Eugene M. (1901-) Physiol. MHM2 MHSE

LANDIS, Walter S. (1891-1944) Chem. ACCE NC33

LANDOLT, Hans H. (1831-1910) Chem. BDOS BEOS
CDZZ HSSO ZZ-7

LANDOLT, Percy E. (1891-1970) Chem. Engr. NC55

LANDRIANI, Marsilio (c.1751-1816) Instr. CDZZ
ZZ-7

LANDSBERG, Georg (1865-1912) Math. CDZZ ZZ-7

LANDSBERG, Grigory S. (1890-1957) Phys. CDZZ
ZZ-7

LANDSBOROUGH, David (1779-1854) Nat. Hist. DNB

LANDSTEINER, Karl (1868-1943) Med. ABES ABET BDOS BEOS BM40 CDZZ NCSD SAIF ZZ-7

LANE, Jonathan H. (1819-1880) Phys. BIOD BM-3 CDZZ NC-3 ZZ-8

LANG, Arnold (1855-1914) Zool. CDZZ ZZ-8

LANG, Karl N. (1670-1741) Paleon. CDZZ ZZ-8

LANG, Walter B. (1890-1973) Geol. NC57

LANG, William D. (1878-1966) Geol.; Paleon. RS12

LANG, William H. (1874-1960) Bot. CDZZ DNB7 RS-7 ZZ-8

LANGE, Carl G. (1834-1900) Med.; Psych. CDZZ ZZ-8

LANGE, Norbert A. (1892-1970) Chem. ACCE

LANGENBECK, Karl (1861-1938) Chem. NC33 NCSA

LANGERHANS, Paul (1847-1888) Anat. ABET CDZZ ZZ-8

LANGEVIN, Paul (1872-1946) Phys. ABES ABET BDOS BEOS CDZZ HSSO ZZ-8

LANGFORD, Nathaniel P. (1832-1911) Cons. WAMB

LANGLEY, John N. (1852-1925) Physiol. BDOS BEOS BHMT CDZZ DNB4 ZZ-8

LANGLEY, John W. (1841-1918) Chem. DAB

LANGLEY, Samuel P. (1834-1906) Aero.; Astrophys. ABES ABET BEOS BM-7 CDZZ DAB GASJ ICFW MPIP MSAJ NC-3 NC15 PAW3 TOWS TPOS WAMB ZZ-8

LANGLOIS, Claude (c.1700-c.1756) Instr. CDZZ ZZ-8

LANGLOIS, Thomas H. (1898-1968) Biol. LACC

LANGMUIR, Irving (1881-1957) Chem.; Phys. ABES ABET ACCE ASIW BDOS BEOS BM45 CB40 CDZZ CSCJ EETD GRCH NCSC NPWC PAW2 RS-4 SMIL WAMB ZZ-8

LANGREN, Michael F. van (c.1600-1675) Engr. CDZZ ZZ-8

LANKESTER, Edwin (1814-1874) Bot.; Nat. Hist. DNB

LANKESTER, Edwin R. (1847-1929) Zool. BDOS BEOS CDZZ DNB4 ZZ-8

LANSBERGE, Philip von (1561-1632) Math.; Astron. CDZZ ZZ-8

LANSDOWNE, J. Fenwick (1937-) Sci. Illus. CB70

LAPHAM, Increase A. (1811-1875) Nat. Hist.; Meteor. BIOD DAB NC-8

LAPICQUE, Louis (1866-1952) Physiol.; Anthro. CDZZ ZZ-8

LAPLACE, Pierre S. de (1749-1827) Astron.; Math. ABES ABET BDOS BEOS CDZZ FNEC GASJ IEAS LISD MELW SOAC TOWS ZZXV

LAPORTE, Otto (1902-1971) Phys. BM50

LAPP, Ralph E. (1917-) Phys. CB55

LAPPARENT, Albert A. de (1839-1908) Geol. CDZZ ZZ-8

LAPWORTH, Arthur (1872-1941) Chem. BDOS BEOS CDZZ ZZ-8

LAPWORTH, Charles (1842-1920) Geol. BDOS BEOS CDZZ ZZ-8

LARAGH, John H. (1924-) Med. NCSL

LARDNER, Dionysius (1793-1859) Sci. Writ. DNB

LARDY, Henry A. (1917-) Biochem. MHM2 MHSE

LARGHI, Bernardino (1812-1877) Med. CDZZ ZZ-8

LARIONOV, Andrei N. (1889-1963) Elec. Engr. SMST

LA RIVE, Arthur A. de (1801-1873) Phys. CDZZ ZZ-8

LA RIVE, Charles G. de (1770-1834) Phys.; Chem. CDZZ ZZ-8

LA RIVERS, Ira (1915-) Entom. BNBR

LARKIN, Edgar L. (1847-1924) Astron. NC20

LARMOR, Joseph (1857-1942) Phys. BEOS CDZZ DNB6 ZZ-8

LA ROCHE, Etienne de (fl. c.1520) Math. CDZZ ZZ-8

LARREY, Dominique J. (1766-1842) Med. BHMT

LARSEN, Esper S. Jr. (1879-1961) Geol. BM37 CDZZ MHM2 MHSE NC45 ZZ-8

LARSON, John A. (1892-) Psychiat. ABES ABET

LARSON, Leonard W. (1898-1974) Med. CB62

LARTET, Edouard A. (1801-1871) Paleon. ABES ABET BEOS CDZZ ZZ-8

LARTET, Louis (1840-1899) Geol. CDZZ ZZ-8

LASHLEY, Karl S. (1890-1958) Psych. BM35 CDZZ RS-5 ZZ-8

LASSELL, William (1799-1880) Astron. ABES ABET BEOS CDZZ DNB IEAS ZZ-8

LASZLO, Daniel (1902-1958) Med. NC43

LATHAM, George H. (1895-1964) Chem. NC51

LATHAM, John (1740-1837) Ornith. DNB HAOA

LATHAM, Roger M. (1914-) Cons. LACC

LATIMER, Lewis H. (1848-1928) Invent. BCST BPSH DANB EBAH HCOK SBPY

LATIMER, Wendell M. (1893-1955) Chem. CDZZ

LATOUR, Cogniard (1777-1849) Phys. BDOS

LATREILLE, Pierre A. (1762-1833) Entom.; Zool. CDZZ ZZ-8

LATROBE, Benjamin H. (1764-1820) Engr. GE-1 TECH

LATTES, Cesare M. (1924-) Phys. CB49

LATTIMORE, Samuel A. (1828-1913) Chem. ACCE NC12

LAU, Hans E. (1879-1918) Astron. CDZZ ZZ-8

LAUCHEN, Georg J. SEE RHETICUS, George J.

LAUDY, Louis H. (1842-1905) Chem. ACCE

LAUE, Max T. von (1879-1960) Phys. ABES ABET BDOS BEOS CDZZ DCPW HSSO POSW RS-6 SAIF ZZ-8

LAUFER, Berthold (1874-1934) Anthro. BM18

LAUFFER, Max A. (1914-) Biophys. NCSL

LAUGER, Paul (1896-) Chem. CB45

LAUGHLIN, Harry H. (1880-1943) Biol. NCSD

LAURENS, Andre du (1558-1609) Anat. CDZZ ZZ-8

LAURENT, Auguste (1807-1853) Chem. ABES ABET BDOS BEOS CDZZ ZZ-8

LAURENT, Matthieu P. (1841-1908) Math. CDZZ ZZ-8

LAURENT, Pierre A. (1813-1854) Math.; Opt. CDZZ ZZ-8

LAURITSEN, Charles C. (1892-1968) Phys. BM46 MHSE NC54

LAURITSEN, Thomas (1915-1973) Phys. NC58

LAUSSEDAT, Aime (1819-1907) Photo. CDZZ ZZ-8

LAVANHA, Joao B. (c.1550-1624) Math. CDZZ ZZ-8

LAVERAN, Charles L. (1845-1922) Med. ABET BEOS BM46 CDZZ ZZ-8

LAVOISIER, Antoine L. (1743-1794) Chem. ABES ABET BDOS BEOS BHMT BMST CDZZ CSCJ EPHG GISA GRCH HLSM HOSS HSSO IFBS LECE LISD MCCW SAIF SMIL TOWS ZZ-8

LAVRENKO, Evgenii M. (1900-) Bot. SMST

LAVRENTEV, Mikhail A. (1900-1980) Math. AO80 SMST

LAVRENTIEV, Boris I. (1892-1944) Physiol. CDZZ ZZ-8

LAVROVSKII, Konstantin P. (1898-) Chem. SMST

LAW, Thomas C. (1880-1962) Chem. NC52

LAWES, John B. (1814-1900) Agr. ABES ABET BDOS BEOS CDZZ ZZ-8

LAWLESS, Theodore K. (1892-1971) Med. BISC GNPA SBPY

LAWRENCE, Charles L. (1882-1950) Engr. ICFW

LAWRENCE, Ernest O. (1901-1958) Phys. ABES ABET BDOS BEOS BM41 CB40 CB52 CDZZ CSCJ DCPW MHM1 MHSE MSAJ MWBR NC48 NCSG POSW TINA WAMB ZZ-8

LAWRENCE, George H. (1910-1978) Bot. NC61

LAWRENCE, George N. (1806-1895) Ornith. BIOD BWCL DAB NC-2 WFBG

LAWRENCE, William (1783-1867) Med. CDZZ ZZ-8

LAWSON, Andrew C. (1861-1952) Geol. CDZZ ZZ-8 BM37

LAWSON, George (1827-1895) Bot. POCS

LAWSON, John (d. 1712) Nat. Hist. BIOD HAOA LHES

LAX, Benjamin (1915-) Phys. BEOS MHM1 MHSE

LAX, Gaspar (1487-1560) Math. CDZZ ZZ-8

LAX, William (1761-1836) Astron. DNB

LAYCOCK, Thomas (1812-1876) Med. BHMT

LAZAREV, Petr P. (1878-1942) Phys. CDZZ ZZ-8

LAZEAR, Jesse W. (1866-1900) Med. ABES ABET BEOS NC15

LEA, Isaac (1792-1886) Zool. ASJD BIOD CDZZ ZZ-8

LEA, Matthew C. (1823-1897) Chem. ACCE BIOD BM-5 DAB NC10

LEACH, Albert E. (1864-1910) Chem. NC19

LEACH, William E. (1790-1836) Nat. Hist. ANHD BWCL DNB WFBG

LEADBETTER, Charles (fl. 1728) Astron. DNB

LEAKE, Chauncey D. (1896-1978) Physiol.; Chem. CB60

LEAKEY, Louis S. (1903-1972) Paleon.; Anthro. ABET BEOS CB66 CDZZ PHLS ZZ-8

LEAKEY, Richard (1944-) Paleon.; Anthro. CB76

LEAMING, Thomas H. (1893-1925) Chem. NC20

LEAR, Edward (1812-1888) Nat. Hist. ANHD

LEAR, William P. (1902-1978) Elec. Engr. CB66 WAMB

LEATHES, John B. (1864-1956) Physiol. RS-4

LEAVENWORTH, Francis P. (1858-1928) Astron. DAB NC-8

LEAVITT, Dudley (1772-1851) Math. DAB

LEAVITT, Henrietta S. (1868-1921) Astron. ABES ABET BEOS CDZZ DAB IDWB IEAS NAW NC25 SLOR ZZ-8

LE BARON, William (1814-1876) Entom. AMEM

LEBEDEV, Aleksandr A. (1903-1969) Phys. SMST

LEBEDEV, Petr N. (1866-1912) Phys. ABES ABET BDOS BEOS CDZZ ZZ-8

LEBEDEV, Sergei V. (1874-1934) Chem. CDZZ ZZ-8

LEBEDINSKY, Vyacheslav V. (1888-1956) Chem. CDZZ ZZ-8

LE BEL, Joseph A. (1847-1930) Chem. ABES ABET BDOS BEOS CDZZ ZZ-8

LEBESQUE, Henri L. (1875-1941) Math. BEOS CDZZ ZZ-8

LE BLANC, Max J. (1865-1943) Chem. CDZZ ZZ-8

LEBLANC, Nicolas (1742-1806) Chem. ABES ABET BDOS BEOS CDZZ GE-1 ZZ-8

LEBLOND, Charles P. (1910-) Anat. MHM1 MHSE

LEBON, Philippe (1767-1804) Invent. BDOS GE-1

LEBOYER, Frederick (1918-) Med. CB82

LE CAT, Claude N. (1700-1768) Med. CDZZ ZZ-8

LE CHATELIER, Henri L. (1850-1936) Chem. ABES ABET BDOS BEOS CDZZ GRCH HSSO ZZ-8

LECLANCHES, Georges (1839-1882) Elec. Engr. BDOS BEOS

LE CLERC, Daniel (1652-1728) Med. BHMT

LE CLERC, Georges L., Comte de Buffon (1707-1788) Nat. Hist. ABES ABET ANHD BDOS BEOS BMST EQSA HAOA HLSM NATJ PHLS ZZ-2

L'ECLUSE, Charles de (1526-1609) Ornith. CDZZ
   ORNS ZZ-8

LECOMTE DU NOUY, Pierre (1883-1947) Biophys.
   NC36

LECONTE, John (1818-1891) Nat. Hist. BIOD BM-3
   CDZZ DAB WFBG ZZ-8

LE CONTE, John E. (1784-1860) Entom. ASJD BIOD

LE CONTE, John L. (1825-1883) Entom. AMEM BM-2
   BWCL DAB WFBG

LE CONTE, Joseph (1823-1901) Nat. Hist.; Geol.
   BIOD MB-6 CDZZ ZZ-8

LE CONTE, Lewis (1782-1835) Nat. Hist. NC11

LECOQ DE BOISBAUDRAN SEE BOISBAUDRAN,
   Paul E. de

LECORNU, Leon F. (1854-1940) Engr. CDZZ ZZ-8

LE DANTEC, Felix (1869-1917) Biol. CDZZ ZZ-8

LEDERBERG, Joshua (1925-) Genet. ABES ABET
   AMJB BEOS CB59 MHM1 MHSE NCSJ PAW2
   WAMB

LEDERMAN, Leon M. (1922-) Phys. MHSE

LEDERMULLER, Martin F. (1719-1769) Nat. Hist.
   ANHD

LEDINGHAM, John C. (1875-1944) Bact. DNB6

LE DOUBLE, Anatole F. (1848-1913) Anat. CDZZ
   ZZ-8

LEDUC, Rene H. (1898-1968) Aero. ICFW

LEDWICH, Thomas H. (1823-1858) Anat. DNB

LEE, Charles A. (1801-1872) Med. DAB

LEE, Leslie A. (1852-1908) Nat. Hist. Nc20

LEE, R. Edwin (1876-1936) Chem. NC30

LEE, Tsung-Dao (1926-) Phys. ABES ABET BEOS
   CB58 MHM1 MHSE PAW2 PBTS POSW WAMB

LEE, William S. (1872-1934) Engr. NC24 TPAE

LEECH, Paul N. (1889-1941) Chem.; Pharm. ACCE

LEEDS, Albert R. (1843-1903) Chem. ACCE

LEEDS, John (1705-1790) Math.; Astron. BIOD DAB

LEEDY, Daniel L. (1912-) Biol. LACC

LEEDY, Haldon A. (1910-) Phys. NCSK

LEEGHWATER, Jan A. (1575-1650) Engr. GE-1
   SAIF

LEES, Edwin (1800-1887) Bot. DNB

LEES, George M. (1898-1955) Geol. DNB7 RS-1

LEET, L. Don (1901-1974) Geol. NC58

LEEUWENHOEK, Anton von (1630-1723) Biol.; Micros.
   ABES ABET ANHD BDOS BEOS BHMT CDZZ
   FBMV GRBW HLSM HOSS LISD MPIP PGFS
   SMIL TOWS ZZ-8

LE FEBVRE, Nicaise (c.1610-1669) Chem. CDZZ
   ZZ-8

LEFEVRE, George (1869-1923) Zool. NC20

LE FEVRE, Jean (c.1652-1706) Astron. CDZZ ZZ-8

LEFFLER, Ross L. (1886-1964) Cons. LACC

LEFFMANN, Henry (1847-1930) Chem. ACCE DAB
   NC25

LEFSCHETZ, Solomon (1884-1972) Math. MHM1
   MHSE NC56 RS19

LEGALLOIS, Julien J. (1770-1814) Physiol. CDZZ
   ZZ-8

LEGENDRE, Adrien M. (1752-1833) Math. ABET
   CDZZ GASJ ZZ-8

LE GENTIL DE LA GALAISIERE, Guillaume (1725-
   1792) Astron. ABET CDZZ ZZ-8

LEGER, Urbain L. (1866-1948) Zool. CDZZ ZZ-8

LE GROS CLARK, Wilfrid E. (1895-1971) Anat.;
   Anthro. BEOS MHM2 MHSE RS19

LEHENBAUER, Philip A. (1881-) Bot. BNBR

LEHMANN, Inge (1888-) Seism. BEOS CB62

LEHMANN, Johann G. (1719-1767) Geol. CDZZ ZZ-8

LEHMANN, Otto (1855-1922) Crystal.; Phys. CDZZ ZZ-8

LEHMER, Derrick N. (1867-1938) Math. NC28

LEHNINGER, Albert L. (1917-) Biochem. MHM2 MHSE

LEIBNIZ, Gottfried W. (1646-1716) Philos.; Math. ABES ABET BDOS BEOS BMST CDZZ HOSS MASW MELW MISU TOWS WTGM ZZ-8

LEIDY, Joseph (1823-1891) Zool.; Paleon. ABFC BHMT BIOD BM-7 CDZZ DAB MADC NC-5 PHLS WAMB ZZ-8

LEIGH, Charles (1662-c.1701) Nat. Hist. DNB

LEIGHTON, Robert B. (1919-) Astron.; Phys. CB66

LEIGHTON, William A. (1805-1889) Bot. DNB

LEIPER, Robert T. (1881-1969) Parasit. RS16

LEISHMAN, William B. (1865-1926) Path. ABES ABET BDOS BEOS DNB4

LEISTER, Claude W. (1893-1963) Zool. NC51

LEITH, Charles K. (1875-1956) Geol. BM33 NC47

LEJWA, Arthur (1895-1972) Biochem. NC57

LELOIR, Luis F. (1906-) Biochem. ABET BEOS MHM2 MHSE

LEMAIRE, Jacques (fl. 1720-1740) Instr. CDZZ ZZ-8

LEMAIRE, Pierre (fl. 1733-1760) Instr. CDZZ ZZ-8

LEMAITRE, Georges E. (1894-1966) Astron. ABES ABET BEOS IEAS

LEMBERG, Max R. (1896-1975) Biochem. RS22

LEMERY, Louis (1766-1743) Chem.; Anat. CDZZ EETD ZZ-8

LEMERY, Nicolas (1645-1715) Chem. BDOS BEOS CDZZ GRCH ZZ-8

LEMMON, John G. (1832-1908) Bot. BIOD BNBR DAB

LEMOINE, Emile M. (1840-1912) Math. CDZZ ZZ-8

LE MONNIER, Louis G. (1717-1799) Bot.; Phys. CDZZ ZZ-8

LE MONNIER, Pierre C. (1715-1799) Astron. CDZZ ZZ-8

LE MOYNE, Jacques (d. 1588) Nat. Hist. HAOA

LENARD, Philipp E. von (1862-1947) Phys. ABES ABET BDOS BEOS CDZZ POSW SUHB ZZ-8

LENG, Charles W. (1859-1941) Entom. AMEM

LENIN, Vladimir I. (1870-1924) Philos. CDZZ OGML ZZ-8

LENNARD-JONES, John E. (1894-1954) Phys.; Chem. BEOS CDZZ RS-1 ZZ-8

LENOIR, Jean J. (1822-1900) Invent. ABES ABET BDOS FNEC SAIF

LENOX-CONYNGHAM, Gerald P. (1866-1956) Geo-phys. RS-4

LENSEN, Serge (1893-1961) Virol. NC46

LENZ, Heinrich F. (1804-1865) Phys. ABES ABET BDOS BEOS CDZZ ZZ-8

LEO THE AFRICAN (c.1485-c.1555) Geog. CDZZ ZZ-8

LEO THE MATHEMATICIAN (c.790-c.870) Math.; Astron. CDZZ ZZ-8

LEODAMUS OF THASOS (fl. c.380 B.C.) Math. CDZZ ZZ-8

LEONARD, Frederick C. (1896-1960) Astron. NC45

LEONARD, Justin W. (1909-) Biol. LACC

LEONARD, Nelson J. (1916-) Chem. MHM2 MHSE

LEONARD, Richard M. (1908-) Cons. LACC

LEONARDO DA VINCI (1452-1519) Anat.; Invent.; Math. ABES ABET ANHD BDOS BHMT BMST CDZZ FNEC GE-1 HLSM HOSS LISD PHLS SAIF SMIL SXWS TOWS ZZ-8

LEONARDO OF PISA SEE FIBONACCI, Leonardo

LEONHARD, Karl C. von (1779-1862) Mineral.; Geol. CDZZ ZZ-8

LEONHARDI, Johann G. (1746-1823) Chem.; Med. CDZZ ZZ-8

LEONICENO, Nicolo (1428-1524) Med. CDZZ ZZ-8

LEONOV, Aleksei (1934-) Astronaut. CB65 IEAS

LEONTOVICH, Mikhail A. (1903-1981) Phys. SMST

LEOPOLD, (Rand) Aldo (1886-1948) Forest.; Cons.
CONS DAB4 GOTH HOCS HSSO LACC PCWA
POEC SFNB WAMB

LEOPOLD, Aldo S. (1913-) Cons. LACC

LEOPOLD, Luna B. (1915-) Meteor.; Geol. LACC
MHSE POEC

LE PAIGE, Constantin (1852-1929) Math. CDZZ ZZ-8

LEPAUTE, Hortense (1723-1788) Astron. IDWB

LEPEKHIN, Ivan I. (1740-1802) Geog.; Nat. Hist.
CDZZ ZZ-8

LE POIVRE, Jacques F. (fl. c.1720) Math. CDZZ ZZ-8

LERCH, Mathias (1860-1922) Math. CDZZ ZZ-8

LEREBOULLET, Dominique A. (1804-1865) Zool.;
Embryol. CDZZ ZZ-8

LE ROY, Charles (1726-1779) Phys.; Meteor. CDZZ
ZZ-8

LE ROY, Edouard (1870-1954) Math. CDZZ ZZ-8

LE ROY, Jean B. (1720-1800) Phys. CDZZ ZZ-8

LESAGE, George L. (1724-1803) Phys. CDZZ ZZ-8

LESLEY, J. Peter (1819-1903) Geol. BIOD BM-8
CDZZ ZZ-8

LESLIE, John (1766-1832) Nat. Philos. CDZZ DNB
MCCW ZZ-8

LESNIEWSKI, Stanislaw (1886-1939) Math. CDZZ
ZZ-8

L'ESPERANCE, Elise (1878-1959) Med. NAWM

LESQUEREUX, Leo (1806-1889) Bot.; Paleon. BIOD
BM-3 CDZZ DAB FHUA MABH NC-9 ZZ-8

LESSEPS, Ferdinand de SEE DE LESSEPS, Ferdinand

LESSON, Rene P. (1794-1849) Nat. Hist.; Exp. ANHD
CDZZ ZZ-8

LESUEUR, Charles A. (1778-1846) Zool. ASJD BIOD
CDZZ DAB NC-8 ZZ-8

LE TENNEUR, Jacques A. (d. c.1653) Math.; Phys.
CDZZ ZZ-8

LETHEBY, Henry (1816-1876) Chem. DNB

LE TONNELIER DE BRETEUIL SEE CHATELET,
Gabrielle E. de

LETTSOM, John C. (1744-1815) Med. BHMT

LEUCIPPUS (fl. 400s B.C.) Philso. ABES CDZZ
ZZ-8

LEUCKART, Karl G. (1822-1898) Zool. ABES ABET
BEOS CDZZ ZZ-8

LEUPOLD, Jacob (1674-1727) Engr. BDOS

LEURECHON, Jean (c.1591-1670) Math. CDZZ ZZ-8

LEURET, Francois (1797-1851) Psychiat.; Anat.
CDZZ ZZ-8

LEUSCHNER, Armin O. (1868-1953) Astron. BM49

LEVADITI, Constantin (1874-1953) Med. CDZZ ZZ-8

LEVAILLANT, Francois (1753-1824) Ornith. ANHD
CDZZ ORNS ZZ-8

LEVENE, Phoebus A. (1869-1940) Biochem. ABES
ABET ACCE BDOS BEOS BM23 CDZZ DAB2
GRCH HLSM NCSE ZZ-8

LEVER, John C. (1811-1858) Med. BHMT

LEVERETT, Frank (1859-1943) Geol. BM23 DAB3

LEVERRIER, Urbain J. (1811-1877) Astron. ABES
ABET BDOS BEOS CDZZ IEAS MGAH ZZ-8

LEVEY, Stanley (1915-1967) Biochem. NC54

LEVI BEN GERSON (1288-1344) Math.; Astron. CDZZ
ZZ-8 GE-1

LEVI, Giuseppe (1872-1965) Anat.; Embryol. CDZZ
ZZ-8

LEVI-CIVITA, Tullio (1873-1941) Phys. CDZZ ZZ-8

LEVI-STRAUSS, Claude (1928-) Anthro. MHSE
EOMH

LEVICH, Veniamin G. (1917-) Chem.; Phys. SMST

LEVIN, Max (1889-) Bact. NCSJ

LEVINE, Philip (1900-) Genet.; Immunol. CB47 MHM1 MHSE

LEVINE, Victor E. (1891-1963) Biochem. NC54

LEVINSON-LESSING, Franz Y. (1861-1939) Geol. CDZZ ZZ-8

LEVINSTEIN, Ivan (1845-1916) Chem. BDOS BEOS

LEVISON, Wallace G. (1846-1924) Invent. NC19

LEVORSEN, Arville I. (1894-1965) Geol. NC50

LEVY, Armand SEE LEVY, Serve-Dieu A.

LEVY, Louise E. (1846-1919) Invent. DAB

LEVY, Maurice (1838-1910) Math.; Engr. CDZZ ZZ-8

LEVY, Serve-Dieu A. (1795-1841) Mineral. CDZZ ZZ-8

LEWIN, William (d. 1796) Nat. Hist. DNB

LEWIS, Enoch (1776-1856) Math. BIOD DAB

LEWIS, Exum P. (1863-1926) Aero. DAB NC20 NC22

LEWIS, George W. (1882-1948) Aero. BM25 ICFW

LEWIS, Gilbert N. (1875-1946) Chem. ABES ABET ACCE BDOS BEOS BM31 CDZZ DAB4 HSSO NC36 WAMB ZZ-8

LEWIS, Harrison F. (1893-) Ornith. DGMT

LEWIS, Howard B. (1887-1954) Biochem. BM44

LEWIS, James SEE SMITHSON, James

LEWIS, Lester C. (1902-1977) Phys. NC60

LEWIS, Margaret A. (1881-1970) Biol. NC58

LEWIS, Tayler (1802-1877) Geol. THOG

LEWIS, Thomas (1881-1945) Med. BHMT CDZZ ZZ-8

LEWIS, Thomas T. (1801-1858) Geol. DNB

LEWIS, Timothy R. (1841-1886) Med. BDOS BEOS CDZZ ZZ-8

LEWIS, W. Bennett (1908-) Phys. MHSE

LEWIS, Walter W. (1881-1976) Elec. Engr. NC59

LEWIS, Warren H. (1870-1964) Anat. BM39

LEWIS, Warren K. (1882-1975) Chem. Engr. HCEF MHSE

LEWIS, William (1708-1781) Chem. CDZZ DNB ZZ-8

LEWIS, William C. (1885-1956) Chem. DNB7 RS-4

LEWIS, Winford L. (1878-1943) Chem. ACCE

LEXELL, Anders J. (1740-1784) Math.; Astron. ABET CDZZ ZZ-8

LEY, Willy (1906-1969) Rocket. ABES ABET CB41 CB53

LEYBENZON, Leonid S. (1879-1951) Engr.; Geophys. CDZZ ZZ-8

LEYBOURN, William (1626-1700) Math. DNB

LEYDEN, Ernst von (1832-1910) Med. BHMT

LEYDIG, Franz von (1821-1908) Anat. CDZZ ZZ-8

L'HERITIER DE BRUTELLE, Charles L. (1746-1800) Bot. CDZZ ZZ-8

L'HERMINIER, Felix L. (1779-1833) Nat. Hist. WFBG

L'HOSPITAL, Guillaume F. de (1661-1704) Math. CDZZ ZZ-8

L'HUILLIER, Simon A. (1750-1840) Math. CDZZ ZZ-8

LHWYD, Edward (1660-1709) Paleon.; Bot. BEOS CDZZ DNB FHUA PHLS ZZ-8

LI, Choh Hao (1913-) Med. ABES ABET BEOS CB63 MFIR MHSE

LI, Min Chiu (1916-) Med. MFIR

LI CHAO-TE (fl. 690) Engr. GE-1

LI CHIEH (fl. 1100) Engr. GE-1

LI CHIH (1192-1279) Math. CDZZ ZZ-8

LI CHUN (fl. 610) Engr. GE-1

LI FANG-HSIEN (fl. 1630) Engr. GE-1

LI PO (fl. 800) Engr. GE-1

LI SHIH-CHUNG (fl. 1059) Engr. GE-1

LIANG JUI (fl. 600) Engr. GE-1

LIANG LING-TSAN (fl. 725) Engr. GE-1

LIBAVIUS, Andreas (c.1540-1616) Alch. ABES ABET
BDOS BEOS CDZZ GRCH SXWS ZZ-8

LIBBY, Willard F. (1908-1980) Chem. ABES ABET
AO80 BEOS CB54 MHM1 MHSE PBTS SCLB
WAMB

LICEAGA, Eduardo (1839-1920) Med. CDZZ ZZ-8

LICHTENBERG, Georg C. (1742-1799) Phys. CDZZ
ZZ-8

LICHTENSTEIN, Martin H. (1780-1857) Zool. BWCL

LIDDEL, Duncan (1561-1613) Math. DNB

LIDDEL, Urner (1905-) Phys. CB51

LIDDLE, Leonard M. (1885-1920) Chem. NC18

LIE, Marius S. (1842-1899) Math. BDOS BEOS CDZZ
ZZ-8

LIEBER, Thomas SEE ERASTUS, Thomas

LIEBERKUHN, Johannes N. (1711-1756) Anat. CDZZ
ZZ-8

LIEBIG, Justus von (1803-1873) Chem. ABES ABET
BEOS BHMT CDZZ FBMV GRCH HLSM HSSO
TOWS YSMS ZZ-8

LIESGANIG, Joseph X. (1719-1799) Astron.; Surv.
CDZZ ZZ-8

LIEUTAUD, Joseph (1703-1780) Anat.; Med. CDZZ
ZZ-8

LIFSHITS, Ilya M. (1917-) Phys. SMST

LIGHT, Sol F. (1886-1947) Entom. AMEM

LIGHTHILL, Michael J. (1924-) Phys. BEOS MHM1
MHSE

LIGNIER, Elie A. (1855-1916) Bot. CDZZ ZZ-8

LILIENTHAL, Otto (1848-1896) Aero. ABES ABET
BDOS ICFW

LILLEHEI, Clarence W. (1918-) Med. CB69 LGIH
MFIR

LILLEY, George (1851-1904) Math. BIOD

LILLIE, Frank R. (1870-1947) Embryol.; Zool. BM30
CDZZ DAB4 NC14 NC36 ZZ-8

LILLY, John C. (1915-) Biophys.; Physiol. CB62
MOS6

LILLY, William (1602-1681) Astrol. DNB

LIM, Robert K. (1896-1969) Physiol. BM51 MHM2
MHSE

LIN, Chia-Chiao (1916-) Math. BEOS

LINACRE, Thomas (c.1460-1524) Med. BDOS BEOS
BHMT CDZZ ZZ-8

LINCECUM, Gideon (1793-1874) Nat. Hist. BIOD
DAB NC25

LINCOLN, Frederick C. (1892-1960) Ornith. LACC

LIND, James (1716-1794) Med. ABES ABET BDOS
BEOS BHMT CDZZ ZZ-8

LIND, Samuel C. (1879-1965) Chem. ACCE NC51

LINDAUER, Martin (1918-) Zool. MHM2 MHSE

LINDBERGH, Charles A. (1902-1974) Aero. ABES
ABET CB54 NC60 NCSE OGML PAW2 TECH
WAMB

LINDBLAD, Bertil (1895-1965) Astron. ABES ABET
BEOS CDZZ IEAS ZZ-8

LINDE, Karl von (1842-1934) Engr. ABES ABET
BDOS BEOS CDZZ MCCW ZZ-8

LINDELOF, Ernst L. (1870-1946) Math. CDZZ ZZ-8

LINDEMANN, Carl L. von (1852-1939) Math. ABES
ABET BEOS CDZZ ZZ-8

LINDEMANN, Frederick A., Lord Cherwell (1886-
1957) Phys. BDOS BEOS CB52 CDZZ DNB7
NBPS SIWG SOSC ZZ-8

LINDENAU, Bernhard A. von (1779-1854) Astron.
CDZZ ZZ-8

LINDENKOHL, Adolph (1833-1904) Ocean. BIOD
DAB

LINDER, David H. (1899-1946) Bot. MABH

LINDERSTROM-LANG, Kaj U. (1896-1959) Chem.
RS-6

LINDGREN, Waldemar (1860-1939) Geol. CDZZ
WAMB ZZ-8

LINDHEIMER, Ferdinand J. (1801-1879) Bot. BIOD
DAB

LINDLEY, John (1799-1865) Bot.; Hort. CDZZ ZZ-8

LINDSAY, James B. (1799-1862) Elec. Sci. DNB1

LINDSAY, Margaret, Lady Huggins (1848-1915)
Astron. SLOR

LINDSAY, R. Bruce (1900-) Phys. MHSE

LINDSAY, William L. (1829-1880) Bot. DNB

LINDSEY, Arthur W. (1894-1963) Entom. AMEM

LINDUSKA, Joseph P. (1913-) Cons. LACC

LINFORD, Maurice B. (1901-1960) Bot. NC48

LINGANE, James J. (1909-) Chem. MHM2 MHSE

LINING, John (1708-1760) Physiol.; Meteor. BIOD

LINK, Edwin A. (1904-1981) Ocean. AO81 CB74
EXDC ICFW

LINK, Heinrich F. (1767-1851) Bot.; Chem. CDZZ
ZZ-8

LINNAEUS, Carl (1707-1778) Bot. ABES ABET ANHD
BDOS BEOS BHMT BMST BWCL CDZZ EQSA
FBMV GISA GRBW HAOA HLSM HNHB LISD
NATJ NEXB ORNS SBCS SGNF TOWS ZZ-8

LINNE, Carl von SEE LINNAEUS, Carl

LINNETT, John W. (1913-1975) Chem. COBC RS23

LINNIK, Vladimir P. (1889-) Phys. SMST

LINNIK, Yurii V. (1915-) Math. SMST

LINSLEY, James H. (1787-1843) Nat. Hist. NC-4

LINSTEAD, Reginald P. (1902-1966) Chem. BEOS
RS14

LINTNER, Joseph A. (1822-1898) Entom. AMEM
BIOD DAB NC-5

LINTON, Edwin (1855-1939) Parasit. NC29

LINTON, Ralph (1893-1953) Anthro. BM31 WAMB

LIOUVILLE, Joseph (1809-1882) Math. ABES ABET
BEOS CDZZ ZZ-8

LIPMANN, Fritz A. (1899-) Biochem. ABES ABET
BEOS CB54 MHM1 MHSE WAMB

LIPPERSHEY, Hans (1587-1619) Opt. ABES ABET
BEOS

LIPPINCOTT, James S. (1819-1885) Hort.; Meteor.
BIOD DAB

LIPPISCH, Alexander M. (1894-1976) Aero. ICFW
NC60

LIPPMANN, Gabriel J. (1845-1921) Phys.; Astron.
ABET BDOS BEOS CDZZ POSW ZZ-8

LIPSCHITZ, Rudolf O. (1832-1903) Math. CDZZ ZZ-8

LIPSCOMB, Guy F. (1884-1958) Chem. NC48

LIPSCOMB, William N. (1919-) Chem. ABET BEOS
MHM2 MHSE PAW2

LISBOA, Joao de (d. c.1525) Nav. CDZZ ZZ-8

LISSAJOUS, Jules A. (1822-1880) Phys. BDOS BEOS
CDZZ ZZ-8

LISTER, Arthur (1830-1908) Bot. DNB2

LISTER, Joseph (1827-1912) Med. ABES ABET BDOS
BEOS BHMT CDZZ DNB3 GEXB LISD MAMR
MMMA MNCS OGML SAIF SMIL TOWS ZZ-8

LISTER, Joseph J. (1786-1869) Opt. ABES ABET
CDZZ ZZ-8

LISTER, Martin (1639-1712) Zool.; Geol. ANHD
CDZZ ZZ-8

LISTER, Samuel C. (1815-1906) Invent. BDOS

LISTER, Thomas (1810-1888) Nat. Hist. DNB

LISTON, Robert (1794-1847) Med. BHMT

LITKE, Fyodor P. (1797-1882) Geog. CDZZ ZZ-8

LITTLE, Arthur D. (1863-1935) Chem. ACCE GRCH NC15

LITTLE, Clarence C. (1888-1971) Biol. MB46 CB44 NCSE

LITTLE, William F. (1880-1976) Elec. Engr. NC59

LITTLEWOOD, John E. (1885-1979) Math. BEOS MHM1 MHSE RS24

LIU HUI (fl. c.250) Math. AMST CDZZ ZZ-8

LIUZZI, Mondino de SEE MONDINO DE LIUZZI

LIVEING, George D. (1827-1924) Chem. DNB4

LIVINGSTON, Burton E. (1875-1948) Bot.; Ecol. CDZZ DAB4 MABH ZZ-8

LIVINGSTON, M. Stanley (1905-) Phys. CB55

LI YEH SEE LI CHIH

LLEWELLYN, R.J. (1915-) Chem. COBC

LLOYD, Curtis G. (1859-1926) Bot. MABH NC25

LLOYD, Dorothy J. (1889-1946) Biochem. DNB6

LLOYD, Francis E. (1868-1947) Bot. MABH

LLOYD, Humphrey (1800-1881) Phys. CDZZ ZZ-8

LLOYD, John A. (1800-1854) Engr. DNB

LLOYD, John U. (1849-1936) Chem. ACCE CDZZ NCSD ZZ-8

LLWYD, Edward SEE LHWYD, Edward

LOBACHEVSKY, Nikolai I. (1793-1856) Math. ABES ABET BDOS BEOS CDZZ OMNM RUSP ZZ-8

L'OBEL, Mathias de (1538-1616) Bot. CDZZ ZZ-8

LOCHHEAD, Allan G. (1890-) Microbiol. MHM1 MHSE

LOCKE, John (1632-1704) Philos. BDOS CDZZ ZZ-8

LOCKE, John (1792-1856) Bot.; Geol. ASJD BIOD DAB NC15

LOCKHART, David (d. 1846) Bot. DNB

LOCKYER, Joseph N. (1836-1920) Astrophys. ABES ABET BDOS BEOS CDZZ DNB3 IEAS SNCB VISC ZZ-8

LOCY, William A. (1857-1924) Zool. DAB NC18

LODGE, Oliver J. (1851-1940) Phys. ABES ABET BDOS BEOS CDZZ EETD MMSB PUNT ZZ-8

LOEB, Edwin M. (1894-) Anthro. NCSJ

LOEB, Jacques (1859-1924) Physiol.; Biol. ABES ABET ABFC BEOS BM13 CDZZ ZZ-8

LOEB, Leo (1869-1959) Med. BM35 CDZZ DODR ZZ-8

LOEB, Morris (1863-1912) Chem. ACCE DAB

LOEB, Robert F. (1895-1973) Med. MHM2 MHSE

LOEFFLER, Friedrich A. (1852-1915) Microbiol.; Med. BHMT CDZZ ZZ-8

LOENING, Grover (1888-1976) Aero. ICFW

LOEWI, Otto (1873-1961) Physiol. ABES ABET BDOS BEOS CDZZ DODR RS-8 ZZ-8

LOEWNER, Charles (1893-1968) Math. CDZZ ZZ-8

LOEWY, Alfred (1873-1935) Math. CDZZ ZZ-8

LOFFLER, Friedrich A. (1852-1915) Bact. ABET BEOS

LOGAN, Henry L. (1896-1975) Engr. NC58

LOGAN, James (1674-1751) Bot.; Opt. BIOD SBCS CDZZ ZZ-8

LOGAN, Myra A. (1909-1977) Med. WPSH

LOGAN, William E. (1798-1875) Geol. CDZZ DNB ZZ-8

LOHEST, (Max) Marie J. (1857-1926) Geol.; Paleon. CDZZ ZZ-8

LOHSE, Wilhelm O. (1845-1915) Astron. CDZZ ZZ-8

LOKHTIN, Vladimir M. (1849-1919) Hydrol. CDZZ ZZ-8

LOMBROSO, Cesare (1835-1909) Forens. Sci. PUNT

LOMONOSOV, Mikhail V. (1711-1765) Chem.; Phys. ABES ABET BDOS BEOS CDZZ GRCH IFBS PFEL RUSP THOG ZZ-8

LONDON, Fritz (1900-1954) Phys.; Chem. ABET BEOS CDZZ NC40 ZZ-8

LONDON, Heinz (1907-1970) Phys. BEOS CDZZ MHM2 MHSE RS17 ZZ-8

LONG, Crawford W. (1815-1878) Med. ABET BEOS BHMT MMMA PAW3

LONG, Cyril N. (1901-1970) Biochem. BM46

LONG, Edmond R. (1890-) Med. DODR

LONG, Franklin A. (1910-) Chem. MHM2 MHSE

LONG, Hugh (1901-) Biochem. NCSG

LONG, John H. (1856-1953) Biochem. ACCE DAB NC19

LONGCOPE, Warfield T. (1877-1953) Med. BM33

LONGINOS MARTINEZ, Jose (d. 1803) Nat. Hist.; Bot. SSNW

LONGOMONTANUS SEE SEVERIN, Christian

LONGSTRETCH, Miers F. (1819-1891) Astron. BM-8

LONGUET-HIGGINS, Hugh C. (1923-) Chem. BEOS COBC MHM2 MHSE

LONGWELL, Chester R. (1887-1975) Geol. BM53

LONICERUS, Adam (1528-1586) Bot. CDZZ ZZ-8

LONITZER, Adam SEE LONICERUS, Adam

LONSDALE, Kathleen Y. (1903-1971) Crystal. BEOS CDZZ COBC IDWB MHM1 MHSE RS21 ZZ-8

LONSDALE, William (1794-1871) Geol. CDZZ DNB ZZ-8

LOOKER, Cloyd D. (1889-1965) Chem. NC52

LOOMIS, Alfred L. (1887-1975) Phys. BM51

LOOMIS, Eben J. (1828-1912) Math.; Astron. NC40

LOOMIS, Elias (1811-1889) Astron.; Meteor. ASJD BEOS BIOD BM-3 CDZZ DAB

LOOMIS, Elmer H. (1861-1931) Phys. DAB NC25

LOOMIS, F. Wheeler (1889-1976) Phys. QPAS

LOOMIS, Frederic B. (1873-1937) Paleon. NC30

LOOMIS, Mahlon (1826-1886) Invent. BIOD EETD

LOQSI (fl. 1290) Engr. GE-1

LORD, Frederick P. (1876-1970) Anat. NC57

LORD, Henry C. (1866-1925) Astron. DAB

LORD, John K. (1818-1872) Nat. Hist. DNB

LORENTZ, Hendrik A. (1853-1928) Phys. ABES ABET BDOS BEOS CDZZ DCPW POSW ZZ-8

LORENZ, Egon (1891-1954) Phys. NC41

LORENZ, Hans (1865-1940) Engr. CDZZ ZZ-8

LORENZ, Konrad Z. (1903-) Ethol. ABET BEOS CB77 CB55 MHSE

LORENZ, Ludwig V. (1829-1891) Phys. CDZZ ZZ-8

LORENZ, Richard (1863-1929) Chem. CDZZ HSSO ZZ-8

LORENZONI, Giuseppe (1843-1914) Astron. CDZZ ZZ-8

LORIA, Gino (1862-1954) Math. CDZZ ZZ-8

LORIN, Rene (1877-1933) Invent. ICFW

LORRY, Anne C. (1726-1783) Med. CDZZ ZZ-8

LOSCHMIDT, Johann J. (1821-1895) Phys.; Chem. ABET CDZZ ZZ-8

LOSSEN, Karl A. (1841-1893) Geol. CDZZ ZZ-8

LOTHROP, Samuel K. (1892-1965) Anthro. BM48

LOTKA, Alfred J. (1880-1949) Math. CDZZ DAB4 IMMO ZZ-8

LOTSY, Jan P. (1867-1931) Bot. CDZZ ZZ-8

LOTZE, Hermann R. (1817-1881) Biol. CDZZ ZZ-8

LOUGEE, Richard J. (1905-1960) Geol. NC48

LOUD, Frank H. (1852-1927) Astron. NC31

LOUIS, Pierre C. (1787-1872) Med. BEOS BHMT DSLP

LOVE, Augustus E. (1863-1940) Math.; Geophys. ABET BEOS CDZZ DNB5 ZZ-8

LOVEJOY, Arthur O. (1873-1962) Philos. CDZZ ZZ-8

LOVEJOY, Esther P. (1870-1967) Med. NAWM

LOVEJOY, Parrish S. (1884-1942) Cons. LACC

LOVELACE, Ada B. (1815-1852) Math. IDWB MEQP

LOVELACE, Benjamin F. (1876-1923) Chem. NC31

LOVELACE, William R. (1907-1965) Med. HIUE ICFW MOS2

LOVELAND, George A. (1863-1940) Meteor. NC31

LOVELL, (Alfred) Bernard (1913-) Astron. ABES ABET BEOS CB59 IEAS MHM1 MHSE MOS8

LOVELL, James A. Jr. (1928-) Astronaut. CB69 IEAS

LOVELL, John H. (1860-1939) Bot.; Entom. CDZZ NC37 ZZ-8

LOVELL, Joseph (1788-1836) Med. BHMT

LOVELL, Robert (c.1630-1690) Nat. Hist. DNB

LOVEN, Sven (1809-1895) Mar. Biol. CDZZ ZZ-8

LOVERING, Joseph (1813-1892) Phys.; Math. BIOD BM-6 NC-6

LOVITS, Johann T. (1757-1804) Chem. CDZZ ZZ-8

LOW, Archibald M. (1888-1956) Engr. MMSB

LOW, George (1747-1795) Nat. Hist. DNB

LOWDERMILK, Walter C. (1888-) Cons. LACC

LOWE, Peter (c.1550-1610) Med. BHMT

LOWE, Thaddeus S. (1832-1913) Aero.; Meteor. DAB MCCW NC-9 WAMB

LOWELL, Francis C. (1775-1817) Invent. ASIW INYG

LOWELL, Percival (1855-1916) Astron. ABES ABET BDOS BEOS CDZZ DAB IEAS NC-8 SLOR WAMB ZZ-8

LOWER, Richard (1631-1691) Med. ABES ABET BDOS BEOS BHMT CDZZ DNB ZZ-8

LOWIE, Robert H. (1883-1957) Anthro. BM44 NC46 WAMB

LOWITZ, J.T. SEE LOVITS, Johann T.

LOWRY, Thomas M. (1874-1936) Chem. BDOS BEOS DNB5

LOWY, Alexander (1889-1941) Electrochem. NC37

LU TAO-LUNG (fl. 1025) Engr. GE-1

LUBBOCK, John, Lord Avebury (1834-1913) Entom.; Anthro. BEOS CDZZ DNB3 ZZ-8

LUBBOCK, John W. (1803-1865) Astron. BEOS CDZZ DNB ZZ-8

LUBBOCK, Richard (1759-1808) Chem. CDZZ ZZ-8

LUC, Jean SEE DE LUC, Jean A.

LUCAS, Francois E. (1842-1891) Math. CDZZ ZZ-8

LUCAS, Frederic A. (1852-1929) Nat. Hist. DAB NC13

LUCAS, Howard J. (1885-1963) Chem. ACCE BM43

LUCAS, Keith (1879-1916) Physiol. BEOS CDZZ DNB3 ZZ-8

LUCIANI, Luigi (1840-1919) Physiol. CDZZ ZZ-8

LUCKIESH, Matthew (1889-) Phys. NCSF

LUCRETIUS (c.95 B.C.-55 B.C.) Philos. ABES ABET BDOS BEOS CDZZ ZZ-8

LUDENDORFF, F.W. Hans (1873-1941) Astron. CDZZ ZZ-8

LUDINGTON, C. Townsend (1896-1968) Aero. NC55

LUDLAM, Henry (1824-1880) Mineral. DNB

LUDLAM, William (1717-1788) Math. DNB

LUDWIG, Karl F. (1816-1895) Physiol. ABES ABET BDOS BEOS BHMT CDZZ GASJ ZZ-8

LUEROTH, Jakob (1844-1910) Math. CDZZ ZZ-8

LUGEON, Maurice (1870-1953) Geol. CDZZ ZZ-8

LUGGER, Otto (1844-1901) Entom. AMEM

LUGININ, Vladimir F. (1834-1911) Chem. CDZZ ZZ-8

LUKASIEWICZ, Jan (1878-1956) Math. CDZZ ZZ-8

LUKENS, Hiram S. (1885-1959) Electrochem. ACCE

LULEK, Ralph N. (1901-1970) Chem. NC56

LULL, Ramon (c.1232-1316) Polym. CDZZ GRCH ZZ-8

LULL, Richard S. (1867-1957) Paleon. MADC NCSA

LULLUS, Raymundus SEE LULL, Ramon

LUMIERE, Louis (1864-1948) Photo. BDOS SAIF

LUMMER, Otto R. (1860-1925) Opt. BEOS CDZZ ZZ-8

LUNA, Emerico (1882-1963) Anat. CDZZ ZZ-8

LUNDEGARDH, Henrik G. (1888-1969) Bot. MHM2 MHSE

LUNDELL, Gustav E. (1886-1935) Chem. NC40

LUNDMARK, Knut (1889-1958) Astron. BEOS

LUNGE, Georg (1839-1923) Chem. CDZZ ZZ-8

LURIA, Salvador E. (1912-) Biol. ABET BEOS CB70 MHM1 MHSE WAMB

LUSH, Jay L. (1896-) Genet. MHSE

LUSITANUS, Amatus (1511-1568) Med. CDZZ ZZ-8

LUSK, Graham (1866-1932) Med. BDOS BEOS BHMT BM21 CDZZ ZZ-8

LUSSAC, Joseph L. SEE GAY-LUSSAC, Joseph L.

LUSTIG, Alessandro (1857-1937) Path.; Bact. CDZZ ZZ-8

LUTHER, C. Robert (1822-1900) Astron. CDZZ ZZ-8

LUTZ, Frank E. (1879-1943) Entom. AMEM DAB3 NC42

LU VALLE, James E. (1912-) Chem. SBPY

LUX, John H. (1918-) Chem. Engr. NCSL

LUXFORD, George (1807-1854) Bot. DNB

LUYTEN, Willem J. (1899-) Astron. MHM2 MHSE

LUZIN, Nikolai N. (1883-1950) Math. CDZZ ZZ-8

LWOFF, Andre M. (1902-) Biol. ABES ABET BEOS MHM1 MHSE

LYALL, Robert (1790-1831) Bot. DNB

LYAPUNOV, Aleksandr M. (1857-1918) Math. CDZZ ZZ-8

LYELL, Charles (1767-1849) Bot. DNB

LYELL, Charles (1797-1975) Geol.; Evol. ABES ABET BDOS BEOS CDZZ DARR DMXE DNB ENCE EQSA FHUA HLSM LISD PHLS TOWS ZZ-8

LYMAN, Benjamin S. (1835-1920) Geol. CDZZ ZZ-8

LYMAN, Carl M. (1903-1969) Biochem. NC56

LYMAN, Chester S. (1814-1890) Astorn.; Geol. BIOD CDZZ DAB NC25 ZZ-8

LYMAN, Theodore (1874-1954) Phys. BDOS BEOS BM30 CDZZ DAB5 ZZ-8

LYNCH, John J. (1894-) Seism. CB46

LYNEN, Feodor (1911-1979) Biochem. ABES ABET BEOS CB67 MHM1 MHSE RS28

LYNN, Eldin V. (1886-1955) Chem. NC44

LYNN, George (1676-1742) Astron. DNB

LYON, G. Albert (1881-1961) Invent. NC49

LYON, Howard (1860-1926) Invent. NC20

LYONET, Pierre (1706-1789) Entom. ANHD CDZZ ZZ-8

LYONS, Henry G. (1864-1944) Geol. DNB6

LYOT, Bernard F. (1897-1952) Astron. ABES ABET
BEOS CDZZ IEAS MHM1 MHSE ZZ-8

LYSENKO, Trofim D. (1898-1976) Biol. ABES ABET
BEOS CB52 EXSB MSFB PAW1 SMST SOVL

LYTTLETON, Raymond A. (1911-) Astrophys.
MHSE

LYULKA, Arkhip M. (1908-) Aero. SMST

LYUSTERNIK, Lazar A. (1899-) Math. SMST

M

MA CHUN (fl. 250) Engr. GE-1

MAANEN, Adriaan van (1884-1946) Astron. CDZZ
ZZ-8

MAAS, Otto (1890-1961) Chem. RS-9

MABERY, Charles F. (1850-1927) Chem. ACCE
DAB NC10

MAC See also MC

MACADAM, John (1827-1865) Chem. DNB

MACALLUM, Archibald B. (1858-1934) Biochem.
CDZZ ZZ-8

MACARTHUR, Robert H. (1930-1972) Ecol. BEOS

MACARTNEY, James (1770-1843) Anat. DNB1

MACAULAY, Francis S. (1862-1937) Math. CDZZ
ZZ-8

MACBRIDE, David (1726-1778) Med. CDZZ ZZ-8

MAC BRIDE, Ernest W. (1866-1940) Embryol. CDZZ
ZZ-8

MAC BRIDE, James F. (1892-) Bot. BNBR

MACBRIDE, Thomas (1848-1934) Bot.; Geol. NC11

MAC CALLUM, George A. (1843-1936) Zool. NC32

MAC CALLUM, William G. (1874-1944) Path. BM23
CB44

MAC CULLAGH, James (1809-1847) Phys. CDZZ
ZZ-8

MAC CULLOCH, John (1773-1835) Geol.; Chem.
CDZZ DNB ZZ-8

MAC CURDY, George G. (1863-1947) Anthro.;
Archaeol. DAB4

MAC DONALD, David K. (1920-1963) Phys. RS10

MAC DONALD, Gordon J. (1929-) Geophys. MHM2
MHSE

MAC DONALD, Hector M. (1865-1935) Math.; Phys.
DNB5

MAC DONALD, Marshall (1835-1895) Ichth. NC13

MAC DOUGAL, Daniel T. (1865-1958) Bot. MABH

MACELWANE, James B. (1883-1956) Geophys. BM31

MACEWEN, William (1848-1924) Med. BDOS BEOS

MACFARLANE, John M. (1855-1943) Bot. NCSD

MAC GILLIVRAY, Alexander D. (1868-1942) Entom.
AMEM

MAC GILLIVRAY, William (1796-1852) Nat. Hist.
BWCL DNB

MACH, Ernst (1838-1916) Phys. ABES ABET BDOS
BEOS CDZZ EGSF FNEC HSSO ICFW SAIF
SMIL TGNH ZZ-8

MACHEBOEUF, Michel (1900-1953) Biochem.
CDZZ ZZ-8

MACHIN, John (d. 1751) Astron. DNB

MACHLIS, Leonard (1915-1976) Bot. NC60

MACIE, Lewis SEE SMITHSON, James

MAC INNES, Duncan A. (1885-1965) Chem. ACCE
BM41

MACINTOSH, Charles (1766-1834) Chem.; Invent.
BDOS BEOS DNG GE-1

MACINTYRE, Sheila (1910-1960) Math. NC48

MACK, Edward Jr. (1893-1956) Chem. ACCE NC43

MACK, Julian E. (1903-1966) Phys. NC51

MACK, Pauline B. (1891-) Chem. CB50

MAC KAY, Andrew (1760-1809) Math. DNB

MAC KAY, James T. (c.1775-1856) Meteor. DNB

MAC KAYE, Benton (1879-1975) Forest. NC61

MAC KENZIE, George (1777-1856) Meteor. DNB

MAC KENZIE, George S. (1780-1848) Mineral. DNB

MACKENZIE, James (1853-1925) Med. BEOS BHMT

MACKENZIE, Morell (1837-1892) Med. BHMT

MACKIN, Joseph H. (1905-1968) Geol. BM45

MACKLIN, Madge T. (1893-1962) Med. NAWM

MAC LANE, Saunders (1909-) Math. MHM1 MHSE

MACLAURIN, Colin (1698-1746) Math. ABET BDOS
BEOS CDZZ DNB ZZ-8

MACLEAN, John (1771-1814) Chem. BIOD CDZZ
DAB ZZ-8

MAC LEAR, Thomas (1794-1879) Astron. AROW
CDZZ DNB ZZ-8

MAC LEAY, Alexander (1767-1848) Entom. DNB

MAC LEAY, William S. (1792-1865) Zool. DNB

MAC LEOD, Colin M. (1909-1972) Med.; Microbiol.
BEOS MHM2 MHSE

MAC LEOD, John J. (1876-1936) Physiol. BDOS
BEOS CDZZ DNB5 ZZ-8

MACLOSKIE, George (1834-1920) Biol. NC19

MACLURE, William (1763-1840) Geol. ASJD BIOD
CDZZ SNAR ZZ-8

MAC MAHON, Percy A. (1854-1919) Math. BEOS
CDZZ DNB4 ZZ-8

MAC MILLAN, Conway (1867-1929) Bot. MABH

MAC MILLAN, William D. (1871-1948) Astron.; Math.
CDZZ ZZ-8

MAC NAUGHTON, Lewis W. (1902-1969) Geol. NC55

MAC NIDER, William (1881-1951) Med. BM32

MACOUN, John (1832-1920) Bot. MABH

MACQUER, Pierre J. (1718-1784) Chem. BDOS
BEOS CDZZ ZZ-8

MACROBIUS, Ambrosius T. (fl. c.400-420) Astron.
CDZZ ZZ-8

MAC WILLIAM, John A. (1857-1937) Med. BHMT

MACY, Icie G. (1892-1984) Chem. NCSH

MACY, Josiah Jr. (1924-) Biophys. WMSW

MADISON, Harold L. (1878-1950) Nat. Hist. NC45

MADISON, James (1749-1812) Astron.; Geol. BIOD

MADLER, Johann H. (1794-1874) Astron. ABET
CDZZ ZZ-9

MAGALOTTI, Lorenzo (1637-1712) Sci. Ed. CDZZ
ZZ-9

MAGATE, Cesare (1579-1647) Med. CDZZ ZZ-9

MAGELLAN, Jean H. (1722-1790) Chem.; Phys.
CDZZ ZZ-9

MAGENDIE, Francois (1783-1855) Physiol. ABES
ABET BDOS BEOS BHMT CDZZ HLSM ZZ-9

MAGGI, Bartolomeo (1477-1617) Math.; Astron.
CDZZ ZZ-9

MAGINI, Giovanni A. (1555-1617) Math.; Astron.
CDZZ ZZ-9

MAGIOTTI, Raffaello (1597-1656) Phys. CDZZ ZZ-9

MAGNENUS, Johann C. (c.1590-1679) Nat. Philos.
CDZZ ZZ-9

MAGNI, Valeriano (1586-1661) Phys. CDZZ ZZ-9

MAGNITSKY, Leonty F. (1669-1739) Math. CDZZ
ZZ-9

MAGNOL, Pierre (1638-1715) Bot. CDZZ ZZ-9

MAGNUS, Heinrich G. (1802-1870) Phys.; Chem.
CDZZ FNEC ZZ-9

MAGNUS, Rudolf (1873-1927) Med. BHMT CDZZ
ZZ-9

MAGUIRE, Bassett (1904-) Bot. BNBR

MAHADEVA (fl. 1316) Astron. CDZZ ZZ-9

MAHALANOBIS, Prasantha C. (1893-1972) Math. RS19

MAHAN, Dennis H. (1802-1871) Engr. BM-2

al-MAHANI, Abu abd Allah (fl. c.860-880) Math.; Astron. CDZZ ZZ-9

MAHAVIRA (fl. c.800s) Math. CDZZ ZZ-9

MAHENDRA SURI (fl. 1370) Astron. CDZZ ZZ-9

MAHESHWARI, Panchanan (1904-1966) Bot. RS13

MAHOMED, Frederick H. (1849-1884) Med. BEOS

MAHONEY, Charles H. (1901-1967) Biol. NC53

MAIER, Michael (1568-1662) Alch. CDZZ ZZ-9

MAIGE, Albert (1872-1943) Bot. CDZZ ZZ-9

MAIGNAN, Emanuel (1601-1676) Phys. CDZZ ESEH ZZ-9

MAILLET, Benoit de (1656-1738) Geol.; Ocean. CDZZ ZZ-9

MAIMAN, Theodore H. (1927-) Phys. ABES ABET BEOS MHM2 MHSE

MAIMON, Moses ben (1135-1204) Med. ABES ABET BEOS BHMT CDZZ ZZ-9

MAIMONIDES SEE MAIMON, Moses ben

MAIN, Robert (1808-1878) Astron. DNB

MAINS, Edwin B. (1890-1968) Bot. NC55

MAIOR, John (1469-1550) Math. CDZZ ZZ-9

MAIR, Jean SEE MAIOR, John

MAIR, Simon SEE MAYR, Simon

MAIRAN, Jean J. (1678-1771) Phys. CDZZ EPHG ZZ-9

MAIRE, Rene C. (1878-1949) Bot. CDZZ ZZ-9

MAIZELS, Montague (1899-1976) Path. RS23

ibn MAJID, Shihab al-Din (fl. 1400s) Nav. CDZZ ZZ-9

MAJOCCHI, Domenico (1849-1929) Med. BHMT

MAJORANA, Ettore (1906-1938) Phys. CDZZ ZZ-9

al-MAJRITI, Abul Qasim (d. c.1007) Astron. CDZZ SCIN ZZ-9

al-MAJUSI, Abul Hasan (d. 994) Med. CDZZ ZZ-9

MAKARANDA (fl. 1478) Astron. CDZZ ZZ-9

MAKAROV, Stepan O. (1849-1904) Ocean. CDZZ ZZ-9

MAKEMSON, Maud W. (1891-) Astron. CB41

MAKSIMOV, Nikolay A. (1880-1952) Bot. CDZZ ZZ-9

MAKSUTOV, Dmitry D. (1896-1964) Opt.; Astron. CDZZ SMST ZZ-9

MALASPINA, Alejandro (1754-1809) Exp. SSNW

MALCOLM, Heather (Contemporary) Ethol. WAGW

MALEBRANCHE, Nicolas (1638-1715) Philos. CDZZ ZZ-9

MALER, Teobert (1842-1917) Archaeol. PAMB

MALESHERBES, Chretien G. de (1721-1794) Agr.; Bot. CDZZ ZZ-9

MALFATTI, Gian F. (1731-1807) Math. CDZZ ZZ-9

MALGAIGNE, Joseph F. (1806-1865) Med. BHMT

MALINA, Frank (1912-1981) Rocket. AO81 ICFW

MALINOVSKI, Aleksandr SEE BOGDANOV, Aleksandr A.

MALINOWSKI, Bronislaw (1844-1942) Anthro. CB41 EOMH

MALL, Franklin P. (1862-1917) Anat.; Embryol. ABFC BM16 CDZZ ZZ-9

MALLARD, (Francois) Ernest (1833-1894) Mineral.; Mng. CDZZ ZZ-9

MALLET, John W. (1832-1912) Chem. ACCE DAB

MALLET, Robert (1810-1881) Seism.; Invent. BEOS CDZZ ZZ-9

MALLINCKRODT, Edward (1845-1928) Chem. ACCE

MALLINCKRODT, Edward Jr. (1878-1967) Chem. ACCE

MALLOCH, John R. (1875-1963) Entom. AMEM

MALOUIN, Paul J. (1701-1778) Chem. CDZZ ZZ-9

MALPIGHI, Marcello (1628-1694) Med. ABES ABET ANHD BDOS BEOS BHMT BMST CDZZ FBMV HEXS HLSM LISD LSCS ZZ-9

MALSBERGER, Henry J. (1902-) Forest. LACC

MALTBY, Margaret E. (1860-1944) Phys. NAW

MALTHUS, Thomas R. (1766-1834) Math. ABES BDOS CDZZ IMMO TOWS ZZ-9

MALTSEV, Anatoly I. (1909-1967) Math. CDZZ SMST ZZ-9

MALUS, Etienne L. (1775-1812) Opt. ABES ABET BEOS CDZZ SOAC ZZ-9

MANARDO, Giovanni (1462-1536) Med. CDZZ ZZ-9

MANDELKERN, Leo (1922-) Chem. MHSE

MANDELSHTAM, Leonid I. (1879-1944) Phys. CDZZ ZZ-9

MANDROKLES OF SAMOS (fl. 512 B.C.) Engr. GE-1

MANFREDI, Eustachio (1674-1739) Astron. CDZZ ZZ-9

MANGELSDORF, Paul C. (1899-) Bot. MHM1 MHSE

MANGIN, Louis A. (1852-1937) Bot. CDZZ ZZ-9

MANILIUS, Marcus (fl. c.10) Astrol. CDZZ ZZ-9

MANLY, Charles M. (1876-1927) Aero. ICFW

MANN, Albert (1883-1962) Bot. MABH

MANN, Frank C. (1887-1962) Med. BM38

MANN, Frederick G. (1897-) Chem. COBC

MANN, Paul B. (1876-1943) Biol. NC42

MANN, William (1817-1873) Astron. DNB

MANN, William M. (1886-1960) Entom. AMEM NC47

MANNESMANN, Reinhard (1856-1922) Metal. BDOS

MANNHEIM, Victor M. (1831-1906) Math. CDZZ ZZ-9

MANSFIELD, Charles B. (1819-1855) Chem. DNB

MANSFIELD, Jared (1759-1830) Math.; Phys. BIOD NC-3

MANSION, Paul (1844-1919) Math. CDZZ ZZ-9

MANSON, Patrick (1844-1922) Med. ABES ABET BDOS BEOS BHMT CDZZ DNB4 ZZ-9

MANSUR ibn ALI ibn IRAQ, Abu Nasr (d. c.1036) Astron. CDZZ ZZ-9

MANTEGAZZA, Paolo (1831-1910) Med.; Anthro. CDZZ ZZ-9

MANTELL, Gideon A. (1790-1852) Paleon.; Geol. ABET CDZZ MADC PHLS ZZ-9

MANTON, Sidnie M. (1902-1979) Zool. BEOS IDWB MHM2 MHSE RS26

MANZO SEE AJIMA NAONOBU

MANZOLINI, Anne (1716-1774) Anat. IDWB

MAPES, Charles V. (1836-1916) Chem. BIOD NC-3

MAPES, James J. (1806-1866) Chem.; Agr. ACCE BIOD

MAPSON, Leslie W. (1907-1970) Biochem. RS18

al-MAQDISI, Shams al-Din Abu (c.946-c.999) Geog. CDZZ ZZ-9

MARALDI, Giacomo F. (1665-1729) Astron. CDZZ ZZ-9

MARCGRAVE, George SEE MARKGRAF, Georg

MARCHAND, Richard F. (1813-1850) Chem. CDZZ ZZ-9

MARCHANT, Jean (1650-1738) Bot. CDZZ ZZ-9

MARCHANT, Nicolas (d. 1678) Bot. CDZZ ZZ-9

MARCHI, Vittorio (1851-1908) Path. CDZZ ZZ-9

MARCHIAFAVA, Ettore (1847-1935) Path.; Anat. CDZZ ZZ-9

MARCHLEWSKI, Leon P. (1869-1946) Chem. CDZZ ZZ-9

MARCI OF KRONLAND, Johannes (1595-1667) Phys.; Med. CDZZ ZZ-9

MARCONI, Guglielmo (1874-1937) Elec. Engr. ABES ABET BDOS BEOS CDZZ EETD FOIF HOSS MGAH MMSB OGML PAW2 POSW SAIF SMIL TOWS ZZ-9

MARCOU, Jules (1824-1898) Geol.; Paleon. BIOD CDZZ ZZ-9

MARCUS, Johannes SEE MARCI OF KRONLAND, Johannes

MARCUS, Rudolph A. (1923-) Chem. MHSE

MARCY, Henry O. (1837-1924) Med. BHMT

MARCY, Oliver (1820-1899) Geol. BIOD

MAREY, Etienne J. (1830-1904) Physiol. ABET BDOS BEOS CDZZ ZZ-9

MARGAI, Milton (1895-1964) Med. CB62

MARGENEAU, Henry (1901-) Phys. QPAS

MARGERIE, Emmanuel M. de (1862-1953) Geol.; Geog. CDZZ ZZ-9

MARGGRAF, Andreas S. (1709-1782) Chem. ABET BDOS BEOS CDZZ GRCH ZZ-9

MARGULES, Max (1856-1920) Meteor.; Phys. CDZZ ZZ-9

MARGULIS, Lynn (1938-) Biol. BEOS

MARIANO, Jacopo SEE TACCOLA, Mariano J.

MARIE, Pierre (1853-1940) Med. BHMT CDZZ ZZ-9

MARIE VICTORIN (Brother) (1885-1944) Bot. MABH

MARIGNAC, Jean C. de (1817-1894) Chem. ABET BDOS BEOS CDZZ ZZ-9

MARINUS (fl. c.450-500) Philos. CDZZ ZZ-9

MARION, Antoine F. (1846-1900) Zool. CDZZ ZZ-9

MARION, Leo E. (1899-1979) Chem. RS26

MARIOTTE, Edme (c.1620-1684) Phys. ABES ABET BDOS BEOS CDZZ ZZ-9

MARIUS, Simon SEE MAYR, Simon

MARK, Edward L. (1847-1946) Zool. NC-9

MARK, Herman F. (1895-) Chem. CB61 MHM1 MHSE

MARKGRAF, Georg (1610-1644) Bot.; Zool. CDZZ HAOA ZZ-9

MARKHAM, Albert H. (1841-1918) Exp. WFBG

MARKHAM, Clements R. (1830-1916) Geog. CDZZ ZZ-9

MARKHAM, Roy (1916-1979) Agr. RS28

MARKOV, Andrei A. (1856-1922) Math. BEOS CDZZ IMMO SMST ZZ-9

MARKOVNIKOV, Vladimir V. (1837-1904) Chem. ABET CDZZ ZZ-9

MARKS, Arthur H. (1874-1939) Chem. ACCE

MARLATT, Charles L. (1863-1954) Entom. AMEM NC13 NC49

MARLIANA, Giovanni (d. 1483) Phys.; Med. CDZZ ZZ-9

MARR, John E. (1857-1933) Geol. DNB5

MARRAT, William (1772-1852) Math. DNB

MARRIAN, Guy F. (1904-1981) Biochem. RS28

MARRIOTT, Williams M. (1885-1936) Biochem. DAB2

MARSDEN, Ernest (1889-1970) Phys. MHM2 MHSE RS17

MARSEL, Charles J. (1921-1964) Chem. Engr. NC51

MARSH, C. Dwight (1855-1932) Biol. NC27

MARSH, George P. (1801-1882) Geog. BIOD BM-6 CONS DAB EAFC GOTH HOCS LACC SFNB

MARSH, James (1794-1846) Chem. BDOS BEOS

MARSH, Othniel C. (1831-1899) Paleon. ABES ABET ABFC BEOS BIOD BM20 CDZZ DAB MSAJ NC-9 NHAH PHLS SNAR WAMB ZZ-9

MARSHAK, Robert E. (1916-) Phys. CB73 MHM2 MHSE

MARSHALL, Abraham L. (1896-1974) Chem. NC58

MARSHALL, Albert E. (1884-1951) Chem. ACCE

MARSHALL, Arthur M. (1852-1893) Nat. Hist. DNB1

MARSHALL, Charles E. (1866-1927) Bact. NC23

MARSHALL, George (1904-) Cons. LACC

MARSHALL, Guy A. (1871-1959) Entom. DNB7 RS-6

MARSHALL, Humphry (1722-1801) Bot. BIOD DAB MABH

MARSHALL, Madison L. (1906-1956) Chem. NC49

MARSHALL, Robert (1901-1939) Cons. EAFC LACC SFNB

MARSHALL, Sheina M. (1896-1977) Mar. Biol. RS24

MARSHAM, Thomas (d. 1819) Entom. DNB

MARSILI, Luigi F. (1658-1730) Nat. Hist. CDZZ ZZ-9

MARSILIUS OF INGHEN (d. 1396) Nat. Philos. CDZZ ZZ-9

MARSTON, Hedley R. (1900-1965) Biochem. RS13

MARTENS, Adolf (1850-1914) Metal. CDZZ ZZ-9

MARTI FRANQUES, Antonio de (1750-1832) Meteor.; Chem. CDZZ ZZ-9

MARTIANUS CAPELLA (fl. 365-440) Sci. Ed. CDZZ ZZ-9

MARTIN OF BOHEMIA SEE BEHAIM, Martin

MARTIN, Archer J. (1910-) Chem. ABES ABET BEOS CB53 COBC MHM1 MHSE

MARTIN, Artemas (1835-1918) Math. DAB NC-2

MARTIN, Benjamin (1704-1782) Instr. CDZZ DNB ZZ-9

MARTIN, Charles J. (1866-1955) Biochem. RS-2

MARTIN, Clyde S. (1884-1963) Forest. LACC

MARTIN, David (1914-1976) Chem. COBC RS24

MARTIN, Henry N. (1848-1896) Physiol. BIOD CDZZ NC12 ZZ-9

MARTIN, Hugh E. (1902-1973) Med. NC57

MARTIN, James S. Jr. (1920-) Astronaut. CB77

MARTIN, John (1789-1869) Meteor. DNB

MARTIN, Matthew (1748-1838) Nat. Hist. DNB

MARTIN, Peter J. (1786-1860) Geol. DNB

MARTIN, Pierre E. (1824-1915) Invent. BDOS

MARTIN, Rudolf (1864-1925) Anthro. CDZZ ZZ-9

MARTIN, William (1767-1810) Nat. Hist. DNB

MARTINEAU, Bryant (1890-) Forest. BNBR

MARTINEZ, Cristomo (1638-1694) Anat. CDZZ ZZ-9

MARTINI, Francesco (1439-1501) Engr. CDZZ ZZ-9

MARTINOVICS, Ignac (1755-1795) Chem. CDZZ ZZ-9

MARTIUS, Karl F. von (1794-1868) Bot.; Anthro. CDZZ ZZ-9

MARTONNE, Emannuel L. de (1873-1955) Geog. CDZZ ZZ-9

MARTYN, David F. (1906-1970) Phys. MHM2 MHSE RS17

MARTYN, John (1699-1768) Bot. DNB

MARTYN, Thomas (1735-1825) Bot. DNB

MARUM, Martin van (1750-1837) Med.; Bot. CDZZ MCCW ZZ-9

MARVEL, Carl S. (1894-) Chem. BEOS MHM1 MHSE

MARVIN, Charles F. (1858-1943) Meteor. DAB3 NC40

MARX, George (1838-1895) Entom. AMEM BIOD

MASAMUNE (fl. 1300) Metal. GE-1

MASCAGNI, Paolo (1755-1815) Anat. CDZZ ZZ-9

MASCART, Eleuthere E. (1837-1908) Phys. CDZZ ZZ-9

MASCHERONI, Lorenzo (1750-1800) Math. CDZZ ZZ-9

MASCHKE, Heinrich (1853-1908) Math. DAB

MASERES, Francis (1731-1824) Math. CDZZ DNB ZZ-9

MASHA ALLAH (fl. 762-815) Astrol. CDZZ ZZ-9

MASIUS, Morton (1883-) Phys. QPAS

MASKELL, Ernest J. (1895-1958) Bot. RS-7

MASKELYNE, Nevil (1732-1811) Astron. ABET BDOS BEOS CDZZ DNB IEAS ZZ-9

MASON, Basil J. (1923-) Meteor. MHSE

MASON, Charles (1728-1786) Astron. CDZZ DNB NC10 WAMB ZZ-9

MASON, David T. (1883-1973) Forest. EAFC LACC

MASON, Donald B. (1898-1968) Anthro. NC54

MASON, Gregory (1889-1968) Anthro. NC54

MASON, Herbert L. (1896-) Bot. BNBR

MASON, James W. (1836-1905) Math. BIOD

MASON, Max (1877-1961) Phys. BM37

MASON, Mayne S. (1890-1977) Elec. Engr. NC59

MASON, Otis T. (1838-1908) Anthro. NC10

MASON, Ronald (1930-) Chem. COBC

MASON, Stanley G. (1914-) Chem. Engr. MHSE

MASON, Thomas G. (1890-1959) Bot. RS-6

MASON, Warren P. (1900-) Phys.; Engr. MHSE

MASON, William H. (1877-1940) Invent. EAFC

MASON, William P. (1853-1937) Chem. ACCE

MASSA, Niccolo (1485-1569) Med. CDZZ ZZ-9

MASSERMAN, Jules H. (1905-) Psychiat. CB80

MASSEVITCH, Alla G. (1918-) Chem. SBPY

MASSIE, Samuel P. (1919-) Chem. SBPY

MASSON, Antoine P. (1806-1860) Phys. CDZZ ZZ-9

MASSON, David O. (1858-1937) Chem. DNB5

MASSON, Francis (1741-1805) Bot. DNB

MASSON, Irvine (1887-1962) Chem. RS-9

MAST, Samuel O. (1871-1947) Bot. CDZZ NC33 ZZ-9

MASTERMAN, Stillman (1831-1863) Meteor.; Astron. BIOD

MASTERS, Maxwell T. (1833-1907) Bot. DNB2

MASTERS, William H. (1915-) Med. CB68

MASTLIN, Michael (1550-1631) Astron. CDZZ ZZ-9

al-MASUDI, Abul Hasan (d. 956/7) Geog. CDZZ SCIN ZZ-9

MATAS, Rodolphe (1860-1957) Med. BHMT

MATHER, Cotton (1863-1728) Med. BIOD SSAH

MATHER, Increase (1639-1723) Astron. BIOD

MATHER, Kenneth (1911-) Genet. BEOS MHM2 MHSE

MATHER, Kirtley F. (1888-1978) Geol. CB51 MHM2 MHSE

MATHER, Stephen T. (1867-1930) Cons. CONS EAFC LACC PCWA WAMB

MATHER, William W. (1804-1859) Geol. ACCE BIOD CDZZ ZZ-9

MATHESON, Robert (1881-1958) Entom. AMEM

MATHESON, William J. (1856-1930) Chem. DAB

MATHEWS, George B. (1861-1922) Math. CDZZ ZZ-9

MATHEWS, Joseph H. (1881-1970) Chem. ACCE

MATHIEU, Emile L. (1835-1890) Math.; Phys. CDZZ ZZ-9

MATRUCHOT, Louis (1863-1921) Bot. CDZZ ZZ-9

MATTEUCCI, Carlo (1811-1868) Physiol.; Phys. CDZZ ZZ-9

MATTHES, Francois E. (1874-1948) Geol. DAB4 WAMB

MATTHEW, William D. (1871-1930) Paleon. DAB

MATTHEWS, Drummond H. (1931-) Geol. BEOS

MATTHEWS, Joseph M. (1874-1931) Chem. DAB

MATTHIAS, Bernard T. (1919-1980) Phys. ABET AO80 BEOS MHM1 MHSE

MATTHIESSEN, Augustus (1831-1870) Chem. CDZZ DNB ZZ-9

MATTHIESSEN, Peter (1927-) Nat. Hist. CB75

MATTILL, Henry A. (1883-1953) Biochem. NC41

MATTIOLI, Pietro A. (1501-1577) Med.; Bot. ANHD CDZZ ZZ-9

MATTOX, Norman T. (1910-1960) Zool. NC48

MATUYAMA, Motonori (1884-1958) Phys.; Geol. BEOS CDZZ ZZ-9

MATZELIGER, Jan Earnest (1852-1889) Invent. BPSH DANB EBAH GNPA HCOK SABL SBPY WAMB

MATZKE, Edwin B. (1902-1969) Bot. NC54

MAUCHLY, John W. (1907-1980) Phys.; Engr.; Comp. ABET AO80

MAUDSLAY, Alfred P. (1850-1931) Archaeol. FAMB

MAUDSLAY, Henry (1771-1831) Engr. BDOS BEOS DNB GE-1

MAUGHAM, William S. (1874-1965) Med. BHMT

MAUGUIN, Charles V. (1878-1958) Crystal.; Mineral. CDZZ ZZ-9

MAUNDER, Edward W. (1851-1928) Astron. ABET BEOS CDZZ ZZ-9

MAUNDER, Elwood R. (1917-) Forest. LACC

MAUPAS, Francois E. (1842-1916) Zool.; Biol. CDZZ ZZ-9

MAUPERTIUS, Pierre L. (1698-1759) Math. ABES ABET BDOS BEOS CDZZ HLSM ZZ-9

MAURER, Julius M. (1857-1938) Meteor.; Astron. CDZZ ZZ-9

MAURI, Ernesto (1791-1836) Bot. WFBG

MAURICEAU, Francois (1637-1709) Med. BHMT

MAURO, Fra (d. 1459) Geog. CDZZ ZZ-9

MAUROLICO, Francesco (1494-1575) Math.; Astron. BMST CDZZ ZZ-9

MAURY, Antonia C. (1866-1952) Astron. BEOS CDZZ IDWB NAWM ZZ-9

MAURY, Carlotta J. (1874-1938) Paleon. NC28

MAURY, Matthew F. (1806-1873) Ocean.; Meteor. ABES ABET BDOS BEOS BIOD CDZZ DAB EXDC EXSG HFGA LISD MSAJ SNAR WAMB ZZ-9

MAVOR, James W. (1883-1963) Biol. NC52

MAWE, John (1764-1829) Mineral. DNB

MAWSON, Douglas (1882-1958) Geol. CDZZ DNB7 RS-5 ZZ-9

MAXCY, Kenneth F. (1889-1966) Med. BM42

MAXIM, Hiram P. (1869-1936) Invent. DAB2

MAXIM, Hiram S. (1840-1916) Invent. ABES ABET BDOS TBTM WAMB

MAXIMOW, Nicolai SEE MAKSIMOV, Nikolay

MAXON, William R. (1877-1948) Bot. NC38

MAXSON, John H. (1906-1966) Geol. NC53

MAXSON, Ralph N. (1879-1943) Chem. NC32

MAXWELL, George H. (1860-1946) Cons. LACC

MAXWELL, James C. (1831-1879) Math.; Phys. ABES ABET BDOS BEOS CAVL CDZZ DNB EETD FNEC GOED GRTH HOSS IFBS SAIF TOWS VTHB ZZ-9

MAY, Robert M. (1936-) Ecol. BEOS

MAYBACH, Wilhelm (1846-1929) Engr. BDOS ICFW

MAYER, Alfred M. (1836-1897) Phys. BIOD BM-8
CDZZ NC13 ZZ-9

MAYER, Christian (1719-1783) Astron. CDZZ ZZ-9

MAYER, Christian G. (1839-1908) Math. CDZZ ZZ-9

MAYER, Jean (1920-) Physiol. CB70

MAYER, Johann T. (1723-1762) Astron. CDZZ ZZ-9

MAYER, Joseph E. (1904-) Chem. MHM1 MHSE

MAYER, Julius R. (1814-1878) Phys. ABES ABET
BDOS BEOS CDZZ MCCW TBSG ZZ-9

MAYER, Maria G. (1906-1972) Phys. ABET BEOS
BM50 CB64 IDWB LLWO MHM1 MHSE NAWM
NC58 POSW WAMB WPSH

MAYER, Rudolph L. (1895-1962) Microbiol. NC47

MAYER-EYMAR, Karl (1826-1907) Paleon. CDZZ
ZZ-9

MAYERNE, Theodore T. de (1573-1655) Med. BHMT

MAYNARD, Charles J. (1845-1929) Nat. Hist. DAB

MAYNARD, George W. (1839-1913) Chem.; Mng.
ACCE

MAYNARD, Leonard A. (1887-1972) Biochem. ACCE
MHM2 MHSE

MAYNARD SMITH, John (1920-) Biol. BEOS

MAYO, Frank R. (1908-) Chem. MHSE

MAYO, Herbert (1796-1852) Med. BHMT CDZZ
DNB ZZ-9

MAYOR, Alfred G. (1868-1922) Zool. DAB NC19

MAYOW, John (1640-1679) Physiol. ABES ABET
BDOS BEOS BHMT CDZZ DNB EPHG ZZ-9

MAYR, Ernst W. (1904-) Biol. BEOS MHM2 MHSE

MAYR, Simon (1570-1624) Astron. ABES ABET
BDOS BEOS CDZZ ZZ-9

MAYWALD, Frederick J. (1870-1937) Chem. NC28

MAZER, Jacob (1885-1954) Phys. NC43

MAZIA, Daniel (1912-) Biol. MHM2 MHSE

al-MAZINI SEE ABU HAMID, al-Gharnati

MAZURKIEWICZ, Stefan (1888-1945) Math. CDZZ
ZZ-9

MAZZINI, Louis Y. (1894-1973) Med. NC58

MC ADAM, John C. (1911-1976) Elec. Engr. NC59

MC ADAM, John L. (1756-1836) Engr. ABES ABET
BDOS BEOS DNB FOIF GE-1 SAIF

MC ADAMS, William H. (1892-1975) Chem. Engr.
HCEF

MC ADIE, Alexander G. (1863-1943) Meteor. DAB3
NC35

MC ARDLE, Richard E. (1899-) Forest. EAFC
LACC

MC ARTHUR, William P. (1814-1850) Surv. BIOD

MC ATEE, Waldo L. (1883-1962) Biol. LACC

MC BAIN, James W. (1882-1953) Chem. NC42

MC BRIDE, James (1784-1817) Bot. NC11

MC BURNEY, Charles (1845-1913) Med. BHMT

MC BURNEY, John W. (1890-1961) Chem. NC49

MC CABE, Warren L. (1899-) Chem. Engr. NCSL

MC CALLEY, Henry (1852-1904) Geol. BIOD

MC CARTHY, John (1927-) Comp. HOPL

MC CARTNEY, Washington (1812-1856) Math. DAB

MC CARTY, Maclyn (1911-) Med. MHM2 MHSE
BEOS

MC CAY, Charles F. (1810-1889) Math. BIOD DAB

MC CLEAN, Frank (1837-1904) Astron. DNB2

MC CLELLAN, George (1796-1847) Med. BHMT

MC CLELLAN, James C. (1908-) Forest. LACC

MC CLENDON, Dorothy (Contemporary) Microbiol.
BISC

MC CLINTOCK, Emory (1840-1916) Math. DAB
NC12

MC CLOSKEY, John M. (1934-) Cons. LACC

MC CLUNG, Clarence E. (1870-1946) Zool. CDZZ
DAB4 NC34 ZZ-9

MC CLURE, Frank T. (1916-1973) Chem. NC57

MC COLL, Hugh (1837-1909) Math. CDZZ ZZ-9

MC COLLOCH, James W. (1889-1929) Entom. NC23

MC COLLUM, Elmer V. (1879-1967) Biochem.
ABES ABET ACCE BEOS BM45 CDZZ NCSC
RS15 ZZ-8

MC CONNELL, Harden M. (1927-) Chem. BEOS
MHM2 MHSE

MC CONNELL, James V. (1925-) Psych. PAW1

MC COOK, Henry C. (1837-1911) Entom. AMEM
DAB

MC CORMICK, Cyrus H. (1809-1884) Invent. AMIH
ASIW BDOS COAC DAB FOIF INYG SAIF
TECH TINA WAMB

MC COWN, John C. (c.1817-1879) Nat. Hist. BWCL

MC COY, Caldwell (1933-) Elec. Engr. BCST

MC COY, David O. (1911-1960) Astron. NC48

MC COY, Elijah (1843-1929) Engr. BCST BPSH
EBAH GNPA HCOK SABL SBPY DANB

MC COY, Frederick (1823-1899) Nat. Hist.; Geol.
DNB1

MC COY, Herbert N. (1870-1945) Chem. ACCE
NCSE

MC CRACKIN, Josephine W. (1838-1920) Cons. NAW

MC CRADY, Edward (1906-) Biol. CB57

MC CREATH, Lesley (1881-1957) Chem. NC47

MC CULLAGH, James (1809-1847) Math. DNB

MC CULLOH, Richard S. (1818-1894) Chem.; Phys.
ACCE BIOD

MC CULLOUGH, C. Rogers (1900-1970) Chem. NC55

MC CUNE, Francis K. (1906-) Elec. Engr. CB61

MC DERMOTT, Eugene (1899-1973) Geol. NC58

MC DERMOTT, Walsh (1909-) Med. MHSE

MC DIVITT, James A. (1929-) Astronaut. CB65

MC DOWELL, Ephraim (1771-1830) Med. BHMT
MMMA

MC DUNNOUGH, James H. (1877-1962) Entom.
AMEM

MC ELVAIN, Samuel M. (1897-1973) Chem. NC58

MC FARLAND, John H. (1859-1948) Cons.; Hort.
DAB4

MC FARLAND, Ross A. (1901-1976) Psych. MHM2
MHSE

MC GEE, William J. (1853-1912) Geol.; Cons. LACC
SASH

MC GLASHAN, Maxwell L. (1924-) Chem. COBC

MC GRAIL, John (1891-1945) Chem. NC38

MC GREGOR, Louis D. (1901-) Cons. LACC

MC GRIGOR, James (1771-1858) Med. BHMT

MC GUIRE, John R. (1916-) Forest. EAFC

MC ILWAIN, Carl E. (1931-) Phys. MHSE

MC INDOO, Norman E. (1881-1956) Entom. AMEM

MC INNES, Alexander G. (1918-1976) Biophys. NC59

MC INTOSH, William C. (1838-1931) Zool. CDZZ
ZZ-9 DNB5

MC KEEVER, Kay (Contemporary) Ethol. WAGW

MC KENNA, Charles F. (1861-1930) Chem. Engr.
ACCE

MC KENNA, Francis E. (1921-1978) Chem. CB66

MC KENZIE, Alexander (1869-1951) Chem. DNB7

MC LAINE, Leonard S. (1887-1943) Entom. AMEM

MC LAUGHLIN, Donald H. (1891-) Geol. NCSK

MC LEAN, Jay (1890-1957) Med. BHMT

MC LENNAN, John C. (1867-1935) Phys. BEOS
DNB5

MC LEOD, James W. (1887-1978) Bact. RS25

MC LINTOCK, William F. (1887-1960) Geol. DNB7

MC MAHON, Charles A. (1830-1904) Geol. DNB2

MC MAHON, Howard O. (1914-) Chem. NCSL

MC MASTER, Le Roy (1879-1946) Chem. NC34

MC MASTER, Philip D. (1891-1973) Physiol. BM50

MC MATH, Robert R. (1891-1962) Astron. BM49
NCSG

MC MEEN, Samuel G. (1864-1934) Elec. Engr. TPAE

MC MICHAEL, John (1904-) Med. MHM2 MHSE

MC MILLAN, Edwin M. (1907-) Phys. ABET BEOS
CB52 DCPW MHM1 MHSE NCSH PAW2 WAMB

MC MURRICH, James P. (1859-1939) Anat. DNB5

MC MURTRIE, William (1851-1913) Chem. ACCE
DAB NC12

MC NAB, William R. (1844-1889) Bot. DNB

MC NAIR, Andrew H. (1909-1978) Geol. NC61

MC NAIR, James B. (1889-) Chem.; Bot. NCSE

MC NARY, Charles L. (1874-1944) Forest. LACC

MC NAUGHT, John (1813-1881) Invent. BDOS

MC NEELY, Eugene J. (1900-1974) Engr. CB62

MC NEILL, James M. (1892-1964) Engr. RS11

MC PHERSON, William (1864-1951) Chem. ACCE

MC QUARRIE, Irvine (1891-1961) Med. DODR

MC SHANE, Edward J. (1904-) Math. MHM1 MHSE

MC TAMMANY, John (1845-1915) Invent. WAMB

MC WEENY, Roy (1924-) Chem. COBC

MEAD, Albert D. (1869-1946) Biol. NC36

MEAD, Margaret (1901-1978) Anthro. CB40 CB51
CWSE CWSN EOMH MHSE NCSI SWWP WAMB
WASM

MEAD, Richard (1673-1754) Med. BHMT

MEAD, Sylvia E. (1935-) Mar. Biol. CB72 IDWB
WPSH

MEAD, Warren J. (1883-1960) Geol. BM35

MEADE, Richard K. (1874-1930) Chem. Engr. ACCE
NC10

MEADE, William (d. 1833) Mineral. BIOD

MEANS, James H. (1885-) Med. DODR

MEARNS, Edgar A. (1856-1916) Nat. Hist. DAB

MEASE, James (1771-1846) Med.; Geol. BIOD DAB

MECHAIN, Pierre F. (1744-1804) Surv.; Astron.
CDZZ ZZ-9

MECHNIKOV, Ilya I. (1845-1916) Bact.; Embryol.
ABES ABET BDOS BEOS BHMT CDZZ HLSM
MAMC PAW2 RUSP TPOS ZZ-9

MECKEL, Johann F. (1781-1833) Anat.; Embryol.
BHMT CDZZ ZZ-9

MEDAWAR, Peter B. (1915-) Biol.; Immunol.
ABES ABET BEOS CB61 MHM1 MHSE PAW2

MEDES, Grace (1886-1967) Chem. ACCE

MEDHURST, George (1759-1827) Engr. DNB

MEDICUS, Friedrich C. (1736-1808) Bot. CDZZ
ZZ-9

MEDINA, Pedro de (1493-1576) Nav. CDZZ ZZ-9

MEDLICOTT, Henry B. (1829-1905) Geol. DNB2

MEDVEDEV, Sergei S. (1891-1970) Chem. SMST

MEDVEDEV, Zhores Z. (1925-) Biol. CB73

MEEHAN, Thomas (1826-1901) Bot.; Hort. BIOD
DAB NC11

MEEK, Fielding B. (1817-1876) Paleon.; Geol. BIOD
BM-4 CDZZ DAB ZZ-9

MEERLOO, Joost A. (1903-1977) Psychiat. CB62

MEES, Carl L. (1853-1932) Phys. NC26

MEES, Charles E. (1882-1960) Chem. BEOS BM42
NC52 RS-7

MEES, Graham C. (1910-1965) Chem. NC52

MEGE MOURIES, Hippolyte (1817-1880) Invent.
BDOS

MEGGERS, Betty Jane (1921-) Anthro. SWWP

MEGGERS, William F. (1888-1966) Phys. BM41
CDZZ NC53 ZZ-9

MEGHNAD, Saha (1893-1956) Spect.; Astrophys.
DNB7

MEHL, Robert F. (1898-1976) Metal.; Chem. MHM2
MHSE

MEIGS, Montgomery C. (1816-1892) Engr. BM-3

MEIKLE, Andrew (1719-1811) Engr. GE-1

MEINERTZHAGEN, Richard (1878-) Ornith. DGMT

MEINESZ, Felix A. SEE VENING MEINESZ, Felix A.

MEINZER, Oscar E. (1876-1948) Hydrol. CDZZ
DAB4 ZZ-9

MEISEL, Maksin N. (1901-) Microbiol. SMST

MEISSNER, Georg (1829-1905) Anat.; Physiol. CDZZ
ZZ-9

MEISTER, Alton (1922-) Biochem. MHM2 MHSE

MEITNER, Lise (1878-1968) Phys. ABES ABET BDOS
BEOS CB45 CDZZ IDWB MHM2 MHSE RS16
WPSH ZZ-9

MELA, Pomponius SEE POMPONIUS MELA

MELANDER, Axel L. (1878-1962) Entom. AMEM

MELDRUM, Charles (1821-1901) Meteor. DNB2

MELENTEV, Lev A. (1908-) Engr. SMST

MELL, Patrick H. (1814-1888) Geol.; Bot. DAB

MELLANBY, Edward (1884-1955) Pharm. BDOS
BEOS CDZZ DNB7 RS-1 ZZXV

MELLANBY, John (1878-1939) Physiol. DNB5

MELLANBY, Kenneth (1908-) Entom. POEC

MELLO, Francisco de (1490-1536) Math. CDZZ ZZ-9

MELLONI, Macedonio (1798-1854) Phys. ABES
ABET BEOS CDZZ ZZ-9

MELLOR, Lewis L. (1889-1961) Opt. NC50

MELNIKOV, Nikolai V. (1909-1980) Mng. AO80

MELNIKOV, Oleg A. (1912-) Astron. SMST

MELSHEIMER, Frederick V. (1749-1814) Entom.
AMEM BIOD DAB

MELTZER, Samuel J. (1851-1920) Physiol.; Pharm.
CDZZ ZZ-9

MELVILL, Thomas (1726-1753) Astron.; Phys. CDZZ
ZZ-9

MELVILLE, Harry W. (1908-) Chem. BEOS COBC
MHM1 MHSE

MENABREA, Luigi F. (1809-1896) Engr. CDZZ ZZ-9

MENAECHMUS (fl. c.350 B.C.) Math. ABET CDZZ
ZZ-9

MENDEL, Bruno (1897-1959) Med. RS-6

MENDEL, (Johann) Gregor (1822-1884) Genet. ABES
ABET ABFC BDOS BEOS CDZZ EQSA FBMV
FMBB HLSM LISD MGAH PAW3 SAIF SMIL
TGNH TOWS ZZ-9

MENDEL, Lafayette B. (1872-1935) Chem. BM18
CDZZ DAB1 NC26 ZZ-9

MENDELEEF, Dmitri I. (1834-1907) Chem. ABES
ABET BDOS BEOS CDZZ CSCJ GRCH HOSS
HSSO IFBS MGAH RUSP SAIF TOWS ZZ-9

MENDELEV SEE MENDELEEF, Dmitri

MENDELEYEV SEE MENDELEEF, Dmitri

MENDELSSOHN, Kurt A. (1906-1980) Phys. AO80

MENDENHALL, Charles E. (1872-1935) Phys. BM18
DAB1

MENDENHALL, Dorothy R. (1874-1964) Med. NAWM

MENDENHALL, Thomas C. (1841-1924) Meteor. BM16
DAB NC10

MENDENHALL, Walter C. (1871-1957) Geol. BM46

MENEGHETTI, Egidio (1892-1961) Pharm. CDZZ ZZ-9

MENELAUS OF ALEXANDRIA (fl. c.100) Math.; Astron. CDZZ ZZ-9

MENGE, Edward J. (1882-1941) Biol. NC45

MENGHINI, Vincenzo A. (1704-1759) Med.; Chem. CDZZ ZZ-9

MENGOLI, Pietro (1625-1686) Math. BDOS BEOS CDZZ ZZ-9

MENIERE, Prosper (1799-1862) Med. BHMT

MENSHUTKIN, Nikolay A. (1842-1907) Chem. CDZZ ZZ-9

MENURET DE CHAMBAUD, Jean J. (1733-1815) Physiol.; Med. CDZZ ZZ-9

MENZEL, Donald H. (1901-1976) Astrophys. ABES ABET BEOS CB56 MHM2 MHSE NC59

MERAY, Hughes C. (1835-1911) Math. CDZZ ZZ-9

MERCATI, Michelle (1541-1593) Med.; Paleon. CDZZ ZZ-9

MERCATOR, Gerardus (1512-1594) Geog. ABES ABET BDOS BEOS CDZZ EETD SAIF ZZ-9

MERCATOR, Nicolaus (c.1619-1687) Math.; Astron. CDZZ ZZ-9

MERCER, James (1883-1932) Math. DNB5

MERCER, John (1791-1866) Chem. BDOS BEOS DNB

MERCK, George (1867-1926) Chem. ACCE

MERCK, George W. (1894-1957) Chem. ACCE

MERGENTHALER, Ottmar (1854-1899) Invent. BDOS MPIP SAIF WAMB

MERICA, Paul D. (1889-1957) Metal. BM33 CDZZ ZZ-9

MERING, Josef von (1849-1908) Med. BHMT

MERIWETHER, W. Delano (1943-) Med. CB78

MERREM, Daniel (1790-1859) Med. BHMT

MERRETT, Christopher (1614-1695) Nat. Hist. CDZZ ZZ-9

MERRIAM, Clinton H. (1855-1942) Biol. BM24 CDZZ DAB3 LACC NC13 ZZ-9

MERRIAM, John C. (1869-1945) Paleon. BM26 CDZZ DAB3 EAFC ZZ-9

MERRIFIELD, Charles W. (1827-1884) Math. DNB

MERRILL, Elmer D. (1876-1956) Bot. BM32 CDZZ MABH NC45 ZZXV

MERRILL, George P. (1854-1929) Geol. CDZZ ZZ-9

MERRILL, Joshua (1820-1904) Chem. DAB NC13

MERRILL, Paul W. (1887-1961) Astron. BEOS BM37 MHM1 MHSE NC49 NCSI

MERRITT, Ernest G. (1865-1948) Phys. NC15

MERSENNE, Marin (1588-1648) Math.; Phys. ABES ABET BEOS CDZZ ZZ-9

MERTON, Thomas R. (1888-1967) Phys. BEOS RS16

MERWIN, Herbert E. (1878-1963) Geol. NC50

MERWIN, Richard E. (1922-1981) Comp. AO81

MERY, Jean (1645-1722) Anat.; Med. CDZZ ZZ-9

MERZ, Charles H. (1874-1940) Elec. Engr. DNB5

MESCHERYAKOV, Mikhail G. (1910-) Phys. SMST

MESELSON, Matthew S. (1930-) Biol. BEOS MHM2 MHSE

MESHCHERSKY, Ivan V. (1859-1935) Phys.; Math. CDZZ ZZ-9

MESMER, Franz A. (1734-1815) Med. ABES ABET BEOS CDZZ MSFB PAW1 ZZ-9

MESNIL, Felix (1868-1938) Biol.; Med. CDZZ ZZ-9

MESSEL, Rudolph (1848-1920) Chem. BDOS BEOS

MESSENGER, Powers S. (1920-1976) Entom. NC59

MESSIER, Charles (1730-1817) Astron. ABES ABET BEOS CDZZ IEAS ZZ-9

MESTRE, Harold de Villa (1884-1939) Biol. NC29

MESYATSEV, Ivan I. (1885-1940) Ocean. CDZZ ZZ-9

METAGENES OF KNOSSOS (fl. 550 B.C.) Engr. GE-1

METCALF, Clell L. (1888-1948) Entom. AMEM NC42

METCALF, Joel H. (1866-1925) Astron. DAB

METCALF, John (1717-1818) Engr. GE-1

METCALF, Maynard C. (1868-1940) Zool. NCSE

METCALF, Zeno P. (1885-1956) Entom. AMEM NC44

METCALFE, Samuel L. (1798-1856) Chem. BIOD DAB

METCHNIKOV, Elie SEE MECHNIKOV, Ilya

METIUS, Adriaen A. (c.1543-1620) Engr. CDZZ ZZ-9

METIUS, Jacob (1580-1628) Instr. BEOS CDZZ ZZ-9

METON (fl. c.420-430 B.C.) Astron. ABES ABET BEOS CDZZ ZZ-9

METTENIUS, Georg H. (1823-1866) Bot. CDZZ ZZ-9

METZ, Charles W. (1889-1975) Zool. MHM2 MHSE

METZGER, Helene (1889-1944) Chem. CDZZ IDWB ZZ-9

MEUSNIER DE LA PLACE, Jean B. (1754-1793) Math.; Phys. CDZZ GE-1 ZZ-9

MEXIA, Ynes E. (1870-1938) Bot. NAW

MEYEN, Franz J. (1804-1840) Bot. CDZZ ZZ-9

MEYER, Christian E. (1801-1869) Paleon. CDZZ ZZ-9

MEYER, Frank N. (1875-1918) Bot. NC20

MEYER, Harry M. Jr. (1932-) Med. MFIR

MEYER, Johann F. (1705-1765) Chem. CDZZ ZZ-9

MEYER, Julius L. (1830-1895) Chem. ABES ABET BDOS BEOS CDZZ ZZ-9

MEYER, Karl (1899-) Biochem. BEOS MHM2 MHSE

MEYER, Karl F. (1884-1974) Bact. BM52

MEYER, Kurt H. (1883-1952) Chem. CDZZ ZZ-9

MEYER, Viktor (1848-1897) Chem. ABES ABET BDOS BEOS CDZZ GRCH HSSO ZZ-9

MEYER, Wilhelm F. (1856-1934) Math. CDZZ ZZ-9

MEYERHOF, Otto F. (1884-1951) Biochem. ABES ABET ACCE BDOS BEOS BHMT BM34 CDZZ DAB5 GJPS HSSO ZZ-9

MEYERHOFF, Howard A. (1899-1982) Geol. NCSK

MEYERSON, Emile (1859-1933) Philos. CDZZ ZZXV

MEYRICK, Edward (1854-1938) Entom. DNB5

MIBELLI, Vittorio (1860-1910) Med. BHMT

MICHAEL SCOT (fl. 1217-1236) Astrol.; Trans. Sci. Lit. CDZZ ZZ-9

MICHAEL, Arthur (1853-1942) Chem. ACCE BM46 CDZZ DAB3 NC15 ZZ-9

MICHAELIS, Leonor (1875-1949) Chem. ABES ABET ACCE BEOS BM31 DAB4

MICHAUD, Howard H. (1902-) Biol.; Sci. Writ. LACC

MICHAUX, Andre (1746-1802) Bot. BIOD CDZZ DAB EAFC LHES MABH ZZ-9

MICHAUX, Francois A. (1770-1855) Bot. BIOD DAB EAFC LHES MABH

MICHEL-LEVY, Auguste (1844-1911) Geol.; Mineral. CDZZ ZZ-9

MICHELI, Pier A. (1679-1737) Bot. CDZZ ZZ-9

MICHELINI, Famiano (1604-1665) Phys. CDZZ ZZ-9

MICHELL, Anthony G. (1870-1959) Engr. RS-8

MICHELL, John (1724-1793) Astron. ABES ABET BEOS CDZZ DNB ZZ-9

MICHELS, Nicholas A. (1891-1969) Anat. NC55

MICHELS, Walter C. (1906-1975) Phys. NC58

MICHELSON, Albert A. (1852-1931) Phys. ABES ABET ASIW BEOS BM19 CDZZ DAB DCPW IEAS MSAJ NC12 NC33 POSW QPAS SAIF SNAR WAMB ZZ-9

MICHENER, Charles D. (1918-) Biol. MHM2 MHSE

MICHENER, Ezra (1794-1887) Nat. Hist. BIOD DAB NC15

MICHIE, Peter S. (1839-1901) Phys.; Engr. BIOD

MICHURIN, Ivan V. (1855-1935) Hort.; Genet. CDZZ ZZXV

MICKEL, Clarence E. (1892-) Entom. NCSH

MIDDAUGH, Paul R. (1920-) Bact. PALF

MIDDENDORF, Alexander T. (1815-1894) Biol. CDZZ WFBG ZZ-9

MIDDLETON, Peter (d. 1781) Chem. ACCE

MIDGLEY, Thomas Jr. (1889-1944) Chem. ABES ABET ACCE BEOS BM23 DAB3 CDZZ GRCH HSSO ZZ-9

MIE, Gustav (1868-1957) Phys. CDZZ ZZ-9

MIELI, Aldo (1879-1950) Chem. CDZZ ZZ-9

MIERS, Henry A. (1858-1942) Mineral. CDZZ DNB6 ZZ-9

MIESCHER, Johann F. (1844-1895) Physiol.; Chem. ABES ABET BEOS CDZZ HLSM ZZ-9

MIGDAL, Arkadii B. (1911-) Phys. SMST

MIKHAILOV, Aleksandr A. (1888-) Astron. SMST

MIKLUKHO-MAKLAY, Mikhail N. (1857-1927) Geol. CDZZ ZZXV

MIKOYAN, Artyom I. (1905-) Aero. SMST

MIKULICZ, Johann von (1850-1905) Med. BHMT

MIKULIN, Aleksandr A. (1895-) Aero. SMST

MILANKOVICH, Milutin (1879-1958) Math. BEOS

MILES, George W. (1868-1939) Chem. NC29

MILES, Manly (1828-1898) Agr.; Zool. BIOD DAB NC15

MILGRAM, Stanley (1933-) Psych. CB79

MILHAM, Willis I. (1874-1957) Astron. NC45

MILHAUD, Gaston (1858-1918) Math. CDZZ ZZ-9

MILKMAN, Louis A. (1895-1951) Med. BHMT

MILL, Hugh R. (1861-1950) Meteor. DNB6

MILL, John S. (1808-1873) Philos. CDZZ ZZ-9

MILLER, Alden H. (1906-1965) Zool. BM43 LACC

MILLER, Arthur M. (1894-1959) Chem. Engr. NC47

MILLER, Banner I. (1917-1976) Meteor. NC59

MILLER, Charles P. (1894-) Med. MHM2 MHSE

MILLER, Dayton C. (1866-1941) Phys. ABES ABET BEOS BM23 CDZZ DAB3 DCPW NC30 ZZ-9

MILLER, Edmund H. (1869-1906) Chem. NC20

MILLER, Edwin C. (1878-1949) Bot. MABH

MILLER, Elmer (1918-1962) Chem. NC50

MILLER, Frederick R. (1881-1967) Physiol. RS15

MILLER, George A. (1863-1951) Math. BM30 CDZZ DAB5 NC16 ZZ-9

MILLER, George A. (1920-) Psych. MHM2 MHSE

MILLER, Harriet M. (1831-1918) Nat. Hist. DAB SFNB

MILLER, Harry W. (1879-1977) Med. CB62

MILLER, Hugh (1802-1856) Geol. BEOS CDZZ DARR HNHB ZZ-9

MILLER, Jacques F. (1931-) Med. ABES ABET BEOS

MILLER, Julian H. (1890-1961) Bot. NC47

MILLER, Neal E. (1909-) Psych. CB74 MHM1 MHSE

MILLER, Olive T. SEE MILLER, Harriet M.

MILLER, Philip (1691-1771) Bot.; Hort. CDZZ ZZ-9

MILLER, Robert L. (1920-1976) Geophys. NC59

MILLER, Stanley L. (1930-) Chem. ABES ABET BEOS MOS6

MILLER, Walter M. (1859-1942) Bot. BNBR

MILLER, Wendell Z. (1892-1958) Geol. NC43

MILLER, William A. (1817-1870) Chem.; Astron. CDZZ DNB ZZ-9

MILLER, William H. (1801-1880) Crystal. ABET CDZZ DNB ZZ-9

MILLER, William L. (1866-1940) Chem. CDZZ ZZ-9

MILLIGAN, Charles H. (1888-) Chem. NCSF

MILLIKAN, Clark B. (1903-1968) Phys.; Math. BM40

MILLIKAN, Robert A. (1868-1953) Phys. ABES ABET ASIW BDOS BEOS BM33 CB40 CB52 CDZZ DAB5 DCPW MMSB POSW QPAS WAMB ZZ-9

MILLINGTON, John (1779-1868) Chem. ACCE

MILLINGTON, Thomas (1628-1704) Med. CDZZ ZZ-9

MILLIONSHCHIKOV, Mikhail D. (1913-) Phys. SMST

MILLON, Auguste N. (1812-1867) Chem.; Agr. CDZZ ZZ-9

MILLS, Bernard Y. (1920-) Phys.; Astron. BEOS

MILLS, Enos A. (1870-1922) Nat. Hist. DAB1 PCWA SFNB

MILLS, James (1876-1950) Chem. NC45

MILLS, Mark M. (1917-1958) Phys. NC48

MILLS, William (1856-1932) Engr. DNB5

MILLS, William H. (1873-1959) Chem. BEOS CDZZ DNB7 RS-6 ZZ-9

MILLSPAUGH, Charles F. (1854-1923) Bot. DAB MABH NC25

MILNE, Edward A. (1896-1950) Math.; Astrophys. ABET BDOS BEOS CDZZ DNB6 MHM1 MHSE ZZ-9

MILNE, John (1850-1913) Seism. ABES ABET BEOS CDZZ ZZ-9

MILNE-EDWARDS, Henri (1800-1885) Zool. CDZZ ZZ-9

MILNER, Isaac (1750-1820) Math. DNB

MILNER, Samuel R. (1875-1958) Phys. RS-5

MILROY, William F. (1855-1942) Med. BHMT

MILSTEIN, Cesar (1927-) Biol. BEOS

MILTON, John (1937-) Ecol. POEC

MINDING, Ernst F. (1806-1885) Math. CDZZ ZZ-9

MINER, Carl S. (1878-1967) Chem. ACCE

MINER, Harlan S. (1864-1938) Chem. NC29

MINETT, Francis C. (1890-1953) Vet. Med. DNB7

MINEUR, Henri (1899-1954) Astron.; Astrophys. CDZZ ZZ-9

MINKOWSKI, Hermann (1864-1909) Math. ABES ABET BDOS BEOS CDZZ EGSF ZZ-9

MINKOWSKI, Oskar (1858-1931) Med.; Chem. BHMT

MINKOWSKI, Rudolph L. (1895-1976) Astron. ABES ABET BEOS

MINNAERT, Marcel G. (1893-1970) Astrophys. CDZZ MHM1 MHSE ZZ-9

MINOKA-HILL, Lillie R. (1876-1952) Med. NAWM

MINOT, Charles S. (1852-1914) Biol. ABFC BM-9 CDZZ DAB NC-6 ZZ-9

MINOT, George R. (1885-1950) Med. ABES ABET BDOS BEOS BHMT BM45 CDZZ ZZ-9

MINTO, Walter (1753-1796) Math. BIOD DAB

M'INTOSH, William SEE MC INTOSH, William

MINTS, Aleksandr L. (1895-) Engr. SMST

MIQUEL, Friedrich A. (1811-1871) Bot. CDZZ ZZ-9

MIRBEL, Charles F. de (1776-1854) Bot. CDZZ ZZ-9

MISES, Richard von (1883-1953) Math. CDZZ ZZ-9

MISLOW, Kurt M. (1923-) Chem. MHSE

MITCHEL, Ormsby M. (1809-1862) Astron. BIOD DAB NC-3

MITCHELL, Elisha (1793-1857) Nat. Hist. BIOD
CDZZ DAB ZZ-9

MITCHELL, George H. (1902-1976) Geol. RS23

MITCHELL, Henry (1830-1902) Surv. BIOD BM20

MITCHELL, James A. (1852-1902) Geol. BIOD

MITCHELL, John (c.1690-1768) Nat. Hist. BIOD
DAB SBCS

MITCHELL, John K. (1793-1858) Chem.; Physiol.
ACCE BIOD DAB

MITCHELL, John W. (1913-) Phys. MHM2 MHSE

MITCHELL, Maria (1818-1889) Astron. ABET BEOS
BIOD CDZZ COAC CWSE DAB HFGA IDWB
NAW NC-5 WAMB ZZ-9

MITCHELL, Peter C. (1864-1945) Zool. DNB6

MITCHELL, Peter D. (1920-) Biochem. ABET BEOS
SOT2

MITCHELL, Samuel A. (1874-1960) Astron. BM36

MITCHELL, Silas W. (1829-1914) Med. BHMT BM32
CDZZ ZZ-9

MITCHELL, Thomas D. (1791-1865) Chem. ACCE

MITCHELL, William (1791-1869) Astron. BIOD DAB
NC11

MITCHELL-HEDGES, Frederick A. (1882-1959)
Archaeol. PAMB

MITCHILL, Samuel L. (1764-1831) Chem.; Nat. Hist.
ABFC ACCE ASJD BIOD DAB NC-4

MITRA, Sisir R. (1890-1963) Phys. RS10

MITSCHERLICH, Eilhardt (1794-1863) Chem.;
Mineral. ABES ABET BDOS BEOS CDZZ GRCH
HSSO ZZ-9

MITTAG-LEFFLER, Magnus G. (1846-1927) Math.
CDZZ ZZ-9

MITTASCH, Alwin (1869-1953) Chem. CDZZ HSSO
ZZ-9

MIVART, St. George J. (1827-1900) Biol.; Nat. Hist.
CDZZ DNB1 ZZ-9

MIYASHIRO, Akiho (1920-) Geol. MHSE

MOBIUS, August F. (1790-1868) Math.; Astron.
ABES ABET BEOS CDZZ ZZ-9

MOBIUS, Karl A. (1825-1908) Zool. CDZZ ZZ-9

MOCINO, Jose M. (1757-1820) Bot. CDZZ ZZ-9

MODJESKI, Ralph (1861-1940) Engr. BM23

MOELWYN-HUGHES, Emyr A. (1905-) Chem. COBC

MOENCH, Conrad (1744-1805) Bot. CDZZ ZZ-9

MOERBEKE, William of (c.1225-c.1285) Math.; Biol.
CDZZ ZZ-9

MOFFETT, James W. (1908-1967) Biol. LACC

MOFFETT, Thomas (1553-1604) Med.; Entom. CDZZ
ZZ-9

MOHL, Hugo von (1805-1872) Biol. ABES ABET
BEOS CDZZ ZZ-9

MOHLER, John F. (1864-1930) Phys. NC42

MOHN, Henrik (1835-1916) Meteor.; Ocean. CDZZ
ZZ-9

MOHOROVICIC, Andrija (1857-1936) Meteor.; Seism.
ABES ABET BEOS CDZZ TGNH ZZ-9

MOHR, Carl F. (1806-1879) Chem.; Geol. CDZZ
HSSO ZZ-9

MOHR, Charles T. (1824-1901) Bot. BIOD DAB
NC26

MOHR, Christian O. (1835-1918) Engr. CDZZ FNEC
ZZ-9

MOHR, Georg (1640-1697) Math. CDZZ ZZ-9

MOHS, Freidrich (1773-1839) Mineral.; Geol. ABES
ABET BDOS BEOS CDZZ ZZ-9

MOISEEV, Nikolay D. (1902-1955) Astron. CDZZ
ZZ-9

MOISSAN, Ferdinand F. (1852-1907) Chem. ABES
ABET BDOS BEOS CDZZ GRCH HSSO NPWC
ZZ-9

MOISSAN, Henri SEE MOISSAN, Ferdinand F.

MOIVRE, Abraham de (1667-1754) Math. BDOS BEOS
CDZZ DNB ZZ-9

MOLARD, Francois E. (1774-1829) Engr. GE-1

MOLDENHAWER, Johann J. (1766-1827) Bot. CDZZ ZZ-9

MOLESCHOTT, Jacob (1822-1893) Med. CDZZ ZZ-9

MOLIN, Fedor E. (1861-1941) Math. CDZZ ZZ-9

MOLINA, Augustin SEE BETANCOURT Y MOLINA, Augustin de

MOLINA, Juan I. (1740-1829) Nat. Hist. CDZZ ZZ-9

MOLL, Friedrich R. (1882-1951) Engr. CDZZ ZZ-9

MOLL, Gerard (1785-1838) Astron.; Phys. CDZZ ZZ-9

MOLLER, Didrik M. (1830-1896) Astron. CDZZ ZZ-9

MOLLIARD, Marin (1866-1944) Bot. CDZZ ZZ-9

MOLLIER, Richard (1863-1935) Engr. CDZZ FNEC ZZ-9

MOLLWEIDE, Karl B. (1774-1825) Astron. CDZZ ZZ-9

MOLODENSKII, Mikhail S. (1909-) Geophys. SMST

MOLYNEUX, Samuel (1689-1728) Astron.; Opt. CDZZ DNB ZZ-9

MOLYNEUX, William (1656-1698) Astron.; Phys. CDZZ ZZ-9

MONAKOW, Constantin von (1853-1930) Med. BHMT

MONARDES, Nicolas B. (1493-1588) Med. CDZZ SBCS ZZ-9

MOND, Ludwig (1839-1909) Chem. BDOS BEOS CDZZ DNB2 ZZ-9

MOND, Robert L. (1861-1938) Chem. DNB5

MONDEVILLE SEE HENRY OF MONDEVILLE

MONDINO DE LUZZI (c.1275-1326) Anat. ABET BEOS CDZZ TALS ZZ-9

MONEY, John (1752-1817) Aero. DNB

MONEYMAKER, Berlen C. (1904-) Geol. NCSK

MONGE, Gaspard (1746-1818) Math. ABET BDOS BEOS CDZZ ZZ-9

MONIZ, Antonio SEE EGAS MONIZ, Antonio

MONNET, Antoine G. (1734-1817) Chem.; Mineral. CDZZ ZZ-9

MONOD, Jacques L. (1910-1976) Biol. ABES ABET BEOS CB71 EDCJ MHM1 MHSE RS23

MONRO, Alexander I (1697-1767) Anat. BDOS BEOS CDZZ ZZ-9

MONRO, Alexander II (1733-1817) Anat. BDOS BEOS CDZZ ZZ-9

MONRO, Alexander III (1773-1859) Anat. BDOS DNB

MONTAGU, George (1751-1815) Nat. Hist. DNB

MONTANARI, Geminiano (1633-1687) Astron.; Geophys. CDZZ ZZ-9

MONTE, Guidobaldo del (1545-1607) Math.; Astron. CDZZ ZZ-9

MONTELIUS, Gustav O. (1843-1921) Archeol. CDZZ ZZ-9

MONTENIER, Jules B. (1895-1962) Chem. NC52

MONTESQUIEU, Charles L. (1689-1755) Philos. CDZZ ZZ-9

MONTGERY, Jacques P. de (1781-1839) Rocket. CDZZ ZZ-9

MONTGOLFIER, Etienne J. (1745-1777) Invent. ABES ABET BDOS CDZZ GE-1 ICFW SAIF ZZ-9

MONTGOLFIER, Michel J. (1740-1810) Invent. ABES ABET BDOS CDZZ GE-1 ICFW SAIF ZZ-9

MONTGOMERY, Deane (1909-) Math. CB57

MONTGOMERY, Edmund D. (1835-1911) Biol. CDZZ ZZ-9

MONTGOMERY, John J. (1858-1911) Invent. NC15

MONTGOMERY, Thomas H. Jr. (1873-1912) Zool. CDZZ DAB NC15 ZZ-9

MONTMORT, Pierre R. de (1678-1719) Math. CDZZ ZZ-9

MONTUCLA, Jean E. (1725-1799) Math. CDZZ ZZ-9

MOODY, Herbert R. (1869-1948) Anat. NC36

MOODY, Paul (1779-1831) Engr.; Invent. GE-1

MOODY, Robert O. (1864-1948) Anat. NC36

MOOK, Maurice A. (1904-1973) Anthro. NC58

MOON, Merl P. (1891-1958) Bact. NC46

MOONEY, James (1861-1921) Anthro. SASH

MOORE, Carl R. (1892-1955) Zool. BM45

MOORE, Clarence L. (1876-1931) Math. DAB

MOORE, Eliakim H. (1862-1932) Math. BM17 CDZZ
DAB1 ZZ-9

MOORE, Emmeline (1872-1963) Biol. LACC

MOORE, Forris J. (1867-1926) Chem. ACCE

MOORE, George E. (1920-) Med. CB68

MOORE, George T. (1871-1956) Bot. NC13 NC47

MOORE, Gideon E. (1842-1895) Chem. ACCE

MOORE, John A. (1915-) Biol. MHM2 MHSE

MOORE, Jonas (1617-1679) Math. DNB

MOORE, Joseph H. (1878-1949) Astron. CDZZ DAB4
NC37 ZZ09

MOORE, Norman (1847-1922) Med. BHMT

MOORE, Norman (1923-) Biol. POEC

MOORE, Raymond C. (1892-1974) Geol.; Paleon.
MHM1 MHSE NC59

MOORE, Richard B. (1871-1931) Chem. ACCE DAB
NC40

MOORE, Robert J. (1892-1947) Chem. ACCE

MOORE, Stanford (1913-) Biochem. ABET BEOS
MHSE

MOORE, Thomas (1821-1887) Bot. DNB

MOORE, Veranus A. (1859-1931) Bact. NC22

MOORE, William (fl. c.1806-1823) Rocket. CDZZ
ZZ-9

MOOREHEAD, Warren K. (1866-1939) Archaeol. NC38

MORAT, Jean P. (1846-1920) Physiol. CDZZ ZZ-9

MORAY, Robert (1608-1673) Chem.; Metal. CDZZ
ZZ-9

MORDELL, Louis J. (1888-1972) Math. BEOS MHM1
MHSE RS19

MORE, Henry (1614-1687) Philos. CDZZ ZZ-9

MORE, Thomas (fl. 1670-1724) Nat. Hist. BIOD
SBCS

MOREAU, Charles (1863-1929) Chem. GRCH

MOREHEAD, John M. (1870-1965) Chem. ACCE

MOREHOUSE, Daniel W. (1876-1941) Astron. NC33

MOREY, George W. (1888-1965) Chem. NC53

MOREY, Samuel (1762-1843) Invent. BIOD GE-1

MORFIT, Campbell (1820-1897) Chem. BIOD DAB

MORGAGNI, Giovanni B. (1682-1771) Anat. ABES
ABET BDOS BEOS BHMT CDZZ ZZ-9

MORGAN, Agnes F. (1884-1968) Chem. ACCE

MORGAN, Anne H. (1882-1966) Zool. NAWM

MORGAN, Augustus de (1808-1871) Math. STYC

MORGAN, Charles E. (1900-1960) Chem. NC48

MORGAN, Conway L. (1852-1936) Psych. CDZZ
ZZ-9

MORGAN, Garret A. (1877-1963) Invent. BCST
BPSH DANB EBAH GNPA HCOK SABL SBPY

MORGAN, George C. (1754-1798) Sci. Writ. DNB

MORGAN, Gilbert T. (1872-1940) Chem. DNB5

MORGAN, Harcourt A. (1867-1950) Entom. NC14
NCSE

MORGAN, Herbert R. (1875-1957) Astron. CDZZ
ZZ-9

MORGAN, John (1735-1789) Chem.; Med. ACCE
BHMT

MORGAN, John H. (1867-1950) Entom. DAB4

MORGAN, Lewis H. (1818-1881) Anthro. BM-6
WAMB

MORGAN, Morien B. (1912-1978) Aero. RS26

MORGAN, Paul W. (1911-) Chem. MHSE

MORGAN, Thomas H. (1866-1945) Genet. ABES
ABET ABFC BDOS BEOS BM33 CDZZ DAB3
FMBB GRBW HLSM MSAJ NC12 NC35 PAW2
TOWS WAMB ZZ-9

MORGAN, William W. (1906-) Astron. ABES ABET
BEOS IEAS MHM2 MHSE

MORGENSTERN, Oskar (1902-1977) Math. IMMO

MORICHINI, Domenico L. (1773-1836) Med.; Chem.
CDZZ ZZ-9

MORIN, Jean B. (1583-1656) Med.; Astrol. CDZZ
ZZ-9

MORISON, Robert (1620-1683) Bot. CDZZ DNB
ZZ-9

MORITA, Akio (1921-) Phys. CB72

MORLAND, Samuel (1625-1695) Math. CDZZ ZZ-9

MORLEY, Edward W. (1838-1923) Chem.; Phys.
ABES ABET ACCE BDOS BEOS CDZZ DAB
WANB ZZ-9

MORLEY, Frank (1860-1937) Math. DAB2 NC15
NC28

MORLEY, Sylvanus G. (1883-1948) Archaeol. DAB4
PAMB

MORO, Antonio L. (1687-1764) Geol. CDZZ ZZ-9

MOROZOV, Georgy F. (1867-1920) Biol.; Ecol.
CDZZ ZZ-9

MORREY, Charles B. Jr. (1907-) Math. MHM1
MHSE

MORRILL, Austin W. (1880-1954) Entom. AMEM

MORRIS, Desmond (1928-) Zool. CB74

MORRIS, Francis O. (1810-1893) Nat. Hist. DNB

MORRIS, James L. (1885-1926) Biochem. NC20

MORRIS, John (1810-1886) Geol. DNB

MORRIS, John G. (1803-1895) Entom. AMEM BIOD

MORRIS, Kelso B. (1909-) Chem. SBPY

MORRIS, Margaretta H. (1797-1867) Entom. BIOD

MORRISON, Harley J. (1866-1950) Chem. NC39

MORRISON, Harold (1890-1963) Entom. AMEM

MORRISON, Philip (1915-) Astrophys. CB81

MORSE, Albert P. (1863-1936) Entom. AMEM NC27

MORSE, Edward S. (1838-1925) Zool. BM17 CDZZ
DAB NC-3 NC24

MORSE, Harmon N. (1848-1920) Chem. NC16

MORSE, Harold M. (1892-1977) Math. CB57 MHM1
MHSE NCSF

MORSE, Harry W. (1873-1936) Chem. ACCE

MORSE, Jedidiah (1761-1826) Geog. CDZZ ZZ-9

MORSE, Philip M. (1903-) Phys. CB48 MHM2
MHSE QPAS

MORSE, Samuel F.B. (1791-1872) Invent. ABES
ABET AMIH ASIW BDOS BEOS COAC COBC
DAB EETD GE-1 HFGA HOSS INYG SAIF
TINA TPAE WAMB

MORSE, William C. (1874-1962) Geol. NC52

MORTILLET, Louis L. de (1821-1898) Anthro.;
Archaeol. ABET CDZZ ZZ-9

MORTON, George H. (1826-1900) Geol. DNB1

MORTON, Harold A. (1890-1958) Chem. NC48

MORTON, Henry (1836-1902) Chem.; Phys. ACCE
BIOD BM-8 DAB NC11

MORTON, John (c.1671-1726) Nat. Hist. CDZZ DNB
ZZ-9

MORTON, Julius S. (1832-1902) Forest. LACC

MORTON, Richard (1637-1698) Med. BHMT

MORTON, Richard A. (1899-1977) Biochem. RS24

MORTON, Samuel G. (1799-1851) Anthro. ASJD BIOD CDZZ DAB ZZ-9

MORTON, William T. (1819-1868) Med. ABES ABET ASIW BDOS BEOS BHMT COAC HFGA MSAJ SMIL PAW3 TBSG YSMS

MORUZZI, Giuseppe (1910-) Physiol. MHM2 MHSE

MOSANDER, Carl G. (1797-1858) Chem. ABES ABET BDOS BEOS CDZZ ZZ-9

MOSELEY, Edwin L. (1865-1948) Nat. Hist. NC41

MOSELEY, Hal W. (1888-1941) Chem. NC30

MOSELEY, Henry (1801-1872) Math. DNB

MOSELEY, Henry G. (1887-1915) Phys. ABES ABET BDOS BEOS CDZZ CSCJ DNB3 ZZ-9

MOSELEY, Henry N. (1844-1891) Nat. Hist. DNB

MOSS, Eugene G. (1877-1949) Chem. NC39

MOSS, Sanford (1872-1949) Aero. ICFW

MOSS, William L. (1876-1957) Med. CDZZ ZZ-9

MOSSBAUER, Rudolph L. (1929-) Phys. ABES ABET BEOS CB62 MHM1 MHSE POSW TGNH

MOSSO, Angelo (1846-1910) Physiol.; Archaeol. CDZZ ZZ-9

MOSSOTTI, Ottaviano F. (1791-1863) Phys. CDZZ ZZ-9

MOTT, Henry A. Jr. (1852-1896) Chem. BIOD NC-3

MOTT, Nevill F. (1905-) Phys. ABET BEOS CAVL MHM1 MHSE PAW2 POSW SOTT

MOTT, Valentine (1785-1865) Med. BHMT

MOTTELSON, Ben R. (1926-) Phys. ABET BEOS MHSE POSW

MOTTIER, David M. (1864-1940) Bot. MABH

MOTTRAM, James C. (1879-1945) Med.; Nat. Hist. CDZZ ZZ-9

MOUCHEZ, Ernest B. (1821-1892) Astron. CDZZ ZZ-9

MOULTON, Forest R. (1872-1952) Astron. ABES ABET BEOS BM41 CB46 CDZZ DAB5 NC43 ZZ-9

MOUTARD, Theodore F. (1827-1901) Engr. CDZZ ZZ-9

MOUTON, Gabriel (1618-1694) Math.; Astron. CDZZ ZZ-9

MOYER, Burton J. (1912-1973) Phys. NC58

MOYES, Henry (1750-1807) Chem. ACCE

MOYLE, Matthew P. (1788-1880) Meteor. DNB

MOYNIHAN, Berkeley G. (1865-1936) Med. BHMT CDZZ ZZ-9

MOZINO, Jose M. (c.1758-1820) Bot. SSNW

MUDGE, Thomas (1717-1794) Invent. BDOS

MUELLER, Erwin W. (1911-1977) Phys. ABES ABET BEOS MHSE

MUELLER, George E. (1918-) Phys. CB64

MUENCH, Carl G. (1887-1971) Invent. NC58

MUHLENBERG, Gotthilf H. (1753-1815) Bot. BIOD DAB NC-9

MUHYIL-DIN al-MAGHRIBI (fl. c.1260) Math.; Astrol. CDZZ ZZ-9

MUIR, John (1838-1914) Nat. Hist.; Geol. CONS DAB EAFC GANC GOTH HOCS LACC NEXB PCWA SFNB TLLW WAMB

MUIR, Matthew M. (1848-1931) Chem. CDZZ ZZ-9

MUIR, Robert (1864-1959) Path. DNB7 RS-5

MUIR, William (1806-1888) Engr. DNB

MULAIK, Stanley B. (1902-) Nat. Hist. LACC

MULDER, Gerardus J. (1802-1880) Chem. ABET CDZZ ZZ-9

MULFORD, Walter (1877-1955) Forest. LACC

MULLER, Franz J. (1740-1825) Mineral. ABES ABET BEOS CDZZ ZZ-9

MULLER, Fritz (1822-1897) Nat. Hist. CDZZ ZZ-9

MULLER, George E. (1850-1934) Psych. CDZZ ZZ-9

MULLER, Gertrude A. (1887-1954) Invent. NAWM

MULLER, Gustav (1851-1925) Astron.; Astrophys. CDZZ ZZ-9

MULLER, Hermann J. (1890-1967) Biol. ABES ABET BDOS BEOS CB47 CDZZ FMBB HLSM MHM1 MHSE NCSH RS14 WAMB ZZ-9

MULLER, Johann SEE REGIOMONTANUS, Johannes

MULLER, Johann H. (1809-1875) Phys. CDZZ ZZ-9

MULLER, Johannes P. (1801-1858) Physiol. ABES ABET BDOS BEOS BHMT CDZZ HLSM ZZ-9

MULLER, John (1699-1784) Math. DNB

MULLER, Otto F. (1730-1784) Biol. ABES ABET ANHD BEOS CDZZ ZZ-9

MULLER, Paul H. (1899-1965) Chem. ABES ABET BEOS CB45 CDZZ MHM1 MHSE ZZ-9

MULLER-BRESLAU, Heinrich (1851-1925) Engr. CDZZ ZZ-9

MULLIKEN, Robert S. (1896-) Chem. ABES ABET BEOS CB67 MHM1 MHSE QPAS WAMB

MULLIKEN, Samuel P. (1864-1934) Chem. ACCE DAB1

MULLIN, Charles E. (1890-1953) Chem. NC41

MUMFORD, David B. (1937-) Math. MHSE

MUNCKE, Georg W. (1772-1847) Phys. CDZZ ZZ-9

MUNIER-CHALMAS, Ernest C. (1843-1903) Paleon. CDZZ ZZ-9

MUNISVARA VISVARUPA (b. 1603) Astron.; Math. CDZZ ZZ-9

MUNJALA (fl. 932) Astron. CDZZ ZZ-9

MUNK, Max (1890-) Aero. ICFW

MUNK, Walter H. (1917-) Geophys. BEOS MHM2 MHSE

MUNROE, Charles E. (1849-1938) Chem. ACCE DAB2 NC-9 NC29

MUNSON, Eneas (1734-1826) Alch. ACCE

MUNSTER, Sebastian (1489-1552) Geog. CDZZ ZZ-9

MUNZ, Philip A. (1892-) Biol. BNBR

MURALT, Johannes von (1645-1733) Med. CDZZ ZZ-9 ZZXV

MURAYAMA, Makio (1912-) Biochem. CB74

MURCHISON, Charles (1830-1879) Med. BHMT

MURCHISON, Roderick I. (1792-1871) Geol. ABES ABET BDOS BEOS CDZZ DNB HNHB ZZ-9

MURDOCK, William (1754-1839) Invent. ABES ABET BDOS DNB GE-1 SAIF

MURIE, Margaret (1890-) Nat. Hist. WAWL

MURIE, Olaus J. (1889-1963) Cons. DGMT EAFC LACC PCWA

MURKE, Franz (1869-1923) Chem. NC20

MURNAGHAN, Francis D. (1893-1976) Math. MHM1 MHSE

MURPHREE, Eger V. (1898-1962) Engr. BM40

MURPHY, George M. (1903-1968) Chem. ACCE NC54

MURPHY, James B. (1884-1950) Biol. BM34 CDZZ ZZ-9

MURPHY, John B. (1857-1916) Med. BHMT

MURPHY, Leonard M. (1916-1974) Seism.; Geophys. NC59

MURPHY, Robert (1806-1843) Math. DNB

MURPHY, Robert C. (1887-1973) Nat. Hist. BWCL LACC NCSF SFNB

MURPHY, Walter J. (1899-1959) Chem. ACCE

MURPHY, William P. (1892-) Med. ABES ABET BEOS

MURRAY, A. Rosemary (1913-) Chem. COBC

MURRAY, Andrew (1812-1878) Nat. Hist. DNB

MURRAY, Elsie (1878-1965) Psych. NC53

MURRAY, George R. (1858-1911) Bot. CDZZ DNB2 ZZ-9

MURRAY, George R. (1865-1938) Med. BHMT

MURRAY, John (d. 1820) Chem.; Phys. DNB

MURRAY, John (1841-1914) Ocean. BDOS BEOS
CDZZ DNB3 EXSG SNCB ZZ-9

MURRAY, Lilian (1871-1959) Med. IDWB

MURRAY, Matthew (1765-1826) Engr. DNB GE-1

MURRAY, Robert SEE MORAY, Robert

MURRAY, Robert G. (1919-) Bact. MHM2 MHSE

MURRELL, William (1853-1912) Med. BHMT

MUSGRAVE, William (1655-1721) Med. BHMT

MUSGRAVE, William K. (1918-) Chem. COBC

MUSHET, David (1772-1847) Metal. CDZZ DNB
GE-1 ZZ-9

MUSHET, Robert F. (1811-1891) Invent. BDOS DNB

MUSHKETOV, Ivan V. (1850-1902) Geol.; Geog.
CDZZ ZZ-9

MUSKHELISHVILI, Nikolai I. (1891-) Math.; Phys.
SMST

MUSPRATT, James (1793-1886) Chem. BDOS BEOS

MUSSCHENBROEK, Petrus van (1692-1761) Phys.
ABET BEOS CDZZ EETD GE-1 ZZ-9

MUTIS Y BOSSIO, Jose C. (1732-1808) Bot.; Astron.
CDZZ ZZXV

MUYBRIDGE, Eadweard (1830-1904) Photo. BDOS
DNB2

MYDDLETON, Hugh (1560-1631) Engr. GE-1

MYDORGE, Claude (1585-1647) Math.; Phys. CDZZ
ZZ-9

MYERS, Thomas (1774-1834) Math. DNB

MYERS, Victor C. (1883-1948) Biochem. NCSC

MYLNE, Robert (1734-1811) Engr. GE-1

MYLNE, William C. (1781-1863) Engr. DNB

MYLON, Claude (c.1618-c.1660) Math. CDZZ ZZ-9

MYSELS, Karol J. (1914-) Chem. MHSE

N

NABRIT, Samuel M. (1905-) Biol. CB63 SBPY

NACHMANSOHN, David (1899-1983) Biochem.
MHM2 MHSE

NADEL, Michael (1901-) Cons. LACC

NAEGELI, Carl W. von (1817-1891) Bot. ABES ABET
BDOS BEOS CDZZ ZZ-9

ibn al-NAFIS, Ala al-Din Abul-Hasan (d. 1288) Med.
CDZZ ZZ-9

NAGAOKA, Hantaro (1865-1950) Phys. ABET CDZZ
ZZ-9

NAGELI, Karl SEE NAEGELI, Carl

NAGESA (fl. c.1630) Astron. CDZZ ZZ-9

NAIR, John H. Jr. (1893-1971) Chem. ACCE

NAIRNE, Edward (1726-1806) Math.; Phys. CDZZ
DNB MCCW ZZ-9

NALIVKIN, Dmitrii V. (1889-) Geol.; Paleon. SMST

NAMETKIN, Sergey S. (1876-1950) Chem. CDZZ
ZZ-9

NAMIAS, Jerome (1910-) Meteor. MHM1 MHSE

NANSEN, Fridtjof (1861-1930) Meteor.; Ocean.
ABET BDOS BEOS CDZZ EXSG ZZXV

NANZAN SEE AJIMA NAONOBU

NAPIER, John (1550-1617) Math. ABES ABET BDOS
BEOS CDZZ HOSS MELW ZZ-9

NAPIER, Robert (1791-1876) Engr. DNB

NARAYANA (fl. 1356) Math. CDZZ ZZ-9

al-NASAWI, Abul-Hasan (fl. 1029-1044) Math. CDZZ
ZZ-9

NASIR al-Din al-Tusi SEE al-TUSI, Sharaf al-Din

NASMYTH, James (1808-1890) Engr.; Astron. BDOS BEOS CDZZ DNB SAIF ZZ-9

NASON, Henry B. (1831-1895) Chem. ACCE BIOD NC-2

NASSAU, Jason J. (1893-1965) Astron. NC57

NATALIS, Stephanus SEE NOEL, Etienne

NATANSON, Wladyslaw (1864-1937) Phys. CDZZ ZZ-9

NATHANS, Daniel (1928-) Microbiol. ABET BEOS MHSE SOT2

NATHORST, Alfred G. (1850-1921) Geol. CDZZ FHUA ZZ-9

NATTA, Giulio (1903-1979) Chem. ABES ABET BEOS CB64 MHM1 MHSE PAW2

NAUDIN, Charles (1815-1899) Hort.; Bot. BDOS BEOS CDZZ HLSM ZZ-9

NAUMAN, Johann A. (1744-1826) Ornith. ORNS

NAUMANN, Alexander (1837-1922) Chem. CDZZ ZZ-9

NAUMANN, Karl F. (1797-1873) Mineral.; Geol. CDZZ ZZ-9

NAUMBERG, Elsie M. (1880-1953) Ornith. NC41

NAUNYN, Bernhard (1839-1925) Med. BHMT

NAUR, Peter (1928-) Comp. HOPL

NAVASHIN, Sergey G. (1857-1930) Biol. CDZZ ZZ10

NAVIER, Claude L. (1785-1836) Engr. CDZZ GE-1 ZZ10

al-NAYRIZI, Abul Abbas al-Fadi (fl. c.897) Math.; Astron. CDZZ ZZ10

NEANDER, Michael (1529-1581) Math.; Med. CDZZ ZZ10

NECKER, Louis A. (1786-1861) Geol.; Mineral. CDZZ ZZ10

NECKHAM, Alexander (1157-1217) Nat. Philos. EETD

NEEDHAM, Dorothy M. (1896-) Biochem. BEOS

NEEDHAM, James G. (1868-1957) Entom. AMEM LACC NCSB

NEEDHAM, John T. (1713-1781) Nat. Hist. ABES ABET BEOS CDZZ ZZ10

NEEDHAM, Joseph (1900-) Biochem. BEOS

NEEL, James van (1915-) Genet. MHM2 MHSE

NEEL, Louis E. (1904-) Phys. ABET BEOS MHM2 MHSE POSW

NE'EMAN, Yuval (1925-) Phys. ABES ABET BEOS MHSE

NEES VON ESENBECK, Christian G. (1776-1858) Bot. CDZZ ZZ10

NEF, John U. (1862-1915) Chem. ABES ABET ACCE BEOS BM34 CDZZ DAB GRCH ZZ10

NEGRETTI, Enrico A. (1817-1879) Instr. DNB

NEGRI, Adelchi (1876-1912) Path. CDZZ ZZ10

NEHRING, Alfred (1845-1904) Paleon.; Zool. CDZZ ZZ10

NEHRLING, Arno H. (1886-1974) Hort. NC58

NEHRLING, Henry (1853-1929) Ornith.; Hort. DAB

NEILE, William (1637-1670) Math. DNB

NEILL, Patrick (1776-1851) Nat. Hist. DNB

NEILSON, James B. (1792-1865) Engr. GE-1

NEISH, Arthur C. (1916-1973) Biochem. RS20

NEISSER, Albert L. (1855-1916) Med. ABET BEOS CDZZ ZZ10

NEKRASOV, Aleksandr I. (1883-1957) Math. CDZZ ZZ10

NEKRASOV, Boris V. (1899-) Chem. SMST

NELSON, Aven (1859-1952) Bot. BNBR

NELSON, DeWitt (1901-) Forest. LACC

NELSON, Edward W. (1855-1934) Nat. Hist. DAB1 NC26

NELSON, Elnathan K. (1870-1940) Chem. NC30

NELSON, Harold R. (1904-1960) Phys. NC45

NELSON, Jesse W. (1874-1958) Forest. LACC

NELSON, John M. (1876-1965) Chem. ACCE HSSO

NELSON, Julius (1858-1916) Biol. DAB

NELSON, Ray (1893-1967) Bot. NC53

NELSON, Richard J. (1803-1877) Engr.; Geol. DNB

NELSON, Thurlow C. (1890-1960) Zool. NC48

NEMESIUS (fl. 390-400) Med. CDZZ ZZ10

NEMORE, Jordanus SEE JORDANUS DE NEMORE

NENCKI, Marceli (1847-1901) Biochem. CDZZ ZZ10

NERI, Antonio (1576-1614) Chem. CDZZ ZZ10

NERNST, (Hermann) Walther (1864-1941) Chem.
ABES ABET BDOS BEOS CDZZ GRCH HSSO
NPWC TOWS ZZXV

NESBIT, John C. (1818-1862) Chem. DNB

NESMEYANOV, Alexander N. (1899-) Chem. CB58
MHM2 MHSE SMST

NESS, Norman F. (1933-) Astrophys. MHSE

NESTOR (c.380-c.450) Med. MMMA

NETTESHEIM SEE AGRIPPA, Heinrich C.

NETTLESHIP, Edward (1845-1913) Med. BHMT

NETTO, Eugen (1848-1919) Math. CDZZ ZZ10

NEUBERG, Carl (1877-1956) Biochem. GJPS

NEUBERG, Joseph (1840-1926) Math. CDZZ
ZZ10

NEUMANN, Carl G. (1832-1925) Math.; Phys. CDZZ
ZZ10

NEUMANN, Caspar (1683-1737) Chem. CDZZ ZZ10

NEUMANN, Franz E. (1798-1895) Mineral.; Phys.
CDZZ ZZ10

NEUMANN, John von SEE VON NEUMANN, Johan

NEUMAYR, Melchior (1845-1890) Paleon.; Geol.
CDZZ ZZ10

NEURATH, Hans (1909-) Biochem. MHM2 MHSE

NEUYMIN, Grigory N. (1886-1946) Astron. CDZZ
ZZ10

NEWALL, Hugh F. (1857-1944) Astrophys. CDZZ
DNB6 ZZ10

NEWALL, Robert S. (1812-1889) Engr.; Astron. DNB

NEWARK, Nathan M. (1910-) Engr. MHM1

NEWBERRY, John S. (1822-1892) Paleon.; Geol.
BIOD BM-6 CDZZ DAB NC-9 ZZ10

NEWBERRY, Spencer B. (1857-1922) Chem. NC20

NEWBOULD, William W. (1819-1886) Bot. DNB

NEWCOMB, Simon (1835-1909) Astron. ABES ABET
BDOS BEOS CDZZ DAB HFGA IEAS NC-7
SNAR WAMB ZZ10

NEWCOMBE, Frederick C. (1858-1927) Bot. MABH

NEWCOMEN, Thomas (1663-1729) Engr. ABES ABET
BDOS BEOS CDZZ GE-1 SAIF ZZ10

NEWELL, Frederick H. (1862-1932) Geol. EAFC
LACC

NEWELL, Homer E. (1915-1983) Phys.; Math. CB54
MOS5

NEWELL, (Brother) Matthias (1854-1939) Bot.; Zool.
WFBG

NEWELL, Norman D. (1909-) Paleon.; Geol. MHM2
MHSE

NEWELL, Wilmon (1878-1943) Entom. AMEM NC36

NEWITT, Dudley M. (1894-1980) Chem. MHM2 MHSE
RS27

NEWLANDS, John A. (1837-1898) Chem. ABES
ABET BDOS BEOS CDZZ ZZ10

NEWMAN, Edward (1801-1876) Nat. Hist. DNB

NEWMARK, Nathan M. (1910-) Engr. MHSE

NEWPORT, George (1803-1854) Entom.; Nat. Hist.
CDZZ DNB ZZ10

NEWSOM, Carroll C. (1904-) Math. CB57

NEWTON, Alfred (1829-1907) Ornith. BEOS DNB2

NEWTON, Edwin T. (1840-1930) Paleon. CDZZ ZZ10

NEWTON, Henry (1845-1877) Geol.; Mng. BIOD

NEWTON, Hubert A. (1830-1896) Astron.; Math.
BIOD BM-4 CDZZ DAB NC-9 ZZ10

NEWTON, Isaac (1642-1727) Phys.; Astron. ABES
ABET ASTR BDOS BEOS CDZZ DCPW DNB
EETD FASP FBSC FMAS FNEC FPHM GASW
GE-1 GEXB GISA GMOP GRTH HOSS ICFW
IEAS IFBS LISD LSCS MAKS MGAH MSCH
OMNM PAW2 PFEL SAIF SGSC SLOR SMIL
STSW TMAL TOWS ZZ10

NEWTON, James (c.1664-1750) Bot. DNB

NEWTON, John (1622-1678) Math.; Astron. DNB

NEWTON, John (1823-1895) Engr. BM-4

NEYMAN, Jerzy (1894-1981) Math. AO81 MHM1
MHSE RS28

NICE, Margaret M. (1883-1974) Ornith. DGMT
NAWM

NICERON, Jean F. (1613-1646) Opt. CDZZ ZZ10

NICHOL, John P. (1804-1859) Astron. DNB

NICHOLAS OF CUSA (1401-1564) Math. BEOS
CCSW CDZZ WTGM ZZ-3

NICHOLAS, John S. (1895-1963) Biol. BM40 CDZZ
NC48 ZZ10

NICHOLS, Edward L. (1854-1937) Phys. BM21 DAB2
NC-4

NICHOLS, Ernest F. (1869-1924) Phys. BM12 CDZZ
DAB NC13 ZZ10

NICHOLS, George E. (1882-1939) Bot. MABH NC29

NICHOLS, James R. (1819-1888) Chem. BIOD DAB
NC-5

NICHOLS, William H. (1852-1930) Chem. ACCE

NICHOLSON, George (1847-1908) Bot. DNB2

NICHOLSON, Henry A. (1844-1899) Biol. DNB1

NICHOLSON, Henry H. (1850-1940) Chem.; Mineral.
NC48

NICHOLSON, John W. (1881-1955) Phys. CDZZ
RS-2 ZZ10

NICHOLSON, Peter (1765-1844) Math. DNB

NICHOLSON, Seth B. (1891-1963) Astron. ABES
ABET BEOS BM42 CDZZ SLOR ZZ10

NICHOLSON, William (1753-1815) Chem. ABES
ABET BEOS CDZZ DNB ZZ10

NICOL, James (1810-1879) Geol. DNB

NICOL, William (1768-1851) Opt.; Paleon. ABET
BDOS BEOS CDZZ ZZ10

NICOLAI, Friedrich B. (1793-1846) Astron. CDZZ
ZZ10

NICOLAUS OF DAMASCUS (b. 64 B.C.) Bot. CDZZ
ZZ10

NICOLET, Marcel (1912-) Astrophys. CB58

NICOLLE, Charles J. (1866-1936) Med. ABES ABET
BDOS BEOS BHMT CDZZ ZZXV

NICOLLE, Eugene D. (1824-1895) Engr. MCCW

NICOLLET, Joseph N. (1786-1843) Astron.; Math.
BIOD DAB WAMB

NICOMACHUS OF GERASA (fl. c.100) Math. CDZZ
ZZ10

NICOMEDES (fl. c.250 B.C.) Math. CDZZ ZZ10

NICOT, Jean (c.1530-1604) Bot. CDZZ ZZ10

NIEBUHR, Carsten (1733-1815) Exp. CDZZ ZZ10

NIEDERLAND, William G. (1904-) Psychiat. CB80

NIELSEN, Harold H. (1903-1973) Phys. NC57

NIELSEN, Niels (1865-1931) Math. CDZZ ZZ10

NIEMANN, Carl G. (1908-1964) Chem. BM40 NC50

NIEPCE, Joseph N. (1765-1833) Invent. ABES ABET
BDOS BEOS CDZZ MPIP SAIF ZZ10

NIER, Alfred O. (1911-) Phys. MHM2 MHSE

NIESTEN, Jean L. (1844-1920) Astron. CDZZ ZZ10

NIEUWENTIJT, Bernard (1654-1718) Math. CDZZ ZZ10

NIEUWLAND, Julius A. (1878-1936) Chem. ABES ABET BDOS BEOS CDZZ DAB2 NC26 ZZ10

NIFO, Agostino (c.1469-1538) Med. CDZZ ZZ10

NIGGLI, Paul (1888-1953) Crystal.; Geol. CDZZ ZZ10

NIGHTINGALE, Florence (1820-1910) Med. BHMT WIWM

NIKITIN, Nikolai I. (1890-) Chem. SMST

NIKITIN, Sergey N. (1851-1901) Geol. CDZZ ZZ10

NIKOLAYEV, Anatoli V. (1902-) Chem. SMST

NIKOLAYEV, Andrian (1929-) Astronaut. CB64 FPSN

NILAKANTHA (c.1444-c.1502) Astron. CDZZ ZZ10

NILSON, Lars F. (1840-1899) Chem. ABES ABET BEOS

NILSSON-EHLE, Herman (1873-1949) Genet. CDZZ ZZ10

NIPHER, Francis E. (1847-1926) Phys. DAB

NIPKOW, Paul (1860-1940) Invent. SAIF

NIRENBERG, Marshall W. (1927-) Biochem. ABES ABET BEOS CB65 EDCJ MHM2 MHSE WAMB

NISSEN, Henry W. (1901-1958) Psych. BM38

NISSL, Franz (1860-1919) Med. CDZZ BHMT ZZ10

NIXON, Henry B. (1857-1916) Math. NC17

NOAD, Henry M. (1815-1877) Electrochem. DNB

NOBEL, Alfred B. (1833-1896) Chem. ABES ABET BDOS BEOS CDZZ IFBS IHMV LLWO OGML POSW TBTM TGNH ZZ10

NOBERT, Friedrich A. (1806-1881) Instr. CDZZ ZZ10

NOBILI, Leopoldo (1784-1835) Phys. BDOS BEOS CDZZ EETD ZZ10

NOBLE, Andrew (1831-1915) Phys. DNB3

NOBLE, Gladwyn K. (1894-1940) Biol. DAB2 NC31

NODDACK, Ida E. (1896-) Chem. ABES ABET BEOS IDWB

NODDACK, Walter (1893-1960) Chem. ABES ABET BEOS CDZZ ZZ10

NOE, Adolphe C. (1873-1939) Paleon. FHUA

NOEL, Etienne (1581-1659) Phys. CDZZ ZZ10

NOETHER, Amalie E. (1882-1935) Math. CDZZ IDWB MASW MEQP WIMO ZZ10

NOETHER, Max (1844-1921) Math. CDZZ ZZ10

NOGUCHI, Hideyo (1876-1928) Microbiol. BEOS BHMT CDZZ DAB WAMB ZZ10

NOGUCHI, Thomas T. (1927-) Forens. Sci. DNFH

NOLLET, Jean A. (1700-1770) Phys. BDOS BEOS CDZZ EETD ESEH ZZ10

NOMURA, Masayasu (1927-) Biol. MHSE

NOORDEN, Carl von (1858-1944) Med. BHMT

NOPSCA, Franz (1877-1933) Paleon. PHLS

NORDEN, Carl L. (1880-1965) Invent. NC52

NORDENSKIOLD, Adolf E. (1832-1901) Geol. BDOS BEOS CDZZ ZZ10

NORDENSKIOLD, Nils E. (1872-1933) Zool. ABET CDZZ ZZ10

NORLUND, Niels E. (1885-) Math. BEOS MHM2 MHSE

NORMAN, Robert (b. c.1560) Nav. ABET BEOS CDZZ EETD ZZ10

NORMANDY, Alphonse R. de (1809-1864) Chem. DNB

NORRIS, James F. (1871-1940) Chem. ACCE BM45 DAB2 NC30

NORRIS, Robert S. (1869-1945) Chem. NC37

NORRISH, Ronald G. (1897-1978) Chem. ABES ABET BEOS COBC MHM1 MHSE RS27

NORTH, Henry B. (1879-1956) Chem. NC45

NORTH, Myles E. (1908-) Ornith. DGMT

NORTHROP, John H. (1891-1981) Biochem. ABES
ABET BEOS CB47 MHM1 MHSE NPWC

NORTHROP, John K. (1895-) Aero. ICFW

NORTHRUP, Edwin F. (1866-1940) Phys. NC38

NORTON, John P. (1822-1852) Chem.; Agr. ACCE
BIOD CDZZ DAB ZZ10

NORTON, Lewis M. (1855-1893) Chem. ACCE HCEF

NORTON, Sidney A. (1835-1918) Chem. ACCE

NORTON, Thomas (c.1437-c.1514) Alch. BEOS

NORTON, Thomas H. (1851-1941) Chem. Engr. ACCE

NORTON, William A. (1810-1883) Astron.; Phys.
BIOD BM-2 NC-9

NORWOOD, Richard (1590-1665) Math.; Surv.
CDZZ ZZ10

NOSTRADAMUS, Michael (1503-1566) Med.; Astrol.
CDZZ ZZ10

NOVARA, Domenico M. (1454-1504) Astron. CDZZ
ZZ10

NOVIKOV, Ivan I. (1916-) Phys. SMST

NOVY, Frederick G. (1864-1957) Bact. BM33 CDZZ
NC54 ZZ10

NOYES, Arthur A. (1866-1936) Chem. ACCE BM31
CDZZ DAB2 NC13 WAMB ZZ10

NOYES, William A. (1857-1941) Chem. ACCE BEOS
BM27 CDZZ DAB3 NC13 NC44 ZZ10

NOYES, William A. Jr. (1898-) Chem. CB47 MHM1
MHSE NCSH

NUMEROV, Boris V. (1891-1943) Astron. CDZZ
ZZ10

NUNEZ SALACIENSE, Pedro (1502-1578) Math.
BMST CDZZ ZZ10

NUSSLET, Ernst K. (1882-1957) Phys. CDZZ FNEC
ZZ10

NUTTALL, George H. (1862-1937) Bact. DNB5

NUTTALL, Josiah (1771-1849) Nat. Hist. DNB

NUTTALL, Thomas (1786-1859) Bot.; Ornith. ABFC
ASJD BIOD BWCL CDZZ DAB DNB EAFC
MABH NC-8 NHAH WFBG YSMS ZZ10

NUTTALL, Zelia (1857-1933) Anthro. POAA

NUTTING, Charles C. (1858-1927) Mar. Biol.; Ornith.
DAB

NYGAARD, Kristen (1926-) Comp. HOPL

NYHOLM, Ronald S. (1917-1971) Chem. COBC
RS18

NYLANDER, Frederick (1820-1880) Bot.; Med.
CDZZ ZZ10

NYLANDER, William (1822-1899) Bot. CDZZ ZZ10

NYQUIST, Harry (1889-1976) Elec. Engr. MHSE

O

OAKLEY, Cyril L. (1907-1975) Bact. RS22

OAKLEY, Kenneth P. (1911-1981) Anthro. AO81
BEOS

OATLEY, Charles (1904-) Elec. Engr. MHSE

OBER, Frederick A. (1849-1913) Ornith. BIOD DAB
NC54

OBERFELL, George G. (1885-1965) Chem. NC53

OBERG, Kalervo (1901-1973) Anthro. NC58

OBERHOLSER, Harry C. (1870-1963) Ornith. BWCL
WFBG

OBERHOLTZER, Ernest C. (1884-1977) Cons. EAFC
LACC

OBERMEIER, O. Hugh (1843-1873) Paleon. CCSW

OBERTH, Hermann J. (1894-) Phys.; Rocket. ABET
BEOS CB57 FPSN HRST IEAS ICFW MOS8
PORS ROPW

OBLAD, Alex G. (1909-) Chem. MHSE

OBRIEMOV, Ivan V. (1894-) Phys. SMST

O'BRIEN, Brian (1898-) Phys. MHM2 MHSE

O'BRIEN, Matthew (1814-1855) Math. DNB

OBRUCHEV, Sergei V. (1891-) Geol. SMST

OBRUCHEV, Vladimir A. (1863-1956) Geol. CDZZ
ZZ10

OBUKHOV, Aleksandr M. (1918-) Geophys. SMST

OCAGNE, Philbert M. d' (1862-1938) Math. CDZZ
ZZ10

OCCHIALINI, Giuseppe P. (1907-) Phys. BEOS

OCHOA, Severo (1905-) Biochem. ABES ABET
BEOS CB62 GJPS MHM1 MHSE NCSL PAW2
WAMB

OCHSENIUS, Carl (1830-1906) Geol. CDZZ ZZ10

OCHSNER, Albert J. (1858-1925) Med. BHMT

OCKHAM, William of (c.1300-1349) Philos. ABES
ABET BDOS CDZZ ZZ10

ODDI, Ruggero (1864-1913) Med. CDZZ ZZ10

ODIERNA, Gionbatista (1597-1660) Astron.; Meteor.
CDZZ ZZ10

ODING, Ivan A. (1896-1964) Metal. SMST

ODINGTON SEE WALTER OF ODINGTON

ODLING, William (1829-1921) Chem. BDOS BEOS
CDZZ ZZ10

OENOPIDES OF CHIOS (fl. 400s B.C.) Astron.; Math.
ABET CDZZ ZZ10

OENSLAGER, George (1873-1956) Chem. ACCE
NCSF

OERSTED, Hans C. (1777-1851) Phys. ABES ABET
BDOS BEOS CDZZ DCPW EETD GASJ GE-1
GOED IFBS VTHB ZZ10

OHAIN, Hans von (1911-) Invent. ICFW

OHM, Georg S. (1789-1854) Phys. ABES ABET BDOS
BEOS CDZZ DCPW EETD ELEC FNEC GOED
MAKS SAIF TOWS VTHB ZZ10

O'KEEFE, John A. (1916-) Phys. ABES ABET BEOS

OKEN, Lorenz (1779-1851) Nat. Hist. ABES ABET
BEOS CDZZ HLSM ZZ10

OKENFUSS, Lorenz SEE OKEN, Lorenz

OKHOTSIMSKII, Dmitrii Y. (1921-) Phys. SMST

OKKELBERG, Peter O. (1880-1960) Zool. NC48

OLAUS MAGNUS (1490-1557) Geog.; Anthro. CDZZ
ZZ10

OLBERS, Heinrich W. (1758-1840) Astron. ABES
ABET BEOS CDZZ IEAS ZZ10

OLDENBERG, Henry (c.1618-1677) Sci. Writ. CDZZ
ZZ10

OLDHAM, John (1779-1840) Engr. DNB

OLDHAM, Richard D. (1858-1936) Geol.; Seism.
BEOS CDZZ ZZ10

OLDHAM, Thomas (1816-1878) Geol. CDZZ DNB
ZZ10

OLDROYD, Tom S. (1853-1932) Conch. NC24

OLDS, Henry W. (1859-1925) Ornith. NC32

OLIPHANT, Marcus L. (1901-) Phys. ABES ABET
BEOS CB51

OLIVE, John R. (1916-1974) Biol. NC58

OLIVER, Andrew (1731-1799) Meteor.; Astron. BIOD
DAB

OLIVER, Bernard M. (1916-) Elec. Engr. MHSE

OLIVER, Francis W. (1864-1951) Paleon. DNB7

OLIVER, George (1841-1915) Physiol. BHMT CDZZ
ZZ10

OLIVER, James A. (1914-1981) Zool. CB66

OLIVER, James E. (1829-1895) Math. BIOD BM-4

OLIVER, Wade W. (1890-1964) Bact. NC53

OLMSTED, Denison (1791-1859) Geol.; Astron. ASJD
BIOD DAB NC-8

OLMSTED, Frederick E. (1872-1925) Forst. EAFC
LACC

OLMSTED, Frederick L. (1822-1903) Cons. CONS EAFC GOTH LACC SFNB

OLNEY, Louis A. (1874-1949) Chem. ACCE NC38

OLNEY, Stephen T. (1812-1878) Bot. MABH NC13

OLSON, Harry F. (1901-1982) Engr. MHSE

OLSON, Sigurd F. (1899-1982) Cons. EAFC LACC

OLSZEWSKI, Karol S. (1846-1915) Chem.; Phys. CDZZ ZZ10

OLUFSEN, Christian F. (1802-1855) Astron. CDZZ ZZ10

OLYMPIODORUS (c.360-c.426) Alch. CDZZ ZZ10

OMALIUS D'HALLOY, Jean B. (1783-1875) Geol. CDZZ ZZ10

OMAR KHAYYAM SEE al-KHAYYAMI, Ghiyath al-Din Abul Fath

OMORI, Fusakichi (1868-1923) Seism. CDZZ ZZ10

O'NEIL, Arthur S. (1879-1926) Chem. NC20

O'NEILL, Eugene F. (1918-) Elec. Engr. CB63

O'NEILL, Gerard K. (1927-) Phys. ABET CB79

ONNES, Heike SEE KAMERLINGH-ONNES, Heike

ONSAGER, Lars (1903-1976) Chem. ABES ABET BEOS CB58 MHM1 MHSE RS24 WAMB

ONTHANK, Karl W. (1890-1967) Cons. EAFC

OORT, Jan H. (1900-) Astron. ABES ABET BEOS CB69 IEAS MHM1 MHSE PBTS RS24 WAMB

OPARIN, Aleksandr I. (1894-1980) Chem. ABES ABET AO81 BEOS SMST

OPIE, Eugene L. (1873-1971) Path. BEOS BHMT MHSE SMST

OPIK, Ernst J. (1893-) Astron. ABET MHSE

OPPEL, Albert (1831-1865) Paleon. CDZZ ZZ10

OPPENHEIM, Samuel (1857-1928) Astron. CDZZ ZZ10

OPPENHEIMER, J. Robert (1904-1967) Phys. ABES ABET BDOS BEOS CB45 CB64 CDZZ GDSP MHM2 MHSE MWBR NBPS NCSG PBTS PPEY PPTY RS14 SAIF SSAH WAMB ZZ10

OPPOLZER, Rheodor R. von (1841-1886) Astron. CDZZ ZZ10

ORBELI, Leon A. (1882-1958) Physiol. CDZZ ZZ10

ORBIGNY, Alcide C. d' (1802-1857) Paleon. CDZZ PHLS ZZ10

ORD, George (1781-1866) Zool. BIOD

ORDWAY, John M. (1823-1909) Chem. ACCE NC-7

ORDWAY, Samuel H. (1900-) Cons. LACC

ORELL, Bernard L. (1914-) Forest. LACC

ORESME, Nicols (c.1320-1382) Math. CDZZ ZZ10

ORIBASIUS (fl. 300s) Med. CDZZ ZZ10

ORLOV, Aleksandr Y. (1880-1954) Astron.; Seism. CDZZ ZZ10

ORLOV, Sergey V. (1880-1958) Astron.; Astrophys. CDZZ ZZ10

ORLOV, Yurii A. (1893-1966) Paleon. SMST

ORMEROD, Eleanor A. (1828-1901) Entom. DNB2

ORMEROD, George W. (1810-1891) Geol. DNB

ORMEROD, William P. (1818-1860) Anat. DNB

ORNSTEIN, Leonard S. (1880-1941) Phys. CDZZ ZZ10

ORR, Hugh (1717-1798) Invent. DNB

ORR, William M. (1866-1934) Math. DNB5

ORTA, Garcia da (c.1500-c.1568) Med. BHMT CDZZ ZZ10

ORTEGA, Juan de (c.1480-c.1568) Math. CDZZ ZZ10

ORTELIUS, Abraham (1527-1598) Geog. BEOS CDZZ ZZ10

ORTON, Edward F. (1829-1899) Geol. BIOD

ORTON, James (1830-1877) Nat. Hist. BIOD CDZZ
DAB ZZ10

ORVILLE, Howard T. (1901-) Meteor. CB56

OSBORN, Fairfield (1887-1969) Nat. Hist.; Cons.
CB49 LACC SFNB WAMB

OSBORN, Henry F. (1857-1935) Paleon.; Anat. ABFC
BEOS BM19 CDZZ DAB1 MADC NC11 NC26
PHLS SFNB WAMB ZZ10

OSBORN, Herbert (1856-1954) Entom. AMEM NC13

OSBORNE, Thomas B. (1859-1929) Chem. ABET
BM14 CDZZ DAB NC15 ZZ10

OSBURN, Raymond C. (1872-1955) Zool. NC46

OSGOOD, Wilfred H. (1875-1946) Zool. NC36

OSGOOD, William F. (1864-1943) Math. CDZZ DAB3
NC13 ZZ10

OSIANDER, Andreas (1498-1552) Sci. Writ. CDZZ
ZZ10

OSLER, Abraham F. (1808-1903) Meteor. DNB2

OSLER, William (1849-1919) Med. ABFC BEOS
BHMT SMIL

OSMOND, Floris (1849-1912) Metal. CDZZ ZZ10

OSTEN SACKEN, Carl R. (1828-1906) Entom. BIOD
DAB

OSTERHOUT, Winthrop J. (1871-1964) Bot. BM44

OSTROGRADSKY, Mikhail V. (1801-1862) Math.
CDZZ ZZ10

OSTROMISLENSKY, Ivan I. (1880-1939) Chem. ACCE
DAB2

OSTWALD, Carl W. (1883-1943) Chem.; Zool. CDZZ
ZZ10

OSTWALD, (Friedrich) Wilhelm (1853-1932) Chem.
ABES ABET BDOS BEOS CDZZ GRCH HSSO
NPWC TOWS ZZXV

OTHMER, Donald F. (1904-) Chem. Engr. MHSE

OTIS, Elisha G. (1811-1861) Invent. ABES ABET
BDOS DAB NC11

OTT, Emil (1902-1963) Chem. ACCE

OTT, Isaac (1847-1916) Physiol. CDZZ ZZ10

OTTO, John C. (1774-1844) Med. BHMT

OTTO, Nikolaus A. (1832-1891) Engr. BDOS FOIF
SAIF

OUDEMANS, Corneille A. (1825-1906) Med.; Bot.
CDZZ ZZ10

OUGHTRED, William (1575-1660) Math. ABES ABET
BEOS CDZZ DNB ZZ10

OUTHIER, Reginald (1694-1774) Astron. CDZZ ZZ10

OVEREND, William G. (1921-) Chem. COBC

OVERHAUSER, Albert W. (1925-) Phys. MHSE

OVERHOLTS, Lee O. (1890-1946) Bot. NC48

OVERSTREET, Roy (1903-1968) Chem. NC54

OVERTON, Charles E. (1865-1933) Physiol.; Pharm.
CDZZ ZZ10

OVERTON, James B. (1869-1951) Bot. MABH

OVIEDO, Gonzalo F. de (1478-1557) Nat. Hist.
SBCS

OWEN, David D. (1807-1860) Geol. BIOD CDZZ
NC-8 ZZ10

OWEN, George (1552-1613) Geol. CDZZ ZZ10

OWEN, Richard (1804-1892) Zool. ABES ABET BDOS
BEOS CDZZ DARR DNB HNHB MADC PHLS
VISC ZZ10

OWINGS, Margaret (Contemporary) Cons. WAWL

OZANAM, Jacques (1640-1717) Math. CDZZ ZZ10

OZERSKY, Aleksandr D. (1813-1880) Mng.; Geol.
CDZZ ZZ10

P

PACCHIONI, Antonio (1665-1726) Med. CDZZ ZZ10

PACINI, Filippo (1812-1883) Anat. CDZZ ZZ10

PACINOTTI, Antonio (1841-1912) Elec. Sci. CDZZ
ZZ10

PACIOLI, Luca (c.1445-1517) Math. ABET BMST CDZZ ZZ10

PACK, Arthur N. (1893-) Forest. LACC

PACK, Charles L. (1857-1937) Forest. EAFC LACC

PACK, Randolph G. (1890-1956) Forest. LACC

PACKARD, Alpheus S. (1839-1905) Entom. AMEM BIOD BM-9 CDZZ DAB NC-3 ZZ10

PACSU, Eugene (1891-1972) Chem. NC56

PADOA, Alessandro (1868-1937) Math. CDZZ ZZ10

PAGANO, Giuseppe (1872-1959) Physiol. CDZZ ZZXV

PAGE, Charles G. (1812-1868) Phys. ASJD BIOD

PAGE, David (1814-1879) Geol. DNB

PAGE, Frederick H. (1885-1962) Aero. ICFW

PAGE, Irvine H. (1901-) Med. MHM1 MHSE

PAGE, Kenneth C. SEE HOGBEN, Lancelot T.

PAGE, Leigh (1884-1952) Phys. DAB5

PAGE, Robert M. (1903-) Phys. CB64

PAGET, James (1814-1899) Med. BHMT

PAINE, John A. (1840-1912) Archaeol.; Bot. DAB

PAINE, Robert T. (1803-1885) Astron. BIOD

PAINE, Thomas O. (1921-) Engr. CB70

PAINLEVE, Paul (1863-1933) Math. CDZZ ZZ10

PAINTER, Theophilus S. (1889-1969) Zool. CDZZ NC55 NCSI ZZ10

PALACHE, Charles (1869-1954) Mineral. BM30

PALADE, George E. (1912-) Biol. ABES ABET BEOS CB67 MHM1 MHSE

PALEY, William (1743-1805) Nat. Philos. CDZZ ZZ10

PALISA, Johann (1848-1925) Astron. CDZZ ZZ10

PALISSY, Bernard (c.1510-1589) Geol. CDZZ SXWS THOG ZZ10

PALLADIN, Aleksandr V. (1885-) Biochem. SMST

PALLADIN, Vladimir I. (1859-1922) Biochem. CDZZ ZZ10

PALLADIO, Andrea (1518-1580) Engr. GE-1

PALLAS, Peter S. (1741-1811) Ornith. CDZZ HAOA ORNS ZZ10

PALLISHER, John (1807-1887) Geog. DNB

PALMEN, Erik H. (1898-) Meteor.; Ocean. MHM1 MHSE

PALMER, Arthur W. (1861-1904) Chem. BIOD

PALMER, Carroll E. (1903-1972) Med. NC56

PALMER, Charles S. (1858-1939) Chem. NC45

PALMER, E. Laurence (1888-1970) Nat. Hist. NC56

PALMER, Edward (1831-1911) Nat. Hist. CDZZ GANC ZZ10

PALMER, Ephraim L. (1888-) Cons. LACC

PALMER, Timothy (1751-1821) Invent. GE-1 INYG

PALMER, Walter W. (1882-1950) Med. DAB4

PALMIERI, Luigi (1807-1896) Geophys.; Meteor. ABET BEOS

PAMBOUR, Francois M. (b. 1795) Engr. CDZZ ZZ10

PAMMEL, Louis H. (1862-1931) Bot. DAB MABH NC10

PAN CHI-HSUN (1521-1595) Engr. GE-1

PANCOAST, Joseph (1805-1882) Med. BHMT

PANDER, Christian H. (1794-1865) Embryol.; Paleon. ABET CDZZ ZZ10

PANETH, Friedrich A. (1887-1958) Chem. ABET BDOS BEOS CDZZ DNB7 RS-6 ZZ10

PANNEKOEK, Antoine (1873-1960) Astron. CDZZ ZZ10

PANOFSKY, Wolfgang K. (1919-) Phys. BEOS CB70 MHM1 MHSE

PANTIN, Carl F. (1899-1967) Zool. BEOS MHM1 MHSE RS14

PANUM, Pater L. (1820-1886) Med. BHMT

PAPADAKIS, Philippos E. (1894-1977) Chem. NC60

PAPANICOLAOU, George N. (1883-1962) Anat. CDZZ NC50 ZZ10

PAPEZ, James W. (1883-1958) Anat. NC48 NCSE

PAPIN, Denis (1647-1712) Phys. ABES ABET BDOS BEOS CDZZ GE-1 ZZ10

PAPPENHEIMER, John R. (1915-) Physiol. BEOS MHM2 MHSE

PAPPUS OF ALEXANDRIA (fl. 320) Math.; Astron. ABET BDOS BEOS CDZZ ZZ10

PARACELSUS (1493-1541) Med.; Alch. ABES ABET BDOS BEOS BHMT MBST CDZZ CSCJ DSLP GRCH HLSM HSSO LISD MMMA NBPS PAW2 SAIF SMIL SXWS TOWS ZZ10

PARAMESVARA (c.1380-c.1460) Astron. CDZZ ZZ10

PARDEE, Arthur B. (1921-) Biochem. BEOS MHM1 MHSE

PARDIES, Ignace G. (1636-1673) Phys. CDZZ ZZ10

PARE, Ambroise (1510-1590) Med. ABES ABET BDOS BEOS BHMT CDZZ MMMA SXWS TOWS ZZ10

PARENAGO, Pavel P. (1906-1960) Astron. CDZZ ZZ10

PARENT, Antoine (1666-1716) Phys. CDZZ ZZ10

PARK, Orlando (1901-1969) Biol. NC55

PARK, Thomas (1908-) Zool. CB63

PARK, William H. (1863-1939) Bact. DAB2

PARKER, Arthur C. (1881-1955) Archaeol. DAB5 NCSC

PARKER, Eugene N. (1927-) Astrophys. ABET MHSE

PARKER, George H. (1864-1955) Zool. BM39 DAB5

PARKER, Herschel C. (1867-1944) Phys. NC14

PARKER, John R. (1884-1972) Entom. NC58

PARKER, Joseph L. (1898-) Engr. SBPY

PARKER, Lansing A. (1912-1965) Forest. LACC

PARKER, Richard E. (1925-) Chem. COBC

PARKER, Willard (1800-1884) Med. BHMT

PARKER, William K. (1823-1890) Anat. DNB

PARKES, Alexander (1813-1890) Chem. ABES ABET BDOS BEOS DNB

PARKES, Samuel (1761-1825) Chem. DNB

PARKHURST, John A. (1861-1925) Astron. CDZZ DAB ZZ10

PARKINSON, James (1755-1824) Med. ABET BEOS BHMT CDZZ ZZ10

PARKINSON, Stephen (1823-1889) Math. DNB

PARKINSON, Sydney (1745-1771) Nat. Hist. CDZZ ZZ10

PARKINSON, Thomas (1745-1830) Math. DNB

PARKMAN, Paul D. (1932-) Med. MFIR

PARKS, Robert J. (1922-) Rocket. CB68 MOS7

PARMELEE, Howard C. (1874-1959) Chem. ACCE

PARMENIDES OF ELEA (c.515 B.C.-c.450 B.C.) Philos. ABES ABET BEOS CDZZ ZZ10

PARMENTIER, Antoine A. (1737-1813) Chem. CDZZ ZZ10

PARNAS, Jakub K. (1884-1949) Biochem. CDZZ ZZ10

PARPART, Arthur K. (1903-1965) Biol. NC51

PARR, Albert E. (1900-) Ocean. CB42 NCSG

PARR, Samuel W. (1857-1931) Chem. ACCE DAB

PARROTT, Percival J. (1873-1953) Entom. NC44

PARRY, Caleb H. (1755-1822) Med. BHMT

PARRY, Charles C. (1823-1890) Bot. BIOD DAB
    MABH NC13

PARSEVAL DES CHENES, Marc A. (1755-1836) Math.
    CDZZ ZZ10

PARSHLEY, Howard M. (1844-1953) Entom. AMEM

PARSON, Alfred L. (1889-) Chem. QPAS

PARSONS, Charles A. (1854-1931) Engr. ABES
    ABET BDOS BEOS FNEC HOSS MMSB SAIF
    SGEC

PARSONS, Charles L. (1867-1954) Chem. ACCE
    NC47

PARSONS, Donald J. (1909-1969) Forens. Sci. NC54

PARSONS, Elsie C. (1875-1941) Anthro. POAA WAMB

PARSONS, James A. Jr. (1900-) Metal. SBPY

PARSONS, John H. (1868-1957) Physiol. DNB7

PARSONS, Laurence (1840-1908) Astron. DNB2

PARSONS, William (1800-1867) Astron. ABET
    BEOS CDZZ IEAS TMAL ZZ10

PARTAIN, Lloyd E. (1906-) Cons. LACC

PARTINGTON, James R. (1886-1965) Chem. BDOS
    BEOS CDZZ ZZ10

PARTRIDGE, Everett P. (1902-1969) Chem. Engr.
    NC55

PASCAL, Blaise (1623-1662) Math. ABES ABET
    BDOS BEOS CDZZ DCPW FNEC GE-1 IFBS
    MASW MELW MISU OMNM TOWS WTGM
    ZZ10

PASCAL, Etienne (1588-1651) Math. CDZZ ZZ10

PASCH, Mortiz (1843-1930) Math. CDZZ ZZ10

PASCHEN, Louis C. (1865-1947) Phys. ABET CDZZ
    ZZ10

PASCOE, Francis P. (1813-1893) Entom. DNB

PASOR, Matthias (1599-1658) Math. DNB

PASTEUR, Louis (1822-1895) Chem. ABES ABET
    BDOS BEOS BHMT CDZZ FBMV FMBB GASJ
    GRCH HLSM HSSO LISD MAMR MGAH MMMA
    MSCH PGFS SAIF SMIL SSDH TOWS ZZ10

PASTOR, Julio R. SEE REY PASTOR, Julio

PATAI, Imre F. (1894-1954) Phys. NC37

PATCH, Edith M. (1876-1954) Entom. AMEM NC18

PATE, Vernon S. (1903-1958) Entom. AMEM

PATEL, C. Kumar (1938-) Phys.; Engr. MHSE

PATON, Boris E. (1918-) Metal. SMST

PATRICK, Ruth (1908-) Ecol. CWSE

PATRIZI, Francesco (1529-1597) Math. CDZZ ZZ10

PATT, Harvey M. (1918-) Physiol. MHM1 MHSE

PATTEN, William (1861-1932) Biol. DAB NC24

PATTERSON, Austin M. (1876-1956) Chem. ACCE

PATTERSON, Carlile P. (1816-1881) Surv. NC-4

PATTERSON, Charles A. (1876-1922) Chem. NC19

PATTERSON, John T. (1878-1960) Zool. BM38

PATTERSON, Robert (1732-1824) Math. ACCE
    BIOD DAB

PATTERSON, Robert (1802-1872) Nat. Hist. DNB

PATTERSON, Robert M. (1787-1854) Chem. ACCE
    BIOD

PATTINSON, Hugh L. (1796-1858) Invent. BDOS DNB

PATTISON, Granville S. (1791-1851) Anat. DNB

PAUL OF AEGINA (fl. 640) Med. CDZZ ZZ10

PAUL OF ALEXANDRIA (fl. c.378) Astron. CDZZ
    ZZ10

PAUL OF VENICE (c.1370-1429) Nat. Philos. CDZZ
    ZZ10

PAUL, Henry M. (1851-1931) Astron. DAB NC10

PAUL, John R. (1893-1971) Med. BM47 MHM2 MHSE

PAUL, Lewis (1730-1759) Engr. GE-1

PAULI, Wolfgang (1900-1958) Phys. ABES ABET
BDOS BEOS CB46 CDZZ DCPW HSSO MHM1
MHSE POSW RS-5 ZZ10

PAULING, Linus C. (1901-) Chem. ABES ABET
BEOS CB49 CB64 EDCJ IFBS MHM1 MHSE
NBPS NCSG PBTS PPEY QPAS WAMB

PAULISA (fl. c.400) Astron. CDZZ ZZ10

PAULLI, Simon (1603-1680) Bot.; Anat. CDZZ ZZ10

PAULY, August (1850-1914) Zool.; Entom. CDZZ
ZZ10

PAUSON, P.L. (1925-) Chem. COBC

PAVLOV, Aleksei P. (1854-1929) Geol. CDZZ ZZ10

PAVLOV, Igor M. (1900-) Metal. SMST

PAVLOV, Ivan P. (1849-1936) Physiol. ABES ABET
BDOS BEOS BHMT CDZZ GRTH LISD PAW2
POPF RUSP SAIF TOWS ZZ10

PAVLOVSKY, Evgenii N. (1884-1965) Zool. SMST

PAVON Y JIMENEZ, Jose A. (1754-1840) Bot. CDZZ
ZZXV

PAVY, Octave B. (1844-1884) Nat. Hist. DAB NC-7

PAWSEY, Joseph L. (1908-1962) Astrophys. RS10

PAYEN, Anselme (1795-1871) Chem. ABES ABET
BEOS CDZZ GRCH ZZ10

PAYKULL, Gustaf (1757-1826) Entom. CDZZ ZZ10

PAYNE-GAPOSCHKIN, Cecilia (1900-1979) Astron.
CB57

PEABODY, George (1795-1869) Paleon. MADC

PEABODY, Raymond A. (1923-1978) Engr. NC61

PEACH, Charles W. (1800-1886) Nat. Hist.; Geol.
DNB

PEACOCK, George (1791-1858) Math. ABET CDZZ
DNB ZZ10

PEACOCK, Thomas B. (1812-1882) Med. BHMT

PEAIRS, Leonard M. (1886-1956) Entom. AMEM

PEALE, Charles W. (1741-1827) Nat. Hist. BIOD
CDZZ COAC DAB HNHB ZZ10

PEALE, Rembrandt (1778-1860) Biol. CDZZ ZZXV

PEALE, Titan R. (1799-1885) Nat. Hist. BIOD
CDZZ DAB ZZ10

PEAN DE SAINT-GILLES, Leon (1832-1862) Chem.
CDZZ ZZ10

PEANO, Giuseppe (1858-1932) Math. ABES ABET
BEOS CDZZ ZZ10

PEARCE, Leonard (1873-1947) Elec. Engr. DNB6

PEARCE, Louise (1885-1959) Med. NAWM

PEARL, Raymond (1879-1940) Biol.; Genet. BM22
CDZZ DAB2 IMMO NC15 WAMB ZZ10

PEARSALL, William H. (1891-1964) Bot. RS17

PEARSE, Arthur S. (1877-1956) Zool. NC47

PEARSON, Egon S. (1895-1980) Math. RS27

PEARSON, George (1751-1828) Chem. CDZZ ZZ10

PEARSON, Gustaf A. (1880-1949) Forest. LACC

PEARSON, Herbert W. (1850-1916) Geol.; Astron.
NC18

PEARSON, Jay F. (1901-1965) Biol. CB53 NC52

PEARSON, Karl (1857-1936) Math. ABET BEOS
CDZZ DNB5 ZZ10

PEARSON, Ralph G. (1919-) Chem. MHSE

PEARSON, Thomas G. (1873-1943) Ornith. DAB3
LACC NC33

PEARY, Robert E. (1856-1920) Exp. ABET MGAH

PEASE, Francis G. (1881-1938) Astron. CDZZ ZZ10

PEASE, Robert N. (1895-1964) Chem. NC50

PEAT, Stanley (1902-1969) Chem. RS16

PEATTIE, Donald C. (1898-1965) Bot. CB40

PECHAM, John (c.1230-1292) Opt.; Math. CDZZ
ZZ10

PECK, Charles H. (1833-1917) Bot. MABH

PECK, Ralph B. (1912-) Engr. MHSE

PECK, William G. (1820-1892) Nat. Hist. AMEM
BIOD DAB

PECKHAM, George W. (1845-1914) Entom. AMEM
DAB NC12

PECKHAM, Stephan F. (1839-1918) Chem. DAB
NC-9

PECORA, William T. (1913-1972) Geol. BM47 MHM2
MHSE

PECQUET, Jean (1622-1674) Anat. BDOS BEOS
CDZZ ZZ10

PEEK, Cuthbert E. (1855-1901) Meteor. DNB2

PEGRAM, George B. (1876-1958) Phys. BM41 NC49
NCSF

PEIERLS, Rudolf E. (1907-) Phys. BEOS MHM2
MHSE

PEIRCE, Benjamin (1809-1880) Math.; Astron. BIOD
CDZZ DAB NC-8 WAMB ZZ10

PEIRCE, Benjamin O. (1854-1914) Math.; Phys. BM-8
CDZZ DAB NC20 QPAS YSMS ZZ10

PEIRCE, Charles S. (1839-1914) Math. CDZZ DAB
NC-8 SNAR WAMB ZZ10

PEIRCE, George J. (1868-1954) Bot. NC41

PEIRCE, James M. (1834-1906) Math. DAB

PEIRESC, Nicolas C. de (1580-1637) Astron. CDZZ
ZZ10

PEKELHARING, Cornelius A. (1848-1922) Chem.;
Med. CDZZ ZZ10

PEKERIS, Chaim L. (1908-) Math. MHSE

PELETIER, Jacques (1517-1582) Math.; Med. CDZZ
ZZ10

PELIGOT, Eugene M. (1811-1890) Chem. BDOS BEOS

PELL, John (1611-1685) Math. CDZZ DNB ZZ10

PELLETIER, Bertrand (1761-1797) Chem. CDZZ
ZZ10

PELLETIER, Pierre J. (1788-1842) Chem. ABES
ABET BDOS BEOS CDZZ ZZ10

PELOUZE, Theophile J. (1807-1867) Chem. CDZZ
ZZ10

PELTIER, Jean C. (1785-1845) Phys. BDOS BEOS
CDZZ EETD ZZ10

PELTON, Lester A. (1829-1918) Invent. FNEC

PEMBERTON, Henry (1694-1771) Phys.; Math.
CDZZ ZZ10

PEMBERTON, Henry (1855-1913) Chem. NC15

PENAUD, Alphonse (1850-1880) Aero. ICFW

PENCK, Albrecht (1858-1945) Geol.; Geomorph.
BEOS CDZZ ZZ10

PENCK, Walther (1888-1923) Geol. CDZZ ZZ10

PENDLETON, Edmund M. (1815-1884) Med.; Chem.
DAB

PENFIELD, Samuel L. (1856-1906) Mineral. BM-6

PENFIELD, Wilder G. (1891-1976) Med. CB68 MHM1
MHSE RS24

PENFOLD, Joseph W. (1907-1973) Cons. EAFC
LACC

PENGELLY, William (1812-1894) Geol. DNB

PENHALLOW, David P. (1854-1910) Bot. NC20

PENNANT, Thomas (1726-1798) Nat. Hist. ANHD
CDZZ DNB HAOA ZZ10

PENNEY, William G. (1909-) Math. BEOS CB53

PENNINGTON, Mary E. (1872-1952) Chem. ACCE
NAWM

PENNOCK, John D. (1860-1921) Chem. NC19

PENNY, Charles L. (1858-1925) Chem. NC17

PENNY, Frederick (1816-1869) Chem. CDZZ ZZ10

PENROSE, Lionel S. (1898-1972) Genet. RS19

PENROSE, Roger (1931-) Math.; Phys. BEOS MHSE

PENSA, Antonio (1874-1970) Anat.; Embryol. CDZZ
ZZXV

PENZIAS, Arno A. (1933-) Astron.; Phys. ABET BEOS MHSE POSW SOT2

PEPYS, William H. (1775-1856) Phys. DNB

PERCIVAL, James G. (1795-1856) Geol. BIOD

PERCIVAL, Thomas (1740-1804) Med. BHMT

PERCY, John (1817-1889) Metal. CDZZ DNB ZZ10

PEREIRA, Benedictus (1535-1610) Phys.; Astron. CDZZ ZZ10

PEREIRA, Duarte P. (c.1460-1533) Nav. CDZZ ZZ10

PEREIRA, Jonathan (1804-1853) Pharm. DNB

PERES, Joseph J. (1890-1962) Math. CDZZ ZZ10

PEREY, Marguerite C. (1909-1975) Chem. BEOS IDWB

PEREZ DE VARGAS, Bernardo (fl. 1560-1570) Astron.; Biol. CDZZ ZZ10

PERGANDE, Theodore (1840-1916) Entom. AMEM

PERKIN, Arthur G. (1861-1937) Chem. DNB5

PERKIN, William H. (1838-1907) Chem. ABES ABET BDOS BEOS CDZZ DNB2 GRCH HOSS MNCS SAIF ZZ10

PERKIN, William H. Jr. (1860-1929) Chem. BDOS BEOS CDZZ DNB4 HSSO ZZ10

PERKINS, Angier M. (c.1799-1881) Engr. DNB

PERKINS, Elisha (1742-1799) Med. MSFB

PERKINS, George H. (1844-1933) Nat. Hist. NC10

PERKINS, Jacob (1766-1849) Engr. GE-1

PERKINS, Loftus (1834-1891) Engr. DNB

PERKINS, (R.) Marlin (1905-) Herp. CB51 SWWP WAMB

PERKINS, Robert C. (1866-1955) Entom.; Zool. DNB7 RS-2

PERLIS, Alan J. (1922-) Comp. HOPL

PERLMANN, Gertrude E. (1912-1974) Biochem. MHSE

PERLZWEIG, William A. (1891-1949) Biochem. NC38

PERON, Francois (1775-1810) Zool.; Nat. Hist. CDZZ ZZ10

PEROT, Jean B. (1863-1925) Phys. CDZZ ZZ10

PERRAULT, Claude (1613-1688) Zool.; Med. ANHD BDOS BEOS CDZZ ZZ10

PERRAULT, Pierre (1611-1680) Nat. Hist. CDZZ ZZ10

PERRIER, Edmond (1844-1921) Zool. CDZZ ZZ10

PERRIER, Georges (1872-1946) Surv. CDZZ ZZ10

PERRIN, Francis H. (1901-) Phys. CB51

PERRIN, Jean B. (1870-1942) Phys. ABES ABET BDOS BEOS CDZZ POSW ZZ10

PERRINE, Charles D. (1867-1951) Astron. ABET CDZZ DAB5 NC13 ZZ10

PERRINE, Henry (1797-1840) Bot. BIOD

PERRONCITO, Edoardo (1847-1936) Parasit.; Bact. CDZZ ZZ10

PERRONET, Jean R. (1708-1794) Engr. BDOS CDZZ GE-1 ZZ10

PERROTIN, Henri J. (1845-1904) Astron. CDZZ ZZ10

PERRY, John H. (1895-1953) Chem. Engr. ACCE

PERRY, Stephen J. (1833-1889) Astron. DNB

PERSEUS (fl. 200s B.C.) Math. CDZZ ZZ10

PERSONNE, Jacques (1816-1880) Chem. CDZZ ZZ10

PERSOON, Christiaan H. (1761-1836) Bot. CDZZ ZZ10

PERSOZ, Jean F. (1805-1868) Chem. CDZZ ZZ10

PERUTZ, Max F. (1914-) Crystal. ABES ABET BEOS CB63 EDCJ MHM1 MHSE

PETAVEL, Joseph E. (1873-1936) Engr.; Phys. DNB5 MMSB

PETER OF COELCHURCH (fl. 1175) Engr. GE-1

PETER PEREGRINUS (fl. c.1269) Phys. ABET BDOS
CDZZ EETD ZZ10

PETER PHILOMEN OF DACIA (fl. 1290-1300) Math.
CDZZ ZZ10

PETER THE PILGRIM SEE PETER PEREGRINUS

PETER, Robert (1805-1894) Chem. BIOD DAB

PETERS, Carl F. (1844-1894) Astron.; Surv. CDZZ
ZZ10

PETERS, Christian A. (1806-1880) Astron. CDZZ
DAB ZZ10

PETERS, Christian H. (1813-1890) Astron. BIOD
CDZZ NC13 ZZ10

PETERS, James L. (1889-1952) Ornith. NC41

PETERS, John P. (1887-1955) Archaeol. BM31

PETERS, Rudolph A. (1889-1982) Biochem. BEOS
MHM1 MHSE

PETERSEN, Julius (1839-1910) Math. CDZZ ZZ10

PETERSEN, Neils F. (1877-1940) Bot. BNBR

PETERSON, Alvah (1888-1972) Entom. NC58

PETERSON, Karl M. (1828-1881) Math. CDZZ ZZ10

PETERSON, Ralph M. (1927-) Forest. EAFC

PETERSON, Roger T. (1908-) Ornith. CB59 DGMT
LACC SWWP WAMB

PETIT, Alexis T. (1791-1820) Phys. ABES ABET BDOS
BEOS CDZZ ZZ10

PETIT, Jean L. (1674-1750) Med. BEOS

PETIT, Pierre (1594-1677) Phys.; Astron. CDZZ ZZ10

PETIVER, James (1663-1718) Bot.; Entom. DNB

PETOSIRIS, Pseudo- (fl. c.110 B.C.-90 B.C.) Astrol.
CDZZ ZZ10

PETRI, Julius R. (1852-1921) Bact. BEOS

PETRIE, (William) Flinders (1853-1942) Archaeol.
ABET CDZZ OGML ZZ10

PETRIE, William (1821-1908) Elec. Sci. DNB2

PETROV, Aleksandr D. (1895-1964) Chem. SMST

PETROV, Georgii I. (1912-) Phys. SMST

PETROV, Nikolai N. (1876-1964) Med. SMST

PETROV, Nikolay P. (1836-1920) Engr. CDZZ ZZ10

PETROV, Vasily V. (1761-1834) Phys.; Chem. CDZZ
ZZ10

PETROVSHY, Ivan G. (1901-1973) Math. CDZZ
SMST ZZ10

PETRUNKEVITCH, Alexander (1875-1964) Entom.
AMEM NCSA SEMK

PETRUS BONUS (fl. c.1323-1330) Alch. CDZZ ZZ10

PETRY, Loren (1887-1970) Bot. NC55

PETRYANOV-SOKOLOV, Igor V. (1907-) Chem.
SMST

PETTENKOFER, Max J. von (1818-1901) Chem.;
Med. ABES ABET BDOS BEOS BHMT CDZZ
TBSG ZZ10

PETTERSSON, Hans (1888-1966) Ocean. CDZZ
EXSG RS12 ZZ10

PETTIGREW, James B. (1834-1908) Anat. DNB2

PETTIGREW, Thomas J. (1791-1865) Med. BHMT

PETTIJOHN, Francis J. (1904-) Geol. MHM2 MHSE

PETTINGILL, Olin S. (1907-) Ornith. DGMT

PETTIT, Ted S. (1914-) Cons. LACC

PETTY, William (1623-1687) Geog. CDZZ ZZ10

PEURBACH, Georg von (1423-1461) Astron.; Math.
ABES ABET BEOS CDZZ ZZXV

PEYER, Johann C. (1653-1712) Physiol. CDZZ ZZ10

PEYSONNEL, Jean A. (1694-1759) Bot.; Zool. CDZZ
ZZ10

PEYVE, Aleksandr V. (1909-) Geol. SMST

PEYVE, Yan V. (1906-) Chem. SMST

PEZARD, Albert (1875-1927) Med. CDZZ ZZ10

PEZENAS, Esprit (1692-1776) Astron.; Phys. CDZZ ZZ10

PFAFF, Johann F. (1765-1825) Math. CDZZ ZZ10

PFAFFMANN, Carl (1913-) Psych. MHM2 MHSE

PFANNMULLER, Julius F. (1889-1961) Chem. NC50

PFEFFER, Wilhelm F. (1845-1920) Bot. ABES ABET BDOS BEOS CDZZ ZZ10

PFEIFFER, Paul (1875-1951) Chem. CDZZ HSSO ZZ10

PFEIFFER, Richard F. (1858-1945) Bact. BDOS BEOS RS-2

PFEIL, Leonard B. (1898-1969) Metal. RS18

PFIFFNER, Joseph J. (1903-1975) Biochem. NC59

PFIZER, Charles (1823-1906) Chem. ACCE

PFLUGER, Eduard F. (1829-1910) Physiol. CDZZ ZZ10

PFUND, August H. (1879-1949) Phys. DAB4 NC37

PHELPS, Almira H. (1793-1884) Sci. Writ. ACCE BIOD

PHELPS, Thomas (fl. 1750) Astron. DNB

PHILINUS OF COS (fl. c.250 B.C.) Med. CDZZ ZZ10

PHILIP, Alexander P. (1770-1851) Med. CDZZ ZZ10

PHILIPS, Peregrine (b. c.1800) Chem. BEOS

PHILLIPS, Arthur M. (1914-) Biol. LACC

PHILLIPS, David C. (1924-) Biophys. BEOS

PHILLIPS, Everett F. (1878-1951) Entom. AMEM

PHILLIPS, Francis C. (1850-1920) Chem. ACCE DAB NC18

PHILLIPS, Horatio (1845-1924) Aero. ICFW

PHILLIPS, John (1800-1874) Geol.; Paleon. CDZZ DNB GENT ZZ10

PHILLIPS, John A. (1822-1887) Geol. DNB

PHILLIPS, John C. (1876-1938) Ornith.; Genet. NC29

PHILLIPS, Paul H. (1898-1977) Biochem. NC60

PHILLIPS, Richard (1778-1851) Chem. DNB

PHILLIPS, Theodore E. (1868-1942) Astron. CDZZ ZZ10

PHILLIPS, William (1775-1828) Geol. CDZZ DNB ZZ10

PHILLIPS, William (1822-1905) Bot. DNB2

PHILO OF BYZANTIUM (fl. c.250 B.C.) Phys. ABET CDZZ GE-1 ZZ10

PHILOLAUS OF CROTONA (fl. c.450 B.C.-400 B.C.) Astron.; Med. ABET BEOS CDZZ ZZ10

PHYSICK, Philip S. (1768-1837) Med. BHMT

PIAGET, Jean (1896-1980) Psych. AO80 MHM2 MHSE POPF

PIANESE, Giuseppe (1864-1933) Anat. CDZZ ZZXV

PIAZZI, Giuseppe (1746-1826) Astron. ABES ABET BDOS BEOS CDZZ IEAS ZZ10

PICARD, Charles E. (1856-1941) Math. CDZZ ZZ10

PICARD, Jean (1620-1682) Astron. ABES ABET BDOS BEOS CDZZ EETD WAMB ZZ10

PICCARD, Auguste (1884-1962) Ocean.; Phys. ABES ABET BDOS BEOS CB47 CDZZ EXDC GDSP ICFW ZZ10

PICCARD, Jacques E. (1922-) Ocean. CB65 EXDC EXSG

PICCARD, Jean F. (1884-1963) Aero. CB47 GDSP NC47

PICCARD, Jeannette (1895-1981) Aero. AO81

PICCOLOMINI, Arcangelo (1525-1586) Anat.; Physiol. CDZZ ZZ10

PICKARD, Robert H. (1874-1949) Chem. DNB6

PICKENS, Andrew L. (1890-1969) Biol. NC55

PICKERING, Charles (1805-1878) Nat. Hist. BIOD DAB

PICKERING, Edward C. (1846-1919) Astron. ABES
ABET BDOS BEOS BM15 CDZZ DAB IEAS
NC-6 WAMB ZZ10

PICKERING, George W. (1904-1980) Med. AO80
MHM2 MHSE RS28

PICKERING, William H. (1858-1938) Astron. ABES
ABET BDOS BEOS CDZZ IEAS NC33 ZZ10

PICKERING, William H. (1910-) Phys. CB58 MHM1
MOS2

PICTET, Ame (1857-1937) Chem. BDOS BEOS

PICTET, Marc A. (1752-1825) Phys. CDZZ SOAC
ZZ10

PICTET, Raoul P. (1846-1929) Phys. ABES ABET
BDOS BEOS CDZZ MCCW ZZ10

PIDDINGTON, Henry (1797-1858) Meteor. DNB

PIERCE, George W. (1872-1956) Phys. BM33 CDZZ
QPAS ZZ10

PIERCE, John R. (1910-) Engr. ABES ABET BEOS
CB61 MHM1 MHSE MOS4 TPAE

PIERCE, Joseph A. (1902-) Math. SBPY

PIERI, Mario (1860-1913) Math. CDZZ ZZ10

PIETTE, Louis E. (1827-1906) Archaeol.; Paleon.
CDZZ ZZ10

PIEZ, Karl A. (1924-) Biochem. MHSE

PIGGOT, Aaron S. (1822-1869) Chem. ACCE

PIGOTT, Edward (1753-1825) Astron. CDZZ DNB
ZZ10

PIGOTT, Nathaniel (d. 1804) Astron. CDZZ DNB
ZZ10

PIKE, Nicolas (1743-1819) Math. BIOD DAB NC20

PILATRE DE ROZIER, Jean F. (1754-1785) Aero.
CDZZ ZZ10

PILLSBURY, John E. (1846-1919) Ocean. DAB

PILLSBURY, Walter B. (1872-1960) Psych. BM37

PILSBRY, Henry A. (1862-1957) Zool. NC47

PINCHERLE, Salvatore (1853-1936) Math. CDZZ
ZZ10

PINCHOT, Gifford (1865-1946) Cons. CONS EAFC
GOTH HOCS LACC PCWA TECH WAMB

PINCUS, Gregory G. (1903-1967) Biol. ABES
ABET BEOS BM42 CB66 CDZZ MHM2 MHSE
ZZ10

PINEDA Y RAMIREZ, Antonio (1753-1793) Nat. Hist.
SSNW

PINEL, Philippe (1745-1826) Med. ABES ABET
BEOS BHMT CDZZ ZZ10

PINGRE, Alexandre G. (1711-1796) Astron. CDZZ
ZZ10

PIPER, Charles V. (1867-1926) Agr. MABH

PIPPARD, Alfred B. (1920-) Phys. BEOS MHM2
MHSE

PIPPARD, Leone (Contemporary) Ethol. WAGW

PIRES, Tome (c.1470-c.1540) Pharm. CDZZ ZZ10

PIRI RAIS, Muhyi al-Din (1470-1554) Geog. CDZZ
ZZ10

PIRI REIS SEE PIRI RAIS

PIRIE, Norman W. (1907-) Microbiol.; Biochem.
BEOS MHSE

PIROGOFF, Nikolai I. (1810-1881) Med. BHMT
CDZZ ZZ10

PIRSSON, Louis V. (1860-1919) Geol. BM34

PISANO, Leonardo SEE FIBONACCI, Leonardo

PISANO, Michael (1923-) Biochem. CHUB

PISO, Willem (c.1611-1678) Med. CDZZ ZZ10

PISTOLKORS, Aleksandr A. (1896-) Elec. Engr.
SMST

PITCAIRN, Archibald (1652-1713) Med. CDZZ ZZ11

PITCHER, Zina (1797-1872) Nat. Hist. BIOD DAB

PITISCUS, Bartholomeo (1561-1613) Math. CDZZ
ZZ11

PITMAN, Isaac (1813-1897) Invent. SAIF

PITOT, Henri (1695-1771) Engr. CDZZ FNEC GE-1 ZZ11

PITT-RIVERS, Augustus H. (1827-1900) Archaeol.; Anthro. CDZZ ZZ11

PITTS, Robert F. (1908-1977) Med. MHM2 MHSE

PITZER, Kenneth S. (1914-) Chem. BEOS CB50 MHM2 MHSE

PIXII, Hippolyte (1808-1835) Elec. Sci. BDOS

PIYP, Boris I. (1906-1966) Volcan. SMST

PLANA, Giovanni (1781-1864) Math.; Astron. CDZZ ZZ11

PLANCK, Max K. von (1958-1947) Phys. ABES ABET BDOS BEOS CDZZ FNEC GISA HOSS HSSO IFBS PAW2 POSW SAIF TOWS ZZ11

PLANT, Thomas L. (1819-1883) Meteor. DNB

PLANTE, Gaston (1834-1889) Phys. ABES ABET BEOS

PLANUDES, Maximum (c.1255-1305) Polym. CDZZ ZZ11

PLASKETT, Harry H. (1893-1980) Astron. AO80 MHSE RS27

PLASKETT, John S. (1865-1941) Astron. ABET BEOS CDZZ DNB6 ZZ11

PLATE, Ludwig H. (1862-1937) Zool. CDZZ ZZ11

PLATEAU, Joseph A. (1801-1883) Phys. CDZZ ZZ11

PLATO (427 B.C.-348/7 B.C.) Philos. ABES ABET BEOS CDZZ EETD GRTH HLSM ZZ11

PLATO OF TIVOLI (fl. c.1100-1150) Math.; Astrol. CDZZ ZZ11

PLATT, Franklin (1844-1900) Geol. BIOD

PLATTER, Felix (1536-1614) Med. CDZZ BHMT ZZ11

PLATTNER, Karl F. (1800-1858) Metal. CDZZ ZZ11

PLATZ, Reinhold (1886-1966) Aero. ICFW

PLAUDE, Karl K. (1897-) Phys. SMST

PLAYFAIR, John (1748-1819) Math.; Phys. BDOS BEOS CDZZ DNB ZZ11

PLAYFAIR, Lyon (1818-1898) Chem. BDOS BEOS CDZZ DNB1 SOSC VISC ZZ11

PLENCIC, Marcus A. (1705-1786) Med. CDZZ ZZ11

PLIMMER, Robert H. (1877-1955) Biochem. DNB7

PLINUS SECUNDUS, Gaius SEE PLINY THE ELDER

PLINY THE ELDER (23-79) Nat. Hist. ABES ABET ANHD BDOS BEOS CDZZ EETD GE-1 HAOA HLSM LISD NATJ ORNS ZZ11

PLOT, Robert (1640-1696) Nat. Hist.; Archaeol. CDZZ ZZ11

PLOTINUS (c.204-270) Philos. CDZZ ZZ11

PLOTZ, Harry (1890-1947) Bact. DAB4

PLUCHE, Noel A. (1688-1761) Sci. Ed. CDZZ ZZ11

PLUCKER, Julius (1801-1868) Math.; Phys. ABES ABET BDOS BEOS CDZZ ZZ11

PLUKENET, Leonard (1642-1706) Bot. DNB

PLUMIER, Charles (1646-1704) Nat. Hist.; Bot. CDZZ ZZ11

PLUMMER, Andrew (c.1698-1756) Med. CDZZ ZZ11

PLUMMER, Henry C. (1875-1946) Astron. CDZZ DNB6 ZZ11

PLUMMER, John T. (1807-1865) Nat. Hist.; Chem. BIOD

POGGENDORFF, Johann C. (1796-1877) Phys. BDOS BEOS CDZZ EETD ZZ11

POGGIALE, Antoine B. (1808-1879) Chem.; Med. CDZZ ZZ11

POGORELOV, Aleksei V. (1919-) Math. SMST

POGSON, Norman R. (1829-1891) Astron. ABES ABET BEOS DNB

POHL, Georg F. (1788-1849) Elec. Sci. ELEC

POINCARE, Jules Henri (1854-1912) Math. ABES ABET BDOS BEOS CDZZ GASJ ZZ11

POINDEXTER, Hildrus A. (1901-) Med. SBPY

POINSOT, Louis (1777-1859) Math. CDZZ ZZ11

POISEUILLE, Jean L. (1799-1869) Physiol.; Phys.
ABET CDZZ FNEC ZZ11

POISSON, Simeon D. (1781-1840) Phys. ABET
BDOS BEOS CDZZ FNEC SOAC ZZXV

POIVRE, Pierre (1719-1786) Bot. CDZZ ZZ11

POLANYI, John C. (1929-) Chem. MHSE

POLANYI, Michael (1891-1976) Chem. BEOS RS23

POLDERVAART, Arie (1918-1964) Geol. NC51

POLENI, Giovanni (1683-1761) Math.; Phys.
CDZZ ZZ11

POLHAMMER, Christopher SEE POLHEM, Christopher

POLHAMUS, Edward (1921-) Aero. ICFW

POLHEM, Christopher (1661-1751) Invent. ABES
ABET BDOS GE-1

POLI, Giuseppe S. (1746-1825) Phys. CDZZ ZZ11

POLIKARPOV, Nikolai (1892-1944) Aero. ICFW

POLINIERE, Pierre (1671-1734) Phys. CDZZ ZZ11

POLITZER, Adam (1835-1920) Med. BHMT

POLLARD, William G. (1911-) Phys. CB53

POLLENDER, Aloys (1800-1879) Med. CDZZ ZZ11

POLLIO, Marcus SEE VIRTRUVIUS

POLLITZER, Sigmund (1859-1937) Med. BHMT

POMERANCHUK, Isaak Y. (1913-1966) Phys. SMST

POMEROY, Kenneth B. (1907-) Forest. LACC

POMMER, Alfred M. (1916-1977) Biochem. NC59

POMPONAZZI, Pietro (1462-1525) Nat. Philos.
CDZZ ZZ11

POMPONIUS MELA (fl. 44) Geog. ABET BEOS
CDZZ ZZ11

PONCELET, Jean V. (1788-1867) Math. ABES ABET
BDOS BEOS CDZZ ZZ11

POND, George C. (1861-1920) Chem. ACCE NC20

POND, John (1767-1836) Astron. BEOS IEAS

PONNAMPERUMA, Cyril A. (1923-) Biochem.
ABES ABET BEOS

PONS, Jean L. (1761-1831) Astron. ABES ABET
BEOS CDZZ ZZ11

PONTECORVO, Guido (1907-) Genet. BEOS
MHM2 MHSE

PONTEDERA, Giulio (1688-1757) Bot. CDZZ ZZ11

PONTEKORVO, Bruno M. (1913-) Phys. SMST

PONTRYAGIN, Lev S. (1908-) Math. SMST

POOL, Judith G. (1919-1975) Physiol. NAWM

POOLE, Daniel A. (1922-) Cons. LACC

POOR, Charles L. (1866-1951) Astron. CDZZ NC14
NC38 ZZ11

POOR, John M. (1871-1933) Astron. NC25

POPE SYLVESTER II SEE GERBERT D'AURILLAC

POPE, Walter (d. 1714) Astron. DNB

POPE, William J. (1870-1939) Chem. ABES ABET
BDOS BEOS CDZZ DNB5 ZZ11

POPENOE, Paul B. (1888-) Biol. CB46

POPKOV, Valerii I. (1908-) Elec. Engr. SMST

POPOV, Aleksandr N. (1840-1881) Chem. CDZZ
ZZ11

POPOV, Aleksandr S. (1859-1906) Phys. ABES ABET
BEOS CDZZ ZZ11

POPOV, Egor SEE POPOV, Yevgenii P.

POPOV, Yevgenii P. (1914-) Engr. MHSE SMST

POPOVICH, Pavel R. (1930-) Astronaut. FPSN

PORCHER, Francis P. (1825-1895) Bot. BIOD DAB

PORETSKY, Platon S. (1846-1907) Math.; Astron. CDZZ ZZ11

PORRETT, Robert (1783-1868) Chem. DNB

PORRO, Ignazio (1801-1875) Surv.; Opt. CDZZ ZZ11

PORTA, Giambattista della (1535-1615) Math. ABET CDZZ GE-1 ZZ11

PORTA, Luigi (1800-1875) Med. CDZZ ZZ11

PORTAL, Antoine (1742-1832) Med. CDZZ ZZ11

PORTER, Charles T. (1826-1910) Engr. NC20 TPAE

PORTER, Eliot (1901-) Ecol.; Photo. CB76

PORTER, George (1920-) Chem. ABES ABET BEOS COBC MHM2 MHSE

PORTER, Jermain G. (1852-1933) Astron. DAB NC13

PORTER, John A. (1822-1866) Chem. BIOD DAB

PORTER, John J. (1880-1956) Chem. NC46

PORTER, Keith R. (1912-) Biol. BEOS MHM1 MHSE

PORTER, Milton B. (1869-1960) Math. NC49

PORTER, Rodney R. (1917-) Biochem. BEOS MHSE PAW2

PORTER, Thomas C. (1822-1901) Bot. BIOD DAB

PORTEVIN, Albert M. (1880-1962) Metal. RS-9 CDZZ ZZ11

PORTIER, Paul (1866-1962) Biol.; Physiol. CDZZ ZZ11

POSEPNY, Franz (1836-1895) Geol. CDZZ ZZ11

POSIDONIUS (c.135 B.C.-c.51 B.C.) Philos. ABET BEOS CDZZ ZZ11

POST, Emil L. (1897-1954) Math. CDZZ MATT ZZ11

POTAIN, Pierre C. (1825-1901) Med. BHMT

POTAMIAN, (Brother) Michael (1847-1917) Sci. Writ. DAB

POTANIN, Grigory N. (1835-1920) Geog. CDZZ ZZ11

POTEAT, William L. (1856-1938) Biol. NC28

POTT, Johann H. (1692-1777) Chem. CDZZ ZZ11

POTT, Percival (1714-1788) Med. BHMT

POTTER, Albert F. (1859-1944) Forest. LACC

POTTER, John P. (1818-1847) Anat. DNB

POTTER, Van Rensselaer (1911-) Biochem. MHM2 MHSE

POTTS, Robert (1805-1885) Math. DNB

POTZGER, John E. (1866-1955) Bot. NC43

POUCHET, Felix A. (1800-1872) Biol.; Nat. Hist. CDZZ HLSM ZZ11

POUGH, Richard H. (1904-) Cons. LACC

POUILLET, Claude S. (1790-1868) Phys. CDZZ ZZ11

POULSEN, Valdemar (1869-1942) Invent. ABES ABET

POULTON, Edward B. (1856-1943) Zool. BEOS DNB6

POUND, James (1669-1724) Astron. DNB

POUND, Robert V. (1919-) Phys. MHM2 MHSE

POURFOUR DU PETIT, Francois (1664-1741) Med. CDZZ ZZ11

POURTALES, Louis F. de (1824-1880) Ocean. BIOD BM-5 CDZZ DAB ZZ11

POWALKY, Karl R. (1817-1881) Astron. CDZZ ZZ11

POWDERMAKER, Hortense (1900-1970) Anthro. NAWM NC55 NCSJ

POWELL, Alan R. (1894-1975) Chem. COBC RS22

POWELL, Baden (1796-1860) Phys. CDZZ DARR ZZ11

POWELL, Cecil F. (1903-1969) Phys. ABES ABET BDOS BEOS CDZZ MHM1 MHSE POSW RS17 ZZ11

POWELL, Hugh (1799-1883) Instr. MNCS

POWELL, John W. (1834-1902) Geol.; Cons. BIOD
BM-8 CDZZ CONS FIFE GKGP LACC PCWA
SASH WAMB ZZ11

POWELL, Richard (1767-1834) Med. BHMT

POWELL, Wilson M. (1903-1974) Phys. NC57

POWER, Frederick B. (1853-1927) Chem. ACCE
CDZZ DAB NC28 ZZ11

POWER, Henry (1623-1668) Micros.; Phys. CDZZ
ZZ11

POWERS, Donald H. (1901-1968) Chem. NC54

POWERS, Edwin B. (1880-1949) Zool. NC38

POYNTING, John H. (1852-1914) Phys. BDOS BEOS
CDZZ DNB3 ZZ11

PRAGER, William (1903-1980) Engr. AO80

PRAIN, David (1857-1944) Bot. DNB6

PRANDTL, Ludwig (1875-1953) Phys. CDZZ FNEC
ICFW RS-1 ZZ11

PRATT, Anne (1806-1893) Bot. DNB

PRATT, Frederick H. (1873-1958) Physiol. CDZZ
ZZ11

PRATT, George D. (1869-1935) Cons. NC29

PRATT, J. Gaither (1910-) Psych. CB64

PRATT, John H. (1809-1871) Math. CDZZ BEOS
ZZ11

PRAUSNITZ, John M. (1928-) Chem. BEOS

PRAXAGORAS OF COS (b. c.340 B.C.) Anat.;
Physiol. ABET BEOS CDZZ ZZ11

PREDVODITELEV, A.S. (1891-) Phys. SMST

PREECE, William H. (1834-1913) Elec. Engr. DNB3

PREGEL, Boris (1893-1976) Engr. NC59

PREGL, Fritz (1869-1930) Chem. ABES ABET
BDOS BEOS CDZZ GRCH NPWC ZZ11

PRELOG, Vladimir (1906-) Chem. ABET BEOS
MHM2 MHSE PAW2

PRESCOTT, Albert B. (1832-1905) Chem. ACCE
BIOD DAB NC13

PRESCOTT, Samuel C. (1872-1962) Bact. NC50
NCSC

PRESL, Karel B. (1794-1852) Bot. CDZZ ZZ11

PRESS, Frank (1924-) Geophys. CB66 MHM2
MHSE

PRESTON, Ann (1813-1872) Med. IDWB

PRESTON, John F. (1883-1967) Forest. LACC

PRESTON, Walter C. (1895-1950) Chem. NC40

PRESTWICH, Joseph (1812-1896) Geol. BEOS CDZZ
DNB1 ZZ11

PREVOST, Isaac B. (1755-1819) Math.; Phys. CDZZ
ZZ11

PREVOST, Jean L. (1790-1850) Physiol.; Embryol.
CDZZ ZZ11

PREVOST, Louis C. (1787-1856) Geol. CDZZ ZZ11

PREVOST, Pierre (1751-1839) Phys. ABES ABET
BEOS CDZZ ZZ11

PREYER, Thierry W. (1841-1897) Physiol. CDZZ
ZZ11

PRICE, Charles C. (1913-) Chem. CB57

PRICE, George M. (1870-1963) Geol. MSFB

PRICE, Overton W. (1873-1914) Forest. EAFC
LACC

PRICHARD, James C. (1786-1848) Anthro. CDZZ
ZZ11

PRIESTLEY, John C. (1879-1941) Physiol.; Med.
CDZZ ZZ11

PRIESTLEY, Joseph (1733-1804) Chem. ABES ABET
ACCE ASIW BDOS BEOS BHMT BIOD BMST
CDZZ CSCJ DAB DNB EETD GRCH HLSM
HOSS HSSO IFBS MCCW NC-6 SAIF SIRC
SMIL SSDH TOWS ZZ11

PRIGOGINE, Ilya (1917-) Chem.; Phys. ABET
BEOS MHSE SOTT

PRIMAN, Jacob (1891-1971) Anat. NC57

PRIME, Temple (1832-1903) Conch. BIOD

PRINGLE, John (1707-1782) Med. BHMT CDZZ
ZZ11

PRINGSHEIM, Alfred (1850-1941) Math. CDZZ
ZZ11

PRINGSHEIM, Ernst (1859-1917) Phys. BDOS BEOS
CDZZ ZZ11

PRINGSHEIM, Nathaniel (1823-1894) Bot. BDOS
BEOS CDZZ ZZ11

PRITCHARD, Andrew (1804-1882) Micros. DNB

PRITCHARD, Charles (1808-1893) Astron.; Astrophys. BDOS BEOS CDZZ DNB ZZ11

PRITCHARD, Fred J. (1874-1931) Bot. NC23

PRITCHARD, Harold W. (1916-) Cons. LACC

PRITCHETT, Henry S. (1857-1939) Astron.; Geol.
DAB2 NC10 NC29

PRIVALOV, Ivan I. (1891-1941) Math. CDZZ ZZ11

PRIVAT DE MOLIERES, Joseph (1677-1742) Phys.;
Math. CDZZ ZZ11

PROCHASKA, Georgius (1749-1820) Anat.;
Embryol. CDZZ ZZ11

PROCHAZKA, George A. (1855-1936) Chem. NC53

PROCHORAV, Aleksandr SEE PROKHOROV, Alexander

PROCLUS (410-485) Math.; Astron. ABET BEOS
CDZZ ZZ11

PROCTOR, John R. (1844-1903) Geol. BIOD

PROCTOR, Richard A. (1837-1888) Astron. ABES
ABET BEOS CDZZ DNB ZZ11

PROFATIUS TIBBON SEE ibn TIBBON, Jacob ben
Machir

PROKHOROV, Alexander M. (1916-) Phys. ABES
ABET BEOS MHM1 MHSE POSW SMST

PRONY, Gaspard F. de (1755-1839) Engr. CDZZ
GE-1 ZZ11

PROSSER, C. Ladd (1907-) Zool. NCSJ

PROTHRO, Johnnie H. (1922-) Med. SBPY

PROUDMAN, Joseph (1888-1975) Math.; Ocean.
BEOS MHM1 MHSE RS22

PROUST, Joseph L. (1754-1826) Chem. ABES ABET
BDOS BEOS CDZZ GRCH ZZ11

PROUT, William (1785-1850) Chem.; Physiol. ABES
ABET BDOS BEOS BHMT CDZZ DNB ZZ11

PROVANCHER, (Abbe) Leon (1820-1892) Entom.
AMEM POCS

PROVENCAL, Jean M. (1781-1845) Zool. SOAC

PROWAZEK, Stanislaus (1875-1915) Microbiol.
CDZZ ZZ11

PRUDDEN, Theophii M. (1849-1924) Bact. BM12
CDZZ ZZ11

PRUNER BEY, Franz I. (1808-1882) Med.; Anthro.
CDZZ ZZ11

PRUTTON, Carl F. (1898-1970) Chem. Engr. NC55

PRUVOST, Pierre (1890-1967) Geol. MHM2 MHSE

PRYANISHNIKOV, Dmitry N. (1865-1948) Chem.;
Bot. CDZZ ZZ11

PRYOR, Alfred R. (1839-1881) Bot. DNB

PRYOR, Karen (Contemporary) Ethol. WAGW

PRZHEVALSKY, Nikolay M. (1839-1888) Geog.
ABET CDZZ ZZ11

PSELLUS, Michael (1018-1078) Philos. CDZZ ZZ11

PTITSYN, Boris V. (1903-1965) Chem. SMST

PTOLEMY, Claudius (c.90-168) Astron. ABES ABET
AMST ASTR BDOS BEOS CDZZ FASP GSAL
IEAS LISD MAKS ZZ11

PUCK, Theodore T. (1916-) Biophys. BEOS MHM2
MHSE

PUERBACH, Georg von (1423-1461) Astron.; Math.
BMST BEOS

PUGH, Evan (1828-1864) Chem. ACCE BIOD DAB

PUGH, William J. (1892-1974) Geol. RS21

PUISEUX, Victor (1820-1883) Math.; Astron. CDZZ ZZ11

PULFRICH, Carl (1858-1927) Phys. CDZZ ZZ11

PULTENEY, Richard (1730-1801) Bot. DNB

PUMPELLY, Raphael (1837-1923) Geol. BM16 CDZZ ZZ11

PUMPHREY, Richard J. (1905-1967) Zool. RS14

PUNNETT, Reginald C. (1875-1967) Genet. CDZZ RS13 ZZ11

PUPIN, Michael I. (1858-1935) Phys. ABES ABET BM19 CDZZ DAB1 NC13 NC26 QPAS TPAE WAMB

PURBACH, Georg von SEE PUERBACH, Georg von

PURCELL, Edward M. (1912-) Phys. ABES ABET BEOS CB54 MHM1 MHSE POSW WAMB WMSW

PURINTON, George C. (1856-1897) Biol. NC-8

PURKINJE, Jan Evangelista (1787-1869) Physiol. ABES ABET BDOS BEOS BHMT CDZZ HLSM ZZ11

PURKYNE, Johannes SEE PURKINJE, Jan Evangelista

PURSH, Frederick (1774-1820) Bot. BIOD CDZZ DAB MABH ZZ11

PURYEAR, Bennet (1826-1914) Chem.; Agr. BIOD

PUSTOVALOV, Leonid V. (1902-) Geol. SMST

PUTNAM, Frederic W. (1839-1915) Anthro.; Nat. Hist. BM16 CDZZ DAB NC-3 ZZ11

PUTNAM, James J. (1846-1918) Med. BHMT

PUTNAM, Mary SEE JACOBI, Mary P.

PUTT, Donald L. (1905-) Aero. MOS7

PYE, David R. (1886-1960) Engr. RS-7

PYKE, Magnus (1908-) Chem. COBC

PYTHAGORAS (c.560 B.C.-c.480 B.C.) Math.; Astron. ABES ABET BDOS BEOS CDZZ FNEC GISA HLSM HOSS IEAS IFBS MELW OMNM WTGM ZZ11

PYTHEAS OF MASSALIA (fl. c.330 B.C.) Geog. ABES ABET BEOS CDZZ ZZ11

Q

al-QABISI, Sbu al-Saqr (fl. c.950) Astrol. CDZZ ZZ11

QADI ZADA al-RUMI (c.1364-c.1436) Math.; Astron. CDZZ ZZ11

al-QALASADI, Abul-Hasan (1412-1486) Math. CDZZ ZZ11

al-QAZWINI, Zakariya ibn Muhammad (c.1203-1283) Geog.; Cosmol. CDZZ ZZ11

QUADRA, Juan F. SEE BODEGA Y QUADRA, Juan F. dela

QUAIN, Jones (1796-1865) Anat. DNB

QUAINTANCE, Altus L. (1870-1958) Entom. AMEM

QUASTEL, Juda H. (1899-) Biochem. MHSE

QUATREFAGES DE BREAU, Jean L. de (1810-1892) Med.; Zool. CDZZ ZZ11

QUAYLE, Henry J. (1876-1951) Entom. AMEM

QUECKENSTEDT, Hans (1876-1918) Med. BHMT

QUEENY, Edgar M. (1897-1968) Chem. ACCE

QUEENY, John F. (1859-1933) Chem. ACCE

QUENSTEDT, Friedrich (1809-1889) Paleon.; Geol. CDZZ ZZ11

QUETELET, Lambert A. (1796-1874) Math. ABES ABET BEOS CDZZ ENCE GASJ IMMO ZZ11

ibn al-QUFF, Amin al-Dawlah (1233-1286) Med. CDZZ ZZ11

al-QUHI, Abu Sahl Wayjan (fl. 970-1000) Math.; Astron. CDZZ ZZ11

QUICK, Armand J. (1894-1978) Biochem. NC61

QUILLAN, Daniel G. (1940-) Math. MHSE

QUIMBY, Edith H. (1891-1982) Biophys. CB49 CWSE CWSN

QUINCKE, Georg H. (1834-1924) Phys. CDZZ ZZ11

QUINCKE, Heinrich I. (1842-1922) Med.　BHMT

QUOY, Jean R. (1790-1869) Zool. ANHD CDZZ
ZZ11

QUSTA ibn LUQA al-BALABAKKI (fl. 860-900) Med.
CDZZ ZZ11

ibn QUTAYBA, Abu Muhammad (828-884) Sci. Ed.
CDZZ ZZ11

QUTB al-Din al-SHIRAZI (1236-1311) Opt.; Astron.
CDZZ SCIN ZZ11

R

RABB, Maurice F. (1932-) Med. BISC

RABELAIS, Francois (1494-1553) Med. CDZZ ZZ11

RABER, Oran L. (1893-1940) Bot. NC31

RABI, Isidor I. (1898-) Phys. ABES ABET AMJB
BEOS CB48 EXSB MHM1 MHSE NCSH PBTS
POSW QPAS WAMB

RABINOVICH, Isaak M. (1886-) Engr. SMST

RABL, Carl (1853-1917) Anat.; Embryol. CDZZ
ZZ11

RABORN, William F. (1905-) Rocket. MOS3

RABOTNOV, Yurii N. (1914-) Phys. SMST

RACKER, Efraim (1913-) Biochem. MHM2 MHSE

RADCLIFFE, John (1650-1714) Med. BHMT

RADEMACHER, Hans (1892-1969) Math. CDZZ
ZZ11

RADL, Emanuel (1873-1942) Philos. CDZZ ZZ11

RADO, Tiber (1895-1965) Math. CDZZ ZZ11

RADON, Johann (1887-1956) Math. CDZZ ZZ11

RAFFLES, Thomas S. (1781-1826) Nat. Hist. CDZZ
ZZ11

RAFINESQUE, Constantine S. (1783-1840) Nat. Hist.
ASJD BIOD CDZZ DAB MABH MSAJ NHAH
WAMB ZZ11

RAGHAVANADA SARMAN (fl. 1591-1599) Astron.
CDZZ ZZ11

RAGSDALE, Randolph D. (1901-) Elec. Engr. SBPY

RAHIYA, Michael J. (1914-1973) Chem. Engr. NC58

RAHN, Otto (1881-1957) Bact. NC49

RAIKES, Humphrey R. (1891-1955) Chem. DNB7

RAINEY, Froelich (1907-) Archaeol. CB67

RAINEY, George (1801-1884) Anat. DNB

RAINS, George W. (1817-1898) Chem. ACCE

RAINWATER, Leo J. (1917-) Phys. ABET BEOS
MHM1 MHSE PAW2 POSW

RAISTRICK, Harold (1890-1971) Biochem. RS18

RALFS, John (1807-1890) Bot. DNB

RAMAN, Chandrasekhara V. (1888-1970) Phys.
ABES ABET BDOS BEOS CB48 CDZZ MHM2
MHSE PAW2 POSW RS17 TOWS ZZ11

RAMANUJAN, Srinivasa (1887-1920) Math. BDOS
BEOS CDZZ ZZ11

RAMAZZINI, Bernardini (1633-1714) Med. BHMT

RAMBERG, Hans (1917-) Geol. MHSE

RAMEE, Pierre de la (1515-1572) Math.; Astron.
BMST CDZZ SXWS ZZ11

RAMELLI, Agostino (1531-1608) Engr. BDOS GE-1

RAMES, Jean B. (1832-1894) Bot.; Geol. CDZZ ZZ11

RAMEY, Estelle R. (1917-) Physiol. CWSN

RAMMELKAMP, Charles H. Jr. (1911-1981) Med.
MHM2 MHSE

RAMMELSBERG, Karl F. (1813-1899) Chem. CDZZ
ZZ11

RAMO, Simon (1913-) Engr. MHM2 MHSE MOS2
NCSK

RAMON, Gaston (1886-1963) Immunol. CDZZ ZZ11

RAMON Y CAJAL, Santiago (1852-1934) Physiol. ABES ABET BDOS BEOS BHMT CDZZ ZZ11

RAMOND DE CARBONNIERES, Louis F. (1755-1827) Geol.; Bot. CDZZ ZZ11

RAMSAUER, Carl W. (1879-1955) Phys. CDZZ ZZXV

RAMSAY, Alexander (1754-1824) Anat. BIOD

RAMSAY, Andrew C. (1814-1891) Geol. CDZZ DNB ZZ11

RAMSAY, David (1749-1815) Med. BHMT

RAMSAY, William (1852-1916) Chem. ABES ABET BDOS BEOS CDZZ DNB3 GASJ GRCH HOSS NPWC PAW2 SNCB ZZ11

RAMSDEN, Jesse (1735-1800) Math.; Phys. BDOS BEOS CDZZ EETD GE-1 ZZ11

RAMSEY, Frank P. (1903-1930) Math. CDZZ ZZ11

RAMSEY, Norman F. (1915-) Phys. CB63 MHM1 MHSE

RAMSEY, Rolla R. (1872-1955) Phys. NC42

RAMUS SEE RAMEE, Pierre de la

RANCHIN, Francois (1560-1641) Med. BHMT

RAND, Isaac (d. 1743) Bot. DNB

RAND, Marie G. (1886-1970) Psych. NAWM

RANDALL, Marle (1888-1950) Chem. NC39

RANDALL, Wyatt W. (1867-1930) Chem. DAB NCSA

RANDERS, Gunnar (1914-) Phys. CB57

RANDOLPH, Charles (1809-1878) Engr. DNB

RANEY, Murray (1885-1966) Chem. NC51

RANGANATHA (fl. 1603) Astron. CDZZ ZZ11

RANKINE, Alexander O. (1881-1956) Phys. CDZZ RS-2 ZZ11

RANKINE, William J. (1820-1872) Engr. ABES ABET BDOS BEOS CDZZ FNEC HSSO ZZ11

RANSOME, Frederick L. (1869-1935) Geol. BM22 DAB1

RANSON, Stephen W. (1880-1942) Med. BM23

RANVIER, Louis A. (1835-1922) Physiol. BEOS CDZZ ZZ11

RANYARD, Arthur C. (1845-1894) Astrophys. CDZZ DNB ZZ11

RAOULT, Francis M. (1830-1901) Chem. ABES ABET BDOS BEOS CDZZ ZZ11

RAPER, John R. (1911-1974) Bot. MHM2 MHSE

RAPHAEL, Ralph A. (1921-) Chem. COBC

RASMUSSEN, Boyd L. (1913-) Forest. LACC

RASMUSSEN, John O. Jr. (1926-) Phys. MHM2 MHSE

RASPAIL, Francois V. (1794-1878) Biol.; Med. CDZZ ZZ11

RASPE, Rudolf E. (1737-1794) Geol. CDZZ ZZ11

RATCLIFFE, John A. (1902-) Phys. BEOS MHM2 MHSE

RATEAU, Auguste C. (1863-1930) Engr. CDZZ ZZ11

RATHBUN, Mary J. (1860-1943) Mar. Biol. NAW

RATHBUN, Richard (1852-1918) Zool. DAB

RATHKE, Martin H. (1793-1860) Embryol.; Anat. CDZZ ZZ11

RATZEL, Frederick (1844-1904) Geog.; Anthro. CDZZ ZZ11

RAU, Phil (1885-1948) Entom. AMEM

RAULIN, Jules (1836-1896) Bot. CDZZ ZZ11

RAUWOLF, Leonhard (1535-1596) Bot. CDZZ ZZ11

RAVENEL, Edmund (1797-1871) Conch. BIOD DAB

RAVENEL, Henry W. (1814-1887) Bot. BIOD DAB MABH NC10

RAVENEL, Mazyck P. (1861-1946) Bact. DAB4 NC38

RAVENEL, St. Julies (1819-1882) Chem. BIOD

RAWCLIFFE, Gordon H. (1910-1979) Elec. Engr. RS27

RAWLINSON, Henry C. (1810-1895) Archaeol. ABES ABET

RAY, Dixie Lee (1914-) Mar. Biol. CB73 CWSE CWSN PPNF SWWP

RAY, John (1627-1705) Nat. Hist. ABES ABET ANHD BDOS BEOS BMST CDZZ DNB FBSC FHUA HAOA HLSM LISD NATJ ORNS ZZ11

RAY, Prafulla C. (1861-1944) Chem. CDZZ ZZ11

RAY, Rose C. (1885-) Ornith. NCSE

RAY, Thomas W. (1883-1958) Biochem. NC48

RAYER, Pierre F. (1793-1867) Med. BHMT

RAYET, Georges A. (1839-1906) Astron. CDZZ ZZ11

RAYLEIGH, Lord SEE STRUTT, John W.

RAYMOND OF MARSEILLES (fl. c.1100-1140) Astron. CDZZ ZZ11

RAYMOND, Percy E. (1879-1952) Paleon. CDZZ ZZ11

RAYNAUD, Maurice (1834-1881) Med. BHMT

RAYTON, Willis M. (1909-1957) Phys. NC46

al-RAZI, Abu Bakr (c.854-925) Med.; Alch. ABES ABET BDOS BEOS BHMT CDZZ GRCH ZZ11

RAZMADZE, Andrei M. (1889-1929) Math. CDZZ ZZ11

RAZUVAEV, Grigorii A. (1895-) Chem. SMST

READ, Herbert H. (1889-1970) Geol. BEOS MHM1 MHSE RS16

READ, John (1884-1963) Chem. RS-9

READ, Nathan (1759-1849) Invent. GE-1

READ, Thomas A. (1913-1966) Phys. NC51

READE, Joseph B. (1801-1870) Chem.; Micros. DNB

READE, Thomas M. (1832-1909) Geol. DNB2

REAUMUR, Rene A. de (1683-1757) Phys. ABES ABET ANHD BDOS BEOS CDZZ GE-1 ZZ11

REBER, Grote (1911-) Elec. Engr. ABES ABET BEOS IEAS TMAL

REBINDER, Pyotr A. (1898-) Chem. SMST

RECHT, Albert W. (1898-1962) Astron. NC48

RECHTIN, Eberhardt (1926-) Elec. Engr. MHSE

RECK, Hans (1886-1937) Volcan.; Paleon. CDZZ ZZ11

RECKLINGHAUSEN, Friedrich von (1833-1910) Med. BHMT

RECLUS, Elisee (1830-1905) Geog. CDZZ ZZ11

RECORDE, Robert (c.1510-1558) Math. CDZZ DNB ZZ11

RECTOR, Thomas M. (1894-1950) Chem. NC41

REDFERN, Peter (1821-1912) Med. BHMT

REDFIELD, Alfred C. (1890-) Biol. LACC

REDFIELD, Caspar L. (1853-1943) Invent. NCSC

REDFIELD, Robert (1897-1958) Anthro. NC44 WAMB

REDFIELD, William C. (1789-1857) Meteor.; Paleon. ABET ASJD BEOS BIOD CDZZ DAB NC-7 ZZ11

REDI, Francesco (1626-1697) Med.; Entom. ABES ABET BDOS BEOS CDZZ ZZ11

REDMAN, John (1722-1808) Med. BHMT

REDMAN, Lawrence V. (1880-1946) Chem. ACCE NC38

REDMAN, Roderick O. (1905-1975) Astron. RS22

REDOUTE, Pierre J. (1759-1840) Bot. CDZZ ZZ11

REDTENBACHER, Ferdinand J. (1809-1863) Engr. CDZZ ZZ11

REECH, Ferdinand (1805-1884) Engr. CDZZ ZZ11

REED, Cordell (1938-) Engr. BCST

REED, Franklin W. (1877-1949) Forest. LACC

REED, Howard S. (1876-1950) Bot. NC40

REED, Thomas B. (1926-) Chem. PALF

REED, Walter (1851-1902) Med. ABES ABET BDOS BEOS BHMT CDZZ COAC HFGA HIUE MMMA NC13 NC33 ZZ11

REES, John K. (1851-1907) Astron. DAB NC11

REES, Mina S. (1902-) Math. CB57

REESE, Charles L. (1862-1940) Chem. ACCE DAB2 NC30

REESIDE, John B. (1889-1958) Geol. BM35

REEVE, Lovell A. (1814-1865) Conch. DNB

REEVES, John (1774-1856) Nat. Hist. DNB

REGAN, Charles T. (1878-1943) Zool. DNB6

REGENER, Erich R. (1881-1955) Phys. CDZZ ZZ11

REGENSTEIN, Lewis (1943-) Cons. AMJB

REGGE, Tullio (1931-) Phys. MHM2 MHSE

REGIOMONTANUS, Johannes (1436-1476) Astron. ABES ABET BDOS BEOS BMST CDZZ ZZ11

REGNAULT, Henri V. (1810-1878) Phys.; Chem. ABES ABET BDOS BEOS CDZZ ZZ11

REHN, James A. (1881-1965) Entom. AMEM

REICH, Ferdinand (1799-1882) Mineral. ABES ABET BEOS

REICHARD, Gladys A. (1893-1955) Anthro. NAWM

REICHELDERFER, Francis W. (1895-1983) Meteor. CB49 MHM2 MHSE

REICHENBACH, Georg F. von (1771-1826) Instr.; Engr. CDZZ GE-1 ZZ11

REICHENBACH, Hans (1891-1953) Philos. of Sci. CDZZ ZZ11

REICHENBACH, Karl L. (1788-1869) Chem. CDZZ ZZ11

REICHERT, Karl B. (1811-1883) Anat.; Embryol. CDZZ ZZ11

REICHSTEIN, Tadeusz (1897-) Chem. ABES ABET BEOS CB51 MHM1 MHSE PAW2

REID, David B. (1805-1863) Chem. DAB

REID, Ernest W. (1897-1966) Chem. NC51

REID, Harry F. (1859-1944) Geophys. ABET BM26 CDZZ ZZ11

REID, John (1809-1849) Anat. DNB

REID, Kenneth A. (1895-1956) Cons. LACC

REIDEMEISTER, Kurt W. (1893-1971) Math. CDZZ ZZ11

REIK, Theodor (1888-1969) Psych. PAW3

REIL, Johann C. (1759-1813) Med. CDZZ ZZ11

REINES, Frederick (1918-) Phys. ABES ABET BEOS

REINHOLD, Erasmus (1511-1553) Math. ABES ABET BEOS CDZZ ZZ11

REINKING, Otto A. (1890-1962) Bot. NC46

REIS, Piri SEE PIRI RAIS, Muhyi al-Din

REISSNER, Eric (1913-) Math.; Engr. MHSE

REITER, Hans (1881-1969) Med. BHMT

RELF, Ernest F. (1888-1970) Phys. RS17

RELHAN, Richard (1754-1823) Bot. DNB

REMAK, Robert (1815-1865) Med. ABES ABET BDOS BEOS BHMT CDZZ ZZ11

REMINGTON, Eliphalet (1793-1861) Invent. WAMB

REMSEN, Ira (1846-1927) Chem. ABET ACCE BDOS BEOS BM14 CDZZ DAB GRCH NC-9 NC37 WAMB ZZ11

RENARD, Alphonse F. (1842-1903) Geol.; Mineral. CDZZ ZZ11

RENAULT, Bernard (1836-1904) Paleon. CDZZ FHUA ZZ11

RENAUT, Joseph L. (1844-1917) Med. CDZZ ZZ11

RENDLE, Alfred B. (1865-1938) Bot. DNB5

RENDU, Henri (1844-1902) Med. BHMT

RENEVIER, Eugene (1831-1906) Geol.; Paleon. CDZZ ZZ11

RENGARTEN, Vladimir P. (1882-) Geol. SMST

RENNELL, James (1742-1830) Geog. CDZZ ZZ11

RENNER, Otto (1883-1960) Bot. RS-7

RENNIE, James (1787-1867) Nat. Hist. DNB

RENNIE, John (1761-1821) Engr. BDOS GE-1

RENSCH, Bernhard (1900-) Biol. MHM2 MHSE

RENSHAW, Arnold (1885-1980) Forens. Sci. AO80

RENSSELAER, Jeremiah van (1793-1871) Med.; Nat. Hist. ASJD

RENTSCHLER, Harvey C. (1881-1949) Phys. NCSD

RENWICK, James (1792-1863) Engr.; Phys. BIOD NC11

REPSOLD, Adolf (1806-1871) Instr. CDZZ ZZ11

REPSOLD, Johann A. (1838-1919) Instr. CDZZ ZZ11

REPSOLD, Johann G. (1770-1830) Instr. CDZZ GE-1 ZZ11

RESPIGHI, Lorenzo (1824-1889) Astron. CDZZ ZZ11

RESSER, Charles E. (1889-1943) Paleon. NC32

RETTGER, Leo F. (1874-1954) Bact. NC42

RETZIUS, Anders A. (1796-1860) Med. ABET BEOS BHMT CDZZ ZZ11

RETZIUS, Magnus G. (1842-1919) Med. BHMT CDZZ ZZ11

REULEAUX, Franz (1829-1905) Engr. CDZZ ZZ11

REUSS, August E. (1811-1873) Paleon. CDZZ ZZ11

REUSS, Franz A. (1761-1830) Mineral.; Geol. CDZZ ZZ11

REUTOV, Oleg A. (1920-) Chem. SMST

REVELLE, Roger (1909-) Ocean. CB57 EXDC MHM2 MHSE PBTS SWWP

REY, Abel (1873-1940) Philos. CDZZ ZZ11

REY, Jean (1582-c.1645) Chem. CDZZ ZZ11

REY PASTOR, Julio (1888-1962) Math. CDZZ ZZ11

REYE, Theodor (1838-1919) Math. CDZZ ZZ11

REYERSON, Lloyd H. (1893-1969) Chem. ACCE NC55

REYNA, Francisco de la (b. c.1520) Physiol. CDZZ ZZ11

REYNOLDS, Doris L. (1899-) Geol. MHM1 MHSE

REYNOLDS, Harris A. (1883-1953) Forest. LACC

REYNOLDS, James E. (1844-1920) Chem. DNB3

REYNOLDS, Orr E. (1920-) Physiol. MOS6

REYNOLDS, Osborne (1842-1912) Engr.; Phys. BDOS BEOS CDZZ DNB3 FNEC ICFW STYC ZZ11

RHAZES SEE al-RAZI, Abu Bakr

RHEITA, Anton M. de (1597-1660) Astron. CDZZ ZZ11

RHETICUS, George J. (1514-1576) Math. ABES ABET BDOS BEOS CDZZ ZZ11

RHINE, Joseph B. (1895-1980) Parapsych. ABES ABET PAW1

RIABOUCHINSKY, Dimitri P. (1882-1962) Phys. ICFW

RIBAUCOUR, Albert (1845-1893) Math.; Engr. CDZZ ZZ11

RIBEIRO SANTOS, Carlos (1813-1882) Engr.; Geol. CDZZ ZZ11

RICARDO, Harry R. (1885-1974) Engr. RS22

RICCATI, Jacopo F. (1676-1754) Math. CDZZ ZZ11

RICCATI, Vincenzo (1707-1775) Math. CDZZ ZZ11

RICCI, Matteo (1552-1610) Math.; Geog. BEOS CDZZ ZZ11

RICCI, Michelangelo (1619-1682) Math. CDZZ ZZ11

RICCI, Ostilio (1540-1603) Math. CDZZ ZZ11

RICCI-CURBASTRO, Gregorio (1853-1925) Math.; Phys. CDZZ ZZ11

RICCIOLO, Giambatista (1598-1671) Astron. ABES ABET BEOS CDZZ ZZ11

RICCO, Annibale (1844-1919) Geophys.; Astrophys. CDZZ ZZ11

RICE, Charles (1841-1901) Pharm.; Chem. BIOD DAB

RICE, Edwin W. (1862-1935) Elec. Engr. DAB1

RICE, John W. (1891-1971) Bact. NC56

RICE, William N. (1845-1928) Geol. DAB NC12

RICH, Arnold R. (1893-1968) Path. BM50

RICH, Willis H. (1885-1972) Biol. NC59

RICHARD OF WALLINGFORD (c.1291-1336) Math.; Astron. BDOS BEOS CDZZ GE-1 ZZ11

RICHARD, Jules A. (1862-1956) Math. CDZZ ZZ11

RICHARD, Louis P. (1795-1849) Math. CDZZ ZZ11

RICHARDS, Alfred N. (1876-1966) Pharm. BM42 RS13

RICHARDS, Dickinson W. (1895-1973) Med. ABET BEOS CB57 MHM1 MHSE MFIR

RICHARDS, Ellen (1842-1911) Chem. ACCE DAB IDWB NAW TECH

RICHARDS, Francis J. (1901-1965) Bot. CDZZ RS12 ZZ11

RICHARDS, Joseph W. (1864-1921) Chem. ACCE

RICHARDS, Rex E. (1922-) Chem.; Biophys. COBC MHSE

RICHARDS, Theodore W. (1868-1928) Chem. ABES ABET ACCE BDOS BEOS BM44 CDZZ DAB GRCH NC12 NPWC WAMB ZZ11

RICHARDS, Thomas W. (1926-) Cons. LACC

RICHARDSON, Archibald R. (1881-1954) Math. RS-1

RICHARDSON, Benjamin W. (1828-1896) Med. BHMT CDZZ ZZ11

RICHARDSON, George F. (c.1796-1848) Geol. DNB

RICHARDSON, John (1787-1865) Nat. Hist.; Exp. DNB

RICHARDSON, Lewis F. (1881-1953) Meteor.; Phys. BEOS DNB7

RICHARDSON, Owen W. (1879-1959) Phys. ABES ABET BEOS CDZZ DNB7 POSW RS-5 ZZ11

RICHARDSON, Richard (1663-1741) Bot. DNB

RICHARDSON, Roland G. (1878-1949) Math. NCSC

RICHE de PRONY, Gaspard SEE PRONY, Gaspard F. de

RICHER, Jean (1630-1696) Astron. ABET BEOS CDZZ ZZ11

RICHET, Charles R. (1850-1935) Physiol. ABET BEOS CDZZ PUNT ZZ11

RICHEY, James E. (1886-1968) Geol. RS15

RICHMANN, Georg W. (1711-1753) Phys. CDZZ ZZ11

RICHMOND, Charles W. (1868-1932) Ornith. DAB WFBG

RICHTER, Burton (1931-) Phys. ABET BEOS CB77 MHSE PAW2 POSW

RICHTER, Charles F. (1900-) Seism. BEOS CB75

RICHTER, Curt P. (1894-) Psych. MHM2 MHSE

RICHTER, Hieronymous T. (1824-1898) Mineral. ABES ABET BEOS

RICHTER, Jeremias B. (1762-1807) Chem. ABET CDZZ ZZ11

RICHTHOFEN, Ferdinand von (1833-1905) Geol. CDZZ ZZ11

RICHTMYER, Floyd K. (1881-1939) Phys. BM22 CDZZ DAB2 NCSB ZZ11

RICKER, William E. (1908-) Biol. LACC

RICKETTS, Howard T. (1871-1910) Path. ABES
ABET BDOS BEOS CDZZ ZZ11

RICKOVER, Hyman G. (1900-) Engr. ABES ABET
EXDC MHM1 MHSE PPJY

RICORD, Philippe (1800-1889) Med. BHMT

RIDDELL, Charles J. (1817-1903) Meteor. DNB2

RIDDELL, John L. (1807-1865) Bot.; Micros. ACCE
BIOD DAB

RIDDLE, Edward (1788-1854) Math.; Astron. DNB

RIDDLE, Oscar (1877-1968) Biol. BEOS BM45 NCSC

RIDE, Sally K. (1951-) Astronaut.; Astrophys. CB83

RIDEAL, Eric K. (1890-1974) Chem. BEOS COBC
MHM1 MHSE RS22

RIDGWAY, Raymond R. (1897-1947) Chem. Engr.
ACCE

RIDGWAY, Robert (1850-1929) Ornith. BM15 BWCL
CDZZ DAB WFBG ZZ11

RIDLEY, Henry N. (1855-1956) Bot.; Geol. RS-3

ibn RIDWAN, Abul-Hasan (998-1061/9) Med. CDZZ
ZZ11

RIECKE, Eduard (1845-1915) Phys. CDZZ ZZ11

RIEDEL, Klaus (1907-1944) Rocket. ICFW

RIEHL, Gustav (1855-1943) Med. BHMT

RIEMANN, Georg F. (1826-1866) Math. ABES ABET
BDOS BEOS CDZZ ZZ11

RIES, Adam (1492-1559) Math.; Mng. CDZZ ZZ11

RIESZ, Frigyes (1880-1956) Math. CDZZ ZZ11

RIGGE, William F. (1857-1927) Astron. DAB

RIGGS, Lorrin A. (1912-) Psych. MHM1 MHSE

RIGHI, Augusto (1850-1920) Phys. ABES ABET
BEOS CDZZ ZZ11

RILEY, Charles V. (1843-1895) Entom. AMEM BIOD
DAB NC-9

RILEY, Harland K. (1905-1972) Hort. NC59

RILEY, William A. (1876-1963) Entom. AMEM NC51

RILLIEUX, Norbert (1806-1894) Engr.; Invent. BCST
BPSH DANB EBAH GNPA HCOK SABL SBPY
TINA

RIMA, Tommaso (1775-1843) Med. CDZZ ZZ11

RINGER, Sydney (1835-1910) Med. ABET BHMT
CDZZ ZZ11

RINGLEB, Friedrich O. (1900-1966) Phys. NC53

RINGWOOD, Alfred E. (1930-) Chem. MHSE

RINMAN, Sven (1720-1792) Metal. CDZZ ZZ11

RIO, Andres M. del (1764-1849) Mineral.; Geol.
CDZZ ZZ11

RIO-HORTEGA, Pio del (1882-1945) Med. CDZZ
ZZ11

RIOLAN, Jean Jr. (1580-1675) Anat.; Med. CDZZ
ZZ11

RIPLEY, S. Dillon (1913-) Zool. CB66

RIQUET DE BONROPOS, Pierre P. (1604-1680) Engr.
GE-1

RISING, Willard B. (1839-1910) Chem. ACCE NC12
NC25

RISNER, Friedrich (d. c.1580) Math.; Opt. CDZZ
ZZ11

RISTORO D'AREZZO (c.1210-c.1283) Nat. Hist.
CDZZ ZZ11

RITCHEY, George W. (1864-1945) Astron. BEOS
CDZZ DAB3 IEAS ZZ11

RITCHEY, Harold (1912-) Chem. Engr.; Rocket.
MOS3

RITCHIE, William (1790-1837) Phys. DNB

RITT, Joseph F. (1893-1951) Math. BM29 CDZZ
ZZ11

RITTENHOUSE, David (1732-1796) Astron.; Instr.
BIOD CDZZ DAB WAMB ZZ11

RITTER, Johann W. (1776-1810) Phys. ABES ABET
BDOS BEOS CDZZ ELEC ZZ11

RITTER, William E. (1856-1944) Zool. DAB3 NC16

RITZ, Walter (1878-1909) Phys. CDZZ ZZ11

RIVA-ROCCI, Scipione (1863-1937) Med. CDZZ ZZ11

RIVERS, Thomas M. (1888-1962) Bact. BM38 NCSE

RIVETT, Albert C. (1885-1961) Chem. RS12 CDZZ ZZ11

RIVIERE DE PRECOURT, Emile V. (1835-1922) Anthro. CDZZ ZZ11

RIVINUS, Augustus SEE BACHMANN, Augustus Q.

RIZNICHENKO, Yurii V. (1911-) Geophys. SMST

ROARK, Ruric C. (1887-1962) Entom. AMEM

ROBB, James C. (1924-) Chem. COBC

ROBBINS, Frederick C. (1916-) Microbiol. ABES ABET BEOS CB55 MHM1 MHSE PAW2 WAMB

ROBBINS, Wilfred W. (1884-1952) Bot. MABH

ROBBINS, William J. (1890-) Bot. CB56

ROBERT OF CHESTER (fl. 1100) Trans. Sci. Lit. BDOS

ROBERT OF LINCOLN SEE GROSSETESTE, Robert

ROBERT, Nicholas L. (1761-1828) Invent. FOIF

ROBERTS, Charlotte F. (1859-1917) Chem. NC19

ROBERTS, Dorothea K. (1861-1942) Astron. NC31

ROBERTS, George E. (1831-1865) Geol. DNB

ROBERTS, Gilbert (1899-1978) Engr. RS25

ROBERTS, Isaac (1829-1904) Astron. CDZZ DNB2 ZZ11

ROBERTS, John D. (1918-) Chem. BEOS MHM2 MHSE

ROBERTS, Louis W. (1913-) Phys. BCST

ROBERTS, Michael (1817-1882) Math. DNB

ROBERTS, Nathan S. (1776-1852) Engr. GE-1

ROBERTS, Richard (1789-1864) Invent. BDOS GE-1

ROBERTS, Richard B. (1910-1980) Biophys. ABET AO80

ROBERTS, Thomas S. (1858-1946) Ornith. NCSE

ROBERTS, Walter O. (1915-) Astrophys. CB60 NCSJ

ROBERTS-AUSTEN, William C. (1843-1902) Metal. BDOS CDZZ ZZ11

ROBERTSON, Abraham (1751-1826) Astron.; Math. DNB

ROBERTSON, Alexander (1896-1970) Chem. RS17

ROBERTSON, Andrew (1883-1977) Engr. RS24

ROBERTSON, Argyll (1837-1909) Med. BHMT

ROBERTSON, Benjamin F. (1873-1943) Phys. NC50

ROBERTSON, Howard P. (1903-1961) Phys. BM51 NC50

ROBERTSON, John (1712-1776) Math. DNB

ROBERTSON, John M. (1900-) Chem. BEOS COBC MHM1 MHSE

ROBERTSON, Joseph H. (1906-) Bot. BNBR

ROBERTSON, Muriel (1883-1973) Bact. RS20

ROBERTSON, Oswald H. (1886-1966) Med. BM42 HIUE

ROBERTSON, Robert (1869-1949) Chem. BEOS DNB6 MMSB

ROBERTSON, Rutherford N. (1913-) Bot. MHM2 MHSE

ROBERVAL, Gilles P. (1602-1675) Math.; Phys. CDZZ ZZ11

ROBESON, Eslanda C. (1896-1965) Anthro. CB45 NAWM

ROBEY, Ashley (1903-1965) Chem. NC52

ROBIE, Thomas (1689-1729) Meteor.; Astron. BIOD SBCS

ROBIN, Charles P. (1821-1885) Biol. CDZZ ZZ11

ROBINET, Jean B. (1735-1820) Nat. Hist. CDZZ ZZ11

ROBINS, Benjamin (1707-1751) Math.; Engr. CDZZ DNB GE-1 ZZ11

ROBINSON, Benjamin L. (1864-1935) Bot. BM17 DAB1 MABH NC12

ROBINSON, Clark S. (1888-1947) Chem. Engr. HCEF

ROBINSON, Glen P. (1923-) Phys. NCSK

ROBINSON, Harold R. (1889-1955) Phys. RS-3

ROBINSON, Horatio (1806-1867) Math. NC-2

ROBINSON, Julia B. (1919-) Math. MATT

ROBINSON, Philip S. (1847-1902) Nat. Hist. DNB2

ROBINSON, Robert (1886-1975) Chem. ABES ABET BEOS COBC MHM1 MHSE NPWC PAW2 RS22

ROBINSON, Roy L. (1883-1952) Forest. DNB7

ROBINSON, Thomas R. (1792-1882) Astron.; Phys. DNB

ROBIQUET, Pierre J. (1780-1840) Chem. CDZZ ZZ11

ROBISON, John (1739-1805) Phys. CDZZ DNB ESEH ZZ11

ROBISON, Robert (1883-1941) Biochem. DNB6

ROBITZEK, Edward H. (1912-) Med. CB53

ROBSON, Stephen (1741-1779) Bot. DNB

ROCHE, Edouard A. (1820-1883) Geophys.; Meteor. ABET BEOS CDZZ ZZ11

ROCK, John (1890-) Med. CB64 LGIH

ROCKEFELLER, John D. Jr. (1874-1960) Cons. LACC

ROCKEFELLER, Laurence S. (1910-) Cons. LACC

ROCKWOOD, Charles G. (1843-1913) Seism. NC16

RODAHL, Kaare (1917-) Physiol. CB56

RODD, Edward H. (1810-1880) Ornith. DNB

RODDY, H. Justin (1856-1943) Nat. Hist. NC47

RODEBUSH, Worth H. (1887-1959) Chem. BM36 NC50

RODGERS, John (1812-1882) Exp. BM-6

RODRIGUES, Joao SEE LUSITANUS, Amatus

ROE, Joseph H. (1892-) Biochem. NCSD

ROEBER, Eugene F. (1867-1917) Chem. ACCE

ROEBLING, John (1806-1869) Invent. INYG

ROEBUCK, John (1718-1794) Chem. BDOS GE-1 SIRC CDZZ ZZ11

ROEDER, Kenneth D. (1908-) Zool. MHM2 MHSE

ROEMER SEE ALSO ROMER

ROEMER, Ferdinand (1818-1891) Geol.; Paleon. CDZZ ZZ11

ROEMER, Friedrich A. (1809-1869) Paleon. CDZZ ZZ11

ROEMER, Olaus (1644-1710) Astron. ABES ABET BDOS BEOS CDZZ HOSS IEAS MGAH SLOR ZZ11

ROENTGEN, Wilhelm SEE RONTGEN, Wilhelm C. von

ROESEL VON ROSENHOF, August J. (1705-1759) Nat. Hist. ANHD CDZZ ZZ11

ROESER, William F. (1901-1964) Phys. NC51

ROGER OF HEREFORD (fl. c.1150-1200) Astron.; Astrol. CDZZ ZZ11

ROGER, Henri L. (1809-1891) Med. BHMT

ROGER, Muriel (1922-1981) Biol. AO81

ROGERS, Allen (1876-1938) Chem. ACCE NCSD

ROGERS, Fairman (1833-1900) Engr. BM-6

ROGERS, Henry D. (1808-1866) Geol. ACCE BIOD CDZZ ZZ11

ROGERS, James B. (1802-1852) Chem. ACCE BIOD DAB NC-8

ROGERS, Leonard (1868-1962) Med. RS-9

ROGERS, Leonard J. (1862-1933) Math. DNB5

ROGERS, Patrick K. (1776-1828) Chem. ACCE

ROGERS, Robert E. (1813-1884) Chem. ACCE BIOD
BM-5 DAB

ROGERS, Thomas A. (1887-1944) Chem. NC33

ROGERS, William A. (1832-1898) Astron.; Phys.
BIOD BM-4 DAB NC-9

ROGERS, William B. (1804-1882) Geol. ACCE BIOD
BM-3 CDZZ ZZ11

ROGET, Peter M. (1779-1869) Med. BHMT

ROGINSKII, Simon Z. (1900-) Chem. SMST

ROGOSINSKI, Werner W. (1894-1964) Math. RS11

ROHAULT, Jacques (1620-1675) Philos. CDZZ ZZ11

ROHN, Karl (1855-1920) Math. CDZZ ZZ11

ROHRBACH, Adolf (1889-1939) Aero. ICFW

ROHWER, Sievert A. (1888-1951) Entom. AMEM
NC39

ROKITANSKY, Carl von (1804-1878) Med. BDOS
BEOS BHMT

ROLANDO, Luigi (1773-1831) Anat.; Physiol. CDZZ
ZZ11

ROLFINCK, Guerner (1599-1673) Chem.; Bot. CDZZ
ZZ11

ROLLE, Michel (1652-1719) Math. CDZZ ZZ11

ROLLESTON, George (1829-1881) Anat.; Zool.
CDZZ ZZ11

ROLLET, Joseph P. (1824-1894) Med. CDZZ ZZ11

ROLLIER, Auguste H. (1874-1954) Med. MMSB

ROMAN, Nancy G. (1925-) Astron. CB60

ROMANES, George J. (1848-1894) Physiol.; Evol.
CDZZ DNB ZZ11

ROMANOFF, Alexis L. (1892-) Zool. CB53 SEMK

ROMANS, Bernard (c.1720-c.1784) Engr.; Nat. Hist.
BIOD DAB

ROMBERG, Moritz H. (1795-1873) Med. BHMT

ROME DE L'ISLE, Jean B. (1736-1790) Crystal.;
Mineral. CDZZ ZZ11

ROMER SEE ALSO ROEMER

ROMER, Alfred S. (1894-1973) Zool.; Paleon. BEOS
BM53 MHM1 MHSE NC61 PHLS RS21

ROMER, Eugeniusz M. (1871-1954) Geog. CDZZ ZZ11

RONALDS, Edmund (1819-1889) Chem. DNB

RONALDS, Francis (1788-1873) Invent.; Meteor.
DNB GE-1

RONDELET, Guillaume (1507-1566) Ichth.; Anat.
ANHD CDZZ ZZ11

RONDELET, Pierre (1517-1564) Nat. Hist. NATJ

RONNE, Finn (1899-1980) Exp. AO80

RONTGEN, Wilhelm C. (1845-1923) Phys. ABES
ABET BDOS BEOS BHMT CDZZ DCPW EETD
HOSS PAW2 POSW SAIF SMIL TMSB TOWS
ZZ11

ROOD, Ogden N. (1831-1902) Phys. BIOD BM-6
CDZZ DAB NC13 ZZ11

ROOD, Paul (1894-1977) Phys. NC60

ROOKE, Lawrence (1622-1662) Astron. CDZZ DNB
ZZ11

ROOMEN, Adriaan van (1561-1615) Math.; Med.
CDZZ ZZ11

ROOSEVELT, Theodore (1858-1919) Nat. Hist. LACC
SFNB

ROOT, L. Eugene (1910-) Aero. MOS5

ROOZEBOOM, Hendrik W. (1856-1907) Chem. ABES
ABET BDOS BEOS CDZZ ZZ11

RORSCHACH, Hermann (1884-1922) Psychiat. ABES
ABET PAW2

ROSA, Daniele (1857-1944) Zool. CDZZ ZZ11

ROSA, Edward B. (1861-1921) Phys. BM16 DAB
NC26

ROSALDO, Michelle Z. (1944-1981) Anthro. AO81

ROSANES, Jakob (1842-1922) Math. CDZZ ZZ11

ROSCOE, Henry E. (1833-1915) Chem. BDOS CDZZ DNB3 VISC ZZ11

ROSE, Caleb B. (1790-1872) Geol. DNB

ROSE, Francis L. (1909-) Chem. COBC

ROSE, Gustav (1798-1873) Mineral.; Crystal. CDZZ ZZ11

ROSE, Heinrich (1795-1864) Chem. CDZZ ZZ11

ROSE, John D. (1911-1976) Chem. RS23

ROSE, Joseph N. (1862-1928) Bot. DAB NC27

ROSE, Mary D. (1874-1941) Med. NAW

ROSE, Morris E. (1911-1967) Phys. NC54

ROSE, Robert E. (1879-1946) Chem. ACCE

ROSE, William C. (1887-) Biochem. ABES ABET BEOS CB53 MHM2 MHSE

ROSEN, Louis (1918-) Phys. MHM1 MHSE

ROSEN, Nils (1706-1773) Med. BHMT

ROSEN, Samuel (1897-) Med. MFIR

ROSENBERG, Hans O. (1879-1940) Astron.; Astrophys. CDZZ ZZ11

ROSENBERGER, Johann K. (1845-1899) Phys. CDZZ ZZ11

ROSENBERGER, Otto A. (1800-1890) CDZZ ZZ11

ROSENBLUETH, Arturo (1900-1970) Physiol. CDZZ ZZ11

ROSENBLUTH, Marshall N. (1927-) Phys. MHM1 ZZ11

ROSENBUSCH, Harry K. (1836-1914) Geol. CDZZ ZZ11

ROSENFELD, Arthur H. (1926-) Phys. DCPW

ROSENGARTEN, George D. (1869-1936) Chem. Engr. ACCE NC35

ROSENHAIN, Johann G. (1816-1887) Math. CDZZ ZZ11

ROSENHAIN, Walter (1875-1934) Metal. CDZZ DNB5 ZZ11

ROSENHEIM, Arthur (1865-1942) Chem. CDZZ ZZ11

ROSENHEIM, Max L. (1908-1972) Med. RS20

ROSENHEIM, Sigmund O. (1871-1955) Chem. DNB7 RS-2

ROSENHOF, August SEE ROESEL VON ROSENHOF, August J.

ROSENTHAL, Adolph H. (1906-1962) Phys. NC47

ROSS, Andrew (c.1800-1859) Instr. MNCS

ROSS, Bennett B. (1864-1930) Chem. NC26

ROSS, Douglas T. (1929-) Comp. HOPL

ROSS, Frank E. (1874-1960) Astron. BM39 CDZZ ZZ11

ROSS, James C. (1800-1862) Exp. WFBG CDZZ ZZ11

ROSS, Malcolm D. (1920-) Aero. MOS4

ROSS, Ronald (1857-1932) Med. ABES ABET BDOS BEOS BHMT CDZZ DNB5 MMSB ZZ11

ROSS, William H. (1909-1975) Phys. NC58

ROSSBY, Carl-Gustaf (1898-1957) Meteor.; Ocean. BEOS BM34 CDZZ MHM1 MHSE ZZ11

ROSSE, Lord SEE PARSONS, William

ROSSETTI, Francesco (1833-1885) Phys. CDZZ ZZ11

ROSSI, Bruno B. (1905-) Phys. ABES ABET BEOS MHM1 MHSE

ROSSINI, Frederick D. (1899-) Chem. BEOS MHM2 MHSE

ROSSITER, Roger J. (1913-1976) Biochem. MHM2 MHSE

ROSSLIN, Eucharius (d. 1526) Med. BHMT

ROSTAN, Leon L. (1790-1866) Med. CDZZ ZZ11

ROSTAND, Jean (1894-) Biol. CB54

ROTCH, Abbot L. (1861-1954) Chem. ACCE

ROTH, Charles F. (1886-1954) Chem. ACCE

ROTH, Filibert (1858-1925) Forest. LACC

ROTH, Justus L. (1818-1892) Geol. CDZZ ZZ11

ROTHMANN, Christoph (d. 1599/1608) Astron. CDZZ ZZ11

ROTHROCK, Addison M. (1903-1971) Phys. NC56

ROTHROCK, Joseph T. (1839-1922) Bot. BNBR DAB EAFC LACC NC19

ROTHSCHILD, Miriam (1908-) Zool.; Parasit. IDWB

ROUELLE, Guillaume F. (1703-1770) Chem.; Geol. BDOS BEOS CDZZ GRCH ZZ11

ROUELLE, Hilaire M. (1718-1779) Chem. BDOS CDZZ ZZ11

ROUELLE, Jean (b. c.1752) Chem.; Nat. Hist. CDZZ ZZ11

ROUGET, Charles M. (1824-1904) Med. BHMT CDZZ ZZ11

ROUGHTON, Francis J. (1899-1972) Physiol. RS19

ROUILLIER, Karl F. (1814-1858) Biol.; Paleon. CDZZ ZZ11

ROUS, Francis P. (1879-1970) Virol. ABES ABET BDOS BEOS BM48 MHM1 MHSE NC55 PAW2 RS17

ROUTH, Edward J. (1831-1907) Math. CDZZ DNB2 ZZ11

ROUX, Pierre P. (1853-1933) Bact. ABET BDOS BEOS CDZZ MAMR ZZ11

ROUX, Wilhelm (1850-1924) Embryol.; Anat. CDZZ HLSM ZZ11

ROVERETO, Gaetano (1870-1952) Geol. CDZZ ZZ11

ROWE, Allan W. (1879-1934) Chem. CDZZ ZZ11

ROWELL, George A. (1804-1892) Meteor. DNB

ROWLAND, Henry A. (1848-1901) Phys. ABES ABET BDOS BEOS BIOD BM-5 CDZZ DAB GASJ HSSO SNAR WAMB ZZ11

ROWLEDGE, Arthur J. (1876-1957) Engr. RS-4

ROWLINSON, John S. (1926-) Chem. COBC

ROWNING, John (1701-1771) Math. CDZZ DNB ZZ11

ROXBURGH, William (1751-1815) Bot. DNB

ROY, Sharat K. (1897-1962) Geol. NC50

ROYCE, Frederick (1863-1933) Engr. OGML

ROYCE, Josiah (1855-1916) Psych. BM33

ROYEN, Snell von SEE SNELL, Willebrord van Roijen

ROZHDESTVENSKY, Dmitry S. (1876-1940) Phys. CDZZ ZZ11

ROZHKOV, Ivan S. (1908-) Geol. SMST

RUBENS, Heinrich (1865-1922) Phys. CDZZ ZZ11

RUBEY, William W. (1898-1974) Geol. BM49 MHM1 MHSE

RUBIN, Theodore I. (1923-) Psych. CB80

RUBNER, Max (1854-1932) Physiol. ABES ABET BEOS BHMT CDZZ ZZ11

RUCKDESCHEL, Carol (Contemporary) Nat. Hist. WAWL

RUDBECK, Olof (1630-1702) Nat. Hist. ABES ABET BDOS BEOS CDZZ ZZ11

RUDDIMAN, Edsel A. (1864-1954) Chem. NC45

RUDENBERG, Reinhold (1883-1961) Elec. Engr. CDZZ ZZ11

RUDGE, Edward (1763-1946) Bot. DNB

RUDIO, Ferdinand (1856-1929) Math. CDZZ ZZ11

RUDOLFF, Christoff (c.1499-c.1545) Math. CDZZ ZZ11

RUDOLPHI, Karl A. (1771-1832) Anat.; Physiol. CDZZ ZZ11

RUE, Warren de la SEE DE LA RUE, Warren

RUEDEMANN, Rudolf (1864-1956) Paleon.; Geol. BM44 CDZZ ZZ11

RUEL, Jean (1474-1537) Med.; Bot. CDZZ ZZ11

RUFFER, Marc A. (1859-1917) Paleon. CDZZ ZZ11

RUFFIN, Edmund (1794-1865) Chem. ACCE BIOD

RUFFINI, Angelo (1864-1929) Embryol. CDZZ ZZ11

RUFFINI, Paolo (1765-1822) Math.; Med. CDZZ ZZ11

RUFFO, Giordano (fl. c.1250) Vet. Med. CDZZ ZZ11

RUFINUS (fl. c.1250-1300) Bot.; Med. CDZZ ZZ11

RUFUS OF EPHESUS (fl. 98-117) Med. BHMT CDZZ ZZ11

RUHMKORFF, Heinrich D. (1803-1877) Invent. BDOS CDZZ EETD ZZ11

RUINI, Carlo (c.1530-1598) Anat.; Vet. Med. CDZZ ZZ11

RUIZ, Hipolito (1754-1816) Bot. CDZZ ZZ11

RULAND, Martin (1569-1611) Med. CDZZ ZZ11

RULEIN VON CALW, Ulrich (1465-1523) Geol.; Mng. CDZZ ZZ11

RUMBAUGH, Lynn H. (1904-1964) Phys. NC51

RUMFORD, Count SEE THOMPSON, Benjamin

RUMOVSKY, Stepan Y. (1734-1812) Astron.; Math. CDZZ ZZ11

RUMPF, Georg E. (1628-1702) Ornith. ANHD ORNS

RUMSEY, James (1743-1792) Invent. TINA

RUNCORN, Stanley K. (1922-) Geophys. BEOS MHSE

RUNGE, Carl D. (1856-1927) Math.; Phys. CDZZ ZZ11

RUNGE, Friedlieb F. (1795-1867) Chem. BDOS BEOS CDZZ GRCH HSSO ZZ11

RUNKLE, John D. (1822-1902) Math.; Engr. BIOD DAB NC-6

RUPERT, Joseph A. (1916-1972) Bot. NC58

RUSBY, Henry H. (1855-1940) Bot. NCSA

RUSCELLI, Girolamo (d. c.1565) Med.; Chem. CDZZ ZZXV

RUSH, Benjamin (1745-1813) Chem.; Med. ACCE BDOS BEOS BHMT BIOD CDZZ COAC GRCH HIUE MMMA ZZ11

RUSH, James (1786-1869) Psych. BIOD

ibn RUSHD, Abul-Walid Muhammad (1126-1198) Astron.; Med. BEOS CDZZ SCIN ZZ12

RUSHTON, William A. (1901-1980) Physiol. BEOS MHM2 MHSE

RUSK, Howard (1901-) Med. LGIH

RUSKA, Ernst A. (1906-) Elec. Engr. ABES ABET

RUSSELL, Alexander (c.1715-1768) Nat. Hist. DNB

RUSSELL, Bertrand A. (1872-1970) Math. ABES ABET BEOS CB51 CDZZ OGML RS19 TOWS ZZ12

RUSSELL, Edward J. (1872-1965) Chem.; Agr. BDOS BEOS CDZZ RS12 ZZXV

RUSSELL, Edward S. (1887-1954) Biol. DNB7

RUSSELL, Elizabeth S. (1913-) Genet. CWSN

RUSSELL, Frederick S. (1897-) Zool. BEOS MHM2 MHSE

RUSSELL, Henry C. (1836-1907) Astron.; Meteor. CDZZ DNB2 ZZXV

RUSSELL, Henry N. (1877-1957) Astron. ABES ABET BEOS BM32 CDZZ IEAS NCSA RS-3 SGAC WAMB ZZ12

RUSSELL, Howard W. (1901-1965) Phys. NC51

RUSSELL, Jane A. (1911-1967) Biochem. NAWM

RUSSELL, Loris S. (1904-) Paleon. MHM2 MHSE

RUSSELL, Richard J. (1895-1971) Geomorph. BM46 MHM2 MHSE

RUSSELL, William J. (1830-1909) Chem. DNB2

RUTHERFORD, Daniel (1749-1819) Chem. ABES
ABET BEOS CDZZ DNB ZZ12

RUTHERFORD, Ernest (1871-1937) Phys.; Chem.
ABES ABET BDOS BEOS CAVL CDZZ CSCJ
DCPW DNB5 GEXB GRCH HOSS HSSO IFBS
MMSB MWBR NPWC OGML PHYS POSW RPTC
SAIF SMIL TOWS ZZ12

RUTHERFORD, William (c.1798-1871) Math. DNB

RUTHERFORD, William (1839-1899) Physiol. DNB1

RUTHERFURD, Lewis M. (1816-1892) Astrophys.
ABET BIOD BM-3 CDZZ DAB NC-6 ZZ12

RUTIMEYER, Karl L. (1825-1895) Paleon. CDZZ
ZZ12

RUTZLER, John E. (1903-1960) Chem. NC47

RUYSCH, Frederick (1638-1731) Med. BHMT CDZZ
ZZ12

RUZICKA, Leopold S. (1887-1976) Chem. ABES
ABET BEOS MHM2 MHSE NPWC RS26

RYAN, Harris J. (1866-1934) Elec. Engr. BM19 TPAE

RYDBERG, Johannes R. (1854-1919) Math.; Phys.
ABET BDOS BEOS CDZZ ZZ12

RYDBERG, Per A. (1860-1931) Bot. DAB NC26

RYDE, John W. (1898-1961) Phys. RS-8

RYE, Edward C. (1832-1885) Entom. DNB

RYLE, Martin (1918-1984) Astron. ABET BEOS
CB73 IEAS MHSE POSW

RYLEY, John (1747-1815) Math. DNB

RYZHKOV, Vitaly L. (1896-) Biol. SMST

S

SABATIER, Armand (1834-1910) Anat. CDZZ ZZ12

SABATIER, Paul (1854-1941) Chem. ABES ABET
BDOS BEOS CDZZ NPWG ZZ12

SABIN, Albert B. (1906-) Virol.; Med. ABES ABET
AMJB BEOS CB58 MFIR MHM1 MHSE SCLB
VACE WAMB

SABIN, Alvah H. (1851-1940) Chem. NC41

SABIN, Florence R. (1871-1953) Med. BHMT
BM34 CB45 CDZZ CWSN DAB5 IDWB NAWM
NC40 WPSH ZZ12 WASM

SABINE, Edward (1788-1883) Phys.; Astron. ABET
BDOS BEOS CDZZ SAIF WFBG ZZ12

SABINE, Paul E. (1879-1958) Phys. CDZZ ZZ12

SABINE, Wallace C. (1868-1919) Phys. ABES ABET
BEOS CDZZ DAB NC15 NC27 SAIF ZZ12

SABOURAUD, Raymond (1864-1938) Med. BHMT

SACCHERI, Girolamo (1667-1733) Phys. ABET
CDZZ ZZ12

SACCO, Luigi (1769-1836) Med. CDZZ ZZ12

SACHS, Julius von (1832-1897) Bot. ABES ABET
BDOS BEOS CDZZ ZZ12

SACKEN, Charles R. (1828-1906) Entom. AMEM

SACROBOSCO, Johannes de (c.1198-1256) Astron.
CDZZ ZZ12

al-SADAFI SEE ibn YUNUS, Abul-Hasan Ali ibn Abd

SADLER, Windham W. (1796-1824) Aero. DNB

SADOVSKII, Mikhail A. (1904-) Phys. SMST

SADRON, Charles L. (1902-) Phys.; Biophys.
BEOS MHM2 MHSE

SADTLER, Samuel P. (1847-1923) Chem. DAB NC-5

SAFFORD, Truman H. (1836-1901) Astron.; Math.
BIOD DAB NC13

SAFFORD, William E. (1859-1926) Bot. DAB MABH
NC20

SAGAN, Carl E. (1934-) Astron. ABES ABET BEOS
CB70 IEAS MOS6

SAGE, Balthazar G. (1740-1824) Metal.; Chem.
CDZZ ZZ12

SAGE, John H. (1847-1925) Ornith. NC20

SAGER, Ruth (1918-) Genet. CB67

SAGNAC, Georges M. (1869-1928) Phys. CDZZ ZZ12

SAHA, Meghnad (1893-1956) Astrophys. BDOS BEOS CDZZ RS-5 ZZ12

ST. ANDRE, Nathanael (1680-1776) Anat. DNB

SAINT-HILAIRE, Augustin F. (1779-1853) Nat. Hist. CDZZ ZZ12

ST. JOHN, Charles E. (1857-1935) Astron.; Phys. BM18 CDZZ DAB1 NC26 ZZ12

SAINT-VENANT, Adhemar J. de (1797-1886) Math. CDZZ GE-1 ZZ12

SAINT VINCENT, Gregorius (1584-1667) Math.; Astron. CDZZ ZZ12

SAINTE-CLAIRE DEVILLE, Henri E. (1818-1881) Chem. ABES ABET BEOS GRCH

SAINTE-MESME SEE L'HOSPITAL, Guillaume F. de

SAKHAROV, Andrei D. (1921-) Phys. ABET CB71 NBPS SMST

SAKHAROV, Vladimir V. (1902-1969) Genet. CDZZ ZZ12

SAKS, Stanislaw (1897-1942) Math. CDZZ ZZ12

SAKS, Vladimir N. (1911-) Geol. SMST

SALA, Angelo (1576-1637) Chem.; Med. CDZZ ZZ12

SALAM, Abdus (1926-) Phys. ABET BEOS POSW SOT3

SALAMAN, Redcliffe N. (1874-1955) Med. RS-1

SALERNITAN, Anatomists (fl. c.1100) Anat. CDZZ ZZ12

SALISBURY, Edward J. (1886-1978) Bot. BEOS MHM1 MHSE RS26

SALISBURY, James H. (1823-1905) Micros.; Med. BIOD

SALISBURY, Richard A. (1761-1829) Bot. DNB

SALISBURY, Rollin D. (1858-1922) Geol. CDZZ ZZ12

SALK, Jonas E. (1914-) Microbiol.; Immunol. ABES ABET AMJB BEOS CB54 FMBB LGIH MFIR MHM1 MHSE PBTS PGFS PPEY SAIF WAMB

SALK, Lee (1926-) Psych. CB79

SALLO, Danys de (1626-1669) Sci. Writ. CDZZ ZZ12

SALMON, George (1819-1904) Math. CDZZ ZZ12

SALMONSEN, Carl J. (1847-1924) Bact. CDZZ ZZ12

SALPETER, Edwin E. (1924-) Astrophys. MHSE

SALTER, John W. (1820-1869) Geol. DNB

SALVIANI, Ippolito (1514-1572) Med. CDZZ ZZ12

SALVIN, Osbert (1835-1898) Nat. Hist. DNB1

SALYER, John C. II (1902-1966) Cons. LACC

al-SAMARQANDI, Najib al-Din (d. 1222) Med. CDZZ ZZ12

al-SAMARQANDI, Shams al-Din (fl. 1276) Math.; Astron. CDZZ ZZ12

al-SAMAWAL, ibn Yahya al-Maghribi (d. c.1180) Math.; Med. CDZZ ZZ12

SAMMET, Jean E. (1928-) Comp. HOPL

SAMOYLOV, Aleksandr F. (1867-1930) Physiol.; Med. CDZZ ZZ12

SAMPSON, Arthur W. (1884-1967) Ecol. NC53

SAMPSON, Harry (1890-) Bot. BNBR

SAMPSON, Ralph A. (1866-1939) Astron. CDZZ DNB5 ZZ12

SAMUELS, Edward A. (1836-1908) Ornith. BIOD DAB

SAMUELSSON, Bengt I. (1934-) Biochem. BEOS

SANARELLI, Giuseppe (1864-1940) Med. CDZZ ZZ12

SANCHEZ, Francisco (1550/1-1623) Med. CDZZ ZZ12

SANCTORIUS, Sanctorius (1561-1636) Med. ABES ABET BDOS BEOS BHMT CDZZ MPIP ZZ12

SANDAGE, Allan R. (1926-) Astron. ABES ABET BEOS

SANDER, Bruno H. (1884-) Geol. MHM1 MHSE

SANDERS, James G. (1880-1957) Entom. NC44

SANDERS, William (1799-1875) Geol. DNB

SANDERSON, Ezra D. (1878-1944) Entom. AMEM CDZZ DAB3 ZZ12

SANDERSON, Ivan T. (1911-1973) Nat. Hist. NC57

SANDERSON, John SEE BURDON-SANDERSON, John S.

SANDHOLZER, Leslie A. (1903-1948) Bact. NC37

SANDHOUSE, Grace A. (1896-1940) Entom. AMEM

SANDSTROM, Ivar (1852-1889) Med. BHMT

SANGER, Charles R. (1860-1912) Chem. ACCE DAB NC28

SANGER, Eugen (1905-1964) Rocket. BEOS ICFW IEAS MOS8

SANGER, Frederick (1918-) Chem. ABES ABET BEOS CB81 MHM1 MHSE

SANIO, Karl G. (1832-1891) Bot. CDZZ ZZ12

SANTORINI, Giovanni D. (1681-1737) Med.; Anat. CDZZ ZZ12

SANTORIO, Santorio SEE SANCTORIUS, Sanctorius

SANTOS-DUMONT, Alberto (1873-1932) Aero. ICFW PAW3

SAPORTA, Louis C. de (1823-1896) Paleon. CDZZ ZZ12

SARETT, Lew (1888-1954) Nat. Hist. NCSA

SARETT, Lewis H. (1917-) Chem. MHM2 MHSE

SARGENT, Charles S. (1841-1927) Bot. BM12 EAFC LACC MABH NC13 NC26

SARGENT, George J. (1885-1965) Chem. ACCE

SARPI, Paolo (1552-1623) Nat. Philos. CDZZ ZZ12

SARS, Michael (1805-1869) Mar. Biol. CDZZ ZZ12

SARTON, George A. (1884-1956) Chem.; Hist. of Sci. CB42 CDZZ ZZ12

SARTWELL, Henry P. (1792-1867) Bot. BIOD DAB

SARYCHEV, Gavriil A. (1763-1831) Hydrol. CDZZ ZZ12

SASSCER, Ernest R. (1883-1955) Entom. AMEM

SATANANDA (fl. 1099) Astron. CDZZ ZZ12

SATCHER, George R. (1926-) Phys. MHSE

SATO NOBUHIRO (1769-1850) Mng. CDZZ ZZ12

SATPAEV, Kanysh I. (1899-1964) Geol. SMST

SAUERBRUCH, Ferdinand (1875-1951) Med. BHMT

SAUGRAIN, Antoine F. (1763-1820) Chem.; Instr. ACCE BIOD DAB

SAUKOV, Aleksandr A. (1902-1964) Geol. SMST

SAULL, William D. (1784-1855) Geol. DNB

SAULT, Richard (d. 1702) Math. DNB

SAUNDERS, Edward (1848-1910) Entom. DNB2

SAUNDERS, Frederick A. (1875-1963) Phys. BM39

SAUNDERS, Howard (1835-1907) Ornith. DNB2

SAUNDERS, William (1835-1914) Entom. AMEM

SAUNDERS, William W. (1809-1879) Entom. DNB

SAUNDERSON, Nicholas (1682-1739) Math. DNB

SAURIN, Joseph (1659-1737) Math. CDZZ ZZ12

SAUSSURE, Horace B. de (1740-1799) Geol.; Bot. ABET BDOS BEOS CDZZ ZZ12

SAUSSURE, Nicolas T. de (1767-1845) Chem.; Bot. CDZZ ZZ12

SAUVAGE, Pierre L. (1785-1857) Engr. GE-1

SAUVAGEAU, Camille F. (1861-1936) Bot. CDZZ ZZ12

SAUVEUR, Albert (1863-1939) Metal. BM22 CDZZ ZZ12

SAUVEUR, Joseph (1653-1716) Phys. CDZZ ZZ12

SAVAGE, John L. (1879-1967) Engr. BM49

SAVAGE, Thomas S. (1804-1880) Zool. BIOD DAB

SAVART, Felix (1791-1841) Phys. CDZZ ZZ12

SAVERY, Thomas (1650-1715) Engr. ABES ABET
BDOS BEOS GE-1

SAVIGNY, Marie J. de (1777-1851) Biol. CDZZ ZZ12

SAVILLE, Marshall H. (1867-1935) Archaeol. DAB1

SAVILLE, Wilson G. (1897-1954) Geophys. NC42

SAWYER, Robert W. (1880-1959) Cons. LACC

SAX, Karl (1892-1973) Biol. MHM1 MHSE NC58

SAXBY, Henry L. (1836-1873) Ornith. DNB

SAXTON, Joseph (1799-1873) Instr. BIOD BM-1
CDZZ ZZ12

SAY, Thomas (1787-1834) Entom.; Conch. AMEM
ANHD ASJD BIOD BWCL CDZZ DAB MSAJ
NHAH WAMB ZZ12

SAYRE, A. Nelson (1901-1967) Geol. NC52

SCALIGER, Joseph J. (1540-1609) Chron. ABES
ABET

SCALIGER, Julius C. (1484-1558) Med.; Bot. CDZZ
ZZ12

SCAMMON, Charles (1825-1911) Nat. Hist. NHAH

SCARPA, Antonio (1752-1832) Med. BHMT CDZZ
ZZ12

SCARTH, George W. (1881-1951) Bot. MABH

SCATCHARD, George (1892-1973) Chem. BM52
MHM1 MHSE

SCHAEBERLE, John M. (1853-1924) Astron. ABET
CDZZ DAB NC26 ZZ12

SCHAEFER, Vincent J. (1906-) Meteor. ABES
ABET BEOS CB48 MHM1 MHSE

SCHAEFFER, John A. (1888-1941) Chem. ACCE

SCHAFER, Edward SEE SHARPEY-SCHAFER,
Edward A.

SCHAFFNER, John H. (1866-1939) Bot. MABH

SCHAIBLE, Philip J. (1899-1971) Biochem. NC57

SCHAIRER, George S. (1913-) Engr. MHM1 MHSE

SCHALLY, Andrew V. (1926-) Med. ABET BEOS
MHSE PAW2 SOTT

SCHARDT, Hans (1858-1931) Geol. CDZZ ZZ12

SCHAUDINN, Fritz R. (1871-1906) Zool. ABES ABET
BDOS BEOS BHMT CDZZ ZZ12

SCHAUS, William (1858-1942) Entom. AMEM

SCHEELE, Karl W. (1742-1786) Chem. ABES ABET
BDOS BEOS BHMT BMST CDZZ GRCH HLSM
HSSO TPOS ZZ12

SCHEER, Alan A. (1923-) Med. CB64

SCHEFFERS, Georg (1866-1945) Math. CDZZ ZZ12

SCHEGK, Jakob (1511-1587) Med. CDZZ ZZ12

SCHEINER, Christoph (1573-1650) Astron. ABES
ABET BEOS CDZZ ZZ12

SCHEINER, Julius (1858-1913) Astron. CDZZ ZZ12

SCHELLING, Frederick W. von (1775-1854) Philos.
CDZZ ZZ12

SCHENCK, Carl A. (1868-1955) Forest. EAFC LACC

SCHERMANN, Raphael (d. 1943) Psych. PUNT

SCHEUCHZER, Johann J. (1672-1733) Geol. BMST
CDZZ FHUA THOG ZZ12

SCHIAPARELLI, Giovanni V. (1835-1910) Astron.
ABES ABET BDOS BEOS CDZZ IEAS ZZ12

SCHICKARD, Wilhelm (1592-1635) Astron.; Math.
CDZZ ZZ12

SCHIEFFELIN, William J. (1866-1955) Chem. ACCE

SCHIFF, Hugo J. (1834-1915) Chem. CDZZ ZZ12

SCHIFF, Moritz (1823-1896) Zool.; Physiol. BDOS
BEOS BHMT CDZZ ZZ12

SCHIFFER, John P. (1930-) Phys. MHSE

SCHIMPER, Andreas F. (1856-1901) Bot. BDOS
BEOS CDZZ ZZ12

SCHIMPER, Karl F. (1803-1867) Bot. CDZZ ZZ12

SCHIMPER, Wilhelm P. (1808-1880) Bot.; Geol.
CDZZ FHUA ZZ12

SCHIRRA, Walter M. (1923-) Astronaut. FPSN
IEAS PMAS WESE

SCHISHKIN, Boris K. (1886-) Bot. SMST

SCHJELLERUP, Hans C. (1827-1887) Astron. CDZZ
ZZ12

SCHLAFLI, Ludwig (1814-1895) Math. CDZZ ZZ12

SCHLEGEL, Hermann (1804-1884) Ornith. ANHD
ORNS

SCHLEIDEN, Jacob M. (1804-1881) Bot. ABES
ABET BDOS BEOS CDZZ HLSM ZZ12

SCHLESINGER, Frank (1871-1943) Astron. BM24
CDZZ DAB3 NC14 NC32 ZZ12

SCHLESSINGER, David (1936-) Microbiol. MHSE

SCHLICH, William (1840-1925) Forest. DNB4

SCHLICK, Moritz (1882-1936) Philos. of Sci. CDZZ
ZZ12

SCHLIEMANN, Heinrich (1822-1890) Archaeol. ABET
CDZZ ZZ12

SCHLOTHEIM, Ernst F. von (1765-1832) Geol.;
Paleon. CDZZ PHLS ZZ12

SCHLUMBERGER, Charles (1825-1905) Paleon.
CDZZ ZZ12

SCHMALHAUSEN, Ivan I. (1884-) Zool. SMST

SCHMELKES, Franz C. (1899-1942) Chem. NC32

SCHMERLING, Philippe C. (1791-1836) Paleon.
CDZZ ZZ12

SCHMIDEL, Casimir C. (1718-1792) Med.; Nat. Hist.
CDZZ ZZ12

SCHMIDT, Bernhard V. (1879-1935) Opt. ABES ABET
BDOS CDZZ SLOR TMAL ZZ12

SCHMIDT, Carl A. von (1840-1929) Geophys.; Astrophys. CDZZ ZZ12

SCHMIDT, Carl L. (1885-1946) Biochem. DAB4
NC34

SCHMIDT, Erhard (1876-1959) Math. CDZZ ZZ12

SCHMIDT, Erich F. (1897-1964) Archaeol. NC51

SCHMIDT, Ernst J. (1877-1933) Mar. Biol. BDOS
BEOS CDZZ ZZ12

SCHMIDT, Gerhard C. (1865-1949) Chem. CDZZ
ZZ12

SCHMIDT, Johann F. (1825-1884) Astron.; Geophys.
CDZZ ZZ12

SCHMIDT, Maarten (1929-) Astron. ABES ABET
BEOS CB66 IEAS

SCHMIDT-NIELSEN, Knut (1915-) Physiol. MHM2
MHSE

SCHMIEDEBERG, Oswald (1838-1921) Med. BHMT

SCHMITT, Francis O. (1903-) Biol. MHM2 MHSE

SCHMITT, Harrison H. (1935-) Geol.; Astronaut.
CB74

SCHMITT, Waldo L. (1887-1977) Zool. NC60

SCHMITZ, Henry (1892-1965) Forest. LACC

SCHNEIDER, Albert (1863-1928) Bot. DAB NC13

SCHNEIDER, Friedrich A. (1831-1890) Zool.; Anat.
CDZZ ZZ12

SCHNEIDERHOHN, Hans (1887-1962) Geol. CDZZ
ZZ12

SCHNYDER, Walter A. (1914-1977) Chem. Engr.
NC59

SCHOENFLIES, Arthur M. (1853-1928) Biochem.
ABES ACCE CDZZ DAB3

SCHOENHEIMER, Rudolf (1898-1941) Biochem.
ABET BEOS GJPS

SCHONBEIN, Christian F. (1799-1868) Chem. ABES
ABET BDOS BEOS CDZZ ELEC HSSO ZZ12

SCHONER, Johannes (1477-1547) Astron.; Geog.
ABET CDZZ ZZ12

SCHONFELD, Eduard (1828-1891) Astron. CDZZ
ZZ12

SCHONHERR, Carl J. (1772-1848) Entom. CDZZ
ZZ12

SCHONLAND, Basil F. (1896-1972) Phys. CDZZ
RS19 ZZ12

SCHONLEIN, Johann L. (1793-1864) Med. BHMT
CDZZ ZZ12

SCHOOLCRAFT, Henry R. (1793-1864) Geol. ASJD
BIOD EOMH CDZZ ZZ12

SCHOONHOVEN, John J. (1884-1936) Biol. NC26

SCHOOTEN, Frans van (c.1615-1660) Math. CDZZ
ZZ12

SCHOPF, James M. (1911-1978) Geol.; Paleon. MHSE

SCHOPF, Johan D. (1752-1800) Nat. Hist. BIOD
DAB

SCHOPFER, William H. (1900-1962) Biol.; Biochem.
CDZZ ZZ12

SCHORLEMMER, Carl (1834-1892) Chem. CDZZ
DNB ZZ12

SCHOTT, Arthur C. (1814-1875) Geol. BIOD

SCHOTT, Charles A. (1826-1901) Geophys. BIOD
BM-8 CDZZ ZZ12

SCHOTT, Gaspar (1608-1666) Math.; Phys. CDZZ
ZZ12

SCHOTT, Lionel O. (1906-1974) Elec. Engr. NC58

SCHOTT, Otto F. (1851-1935) Chem. CDZZ ZZ12

SCHOTTKY, Friedrich H. (1851-1935) Math. CDZZ
ZZ12

SCHOUTE, Pieter H. (1846-1923) Math. CDZZ ZZ12

SCHOUTEN, Jan A. (1883-1971) Math. CDZZ ZZ12

SCHOUW, Joakim F. von (1789-1852) Zool. CDZZ
ZZ12

SCHREIBERS, Karl F. von (1775-1852) Zool. CDZZ
ZZ12

SCHREINER, Oswald (1875-1965) Chem. ACCE
NCSE

SCHRENCK-NOTZIG, Albert von (1862-1929) Med.
PUNT

SCHRIEFFER, John R. (1931-) Phys. ABET BEOS
MHSE POSW WAMB

SCHRIEVER, Bernard A. (1910-) Rocket. FPSN
MOS1

SCHRODER, Friedrich W. (1841-1902) Math. CDZZ
ZZ12

SCHRODINGER, Erwin (1887-1961) Phys. ABES
ABET BDOS BEOS CDZZ POSW RS-7 TOWS
ZZ12

SCHROEDER VAN DER KOK, Jacobus L. (1797-1862)
Med. CDZZ ZZ12

SCHROETER, Heinrich E. (1829-1892) Math. CDZZ
ZZ12

SCHROTER, Johann H. (1745-1816) Astron. CDZZ
ZZ12

SCHROTTER, Anton von (1802-1875) Chem. BDOS
BEOS CDZZ ZZ12

SCHUBERT, Ernst (1813-1873) Astron. BIOD

SCHUBERT, Hermann C. (1848-1911) Math. CDZZ
ZZ12

SCHUCHERT, Charles (1858-1942) Paleon. BM27
CDZZ DAB3 ZZ12

SCHULTE, Hermann (1876-1932) Anat. NC23

SCHULTZ, Adolph H. (1891-1976) Anthro. MHM1
MHSE

SCHULTZ, Alfred R. (1876-1943) Geol. NC41

SCHULTZ, Carl E. (1909-1966) Invent. NC51

SCHULTZ, Edwin W. (1887-) Bact. NCSE

SCHULTZ, Jack (1904-1971) Genet. BM47

SCHULTZ, Leonard P. (1901-) Ichth. NCSJ

SCHULTZE, Max J. (1825-1874) Anat. ABES ABET
BDOS BEOS CDZZ ZZ12

SCHULZ, George J. (1925-1976) Phys. MHSE

SCHULZ, William F. (1872-1956) Phys. NC45

SCHULZE, Franz F. (1815-1873) Chem.; Microbiol. CDZZ ZZ12

SCHUMACHER, Heinrich C. (1780-1850) Astron. CDZZ ZZ12

SCHUMACHER, Jan P. (1891-1975) Geophys. NC59

SCHUMANN, Victor (1841-1913) Photo. CDZZ ZZ12

SCHUMB, Walter C. (1892-1967) Chem. ACCE

SCHUNCK, Henry E. (1820-1903) Chem. CDZZ DNB2 ZZ12

SCHUR, Issai (1875-1941) Math. CDZZ ZZ12

SCHURZ, Carl (1829-1906) Cons. LACC

SCHUSTER, Arthur (1851-1934) Phys. BEOS CDZZ DNB5 STYC ZZ12

SCHWABE, Samuel H. (1789-1875) Astron. ABES ABET BDOS BEOS CDZZ SLOR ZZ12

SCHWANN, Theodor A. (1810-1882) Physiol. ABES ABET BDOS BEOS BHMT CDZZ HLSM ZZ12

SCHWARDT, Herbert H. (1903-1962) Entom. AMEM

SCHWARTZ, George (1908-) Biol. SWWP

SCHWARTZ, Jules I. (1927-) Comp. HOPL

SCHWARTZ, Robert S. (1921-1964) Chem. NC50

SCHWARZ, Eugene A. (1844-1928) Chem. AMEM BIOD DAB NC29

SCHWARZ, Herbert F. (1883-1960) Entom. AMEM

SCHWARZ, Hermann A. (1843-1921) Math. CDZZ ZZ12

SCHWARZENBACH, Gerold K. (1904-1978) Chem. MHM2 MHSE

SCHWARZSCHILD, Karl (1873-1916) Astron. ABET BEOS CDZZ IEAS ZZ12

SCHWARZSCHILD, Martin (1912-) Astron. CB67 CHUB MHSE

SCHWEET, Richard S. (1918-1967) Biochem. NC53

SCHWEIGGER, Johann S. (1779-1857) Phys. ABES ABET BEOS CDZZ EETD ZZ12

SCHWEIKART, Ferdinand K. (1780-1859) Math. CDZZ ZZ12

SCHWEINITZ, Emil A. de (1864-1904) Biochem. BIOD DAB

SCHWEINITZ, Lewis D. von (1780-1834) Bot. BIOD DAB MABH NC-8

SCHWENDENER, Simon (1829-1919) Bot. CDZZ ZZ12

SCHWINGER, Julian S. (1918-) Phys. ABES ABET BEOS CB67 MHM1 MHSE WAMB WMSW

SCILLA, Agostino (1629-1700) Geol. CDZZ ZZ12

SCLATER, Philip L. (1829-1913) Ornith. ANHD CDZZ WFBG ZZ12

SCOT, Michael SEE MICHAEL SCOT

SCOTT, Blanche S. (1892-1970) Aero. PAW2

SCOTT, Charles F. (1864-1944) Elec. Engr. TPAE

SCOTT, Charlotte A. (1858-1931) Math. IDWB NAW

SCOTT, David A. (1892-1971) Chem. RS17

SCOTT, David R. (1932-) Astronaut. CB71 IEAS

SCOTT, Dukinfield H. (1854-1934) Bot.; Paleon. BEOS CDZZ FHUA ZZ12

SCOTT, Elmer J. (1916-1975) Phys. NC59

SCOTT, Hugh (1885-1960) Entom. RS-7

SCOTT, John W. (1871-1956) Zool. LACC

SCOTT, Peter M. (1909-) Ornith. CB68

SCOTT, Robert F. (1868-1912) Exp. ABES ABET

SCOTT, Russell B. (1902-1967) Phys. NC54

SCOTT, Thomas G. (1912-) Zool. LACC

SCOTT, Wilfred W. (1876-1932) Chem. ACCE

SCOTT, William B. (1858-1947) Paleon. BM25 CDZZ DAB4 NC36 ZZ12

SCOTT, Winfield (1854-1919) Chem. NC19

SCOTUS, John D. SEE DUNS SCOTUS, John

SCOULER, John (1804-1871) Nat. Hist. DNB

SCOVELL, Josiah T. (1841-1915) Chem.; Mineral.
NC16

SCOVELL, Melville A. (1855-1912) Chem. ACCE
DAB NC15

SCROPE, George J. (1797-1876) Geol. CDZZ DNB
ZZ12

SCUDDER, Samuel H. (1837-1911) Entom. AMEM
CDZZ DAB NC-3 NC24 ZZ12

SEABORG, Glenn T. (1912-) Chem. ABES ABET
BEOS CB48 CB61 MHM1 MHSE NCSH PAW2
PBTS PPEY PPJY PPKY PPTY WAMB WMSW

SEABURY, George J. (1844-1909) Chem. DAB

SEAMAN, Elwood A. (1916-) Ichth. LACC

SEAMANS, Robert C. Jr. (1918-) Phys. CB66 MHM2
MHSE MOS5

SEARES, Frederick H. (1873-1964) Astron. BM39
CDZZ NCSA ZZ12

SEARLE, Arthur (1837-1920) Astron. DAB NC18
NC19

SEARLE, George F. (1864-1954) Phys. RS-1

SEARS, Ernest R. (1910-) Genet. MHM2 MHSE

SEARS, Harry J. (1885-1962) Bact. NC49

SEARS, Paul B. (1891-) Ecol. BEOS CB60 LACC
MHM2 MHSE NCSJ SFNB

SEASHORE, Carl E. (1866-1949) Psych. BM29

SEATON, Edward C. (1815-1880) Immunol. DNB

SECCHI, Pietro A. (1818-1878) Astron. ABES ABET
BDOS BEOS CDZZ ZZ12

SECHENOV, Ivan M. (1829-1905) Physiol.; Chem.
CDZZ ZZ12

SECHLER, Ernest E. (1905-1979) Aero. ICFW

SEDERHOLM, Johannes J. (1863-1934) Geol. CDZZ
ZZ12

SEDGWICK, Adam (1785-1873) Geol. ABES ABET
BDOS BEOS CDZZ DARR DNB ZZ12

SEDGWICK, Adam (1854-1913) Zool. DNB3

SEDGWICK, William T. (1855-1921) Med. BHMT DAB

SEDOV, Georgy Y. (1877-1914) Exp. CDZZ ZZ12

SEDOV, Leonid I. (1907-) Phys. MHM2 MHSE SMST

SEE, Thomas J. (1866-1962) Astron. CDZZ NC13
ZZ12

SEEBECK, Thomas J. (1770-1831) Phys. ABES ABET
BEOS CDZZ SAIF ZZ12

SEEBOHM, Henry (1832-1895) Ornith. DNB

SEELEY, Harry G. (1839-1909) Paleon. DNB2 MADC

SEELEY, Walter J. (1894-1974) Elec. ENgr. NC58

SEELIGER, Hugo von (1849-1924) Astron. CDZZ ZZ12

SEFSTROM, Nils G. (1787-1945) Chem. ABES ABET
BEOS

SEGNER, Janos A. von (1704-1777) Math.; Phys.
CDZZ ZZ12

SEGRE, Corrado (1863-1924) Math. CDZZ ZZ12

SEGRE, Emilio G. (1905-) Phys. ABES ABET
BEOS CB60 DCPW MHM1 MHSE POSW WAMB

SEGUIN, Armand (1767-1835) Chem.; Physiol. CDZZ
ZZ12

SEGUIN, Laurent (1883-1944) Aero. ICFW

SEGUIN, Louis (1869-1918) Aero. ICFW

SEGUIN, Marc (1786-1875) Engr.; Phys. BDOS CDZZ
GE-1 ZZ12

SEIBERG, Florence B. (1897-) Biochem. CB42
NCSG

SEIBERT, Howard F. (1912-1973) Chem. NC58

SEIDEL, Philipp L. von (1821-1896) Astron.; Math.
CDZZ ZZ12

SEIDELL, Atherton (1878-1961) Chem. ACCE

SEIL, Harvey A. (1882-1951) Chem. NC38 NC44

SEITZ, Frederick (1911-) Phys. CB56 MHM2 MHSE

SEKERA, Zdenek (1908-) Phys.; Meteor. MHM2 MHSE

SEKI, Takakazu (c.1642-1708) Math. CDZZ ZZ12

SELBY, Prideaux J. (1788-1867) Nat. Hist. DNB

SELDEN, George B. (1846-1922) Invent. ASIW WAMB

SELEUCUS (fl. c.190 B.C.) Astron. ABES ABET BEOS

SELIKOFF, Irving J. (1915-) Med. MFIR

SELLERS, Matthew B. (1869-1932) Aero. DAB NC15

SELWYN, Alfred R. (1924-1902) Geol. CDZZ DNB2 ZZ12

SELYE, Hans (1907-1982) Med. CB53

SEMENOV, Nikolai N. (1896-) Chem. ABES ABET BEOS CB57 MHM1 MHSE SMST

SEMMELWEIS, Ignaz P. (1818-1865) Med. ABES ABET BDOS BEOS BHMT CDZZ MAMR MMMA ZZ12

SEMON, Richard W. (1859-1918) Zool.; Anat. CDZZ ZZ12

SEMON, Waldo L. (1898-) Chem. CB40

SEMPER, Carl G. (1832-1893) Zool. CDZZ ZZ12

SEMPLE, Hugh (1596-1654) Math. DNB

SEMYONOV-TYAN-SHANSKY, Petr P. (1827-1914) Geog. CDZZ ZZ12

SENAC, Jean B. (c.1693-1770) Anat.; Physiol. CDZZ ZZ12

SENARMONT, Henri H. de (1808-1862) Crystal. CDZZ ZZ12

SENDERENS, Jean B. (1856-1936) Chem. BDOS

SENDIVOGIUS, Michael (1566-1636) Alch. CDZZ ZZ12

SENEBIER, Jean (1742-1809) Physiol. CDZZ ZZ12

SENECA, Lucius A. (c.4 B.C.-A.D. 65) Phys.; Meteor. CDZZ ZZ12

SENEFELDER, Aloys (1771-1834) Invent. GE-1 SAIF

SENNERT, Daniel (1572-1637) Med. CDZZ ZZ12

SENNETT, George B. (1840-1900) Ornith. BIOD DAB NC14

SEQUARD, Charles SEE BROWN-SEQUARD, Charles E.

SERENUS (fl. c.300) Math. CDZZ ZZ12

SERGENT, Edmond (1876-1969) Med. CDZZ ZZ12

SERRE, Jean P. (1926-) Math. BEOS

SERRES, Antoine E. (1786-1868) Anat.; Embryol. CDZZ ZZ12

SERRES, Olivier de (1539-1619) Agr. CDZZ ZZ12

SERRES DE MESPLES, Marcel P. de (1780-1862) Zool.; Geol. CDZZ ZZ12

SERRET, Joseph A. (1819-1885) Math. CDZZ ZZ12

SERTOLI, Enrico (1842-1910) Physiol. CDZZ ZZ12

SERTURNER, Friedrich W. (1783-1841) Pharm. ABET BDOS BEOS CDZZ ZZ12

SERULLAS, Georges S. (1774-1832) Chem. CDZZ ZZ12

SERVETUS, Michael (1511-1553) Med. ABES ABET BDOS BEOS BHMT CDZZ HLSM TBSG ZZ12

SERVOIS, Francois J. (1767-1837) Math. CDZZ ZZ12

SESHADRI, Thiruvenkata R. (1900-1975) Chem. RS25

SESSE Y LACASTA, Martin de (1751-1808) Bot. CDZZ SSNW ZZ12

SESSIONS, Kate O. (1857-1940) Hort. NAW

SESTINI, Benedict (1816-1890) Astron.; Math. BIOD DAB

SETCHELL, William A. (1864-1943) Bot. BM23 DAB3 MABH NC32 CDZZ ZZ12

SETON, Ernest T. (1860-1946) Nat. Hist. CB43 DAB4 EAFC GANC LACC NC36 SFNB

SETZLER, Frank M. (1902-1975) Anthro. NC58

SEVERGIN, Vasily M. (1765-1826) Mineral.; Chem. CDZZ ZZ12

SEVERI, Francesco (1879-1961) Math. CDZZ ZZ12

SEVERIN, Christian (1562-1647) Astron. CDZZ ZZ12

SEVERIN, Sergei E. (1901-) Biochem. SMST

SEVERINO, Marco A. (1580-1656) Med. CDZZ ZZ12

SEVERINUS, Petrus (1542-1602) Chem.; Med. CDZZ ZZ12

SEVERNYI, Andrei B. (1913-) Astron. SMST

SEVERTSOV, Aleksey N. (1866-1936) Anat.; Evol. CDZZ ZZ12

SEVERUD, Fred N. (1899-) Engr. MHSE

SEWARD, Albert C. (1863-1941) Paleon. BEOS CDZZ DNB6 PHLS ZZ12

SEWELL, Robert B. (1880-1964) Zool. RS11

SEXTUS EMPIRICUS (fl. c.200) Med. CDZZ ZZ12

SEYBERT, Adam (1773-1825) Chem.; Mineral. DAB NC-4

SEYBERT, Henry (1801-1883) Mineral. ASJD BIOD

SEYFERT, Carl K. (1911-1960) Astron. BEOS

SEZAWA, Katsutada (1895-1944) Math.; Seism. CDZZ ZZ12

SHABANOVA, Anna (1848-1932) Med. IDWB

SHAFFER, Philip A. (1881-1960) Biochem. BM40

SHAKERLEY, Jeremy (1626-c.1655) Astron. CDZZ DNB ZZ12

SHAKHOV, Feliks N. (1894-) Geol. SMST

SHALER, Nathaniel S. (1841-1906) Geol. CDZZ ZZ12

SHALNIKOV, Aleksandr I. (1905-) Phys. SMST

SHAMEL, Archibald D. (1878-1956) Bot. NC46

SHANK, John J. (1898-1949) Chem. NC38

SHANKLIN, John F. (1903-) Forest. LACC

SHANKS, William (1812-1882) Math. ABET CDZZ ZZ12

SHANNON, Claude E. (1916-) Math. ABET BEOS MHM1 MHSE TPAE WMSW

SHANNON, Hugh S. (1872-1932) Chem. NC24

SHANNON, James A. (1904-) Med.; Physiol. CB65

SHANNON, Raymond C. (1894-1945) Entom. AMEM

SHAPLEY, Harlow (1885-1972) Astron. ABES ABET BEOS BM49 CB41 CDZZ IEAS MHM1 MHSE NCSC WAMB ZZ12

SHAPOSHNIKOV, Vladimir N. (1884-1968) Microbiol. SMST

SHARONOV, Vsevold V. (1901-1964) Astron.; Geophys. CDZZ ZZ12

SHARP, Aaron J. (1904-) Bot. NCSK

SHARP, Abraham (1651-1742) Math. DNB

SHARP, Clayton H. (1869-1942) Engr. NC31

SHARP, Dallas L. (1870-1929) Nat. Hist. DAB

SHARP, David W. (1931-) Chem. COBC

SHARP, Lester W. (1887-1961) Bact. NC51

SHARP, Robert P. (1911-) Geol. MHSE

SHARP, Samuel (1814-1882) Geol. DNB

SHARPE, Daniel (1806-1856) Geol. DNB

SHARPE, Joseph A. (1907-1952) Phys. NC39

SHARPE, Richard B. (1847-1909) Ornith. DNB2

SHARPEY, William (1802-1880) Anat.; Physiol. CDZZ DNB ZZ12

SHARPEY-SCHAFER, Edward A. (1850-1935) Physiol. ABES ABET BDOS BEOS BHMT CDZZ ZZ12

SHARROCK, Robert (1630-1684) Bot. CDZZ ZZ12

SHATALOV, Vladimir A. (1927-) Astronaut. IEAS

ibn al-SHATIR, Ala al-Din (c.1305-c.1375) Astron. CDZZ ZZ12

SHATTUCK, Lemuel (1793-1859) Med. BHMT

SHATTUCK, Lydia W. (1822-1889) Bot. BIOD NAW

SHATUNOVSKY, Samuel O. (1859-1929) Math. CDZZ ZZ12

SHAW, Earl (1937-) Phys. BISC

SHAW, Evelyn (1927-) Mar. Biol. CHUB

SHAW, Frederick W. (1882-1945) Bact. NC36

SHAW, George (1751-1813) Nat. Hist. DNB

SHAW, Leon I. (1885-1962) Chem. NC51

SHAW, Peter (1694-1764) Chem. CDZZ ZZ12

SHAW, Trevor I. (1928-1972) Zool.; Physiol. RS20

SHAW, William N. (1854-1945) Meteor.; Phys. BDOS BEOS CDZZ DNB6 ZZ12

SHAYN, Grigory A. (1892-1956) Astrophys. CDZZ ZZ12

SHCHELKIN, Kirill I. (1911-) Phys. SMST

SHCHERBAKOV, Dmitrii I. (1893-1966) Geol. SMST

SHEAR, Cornelius L. (1865-1956) Bot. NC48

SHEAR, Murray J. (1899-1983) Med. MFIR

SHEAR, Leslie (1880-1945) Archaeol. NC42

SHEARD, Charles (1883-1963) Biophys. NCSE

SHECUT, John L. (1770-1836) Bot. BIOD DAB

SHEDLOVSKY, Theodore (1898-1976) Chem. BM52

SHEEHAN, John C. (1915-) Chem. MHM2 MHSE

SHEEPSHANKS, Richard (1794-1855) Astron. DNB

SHELDON, Charles (1867-1928) Cons. LACC

SHELDON, John L. (1865-1947) Bot. MABH

SHELFORD, Victor E. (1877-1968) Ecol. LACC

SHEMIN, David (1911-) Biochem. ABES ABET BEOS MHM2 MHSE

SHEMYAKIN, Mikhail M. (1908-1970) Chem. MHM2 MHSE SMST

SHEN KUA (1031-1095) Polym. BEOS CDZZ GE-1 ZZ12

SHENSTONE, Allen G. (1893-1980) Phys. RS27

SHEPARD, Alan B. (1923-) Astronaut. CB61 FPSN IEAS MOS3 PMAS WESE

SHEPARD, Charles U. (1804-1886) Mineral. ASJD BIOD

SHEPARD, Francis P. (1897-) Geol. BEOS MHM2 MHSE

SHEPARD, James H. (1850-1918) Chem. BIOD DAB NC17

SHEPHERD, Antony (1721-1796) Astron. DNB

SHEPPARD, Percival A. (1907-1977) Meteor. RS25

SHEPPARD, Phillip M. (1921-1976) Genet. BEOS RS23

SHEPPARD, Samuel E. (1882-1948) Chem. ACCE DAB4 NC52

SHERARD, James (1666-1738) Bot. DNB

SHERARD, William (1659-1728) Bot. CDZZ DNB ZZ12

SHERMAN, Frank D. (1860-1916) Math. DAB

SHERMAN, Henry C. (1875-1955) Biochem. ABES ABET ACCE BEOS BM46 NC45

SHERMAN, James M. (1890-1956) Bact. NC47

SHERMAN, John (1613-1685) Math. BIOD DAB NC-7

SHERRARD, Thomas H. (1874-1941) Forest. LACC

SHERRILL, Mary L. (1888-1968) Chem. ACCE

SHERRINGTON, Charles S. (1857-1952) Med. ABES ABET BDOS BEOS BHMT CDZZ DNB7 ZZ12

SHERTS, J. Hervey (1892-1969) Chem. NC55

SHERWOOD, Thomas K. (1903-1976) Chem. Engr. HCEF MHM1 MHSE

SHEVYAKOV, Lev D. (1889-1963) Mng. SMST

SHIBUKAWA, Harumi (1639-1715) Astron. CDZZ ZZ12

SHIELDS, George O. (1846-1925) Cons. LACC

SHIH CHI (fl. 300 B.C.) Engr. GE-1

SHIH LU (fl. 220 B.C.) Engr. GE-1

SHILOV, Nikolay A. (1872-1930) Chem. CDZZ ZZ12

SHIMEK, Bohumil (1861-1937) Ecol. MABH

SHIMER, Edward B. (1888-) Metal. NCSF

SHIPLEY, Arthur E. (1861-1927) Zool. DNB4

SHIPLEY, Thomas (1861-1930) Engr. MCCW

SHIPPEN, William Jr. (1736-1808) Med. BHMT

SHIRAKATSI, Anania (c.620-c.685) Math.; Geog. CDZZ ZZ12

SHIRANE, Gen (1924-) Phys. MHSE

al-SHIRAZI SEE QUTB al-DIN al-SHIRAZI

SHIRKOV, Dmitrii V. (1928-) Phys. SMST

SHIRLEY, Hardy L. (1900-) Forest. LACC

SHIZUKI, Tadao (1760-1806) Nat. Philos. CDZZ ZZ12

SHKLOVSKII, Iosif S. (1916-) Astrophys. ABET

SHMALHAUZEN, Ivan I. (1884-1963) Biol. CDZZ ZZ12

SHNIRELMAN, Lev G. (1905-1938) Math. CDZZ ZZ12

SHOCKLEY, William B. (1910-) Phys. ABES ABET BEOS CB53 MHM1 MHSE MOS4 POSW PPNF TINA WAMB

SHOEMAKER, Carl D. (1872-1969) Cons. LACC

SHOEMAKER, Eugene M. (1928-) Geol. CB67

SHOENBERG, David (1911-) Phys. MHM2 MHSE

SHOHAT, James A. (1886-1944) Math. NC33

SHOKALSKY, Yuly M. (1856-1940) Ocean.; Geog. CDZZ ZZ12

SHOLES, Christopher (1819-1890) Invent. AMIH INYG MPIP SAIF WAMB

SHONLE, Horace A. (1892-1947) Chem. NC36

SHOPE, Richard E. (1901-1966) Med. BM50 CB63

SHORE, William T. (1840-1905) Geol. DNB2

SHORT, Charles W. (1794-1863) Bot. BIOD DAB

SHORT, James (1710-1768) Opt. CDZZ ZZ12

SHRAPNEL, Henry (1761-1842) Invent. BDOS DNB

SHREVE, Forrest (1878-1950) Bot. MABH NC40

SHREVE, R. Norris (1885-1975) Chem. Engr. NC58

SHTEINFELD, Ari A. (1905-1980) Rocket. AO80

SHTERN, Lina S. (1878-1968) Physiol. SMST

SHTOKMAN, Vladimir B. (1909-1968) Ocean. CDZZ ZZ12

SHUBNIKOV, Aleksei V. (1887-1970) Crystal. SMST

SHUFELDT, Robert W. (1850-1907) Biol.; Zool. NC-6

SHUIKIN, Nikolai I. (1898-1968) Chem. SMST

SHUJA ibn Aslam SEE ABU KAMIL, Shuja ibn Aslam

SHULAIKIN, Vasili V. (1895-) Geophys. SMST

SHULL, Aaron F. (1881-1961) Genet.; Evol. CDZZ ZZ12

SHULL, Clifford G. (1915-) Phys. BEOS MHM1 MHSE

SHULL, George H. (1874-1954) Bot.; Genet. DAB5 NCSA

SHULTZ, John E. (1914-1973) Engr.; Rocket. NC56

SHUMAN, Royal L. (1879-1957) Chem. NC46

SHUMARD, Benjamin F. (1820-1869) Geol.; Paleon. BIOD

SHUMWAY, Norman E. (1923-) Med. DNFH

SHUTTLEWORTH, Robert J. (1810-1874) Bot.; Conch. DNB

SIBLY, (Thomas) Franklin (1883-1948) Geol. DNB6

SIBTHROP, John (1758-1796) Bot. DNB

SIDGWICK, Nevil V. (1873-1952) Chem. ABES ABET BDOS BEOS CDZZ DNB7 GRCH HSSO ZZ12

SIEBOLD, Charlotte von (1761-1859) Med. WIWM

SIEBOLD, Karl T. von (1804-1885) Zool.; Parasit. ABET BEOS CDZZ ZZ12

SIEDENTOFF, Henry F. (1872-1940) Phys. CDZZ ZZ12

SIEDLECKI, Michael (1873-1940) Zool. CDZZ ZZ12

SIEGBAHN, Karl Manne (1886-1978) Phys. ABES ABET BEOS MHM2 MHSE POSW

SIEGEL, Carl L. (1896-1981) Math. AO81

SIEGEMUNDIN, Justine D. (1650-1705) Med. WIWM

SIEMENS, Charles W. (1823-1883) Invent. ABES ABET BDOS CDZZ DNB SAIF VTHB ZZ12

SIEMENS, Ernst W. von (1816-1892) Elec. Sci. BDOS CDZZ EETD FNEC VTHB ZZ12

SIEMENS, Friedrich (1826-1904) Invent. BDOS

SIEMENS, William SEE SIEMENS, Charles W.

SIERPINSKI, Waclaw (1882-1969) Math. CDZZ ZZ12

SIGAUD DE LAFOND, Joseph A. (1730-1810) Phys. CDZZ ZZ12

SIGER OF BRABANT (c.1240-1281/4) Philos. CDZZ ZZ12

SIGORGNE, Pierre (1719-1809) Phys. CDZZ ZZ12

SIGUENZA Y GONGORA, Carlos de (1645-1700) Math.; Astron. CDZZ ZZ12

al-SIJZI, Abu Said Ahmad (c.945-c.1020) Math.; Astron. CDZZ ZZ12

SIKORSKY, Igor I. (1889-1972) Aero. ICFW MHM1 MHSE SAIF TBTM WAMB

SILCOX, Ferdinand A. (1882-1939) Forest. EAFC

SILLIMAN, Benjamin (1779-1864) Chem.; Mineral. ABES ABET ACCE ASJD BDOS BEOS BIOD BM-1 CDZZ DAB GRCH HSSO WAMB ZZ12

SILLIMAN, Benjamin Jr. (1816-1885) Chem.; Geol. ACCE BIOD BM-7 CDZZ NC-2 WAMB ZZ12

SILVER, Arthur E. (1879-1975) Elec. Engr. NC58

SILVERMAN, Alexander (1881-1962) Chem. ACCE NC16 NCSD

SIM, G.A. (1929-) Chem. COBC

SIMER, Parke H. (1897-1972) Anat. NC56

SIMHA, Robert (1912-) Chem. MHSE

SIMMONS, Hexleton E. (1885-1954) Chem. ACCE

SIMMONS, James S. (1890-1954) Bact. DAB5

SIMMS, Denton H. (1912-) Cons. LACC

SIMON DE PHARES (c.1450-c.1500) Astrol. CDZZ ZZ12

SIMON, Francis E. (1893-1956) Phys. ABET BDOS BEOS CDZZ DNB7 RS-4 ZZ12

SIMON, John (1816-1904) Med. BHMT

SIMON, William (1844-1916) Chem. ACCE NC17

SIMONS, Howard P. (1907-1972) Chem. Engr. NC58

SIMONSEN, John L. (1884-1957) Chem. DNB7 RS-5

SIMPLICUS (c.500-c.534) Philos. CDZZ ZZ12

SIMPSON, Charles T. (1846-1932) Nat. Hist. DAB1 NC23

SIMPSON, George C. (1878-1965) Meteor. BDOS BEOS MMSB RS11

SIMPSON, George G. (1902-) Biol.; Paleon. BEOS CB64 MHM2 MHSE WAMB

SIMPSON, James Y. (1811-1870) Med. ABES ABET BDOS BEOS BHMT

SIMPSON, John W. (1914-) Engr. MHSE

SIMPSON, Joanne (1923-) Meteor. CWSN

SIMPSON, Maxwell (1815-1902) Chem. DNB2

SIMPSON, Nathaniel (1599-1642) Math. DNB

SIMPSON, Thomas (1710-1761) Math. CDZZ DNB
ZZ12

SIMS, James M. (1813-1883) Med. BHMT DSLP

SIMS, John (1749-1831) Bot. DNB

SIMSON, Robert (1687-1768) Math. CDZZ DNB
ZZ12

ibn SINA, Abu Ali SEE AVICENNA

SINAN ibn THABIT ibn QURRA, Abu Said (c.880-943)
Math.; Astron. CDZZ ZZ12

SINCLAIR, Andrew (d. 1861) Nat. Hist. DNB

SINGER, Isaac M. (1811-1875) Invent. ASIW BDOS
INYG WAMB

SINGER, S. Fred (1924-) Phys. CB55

SINK, M. Virginia (1913-) Engr. CB64

SINKFORD, Jeanne C. (1933-) Physiol.; Dent.
SBPY

SINNOTT, Edmund W. (1888-1968) Bot. CB48 MHM1
MHSE NCSH

SINNOTT, John A. (1884-1956) Med. RS-2

SINSHEIMER, Robert (1920-) Biophys. CB68

SIPLE, Paul A. (1908-) Biol. CB57 MASY

SIRI, William E. (1919-) Cons. LACC

SISAKYAN, Norair M. (1907-1966) Biochem. SMST

SITTER, Willem de (1872-1934) Astron. ABES ABET
BEOS CDZZ ZZ12

SITTERLY, Bancroft (1895-1977) Phys.; Astron.
NC59

SITTERLY, Charlotte M. (1898-) Astrophys. CB62

SKINNER, Aaron N. (1845-1918) Astron. DAB NC20

SKINNER, B(urrhus) F. (1904-) Psych. CB64 CB79
MFIR MHSE POPF

SKINNER, Henry (1861-1926) Entom. AMEM

SKOBELTSYN, Dmitrii V. (1892-) Phys. SMST

SKODA, Josef (1805-1881) Med. BEOS BHMT
CDZZ ZZ12

SKOLEM, Albert T. (1887-1963) Math. CDZZ ZZ12

SKOTTSBERG, Carl J. (1880-1963) Bot. RS10

SKRAUP, Zdenko H. (1850-1910) Chem. BDOS BEOS
CDZZ ZZ12

SKRYABIN, Konstantin I. (1878-1972) Biol. CDZZ
SMST ZZ12

SKUTCH, Alexander (1904-) Ornith.; Bot. DGMT

SLACK, Charles M. (1901-1970) Phys. NC56

SLATER, John C. (1900-1976) Phys. BM53 MHSE
QPAS

SLATER, Samuel (1768-1835) Invent. ASIW FOIF
GE-1 INYG WAMB YSMS

SLAUGHT, Herbert E. (1861-1937) Math. NC28

SLAVSON, Samuel R. (1891-) Med. MFIR

SLAYTER, Games (1896-1964) Invent. NC50

SLAYTON, Donald K. (1924-) Astronaut. CB76
IEAS PMAS WESE

SLICHTER, Charles P. (1924-) Phys. MHSE

SLICHTER, Louis B. (1896-1978) Geophys. MHM2
MHSE

SLINGERLAND, Mark V. (1864-1909) Entom. AMEM
NC13

SLIPHER, Earl C. (1883-1964) Astron. CDZZ ZZ12

SLIPHER, Vesto M. (1875-1969) Astron. ABES ABET
BEOS BM52 CDZZ IEAS WAMB ZZ12

SLOANE, Hans (1660-1753) Med. BHMT CDZZ
ZZ12

SLOSSON, Edwin E. (1865-1929) Chem. DAB NC32

SLUSE, Rene F. de (1622-1685) Math. CDZZ ZZ12

SLUTSKY, Evgeny E. (1880-1948) Math. CDZZ
ZZ12

SLYE, Maud C. (1869-1954) Med. NAWM

SLYKE, Donald van SEE VAN SLYKE, Donald D.

SMADEL, Joseph E. (1907-1963) Med. CB63

SMALE, Stephen (1930-) Math. MHSE MHM2

SMALL, John K. (1869-1938) Bot. MABH

SMALL, Lyndon F. (1897-1957) Chem. ACCE BM33
NC44

SMALLEY, Frank N. (1874-1921) Chem. NC19

SMALLWOOD, Charles (1812-1872) Meteor. DNB

SMALLWOOD, William M. (1873-1949) Zool. NC42

SMEATON, John (1724-1792) Engr. BDOS CDZZ
GE-1 ZZ12

SMEKAL, Adolf G. (1895-1959) Phys. CDZZ ZZ12

SMELLIE, William (1697-1763) Med. BEOS BHMT

SMIRNOV, Nikolai V. (1900-1966) Math. SMST

SMIRNOV, Vasili I. (1899-) Metal. SMST

SMIRNOV, Vasili S. (1915-) Metal. SMST

SMIRNOV, Vladimir I. (1899-) Math. SMST

SMIRNOV, Vladimir I. (1910-) Geol. MHM2 MHSE
SMST

SMITH, Albert W. (1862-1927) Chem. NC24

SMITH, Alexander (1865-1927) Chem. NC24

SMITH, Anthony W. (1906-) Cons. LACC

SMITH, Burnett (1877-1958) Geol. NC47

SMITH, Cyril S. (1903-) Metal. MHM2 MHSE

SMITH, Daniel B. (1792-1883) Chem. ACCE

SMITH, Edgar F. (1854-1928) Chem. ACCE BM17
CDZZ DAB GRCH HSSO NC13 ZZ12

SMITH, Edward (1818-1874) Med. CDZZ ZZ12

SMITH, Edward S. (1894-1971) Geol. NC57

SMITH, Erminnie P. (1836-1886) Geol.; Anthro.
BIOD POAA

SMITH, Ernest L. (1904-) Chem. COBC

SMITH, Erwin F. (1854-1927) Bot.; Bact. BM21
CDZZ DAB MABH ZZ12

SMITH, Franklin (1857-1942) Zool. NC31

SMITH, Gilbert M. (1885-1959) Bot. BM36 NC47

SMITH, Glen A. (1880-1958) Cons. LACC

SMITH, Grafton E. SEE ELLIOT SMITH, Grafton

SMITH, Hamilton L. (1818-1903) Astron.; Micros.
BIOD NC12

SMITH, Hamilton O. (1931-) Bact.; Genet. ABET
BEOS MHSE SOT2

SMITH, Harry L. (1894-1975) Phys. NC58

SMITH, Harry S. (1883-1957) Entom. AMEM NC46

SMITH, Herbert A. (1866-1944) Forest. LACC

SMITH, Herbert D. (1894-1959) Entom. NC48

SMITH, Homer W. (1895-1962) Physiol.; Evol. BM39
CDZZ ZZ12

SMITH, James (1740-1812) Chem. ACCE

SMITH, James E. (1759-1828) Bot. ANHD CDZZ
DNB ZZ12

SMITH, James H. (1829-1901) Math. DNB2

SMITH, James P. (1864-1931) Paleon.; Geol. BM38
DAB

SMITH, John B. (1858-1912) Entom. AMEM DAB
NC15

SMITH, John B. (1894-1976) Chem. NC61

SMITH, John L. (1818-1883) Chem.; Mineral. ACCE
ASJD BIOD BM-2 DAB NC-6

SMITH, Kenneth M. (1892-1981) Virol. RS28

SMITH, LeRoy H. (1897-1954) Chem. NC44

SMITH, Lincoln G. (1912-1972) Phys. NC58

SMITH, Lloyd P. (1903-) Phys. NCSI

SMITH, Nathan (1762-1829) Med. BHMT

SMITH, Philip E. (1884-1970) Anat.; Med. ABET CDZZ ZZ12

SMITH, Robert (1689-1768) Phys. CDZZ DNB ZZ12

SMITH, Robert A. (1817-1884) Chem. CDZZ DNB ZZ12

SMITH, Robert A. (1909-1980) Phys. AO80 RS28

SMITH, Sidney I. (1843-1926) Zool. BM14 CDZZ ZZ12

SMITH, Theobald (1859-1934) Microbiol. ABET BDOS BEOS BHMT BM17 CDZZ DAB1 WAMB ZZ12

SMITH, Thomas (1883-1969) Phys. RS17

SMITH, Thomas P. (c.1776-1802) Chem. ACCE

SMITH, Warren D. (1880-1950) Geol. NC41

SMITH, William (1769-1939) Geol. ABET BEOS CDZZ DNB GE-1 HLSM LISD NC41 ZZ12

SMITH, William A. (1878-1933) Chem. ACCE

SMITH, William W. (1875-1956) Bot. RS-3

SMITH, Wilson (1897-1965) Microbiol. CDZZ RS12 ZZ12

SMITHELS, Arthur (1860-1939) Chem. CDZZ DNB5 ZZ12

SMITHSON, James (1765-1829) Chem. BDOS BEOS CDZZ ZZ12

SMITS, Andreas (1870-1948) Chem. CDZZ ZZ12

SMOLLETT, Tobias (1721-1771) Med. BHMT

SMOLUCHOWSKI, Marian (1872-1917) Phys. CDZZ ZZ12

SMYTH, Charles P. (1819-1900) Astron. CDZZ DNB1 MCCW ZZ12

SMYTH, Charles P. (1895-) Chem. MHM2 MHSE

SMYTH, David H. (1908-1979) Physiol. RD27

SMYTH, Warington W. (1817-1890) Geol.; Mineral. DNB

SMYTH, William (1797-1868) Math. BIOD

SNEL, Willebrord (1580-1626) Math. ABES ABET BDOS BEOS CDZZ DCPW ZZ12

SNELL, Ebenezer S. (1801-1876) Math.; Phys. BIOD

SNELL, Esmond E. (1914-) Biochem. MHM2 MHSE

SNELL, Foster D. (1898-1980) Chem. CB43

SNELL, George D. (1903-) Genet. ABET BEOS MHSE

SNELL, John F. (1869-1938) Elec. Engr. DNB5 MMSB

SNELL VAN ROYEN, Willebrord SEE SNEL, Willebrord

SNELUS, George J. (1837-1906) Metal. DNB2

SNIESZKO, Stanislas (1902-) Biol. LACC

SNODGRASS, Robert E. (1875-1962) Entom. AMEM NC49

SNOW, Charles P. (1905-1980) Phys. AO80 CB61

SNOW, Francis H. (1850-1908) Entom. AMEM DAB

SNOW, George R. (1897-1969) Bot. RS16

SNOW, Harold R. (1895-1957) Chem. NC46

SNOW, John (1813-1858) Med. ABET BEOS BHMT CDZZ ZZ12

SNYDER, Solomon H. (1938-) Pharm. BEOS

SNYDER, Thomas E. (1885-1970) Entom. NC56

SOBOLEV, Sergei L. (1908-) Math.; Phys. SMST

SOBOLEV, Victor V. (1915-) Astron. SMST

SOBOLEV, Vladimir S. (1908-) Geol.; Mineral. MHM2 MHSE SMST

SOBRERO, Ascanio (1812-1888) Chem. ABES ABET BDOS BEOS

SODERBERG, C. Richard (1895-1979) Engr. CB58 NC61

SODDY, Frederick (1877-1956) Chem. ABES ABET BDOS BEOS CDZZ DNB7 GRCH HSSO MWBR NPWC ZZ12

SOEMMERING, Samuel T. von (1755-1830) Anat. CDZZ WFBG ZZ12

SOHNCKE, Leonhard (1842-1897) Crystal.; Phys. CDZZ ZZ12

SOKHOTSKY, Yulian K. (1842-1927) Math. CDZZ ZZ12

SOKOLOFF, Louis (1921-) Physiol. BEOS

SOKOLOV, Boris S. (1914-) Geol.; Paleon. SMST

SOKOLOV, Dmitry I. (1788-1852) Geol. CDZZ ZZ12

SOLANDER, Daniel C. (1736-1782) Nat. Hist. ANHD CDZZ DNB ZZ12

SOLANDT, Omond M. (1909-) Med. CB74

SOLDANI, Ambrogio (1736-1808) Geol. CDZZ ZZ12

SOLDNER, Johann G. von (1776-1833) Astron. CDZZ ZZ12

SOLE, William (1741-1802) Bot. DNB

SOLEIL, Jean B. (1798-1878) Instr. CDZZ ZZ12

SOLLAS, William J. (1849-1936) Geol.; Paleon. CDZZ DNB5 ZZ12

SOLLY, Edward (1819-1886) Chem. DNB

SOLMS-LAUBACH, Hermann G. (1842-1915) Bot.; Paleon. FHUA

SOLVAY, Ernest (1838-1922) Chem. ABES ABET BDOS BEOS CDZZ GRCH ZZ12

SOMERVILLE, Mary F. (1780-1872) Math. BEOS CDZZ DNB IDWB MEQP WIMO ZZ12

SOMMER, Hugo H. (1896-1953) Dairy Sci. NC42

SOMMERFELD, Arnold J. (1868-1951) Phys. ABES ABET BDOS BEOS CB50 CDZZ HSSO ZZ12

SOMMERING, Samuel SEE SOEMMERING, Samuel T. von

SOMMERVILLE, Duncan M. (1879-1934) Math. CDZZ ZZ12

SOMMERVILLE, Mary SEE SOMERVILLE, Mary F.

SOMOV, Osip I. (1815-1876) Math. CDZZ ZZ12

SONDHEIMER, Franz (1926-1981) Chem. AO81 BEOS COBC MHSE RS28

SONES, F. Mason (1919-) Med. MFIR

SONIN, Nikolay Y. (1849-1915) Math. CDZZ ZZ12

SONNEBORN, Tracy M. (1905-1981) Genet. BEOS MHM1 MHSE RS28

SONNERAT, Pierre (1748-1814) Nat. Hist. CDZZ ZZ12

SOPER, J. Dewey (1893-) Nat. Hist. DGMT

SORANUS OF EPHESUS (fl. 100s) Med. CDZZ ZZ12

SORBY, Henry C. (1826-1908) Geol.; Biol. BDOS BEOS CDZZ DNB2 ZZ12

SORENSEN, Soren P. (1868-1939) Chem. ABES ABET BDOS BEOS CDZZ HSSO ZZ12

SOSIGENES (fl. c.50 B.C.) Astron. ABES ABET BDOS BEOS CDZZ ZZ12

SOSKE, Joshua L. (1903-1966) Geophys. NC53

SOTCHAVA, Viktor B. (1905-) Bot. SMST

SOTO, Domingo de (c.1494-1560) Nat. Philos. CDZZ ZZ12

SOUFFLOT, Jacques G. (1713-1780) Engr. BDOS

SOULAVIE, Jean L. (1752-1813) Geol. BMST CDZZ ZZ12

SOULE, George (1834-1926) Math. DAB

SOULEYET, Louis F. (1811-1852) Zool. CDZZ ZZ12

SOUPART, Pierre (1923-1981) Physiol. AO81

SOUTH, James (1785-1867) Astron. CDZZ DNB ZZ12

SOUTHALL, James P. (1871-1962) Phys. NC50

SOUTHAM, Chester M. (1919-) Med. SCLB

SOUTHWELL, Thomas (1831-1909) Nat. Hist. DNB2

SOUTHWORTH, George C. (1890-1972) Phys. TPAE

SOWERBY, George B. (1788-1854) Conch. DNB

SOWERBY, James (1757-1822) Nat. Hist.; Geol. CDZZ DNB PHLS ZZ12

SOWERBY, James (1787-1871) Nat. Hist. DNB

SPALDING, Volney M. (1849-1918) Bot. DAB MABH

SPALLANZANI, Lazzaro (1729-1799) Biol. ABES ABET BDOS BEOS BHMT BMST CCSW CDZZ HLSM ZZ12

SPARKS, William J. (1904-1976) Chem. NC59

SPARRE, Fin (1879-1944) Chem. NC33

SPATH, Ernst (1886-1946) Chem. GRCH

SPATH, Leonhard F. (1882-1957) Paleon. RS-3

SPEDDING, Frank H. (1902-) Chem. ABES ABET BEOS MHM2 MHSE

SPEED, Carleton D. (1903-1970) Geol. NC55

SPEMANN, Hans (1869-1941) Zool. ABES ABET BDOS BEOS CDZZ HLSM ZZ12

SPENCE, David (1881-1957) Chem. ACCE NC46

SPENCE, Kenneth W. (1907-1967) Psych. MHM1 MHSE

SPENCE, Peter (1806-1883) Chem. BEOS

SPENCE, Robert (1905-1976) Chem. COBC RS23

SPENCER, Donald C. (1912-) Math. MHM1 MHSE

SPENCER, George J. (1888-1966) Entom. AMEM

SPENCER, Guilford L. (1858-1925) Chem. ACCE

SPENCER, Herbert (1820-1903) Biol.; Psych. ABES ABET BDOS BEOS CDZZ DARR ZZ12

SPENCER, Leonard J. (1870-1959) Mineral. CDZZ DNB7 RS-7 ZZ12

SPENCER, Walter B. (1860-1929) Biol. DNB4

SPENCER, William G. (1790-1866) Math. DNB

SPENCER, William K. (1878-1955) Paleon. RS-2

SPENCER JONES, Harold SEE JONES, Harold S.

SPERANSKII, Georgi N. (1873-1969) Med. SMST

SPERR, Frederick W. (1885-) Chem. NCSA

SPERRY, Elmer A. (1860-1930) Invent. ABES ABET BDOS BEOS BM28 CDZZ ICFW MASY WAMB ZZ12

SPERRY, Roger W. (1913-) Med. BEOS MHM2 MHSE

SPERTI, George S. (1900-) Elec. Engr. CB40

SPEUSIPPUS (c.408 B.C.-339 B.C.) Philos. CDZZ ZZ12

SPHUJIDHVAJA (fl. 269) Astrol. CDZZ ZZ12

SPIEGEL, Adriaan van den (1578-1625) Bot.; Anat. CDZZ ZZ12

SPIEGELMAN, Sol (1914-) Biol. BEOS CB80

SPIELMAN, Marvin A. (1906-1957) Chem. NC46

SPILHAUS, Athelston (1911-) Meteor.; Ocean. CB65

SPILLMAN, William J. (1863-1931) Agr.; Math. DAB

SPILSBURY, Bernard H. (1877-1947) Forens. Sci. DNB6

SPINDEN, Herbert J. (1879-1967) Archaeol. PAMB

SPITSYN, Viktor T. (1902-) Chem. SMST

SPITZ, Armand N. (1904-1971) Astron. NC56

SPITZER, Lyman Jr. (1914-) Astrophys. ABES ABET BEOS CB60 MHM1 MHSE

SPIX, Johann B. von (1781-1826) Zool. CDZZ ZZ12

SPOEHR, Herman A. (1885-1954) Chem. NC43

SPOERER, Gustav F. (1822-1895) Astron. BDOS BEOS CDZZ ZZ12

SPORN, Philip (1896-) Engr. CB66 TPAE

SPORUS OF NICEA (fl. c.250-300) Math. CDZZ ZZ12

SPOTTISWOODE, William (1825-1883) Math.; Phys. DNB

SPRAGUE, Frank J. (1857-1934) Engr. DAB1 TPAE WAMB

SPRAGUE, George F. (1902-) Genet. MHSE

SPRAT, Thomas (1635-1713) Sci. Hist. CDZZ ZZ12

SPRENGEL, Christian K. (1750-1816) Bot. ABET CDZZ ZZ12

SPRENGEL, Hermann J. (1834-1906) Invent. BDOS DNB2

SPRENGEL, Kurt P. (1766-1833) Bot. CDZZ ZZ12

SPRING, Frank S. (1907-) Chem. COBC

SPRING, Walthere V. (1848-1911) Chem.; Phys. CDZZ ZZ12

SPRINGER, Frank (1848-1927) Paleon. DAB

SPRINGWALL, Harold D. (1910-) Chem. COBC

SPRUCE, Richard (1817-1893) Bot. CDZZ DNB ZZ12

SPRUNG, Adolf F. (1848-1909) Meteor. CDZZ ZZ12

SPRUNT, Alexander J. (1898-1973) Ornith. DGMT

SPURR, Stephen H. (1918-) Forest. LACC

SPURZHEIM, Johann C. (1776-1832) Psychiat. CDZZ ZZ12

SQUIBB, Edward R. (1819-1900) Chem.; Pharm. BIOD COAC DAB NC19

SQUIER, George O. (1865-1934) Elec. Engr. BM20 DAB NC24 TPAE

SQUIRE, Herbert B. (1909-1961) Phys. RS-8

SRETENSKII, Leonid N. (1902-) Math. SMST

SRIDHARA (fl. 800s) Math. CDZZ ZZ12

SRIPATI (fl. 1039-1056) Astron.; Math. CDZZ ZZ12

ST. SEE SAINT

STACEY, Maurice (1907-) Chem. COBC

STACK, John (1906-1976) Aero. ICFW

STACKEL, Paul G. (1862-1919) Math. CDZZ ZZ12

STACKHOUSE, John (1742-1819) Bot. DNB

STADLER, Lewis J. (1896-1954) Genet. BM30 NC45

STAFFORD, Thomas P. (1930-) Astronaut. CB77 IEAS

STAHL, Franklin W. (1910-) Biol. BEOS

STAHL, Georg E. (1660-1734) chem. ABES ABET BDOS BEOS BHMT BMST CDZZ HLSM ZZ12

STAHR, Elvis J. (1916-) Cons. LACC

STAINTON, Henry T. (1822-1892) Entom. DNB

STAKMAN, Elvin C. (1885-1979) Agr.; Bot. CB49

STALLO, Johann B. (1823-1900) Philos. of Sci. BIOD CDZZ DAB ZZ12

STAMLER, Jeremiah (1919-) Med. SCLB

STAMPIOEN, Jan J. (1610-1689) Math. CDZZ ZZ12

STANHOPE, Charles (1753-1816) Invent. GE-1

STANIER, Roger Y. (1916-) Biol. MHM2 MHSE

STANIER, William A. (1876-1965) Engr. RS12

STANLEY, Francis E. (1849-1918) Invent. BDOS WAMB

STANLEY, Freelan (1849-1940) Invent. WAMB

STANLEY, Herbert M. (1903-) Chem. COBC

STANLEY, Wendell M. (1904-1971) Biochem. ABES ABET ACCE BEOS CB47 FMBB MHM1 MHSE NC57 NCSG NPWC PGFS TMSB WAMB

STANLEY, William (1858-1916) Engr. TPAE

STANLEY, William F. (1829-1909) Instr. DNB2

STANNER, William C. (1905-1981) Anthro. AO81

STANNIUS, Hermann F. (1808-1883) Anat.; Physiol. CDZZ ZZ12

STANTON, Thomas E. (1865-1931) Engr. CDZZ ZZ12

STANTON, Timothy W. (1860-1953) Geol. NC40

STAPLEDON, Reginald G. (1882-1960) Agr. RS-7

STAPP, John P. (1910-) Med. CB59

STARIK, Josif E. (1902-1964) Chem. SMST

STARK, Johannes (1874-1957) Phys. ABET BDOS
BEOS CDZZ POSW SUHB ZZ12

STARKEY, George (1627-1665) Chem. ACCE CDZZ
ZZ12

STARKS, Edwin C. (1867-1932) Zool. DAB1 NC24

STARLING, Ernest H. (1866-1927) Physiol. ABES
ABET BDOS BEOS BHMT CDZZ DNB4 ZZ12

STARR, Chauncey (1912-) Phys. CB54 MHM1
MHSE

STARR, Victor P. (1909-1976) Meteor. MHM2 MHSE

STAS, Jean S. (1813-1891) Chem. ABES ABET
BDOS BEOS CDZZ ZZ12

STASZIC, Stanislaw W. (1755-1826) Geol. CDZZ
ZZXV

STATZ, Hermann (1928-) Phys. CB58

STAUDINGER, Hermann (1881-1965) Chem. ABES
ABET BDOS BEOS CB54 CDZZ HSSO MHM1
MHSE ZZ13

STAUDT, Karl G. von (1798-1867) Math. CDZZ ZZ13

STEACIE, Edgar W. (1900-1962) Chem. CB53 CDZZ
RS10 ZZ13

STEAD, John E. (1851-1923) Metal.; Chem. CDZZ
ZZ13

STEARNS, Joyce C. (1893-1948) Phys. NC37

STEARNS, Robert E. (1827-1909) Zool.; Paleon.
DAB

STEBBING, Thomas R. (1835-1926) Zool. CDZZ
ZZ13

STEBBINS, George L. (1906-) Bot. BEOS MHM2
MHSE

STEBBINS, James H. Jr. (1857-1932) Chem. ACCE

STEBBINS, Joel (1878-1966) Astron. BM49

STECHKIN, Boris S. (1891-1969) Aero. SMST

STECKBECK, Walter (1880-1956) Bot. NC47

STEDMAN, Edgar (1890-1975) Biochem. RS22

STEDMAN, John M. (1864-1949) Entom. NC41

STEELE, Joel D. (1836-1886) Sci. Writ. ACCE BIOD

STEELL, Graham (1851-1942) Med. BHMT

STEENBOCK, Harry (1886-1953) Biochem. NCSF

STEENSEN, Niels SEE STENO, Nicolaus

STEENSTRUP, Johannes J. (1813-1897) Zool. BDOS
BEOS CDZZ ZZ13

STEFAN, Josef (1835-1893) Phys. ABES ABET
BDOS BEOS CDZZ ZZ13

STEIN, Earl R. (1886-1957) Chem. Engr. NC48

STEIN, Johan W. (1871-1951) Astron. CDZZ ZZ13

STEIN, Richard S. (1925-) Chem. MHSE

STEIN, William H. (1911-1980) Biochem. ABET AO80
BEOS MHSE

STEINER, Jakob (1796-1863) Math. CDZZ ZZ13

STEINER, Lewis H. (1827-1892) Chem. ACCE

STEINHAUS, Edward A. (1914-1968) Microbiol. BM44
CB55

STEINHEIL, Karl A. (1801-1870) Phys.; Astron. CDZZ
ZZ13

STEINITZ, Ernst (1871-1928) Math. CDZZ ZZ13

STEINMAN, David B. (1886-1960) Engr. MHM1
MHSE WAMB

STEINMETZ, Charles P. (1865-1923) Elec. Engr.
ABES ABET CDZZ DAB EETD NC23 TPAE
WAMB ZZ13

STEJNEGER, Leonhard H. (1851-1943) Nat. Hist.
BM24 CDZZ DAB3 NC14 ZZ13

STEKEL, Wilhelm (1868-1940) Psych. PAW3

STEKLOV, Vladimir A. (1864-1926) Math. CDZZ ZZ13

STELLER, Georg W. (1709-1746) Nat. Hist. CDZZ WFBG ZZ13

STELLUTI, Francesco (1577-1652) Micros. ANHD CDZZ ZZ13

STENHOUSE, John (1809-1880) Chem. DNB

STENO, Nicolaus (1638-1686) Anat.; Geol. ABES ABET BDOS BEOS BHMT BMST CDZZ FHUA HLSM ZZ13

STENSEN, Niels SEE STENO, Nicolaus

STEPANOV, Vyacheslav V. (1889-1950) Math. CDZZ ZZ13

STEPHAN, Edouard J. (1837-1923) Astron. CDZZ ZZ13

STEPHANUS OF ALEXANDRIA (fl. c.600-650) Math.; Alch. CDZZ ZZ13

STEPHEN OF ANTIOCH (fl. c.1100-1150) Trans. Sci. Lit. CDZZ ZZ13

STEPHENS, Edwin S. (1881-1948) Cons. LACC

STEPHENS, James F. (1792-1852) Entom. DNB

STEPHENSON, George (1781-1848) Engr. ABES ABET BDOS BEOS FNEC GE-1 SAIF

STEPHENSON, Marjory (1885-1948) Biochem. DNB6

STEPHENSON, Robert (1803-1859) Engr. BDOS

STEPHENSON, Thomas A. (1898-1961) Zool. RS-8

STEPLING, Joseph (1716-1778) Astron.; Phys. CDZZ ZZ13

STEPTOE, Patrick C. (1913-) Med. CB79 DNFH

STERN, Curt (1902-1981) Genet. AO81 BEOS MHM1 MHSE

STERN, Otto (1888-1969) Phys. ABES ABET BEOS BM43 CDZZ MHM1 MHSE POSW WAMB ZZ13

STERNBERG, George M. (1838-1915) Med. BHMT HIUE WAMB

STERNBERG, Kaspar M. von (1761-1838) Bot.; Paleon. CDZZ FHUA PHLS ZZ13

STERNBERG, Pavel K. (1865-1920) Astron. CDZZ ZZ13

STETSON, Henry C. (1900-1955) Geol. DAB5

STEVENS, Edward (1755-1834) Med. CDZZ ZZ13

STEVENS, John (1749-1838) Invent. AMIH FOIF GE-1 INYG TINA WAMB

STEVENS, Nettie M. (1861-1912) Biol.; Genet. IDWB NAW RPTC

STEVENS, Robert L. (1787-1856) Invent. AMIH GE-1 INYG WAMB

STEVENS, Stanley S. (1906-1973) Physiol. BM47 MHM1 MHSE

STEVENS, Thomas S. (1900-) Chem. COBC

STEVENSON, Matilda E. (1850-1915) Anthro. POAA

STEVENSON, Thomas (1818-1887) Engr.; Meteor. DNB

STEVENSON, Thomas (1838-1908) Toxicol. DNB2

STEVER, Horton G. (1916-) Phys. CB81 MHM1 MHSE

STEVIN, Simon (1548-1620) Math. ABES ABET BDOS BEOS BMST CDZZ GE-1 LSHS SXWS ZZ13

STEWARD, Frederick C. (1904-) Bot. MHM2 MHSE

STEWART, Andrew (1867-1942) Chem. NC30

STEWART, Balfour (1828-1887) Phys. ABES ABET BEOS CDZZ DNB ZZ13

STEWART, Charles (1840-1907) Anat. DNB2

STEWART, David (1813-1899) Chem. ACCE

STEWART, Frederick H. (1916-) Geol. MHM2 MHSE SIWG

STEWART, George N. (1860-1930) Physiol. CDZZ ZZ13

STEWART, George W. (1876-1956) Phys. BM32

STEWART, Harris B. (1922-) Ocean. CB68

STEWART, Margaret (1927-) Herp. WAWL

STEWART, Matthew (1717-1785) Math.; Astron. CDZZ ZZ13

STEWART, Norman H. (1885-1970) Biol. NC55

STEWART, Thomas D. (1890-1955) Chem. NC47

STEWART, Thomas O. (1901-) Anthro. MHM2 MHSE

STIEGLITZ, Julius O. (1867-1937) Chem. ACCE BM21 DAB2 NC15 NC27

STIELTJES, Thomas J. (1856-1894) Math. CDZZ ZZ13

STIFEL, Michael (c.1487-1567) Math. BMST CDZZ ZZ13

STILES, Charles W. (1867-1941) Zool. CDZZ DAB3 NCSD ZZ13

STILES, George W. (1877-1970) Bact. NC57

STILES, Karl A. (1895-1968) Zool. NC54

STILES, Walter (1886-1966) Bot. RS13

STILL, George F. (1868-1941) Med. BHMT

STILLE, Alfred (1813-1900) Med. BHMT

STILLE, Wilhelm H. (1876-1966) Geol. CDZZ ZZ13

STILLINGFLEET, Benjamin (1702-1771) Nat. Hist. DNB

STILLMAN, John M. (1852-1923) Chem. ACCE NC20

STILLMAN, Thomas B. (1852-1915) Chem. Engr. ACCE DAB

STILLWELL, Lewis B. (1863-1941) Elec. Engr. BM34

STIMPSON, William (1832-1872) Mar. Biol. BIOD BM-8 CDZZ DAB ZZ13

STINE, Charles M. (1882-1954) Chem. Engr. ACCE CB40 CDZZ DAB5 NC47 NCSE ZZ13

STIRLING, James (1692-1779) Math. CDZZ DNB ZZ13

STIRLING, Matthew W. (1896-1975) Anthro. NC58

STIRLING, Robert (1790-1878) Invent. FNEC

STOCK, Alfred (1876-1946) Chem. ABES ABET BEOS CDZZ GRCH ZZ13

STOCK, Chester (1892-1950) Biochem.; Paleon. BM27 CDZZ NCSJ ZZ13

STOCKARD, Charles R. (1879-1939) Biol. DAB2 NC30

STOCKDALE, Paris B. (1896-1962) Geol. NC52

STODDARD, Herbert L. (1889-1970) Ornith. DGMT LACC

STODDARD, John F. (1825-1873) Math. BIOD

STODDARD, John T. (1852-1919) Chem. ACCE DAB

STODOLA, Aurel B. (1859-1942) Engr. CDZZ ZZ13

STOKER, James J. (1905-) Math. MHM2 MHSE

STOKES, Adrian (1887-1927) Bact. BEOS

STOKES, George G. (1819-1903) Math.; Phys. ABES ABET BDOS BEOS CDZZ FNEC ZZ13

STOKES, Rufus (1924-) Invent. BCST

STOKES, William (1804-1878) Med. BHMT

STOLETOV, Aleksandr G. (1839-1896) Phys. CDZZ ZZ13

STOLL, Arthur (1887-1971) Chem. RS18

STOLZ, Otto (1842-1905) Math. CDZZ ZZ13

STOMMEL, Henry M. (1920-) Ocean. MHSE

STONE, Constance (1856-1902) Med. IDWB

STONE, Edward J. (1831-1897) Astron. AROW DNB

STONE, Francis G. (1925-) Chem. COBC

STONE, Marshall H. (1903-) Math. MHM2 MHSE

STONE, Ormond (1847-1933) Astron. DAB1 NC-6

STONE, Wilson S. (1907-1968) Genet. BM52

STONE, Witmer (1866-1939) Nat. Hist. DAB2

STONELEY, Robert (1894-1976) Seism. RS22

STONER, Edmund C. (1899-1968) Phys. MHM2 MHSE RS15

STONEY, George J. (1826-1911) Phys. ABES ABET BDOS BEOS CDZZ DNB2 ZZ13

STOPES, Marie C. (1880-1958) Bot. FHUA

STOPFORD, John S. (1888-1961) Anat. RS-7

STORER, David H. (1804-1891) Ichth. ASJD DAB BIOD

STORER, Francis H. (1832-1914) Chem. ACCE DAB NC11

STORER, John H. Jr. (1888-1976) Cons. NC58 NC59

STOREY, Harold H. (1894-1969) Agr. RS15

STORMER, Frederick C. (1874-1957) Math. CDZZ RS-4 ZZ13

STORMS, Harrison A. (1915-) Aero. CB63 MOS4

STORY, Richard H. (1910-) Astron. AROW

STORY, William E. (1850-1930) Math. DAB NC24

STOTT, Louis L. (1906-1964) Invent. NC51

STOUGHTON, Bradley (1873-1959) Chem. ACCE

STOUT, Gilbert L. (1898-1963) Bot. NC51

STRABO (63 B.C.-A.D. 25) Geog. ABES ABET BEOS CDZZ ZZ13

STRACHEY, John (1671-1743) Geol. CDZZ ZZ13

STRACHEY, William (fl. 1609-1618) Ornith. HAOA

STRAHL, William E. (1919-1974) Chem. Engr. NC58

STRAKHOV, Nikolai M. (1900-) Geol. SMST

STRANGE, Alexander (1818-1876) Astron. SOSC

STRASBURGER, Eduard A. (1844-1912) Bot. ABES ABET BDOS BEOS CDZZ ZZ13

STRASSMANN, Fritz (1902-) Chem. ABES ABET BEOS MHM2 MHSE

STRATO OF LAMPSACUS (c.340 B.C.-c.270 B.C.) ABES ABET BEOS CDZZ HLSM ZZ13

STRATTON, Frederick J. (1881-1960) Astron. CDZZ DNB7 RS-7 ZZ13

STRATTON, George M. (1865-1957) Psych. BM35

STRATTON, Julius A. (1901-) Elec. Engr. CB63

STRATTON, Samuel W. (1861-1931) Phys.; Elec. Engr. BM17 WAMB

STRATTON-PORTER, Gene (1863-1924) Nat. Hist. SFNB

STRAUS, William L. (1900-) Anat.; Anthro. MHM2 MHSE

STRECKER, Ferdinand H. (1836-1901) Entom. AMEM BIOD

STREETE, Thomas (1622-1689) Astron. CDZZ ZZ13

STREETER, George L. (1873-1948) Anat.; Embryol. BM28 CDZZ NC37 ZZ13

STRELETSKII, Nikolai S. (1885-1967) Engr. SMST

STRELKOV, Petr G. (1899-1968) Phys. SMST

STRETCH, Richard H. (1837-1926) Entom. AMEM

STRICKLAND, Hugh E. (1811-1853) Nat. Hist. DNB

STRIEBY, Maurice E. (1893-1975) Invent. TPAE

STRINGFELLOW, John (1799-1883) Aero. GE-1 ICFW

STRINGHAM, Washington I. (1847-1909) Math. DAB

STRODE, Thomas (fl. 1642-1688) Math. DNB

STROHMEYER, Friedrich (1776-1835) Chem. ABES ABET BEOS

STROMBERG, Gustaf B. (1882-1962) Astron. CDZZ ZZ13

STROMGREN, Bengt G. (1908-) Astron. BEOS MHM1 MHSE

STROMGREN, Svante E. (1870-1947) Astron. CDZZ ZZ13

STROMINGER, Jack L. (1925-) Biochem. MHSE

STRONG, Harriet W. (1844-1929) Agr. NAW

STRONG, Lee A. (1886-1941) Entom. NC33

STRONG, Richard P. (1872-1948) Biol. NCSA

STRONG, Theodore (1790-1869) Math. ASJD BIOD
BM-2 DAB NC-9

STRONG, William W. (1883-1955) Phys. NCSE

STROUD, Richard H. (1918-) Cons. LACC

STROWD, Wallace H. (1889-1946) Chem. NC34

STROWGER, Almon B. (1839-1902) Invent. EETD

STRUGHOLD, Hubertus (1898-) Med. CB66 ICFW
MOS4

STRUMINSKII, Vladimir V. (1914-) Engr. SMST

STRUMPELL, Adolph von (1853-1925) Med. BHMT

STRUSS, Jozef (1510-1568) Med. CDZZ ZZ13

STRUTHERS, John (1823-1899) Anat. DNB1

STRUTHERS, Parke H. (1891-) Zool. NCSD

STRUTT, John W., Lord Rayleigh (1842-1919) Phys.
ABES ABET BDOS BEOS CAVL CDZZ DNB3
FNEC POSW STYC ZZ13

STRUTT, Robert J. (1875-1947) Phys. CDZZ DNB6
ZZ13

STRUVE, Friedrich G. von (1793-1864) Astron.
ABES ABET BDOS BEOS CDZZ IEAS ZZ13

STRUVE, George O. (1886-1933) Astron. CDZZ
IEAS ZZ13

STRUVE, Gustav W. (1858-1920) Astron. CDZZ
ZZ13

STRUVE, Karl H. (1854-1920) Astron. CDZZ IEAS
ZZ13

STRUVE, Otto (1897-1963) Astron. ABES ABET
BEOS CB49 CDZZ MHM1 MHSE PBTS RS10
WAMB ZZ13

STRUVE, Otto W. (1819-1905) Astron. CDZZ IEAS
ZZ13

STRYER, Lubert (1938-) Biol. MHSE

STUART, Alexander (1673-1742) Physiol. CDZZ
ZZ13

STUART, Charles A. (1893-1962) Bact. NC52

STUART, Miranda (c.1795-1865) Med. IDWB WIWM

STUART, Robert Y. (1883-1933) Forest. EAFC
LACC

STUBBLEFIELD, Nathan B. (1859-1928) Invent. EETD

STUBBS, William C. (1843-1924) Agr. NC24

STUCKY, Charles J. (1896-1938) Biochem. NC29

STUDER, Bernhard (1794-1887) Geol. CDZZ ZZ13

STUDY, Eduard (1862-1930) Math. CDZZ ZZ13

STUHLINGER, Ernst (1913-) Phys.; Astronaut.
CB57 ICFW

STULL, Wilfred (1877-1937) Chem. NC29

STUMM, Erwin C. (1908-1969) Geol. NC54

STURGEON, William (1783-1850) Phys. ABES ABET
BDOS BEOS CDZZ DNB EETD GE-1 ZZ13

STURM, Charles F. (1803-1855) Math.; Phys. CDZZ
ZZ13

STURM, Friedrich O. (1841-1919) Math. CDZZ ZZ13

STURTEVANT, Alfred H. (1891-1970) Genet. ABET
BEOS CDZZ MHM1 MHSE ZZ13

STURTEVANT, Edward L. (1842-1898) Bot. BIOD

STYRIKOVICH, Mikhail A. (1902-) Engr. SMST

SUBBOTIN, Mikhail F. (1893-1966) Astron. CDZZ
SMST ZZ13

SUCHTEN, Alexander (c.1520-1590) Chem.; Med.
CDZZ ZZ13

SUCKSMITH, Willie (1896-1981) Phys. RS28

SUDHOFF, Karl F. (1853-1938) Med. CDZZ ZZ13

SUDWORTH, George B. (1864-1927) Forest. LACC

SUESS, Eduard (1831-1914) Geol. ABET BEOS CDZZ
ZZ13

al-SUFI, Abul-Husayn (903-986) Astron. CDZZ ZZ13

SUGDEN, Samuel (1892-1950) Chem. BDOS BEOS

SUITS, Chauncey G. (1905-) Phys. CB50 MHM1 MHSE

SUKACHYEV, Vladimir N. (1880-1967) Bot. SMST

SULLIVAN, Eugene C. (1872-1962) Chem. ACCE

SULLIVANT, William S. (1803-1873) Bot. BIOD BM-1 DAB MABH NC-8

SUMNER, Francis B. (1874-1945) Biol. BM25 CDZZ DAB3 NC34 ZZ13

SUMNER, James B. (1887-1955) Biochem. ABES ABET ACCE BDOS BEOS CB47 CDZZ DAB5 MHM1 MHSE NC46 NPWC WAMB ZZ13

SUMNER, Thomas H. (1807-1851) Nav. YSMS

SUNDMAN, Karl F. (1873-1949) Astron. CDZZ ZZ13

SURFACE, Frank M. (1882-1965) Biol. NC54

SURINGER, Willem F. (1832-1898) Bot. CDZZ ZZ13

SU SUNG (1020-1101) Invent. BEOS GE-1

SUSRUTA (fl. c.100 B.C.) Med. OGIV

SUTER, Heinrich (1848-1922) Math. CDZZ ZZ13

SUTHERLAND, Earl W. (1915-1974) Physiol. ABET BEOS BM49 MHSE

SUTHERLAND, Gordon (1907-1980) Phys. RS28

SUTHERLAND, William (1859-1911) Chem.; Phys. CDZZ ZZ13

SUTTON, George M. (1898-) Ornith. DGMT

SUTTON, Leslie E. (1906-) Chem. COBC

SUTTON, Oliver G. (1903-1977) Phys. RS24

SUTTON, Walter S. (1877-1916) Biol.; Med. ABET CDZZ ZZ13

SUYYA (fl. 860) Engr. GE-1

SVEDA, Michael (1912-) Chem. CB54

SVEDBERG, Theodor H. (1884-1971) Chem. ABES ABET BEOS CDZZ NPWC RS18 ZZ13

SVEDELIUS, Nils E. (1873-1960) Biol. CDZZ RS-7 ZZ13

SVERDRUP, Harald U. (1888-1957) Ocean. CDZZ MHM1 MHSE ZZ13

SVETOVIDOV, Anatoli N. (1903-) Ichth. SMST

SWAIM, Verne F. (1886-1954) Phys. NC46

SWAIN, Francis E. (1910-1971) Elec. Engr. NC58

SWAIN, George F. (1857-1931) Engr. BM17

SWAIN, Robert E. (1875-1961) Chem. NC57

SWAINE, James M. (1879-1955) Entom. AMEM

SWAINSON, William (1789-1855) Zool. ANHD BWCL CDZZ DNB ZZ13

SWALES, Bradshaw H. (1874-1928) Ornith. NC23

SWALLOW, George C. (1817-1899) Geol. BIOD

SWAMMERDAM, Jan (1637-1680) Biol. ABES ABET BDOS BEOS BHMT BMST CDZZ HLSM LSHS ZZ13

SWAN, Joseph (1791-1874) Anat. DNB

SWAN, Joseph W. (1828-1914) Phys.; Chem. ABES ABET BDOS BEOS DNB3 EETD SAIF

SWANK, Wendell G. (1917-) Ecol. LACC

SWANN, Ralph C. (1912-1967) Chem. NC54

SWANN, William F. (1884-1962) Phys. CB41 CB60 CDZZ NC53 ZZ13

SWANSON, Gustav A. (1910-) Zool. LACC

SWANTON, John R. (1873-1958) Anthro. BM34

SWART, Gilbert H. (1903-1965) Chem. ACCE

SWARTS, Frederic J. (1866-1940) Chem. CDZZ ZZ13

SWARTZ, Olof (1760-1818) Bot. CDZZ ZZ13

SWASEY, Ambrose (1846-1937) Engr.; Invent. BM22

SWEDENBORG, Emanuel (1688-1772) Geol.; Physiol. BDOS BHMT CDZZ ZZ13

SWEET, Robert (1783-1835) Hort. DNB

SWENSON, Magnus (1854-1936) Chem. ACCE

SWEZEY, Otto H. (1869-1959) Entom. AMEM NC50

SWIETEN, Gerard van (1700-1772) Med. CDZZ ZZ13

SWIFT, Ernest H. (1897-1968) Chem. MHM2 MHSE NC56

SWIFT, Lewis (1820-1913) Astron. DAB NC-4

SWIFT, Lloyd W. (1904-) Cons. LACC

SWINBURNE, James (1858-1958) Elec. Engr. BDOS DNB7 RS-5

SWINDEN, Jan H. van (1746-1823) Phys.; Meteor. CDZZ ZZ13

SWINDIN, Norman (1880-1976) Chem. Engr. HCEF

SWINDLER, Mary H. (1884-1967) Archaeol. NAWM NC54

SWINESHEAD, Richard (fl. c.1340-1355) Nat. Philos. CDZZ ZZ13

SWINGLE, Homer S. (1902-) Biol. LACC

SWINGLE, Walter T. (1871-1952) Bot. MABH NC54

SWINGS, Polidore (1906-) Astrophys. CB54 MHM2 MHSE

SWINTON, Alan A. (1863-1930) Elec. Engr. DNB4

SWOPE, Henrietta H. (1902-1980) Astron. AO80

SYDENHAM, Thomas (1624-1689) Med. ABET BDOS BEOS BHMT CDZZ ZZ13

SYKES, Kebel W. (1921-) Chem. COBC

SYKES, William H. (1790-1872) Nat. Hist. DNB

SYLOW, Peter L. (1832-1918) Math. CDZZ ZZ13

SYLVESTER II, Pope SEE GERBERT D'AURILLAC

SYLVESTER, James J. (1814-1897) Math. BDOS BEOS BIOD CDZZ DAB DNB MASW ZZ13

SYLVIUS, Franciscus (1614-1672) Med. ABES ABET BDOS BEOS CDZZ HLSM ZZ13

SYLVIUS, Jacobus SEE DUBOIS, Jacques

SYME, James (1799-1870) Med. BHMT

SYMINGTON, William (1763-1831) Engr. DNB GE-1

SYMMER, Robert (c.1707-1763) Elec. Sci. CDZZ ESEH ZZ13

SYMMES, John C. (1780-1829) Astron. MSFB

SYMONDS, William S. (1818-1887) Geol. DNB

SYMONS, George J. (1838-1900) Meteor. DNB1

SYNESIUS OF CYRENE (c.370-c.414) Astron.; Phys. CDZZ ZZ13

SYNGE, Richard L. (1914-) Chem. ABES ABET BEOS CB53 MHM1 MHSE

SYRKIN, Yakov K. (1894-) Chem. SMST

SZASZ, Otto (1884-1952) Math. NC41

SZASZ, Thomas (1920-) Psychiat. AMJB

SZEBELLEDY, Laszlo (1901-1944) Chem. CDZZ ZZ13

SZENT-GYORGYI, Albert (1893-) Biochem. ABES ABET BEOS CB55 MHM2 MHSE WAMB

SZILARD, Leo (1898-1964) Phys.; Biol. ABES ABET BEOS BM40 CB47 CDZZ MHM1 MHSE HSSO PPTY WAMB ZZ13

SZILY, Pal (1878-1945) Chem. CDZZ ZZ13

SZWARC, Michael (1909-) Chem. MHM2 MHSE

T

al-TABARI, Abul-Hasan Ahmad (c.920-c.980) Philos.; Med. CDZZ ZZ13

al-TABARI, Abul-Hasan Ali ibn Sahl (c.808-c.861) Med. CDZZ ZZ13

TABOR, John (b. 1667) Med. CDZZ ZZ13

TABOR, Paul (1893-) Agr. LACC

TACCHINI, Pietro (1838-1905) Astron.; Meteor. CDZZ ZZ13

TACCOLA, Mariano (1381-1453) Engr. CDZZ GE-1 ZZ13

TACHENIUS, Otto (fl. 1650-1670) Chem. CDZZ ZZ13

TACQUET, Andreas (1612-1660) Math. CDZZ ZZ13

TAGGART, Walter T. (1872-1938) Chem. NC29

TAGLIACOZZI, Gaspare (1545-1599) Med. BHMT

TAINTER, Charles S. (1854-1940) Phys. NC29

TAIT, Peter G. (1831-1901) Phys.; Math. CDZZ DNB2 ZZ13

TAIT, Robert L. (1854-1899) Med. BHMT

TAKAMINE, Jokichi (1854-1922) Chem. ABES ABET ACCE BDOS BEOS DAB NC40

TALBOT, Henry P. (1864-1927) Chem. ACCE DAB

TALBOT, William H. (1800-1877) Invent.; Photo. ABES ABET BDOS BEOS CDZZ ENCE HOSS SAIF ZZ13

TALCOTT, Andrew (1797-1883) Engr.; Astron. GE-1

TALCOTT, Lucy (1899-1970) Archaeol. NC54

TALIAFERRO, William H. (1895-1973) Parasit. NCSF NC58

TALMUD, David L. (1900-) Chem. SMST

TAMARKIN, Jacob D. (1888-1945) Math. DAB3

TAMIYA, Hiroshi (1903-) Biol.; Biochem. MHM2 MHSE

TAMM, Igor Y. (1895-1971) Phys. ABES ABET BEOS CDZZ MHM1 MHSE PAW2 POSW SMST ZZ13

TAMMANN, Gustav H. (1861-1938) Chem. CDZZ HSSO ZZ13

TANANAEV, Ivan V. (1904-) Chem. SMST

TANBERG, Arthur P. (1885-1963) Chem. NC51

TANFILEV, Gavriil I. (1857-1928) Geog.; Soil Sci. CDZZ ZZ13

TANNER, John H. (1861-1940) Math. NC29

TANNERY, Jules (1848-1910) Math. CDZZ ZZ13

TANNERY, Paul (1843-1904) Sci. Hist. CDZZ ZZ13

TANQUARY, Maurice E. (1881-1944) Entom. NC34

TANSLEY, Arthur G. (1871-1955) Bot. BDOS BEOS DNB7 RS-3

TANZER, Helen H. (1876-1961) Archaeol. NCSG

TAO HSUN (fl. 1250) Engr. GE-1

TARBELL, Dean S. (1913-) Chem. MHM2 MHSE

TARDE, Jean (c.1561-1636) Astron.; Geog. CDZZ ZZ13

TARGIONI TOZZETTI, Giovanni (1712-1783) Nat. Hist. CDZZ ZZ13

TARLTON, Robert J. (Contemporary) Invent. NTBM

TARSHIS, Maurice S. (1912-1974) Microbiol.; Immunol. NC58

TARSKI, Alfred (1902-) Math. BEOS

TARTAGLIA, Niccolo (1500-1557) Math. ABES ABET BDOS BEOS CDZZ ZZ13

TARZWELL, Clarence M. (1907-) Biol. LACC

TASCHER, Wendell R. (1898-1964) Cons. LACC

TASHIRO, Shiro (1883-1963) Biochem. CDZZ ZZ13

TATE, Alexander N. (1837-1892) Chem. DNB

TATE, George (1805-1871) Nat. Hist. DNB

TATE, George H. (1894-1953) Zool. DAB5 NC44

TATE, John T. (1889-1950) Phys. BM47 DAB4 QPAS

TATE, Thomas (1807-1888) Math. DNB

TATLOW, John C. (1923-) Chem. COBC

TATTERFIELD, Frederick (1881-1959) Chem. DNB7

TATUM, Edward L. (1909-1975) Biochem.; Genet.
ABES ABET BEOS CB59 MHM1 MHSE NCSJ
PAW2 WAMB

TAUB, James M. (1918-) Metal. MHM1 MHSE

TAUBE, Henry (1915-) Chem. BEOS MHM1 MHSE

TAUBER, Alfred (1866-1942) Math. CDZZ ZZ13

TAURINUS, Franz A. (1794-1874) Math. CDZZ ZZ13

TAUSSIG, Helen B. (1898-) Med. IDWB MFIR
MHM1 MHSE

TAYLOR, Albert H. (1879-1962) Phys. CB45

TAYLOR, Brook (1685-1731) Math. BDOS BEOS
CDZZ DNB ZZ13

TAYLOR, Charles V. (1885-1946) Biol. BM25 CDZZ
ZZ13

TAYLOR, Charlotte (1806-1861) Entom. BIOD DAB

TAYLOR, David W. (1864-1940) Engr. BM22

TAYLOR, Edward W. (1891-1980) Opt. RS27

TAYLOR, Frank B. (1860-1938) Geol. CDZZ ZZ13

TAYLOR, Frank S. (1897-1956) Chem. DNB7

TAYLOR, Fred (1910-1978) Chem. NC60

TAYLOR, Frederick W. (1856-1915) Engr. ABES
ABET CDZZ WAMB ZZ13

TAYLOR, Geoffrey I. (1886-1975) Math. BEOS
MHM2 MHSE RS22

TAYLOR, Guy B. (1888-1972) Chem. ACCE

TAYLOR, Henry M. (1842-1927) Math. DNB4

TAYLOR, Hugh S. (1890-1974) Chem. BEOS MHM2
MHSE RS21

TAYLOR, James (1753-1825) Engr. DNB

TAYLOR, James H. (1909-1968) Geol. RS14

TAYLOR, John E. (1837-1895) Sci. Writ. DNB

TAYLOR, Lawnie (1902-) Phys. BCST

TAYLOR, Lucy (1833-1910) Dent. NAW

TAYLOR, Maurice C. (1894-1959) Chem. NC49

TAYLOR, Moddie D. (1912-1976) Chem. NC59

TAYLOR, Richard C. (1789-1851) Geol. BIOD

TAYLOR, Theodore B. (1925-) Phys. CB76 MHM1
MHSE

TAYLOR, Thomas G. (1804-1848) Astron. DNB

TAYLOR, Thomas W. (1895-1953) Chem. DNB7

TAYLOR, Walter P. (1888-) Cons. DGMT LACC

TAYLOR, William C. (1886-1958) Chem. NC49

TAYLOR, William H. (1835-1917) Chem. NC18

TAYLOR, William R. (1895-) Bot. MHM2 MHSE

TEALE, Edwin W. (1899-1980) Nat. Hist. AO80
CB61 SWWP

TEALL, Jethro J. (1849-1924) Geol. CDZZ DNB4
ZZ13

TEDDER, John M. (1926-) Chem. COBC

TEDESCHE, Leon G. (1878-1956) Bact. NC46

TEED, Cyrus R. (1839-1908) Astron. MSFB

TEEPLE, John E. (1874-1931) Chem. GRCH

TEICHMANN, Ludwik K. (1823-1895) Anat. CDZZ
ZZ13

TEILHARD DE CHARDIN, Pierre (1881-1955) Paleon.;
Geol. CDZZ ZZ13

TEISSERENC DE BORT, Leon (1855-1913) Meteor.
ABES ABET BEOS

TELESIO, Bernardino (1509-1588) Nat. Philos. CDZZ
ZZ13

TELFAIR, Charles (c.1777-1833) Nat. Hist. DNB

TELFORD, Thomas (1757-1834) Engr. BDOS BEOS
DNB GE-1

TELKES, Maria de (1900-) Chem. CB50

TELLER, Edward (1908-) Phys. ABES ABET AMJB
BEOS CB54 CB83 MHM2 MHSE MOS2 NBPS
PPEY PPKY PPTY WAMB

TELLIER, Charles (1828-1913) Engr. MCCW

TEMIN, Howard M. (1934-) Virol. ABET BEOS MHSE

TEMMINCK, Coenraad J. (1778-1858) Ornith. ANHD ORNS

TEMPLE, Lewis (1800-1825) Invent. EBAH

TEMPLETON, John (1766-1825) Nat. Hist. DNB

TEN RHYNE, Willem (1647-1700) Med.; Bot. CDZZ ZZ13

TENNANT, Charles (1768-1838) Chem. BDOS BEOS

TENNANT, James (1808-1881) Mineral. DNB

TENNANT, Smithson (1761-1815) Chem. ABES ABET BDOS BEOS CDZZ DNB ZZ13

TENNENT, David H. (1873-1941) Biol. BM26 CDZZ NC36 ZZ13

TERENIN, Aleksandr N. (1896-1967) Chem. SMST

TERENTEV, Aleksandr P. (1891-1970) Chem. SMST

TERESHKOVA, Valentine V. (1937-) Astronaut. CB63 IEAS

TERMAN, Frederick E. (1900-) Engr. MHM1 MHSE TPAE

TERMAN, Lewis M. (1877-1956) Psych. BM33

TERMIER, Pierre (1859-1930) Geol.; Geophys. CDZZ ZZ13

TERRY, Ethel M. (1887-1963) Chem. ACCE

TERRY, Robert W. (1892-1949) Chem. NC47

TESCHEMACHER, James E. (1790-1853) Geol.; Bot. BIOD

TESLA, Nikola (1856-1943) Elec. Engr. ABES ABET BDOS BEOS CDZZ DAB3 EETD FNEC PAW1 SAIF TBTM TPAE VTHB WAMB ZZ13

TESTUT, Jean L. (1849-1925) Anat.; Anthro. CDZZ ZZ13

TEXTOR, Oscar (1860-1937) Chem. NC32

THABIT ibn QURRA, al-Sabi (836-901) Math.; Astron. ABET CDZZ SCIN ZZ13

THACHER, James (1754-1844) Med. BHMT

THALER, William J. (1925-) Phys. CB60

THALES (624 B.C.-546 B.C.) Philos. ABES ABET AMST BDOS BEOS CDZZ EETD GISA ZZ13

THAN, Karoly (1834-1908) Chem. CDZZ ZZ13

THAN STON RGYAL PO (1385-1464) Engr. GE-1

THAXTER, Roland (1858-1932) Bot. BM17 CDZZ DAB MABH NC30 ZZ13

THAYER, John E. (1862-1933) Ornith. BWCL NC33

THAYER, Sidney A. (1902-1969) Biochem. NC54

THAYER, William S. (1864-1932) Med. CDZZ ZZ13

THEAETETUS (c.417 B.C.-369 B.C.) Math. ABET CDZZ ZZ13

THEGE, Miklos SEE KONKOLY THEGE, Miklos von

THEILER, Max (1899-1972) Med.; Virol. ABES ABET BEOS CB52 MHM1 MHSE VACE

THEKAEKARA, Matthew P. (1914-) Phys. CB74

THEMISTIUS (c.318-c.388) Philos. CDZZ ZZ13

THENARD, Louis J. (1777-1857) Chem. ABES ABET BDOS BEOS CDZZ GRCH SOAC ZZ13

THEODORIC OF CERVIA (1205-c.1296) Med. BHMT

THEODORIC OF FREIBERG SEE DIETRICH VON FREIBERG

THEODORUS OF CYRENE (c.465 B.C.-399 B.C.) Math. CDZZ ZZ13

THEODOSIUS OF BITHYNIA (fl. c.200 B.C.) Math.; Astron. CDZZ ZZ13

THEON OF ALEXANDRIA (fl. c.350-c.400) Math.; Astron. CDZZ ZZ13

THEON OF SMYRNA (fl. c.110) Math.; Astron. CDZZ ZZ13

THEOPHILUS (fl. c.1100-1130) Metal.; Chem. CDZZ GE-1 ZZ13

THEOPHRASTUS (c.370 B.C.-c.285 B.C.) Bot. ABES ABET BDOS BEOS CDZZ EETD HLSM LISD ZZ13

THEORELL, Axel H. (1903-1982) Biochem. ABES ABET BEOS CB56 MHM1 MHSE

THEORELL, Hugo SEE THEORELL, Axel H.

THEUDIUD OF MAGNESIA (fl. 300s B.C.) Math. CDZZ ZZ13

THEVENOT, Melchisedech (c.1620-1692) Trans. Sci. Lit. CDZZ ZZ13

THIELE, Friedrich K. (1865-1918) Chem. BDOS BEOS CDZZ HSSO ZZ13

THIELE, Thorvald N. (1838-1910) Astron.; Math. CDZZ ZZ13

THIERRY OF CHARTRES (c.1080-c.1155) Philos. CDZZ ZZ13

THIERSCH, Carl (1822-1895) Med. BHMT

THIESSEN, Gilbert (1905-1966) Chem. NC53

THIESSEN, Reinhardt (1867-1938) Chem. NC28

THIMANN, Kenneth V. (1904-) Bot. MHM2 MHSE

THIMONNIER, Bartholome (1793-1857) Invent. GE-1

THIOUT, Antoine (1692-1767) Instr. BDOS

THIRSK, Harold R. (1915-) Chem. COBC

THIRY, Paul H. SEE HOLBACH, Paul H. d'

THISELTON-DYER, William T. (1843-1928) Bot. CDZZ DNB4 ZZ13

THODAY, David (1883-1964) Bot. RS11

THODE, Henry G. (1910-) Chem. MHM2 MHSE

THOLLON, Louis (1829-1887) Phys. CDZZ ZZ13

THOM, Alexander (1894-) Engr. BEOS

THOM, Charles (1872-1956) Bot. BM38 NC44

THOMAS OF CANTIMPRE (c.1186/1210-1276/94) Nat. Hist. CDZZ ZZ13

THOMAS, Andrew (1932-) Med. BISC

THOMAS, Charles A. (1895-1962) Entom. AMEM

THOMAS, Charles A. (1900-1982) Chem. CB50

THOMAS, Cyrus (1825-1910) Anthro.; Entom. DAB NC13

THOMAS, Herbert H. (1876-1935) Geol. DNB5

THOMAS, Hugh H. (1885-1962) Paleon. CDZZ FHUA MHM2 MHSE RS-9 ZZ13

THOMAS, Hugh O. (1834-1891) Med. BHMT

THOMAS, John W. (1880-1951) Chem. ACCE

THOMAS, Lewis (1913-) Biol. CB75 EXSB

THOMAS, Meirion (1894-1977) Bot. RS24

THOMAS, Sidney G. (1850-1885) Metal. BDOS BEOS CDZZ DNB SNCB ZZ13

THOMAS, Stanley J. (1889-1960) Bact. NC47

THOMAS, Tracy Y. (1899-) Math. MHM1 MHSE

THOMAZ, Alvaro (fl. 1509-1513) Phys.; Math. CDZZ ZZ13

THOMPSON, Almon H. (1839-1906) Engr. BIOD

THOMPSON, Benjamin, Count Rumford (1753-1814) Phys. ABES ABET ASIW BDOS BEOS BIOD CDZZ DAB FNEC GISA HOSS MCCW MSAJ SAIF SSDH TINA WAMB YSMS ZZ13

THOMPSON, D'Arcy W. (1860-1948) Nat. Hist. BEOS CDZZ DNB6 ZZ13

THOMPSON, Edward H. (1856-1935) Exp.; Archaeol. DAB1

THOMPSON, Harold W. (1908-) Chem. BEOS COBC MHM2 MHSE

THOMPSON, Homer C. (1885-1976) Hort. NC59

THOMPSON, John G. (1932-) Math. MHSE

THOMPSON, John V. (1779-1847) Nat. Hist. CDZZ DNB ZZ13

THOMPSON, Kenworthy J. (1881-1933) Chem. NC29

THOMPSON, Louis T. (1891-) Phys. NCSH

THOMPSON, Marvin R. (1905-1969) Pharm. NC55

THOMPSON, Silvanus P. (1851-1916) Phys. CDZZ DNB3 ZZ13

THOMPSON, Stanley G. (1912-1976) Chem. MHM1 MHSE

THOMPSON, Thomas G. (1888-1961) Ocean. BM43

THOMPSON, William (1805-1852) Nat.Hist. DNB

THOMPSON, William F. (1888-1965) Biol. LACC NC52

THOMPSON, William R. (1887-1972) Entom. RS19

THOMPSON, Zadock (1796-1856) Nat. Hist.; Math. BIOD DAB

THOMSEN, Christian J. (1788-1865) Archaeol. ABES ABET CDZZ ZZ13

THOMSEN, Hans P. (1826-1909) Chem. ABES ABET BEOS CDZZ ZZ13

THOMSON, Allen (1809-1884) Embryol.; Evol. DNB VISC

THOMSON, Arthur (1861-1933) Biol.; Zool. MMSB

THOMSON, Charles W. (1830-1882) Zool. ABES ABET BDOS BEOS CDZZ DNB EXSG SNCB WFBG ZZ13

THOMSON, Elihu (1853-1937) Chem. ABET ACCE BEOS BM21 CDZZ DAB2 EETD TPAE WAMB ZZ13

THOMSON, F. Dupont (1869-1959) Engr. NC49

THOMSON, George P. (1892-1975) Phys. ABES ABET BEOS CB47 MHM1 MHSE POSW RS23

THOMSON, James (1786-1849) Math. DNB

THOMSON, James (1822-1892) Phys. BDOS

THOMSON, Joseph J. (1856-1940) Phys. ABES ABET BDOS BEOS CAVL CDZZ CSCJ DCPW DNB5 EETD HOSS HSSO MWBR PAW2 POSW SAIF SMIL TOWS ZZ13

THOMSON, Robert B. (1870-1947) Bot. MABH

THOMSON, Robert W. (1822-1873) Engr. ABES ABET

THOMSON, Thomas (1773-1852) Chem. CDZZ DNB ZZ13

THOMSON, Thomas (1817-1878) Nat. Hist. DNB

THOMSON, William, Lord Kelvin (1824-1907) Math.; Phys. ABES ABET BDOS BEOS CDZZ DNB2 EETD GASJ GOED HSSO MAKS MCCW SAIF SNCB TOWS VISC ZZ13

THORN, George W. (1906-) Med. MHM2 MHSE

THORNDIKE, Edward L. (1874-1949) Psych. BM27

THORNE, Kip (1940-) Phys. BEOS

THORNTON, Henry G. (1892-1977) Soil Sci. RS23

THORNTON, William (1761-1828) Med. BHMT WAMB

THORP, Frank H. (1864-1932) Chem. Engr. HCEF

THORPE, Jocelyn F. (1872-1940) Chem. CDZZ ZZ13

THORPE, Thomas E. (1845-1925) Chem. BDOS BEOS CDZZ DNB4 ZZ13

THOUIN, Andre (1747-1824) Bot. CDZZ ZZ13

THOULESS, David J. (1934-) Phys. MHSE

THREFALL, Richard (1861-1932) Phys.; Chem. Engr. DNB5

THRELKELD, Caleb (1676-1728) Bot. DNB

THUE, Axel (1863-1922) Math. CDZZ ZZ13

THUNBERG, Carl P. (1743-1828) Bot. BDOS BEOS CDZZ ZZ13

THUNBERG, Thorsten L. (1873-1952) Physiol. CDZZ ZZ13

THURBER, George (1821-1890) Bot. BIOD DAB

THURET, Gustave A. (1817-1875) Bot. CDZZ ZZ13

THURNEYSSER, Leonhard (1531-1596) Alch. CDZZ ZZ13

THURNMAN, John (1810-1873) Psychiat. CDZZ ZZ13

THURSTON, Robert H. (1839-1903) Engr. CDZZ ZZ13

THURSTONE, Louis L. (1887-1955) Psych. BM30

THWAITES, George H. (1811-1882) Bot.; Entom. DNB

THYMARIDAS (fl. 300s B.C.) Math. CDZZ ZZ13

ibn TIBBON, Jacob ben Machir (1236-1305) Astron. CDZZ ZZ13

ibn TIBBON, Moses ben Samuel (1240-1283) Med. CDZZ ZZ13

TIDESTROM, Ivar F. (1864-1956) Bot. BNBR

TIEDEMANN, Friedrich (1781-1861) Anat.; Physiol. CDZZ ZZ13

TIEGHEM, Philippe van (1839-1914) Bot. CDZZ ZZ13

TIEGS, Oscar W. (1897-1956) Biol. RS-3

TIEMANN, Johann C. (1848-1899) Chem. BDOS BEOS CDZZ ZZ13

TIETZ, Johann SEE TITIUS, Johann D.

al-TIFASHI, Shihab al-Din (1184-1253) Mineral. CDZZ ZZ13

TIFFANY, Hanford (1894-1965) Bot. NC52

TIFFENEAU, Marc (1873-1946) Chem. GRCH

TIGER, Lionel (1937-) Anthro. CB81

TIKHONOV, Andrei N. (1906-) Math.; Geophys. SMST

TIKHONRAVOV, Mikhail K. (1900-1974) Rocket. IEAS

TIKHOV, Gavriil A. (1875-1960) Astrophys. CDZZ ZZ13

TILAS, Daniel (1712-1772) Geol.; Mng. CDZZ ZZ13

TILDEN, William A. (1842-1926) Chem. BDOS BEOS CDZZ ZZ13

TILGHMAN, Richard A. (1824-1899) Chem. BIOD DAB

TILLET, Mathieu (1714-1791) Agr.; Chem. CDZZ ZZ13

TILLETT, William S. (1892-1974) Med. MHM2 MHSE

TILLEY, Cecil E. (1894-1973) Geol. MHM2 MHSE RS20

TILLEY, Norman N. (1892-1962) Geog. ZZ13

TILLO, Aleksey A. (1839-1900) Geog. CDZZ ZZ13

TILLOCH, Alexander (1759-1825) Nat. Philos. CDZZ ZZ13

TILLOTSON, Edwin W. (1884-1956) Chem. ACCE

TILLY, Joseph M. de (1837-1906) Math. CDZZ ZZ13

ibn al-TILMIDH, Amin al-Dawla (c.1073-1165) Med. CDZZ ZZ13

TILTON, James (1745-1822) Med. BHMT

TIMIRYAZEV, Kliment A. (1843-1920) Bot. CDZZ ZZ13

TIMOFEEV, Pyotr V. (1902-) Elec. Engr. SMST

TIMOSHENKO, Stephen P. (1878-1972) Engr. BM53 FNEC RS19

TINBERGEN, Nikolaas (1907-) Zool. ABET BEOS CB75 MHM2 MHSE

TING, Samuel C. (1936-) Phys. ABET BEOS MHSE PAW2 POSW

TINKHAM, Michael (1928-) Phys. MHSE

TINNERMAN, Albert H. (1879-1961) Invent. NC52

TINSEAU D'AMONDANS, Charles de (1748-1822) Math. CDZZ ZZ13

TISELIUS, Arne W. (1902-1971) Biochem. ABES ABET BDOS BEOS CB49 CDZZ MHM1 MHSE NPWC PAW2 RS20 ZZ13

TISHLER, Max (1906-) Chem. BEOS CB52 MHM2 MHSE

TISSERAND, Francois F. (1845-1896) Astron. CDZZ ZZ13

TISSOT, Simon A. (1728-1797) Med. BHMT

TITCHMARSH, Edward C. (1899-1963) Math. CDZZ RS10 ZZ13

TITIUS, Johann D. (1729-1796) Astron.; Phys. ABET CDZZ ZZ13

TITOV, Gherman (1935-) Astronaut. CB62 FPSN IEAS

TITUS, Rolla W. (1884-1956) Chem. NC45

TIZARD, Henry T. (1885-1959) Chem. BDOS BEOS CB49 DNB7 RS-7 SIWG SOSC

TIZARD, Thomas H. (1839-1924) Ocean. DNB4

TOBIAS, Cornelius A. (1918-) Biophys. MHM2 MHSE

TODD, Alexander R. (1907-) Chem. ABES ABET BEOS CB58 COBC MHM1 MHSE PAW2

TODD, Charles (1826-1910) Astron. DNB2

TODD, Charles (1869-1957) Med. RS-4

TODD, David P. (1855-1939) Astron. NC-7 NC28

TODD, Henry D. (1838-1907) Math. NC19

TODD, Thomas W. (1885-1938) Anat.; Anthro. DAB2

TODHUNTER, Isaac (1820-1884) Math. CDZZ DNB ZZ13

TOEPLITZ, Otto (1881-1940) Math. CDZZ ZZ13

TOFTOY, H.N. (1903-) Rocket. MOS3

TOKUGAWA YOSHIMUNE (1684-1751) Instr. GE-1

TOLANSKY, Samuel (1907-1973) Phys. MHM2 MHSE RS20

TOLMAN, Edward C. (1886-1959) Psych. BM37

TOLMAN, Richard C. (1881-1948) Chem.; Phys. ACCE BM27 CDZZ QPAS ZZ13

TOMBAUGH, Clyde W. (1906-) Astron. ABES ABET BEOS IEAS STSW

TOMLINSON, Charles (1808-1897) Sci. Writ. DNB

TOMONAGA, Sin-itiro (1906-1979) Phys. ABES ABET BEOS MHM1 MHSE POSW

TOMPION, Thomas (c.1639-1713) Instr. BDOS

TOMPKINS, Frederick C. (1910-) Chem.; Phys. COBC

TONDORF, Francis A. (1870-1929) Seism. DAB

TOPCHIEV, Aleksandr V. (1907-1962) Chem. BDOS BEOS

TOPLEY, William (1841-1894) Geol. DNB

TOPLEY, William W. (1886-1944) Bact. DNB6

TOROPOV, Nikita A. (1908-1968) Chem. SMST

TORPORLEY, Nathaniel (1564-1632) Math. DNB

TORRE, Marcantonio della (1481-1511) Med. CDZZ ZZ13

TORRE-BUENO, Jose R. de la (1871-1948) Entom. AMEM

TORRES QUEVEDO, Leonardo (1852-1936) Engr. CDZZ ZZ13

TORREY, Bradford (1843-1912) Ornith. BIOD DAB SFNB

TORREY, John (1796-1873) Chem. ABFC ACCE ASJD BEOS BIOD BM-1 CDZZ DAB MABH WAMB ZZ13

TORRICELLI, Evangelista (1608-1647) Phys. ABES ABET BDOS BEOS CDZZ DCPW FNEC HOSS SAIF TOWS ZZ13

TORRIGIANO, Pietro SEE TURISANUS

TOSCANELLI DAL POZZO, Paolo (1397-1482) Astron.; Geog. ABET BEOS CDZZ ZZ13

TOTTEN, Joseph G. (1788-1864) Engr. BM-1 DAB

TOULMIN, George H. (1754-1817) Geol. CDZZ ZZ13

TOUMEY, James W. (1865-1932) Forest. LACC

TOURNEFORT, Joseph P. de (1656-1708) Bot.; Med. BMST CDZZ ZZ13

TOUSEY, Richard (1908-) Phys. BEOS MHM1 MHSE

TOWELL, William E. (1916-) Forest. LACC

TOWER, Olin F. (1872-1945) Chem. ACCE NCSC

TOWN, Ithiel (1784-1844) Engr. GE-1

TOWNELEY, Richard (1629-1707) Nat. Philos. CDZZ
ZZ13

TOWNES, Charles H. (1915-) Phys. ABES ABET
BEOS DCPW MHM1 MHSE MOS5 NTBM POSW
SAIF SCLB TINA WAMB

TOWNLEY, Sidney D. (1867-1946) Astron. NC42

TOWNSEND, Charles H. (1863-1944) Entom. AMEM
WFBG

TOWNSEND, John K. (1809-1851) Ornith. BIOD DAB
WFBG

TOWNSEND, John S. (1868-1957) Phys. BDOS BEOS
CDZZ DNB7 RS-3 ZZ13

TOWNSEND, Joseph (1739-1816) Geol.; Med. CDZZ
DNB ZZ13

TOWNSEND, Oliver H. (1917-1969) Phys. NC55

TOWNSEND, Richard (1821-1884) Math. DNB

TOWNSHEND, Charles (1674-1738) Agr. BDOS

TOWSON, John T. (1804-1881) Sci. Writ. DNB

TOZZER, Alfred M. (1877-1954) Anthro. BM30

TOZZI, Don Bruno (1656-1743) Bot. CDZZ ZZ13

TRACY, Clarissa T. (1818-1905) Bot. BIOD

TRADESCANT, John (1570/5-1638) Nat. Hist. CDZZ
DNB ZZ13

TRAGUS, Hieronymus SEE BOCK, Jerome

TRAILL, Thomas S. (1781-1862) Zool. WFBG

TRAIN, Percy (1877-1942) Bot. BNBR

TRAIN, Russell (1920-) Cons. LACC

TRAPEZNIKOV, Vadim A. (1905-) Elec. Engr. SMST

TRASK, John B. (1824-1879) Geol. BIOD

TRAUBE, Ludwig (1818-1876) Med. BHMT

TRAUBE, Moritz (1826-1894) Chem. BDOS BEOS
CDZZ ZZ13

TRAUTMAN, Milton B. (1899-) Zool. LACC

TRAUTWINE, John C. (1810-1883) Engr. BIOD

TRAVERS, Benjamin (1783-1858) Med. BHMT

TRAVERS, Morris W. (1872-1961) Chem. ABET
BDOS BEOS CDZZ RS-9 ZZ13

TREADWELL, Daniel (1791-1872) Phys.; Invent.
BIOD

TREBRA, Friedrich W. von (1740-1819) Mng. CDZZ
ZZ13

TREDGOLD, Thomas (1788-1829) Engr. GE-1

TREFETHEN, James B. (1916-) Cons. LACC

TREFOUEL, Jacques (1897-1977) Chem. MHM2
MHSE

TRELEASE, William (1857-1945) Bot. BM35 CDZZ
DAB3 MABH NC11 ZZ13

TREMBLEY, Abraham (1710-1784) Zool. ANHD
BMST CDZZ ZZ13

TRENDELENBURG, Friedrich (1844-1924) Med.
BHMT

TRENEER, Joseph M. (1881-1968) Chem. NC54

TRESAQUET, Pierre (1716-1794) Engr. BDOS GE-1

TREUB, Melchior (1851-1910) Bot. CDZZ ZZ13

TREVAN, John W. (1887-1956) Physiol. RS-3

TREVELYAN, Walter C. (1797-1879) Nat. Hist. DNB

TREVIRANUS, Ludolph C. (1779-1864) Bot. CDZZ
ZZ13

TREVISAN, Bernard (1406-1490) Chem. CSCJ

TREVITHICK, Richard (1771-1833) Invent. ABES
ABET BDOS FNEC GE-1 MCCW

TRIANA, Jose G. (1826-1890) Bot. CDZZ ZZ13

TRICE, Virgil G. (1926-) Chem. Engr. BCST

TRIMEN, Henry (1843-1896) Bot. DNB

TRIMMER, Joshua (1795-1857) Geol. DNB

TRISMEGISTUS SEE HERMES TRISMEGISTUS

TRISTRAM, Henry B. (1822-1906) Nat. Hist. DNB2

TROFIMUK, Andrei A. (1911-) Geol. MHM2
MHSE SMST

TROJA, Michele (1747-1827) Med. CDZZ ZZ13

TROLAND, Leonard T. (1889-1932) Psych.; Phys.
DAB

TROMMSDORFF, Johann B. (1770-1837) Chem.
CDZZ ZZ13

TROOST, Gerard (1776-1850) Geol.;Mineral. ASJD
BIOD CDZZ ZZ13

TROOST, Louis J. (1825-1911) Chem. CDZZ ZZ13

TROOSTWIJK, Adriaan P. van (1752-1837) Chem.
CDZZ ZZ13

TROPFKE, Johannes (1866-1939) Math. CDZZ ZZ13

TROSHIN, Afanasii S. (1912-) Med. SMST

TROST, Barry M. (1941-) Chem. MHSE

TROTTER, Mildred (1899-) Anat. MHM1 MHSE

TROTTER, Wilfred B. (1872-1939) Physiol. DNB5

TROUGHTON, Edward (1753-1836) Phys. CDZZ
DNB GE-1 ZZ13

TROUP, Robert S. (1874-1939) Forest. DNB5

TROUSSEAU, Armand (1801-1867) Med. BHMT

TROUTON, Frederick T. (1863-1922) Phys. CDZZ
ZZ13

TROUVELOT, Etienne L. (1827-1895) Nat. Hist.;
Astron. CDZZ ZZ13

TROWBRIDGE, Augustus (1870-1934) Phys. BM18
DAB NCSC

TROWBRIDGE, Charles C. (1870-1918) Phys. NC18

TROWBRIDGE, John (1843-1923) Phys. BM14
CDZZ DAB NC23 ZZ13

TROWBRIDGE, William P. (1825-1892) Geophys.;
Engr. BIOD BM-3 DAB

TROXELL, Edward L. (1884-1972) Paleon.; Geol.
NC57

TRUAX, Robert C. (1917-) Rocket. MOS2

TRUE, Frederick W. (1858-1914) Zool. DAB NC19

TRUE, Rodney H. (1866-1940) Bot. MABH

TRUEMAN, Arthur E. (1894-1956) Paleon. DNB7
RS-4

TRULLI, Giovanni (1598-1661) Med. CDZZ ZZ13

TRUMBULL, Gurdon (1841-1903) Ornith. BIOD

TRUMBULL, James H. (1821-1897) Philos. BM-7

TRUMPINGTON, Todd of SEE TODD, Alexander R.

TRUMPLER, Robert J. (1886-1956) Astron. ABES
ABET BEOS CDZZ NC54 ZZ13

TRUOG, Emil (1884-1969) Agr. MASY

TRYON, George W. (1838-1888) Conch. BIOD DAB

TSAI LUN (c.50-c.118) Invent. ABES ABET

TSAO, George T. (1931-) Chem. Engr. PALF

TSCHERMAK, Gustav (1836-1927) Geol. CDZZ ZZ13

TSCHERMAK VON SEYSENEGG, Erich (1871-1962)
Bot.; Genet. ABET CDZZ HLSM ZZ13

TSCHIRNHAUS, Ehrenfried W. (1651-1708) Math.;
Phys. CDZZ ZZ13

TSCHOPIK, Harry (1915-1956) Entom. NC45

TSERASKY, Vitold K. (1849-1925) Astron. CDZZ
ZZ13

TSIOLKOVSKY, Konstantin E. (1857-1935) Phys.;
Astronaut. ABES ABET BEOS CDZZ FPSN
HRST ICFW IEAS MOS1 PAW2 PORS ROPW
RUSP ZZ13

TSITSIN, Nikolai V. (1898-) Bot. SMST

TSU CHUNG-CHIH (c.429-c.500) Math. CDZZ ZZ13

TSUNG-DAO LEE SEE LEE, Tsung-Dao

TSVET, Mikhail S. (1872-1919) Bot. ABES ABET
BDOS BEOS CDZZ ZZ13

TUBBS, Francis R. (1907-1980) Hort. AO80

TUCKER, Richard H. (1859-1952) Astron. NC18 NC41

TUCKER, Willis G. (1849-1922) Chem. ACCE NC28

TUCKERMAN, Edward (1817-1886) Bot. BIOD BM-3 DAB NC-5

TUCKERMAN, Frederick (1857-1929) Anat.; Nat. Hist. DAB

TUCKERMAN, Louis B. (1879-1962) Phys. NC50

TUDOROVSKII, Aleksandr I. (1875-1964) Phys. SMST

ibn TUFAYL, Abu Bakr (c.1109-1185) Med. CDZZ ZZ13

TULASNE, Louis R. (1815-1885) Bot. CDZZ ZZ13

TULL, Jethro (1674-1741) Invent. BDOS BEOS GE-1

TULP, Nicholas (1593-1674) Med.; Anat. BHMT CDZZ ZZ13

TUMANOV, Ivan I. (1894-) Bot. SMST

TUNISON, Abram V. (1909-1971) Cons. LACC

TUNSTALL, Cuthbert (1474-1559) Math. CDZZ ZZ13

TUNSTALL, Marmaduke (1743-1790) Nat. Hist. DNB

TUOMEY, Michael (1805-1857) Geol. BIOD

TUPOLEV, Andrey N. (1888-1972) Aero. CDZZ SMST ZZ13

TURCK, Fenton B. (1857-1932) Biol. NC25

TURCK, Ledwig (1810-1868) Med. CDZZ ZZ13

TURGOT, Etienne F. (1721-1788) Bot.; Agr. CDZZ ZZ13

TURING, Alan M. (1912-1954) Math. ABET BEOS CDZZ RS-1 ZZ13

TURISANUS (fl. 1302-1319) Med. TALS

TURNBULL, Herbert W. (1885-1961) Math. RS-8

TURNBULL, Hubert M. (1875-1955) Path. RS-3

TURNER, Charles H. (1867-1923) Entom. AMEM BISC DANB SBAH SBPY

TURNER, Daniel (1667-1740) Med. BHMT

TURNER, Dawson (1775-1858) Bot. DNB

TURNER, Edward (1796-1837) Chem. CDZZ DNB ZZ13

TURNER, Eustace E. (1893-1966) Chem. RS14

TURNER, Herbert H. (1861-1930) Astron.; Seism. BEOS CDZZ DNB4 ZZ13

TURNER, Louis A. (1898-1977) Phys. NC60

TURNER, Peter (1586-1652) Math. CDZZ DNB ZZ13

TURNER, Richard B. (1916-1971) Chem. BM53

TURNER, Thomas W. (1877-1978) Biol. NC61 SBPY

TURNER, William (c.1508-1568) Nat. Hist.; Med. BDOS BEOS CDZZ HAOA ORNS ZZ13

TURNER, William (1832-1916) Anat. CDZZ DNB3 ZZ13

TURNER, William E. (1881-1963) Chem. RS10 CDZZ ZZ13

TURPIN, Pierre J. (1775-1840) Bot. CDZZ ZZ13

TURQUET DE MAYERNE, Theodore (1573-1655) Med.; Chem. CDZZ ZZ13

TURRENTINE, John W. (1880-1966) Chem. ACCE

TURRILL, William B. (1890-1961) Bot. RS17

TURRO, Nicholas (1939-) Chem. MHSE

TURTON, William (1762-1835) Conch. DNB

al-TUSI, Muhammad (1201-1274) Astron.; Math. CDZZ SCIN ZZ13

al-TUSI, Sharaf al-Din (d. c.1213) Astron.; Math. CDZZ ZZ13

TUTTLE, Charles W. (1829-1881) Astron. BIOD DAB

TUTTLE, Fordyce E. (1903-1969) Photo. NC54

TUTTLE, O. Frank (1916-) Geol. MHSE

TUTTON, Alfred E. (1864-1938) Crystal. CDZZ DNB5 ZZ13

TUVE, Merle A. (1901-1982) Phys. BEOS MHM1 MHSE

TWENHOFEL, William H. (1875-1957) Geol. CDZZ NC45 ZZ13

TWINING, Alexander C. (1801-1884) Invent.; Engr. BIOD DAB NC19

TWITTY, Victor C. (1901-1967) Zool. MHM2 MHSE

TWORT, Frederick W. (1877-1950) Bact. ABES ABET BDOS BEOS CDZZ ZZ13

TWYMAN, Frank (1876-1959) Elec. Engr. RS-5

TYCHO BRAHE SEE BRAHE, Tycho

TYLOR, Alfred (1824-1884) Geol. DNB

TYNDALL, Arthur M. (1881-1961) Phys. RS-8

TYNDALL, John (1820-1893) Phys. ABES ABET BDOS BEOS BHMT CDZZ DNB HLSM STYC VISC ZZ13

TYRRELL, Joseph B. (1858-1957) Geol.; Mng. CDZZ ZZ13

TYSON, Edward (c.1650-1708) Anat.; Med. ANHD CDZZ ZZ13

TYSON, Philip T. (1799-1877) Geol.; Chem. BIOD NC13

TYZZER, Ernest E. (1875-1965) Path. BM49

U

UBALDO, Guido SEE MONTE, Guidobaldo

UBBELOHDE, Alfred R. (1907-) Chem. COBC

UDALL, Stewart L. (1920-) Cons. LACC

UDY, Marvin J. (1892-1959) Metal. ACCE

UEXKULL, Jakob J. von (1864-1944) Biol. CDZZ ZZXV

UHLENBECK, George E. (1900-) Phys. ABES ABET BEOS DCPW

UHLER, Philip R. (1835-1913) Entom. AMEM DAB NC-8

UKHTOMSKY, Alexei A. (1875-1942) Physiol. CDZZ ZZ13

ULAM, Stanislaw M. (1909-1984) Math. MHM2 MHSE

ULKE, Henry (1821-1910) Entom. AMEM

ULLOA Y DE LA TORRE GIRAL, Antonio de (1716-1795) Nat. Hist. CDZZ ZZ13

ULRICH OF STRASBOURG (d. 1278) Nat. Philos. CDZZ ZZ13

ULRICH, Edward O. (1857-1944) Paleon. BM24 CDZZ DAB3 NC33 ZZ13

ULSTAD, Philippe (fl. c.1500-1520) Med. Alch. CDZZ ZZ13

ULUGH BEG (1394-1449) Astron. ABET BEOS CDZZ ZZ13

UMAR ibn al-FARRUKHAN al-TABARI (fl. 762-812) Astrol.; Astron. CDZZ ZZ13

al-UMAWI, Abu Abdallah Yaish (fl. 1300s) Math. CDZZ ZZ13

UNANUE, Jose H. (1755-1833) Nat. Hist. CDZZ ZZ13

UNDERHILL, Frank P. (1877-1932) Chem. NC25

UNDERWOOD, Eric J. (1905-1980) Agr. RS27

UNDERWOOD, Lucien M. (1853-1907) Bot. DAB NC12

UNDERWOOD, Newton (1906-1973) Phys. NC58

UNDERWOOD, William L. (1864-1929) Nat. Hist. NC23

UNGER, Franz (1800-1870) Bot. CDZZ ZZ13

UNI (fl. c.2350 B.C.) Engr. GE-1

UNNA, Paul G. (1850-1929) Med. BHMT

UNSOLD, Albrecht O. (1905-) Astrophys. MHM1 MHSE

UNVERDORBEN, Otto (1806-1873) Chem. BDOS BEOS

UNWIN, William C. (1838-1938) Engr. DNB5

UNZER, Johann A. (1727-1799) Physiol.; Med. CDZZ ZZ13

UPSON, Ralph H. (1888-1968) Aero. NC54

UPTON, Arthur C. (1923-) Path. MHM1 MHSE

UPTON, Winslow (1853-1914) Astron. DAB NC12

al-UQLIDISI, Abul-Hasan Ahmad (fl. 952-953) Math. CDZZ ZZ13

URBACH, Erich (1893-1946) Med. BHMT

URBAIN, Georges (1872-1938) Chem. ABES ABET BDOS BEOS CDZZ ZZ13

URE, Andrew (1778-1857) Chem. BDOS BEOS CDZZ DNB ZZ13

URE, David (d. 1798) Geol. DNB

UREY, Harold C. (1893-1981) Chem. ABES ABET AO81 BEOS CB41 CB60 IEAS MHM1 MHSE MOS6 MWBR NCSE NPWC PBTS PPTY WAMB

URYSON, Pavel S. (1898-1924) Math. CDZZ ZZ13

USHAKOV, Sergei N. (1893-) Chem. SMST

USSHER, Henry (d. 1790) Astron. DNB

UVAROV, Boris P. (1889-1970) Entom. RS17

UYEDA, Seiya (1929-) Geophys. MHSE

V

VAGNER, Egor E. (1849-1903) Chem. CDZZ ZZ13

VAILLANT, Leon L. (1834-1914) Ichth.; Herp. CDZZ ZZ13

VAILLANT, Sebastien (1669-1722) Bot. CDZZ ZZ13

VALDEN, Pavel SEE WALDEN, Paul

VALENCIENNES, Achille (1794-1865) Zool. CDZZ ZZ13

VALENTIN, Gabriel G. (1810-1883) Embryol.; Anat. ABET BHMT CDZZ ZZ13

VALENTINE, Basil (1394-c.1470) Alch. CDZZ MMMA ZZ13

VALERIO, Luca (1552-1618) Math. CDZZ ZZ13

VALKO, Emery (1902-1975) Chem. NC59

VALLEE-POUSSIN, Charles J. de la (1866-1962) Math. CDZZ ZZ13

VALLISNERI, Antonio (1661-1730) Biol.; Med. BDOS BEOS CDZZ WFBG ZZ13

VALLOIS, Henri V. (1889-) Anthro.; Paleon. MHM1 MHSE

VALMONT DE BOMARE, Jacques C. (1731-1807) Mineral.; Nat. Hist. CDZZ ZZ13

VALSALVA, Anton M. (1666-1723) Anat. BHMT CDZZ ZZ13

VALTURIO, Roberto (1405-1475) Engr.; Sci. Ed. CDZZ ZZ13

VALVERDE, Juan de (c.1520-c.1588) Med.; Anat. CDZZ ZZ13

VAN ALLEN, James A. (1914-) Phys. ABES ABET BEOS CB59 FPSN IEAS MHM1 MHSE MOS1 PBTS PPKY SCLB TGNH WAMB WMSW

VAN BENEDEN, Edouard SEE BENEDEN, Edouard van

VANCE, Samuel (1749-1821) Math.; Astron. DNB

VAN CLEAVE, Harley J. (1886-1953) Zool. NC44

VAN DE GRAAFF, Robert J. (1901-1967) Phys. ABES ABET BDOS BEOS CDZZ MHM2 MHSE ZZ13

VAN DE HULST, Hendrik C. (1918-) Astron. ABES ABET BEOS MHM2 MHSE

VAN DE KAMP, Peter (1901-) Astron. ABES ABET BEOS IEAS

VAN DEN HOVE, Maarten SEE HORTENSIUS, Martinus

VAN DEPOELE, Charles J. (1846-1892) Elec. Engr. DAB WAMB

VANDERMONDE, Alexander T. (1735-1796) Math. CDZZ ZZ13

VAN DER WAALS, Johann D. (1837-1923) Phys. ABES ABET BDOS BEOS CDZZ GRCH POSW SAIF ZZ14

VAN DER WEYDE, Peter H. (1813-1893) Chem. MCCW

VAN DEUSEN, Hobart M. (1910-1976) Zool. NC60

VAN DUZEE, Eduard P. (1861-1940) Entom. AMEM

VAN DYKE, Edwin C. (1869-1952) Entom. AMEM

VANE, John R. (1927-) Pharm. BEOS

VAN HELMONT, Johann B. (1579-1644) Chem.; Med. ABES ABET BDOS BEOS BHMT BMST CDZZ ESCS GRCH ZZ-6

VAN HISE, Charles R. (1857-1918) Geol. CDZZ WAMB ZZ13

VAN HOVE, Leon C. (1924-) Phys. MHM1 MHSE

VANINI, Giulio C. (1585-1619) Philos. CDZZ ZZ13

VAN LAWICK-GOODALL, Jane SEE GOODALL, Jane

VAN LEEUWENHOEK, Anton SEE LEEUWENHOEK, Anton van

VAN MAANEN, Adriaan (1884-1946) Astron. BEOS

VAN NAME, Ralph G. (1877-1961) Chem. NC49

VAN NIEL, Cornelius B. (1897-) Microbiol. MHM2 MHSE

VANNIKOV, Boris (1897-) Engr. NBPS

VAN OOSTEN, John (1891-1966) Ichth. LACC NC51

VAN ORSTRAND, Charles E. (1870-1959) Geophys. NC49 NCSD

VAN RENSSELAER, Jeremiah (1793-1871) Geol. BIOD

VAN SLYKE, Donald D. (1883-1971) Chem.; Physiol. ACCE BM48 CB43 CDZZ MHM1 MHSE NC56 ZZ13

VAN STONE, Nathan E. (1890-1971) Chem. NC57

VAN STRATEN, Florence (1913-) Chem. CWSE

VAN SWIETEN, Gerhard (1700-1772) Med. BHMT

VAN TAMELEN, Eugene E. (1925-) Chem. MHSE

VAN'T HOFF, Jacobus H. (1852-1911) Chem. ABES ABET BDOS BEOS BHMT CDZZ GRCH HSSO NPWC ZZ13

VANUXEM, Lardner (1792-1848) Geol. ASJD BIOD CDZZ ZZ13

VAN VLECK, Edward B. (1863-1943) Math. BM30 DAB3 NCSA

VAN VLECK, John H. (1899-1980) Phys. ABET AO80 BEOS MHM2 MHSE PAW2 POSW QPAS SOTT

VAN ZWALUWENBURG, R. (1891-1970) Entom. NC 58

VAQUEZ, Louis H. (1860-1936) Med. BHMT

VARAHAMIHIRA (499-587) Astron.; Astrol. CDZZ OGIV ZZ13

VARENIUS, Bernhardus (1622-1650) Geog. BEOS CDZZ ZZ13

VARENTSOV, Mikhail I. (1902-) Geol. SMST

VARIAN, Russell H. (1898-1959) Phys. NC49 TPAE

VARIAN, Sigurd F. (1901-1961) Invent. TPAE

VARIGNON, Pierre (1654-1722) Math. CDZZ ZZ13

VARLEY, Cromwell F. (1828-1883) Elec. Engr. DNB

VAROLIO, Constanzo (1543-1575) Med. BDOS BEOS CDZZ ZZ13

VARRO, Marcus T. (116 B.C.-27 B.C.) Polym. CDZZ ZZ13

VASEY, George (1822-1893) Bot. BIOD DAB MABH

VASSALE, Giulio (1862-1913) Med. CDZZ ZZ13

VASTARINI-CRESI, Giovanni (1870-1924) Anat.
CDZZ ZZ13

VATESVARA (b. 880) Astron. CDZZ ZZ13

VAUBAN, Sebastien L. (1633-1707) Engr. BDOS
CDZZ GE-1 ZZ13

VAUCANSON, Jacques de (1709-1782) Invent. BDOS
GE-1

VAUCHER, Jean P. (1763-1841) Bot. CDZZ ZZ13

VAUGHAN, Daniel (c.1818-1879) Astron.; Math.
BIOD DAB NC13

VAUGHAN, Ernest J. (1901-) Chem. COBC

VAUGHAN, John (1775-1807) Chem. ACCE

VAUGHAN, Thomas W. (1870-1952) Geol.; Ocean.
BM32 DAB5

VAUGHAN, Victor C. (1851-1929) Chem. ACCE
DAB

VAUQUELIN, Louis N. (1762-1829) Chem. ABES
ABET BDOS BEOS CDZZ ZZ13

VAUX, Henry J. (1912-) Forest. LACC

VAVILOV, Nikolai I. (1887-1943) Bot.; Genet. ABET
BDOS BEOS CDZZ ZZXV

VAVILOV, Sergey I. (1891-1951) Phys. CDZZ ZZ13

VAVRA, A. Stephen (1869-1947) Bot. NC36

VDOVENKO, Viktor M. (1907-) Chem. SMST

VEBLEN, Oswald (1880-1960) Math. CDZZ NCSF
WAMB ZZ13

VEEZEY, William E. (1883-1958) Chem. ACCE
NC47

VEGA, Garcilaso de la (c.1537-c.1616) Nat. Hist.
HAOA

VEITCH, Herry J. (1840-1929) Hort. DNB4

VEJDOVSKY, Frantisek (1849-1939) Zool. CDZZ
ZZXV

VEKSHINSKII, Sergei A. (1896-) Phys. SMST

VEKSLER, Vladimir I. (1907-1966) Phys. ABES
ABET BEOS CB65 CDZZ SMST ZZ13

VEKUA, Ilya N. (1907-) Math. SMST

VELIKANOV, Mikhail A. (1879-1964) Phys. SMST

VELIKOVSKY, Immanuel (1895-1979) Psych.; Sci.
Writ. CB57 MSFB PAW1

VELLEY, Thomas (1748-1806) Bot. DNB

VELLOZO, Jose M. (1742-1811) Bot. CDZZ ZZ13

VELPEAU, Alfred (1795-1867) Med. BHMT

VENABLE, Charles S. (1827-1900) Math. BIOD DAB

VENABLE, Francis P. (1856-1934) Chem. ACCE
NC10 NC28

VENDELINUS SEE WENDELIN, Gottfried

VENEL, Gabriel F. (1723-1775) Chem.; Med. CDZZ
ZZ13

VENETZ, Ignatz (1788-1859) Engr.; Glaciol. ABET
CDZZ ZZ13

VENING MEINESZ, Felix A. (1887-1966) Geophys.
BDOS BEOS CDZZ MHM1 MHSE RS13 ZZ13

VENN, John (1834-1923) Math. ABET CDZZ ZZ13

VENNESLAND, Birgit (1913-) Biochem. MHSE

VENTURI, Gioganni B. (1746-1822) Phys. FNEC

VERANTIUS, Faustus (1551-1617) Engr. CDZZ
GE-1 ZZ13

VERDET, Marcel E. (1824-1866) Phys. CDZZ ZZ13

VER EECKE, Paul (1867-1959) Math. CDZZ ZZ13

VERESCHAGIN, Leonid F. (1909-) Phys. SMST

VERHOOGEN, John (1912-) Geophys. MHM2 MHSE

VERHULST, Pierre F. (1804-1849) Math. CDZZ
IMMO ZZ13

VERMUYDEN, Cornelius (1590-1677) Engr. BDOS
GE-1

VERNADSKY, Vladimir I. (1863-1945) Mineral.
ABET CDZZ ZZ13

VERNEUIL, Philippe E. de (1805-1873) Geol.; Paleon.
CDZZ ZZ13

VERNEY, Ernest B. (1894-1967) Pharm. RS16

VERNIER, Pierre (1584-1637) Engr.; Instr. ABET
  BDOS BEOS CDZZ ZZ13

VERNON, Arthur A. (1902-1973) Chem. NC58

VERNOV, Sergei N. (1910-) Phys. SMST

VERONESE, Giuseppe (1854-1917) Math. CDZZ ZZ13

VERREAUX, Jules P. (1807-1873) Exp. WFBG

VERRILL, Addison E. (1839-1926) Zool. BM14
  CDZZ DAB NC-3 ZZ14

VERVILLE, Alfred (1890-1970) Aero. ICFW

VERWORN, Max (1863-1921) Physiol. CDZZ ZZ14

VERY, Frank W. (1852-1927) Astron. NC12

VESALIUS, Andreas (1514-1564) Anat. ABES ABET
  BDOS BEOS BHMT CDZZ HEXS HLSM LISD
  MMMA SMIL SXWS TBSG TOWS ZZ14

VESEY, Louis de SEE XANTUS, John

VESLING, Johann (1598-1649) Anat.; Bot. CDZZ
  ZZ14

VESSIOT, Ernest (1865-1952) Math. CDZZ ZZ14

VESTINE, Ernest H. (1906-1968) Phys. BM51

VICAT, Louis J. (1786-1861) Engr. GE-1

VICKERY, Hubert B. (1893-1978) Biochem. MHM2
  MHSE

VICQ D'AZYR, Felix (1748-1794) Anat.; Med. CDZZ
  ZZ14

VIDAL, Emil (1825-1893) Med. BHMT

VIEHOEVER, Arno (1885-1969) Pharm. NC55

VIEILLOT, Louis J. (1748-1831) Ornith. HAOA

VIERECK, Henry L. (1881-1931) Entom. AMEM

VIETA, Franciscus SEE VIETE, Francois

VIETE, Francois, (1540-1603) Math. ABES ABET
  BDOS BEOS BMST CDZZ MELW SXWS ZZ14

VIEUSSENS, Raymond de (1635-1715) Anat.; Med.
  BHMT CDZZ ZZ14

VIGANI, John F. (1650-1713) Chem.; Pharm. CDZZ
  ZZ14

VIGNOLES, Charles B. (1793-1875) Engr. GE-1

VIGO, Giovanni da (1450-1525) Med. CDZZ ZZ14

VIGORS, Nicholas A. (1785-1840) Zool. DNB

VIJAYANANDA (fl. 966) Astron. CDZZ ZZ14

VILLALPANDO, Juan B. (1552-1608) Math.; Archit.
  CDZZ ZZ14

VILLARD, Paul U. (1860-1934) Phys. ABES ABET
  CDZZ ZZ14

VILLARD DE HONNECOURT (b. c.1190) Archit.
  CDZZ ZZ14

VILLARI, Emilio (1836-1904) Phys. CDZZ ZZ14

VILLEMIN, Jean A. (1827-1892) Med. BDOS BEOS

VILMORIN, Pierre L. de (1816-1860) Bot. CDZZ
  ZZ14

VINCENT OF BEAUVAIS (c.1190-c.1264) Sci. Writ.
  CDZZ ZZ14

VINE, Frederick J. (1939-) Geol. BEOS

VINES, Sydney H. (1849-1934) Bot. DNB5

VINOGRAD, Jerome R. (1913-1976) Chem. MHSE

VINOGRADOV, Aleksandr P. (1895-1975) Geol.
  SMST

VINOGRADOV, Ivan M. (1891-1983) Math. BEOS
  SMST

VINOGRADSKY, Sergey N. (1856-1953) Microbiol.
  CDZZ ZZ14

VIOLLE, Jules L. (1841-1923) Phys. CDZZ ZZ14

VIRCHOW, Rudolf C. (1821-1902) Path. ABES
  ABET BDOS BEOS BHMT CDZZ DSLP ZZ14

VIREY, Julien J. (1775-1846) Nat. Hist. CDZZ ZZ14

VIRTANEN, Artturi I. (1895-1973) Biochem. ABES
  ABET BEOS CDZZ MHM1 MHSE NPWC ZZ14

VISHNIAC, Roman (1897-) Microbiol.; Zool. AMJB CB67 SEMK

VISHNIAC, Wolf (1922-1973) Biochem. MOS6

VISSCHER, Maurice B. (1901-) Physiol. MHM2 MHSE

VISVARUPA SEE MUNISVARA VISVARUPA

VITALI, Giuseppe (1875-1932) Math. CDZZ ZZ14

VITRUVIUS (c.70 B.C.-25 B.C.) Archit. ABES ABET BDOS CDZZ SMIL ZZXV

VIVES, Juan L. (1492-1540) Philos.; Psych. CDZZ ZZ14

VIVIANI, Vincenzo (1622-1703) Math. ABES ABET BEOS CDZZ ZZ14

VIZE, Vladimir Y. (1886-1954) Ocean.; Meteor. CDZZ ZZ14

VLACK, Adriaan (1600-1666/7) Math. CDZZ ZZ14

VLACQ, Adriaan SEE VLACK, Adriaan

VLASOV, Kuzma A. (1905-1964) Geol. SMST

VOEVODSKII, Vladislav V. (1917-) Chem. SMST

VOEYKOV, Aleksandr I. (1842-1916) Geog.; Climat. CDZZ ZZ14

VOGEL, Hermann K. (1842-1907) Astron. ABES ABET BEOS CDZZ ZZ14

VOGT, Carl (1817-1895) Zool.; Biol. ANHD CDZZ ZZ14

VOGT, Johan H. (1858-1932) Geol. CDZZ ZZ14

VOGT, Louis F. (1880-1952) Chem. ACCE

VOGT, Thorolf (1888-1958) Geol. CDZZ ZZ14

VOGT, William (1902-1968) Cons. HOCS LACC

VOIGT, Johann C. (1752-1821) Geol.; Mng. CDZZ ZZ14

VOIGT, Woldemar (1850-1919) Phys. CDZZ ZZ14

VOIT, Carl von (1831-1908) Physiol. ABES ABET BHMT CDZZ ZZ14

VOLCK, William H. (1879-1943) Entom. AMEM

VOLFKOVICH, Semen I. (1896-) Chem. SMST

VOLHARD, Jacob (1834-1910) Chem. HSSO

VOLKMANN, Paul O. (1856-1938) Phys. CDZZ ZZ14

VOLNEY, Constantin F. de (1757-1820) Geog. CDZZ ZZ14

VOLSKII, Anton N. (1897-1966) Metal. SMST

VOLTA, Alessandro G. (1745-1827) Phys. ABES ABET BDOS BEOS CDZZ DCPW EETD ELEC ESEH FNEC FPHM GASJ GE-1 GOED HOSS IFBS LECE PAW2 SAIF TPOS VTHB ZZ14

VOLTAIRE, Francois M.A. de (1694-1778) Sci. Hist. ABES ABET CDZZ ZZ14

VOLTERRA, Vito (1860-1940) Math. CDZZ IMMO ZZ14

VOLTZ, Philippe L. (1785-1840) Geol. CDZZ ZZ14

VON BRAUN, Wernher (1912-1977) Rocket. ABES ABET BEOS FPSN GDSP HRST ICFW IEAS MHM1 MHSE MOS1 PBTS PPEY PPKY SAIF WAMB

VON ENGELN, Oskar D. (1880-1965) Geol. NC54

VON EULER, Ulf S. (1904-1983) Physiol. ABET

VON GRAEFE, Albrecht (1828-1870) Med. BHMT

VON HAGEN, Victor W. (1908-) Nat. Hist. CB42

VON KARMAN, Theodore SEE KARMAN, Theodore von

VONNEGUT, Bernard (1914-) Phys. ABES ABET BEOS

VON NEUMANN, Johan (1903-1957) Math.; Comp. ABES ABET BEOS BM32 CB55 CDZZ FMAS IMMO MATT MELW MHM1 MHSE MOS1 NC46 WAMB ZZ14

VON ROSENSTEIN, Nils R. SEE ROSEN, Nils

VON SOCHOCKY, Sabin A. (1882-1928) Chem. ACCE

VONSOVSKII, Sergei V. (1910-) Phys. SMST

VON For Other Names with Von SEE Second Element of Name.

VORHEES, Edward B. (1856-1911) Chem. DAB NC13

VORONIN, Mikhail S. (1838-1903) Bot. CDZZ ZZ14

VORONY, Georgy F. (1868-1908) Math. CDZZ ZZ14

VOROZHTSOV, Nikolai N. (1907-) Chem. SMST

VOSMAER, Aernout (1720-1799) Nat. Hist. ANHD

VOUGHT, Chance M. (1890-1930) Aero. DAB WAMB

VREELAND, Frederick K. (1874-1964) Invent. NC51

VRIES, Hugo de (1848-1935) Genet.; Evol. ABES BDOS BEOS CDZZ HLSM ZZ14

VUL, Bentsion M. (1903-) Phys. SMST

VVEDENSKY, Nikolay E. (1852-1922) Physiol. CDZZ ZZ14

VYSHNEGRADSKY, Ivan A. (1831-1895) Engr. CDZZ ZZ14

VYSOTSKY, Georgy N. (1865-1940) Soil Sci.; Forest. CDZZ ZZ14

W

WAAGE, Peter (1833-1900) Chem.; Mineral. ABES ABET BDOS BEOS CDZZ ZZ14

WAALS, Johannes SEE VAN DER WAALS, Johannes D.

WACHSMUTH, Charles (1829-1896) Paleon. BIOD DAB NC-7

WACKENRODER, Heinrich W. (1798-1854) Pharm. CDZZ ZZ14

WADDINGTON, Conrad H. (1905-1975) Biol. BEOS CB62 MHM2 MHSE RS23

WADDINGTON, Thomas C. (1930-) Chem. COBC

WADE, Joseph S. (1880-1961) Entom. AMEM NC49

WADE, Walter (d. 1825) Bot. DNB

WADIA, Darashaw N. (1883-1969) Geol. RS16

WADSWORTH, Frank L. (1866-1936) Astrophys. NC13 NC26

ibn WAFID, Abu al-Mutarrif (fl. c.1008-1075) Pharm. CDZZ ZZ14

WAGER, Laurence R. (1904-1965) Geol. RS13

WAGNER, Rudolph (1805-1864) Anat.; Physiol. CDZZ ZZ14

WAGNER, Theodore B. (1869-1936) Chem. NC27

WAGNER, William (1796-1885) Paleon. BIOD

WAGNER-JUAREGG, Julius (1857-1940) Psychiat. ABET BEOS CDZZ PAW2 ZZ14

WAHL, William H. (1848-1909) Sci. Writ. ACCE

WAHLENBERG, Goran (1780-1851) Bot. CDZZ ZZ14

ibn WAHSHIYYA, Abu Bakr Ahmad (c.860-c.935) Agr. CDZZ ZZ14

WAIDNER, Charles W. (1873-1922) Phys. DAB

WAILES, Benjamin L. (1797-1862) Nat. Hist. BIOD DAB

WAIN, Ralph L. (1911-) Chem. COBC

WAITE, Frederick C. (1870-1956) Med. NC44

WAKELAND, Claude (1888-1960) Entom. AMEM

WAKEMAN, A. Maurice (1897-1929) Med. NC25

WAKIL, Salih J. (1927-) Biochem. MHSE

WAKLEY, Thomas (1795-1862) Med. BHMT

WAKSMAN, Selman A. (1888-1973) Bact. ABES ABET BEOS CB46 MFIR MHM1 MHSE WAMB WMSW

WALCH, Johann E. (1725-1778) Paleon. CDZZ ZZ14

WALCOTT, Charles D. (1850-1927) Geol.; Paleon. BM39 CDZZ DAB PHLS WAMB ZZ14

WALCOTT, Frederic C. (1869-1949) Cons. LACC

WALCOTT, Mary M. (1860-1940) Nat. Hist. NAW

WALD, Abraham (1902-1950) Math. CDZZ ZZ14

WALD, Frantisek (1861-1930) Chem. CDZZ ZZ14

WALD, George (1906-) Biol.; Biochem. ABES
ABET AMJB BEOS CB68 MHM1 MHSE

WALDBAUER, Louis J. (1896-1959) Chem. NC47

WALDEN, Paul (1863-1957) Chem. ABES ABET
BDOS BEOS CDZZ ZZ14

WALDEN, Percy T. (1869-1943) Chem. NC31

WALDEYER-HARTZ, Wilhelm H. von (1836-1921)
Anat. ABET BDOS BEOS CDZZ ZZ14

WALDSEEMULLER, Martin (1470-1518) Geog. ABET
CDZZ ZZ14

WALES, William (c.1734-1798) Math. DNB

WALFORD, Lionel A. (1905-) Biol. LACC

WALKER, Alexander (1779-1852) Physiol. CDZZ
ZZ14

WALKER, Charles V. (1812-1882) Elec. Engr. DNB

WALKER, Edmund M. (1877-1969) Zool. MHM1
MHSE

WALKER, Francis A. (1840-1897) Math. BM-5 WAMB

WALKER, Gilbert T. (1868-1958) Meteor. DNB7
RS-8

WALKER, James (1863-1935) Chem. BDOS BEOS
DNB5

WALKER, John (1731-1803) Geol.; Bot. CDZZ ZZ14

WALKER, John (1759-1830) Med. DNB

WALKER, John (1780-1859) Invent. BDOS

WALKER, John C. (1893-) Bot. MHM2

WALKER, Norma F. (1893-) Biol. CB57

WALKER, Sears C. (1805-1853) Astron.; Math.
BIOD DAB NC-8

WALKER, William H. (1869-1934) Chem. Engr. HCEF

WALL, Frederick T. (1912-) Chem. MHM2 MHSE

WALL, Leo A. (1918-1972) Chem. ACCE NC56

WALLACE, Alfred R. (1823-1913) Nat. Hist. ABES
ABET BDOS BEOS CDZZ DARR DMXE DNB3
GRBW HLSM HNHB NEXB SSDH ZZ14

WALLACE, Charles F. (1885-1964) Invent. NC51

WALLACE, John C. (1925-) Microbiol. SBPY

WALLACE, Robert J. (1868-1945) Phys. NC35

WALLACE, Thomas (1891-1965) Hort. RS12

WALLACE, William (1768-1843) Math. CDZZ DNB
ZZ14

WALLACH, Otto (1847-1931) Chem. ABES ABET
BDOS BEOS CDZZ GRCH NPWC ZZ14

WALLACH, Roger N. (1882-1941) Chem. NC31

WALLER, Augustus D. (1856-1922) Med. BHMT

WALLER, Augustus V. (1816-1870) Med. BHMT
CDZZ DNB ZZ14

WALLER, Wilhelmine S. (1914-) Cons. NCSM

WALLERIUS, Johan G. (1709-1785) Chem.; Mineral.
CDZZ ZZ14

WALLICH, George C. (1815-1899) Med.; Zool. CDZZ
ZZ14

WALLICH, Nathaniel (1786-1854) Bot. DNB

WALLING, Cheves T. (1916-) Chem. MHM2 MHSE

WALLINGFORD, Richard SEE RICHARD OF
WALLINGFORD

WALLIS, Barnes N. (1887-1979) Engr.; Aero. BEOS
ICFW RS27

WALLIS, John (1616-1703) Math. ABES ABET BDOS
BEOS CDZZ DNB ZZ14

WALLIS, William E. (1908-) Geophys. SWWP

WALLS, Henry J. (1907-) Chem. COBC

WALSCHAERTS, Egide (1820-1901) Engr. BDOS

WALSH, Arthur D. (1916-1977) Chem. COBC RS24

WALSH, Benjamin D. (1808-1869) Entom. AMEM
BIOD DAB

WALSH, Joseph L. (1895-1973) Math. MHM1 MHSE

WALSH, William B. (1920-) Med. CB62

WALSHE, Francis M. (1885-1973) Med. RS20

WALTER OF ODINGTON (fl. c.1280-1330) Alch. CDZZ ZZ14

WALTER, Philippe (1810-1847) Chem. BDOS CDZZ ZZ14

WALTER, Thomas (c.1740-1789) Bot. BIOD DAB

WALTER, William G. (1910-) Med. ABES ABET BEOS

WALTON, Ernest T. (1903-) Phys. ABES ABET BEOS CB52 MHM1 MHSE POSW

WALTON, Izaak (1593-1683) Zool. CDZZ DNB ZZ14

WANG CHENG (fl. 1627) Engr. GE-1

WANG CHING (fl. 70) Engr. GE-1

WANG HSI-SHAN (1628-1682) Astron. CDZZ ZZ14

WANGENSTEEN, Owen H. (1898-1981) Med. MHM1 MHSE

WANGERIN, Albert (1844-1933) Math. CDZZ ZZ14

WANKEL, Felix (1902-) Engr. NTBM SAIF

WANKLYN, James A. (1834-1906) Chem. CDZZ DNB2 ZZ14

WANSBROUGH-JONES, Owen H. (1905-) Chem. COBC

WARBURG, Emil G. (1846-1931) Phys. CDZZ ZZ14

WARBURG, Otto H. (1883-1970) Biochem. ABES ABET BEOS CDZZ GJPS MHM2 MHSE RS18 ZZ14

WARBURTON, Fred W. (1898-1969) Phys. NC54

WARD, Calvin H. (1933-) Bot. CHUB

WARD, Harry M. (1854-1906) Bot. DNB2

WARD, Henry A. (1834-1906) Nat. Hist. DAB NC28

WARD, Henry B. (1865-1945) Parasit. DAB3 LACC NC13 NC35

WARD, James C. (1843-1880) Geol. DNB

WARD, Joshua (1685-1761) Chem. BDOS BEOS

WARD, Lauriston (1882-1960) Archaeol. NC48

WARD, Lester F. (1841-1923) Paleon. FHUA

WARD, Nathaniel B. (1791-1868) Bot. DNB

WARD, Richard H. (1837-1917) Micros. DAB

WARD, Seth (1617-1689) Astron. CDZZ ZZ14

WARDER, John A. (1812-1883) Forest.; Hort. BIOD LACC

WARDER, Robert B. (1848-1905) Chem. BIOD

WARDLAW, Claude W. (1901-) Bot. MHM2 MHSE

WARDLAW, William (1892-1958) Chem. DNB7

WARGENTIN, Pehr W. (1717-1783) Astron. CDZZ ZZ14

WARING, Edward (1734-1798) Math. CDZZ DNB ZZ14

WARING, P. Alston (1895-1978) Cons. NC61

WARING, William G. (1847-1935) Metal. ACCE

WARINGTON, Robert (1807-1867) Chem. DNB

WARMING, Johannes E. (1841-1924) Bot. CDZZ ZZ14

WARNER, John (c.1673-1760) Hort. DNB

WARNER, John C. (1897-) Chem. CB50 MHM2 MHSE

WARNER, Lucien C. (1841-1925) Chem. ACCE

WARNER, Richard (c.1713-1775) Bot. DNB

WARNER, Roger S. Jr. (1920-) Chem. Engr. MOS5

WARNER, William R. (1836-1901) Chem. NC-2

WARREN, Cyrus M. (1824-1891) Chem. BIOD DAB NC10

WARREN, Gouverneur K. (1830-1882) Engr.; Geol. BIOD BM-2

WARREN, John (1753-1815) Med. BHMT YSMS

WARREN, John C. (1778-1856) Anat.; Paleon. BHMT BIOD

WARREN, Joseph III (1741-1775) Med. BHMT

WARREN, Shields (1898-1980) Path. AO80 BEOS MHM1 MHSE

WASHBURN, E. Roger (1899-1967) Chem. NC55

WASHBURN, Edward W. (1881-1934) Chem. ACCE BM17 CDZZ DAB ZZ14

WASHBURN, Frank S. (1860-1922) Chem. ACCE NC32

WASHBURN, H. Bradford (1910-) Exp. CB66

WASHBURN, Margaret F. (1871-1939) Psych. BM25 CWSE

WASHINGTON, Henry S. (1867-1934) Geol. ACCE CDZZ ZZ14

WASHKEN, Edward (1912-1967) Chem. NC53

WASSERBURG, Gerald J. (1927-) Geol. MHSE

WASSERMAN, August P. von (1866-1925) Bact. ABES ABET BDOS BEOS BHMT CDZZ ZZXV

WASSON, Theron (1887-1970) Geol. NC55

WATERHOUSE, Benjamin (1754-1846) Med. BHMT BIOD COAC

WATERHOUSE, George R. (1810-1888) Nat. Hist. DNB

WATERMAN, Alan T. (1892-1967) Phys. CB51 NC53

WATERMAN, Richard A. (1914-1971) Anthro. NC57

WATERS, Aaron C. (1905-) Geol. MHM2 MHSE

WATERS, William A. (1903-) Chem. COBC

WATERSTON, John J. (1811-1883) Phys.; Chem. BDOS BEOS CDZZ ZZ14

WATERTON, Charles (1782-1865) Nat. Hist. CDZZ DNB HNHB NATJ SGNF ZZ14

WATKINS, George B. (1895-1966) Chem. Engr. NC53

WATSON, Clarence W. (1894-) Cons. LACC

WATSON, David M. (1886-1973) Zool. BEOS RS20

WATSON, George N. (1886-1965) Math. CDZZ RS12 ZZ14

WATSON, Henry W. (1827-1903) Math. DNB2

WATSON, Hewett C. (1804-1881) Evol.; Phren. CDZZ DNB ZZ14

WATSON, James C. (1838-1880) Astron. BIOD BM-3 DAB NC-7

WATSON, James D. (1928-) Biochem. ABES ABET BEOS EDCJ FMBB HLSM MHM1 MHSE SAIF WAMB

WATSON, John B. (1878-1958) Psych. ABES ABET POPF

WATSON, Malcolm (1873-1955) Med. DNB7

WATSON, Peter W. (1761-1830) Bot. DNB

WATSON, Richard (1737-1816) Chem. CDZZ ZZ14

WATSON, Sereno (1826-1892) Bot. BIOD BM-5 BNBR CDZZ DAB MABH ZZ14

WATSON, Thomas A. (1854-1934) Invent. WAMB

WATSON, William (1715-1787) Phys.; Bot. BDOS BEOS BMST CDZZ DNB EETD ESEH ZZ14

WATSON-WATT, Robert A. (1892-1973) Phys. ABES ABET BDOS CB45 EETD GDSP HOSS RS21 SAIF

WATT, George (1820-1893) Chem. ACCE

WATT, James (1736-1819) Invent.; Engr. ABES ABET BDOS BEOS CDZZ DNB FNEC FOIF GE-1 GEXB HOSS LECE MGAH MPIP SAIF SIRC SMIL VTHB ZZ14

WATT, Kenneth (1929-) Ecol. POEC

WATT, Robert E. (1774-1819) Med. BHMT

WATTS, Chester B. (1889-1971) Astron. NC57

WATTS, Henry (1815-1884) Chem. DNB

WATTS, Lyle F. (1890-1962) Forest. EAFC

WATTS, Oliver P. (1865-1953) Electrochem. ACCE

WAUGH, John S. (1929-) Chem. MHSE

WAYBURN, Edgar (1906-) Cons. LACC

WAYNE, Arthur T. (1863-1930) Ornith. DAB

al-WAZZAN al-ZAYYATI SEE LEO THE AFRICAN

WEATHERBEE, Roger (Contemporary) Engr. CHUB

WEATHERBY, Charles A. (1875-1949) Bot. NC38

WEATHERWAX, James L. (1884-1965) Phys. NC51

WEAVER, Ira A. (1871-1965) Invent. NC52

WEAVER, Richard L. (1911-1964) Cons. LACC

WEBB, Harold (1884-) Phys. QPAS

WEBB, Philip B. (1793-1854) Bot. DNB

WEBB, Thomas W. (1806-1885) Astron. DNB

WEBB, Wilse B. (1920-) Med. CHUB

WEBBER, Herbert J. (1865-1946) Bot. DAB4 MABH
   NC17

WEBER, Ernst (1901-) Engr. MHM1 MHSE

WEBER, Ernst H. (1795-1878) Anat.; Physiol. ABES
   ABET BEOS BHMT CDZZ ZZ14

WEBER, Hans H. (1896-1974) Physiol. MHM2 MHSE

WEBER, Harold C. (1895-) Chem. Engr. HCEF

WEBER, Heinrich (1842-1913) Math. CDZZ ZZ14

WEBER, Henry A. (1845-1912) Chem. ACCE DAB
   NC19

WEBER, Max W. (1852-1937) Zool. CDZZ ZZ14

WEBER, Wilhelm E. (1804-1891) Phys. ABES ABET
   BDOS BEOS CDZZ EETD FNEC GOED VTHB
   ZZ14

WEBRE, Alfred L. (1881-1963) Chem. ACCE

WEBSTER, Arthur G. (1863-1923) Phys. BM18 DAB
   NC13 QPAS

WEBSTER, David L. (1888-1976) Phys. BM53 NCSA
   QPAS

WEBSTER, Francis M. (1849-1916) Entom. AMEM
   NC13

WEBSTER, John (1610-1682) Chem.; Med. CDZZ
   ZZ14

WEBSTER, John W. (1793-1850) Chem. ACCE ASJD
   BIOD HSSO

WEBSTER, Leslie T. (1894-1943) Path. NC32

WEBSTER, Thomas (1773-1844) Geol. CDZZ DNB
   ZZ14

WEDDERBURN, Joseph H. (1882-1948) Math. CDZZ
   ZZ14

WEDEL, Georg W. (1645-1721) Med.; Chem. CDZZ
   ZZ14

WEDGWOOD, Josiah (1730-1795) Chem. BDOS GE-1
   CDZZ SIRC ZZ14

WEDGWOOD, Thomas (1771-1805) Photo. BDOS

WEED, Clarence M. (1864-1947) Nat. Hist. NC41

WEED, Lewis H. (1886-1952) Anat. DAB5

WEEDON, Basil C. (1923-) Chem. COBC

WEEKS, Lewis G. (1893-1977) Geol. NC59

WEGEFORTH, Harry M. (1882-1941) Zool. NC42

WEGENER, Alfred L. (1880-1930) Meteor.; Geophys.
   ABES ABET BDOS BEOS CDZZ ZZ14

WEHMEYER, Louis E. (1897-1971) Bot. NC57

WEHNELT, Arthur R. (1871-1944) Phys. CDZZ ZZ14

WEHRLE, Lawrence P. (1887-1950) Entom. NC39

WEI MENG-PIEN (fl. 340) Engr. GE-1

WEICHSELBAUM, Anton (1845-1920) Path. CDZZ
   ZZ14

WEICK, Fred E. (1899-) Aero. ICFW

WEICKER, Theodore (1861-1940) Chem. NC29

WEIDENREICH, Franz (1873-1948) Anthro. DAB4

WEIDLEIN, Edward R. (1887-1983) Chem. CB48
   NCSC

WEIERSTRASS, Karl W. (1815-1897) Math. ABET BDOS BEOS CDZZ WTGM ZZ14

WEIGEL, Christian E. (1748-1831) Chem. CDZZ ZZ14

WEIGEL, Valentin (1533-1588) Philos. CDZZ ZZ14

WEIGERT, Carl (1845-1904) Med. BHMT CDZZ ZZ14

WEIGHTMAN, William (1813-1904) Chem. BIOD DAB

WEIL, Alfred J. (1900-1975) Microbiol. NC58

WEIL, Andre (1906-) Math. BEOS

WEINBERG, Alvin M. (1915-) Phys. CB66 MHM1 MHSE

WEINBERG, Robert A. (1942-) Biochem. CB83

WEINBERG, Steven (1933-) Phys. ABET BEOS MHSE POSW SOT3

WEINBERG, Wilhelm (1862-1937) Genet. CDZZ ZZ14

WEINGARTEN, Julius (1836-1910) Math. CDZZ ZZ14

WEISBERG, Mark (1890-1963) Chem. NC51

WEISEL, Torsten N. (1924-) Physiol. BEOS

WEISMENN, August F. (1834-1914) Zool. ABES ABET BDOS CDZZ HLSM ZZ14

WEISS, Christian S. (1780-1856) Crystal.; Mineral. CDZZ ZZ14

WEISS, Edmund (1837-1917) Astron. CDZZ ZZ14

WEISS, Emil (1893-) Bact. NCSF

WEISS, Joseph J. (1905-) Chem. COBC

WEISS, Paul A. (1898-) Biol. CB70 MHM2 MHSE

WEISS, Pierre (1865-1940) Phys. ABET CDZZ ZZ14

WEISS, Richard A. (1910-1974) Phys. NC58

WEISSBACH, Herbert (1932-) Biochem. MHSE

WEISSKOPF, Victor F. (1908-) Phys. AMJB CB76 MHM2 MHSE

WEISZ, Paul B. (1919-) Chem. Engr. MHSE

WEIZMANN, Chaim (1874-1952) Biochem. ABES ABET CB42 CB48 CDZZ HSSO ZZ14

WEIZSACKER, Carl F. von (1912-) Astron. ABES ABET IEAS

WELCH, Paul S. (1882-1959) Limn. LACC

WELCH, William H. (1850-1934) Bact. ABFC BDOS BHMT BM22 CDZZ ZZ14

WELD, Julia T. (1887-1973) Med. NC58

WELDON, Walter (1832-1885) Chem. BDOS BEOS DNB

WELDON, Walter F. (1860-1906) Evol.; Biol. CDZZ DNB2 ZZ14

WELLER, Thomas H. (1915-) Virol. ABES ABET BEOS CB55 MHM1 MHSE PAW2 WAMB

WELLMAN, Victor E. (1903-1964) Chem. NC51

WELLMAN, Walter (1858-1934) Aero.; Exp. DAB

WELLS, Charlotte F. (1814-1901) Phren. NAW

WELLS, David A. (1828-1898) Chem.; Geol. BIOD

WELLS, Edward (1667-1727) Math. DNB

WELLS, Harry G. (1875-1943) Path. BM26 CDZZ ZZ14

WELLS, Horace (1815-1848) Med. BDOS BEOS PAW3

WELLS, Samuel R. (1820-1875) Phren. BIOD

WELLS, Webster (1851-1916) Math. NC17

WELLS, William C. (1757-1817) Phys.; Physiol. BHMT BIOD CDZZ DAB ZZ14

WELSBACH, Carl A. von (1858-1929) Invent. BDOS

WELSH, Edward C. (1909-) Aero. MOS7

WELSH, John (1824-1859) Meteor. DNB

WELWITSCH, Friedrich M. (1807-1872) Bot. DNB

WENDELIN, Gottfried (1580-1667) Astron.; Meteor. ABES ABET BEOS CDZZ ZZ14

WENDT, Gerald L. (1891-1973) Chem. CB40 NC58

WENHAM, Francis H. (1824-1908) Aero. ICFW

WENNER-GREN, Axel L. (1881-1961) Invent. BDOS

WENT, Friedrich A. (1863-1935) Bot. CDZZ ZZ14

WENT, Frits W. (1903-) Bot. MHM1 MHSE

WENTE, Edward C. (1889-1972) Phys. NC56

WENZEL, Carl F. (1740-1793) Chem. BDOS BEOS

WEPFER, Johann J. (1620-1689) Med. BHMT CDZZ ZZ14

WERKMAN, Chester H. (1893-1962) Bact. BM44 NC49

WERLHOF, Paul G. (1699-1767) Med. BHMT

WERNER, Abraham G. (1750-1817) Geol.; Mineral. ABES ABET BDOS BEOS CDZZ ZZ14

WERNER, Alfred (1886-1919) Chem. ABES ABET BDOS BEOS CDZZ GRCH HSSO NPWC ZZ14

WERNER, Alfred E. (1911-) Chem. COBC

WERNER, Johann (1468-1528) Astron.; Math. BMST CDZZ ZZ14

WERNICKE, Carl (1848-1905) Med. BEOS CDZZ ZZ14

WERTHEIM, Ernst (1864-1920) Med. CDZZ ZZ14

WERTZ, Augustus S. (1896-1978) Engr. NC61

WESSEL, Caspar (1745-1818) Surv.; Math. CDZZ ZZ14

WEST, Benjamin (1730-1813) Astron. BIOD DAB NC-8

WEST, Clarence J. (1886-1953) Chem. ACCE

WEST, Thomas S. (1927-) Chem. COBC

WEST, Tristram F. (1911-) Chem. COBC

WEST, William (d. 1851) Chem. GENT

WESTHEIMER, Frank H. (1912-) Chem. MHM2 MHSE

WESTINGHOUSE, George (1846-1914) Engr.; Invent. ABES ABET AMIH BDOS BEOS HFGA IHMV SGEC SMIL WAMB

WESTON, Richard (1591-1652) Agr. BDOS

WESTWOOD, John O. (1805-1893) Nat. Hist. ANHD DNB

WESTWOOD, Richard W. (1896-1961) Cons. LACC

WETHERILL, Charles M. (1825-1871) Chem. ACCE BIOD DAB NC13

WETHERILL, Samuel (1821-1890) Chem. Engr. ACCE

WETMORE, Alexander (1766-1813) Ornith. BWCL

WETMORE, Alexander (1886-1978) Ornith.; Biol. CB48

WETMORE, Ralph H. (1892-) Bot. MHM1 MHSE

WEXLER, Harry (1911-1962) Meteor. MHM1 MHSE NC53

WEYL, Hermann (1885-1955) Math. BEOS CDZZ DAB5 RS-3 ZZ14

WEYLE, Fritz J. (1915-1977) Math. NC59

WHARTON, George (1617-1681) Astron. CDZZ ZZ14

WHARTON, Thomas (1614-1673) Anat.; Med. BDOS BEOS CDZZ ZZ14

WHATELY, Richard (1787-1863) Math. CDZZ ZZ14

WHEATSTONE, Charles (1802-1875) Phys. ABES ABET BDOS BEOS CDZZ EETD ZZ14

WHEELER, Anna P. (1883-1966) Math. NAWM

WHEELER, George M. (1842-1905) Engr.; Surv. BIOD

WHEELER, Harold A. (1903-) Elec. Engr. MHM1 MHSE

WHEELER, John A. (1911-) Phys. ABET BEOS CB70 MHM2 MHSE

WHEELER, Robert E. (1890-1976) Archaeol. RS23

WHEELER, Thomas (1754-1847) Bot. DNB

WHEELER, William M. (1865-1937) Entom. AMEM BM19 CDZZ DAB2 NC27 ZZ14

WHETZEL, Herbert H. (1877-1944) Bot. DAB3

WHEWELL, William (1794-1866) Astron.; Sci. Hist.
ABET BEOS CDZZ DARR DNB GENT ZZ14

WHIDDINGTON, Richard (1885-1970) Phys. RS17

WHIFFEN, David H. (1922-) Chem. COBC

WHINFIELD, John R. (1901-1966) Invent. BDOS

WHINNERY, John R. (1916-) Engr. BDOS MHSE

WHIPPLE, Amiel W. (1816-1863) Engr. BIOD

WHIPPLE, Fred L. (1906-) Astron. ABES ABET
BEOS CB52 IEAS MHM1 MHSE MOS2 WMSW

WHIPPLE, George C. (1866-1924) Biol. LACC

WHIPPLE, George H. (1878-1976) Path. ABES ABET
BEOS DODR MHM2

WHIPPLE, George M. (1842-1893) Phys. DNB

WHIPPLE, Squire (1804-1888) Engr. BIOD

WHISTLER, Daniel (1619-1684) Med. BHMT

WHISTON, William (1667-1752) Math.; Cosmol.
BEOS CDZZ ZZ14

WHITAKER, Douglas M. (1904-) Biol. CB51

WHITAKER, Milton C. (1870-1963) Chem. Engr.
NC50

WHITBY, George S. (1887-1972) Chem. ACCE NC58

WHITBY, Lionel E. (1895-1956) Med. DNB7

WHITCOMB, Richard T. (1921-) Aero. ICFW MHSE

WHITCOMB, William H. (1880-1957) Chem. NC44

WHITE, Alfred H. (1873-1953) Chem. Engr. ACCE
NC49

WHITE, Canvass (1790-1834) Engr. GE-1

WHITE, Charles (1728-1813) Med. CDZZ ZZ14

WHITE, Charles A. (1826-1910) Geol.; Paleon. BM-7
DAB

WHITE, Charles D. (1862-1935) Geol. BM17 CDZZ
DAB1 FHUA WAMB ZZ14

WHITE, Edward H. (1930-1967) Astronaut. CB65
IEAS

WHITE, Francis B. (1842-1894) Bot. DNB

WHITE, Gilbert (1720-1793) Zool.; Bot. BDOS BEOS
CDZZ DNB NATJ SGNF ZZ14

WHITE, Gilbert F. (1911-) Cons. LACC

WHITE, Henry C. (1848-1927) Chem. DAB

WHITE, Henry S. (1861-1943) Math. BM25 NC33

WHITE, Howard J. (1884-1963) Chem. NC50

WHITE, Israel C. (1848-1927) Geol. CDZZ ZZ14

WHITE, Michael J. (1910-) Genet. MHM2 MHSE

WHITE, Robert M. (1923-) Meteor. CB64

WHITE, Thomas (1593-1676) Nat. Philos. CDZZ
ZZ14

WHITE, Walter P. (1867-1946) Phys. NC33

WHITEHEAD, Alfred N. (1861-1947) Math. ABES
ABET BDOS BEOS CDZZ DAB4 DNB6 NC37
WAMB ZZ14

WHITEHEAD, John (1860-1899) Ornith. DNB

WHITEHEAD, John B. (1872-1954) Engr. BM37

WHITEHEAD, John H. (1904-1960) Math. CDZZ
DNB7 ZZ14

WHITEHEAD, Robert (1823-1905) Invent. BDOS

WHITEHURST, John (1713-1788) Geol. CDZZ ZZ14

WHITESIDES, George (1939-) Chem. MHSE

WHITE-STEVENS, Robert H. (1912-1978) Agr. NC61

WHITFIELD, Robert P. (1828-1910) Paleon.; Geol.
CDZZ DAB ZZ14

WHITING, Mark C. (1925-) Chem. COBC

WHITING, Sarah (1847-1927) Phys.; Astron. IDWB
NAW

WHITMAN, Charles O. (1842-1910) Biol. BM-7
CDZZ DAB NC11 ZZ14

WHITMAN, Walter G. (1885-1974) Chem. Engr. HCEF

WHITMORE, Frank C. (1887-1947) Chem. ACCE BM28 DAB4 HSSO NC39

WHITNEY, Asa (1791-1874) Engr. GE-1

WHITNEY, Eli (1765-1825) Invent. ABES ABET ASIW BDOS COAC FOIF GE-1 HFGA INYG NC-4 SAIF SMIL TECH TINA WAMB YSMS

WHITNEY, Hassler (1907-) Math. MHSE

WHITNEY, Josiah D. (1819-1896) Geol.; Chem. ACCE BIOD CDZZ DAB WAMB WFBG ZZ14

WHITNEY, Mary W. (1847-1921) Astron. DAB IDWB NAW

WHITNEY, Willis R. (1868-1958) Chem. ACCE BM34 NC15 NC46

WHITTAKER, Edmund T. (1873-1956) Math. BDOS BEOS CDZZ DNB7 MHM2 MHSE RS-2 ZZ14

WHITTARD, Walter F. (1902-1966) Geol. RS12

WHITTEMORE, Laurens E. (1892-) Elec. Engr. TPAE

WHITTLE, Frank (1907-) Engr. BEOS GDSP HOSS ICFW MHM1 MHSE SAIF

WHITTLESEY, Charles (1808-1886) Geol. BIOD

WHITWORTH, Joseph (1803-1887) Engr. BDOS FNEC SAIF

WHYBURN, Gordon T. (1904-1969) Math. MHM1 MHSE

WHYTLAW-GRAY, Robert (1877-1958) Chem. CDZZ RS-4 ZZ14

WHYTT, Robert (1714-1766) Med. BDOS BEOS BHMT CDZZ ZZ14

WIBERG, Egon (1901-) Chem. HSSO

WICH, Francis C. (1875-1941) Phys. NC34

WICKERSHEIMER, Ernest (1880-1965) Med. CDZZ ZZ14

WICKHAM, Henry F. (1866-1933) Entom. AMEM

WICKSON, Edward J. (1848-1923) Hort. DAB NC18

WIDAL, Fernand (1862-1929) Med. BHMT

WIDMAN, Johannes (c.1462-c.1498) Math. CDZZ ZZ14

WIDMANNSTATTEN, Aloys J. von (1754-1849) Mineral. CDZZ ZZ14

WIEBE, Gustav A. (1899-1975) Genet. NC58

WIECHERT, Emil (1861-1928) Phys.; Geophys. ABET CDZZ ZZ14

WIECHMANN, Ferdinand G. (1858-1919) Chem. ACCE DAB

WIED, Maximilian Zu (1782-1867) Nat. Hist. CDZZ WFBG ZZ14

WIEDEMANN, Gustav H. (1826-1899) Phys.; Chem. CDZZ ZZ14

WIEDEMANN, H. Edmund (1882-1976) Chem. NC60

WIEDERSHEIM, Robert (1848-1923) Anat.; Embryol. CDZZ ZZ14

WIEGAND, Karl M. (1873-1942) Bot. MABH

WIEGLEB, Johann C. (1732-1800) Chem. CDZZ ZZ14

WIELAND, George R. (1865-1953) Paleon. DAB5 NC39

WIELAND, Heinrich O. (1877-1957) Chem. ABES ABET BDOS BEOS CDZZ GRCH HSSO NPWC RS-4 PAW2 ZZ14

WIELAND, Melchior (c.1520-1589) Bot. CDZZ ZZ14

WIELEITNER, Heinrich (1874-1931) Math. CDZZ ZZ14

WIEN, Wilhelm C. (1864-1928) Phys. ABES ABET BDOS BEOS CDZZ DCPW POSW ZZ14

WIENER, Alexander S. (1907-1976) Med. CB47 MHM1 MHSE

WIENER, Ludwig C. (1826-1896) Math.; Phys. CDZZ ZZ14

WIENER, Norbert (1894-1964) Math. ABES ABET BDOS BEOS CB50 CDZZ FMAS GRTH MHM1 MHSE WAMB ZZ14

WIENER, Otto (1862-1927) Phys. CDZZ ZZ14

WIESNER, Jerome B. (1915-) Elec. Engr. CB61 PPKY

WIESNER, Julius von (1838-1916) Bot. CDZZ ZZ14

WIGAND, Albert J. (1821-1886) Bot. CDZZ ZZ14

WIGG, Lilly (1749-1828) Bot. DNB

WIGGERS, Carl J. (1883-1963) Physiol. BM48

WIGGLESWORTH, Vincent B. (1899-) Biol. BEOS MHM1 MHSE

WIGHT, Robert (1796-1872) Bot. DNB

WIGHT, Sedgwick N. (1879-1968) Invent. NC54

WIGNER, Eugene P. (1902-) Phys. ABES ABET BEOS CB53 MHM1 MHSE NCSJ POSW WAMB

WIGNER, George W. (1842-1884) Chem. DNB

WILBRAND, Johann B. (1779-1846) Physiol. CDZZ ZZ14

WILBUR, Ray L. (1875-1949) Med. BHMT

WILCKE, Johan C. (1732-1796) Phys. BDOS BEOS CDZZ ZZ14

WILCZYNSKI, Ernest J. (1876-1932) Math. BM16 CDZZ DAB ZZ14

WILD, Heinrich (1833-1902) Meteor. CDZZ ZZ14

WILD, John P. (1923-) Astron. BEOS

WILD, Lewis H. (1875-1964) Entom. AMEM

WILDER, Harris H. (1864-1928) Zool. DAB

WILDER, Raymond L. (1896-1982) Math. MHM1 MHSE

WILDER, Russell M. (1885-1959) Med. DODR NC45

WILDT, Rupert (1905-1976) Astron. ABES ABET BEOS

WILEY, Harvey W. (1844-1930) Chem. ACCE CDZZ DAB GRCH NC-9 WAMB ZZ14

WILEY, Samuel W. (1878-1932) Chem. NC23

WILHELM IV, Landgrave of Hesse (1532-1592) Astron. CDZZ ZZ14

WILHELM, Richard H. (1909-1968) Chem. Engr. MHM2 MHSE

WILHELMY, Ludwig F. (1812-1864) Phys.; Chem. CDZZ ZZ14

WILKERSON, Vernon A. (1905-) Biochem. SBPY

WILKES, Charles (1798-1877) Geophys.; Astron. BIOD EXDC NHAH

WILKINS, (George) Hubert (1888-1958) Nat. Hist. DNB7

WILKINS, J. Ernest (1923-) Phys. BCST

WILKINS, John (1614-1672) Math. ABET BDOS BEOS CDZZ FBSC ZZ14

WILKINS, Maurice H. (1916-) Biophys. ABES ABET BEOS EDCJ MHM1 MHSE

WILKINS, Robert W. (1906-) Med. ABES ABET BEOS MHM2 MHSE

WILKINS, T. Russell (1891-1940) Phys. NCSD

WILKINSON, Charles S. (1843-1891) Geol. DNB

WILKINSON, David (1771-1852) Invent. FOIF

WILKINSON, Denys H. (1922-) Phys. BEOS MHM2

WILKINSON, Geoffrey (1921-) Chem. ABET BEOS COBC MHSE

WILKINSON, John (1728-1808) Invent. BDOS GE-1

WILKS, Samuel S. (1906-1964) Math. CDZZ ZZ14

WILLAN, Robert (b. 1757) Med. BHMT

WILLARD, Bradford (1894-1973) Geol. NC58

WILLARD, John E. (1908-) Chem. MHM1 MHSE

WILLARD, Julius T. (1862-1950) Chem. NCSC

WILLCOX, William H. (1870-1941) Forens. Sci. DNB6

WILLDENOW, Karl L. (1765-1812) Bot. CDZZ ZZ14

WILLETT, Hurd C. (1903-) Meteor. MHM1 MHSE

WILLIAM OF AUVERGNE (c.1185-1249) Philos. CDZZ ZZ14

WILLIAM OF OCKHAM SEE OCKHAM, William of

WILLIAM OF SAINT-CLOUD (fl. c.1290) Astron. CDZZ ZZ14

WILLIAM OF SHERWOOD (fl.1200s) Philos. CDZZ ZZ14

WILLIAM THE ENGLISHMAN (fl. 1200s) Astron. CDZZ ZZ14

WILLIAMS, Anna W. (1863-1954) Bact. NAWM

WILLIAMS, Carrington B. (1889-1981) Entom. RS28

WILLIAMS, Carroll M. (1916-) Biol. MHM2 MHSE

WILLIAMS, Charles H. (1829-1910) Chem. DNB2

WILLIAMS, Daniel H. (1856-1931) Med. BISC BPSH GBAR GNPA HCOK SABL SBAH SBPY

WILLIAMS, David (1792-1850) Geol. DNB

WILLIAMS, Donald A. (1905-) Cons. LACC

WILLIAMS, Evan J. (1903-1945) Phys. BDOS BEOS

WILLIAMS, Frederic C. (1911-1977) Elec. Engr. MHM2 MHSE RS24

WILLIAMS, George H. (1856-1894) Mineral. BIOD

WILLIAMS, Henry S. (1847-1918) Geol.; Paleon. CDZZ DAB ZZ14

WILLIAMS, James S. (1896-1957) Geol. NC46

WILLIAMS, John H. (1908-1966) Phys. BM42 CB60

WILLIAMS, John W. (1898-) Chem. MHM2 MHSE

WILLIAMS, Joseph L. (1936-) Chem. SBPY

WILLIAMS, Leslie H. (1903-) Chem. COBC

WILLIAMS, Luther S. (1940-) Biol. SBPY

WILLIAMS, Norman C. (1917-1968) Geol. NC54

WILLIAMS, O.S. (1921-) Aero. BCST

WILLIAMS, Raymond L. (1927-) Chem. COBC

WILLIAMS, Richard T. (1909-1979) Biochem. RS28

WILLIAMS, Robert R. (1886-1965) Chem. ABES ABET BEOS CB51 CDZZ MASY MHM1 MHSE NC58 ZZ14

WILLIAMS, Robley C. (1908-) Biol. ABES ABET BEOS MHM2 MHSE

WILLIAMS, Roger J. (1893-) Biochem. CB57 MHM2 MHSE

WILLIAMS, Roswell C. Jr. (1869-1946) Entom. AMEM NC42

WILLIAMS, Samuel (1743-1817) Astron. NC-1

WILLIAMS, Trevor I. (1921-) Chem. COBC

WILLIAMSON, Alexander W. (1824-1904) Chem. ABES ABET BDOS BEOS CDZZ DNB2 ZZ14

WILLIAMSON, Edward B. (1877-1933) Entom. AMEM

WILLIAMSON, Hugh (1735-1819) Astron.; Climat. BIOD DAB

WILLIAMSON, John T. (1907-1958) Geol. DNB7

WILLIAMSON, William C. (1816-1895) Bot.; Geol. BDOS BEOS CDZZ DNB FHUA ZZ14

WILLIS, Bailey (1857-1949) Geol. BM35 CDZZ DAB4 NC37 ZZ14

WILLIS, John C. (1868-1958) Bot. RS-4

WILLIS, Robert (1800-1875) Engr.; Archaeol. CDZZ ZZ14

WILLIS, Thomas (1621-1675) Anat.; Med. ABET BDOS BEOS BHMT CDZZ ZZ14

WILLISEL, Thomas (d. c.1675) Nat. Hist. DNB

WILLISTON, Samuel W. (1851-1918) Paleon.; Entom. AMEM CDZZ DAB NC30 ZZ14

WILLS, Albert P. (1873-1937) Phys. NC27

WILLSON, Thomas L. (1860-1915) Chem. ACCE

WILLSTATTER, Richard (1872-1942) Chem. ABES ABET BDOS BEOS CDZZ GJPS GRCH HSSO NPWC PAW2 ZZ14

WILLUGHBY, Francis (1635-1672) Nat. Hist. ANHD CDZZ DNB HAOA ZZ14

WILMOT, Sainthill E. (1852-1929) Forest. DNB4

WILSING, Johannes (1856-1943) Astron. CDZZ ZZ14

WILSON, Alexander (1714-1786) Astron. CDZZ ZZ14

WILSON, Alexander (1766-1813) Ornith. ANHD BEOS BWCL BIOD CDZZ DAB DNB EQSA FIFE GANC HAOA LHES NC-7 NHAH WAMB WFBG ZZ14

WILSON, Alexander P. (1770-1851) Med. BHMT

WILSON, Benjamin (1721-1788) Elec. Sci. CDZZ ESEH ZZ14

WILSON, Cecil L. (1912-) Chem. COBC

WILSON, Charles B. (1861-1941) Biol. NC30

WILSON, Charles T. (1869-1959) Phys. ABES ABET BDOS CDZZ DNB7 DCPW MWBR POSW RS-6 STYC ZZ14

WILSON, David W. (1889-1965) Biochem. BM43

WILSON, Edgar B. (1908-) Chem. MHM2 MHSE

WILSON, Edmund B. (1856-1939) Biol. ABET ABFC BEOS BM21 CDZZ DAB2 NC13 RPTC ZZ14

WILSON, Edward A. (1872-1912) Nat. Hist. DNB3

WILSON, Edward O. (1929-) Biol. BEOS CB79 MHSE POEC

WILSON, Edwin B. (1879-1964) Math. BM43 CDZZ DAB2 ZZ14

WILSON, Ernest H. (1876-1930) Bot. DAB

WILSON, George (1818-1859) Chem. DNB

WILSON, Harold A. (1874-1964) Phys. RS11

WILSON, Henry V. (1863-1939) Biol. BM35 NC28

WILSON, James (1795-1856) Zool. DNB

WILSON, James M. (1836-1931) Math.; Astron. DNB5

WILSON, John (1741-1793) Math. CDZZ ZZ14

WILSON, John A. (1890-1942) Chem. NCSC

WILSON, John T. (1908-) Geol. BEOS CB73 MHSE

WILSON, Kenneth G. (1936-) Phys. CB83

WILSON, Morley E. (1882-) Geol. MHM1 MHSE

WILSON, Ralph E. (1886-1960) Astron. BM36

WILSON, Robert (1803-1882) Engr. DNB

WILSON, Robert E. (1893-1964) Chem. Engr. ACCE NC52

WILSON, Robert W. (1936-) Astrophys.; Astron. ABET BEOS MHSE POSW SOT2

WILSON, S.A. Kinnier (1878-1937) Med. BHMT

WILSON, Volney C. (1910-) Phys. CB58 WMSW

WILSON, William (1799-1871) Bot. DNB

WILSON, William E. (1851-1908) Astron.; Phys. DNB2

WINCH, Nathaniel J. (c.1769-1838) Bot. DNB

WINCHELL, Alexander (1824-1891) Geol. BIOD CDZZ NC-6 NC16 ZZ14

WINCHELL, Alexander N. (1874-1958) Geol. CDZZ NC46 ZZ14

WINCHELL, Horace V. (1865-1923) Geol.; Mng. CDZZ ZZ14

WINCHELL, Newton H. (1839-1914) Geol. CDZZ ZZ14

WINDAUS, Adolf O. (1876-1959) Chem. ABES ABET BDOS BEOS CDZZ HSSO NPWC ZZ14

WINDHAUSEN, Franz (1829-1904) Engr. MCCW

WING, Vincent (1619-1668) Astron. CDZZ DNB ZZ14

WINGATE, Edmund (1596-1656) Math. DNB

WINGE, Ojvind (1886-1964) Genet. RS10

WINKLER, Clemens A. (1838-1904) Chem. ABES ABET BDOS BEOS CDZZ HSSO ZZ14

WINKLER, Johann H. (1703-1770) Rocket. EETD

WINKLER, Lajos W. (1863-1939) Chem. CDZZ ZZ14

WINLOCK, Joseph (1826-1875) Astron.; Math. BIOD BM-1 CDZZ DAB NC-9 ZZ14

WINLOCK, William C. (1859-1896) Astron. BIOD
NC-9

WINSLOW, Jacob (1669-1760) Anat. CDZZ ZZ14

WINSOR, Frederick SEE WINZER, Frederick A.

WINSTEIN, Saul (1912-1969) Chem. ACCE BM43
MHSE

WINTERBOTTOM, Thomas M. (1766-1859) Med.
BHMT

WINTERSTEINER, Oskar P. (1898-1971) Chem.
MHM2 MHSE

WINTHROP, John (1714-1779) Astron.; Phys. BIOD
CDZZ DAB NC-7 SBCS WAMB ZZ14

WINTHROP, John Jr. (1605-1676) Chem.; Med. ACCE
BIOD CDZZ ZZ14

WINTNER, Aurel (1903-1958) Math. CDZZ ZZ14

WINTON, Andrew L. (1864-1946) Chem. NC35

WINTRINGHAM, William T. (1904-1976) Engr. NC61

WINZER, Frederick A. (1763-1830) Invent. BDOS

WIRTH, Conrad L. (1899-) Cons. LACC

WISEMAN, Richard (c.1621-1676) Med. BHMT

WISLICENUS, Johannes (1835-1902) Chem. ABES
ABET BDOS BEOS CDZZ HSSO ZZ14

WISLIZENUS, Frederick A. (1810-1889) Meteor.;
Nat. Hist. BIOD

WISLOCKI, George B. (1892-1956) Anat. NC45

WISSER, Edward H. (1895-1970) Geol. NC56

WISSLER, Clark (1870-1947) Anthro. DAB4

WISTAR, Caspar (1761-1818) Anat. BHMT BIOD
CDZZ ZZ14

WITCHELL, Edwin (1823-1887) Geol. DNB

WITEBSKY, Ernest (1901-1969) Bact. NC56

WITELO (c.1230-c.1275) Opt.; Nat. Philos. CDZZ
ZZ14

WITHAM, Henry (1779-1844) Geol.; Paleon. CDZZ
ZZ14

WITHERING, William (1741-1799) Med.; Bot. ABET
BDOS BEOS BHMT CDZZ DNB ZZ14

WITHROW, James R. (1878-1953) Chem. Engr. ACCE

WITHROW, Robert B. (1904-1958) Biophys. NC47

WITT, Jan de (1625-1672) Math. CDZZ ZZ14

WITT, Otto N. (1853-1932) Chem. GRCH

WITTEMANN, Charles R. (1884-1967) Aero. NC54

WITTGENSTEIN, Ludwig (1889-1951) Philos. CDZZ
ZZ14

WITTHAUS, Rudolph A. (1846-1915) Chem. ACCE
DAB

WITTICH, Paul (c.1555-1587) Math. CDZZ ZZ14

WITTIG, Georg F. (1897-) Chem. ABET MHSE
SOT3

WOEPCKE, Franz (1826-1864) Math. CDZZ ZZ14

WOHLER, August (1819-1914) Engr. CDZZ ZZ14

WOHLER, Friedrich (1800-1882) Chem. ABES ABET
BDOS BEOS CDZZ CSCJ GISA GRCH HLSM
HSSO SAIF SMIL ZZ14

WOLCOTT, George N. (1889-1965) Entom. NC55

WOLD, Peter I. (1881-1945) Phys. NC34

WOLF, Charles J. (1827-1918) Astron.; Sci. Hist.
CDZZ ZZ14

WOLF, Emil (1922-) Phys. MHSE

WOLF, Fred W. (1837-1912) Engr. MCCW

WOLF, Johann R. (1816-1893) Astron.; Sci. Writ.
BEOS CDZZ ZZ14

WOLF, Joseph (1820-1899) Nat. Hist.; Sci. Illus.
ANHD

WOLF, Maximilian F. (1863-1932) Astron. ABES
ABET BDOS BEOS CDZZ ZZ14

WOLF, Rudolf (1816-1893) Astron. IEAS

WOLFE, Hugh C. (1905-) Phys. CB50

WOLFF, Christian (1679-1754) Philos. CDZZ ZZ14

WOLFF, Julius (1836-1902) Med. BHMT

WOLFF, Kaspar F. (1733-1794) Biol. ABES ABET
BDOS BEOS BHMT CDZZ HLSM TBSG ZZXV

WOLFGANG, Richard L. (1928-1971) Chem. ACCE

WOLFROM, Melville L. (1900-1969) Chem. ACCE
BM47 MHM2 MHSE

WOLLASTON, Alexander F. (1875-1930) Nat. Hist.
DNB4

WOLLASTON, Francis (1731-1815) Astron. CDZZ
ZZ14

WOLLASTON, Francis J. (1762-1823) Nat. Philos.
DNB

WOLLASTON, William H. (1766-1828) Chem.; Opt.
ABES ABET BDOS BEOS CDZZ DNB EETD
ZZ14

WOLLE, Francis (1817-1893) Bot. MABH

WOLLSTEIN, Martha (1868-1939) Path. NAW

WOLMAN, Abel (1892-) Engr. CB57 MHSE

WOLSTENHOLME, Joseph (1829-1891) Math. DNB

WOLTMAN, Reinhard (1757-1837) Phys. CDZZ ZZ14

WOOD, Alphonso (1810-1881) Bot. NC14

WOOD, Edward S. (1846-1905) Chem. ACCE BIOD
DAB

WOOD, Frank E. (1859-1945) Biol. NC34

WOOD, Harland G. (1907-) Biochem. MHM2 MHSE

WOOD, Horatio C. (1841-1920) Pharm.; Med. BM33
CDZZ ZZ14

WOOD, James (1760-1839) Math. DNB

WOOD, Jay P. (1889-1967) Geol. NC53

WOOD, John G. (1827-1889) Nat. Hist. ANHD

WOOD, Richard D. (1918-1977) Bot. NC59

WOOD, Robert (c.1622-1685) Math. DNB

WOOD, Robert W. (1868-1955) Phys. BDOS BEOS
CDZZ HSSO NC14 NC46 RS-2 ZZ14

WOOD, Searles V. (1798-1880) Geol. DNB

WOOD, Searles V. (1830-1884) Geol. DNB

WOOD, William (1745-1808) Bot. DNB

WOOD, William (1774-1857) Zool. DNB

WOOD, William B. (1910-1971) Bact. BM51 MHM2
MHSE NC56

WOODBRIDGE, Richard G. Jr. (1886-1946) Chem.
ACCE

WOODHOUSE, James (1770-1809) Chem. ACCE
BIOD DAB

WOODHOUSE, Robert (1773-1827) Math. CDZZ
DNB ZZ14

WOODHOUSE, Samuel W. (1821-1904) Ornith. BIOD

WOODRING, Wendell P. (1891-) Geol.; Paleon.
MHM1 MHSE

WOODRUFF, John G. (1898-1971) Geol. NC56

WOODRUFF, Lorande L. (1879-1947) Biol. BM52
DAB4

WOODS, Albert F. (1866-1948) Bot. NC46

WOODS, Donald D. (1912-1964) Biochem. RS11

WOODS, Frederick A. (1873-1939) Biol. NC33

WOODS, Granville T. (1856-1910) Invent. BCST
BPSH BISC EBAH DANB GNPA HCOK SBPY

WOODS, Henry (1868-1952) Paleon. DNB7

WOODS, Joseph (1776-1864) Bot. DNB

WOODS, Julian E. (1832-1889) Geol.; Nat. Hist. DNB

WOODS, Robert J. (1904-1956) Aero. ICFW

WOODVILLE, William (1752-1805) Bot. DNB

WOODWARD, Arthur S. (1864-1944) Paleon. BEOS
DNB6 MMSB PHLS

WOODWARD, Hugh B. (1885-1968) Forest. LACC

WOODWARD, John (1665-1728) Paleon.; Geol.
BEOS CDZZ DNB FHUA PHLS ZZ14

WOODWARD, Joseph J. (1833-1884) Med. BM-2 NC11

WOODWARD, Robert B. (1917-1979) Chem. ABES ABET BEOS CB52 HSSO MHM1 MHSE PBTS RS27 WAMB

WOODWARD, Robert S. (1849-1924) Math. CDZZ ZZ14

WOODWARD, Samuel (1790-1838) Geol. DNB

WOODWARD, Samuel P. (1821-1865) Nat. Hist. DNB

WOODWELL, George M. (1928-) Ecol. CHUB

WOODWORTH, Charles W. (1865-1940) Entom. AMEM

WOODWORTH, Ronert S. (1869-1962) Psych. BM39

WOOLDRIDGE, Dean E. (1913-) Engr. SCLB

WOOLF, Arthur (1766-1837) Engr. GE-1

WOOLLEY, Charles L. (1880-1960) Archaeol. ABET CDZZ ZZ14

WOOLLEY, Richard (1906-) Astron. IEAS

WOOLRIDGE, Sidney W. (1900-1963) Geog. RS10

WOOTEN, Benjamin A. (1891-1974) Phys. NC36

WORCESTER, Dean C. (1866-1924) Bot.; Zool. NC20

WORK, Lincoln T. (1898-1968) Chem. Engr. ACCE

WORM, Ole (1588-1654) Nat. Hist. ANHD CDZZ ZZ14

WORMALL, Arthur (1900-1964) Biochem. RS12

WORMLEY, Theodore G. (1826-1897) Chem. ACCE NC13

WORRALL, David E. (1886-1944) Chem. NC33

WORSAAE, Jens J. (1821-1885) Archaeol. CDZZ ZZ14

WORTHEN, Amos H. (1813-1888) Geol. BIOD BM-3

WORTHEN, Thomas W. (1845-1927) Math. NC27

WORTHING, Archie G. (1881-1949) Phys. NC41

WORTMAN, (Leo) Sterling (1923-1981) Bot.; Genet. AO81

WOTTON, Edward (1492-1555) Med.; Nat. Hist. CDZZ DNB ZZ14

WOULFE, Peter (1727-1803) Chem. CDZZ DNB ZZ14

WRATHER, William E. (1883-1963) Geol. NC52

WREN, Christopher (1632-1723) Math.; Anat. BDOS BHMT CDZZ LSCS ZZ14

WRIGHT, Albert A. (1846-1905) Geol.; Nat. Hist. BIOD

WRIGHT, Almroth E. (1861-1947) Path.; Bact. BEOS CDZZ DNB6 MAMR ZZ14

WRIGHT, Arthur W. (1836-1915) Phys. BM15 NC13

WRIGHT, Benjamin (1770-1842) Engr. GE-1

WRIGHT, Charles (1811-1885) Bot. BIOD DAB WFBG

WRIGHT, Chauncey (1830-1875) Philos. of Sci.; Math. BIOD WAMB

WRIGHT, Edward (1561-1615) Math. CDZZ DNB ZZ14

WRIGHT, Edward P. (1834-1910) Nat. Hist. DNB2

WRIGHT, Frederick E. (1877-1953) Geophys. BM29 CDZZ ZZ14

WRIGHT, Hamilton K. (1867-1917) Med. DAB NC22

WRIGHT, Irving S. (1910-) Med. CB68

WRIGHT, Jane C. (1920-) Med. WPSH

WRIGHT, Louis T. (1891-1952) Med. BPSH SBPY

WRIGHT, Mabel O. (1859-1934) Nat. Hist. LACC NC12 SFNB

WRIGHT, Orville (1871-1948) Aero.; Invent. ABES ABET ASIW BDOS BM25 CB46 CDZZ COAC DAB4 FOIF GASW GEXB HFGA ICFW MGAH NC14 OGML PAW3 SAIF SMIL TINA WAMB ZZ14

WRIGHT, Ralph G. (1875-1954) Chem. ACCE NC40

WRIGHT, Sewall (1889-) Genet. BEOS MHM1 MHSE

WRIGHT, Sydney L. (1896-1970) Chem. NC55

WRIGHT, Thomas (1711-1786) Astron. CDZZ ZZ14

WRIGHT, Thomas (1809-1884) Geol. ABET DNB

WRIGHT, Wilbur (1867-1912) Aero.; Invent. ABES
ABET ASIW BDOS CDZZ COAC DAB FOIF
GASW GEXB HFGA ICFW MGAH NC14 OGML
PAW3 SAIF SMIL TINA WAMB ZZ14

WRIGHT, William H. (1871-1959) Astron. BM50
CDZZ NC60 ZZ14

WRINCH, Dorothy M. (1894-) Biochem. BEOS
CB47

WROBLEWSKI, Zygmunt F. von (1845-1888) Phys.
ABET BDOS BEOS CDZZ ZZ14

WU, Chien-Shiung (1912-) Phys. BEOS CB59
CWSE CWSN DCPW MHM1 MHSE WASM

WU, Hsien (1893-1959) Biochem. CDZZ NC44 ZZ14

WULFF, Georg (1863-1925) Crystal. CDZZ ZZ14

WUNDERLICH, Carl R. (1815-1877) Med. ABES
ABET BEOS

WUNDT, Wilhelm M. (1832-1920) Psych. ABES
ABET CDZZ POPF ZZ14

WURTZ, Charles A. (1817-1884) Chem. ABET BDOS
BEOS CDZZ GRCH ZZ14

WURTZ, Henry (1828-1910) Chem. BIOD DAB NC-7

WWEDENSKY, Boris A. (1893-) Phys. SMST

WYCKOFF, Ralph W. (1897-1975) Crystal.; Biophys.
ABES ABET BEOS MHM2 MHSE

WYCKOFF, Stephen N. (1891-1959) Forest. NC46

WYLIE, Robert B. (1870-1959) Bot. NC50

WYMAN, Jeffries (1814-1874) Anat. ASJD BIOD
BM-2 NC-2 CDZZ ZZ14

WYNKOOP, Frederick (1885-1972) Chem. NC57

WYNKOOP, Gillett (1865-1930) Chem. NC23

WYNNE-EDWARDS, Vero C. (1906-) Zool. BEOS

WYNNE-JONES, William F. (1903-) Chem. COBC

X

XANTOS, Janos SEE XANTUS, John

XANTUS, John (1825-1894) Ornith. BIOD BWCL
DAB WFBG

XENOCRATES OF CHALCEDON (396/5 B.C.-314/3
B.C.) Philos.; Math. CDZZ ZZ14

XENOPHANES (c.570 B.C.-c.480 B.C.) Philos. ABES
ABET BEOS CDZZ HLSM ZZ14

Y

YAGODA, Herman (1908-1964) Chem.; Phys. NC50

YAHYA ibn ABI MANSUR (d. 832) Astron. CDZZ
ZZ14

YAKOVLEV, N.N. (1870-1966) Geol.; Paleon. SMST

YALOW, Rosalyn S. (1921-) Med. ABET AMJB
BEOS CB78 IDWB LLWO MHSE PAW2 SOTT
WPSH

YANDELL, Lunsford P. (1805-1878) Paleon. BIOD
DAB

YANG CHENG YEN (fl. 200 B.C.) Engr. GE-1

YANG HUI (fl. c.1261-1275) Math. CDZZ ZZ14

YANG, Chen Ning (1922-) Phys. ABES ABET BEOS
CB58 MHM1 MHSE PAW2 PBTS POSW WAMB

YANNEY, Benjamin F. (1859-1958) Math. NC49

YANOFSKY, Charles (1925-) Biol. BEOS MHM2
MHSE

YANSHIN, Aleksandr L. (1911-) Geol. SMST

YANUSOV, Sabir Y. (1909-) Chem. SMST

YAQUB ibn TARIQ (fl. c.750-c.800) Astron. CDZZ
ZZ14

YAQUT al-HAMAWI al-RUMI, Shihab Aldin (1179-
1229) Geog. CDZZ ZZ14

YARD, Robert S. (1861-1945) Cons. LACC

YARNALL, Mordecai (1816-1879) Astron. BIOD

YARRANTON, Andrew (1616-1684) Engr. GE-1

YARRELL, William (1784-1856) Zool. DNB

YASUAKI, Aida SEE AIDA YASUAKI

YATIVRSABHA (fl. 500s) Cosmol.; Math. CDZZ ZZ14

YAVANESVARA (fl. c.150) Astrol.; Astron. CDZZ ZZ14

YEAGER, Charles E. (1923-) Aero. MOS1

YEATES, William S. (1856-1908) Geol.; Mineral. BIOD

YEGOROV, Boris B. (1937-) Med.; Astronaut. CB68 IEAS

YELISEYEV, Alexei S. (1934-) Astronaut. IEAS

YEO, Gerald F. (1845-1909) Physiol. DNB2

YERBY, Alonzo S. (1921-) Med. SBPY

YERKES, Robert M. (1876-1956) Psych. BM38 ABET NC43 CDZZ ZZ14

YERSIN, Alexandre E. (1863-1943) Med.; Bact. BEOS CDZZ ZZ14

YERUSHALMY, Jacob (1904-) Math. CB58

YEVELE, Henry (c.1320-1400) Engr. GE-1

YI CHON (1376-1451) Instr. GE-1

YING SHUN-CHEN (fl. 1071) Engr. GE-1

YODER, Hatten S. Jr. (1921-) Geophys. MHM2 MHSE

YORK, Herbert F. (1921-) Phys. CB58 MHM1 MHSE

YORKE, Philip J. (1799-1874) Chem. DNB

YOUDEN, William J. (1900-1971) Math. CDZZ ZZ14

YOUMANS, Edward L. (1821-1887) Sci. Writ. ACCE BIOD NC-2

YOUMANS, William J. (1838-1901) Sci. Writ. BIOD

YOUNG, Aaron (1819-1898) Bot. BIOD

YOUNG, Abran Van Eps (1852-1926) Chem. ACCE

YOUNG, Andrew H. (1852-1926) Bot.; Chem. NC22

YOUNG, Arthur (1741-1820) Agr. BDOS

YOUNG, Augustus (1785-1857) Geol. NC-3

YOUNG, Benjamin P. (1887-1958) Zool. NC47

YOUNG, Charles A. (1834-1908) Astron. ABET BM-7 DAB NC-6 CDZZ ZZ14

YOUNG, Christopher A. (1912-1978) Engr.; Meteor. RS25

YOUNG, David (1781-1852) Astron. DAB

YOUNG, Grace C. (1868-1970) Math. MEQP

YOUNG, Harry C. (1888-1970) Bot. NC56

YOUNG, James (1811-1883) Chem. Engr. BDOS BEOS DNB

YOUNG, John P. (1873-1957) Bot. NC47

YOUNG, John R. (1782-1804) Physiol. CDZZ ZZ14

YOUNG, John R. (1799-1885) Math. DNB

YOUNG, John W. (1879-1932) Math. DAB NC23 CDZZ ZZ14

YOUNG, John W. (1930-) Astronaut. CB65 IEAS

YOUNG, John Z. (1907-) Physiol. MHM2 MHSE

YOUNG, Raymond M. (1911-1970) Microbiol. NC56

YOUNG, Stanley P. (1889-1969) Biol. DGMT LACC

YOUNG, Sydney (1857-1937) Chem. CDZZ DNB5 ZZ14

YOUNG, Thomas (1773-1829) Phys.; Med. ABES ABET BDOS BEOS BHMT CDZZ DCPW DNB ENCE FNEC HOSS STYC ZZ14

YOUNG, William H. (1863-1942) Math. CDZZ DNB6 ZZ14

YOWELL, Everett I. (1870-1959) Astron. NC47

YUKAWA, Hideki (1907-1981) Phys. ABES ABET
AO81 BEOS CB50 DCPW MHM1 MHSE PAW2
POSW

YULE, George U. (1871-1951) Math. CDZZ ZZ14

ibn YUNUS, Abul-Hasan Ali ibn Abd (d. 1009) Astron.;
Math. CDZZ ZZ14

YUTZY, Henry C. (1910-1966) Chem. NC52

Z

ZABARELLA, Jacopo (1533-1589) Nat. Philos. CDZZ
ZZ14

ZACH, Franz X. von (1754-1832) Surv.; Astron.
CDZZ ZZ14

ZACHARIAS, Jerrold (1905-) Phys. CB64 WMSW

ZACUTO, Abraham bar Samuel (c.1450-c.1522)
Astrol.; Astron. CDZZ ZZ14

ZAHM, Albert F. (1862-1954) Aero. ICFW

ZAHNISER, Howard C. (1906-1964) Cons. EAFC
LACC NC50

al-ZAHRAWI, Abul-Qasim Khalaf (c.936-1013) Med.
CDZZ ZZ14

ZALESSKY, Mikhail D. (1877-1946) Paleon. FHUA

ZALUZANSKY DE ZALUZAN, Adam (c.1558-1613)
Bot.; Med. CDZZ ZZ14

ZAMBECCARI, Giuseppe (1655-1728) Med. CDZZ
ZZ14

ZAMBONINI, Ferruccio (1880-1932) Chem.; Mineral.
CDZZ ZZ14

ZANETTI, J. Enrique (1885-1974) Chem. NC58

ZANOTTI, Eustachio (1709-1782) Astron.; Math.
CDZZ ZZ14

ZANSTRA, Herman (1894-1972) Astrophys. MHM2
MHSE

ZARANKIEWICZ, Kazimierz (1902-1959) Math.
CDZZ ZZ14

ZARISKI, Oscar (1899-) Math. MHSE

al-ZARQALI, Abu Ishaw Ibrahim (d. 1100) Astron.
CDZZ ZZ14

ZAVADOVSKY, Mikhail M. (1891-1957) Biol. CDZZ
ZZ14

ZAVALISHIN, Dmitrii A. (1900-1968) Elec. Engr.
SMST

ZAVARZIN, Aleksey A. (1886-1945) Biol.; Embryol.
CDZZ ZZ14

ZAVENYAGIN, Avraami (1901-) Engr. NBPS

ZAVOISKII, Evgenii K. (1907-) Phys. SMST

ZAWADZKI, Eduard S. (1914-1967) Path. NC53

ZAYMOVSKII, Aleksandr S. (1905-) Metal. SMST

al-ZAYYATI al-CHARNATI SEE LEO THE AFRICAN

ZECHMEISTER, Laszlo (1889-1972) Chem. NC57

ZEEMAN, Pieter (1865-1943) Phys. ABES ABET
BDOS BEOS CDZZ POSW ZZ14

ZEILLER, Rene C. (1847-1915) Paleon. CDZZ ZZ14

ZEISBERG, Frederick C. (1888-1938) Chem. ACCE
NC33

ZEISE, William C. (1789-1847) Chem. CDZZ ZZ14

ZEISS, Carl (1816-1888) Opt. BDOS SAIF

ZEJSNER, Ludwik (1805-1871) Geol.; Paleon. CDZZ
ZZXV

ZELDOVICH, Yakov B. (1914-) Phys. SMST

ZELENY, Charles (1878-1939) Zool. NC42

ZELENY, John (1872-1951) Phys. NC40

ZELINSKY, Nikolay D. (1861-1953) Chem. CDZZ
ZZ14

ZEMPLEN, Geza (1883-1956) Chem. CDZZ ZZ14

ZENKEVICH, Lev A. (1889-1970) Ocean. SMST

ZENO OF CITIUM (c.335 B.C.-263 B.C.) Philos.
CDZZ ZZ14

ZENO OF ELEA (c.490 B.C.–c.425 B.C.) Philos.; Math. ABES ABET BEOS CDZZ ZZ14

ZENO OF SIDON (c.150 B.C.–c.70 B.C.) Philos.; Math. CDZZ ZZ14

ZENODORUS (fl. c.200 B.C.) Math. CDZZ ZZ14

ZEPPELIN, Ferdinand von (1838-1917) Invent.; Aero. ABES ABET BDOS ICFW SAIF

ZERBAN, Frederick W. (1880-1956) Chem. ACCE

ZERMELO, Ernst F. (1871-1953) Math. CDZZ ZZ14

ZERNICKE, Frits (1888-1966) Phys. ABES ABET BDOS BEOS CB55 CDZZ MHM1 MHSE POSW RS13 ZZ14

ZERNOV, Dmitrii V. (1907-) Phys. SMST

ZEUNER, Gustav A. (1828-1907) Engr.; Phys. CDZZ ZZ14

ZEUSCHNER, Ludwik SEE ZEJSNER, Ludwik

ZEUTHEN, Hieronymus G. (1839-1920) Math. CDZZ ZZ14

ZHAVORONKOV, Nikolai M. (1907-) Chem. Engr. SMST

ZHUKOVSKI, Nikolai Y. (1847-1921) Phys.; Math. CDZZ ICFW ZZ14

ZHURKOV, Serafim N. (1905-) Phys. SMST

ZIEGLER, Karl (1898-1973) Chem. ABES ABET BEOS HSSO MHM1 MHSE PAW2 RS21

ZILKER, Charles (1864-1946) Engr. MCCW

ZIM, Herbert S. (1909-) Sci. Writ. CB56

ZIMMERLI, William F. (1888-1972) Chem. NC58

ZIMMERMAN, Gordon K. (1910-) Cons. LACC

ZIMMERMAN, Percy W. (1884-1958) Bot. NCSD

ZINDER, Norton D. (1928-) Microbiol. BEOS MHM2 MHSE

ZINGHER, Abraham (1885-1927) Bact. NC26

ZININ, Nikolay N. (1812-1880) Chem. CDZZ ZZ14

ZINN, Donald J. (1911-) Ecol. LACC

ZINN, Justin (1903-1966) Geol. NC51

ZINN, Walter H. (1906-) Phys. ABES ABET BEOS CB55

ZINSSER, Hans (1878-1940) Bact. BHMT BM24 DAB2 NC36 CDZZ WAMB ZZ14

ZINTL, Eduard (1898-1941) Chem. HSSO

ZIOLKOVSKY, Konstantin SEE TSIOLKOVSKY, Konstantin E.

ZIRKEL, Ferdinand (1838-1912) Geol.; Mineral. CDZZ ZZ14

ZITTEL, Karl A. von (1839-1904) Paleon. CDZZ PHLS ZZ14

ZIVNUSKA, John A. (1916-) Forest. LACC

ZOLLNER, Johann K. (1834-1882) Astrophys. CDZZ ZZ14

ZOLOTAREV, Egor I. (1847-1878) Math. CDZZ ZZ14

ZON, Raphael (1874-1956) Forest. EAFC LACC

ZONCA, Vittorio (1568-1603) Engr. GE-1

ZONS, Frederick W. (1885-1960) Chem. Engr. NC48

ZOSIMUS OF PANOPOLIS (fl. c.300) Alch. ABET BEOS CDZZ ZZ14

ZSIGMONDY, Richard A. (1865-1929) Chem. ABES ABET BDOS BEOS CDZZ NPWC ZZ14

ZUBOV, Nikolay N. (1885-1960) Ocean. CDZZ ZZ14

ZUBOV, Vasily P. (1899-1963) Sci. Hist. CDZZ ZZ14

ZUCCHI, Nicolo (1586-1670) Math. CDZZ ZZ14

ZUCKERMAN, Solly (1904-) Zool.; Anat. BEOS CB72 SIWG

Ibn ZUHR, Abu Marwan (c.1092-1162) Med. CDZZ ZZ14

ZVEREV, Mitrofan S. (1903-) Astron. SMST

ZVONKOV, Vasilii V. (1891-1965) Engr. SMST

ZWELFER, Johann (1618-1668) Pharm.; Chem. CDZZ
ZZ14

ZWICKY, Fritz (1898-1974) Astrophys. ABES ABET
BEOS CB53 IEAS

ZWORYKIN, Vladimir K. (1889-1982) Phys. ABES
ABET BEOS CB49 EETD MASY MHM1 MHSE
MPIP TINA TPAE WAMB

ZYGMUND, Antoni (1900-) Math. MHM2 MHSE

List of Scientists
by Field

AERONAUTICS

Ackert, J.
Ader, C.
Alford, W.
Andree, S.
Armstrong, H.
Arnstein, K.
Bacon, J.
Bechereau, L.
Bellanca, G.
Blanchard, J.
Bleriot, L.
Brequet, L.
Bryan, G.
Busemann, A.
Caldwell, F.
Camm, S.
Cayley, G.
Chadwick, R.
Chanute, O.
Cheryk, J.
Cierva y Codornice, J.
Clark, V.
Coanda, H.
Coxwell, H.
Crossfield, A.
Curtiss, G.
De Haviland, G.
Doolittle, J.
Dornier, C.
Dougherty, D.
Douglas, D.
Draper, C.
Dunne, J.
Durant, C.
Durr, L.
Ebel, W.
Fairey, C.
Fales, E.
Farman, H.
Farman, M.
Fink, F.
Flettner, A.
Foche, H.
Fokker, A.
Gale, G.
Gates, S.
Giffard, H.
Gilruth, R.
Glauert, H.
Goett, H.
Green, C.
Hargrave, L.
Heinemann, E.
Henson, W.
Herring, A.
Hill, G.
Hinton, W.
Hoff, N.
Holder, D.
Horten, R.
Horten, W.
Hunsaker, J.
Ide, J.
Jacobs, E.
Jeffries, J.

Johnson, C.L.
Jones, R.
Julliot, H.
Junkers, H.
Karman, T.
Kindelberger, J.
King, S.
Klemin, A.
Kotcher, E.
Kutta, M.
Lachmann, G.
LaMountain, J.
Langley, S.
Leduc, R.
Lewis, G.
Lilienthal, O.
Lindbergh, C.
Lippisch, A.
Loening, G.
Lowe, T.
Ludington, C.
Lyulka, A.
Manly, C.
Mikoyan, A.
Mikulin, A.
Money, J.
Morgan, M.
Moss, S.
Munk, M.
Northrop, J.
Page, F.
Penaud, A.
Phillips, H.
Piccard, J.
Pilatre de Rozier, J.
Platz, R.
Polhamus, E.
Polikarpov, N.
Putt, D.
Rohrbach, A.
Root, L.
Ross, M.
Sadler, W.
Santos-Dumont, A.
Scott, B.
Sechler, E.
Seguin, L.
Sellers, M.
Sikorsky, I.
Stack, J.
Stechkin, B.
Storms, H.
Stringfellow, J.
Tupolev, A.
Upson, R.
Verville, A.
Vought, C.
Wallis, B.
Weick, F.
Wellman, W.
Welsh, E.
Wenham, F.
Whitcomb, R.
Williams, O.S.
Wittlemann, C.
Woods, R.
Wright, O.

Wright, W.
Yakovlev, A.
Yeager, C.
Zahm, A.
Zeppelin, F.

AGRICULTURE

(See also
Horticulture)

Abbott, H.
Armsby, H.
Arnett, E.
Atwater, W.
Awwam abu Zakariyya
Bailey, J.
Bakewell, R.
Bassi, A.
Blackman, G.
Boerma, A.H.
Bolotov, A.
Boussingault, J.
Boyd Orr, J.
Brewer, W.
Brown. L.
Browne, D.
Browning, G.
Cadet de Vaux, A.
Campbell, T.
Clawson, M.
Clemson, T.
Clinton, G.
Cobb, N.
Coke, T.
Duley, E.
Fleming, C.
Headley, F.
Hilgard, E.W.
Hill, R.
Hutton, J.
Jefferson, T.
Judd, O.
Keen, B.A.
Lawes, J.
Malesherbes, C.
Mapes, J.
Markham, R.
Miles, M.
Millon, A.
Norton, J.
Piper, C.
Puryear, B.
Russell, E.
Serres, O.
Slater, W.
Spillman, W.
Stakman, E.
Stapledon, R.
Storey, H.
Strong, H.
Stubbs, W.
Tabor, P.
Tillet, M.
Townshend, C.

Truog, E.
Underwood, E.
Wahshiyya, A.
Weston, R.
White-Stevens, R.
Young, A.

ALCHEMY

Adam of Bodenstein
Amili, B.
Ashton, T.
Balsamo, G.
Bernard Trevisan
Blomefield, M.
Brewster, J.
Bulkeley, G.
Danforth, S.
Despegnet, J.
Dorn, G.
Flamel, N.
Fludd, R.
Gohory, J.
Hitchcock, E.
Jabir ibn Hayyan
Kelley, E.
Khunrath, H.
Ko Hung
Libavius
Munson, E.
Olympiodorus
Paracelsus
Petrus Bonus
Rhazes
Sendivogius, M.
Stephanus of Alexandria
Thurneysser, L.
Ulstad, P.
Valentine, B.
Walter of Odington
Zosimus of Panopolis

ANATOMY

Achillini, A.
Albinus, B.
Albinus, C.
Albinus, F.
Alcmaeon of Crotona
Allen, E.
Allen, H.
Allis, E.
Aranzio, G.
Aselli, G.
Atkinson, W.B.
Baillie, M.
Barclay, J.
Barr, M.L.
Bartelmez, G.
Bartholin, E.
Bassini, E.
Bauhin, G.
Beccari, N.

Bell, C.
Bell, J.
Benedetti, A.
Benivieni, A.
Bensley, R.R.
Bichat, M.F.
Bidder, F.H.
Bidloo, G.
Bilharz, T.
Billroth, C.
Bischoff, T.L.
Black, D.
Blainville, H.M.
Bloom, W.
Bolk, L.
Breschet, G.
Brodel, M.
Brookes, J.
Brookover, C.
Buissiere, P.
Caldani, L.
Canano, G.
Carey, E.
Carpue, J.
Casseri, G.
Castaldi, L.
Cheselden, W.
Chiarugi, G.
Clark, E.
Clark, W.
Clarke, J.
Clift, W.
Cobb, W.
Coghill, G.
Collignon, C.
Collins, S.
Colombo, M.
Corti, A.
Cowdry, E.
Cruikshank, W.
Cruveilhier, J.
Danforth, C.
Darling, W.
Dart, R.
Darwin, G.
Detweiler, S.
Draper, J.
Drummond, J.
Duckworth, W.
DuHamel, J.
Duval, M.
Duverney, J.
Ebel, J.
Eberth, C.
Elliott Smith, G.
Engle, E.
Estienne, C.
Eustachio, B.
Evans, H.
Fallopius, G.
Farris, E.
Ferrein, A.
Flemming, W.
Flint, J.
Flood, V.
Fritsch, G.
Fyfe, A.

Gagliardi, D.
Galeazzi, D.
Galvani, L.
Gaysant, L.
Gegenbaur, K.
Glaser, J.
Godman, J.
Goodrich, E.
Goodsir, J.
Goss, C.
Graaf, R.
Grainger, R.
Grant, R.
Gratiolet, L.
Gray, H.
Gudernatschi, J.
Guidi, G.
Gulliver, G.
Haller, A.
Harlan, R.
Harris, G.
Heidenhain, M.
Heister, L.
Henle, F.
Henry, J.L.
Herophilos
Highmore, N.
His, W.
Hoeven, J.
Hooker, D.
Horne, J.
Horner, W.E.
Houston, J.
Huber, G.
Huber, J.
Hundt, M.
Hunter, W.
Huschke, E.
Hyrtl, J.
Innes, J.
Jackson, J.B.
Jayne, H.
Jones, F.W.
Keill, J.
Keith, A.
Kidd, J.
Knisely, M.
Knox, R.
Kielmeyer, C.
Lamb, D.
Langerhans, P.
Laurens, A.
Leblond, C.
LeDouble, A.
Ledwich, T.
LeGros Clark, W.
Lemery, L.
Leonardo da Vinci
Leuret, F.
Levi, G.
Lewis, W.H.
Leydig, F.
Lieberkuhn, J.
Lieutaud, J.
Lord, F.

Luna, E.
Macartney, J.
Mall, F.
Manzolini, A.
Marchiafava, E.
Martinez, C.
Mascagni, P.
McMurrich, J.
Meckel, J.
Meissner, G.
Mery, J.
Michels, N.
Mondino de Luzzi
Monro, A.
Monro, A. II
Monro, A. III
Moody, R.
Morgagni, G.
Ormerod, W.
Osborn, H.F.
Pacini, F.
Papanicolaou, G.
Papez, J.
Parker, W.
Pattison, G.
Paulli, S.
Pensa, A.
Pettigrew, J.
Pianese, G.
Piccolomini, A.
Potter, J.
Praxagoras of Cos
Priman, J.
Prochaska, G.
Quain, J.
Rabl, C.
Rainey, G.
Ramsay, A.
Rathke, M.
Reichert, K.
Reid, J.
Riolan, J.
Rolando, L.
Rolleston, G.
Rondelet, G.
Roux, W.
Rudolphi, K.
Ruini, C.
Sabatier, A.
St. Andre, N.
Salernitan, A.
Santorini, G.
Schneider, F.
Schulte, H.
Schultza, M.
Semon, R.
Senac, J.
Serres, J.
Serres, A.
Severtsov, A.
Sharpey, W.
Simer, P.
Smith, P.
Soemmering, S.
Speigel, A.
Stannius, H.
Steno, N.

Stewart, C.
Stopford, J.
Straus, W.
Streeter, G.
Struthers, J.
Swan, J.
Teichmann, L.
Testut, J.
Tiedemann, F.
Todd, T.
Trotter, M.
Tuckerman, F.
Tulp, N.
Turner, W.
Tyson, E.
Valentin, G.
Valsalva, A.
Valverde, J.
Vastarini-Cresi, G.
Vesalius, A.
Vesling, J.
Vicq d'Azyr, F.
Vieussens, R.
Wagner, R.
Waldeyer-Hartz, W.
Warren, J.
Weber, E.
Weed, L.
Wharton, T.
Wiedersheim, R.
Willis, T.
Winslow, J.
Wislocki, G.
Wistar, C.
Wren, C.
Wyman, J.
Zuckerman, S.

ANTHROPOLOGY

Anuchin, D.
Ardrey, R.
Baer, K.
Bastian, A.
Bateson, G.
Beddoe, J.
Benedict, R.
Black, D.
Blanc, A.
Blumenbach, J.
Boaz, F.
Brainerd, G.
Breuil, H.
Broca, P.
Burrows, E.
Carey, H.
Christy, H.
Coon, C.
Delaney, M.
Deloria, E.
Densmore, F.
Dixon, R.
Dorsey, G.
Eiseley, L.
Evans, C.

Farb, P.
Fejos, P.
Fewkes, J.
Fletcher, A.
Frazer, J.
Galton, F.
Gibbs, G.
Hallowell, A.
Herskovits, M.
Holmes, W.
Hooton, E.
Howells, W.
Howitt, A.
Hrdlicka, A.
Hunt, J.
Hurston, Z.
Jones, F.W.
Keith, A.
Kerr, A.
Kluckhohn, C.
Krasheninnikov, S.
Kroeber, A.
Krogman, W.
LaFarge, O.
Lapicque, L.
Laufer, B.
Leakey, L.
LeGros Clark, W.
Levi-Strauss, C.
Loeb, E.
Lothrop, S.
Lowie, R.
Lubbock, J.
MacCurdy, G.
Malinowski, B.
Mantegazza, P.
Martin, R.
Martius, K.
Mason, O.
McClintock, W.
Mead, M.
Meggers, B.
Mook, M.
Mooney, J.
Morgan, L.
Martillet, L.
Morton, S.
Nuttall, Z.
Oakley, K.
Oberg, K.
Olaus, M.
Parsons, E.
Pitt-Rivers, A.
Powdermaker, H.
Prichard, J.
Pruner bey, F.
Putnam, F.
Ratzel, F.
Redfield, R.
Reichard, G.
Riviere de Precourt, E.
Robeson, E.
Rosaldo, M.
Schultz, A.
Setzler, F.
Smith, E.P.
Stanner, W.

Stevenson, M.
Stewart, T.O.
Stirling, M.
Straus, W.
Swanton, J.
Testut, J.
Thomas, C.
Tiger, L.
Todd, T.
Tozzer, A.
Vallois, H.
Waterman, R.
Weidenreich, F.
Wissler, C.

ANTIQUARIANISM

Folkes, M.

ARBORICULTURE

Evelyn, J.

ARCHAEOLOGY

Blom, F.
Breasted, J.
Carey, H.
Clark, J.
Cummings, B.
Dechelette, J.
Detweiler, A.
Duell, P.
Eisen, G.
Fewkes, J.
Fisher, C.
Frere, J.
Gates, W.
Glueck, N.
Goldman, H.
Gordon, C.
Hamilton, W.
Hansen, H.
Hay, C.
Haynes, H.
Hewett, E.
Kidder, A.
MacCurdy, G.
Maler, T.
Maudslay, A.
Mitchell-Hedges, F.
Montelius, G.
Moorehead, W.
Morley, S.
Mortillet, L.
Mosso, A.
Paine, J.
Parker, A.
Peters, J.P.
Petrie, F.
Pitt-Rivers, A.
Plot, R.

Rainey, R.
Rawlinson, H.
Saville, M.
Schliemann, H.
Schmidt, E.
Shear, T.
Spinden, H.
Swindler, M.
Talcott, L.
Tanzer, H.
Thompson, E.
Thomsen, C.
Ward, L.
Wheeler, R.
Willis, R.
Woolley, C.
Worsaae, J.

ARCHITECTURE

Villalpando, J.
Villard de Honnecourt
Vitruvius

ASTROLOGY

Abu Ma Shar, B.
Ailly, P.
Andrews, W.
Argoli, A.
Blagrave, J.
Dominicus de Clavasio
Firmicus Maternus
Gadbury, J.
Grisogono, F.
Johannes Lauratius de Fundus
Lilly, W.
Masha Allah
Michael Scot
Morin, J.
Muhyil-Din al-Maghribi
Nastradamus, M.
Paul of Alexandria
Pereira, B.
Petrosiris, P.
Plato of Tivoli
Qabisi, S.
Roger of Hereford
Simon de Phares
Sphujidhvaja
Umar ibn al-Farakhan
Varahamihira
Yavanesvara
Zacuta, A.

ASTRONAUTICS

(See also
Rocketry)

Aldrin, E.
Allen, H.

Anders, W.
Armstrong, J.
Armstrong, N.
Bean, A.
Belyayev, P.
Borman, F.
Buckley, E.
Carpenter, M.
Cernan, E.
Collins, M.
Conrad, C.
Cooper, L.
Duke, C.
Esnault-Pelterie, R.
Feoktistov, K.
Freitag, R.
Gagarin, Y.
Glenn, J.
Grissom, V.
Komarov, V.
Leonov, A.
Lovell, J.A.
Martin, J.
McDivitt, J.
Popovich, P.
Ride, S.
Schirra, W.
Schmitt, H.
Scott, D.
Shatalov, V.
Shepard, A.
Slayton, D.
Stafford, T.
Stuhlinger, E.
Titov, G.
Tsiolkovsky, K.
White, E.
Yegorov, B.
Yeliseyev, A.
Young, J.

ASTRONOMY

Abbot, C.
Abetti, A.
Abney, A.
Abraham Bar Hiyya Ha-Nasi
Abul-Wafa al Buzjani
Acyuta Pisarati
Adams, J.C.
Adams, W.S.
Agassiz, G.R.
Airy, G.
Aitken, R.
Albrecht, C.
Alden, H.
Alembert, J.
Alexander, S.
Alfonso el Sabio
Aller, L.H.
Alter, D.
Anamimander of Militos
Anderson, J.A.
Andoyer, H.
Andre, C.L.
Angelus, J.

Anthelme, V.
Antoniade, E.
Apian, P.
Arago, D.F.
Aratus of Soli
Argelander, F.
Argoli, A.
Aristarchus of Samos
Aristyllus
Arrets, H.L.
Aryabhata I
Aryabhata II
Asada Goryu
Aubert, A.
Autolycus
Auwers, A.
Auzout, A.
Baade, W.H.
Babcock, H.D.
Babcock, H.W.
Backlund, J.O.
Bailey, S.I.
Bailly, J.
Baily, F.
Bainbridge, J.
Ball, R.
Ball, W.
Banachiewicz, T.
Banneker, B.
Banu Musa, al-Hasan
Banu Musa, Ahmad
Banu Musa, Muhammad
Baranzano, G.
Barbier, J.E.
Barnard, E.E.
Barnard, F.A.
Barnes, W.L.
Barocius, F.
Barrett, S.B.
Battani, A.
Baxendell, J.
Bayer, J.
Bayly, W.
Beals, C.
Beaufoy, M.
Beer, W.
Bell, J.
Benzenberg, J.
Bernard of Le Treile
Bernard of Verdun
Bernoulli, J.
Berti, G.
Bessel, F.W.
Bevans, J.
Bhaskara I
Bhaskara II
Biddle, O.
Biela, W.
Bigelow, F.H.
Bigourdan, C.G.
Billy, J.
Birmingham, J.
Birt, W.R.
Biruni, A.
Bishop, G.
Bitruji al-Ishbili, A.
Blake, F.

Blazhko, S.
Bliss, N.
Bochart de Saron, J.
Boguslavsky, P.
Bok, B.
Bond, G.
Bond, W.
Boss, L.
Bouilliau, I.
Bouvard, A.
Bowditch, N.
Bradley, J.
Brahe, T.
Brahmadeva
Brahmagupta
Brandes, H.
Brattle, T.
Bredekhin, F.
Bredon, S.
Breen, J.
Bremiker, C.
Brendel, O.
Brinkley, J.
Brisbane, T.
Brooke, J.
Brooks, W.
Brouwer, D.
Brown, J.
Brown, R.
Bruhl, J.
Bruhns, K.
Brunnow, F.
Brytte, W.
Buot, J.
Burbidge, E.
Burbidge, M.
Burg, J.
Burgi, J.
Burnham, S.
Burray, C.
Burrith, E.
Burton, C.
Busch, A.
Calandrelli, G.
Calandrelli, I.
Calcagnini, C.
Caldas, F.
Caldecott, J.
Callandreau, P.
Callippus
Campani, G.
Campanus of Novara
Capra, B.
Carrington, R.
Cassini, J.
Cassini de Thury, C.F.
Castelli, B.
Caswell, A.
Catton, T.
Celsius, A.
Challis, J.
Chandler, S.
Chandrasekhar, S.
Chang Heng
Chappe d'Auteroche, J.
Chary, C.
Chase, M.

Chaucer, G.
Chauvenet, W.
Chester, R.
Chevallier, T.
Christie, W.
Christmans, J.
Clap, T.
Clark, A.
Clark, A.G.
Clark, G.B.
Claude, F.
Clausen, T.
Clavius, C.
Clemence, G.
Cleomodes
Comas Sola, J.
Common, A.
Comrie, L.
Comstock, G.
Conon of Samos
Cooper, E.
Copeland, R.
Copernicus, N.
Cosserat, E.
Cotes, R.
Cowell, P.
Crabtree, W.
Crawford, R.
Crommelin, A.
Cunitz, M.
Curley, J.
Curtis, H.
Curtiss, R.
Cysat, J.
Dalence, J.
Danjon, A.
D'Arcy, P.
Dasypodius, C.
Davidson, C.
Davidson, G.
Davis, C.
Dawes, W.
Day, E.
Delambre, J.
De la Rue, W.
De la Sabiliere, M.
Delisle, J.
Delporte, E.
Dembowski, E.
Denisse, J.
Deslandres, H.
Dinakara
Dionis du Sejour, A.
Dixon, J.
Dolbear, A.
Dollfus, A.
Donati, G.B.
Dondi, G.
Donkin, W.
Doolittle, C.
Doolittle, E.
Doppelmayr, J.
Doppler, C.
Dorffel, G.
Dositheus
Douglass, A.
Downing, A.

Drake, F.
Draper, H.
Drew, J.
Dreyer, J.
Dudith, A.
Dugan, R.
Dumee, J.
Dunbar, W.
Duncan, J.
Duner, N.
Dunlop, J.
Dunthorne, R.
Dyson, F.
Eastman, J.
Easton, C.
Eddington, A.
Eichelberger, W.
Elkin, W.
Ellery, R.
Ellis, W.
Emanuelli, P.
Encke, J.
Erastosthenes
Esclangon, E.
Euctemon
Eudoxus
Ezra, A.
Fabricius, D.
Fabry, H.
Fazari, M.
Ferguson, J.
Feuille, L.
Fine, O.
Fink, T.
Fisher, G.
Flammarion, N.
Flamsteed, J.
Fleming, W.
Flint, A.
Folger, W.
Fouchy, J.
Fox, P.
Franklin, K.
Freeman, T.
Freundlich, E.
Friend, C.
Frost, E.
Fusoris, J.
Fuss, N.
Gaillot, A.
Galilei, G.
Galle, J.
Ganesa
Gargrave, G.
Gasciogne, W.
Gassendi, P.
Gellibrand, H.
Geminus
Gerard of Silteo
Giles of Lessines
Giles of Rome
Gill, D.
Gillis, J.
Glaisher, J.
Godfrey, T.
Godin, L.
Gold, T.

Goodricke, J.
Gore, J.
Gould, B.
Graff, K.
Graham, J.
Grant, J.
Grant, R.
Green, F.
Green, W.
Greenstein, J.
Gregory, D.
Gregory, J.
Grew, T.
Grimaldi, F.
Grossman, E.
Habash al-Hassib, A.
Hall, A.
Halley, E.
Halm, J.
Halton, I.
Hamilton, J.
Hanburry Brown, R.
Hansen, P.
Hansky, A.
Hansteen, C.
Harding, C.
Haridatta II
Harkness, W.
Harrington, M.
Harshman, W.
Hartmann, J.
Hartwig, E.
Hawkins, G.
Haytham, A.
Heckmann, O.
Hedrick, H.
Hell, M.
Hellins, J.
Helmert, F.
Henderson, T.
Henry Bate
Henry, P.
Henry, P.M.
Heracleides
Herget, P.
Hermann the Lame
Herrick, E.
Herrick, S.
Herschel, A.
Herschel, C.
Herschel, J.
Herschel, W.
Hertzsprung, E.
Hevelius, J.
Hewish, A.
Hicetas of Syracuse
Hill, G.
Hill, T.
Hind, J.
Hinks, A.
Hipparchus
Hippocrates of Chios
Hirst, W.
Hitchins, M.
Hoek, M.
Holden, E.
Holden, M.

Hopkins, A.
Horn d'Arturo, G.
Hornsby, T.
Horrebow, C.
Horrocks, J.
Hortensius, M.
Houel, G.
Hough, G.
Howe, H.
Hoyle, F.
Hubbard, J.S.
Hubble, E.
Hufnagel, L.
Humason, M.
Hussey, W.
Huygens, C.
Hypsicles
Ibrahim ibn Sinan ibn Thabit
Idelson, N.
Innes, R.
Ino, T.
Jabir ibn Aflah al-Ishbili, A.
Jacob, W.S.
Jacoby, H.
Jagannatha
Jawhari, A.
Jayasimha
Jayyani, A.
Jeans, J.
Jeaurat, E.
Jeffreys, H.
John of Gmunden
John of Ligneres
John of Murs
John of Saxony
John of Sicily
John Simonis
Johnson, M.J.
Joly, C.
Jones, H.S.
Jordan, F.
Joy, A.
Kaiser, F.
Kamalakara
Kanaka
Kapteyn, J.
Kashi, G.
Kauvaysky, V.
Keckermann, B.
Keeler, J.
Keenan, P.
Kelly, P.
Kendall, E.
Kepler, J.
Kesava
Khalili, S.
Khayyami, G.
Khazin, A.
Khazini, A.
Khujandi, A.
Khwarizmi, A.
Kiddinu
Kimura, H.
King, E.
Kirch, G.
Kirkwood, D.
Klein, H.

Klumpke, D.
Kohoutek, L.
Konkoly Thege, M.
Kopal, Z.
Kostinsky, S.
Kovalsky, M.
Kozyrev, N.
Kraft, R.
Kramp, C.
Kratzer, N.
Krsna
Kuiper, G.
Kuo Shou-Ching
Kushyar ibn Labban ibn Bashahri
Lacaille, N.
Lagrange, J.
LaHire, G.
LaHire, P.
Lalande, J.
Lalla
Lallemand, A.
Lamont, J.
Lansberge, P.
Laplace, P.
Larkin, E.
Lassell, W.
Lau, H.
Lax, W.
Leadbetter, C.
Leavenworth, F.
Leavitt, H.
Leeds, J.
LeFevre, J.
LeGentil de la Galaisiere, G.
Leighton, R.
Lemaitre, G.
LeMonnier, P.
Leo the Mathematician
Leonard, F.
Lepaute, H.
Leuschner, A.
Leverrier, U.
Levi ben Gerson
Lexell, A.
Liesganig, J.
Lindblad, B.
Lindenau, B.
Lindsay, B.
Lippmann, G.
Lohse, W.
Longstretch, M.
Loomis, E.
Lord, H.
Lorenzoni, G.
Loud, F.
Lovell, B.
Lowell, P.
Lubbock, J.W.
Ludendorff, F.
Lundmark, K.
Luther, C.
Luyten, W.
Lyman, C.
Lynn, G.
Lyot, B.
Maanen, A.
Machin, J.

Maclear, T.
Macmillan, W.
Macrobius, A.
Madison, J.
Madler, J.
Magini, G.
Mahadeva
Mahani, A.
Mahendra Suri
Main, R.
Majriti, A.
Makaranda
Mademson, M.
Maksutov, D.
Manfredi, E.
Mann, W.
Mansur ibn Ali ibn Iraq
Maraldi, G.D.
Maraldi, G.F.
Marius, S.
Maskelyne, N.
Mason, C.
Masterman, S.
Mastlin, M.
Mather, I.
Maunder, E.
Maurer, J.
Maurolico, F.
Maury, A.
Mayer, C.
Mayr, S.
McClean, F.
McCoy, D.
McMath, R.
Mechain, P.
Melnikov, O.
Melvill, T.
Menelaus of Alexandria
Mercator, N.
Merrill, P.
Messier, C.
Metcalf, J.
Meton
Michell, J.
Mikhailov, A.
Milham, W.
Miller, W.A.
Mills, B.
Mineur, H.
Minkowski, R.
Mitchel, O.
Mitchell, M.
Mitchell, W.
Mobius, A.
Moiseev, N.
Moll, G.
Moller, D.
Mollweide, K.
Molyneux, S.
Montanari, G.
Monte, G.
Moore, J.H.
Morehouse, D.
Morgan, H.R.
Morgan, W.
Mouchez, E.
Moulton, F.

Mouton, G.
Muller, G.
Munisvara Visvarupa
Munjala
Mutisy Bossio, J.
Nagesa
Nasmyth, J.
Nassay, J.
Nayrizi, A.
Neuymin, G.
Newall, R.
Newcomb, S.
Newton, H.A.
Newton, I.
Newton, J.
Nichol, J.
Nicholson, S.
Nicolai, F.
Nicollet, J.
Niesten, J.
Nilakantha
Norton, W.
Novard, D.
Numerov, B.
Odierna, G.
Oenopides of Chios
Olbers, H.
Olmsted, D.
Olufsen, C.
Oort, J.
Opik, E.
Oppenheim, S.
Oppolzer, T.
Orlov, S.
Outhier, R.
Paine, R.
Palisa, J.
Pannekoek, A.
Pappus
Paramesvara
Parenago, P.
Parkhurst, J.
Parsons, L.
Parsons, W.
Paul, H.
Paulisa
Payne-Gaposchkin, C.
Pearson, H.
Pease, F.
Peirce, B.
Peiresc, N.
Penzias, A.
Perez de Vargas, B.
Perrine, C.
Perrotin, H.
Perry, S.
Peters, C.A.
Peters, C.H.
Petit, P.
Peurbach, G.
Pezenas, E.
Phelps, T.
Phillips, T.
Philolaus of Crotona
Piazzi, G.
Picard, J.
Pickering, E.

Pickering, W.
Pigott, E.
Pigott, N.
Pingre, A.
Plana, G.
Plaskett, H.
Plaskett, J.
Plummer, H.
Pogson, N.
Pond, J.
Pons, J.
Poor, C.
Poretsky, P.
Porter, J.
Pound, J.
Powalky, K.
Pritchard, C.
Pritchett, H.
Proclus
Proctor, R.
Ptolemy, C.
Puerbach, G.
Puiseux, V.
Pythagoras
Qadi al-Din al-Shirazi
Raghavananda Sarman
Ramee, P.
Ranganatha
Rayet, G.
Raymond of Marseilles
Recht, A.
Redman, R.
Rees, J.
Regiomontamus, J.
Respighi, L.
Riccioli, G.
Richard of Allingford
Richer, J.
Riddle, E.
Rigge, W.
Ritchey, G.
Rittenhouse, D.
Roberts, D.
Roberts, I.
Robertson, A.
Robie, T.
Robinson, T.
Roemer, O.
Roger of Hereford
Rogers, W.A.
Roman, N.
Rooke, L.
Rosenberg, H.
Rosenberger, O.
Ross, F.
Rothmann, C.
Rumovsky, S.
Rushd, A.
Russell, H.C.
Russell, H.N.
Ryle, M.
Sabine, E.
Sacrobosco, J.
Safford, T.
Sagan, C.
St. John, C.
St. Vincent, G.

Samarqandi, S.
Sampson, R.
Sandage, A.
Satananda
Schaeberle, J.
Scheiner, C.
Scheiner, J.
Schiaparelli, G.
Schickard, W.
Schjellerup, H.
Schlesinger, F.
Schmidt, N.
Schoner, J.
Schonfeld, E.
Schroter, J.
Schubert, E.
Schumacher, H.
Schwabe, S.
Schwarzschild, M.
Seares, F.
Searle, A.
Secchi, P.
See, T.
Seeliger, H.
Seidell, P.
Seleucus
Sestini, B.
Severin, C.
Seyfert, C.
Shakerley, J.
Shapley, H.
Sharonov, V.
Shatir, A.
Sheepshanks, R.
Shepherd, A.
Shibukawa, H.
Suguenza y Gongora, C.
Sijzi, A.
Sinan ibn Thabit ibn Qurra
Sitterly, B.
Sittler, W.
Skinner, A.
Slipher, E.
Slipher, V.
Smith, H.
Smyth, C.
Sobolev, V.
Soldner, J.
Sosigenes
South, J.
Spitz, A.
Spoerer, G.
Sripati
Stebbins, J.
Stein, J.
Steinheil, K.
Stephan, E.
Stepling, J.
Sternberg, P.
Stewart, M.
Stone, O.
Strange, A.
Stratton, F.
Streete, T.
Stromberg, G.
Stromgren, S.
Struve, F.

Struve, G.O.
Struve, G.W.
Struve, K.
Struve, O.
Struve, O.W.
Subbotin, M.
Sufi, A.
Sundman, K.
Swift, L.
Swope, H.
Symmes, J.
Synesius of Cyrene
Tacchini, P.
Talcott, A.
Tarde, J.
Taylor, T.G.
Teed, C.
Thabit ibn Qurra
Theodosius of Bithynia
Theon of Alexandria
Thiele, T.
Tibbon, J.
Tisserand, F.
Titius, J.
Todd, C.
Todd, D.
Tombaugh, C.
Toscanelli dal Pozzo, P.
Townley, S.
Trouvelot, E.
Trumpler, R.
Tserasky, V.
Tucker, R.
Turner, H.
Tusi, M.
Tusi, S.
Tuttle, C.
Ulugh Beg
Umar ibn al-Farrukhan
Upton, W.
Ussher, H.
Vance, S.
Van de Hulst, H.
Van de Kamp, P.
Van Maanen, A.
Varahamihira
Vatesvara
Vaughan, D.
Very, F.
Vijayananda
Vogel, H.
Walker, S.
Wang Hsi-Shan
Ward, S.
Wargentin, P.
Warson, J.C.
Watts, C.
Webb, T.
Weiss, E.
Weizsacker, C.
Wendelin, G.
Werner, J.
West, B.
Wharton, G.
Whewell, W.
Whipple, F.
Whiting, S.

Whitney, M.
Wild, J.
Wildt, R.
Wilhelm IV
Wilkes, C.
William of St. Cloud
William the Englishman
Williams, S.
Williamson, H.
Wilsing, J.
Wilson, A.
Wilson, J.M.
Wilson, R.
Wilson, W.
Wing, V.
Winlock, J.
Winthrop, J.
Wolf, C.
Wolf, J.
Wolf, R.
Wollaston, F.
Woolley, R.
Wright, H.
Wright, T.
Wright, W.
Yahya ibn Abi Mansur
Yaqub ibn Tariq
Yarnall, M.
Yavanesvara
Young, C.
Yowell, E.
Yunus, A.
Zach, F.
Zacuto, A.
Zanotti, E.
Zarqali, A.

ASTROPHYSICS

Ambartsumian, V.
Belopolsky, A.
Biermann, L.
Bowen, I.
Burbidge, G.
Carruthers, G.
Delaunay, C.
Eckert, W.
Emden, R.
Fesenkov, V.
Fowler, A.
Friedman, H.
Gaillot, A.
Gerasimovich, B.
Hale, G.
Hamy, M.
Hirayama, K.
Huggins, W.
Hynek, J.
Johnson, F.S.
Kiess, C.
King-Hele, D.
Langley, S.
Lockyer, J.
Lyttleton, R.
Massevitch, A.

Meghnad, S.
Menzel, D.
Milne, E.
Mineur, H.
Minnaert, M.
Morrison, P.
Muller, G.
Ness, N.
Newall, H.
Nicolet, M.
Orlov, S.
Parker, E.
Pawsey, J.
Pritchard, C.
Ranyard, A.
Ricco, A.
Roberts, W.
Rosenberg, H.
Rutherfurd, L.
Saha, M.
Salpeter, E.
Schmidt, C.
Shayn, G.
Shklovskii, I.
Sitterly, C.
Spitzer, L.
Swings, P.
Tikhov, G.
Unsold, A.
Vogel, H.W.
Wadsworth, F.
Wilson, R.W.
Zanstra, H.
Zollner, J.
Zwicky, F.

AVIATION

(See Aeronautics)

BACTERIOLOGY

Anderson, J.
Andrewes, F.
Arkwright, J.
Arnold, L.
Bastian, H.
Bayne-Jones, S.
Bedson, S.
Berberian, D.
Bergey, D.
Bordet, J.
Braun, W.
Browning, C.
Buchner, H.
Bulloch, W.
Bunting, M.
Burn, C.
Calmette, A.
Carroll, J.
Chamberland, C.
Cheyne, W.
Clifton, C.
Cohen, B.

Cohn, F.
Colebrook, L.
Detre, L.
Dixon, S.
Dunham, E.
Ebel, J.
Ehrlich, P.
Endres, J.
Engelbrecht, M.
Evans, A.
Fasting, G.
Fay, A.
Felix, A.
Fellers, C.
Felton, L.
Fildes, P.
Fitz Randolph, R.
Fleming, A.
Flexner, S.
Ford, W.
Frankland, P.
Fred, E.
Frost, W.
Gaffsky, G.
Garey, J.
Gay, F.
Gee, H.
Glenny, A.
Gordon, M.
Gorham, F.
Gorini, L.
Gram, H.
Greaves, J.
Griffith, F.
Haffkine, W.
Hansen, G.
Hazen, E.
Heilman, F.
Henrici, A.
Hershey, A.
Hill, J.H.
Hirszfeld, L.
Hitchens, A.
Ivler, D.
Jay, J.
Jordan, E.
Kellerman, K.
Kendall, A.
Kitasato, S.
Lancefield, R.
Ledingham, J.
Levin, M.
Loffler, F.
Lustig, A.
Marshall, C.
Mechnikov, I.
Meyer, K.
Middaugh, P.
Moon, M.
Moore, V.
Murray, R.
Novy, F.
Nuttall, G.
Oakley, C.
Oliver, W.
Park W.
Perroncito, E.
Petri, J.

Pfeiffer, R.
Plotz, H.
Prescott, S.
Prudden, T.
Rahn, O.
Ravenel, M.
Rettger, L.
Rice, J.
Rivers, T.
Robertson, M.
Roux, P.
Salmonsen, C.
Sandholzer, L.
Schultz, E.
Sears, H.
Sharp, W.
Shaw, F.
Sherman, J.
Simmons, J.
Smith, E.F.
Smith, H.O.
Stiles, G.
Stokes, A.
Stuart, C.
Tedesche, L.
Thomas, S.J.
Topley, W.
Twort, F.
Waksman, S.
Wassermann, A.
Weiss, E.
Welch, W.
Werkman, C.
Williams, A.
Witebsky, E.
Wood, W.
Wright, A.
Yersin, A.
Zingher, A.
Zinsser, H.

BIOCHEMISTRY

Abel, J.
Abraham, E.
Alsberg, C.
Ames, B.
Anderson, R.
Anfinsen, C.
Arber, W.
Arnon, D.
Asimov, I.
Bach, A.N.
Bailey, K.
Ball, E.G.
Balls, A.
Barker, H.A.
Bechamp, P.
Belozersky, A.
Benedict, S.R.
Berg, P.
Bergmann, M.
Bergstrom, S.
Bertrand, G.
Bloch, K.

Boyd, W.
Boyer, H.
Braunstein, A.
Brown, R.
Butler, J.
Cannan, R.
Cannon, L.
Carter, H.
Chain, E.
Chargaff, E.
Cohen, S.
Cohn, E.
Cohn, W.
Conway, E.
Cori, C.
Cori, G.
Coulson, E.
Craig, F.
Crick, F.
Dakin, H.
Dam, H.
Davidson, J.
DeDuve, C.
DeLuca, L.
Dodds, E.
Doisy, E.
Domagk, G.
Dorset, M.
Drummond, J.
Duclaux, E.
DuVigneaud, V.
Ebashi, S.
Edelman, G.
Edsall, J.
Ehrenstein, M.
Eley, D.
Elvehjem, C.
Emerson, G.
Engelhardt, W.
Euler-Chelpin, H.
Farmer, C.
Ferdman, D.
Ferguson, M.
Fischer, E.
Fischer, H.O.
Folin, O.
Fox, S.
Fraenkel-Conrat, H.
Frey, C.
Fruton, J.
Funk, C.
Galeazzi, D.
Garrod, A.
Geiger, E.
Gibson, R.
Gies, W.
Gillespie, L.
Gortner, R.
Goulian, M.
Graham, H.
Green, D.
Greenstein, J.
Griffith, W.
Gulland, J.
Gyorgy, P.

Haagen-Smit, A.
Haldane, J.
Halliburton, W.
Handler, P.
Harden, A.
Herington, C.
Harrow, B.
Hart, E.
Hassid, W.
Hastings, A.
Haurowitz, F.
Hazen, E.
Herter, C.
Hoagland, C.
Hoagland, M.
Hofmann, K.
Holley, R.
Hopkins, F.
Hoppe-Seyler, F.
Horbaczewski, J.
Horecker, B.
Hughes, J.
Ingram, V.
Jacobs, W.
Jodidi, S.
Jencks, W.
Johnson, T.B.
Kabat, E.
Kamen, M.
Kamm, O.
Keilin, D.
Kendall, E.
Kendrew, J.
Kennedy, E.
Kermack, W.
Kidder, G.
Killian, J.
King, C.G.
Kirk, P.
Kluyver, A.
Koch, F.
Koch, R.
Kornberg, A.
Kramer, B.
Kraybill, H.
Krebs, H.
Krewson, C.
Kursanov, A.
Kuzin, A.
Lardy, H.
Lehninger, A.
Lejwa, A.
Leloir, L.
Lemberg, M.
Levene, P.
Levey, S.
Levine, V.
Lewis, H.
Lipmann, F.
Lloyd, D.
Long, C.
Long, H.
Long, J.
Lyman, C.
Lynen, F.
Macallum, A.
Macheboeuf, M.

Mapson, L.
Marrian, G.F.
Marriott, W.
Marston, H.
Martin, C.
Mattill, H.
Maynard, L.
McCollum, E.
Meister, A.
Meyer, K.
Meyerhof, O.
Mitchell, P.
Moore, S.
Morris, J.L.
Morton, R.
Murayama, M.
Nachmansohn, D.
Needham, D.
Needham, J.
Neish, A.
Nencki, M.
Neuberg, C.
Neurath, H.
Nirenberg, M.
Northrop, J.
Ochoa, S.
Palladin, V.
Pardee, A.
Parnas, J.
Perlmann, G.
Perlzweig, W.
Peters, R.
Pfiffner, J.
Phillips, P.
Piez, K.
Pirie, N.
Pisano, M.
Plimmer, R.
Pommer, A.
Ponnamperuma, C.
Porter, R.
Potter, V.
Quastel, J.
Quick, A.
Racker, E.
Raistrick, H.
Ray, T.
Robison, R.
Roe, J.
Rose, W.
Rossiter, R.
Russell, J.
Samuelsson, B.
Schaible, P.
Schmidt, C.L.
Schoenheimer, R.
Schopfer, W.
Schweet, R.
Schweinitz, E.
Seibert, F.
Severin, S.
Shaffer, P.
Shemin, D.
Sherman, H.
Sisakyan, N.
Snell, E.
Stanley, W.

Stedman, E.
Steenbock, H.
Stein, W.
Stephenson, M.
Stock, C.
Strominger, J.
Stucky, C.
Sumner, J.
Szent-Gyorgyi, L.
Tamiya, H.
Tashiro, S.
Tatus, E.
Thayer, S.
Theorell, A.
Tiselius, A.
Vennesland, B.
Vertanen, A.
Vishniac, W.
Wakil, S.
Wald, G.
Warburg, O.
Watson, J.D.
Weinberg, R.
Weissbach, H.
Wilkerson, V.
Wilkins, M.
Williams, R.J.
Williams, R.T.
Wilson, D.
Wood, H.
Woods, D.
Wormall, A.
Wrinch, D.
Wu, H.

BIOLOGY

(See also
Microbiology)

Aldrovandi, U.
Alexander of Myndos
Allee, W.
Allen, D.
Ancel, P.
Artedi, P.
Astaurov, B.
Avakyan, A.
Avery, O.T.
Ayala, F.
Baer, K.E.
Baglivi, G.
Bailey, J.W.
Balbiano, E.
Barski, G.
Becquerel, P.
Belding, D.
Bennet-Clark, T.
Bennett, H.S.
Bennett, L.J.
Benzer, S.
Berg, C.O.
Bexon, G.
Bidloo, G.
Bigelow, M.A.
Bittner, J.J.

Bolos of Mendes
Bolotov, A.
Bonner, J.
Bonnet, C.
Bory de St. VIncent, J.
Bouin, P.A.
Boveri, T.
Brachet, J.
Bradbury, O.
Braun, A.
Brenner, S.
Bristol, C.
Brown, C.J.
Brown, C.L.
Brown, D.
Burnett, W.
Cahalane, V.
Carlander, K.
Carson, R.
Castle, W.
Caullery, M.
Chambers, P.
Chambers, R.
Chaney, L.
Chang, M.
Claude, A.
Clausen, J.
Cobb, N.
Cocke, E.
Coe, W.
Conklin, E.
Conrad, G.
Cook, O.
Cottam, C.
Coulter, S.
Creaser, C.
Cuenot, L.
Darlington, C.
Darnell, J.
Dausset, J.
Davaine, C.
Day, A.
Day, E.
DeBeer, G.
DeDuve, C.
Delage, Y.
Delbruck, M.
Delile, A.
Dennis, D.
Dethier, V.
Dobzhansky, T.
Downing, E.
Driesch, H.
Dubinin, N.
Duran Reynals, F.
Dutton, J.
Ehrenberg, C.
Ehrlich, P.
Einarsen, A.
Ephrussi, B.
Errera, L.
Faure Fremiet, E.
Fell, H.
Fiessinger, N.
Fol, H.
Fontana, F.
Franklin, R.

Fuller, J.
Gabrielson, I.
Galloway, T.
Gardiner, E.
Garnjobst, L.
Geddes, P.
Gee, N.
Giard, A.
Gilbert, W.
Glass, H.
Gowen, J.
Gray, L.
Green, J.
Greenman, M.
Gregory, W.
Gurvich, A.
Hall, R.W.
Hamilton, W.
Hammerling, J.
Hammett, F.
Harrar, J.
Harrison, R.
Hartley, P.
Harvey, E.
Hazzard, A.
Henderson, D.
Herrera, A.
Herrick, F.
Hertwig, K.
Hile, R.
Hogben, L.
Hopfield, J.
Hotchkiss, R.
Hubbs, C.
Hudson, J.
Huntsman, A.
Hutton, R.
Huxley, H.
Huxley, J.
Hylander, C.
Ivanov, I.
Jacob, F.
Jaeger, E.
Jamieson, W.
Jenkins, R.
Johannsen, W.
Johnson, M.W.
Kalmbach, E.
Kammerer, P.
Katchalski, E.
Kellogg, J.
Kidder, G.
Kleczkowski, A.
Kleinenberg, N.
Knowles, F.
Koelliker, R.
Kunkel, B.
Langlois, T.
Laughlin, H.
LeDantec, F.
Leedy, D.
Leeuwenhoek, A.
Leonard, J.
Lewis, M.
Little, C.
Loeb, J.
Lotze, H.

Luria, S.
Lwoff, A.
Lysenko, T.
Macloskie, G.
Mahoney, C.
Mann, P.
Margulis, L.
Marsh, C.
Maupas, F.
Mavor, J.
Maynard Smith, J.
Mayr, E.
Mazia, D.
McAtee, W.
McCrady, E.
Mead, A.
Medawar, P.
Medvedev, Z.
Menge, E.
Merriam, C.
Meselson, M.
Mesnil, F.
Mestre, H.
Michaud, H.
Michener, C.
Middendorf, A.
Milstein, C.
Minot, C.
Mivart, S.G.
Moerbeke, W.
Moffett, J.
Mohl, H.
Monod, J.
Montgomery, E.
Moore, E.
Moore, J.A.
Moore, N.
Morozov, G.
Muller, O.
Munz, P.
Murphy, J.
Nabrit, S.
Navashin, S.
Nelson, J.
Nicholas, J.
Nicholson, H.
Noble, G.
Nomura, M.
Olive, J.
Palade, G.
Park, O.
Parpart, A.
Patten, W.
Peale, R.
Pearl, R.
Pearson, J.
Perez de Vargas, B.
Phillips, A.
Pickens, A.
Pincus, G.
Popenoe, P.
Porter, K.
Portier, P.
Poteat, W.
Pouchet, F.
Purinton, G.
Raspail, F.

Redfield, A.
Rensch, B.
Rich, W.
Ricker, W.
Riddle, O.
Robin, C.
Roger, M.
Rostandi, J.
Rouillier, K.
Russell, E.
Ryzhkov, V.
Savigny, M.
Sax, K.
Schmitt, F.
Schoonhoven, J.
Schopfer, W.
Schouw, J.
Schwartz, G.
Shmalhauzen, I.
Shufeldt, R.
Simpson, G.G.
Siple, P.
Skryabin, K.
Snieszko, S.
Sorby, H.
Spallanzani, L.
Spencer, H.
Spencer, W.
Spiegelman, S.
Stahl, F.
Stanier, R.
Stevens, N.
Stewart, N.
Stockard, C.
Strong, R.
Stryer, L.
Sumner, F.
Surface, F.
Sutton, W.
Svedelius, N.
Swammerdam, J.
Swingle, H.
Szilard, L.
Tamiya, H.
Tarzwell, C.
Taylor, C.V.
Thompson, W.
Thomas, L.
Thomson, A.
Tiegs, O.
Treviranus, G.
Turck, E.
Turner, T.
Uexkull, J.
Vallisnieri, A.
Waddington, C.
Wald, G.
Walford, L.
Walker, N.
Weiss, P.
Weldon, W.F.
Wetmore, A.
Whipple, G.
Whitaker, D.
Whitman, C.
Wigglesworth, V.
Williams, C.
Williams, R.

Wilson, C.
Wilson, E.B.
Wilson, E.O.
Wilson, H.
Wolff, K.
Wood, F.
Woodruff, L.
Woods, F.
Yanofsky, C.
Young, S.
Zavodsky, M.
Zavarzini, A.

BIOPHYSICS

Adair, G.
Baldes, E.
Bovie, W.
Branson, H.
Burton, A.
Chance, B.
Cole, K.
Elkind, M.
Frank, G.
Fry, W.
Hanson, E.
Hartline, H.
Hecht, S.
Hill, T.
Hodgkin, A.
Hoffman, J.
Hollaender, A.
Katzir, E.
Kersten, H.
Konstantinov, R.
Lauffer, M.
Lecomte du Nouy, P.
Lilly, J.
Macy, J.
McInnes, A.
Phillips, D.
Puck, T.
Quimby, E.
Richards, R.
Roberts, R.
Sadron, C.
Sheard, C.
Sinsheimer, R.
Tobias, C.
Withrow, R.
Wyckoff, R.

BOTANY

Abbot, C.
Abel, C.
Acharius, E.
Agardh, C.
Aiton, W.
Alexander, A.
Alexopoulos, C.
Allen, C.E.
Allen, T.F.

Allman, W.
Alpini, P.
Ames, O.
Anderson, A.P.
Anderson, E.S.
Anderson, T.
Anguillara, L.
Arber, A.
Archer, W.
Arnon, D.
Arnott, G.
Arthur, J.
Atkinson, G.
Babington, C.
Bachman, A.
Bailey, I.W.
Bailey, L.H.
Bailey, W.W.
Baker, J.
Baldwin, W.
Balfour, A.
Balfour, I.B.
Balfour, J.H.
Balls, W.
Banister, J.
Banks, J.
Barber, H.
Barnes, C.
Barnhart, J.
Bartholomew, E.
Barton, B.
Barton, W.
Bartram, J.
Bartram, W.
Bauer, F.
Baukin, J.
Baxter, W.
Baytar al-Malaqi, D.
Beal, W.
Beijerinck, M.
Belon, P.
Bennet-Clark, T.
Bennett, A.
Bennett, J.
Bentham, G.
Bentley, R.
Berkeley, M.
Bernard, N.
Bertrand, C.
Bertrand, P.
Bessey, C.
Billings, W.
Bischoff, G.
Blackman, F.
Blair, P.
Blakeslee, A.
Blinks, L.
Blomquist, H.
Bobart, J.
Bock, J.
Bohler, J.
Bolley, H.
Bonnier, G.
Borlaug, N.
Borrer, W.
Borthwick, H.
Bose, J.

Bower, F.
Brickenridge, W.
Bradley, R.
Brainerd, E.
Brandegee, M.
Brandegee, T.
Brandis, D.
Braun, A.
Brefield, J.
Bridges, R.
Brian, P.
Brigham, W.
Britten, J.
Britton, E.
Britton, N.
Bromfield, W.
Broussonet, P.
Brown, J.W.
Brown, R.
Brown, W.
Brown, W.H.
Browne, W.
Brunfels, O.
Buckley, S.
Buddle, A.
Buller, A.
Burbidge, F.
Burnett, G.
Burrill, T.
Buxton, R.
Cain, S.
Caldas, F.
Caldis, P.
Camerarius, R.
Campbell, D.
Candolle, A.
Candolle, A.P.
Carruthers, W.
Castillo, J.
Catesby, M.
Cavanilles, A.
Cels, J.
Cervantes, V.
Cesalpino, A.
Cesi, F.
Chamberlain, C.
Chamisso, A.
Champion, J.
Chapman, A.
Chase, A.
Cheadle, V.
Chesnut, V.
Chodat, R.
Christensen, J.
Clark, H.
Clark, W.
Clayton, J.
Cleland, R.
Clinton, G.
Clokey, I.
Cohn, F.
Coker, W.
Colden, C.
Colden, J.
Coleman, W.
Collins, F.
Combes, R.

Constance, L.
Cook, M.
Cooper, J.
Cooper, W.
Cordus, E.
Corner, E.
Correns, K.
Corti, B.
Costantin, J.
Couch, J.
Coulter, J.
Coville, F.
Cowles, H.
Coyte, W.
Creevey, C.
Crocker, W.
Crosfield, G.
Cunningham, A.
Cunningham, G.
Cunningham, J.
Curtis, C.
Curist, M.
Curtis, O.
Curtis, W.
Cutler, M.
Dahl, A.
Dalzell, N.
Dancer, T.
Daniell, W.
Darlington, H.
Darlington, W.
Darwin, E.
Darwin, F.
Davidson, A.
Davies, H.
Davis, B.
DeBary, A.
Deering, G.
Devaux, H.
Dewey, C.
Dick, R.
Dickson, A.
Dickson, J.
Dillenius, J.
Dixon, H.
Dodart, D.
Dodge, B.
Dodoens, R.
Dombey, J.
Don, G.
Doody, S.
Draparnaud, J.
Drowne, S.
Druce, G.
Dudley, W.
Duggar, B.
Duhamel, H.
Durand, E.
Eastwood, A.
Eaton, D.
Edgeworth, M.
Eichler, A.
Elliott, S.
Ellis, J.
Elwes, H.
Emerson, R.
Engelmann, G.

Engler, H.
Errera, L.
Esau, K.
Evans, A.
Everhart, B.
Ewart, A.
Eykhfeld, I.
Fairchild, D.
Falconer, H.
Farlow, W.
Farmer, J.
Fee, A.
Ferguson, M.
Ferguson, W.
Fernald, M.
Feuillee, L.
Fielding, H.
Florin, R.
Forsskal, P.
Forster, E.
Forster, T.
Fortune, R.
Fraser, J.
Frederick, L.
Freeman, E.
French, C.
Frey-Wyssling, A.
Fries, E.
Fritsch, F.
Fuchs, L.
Furbish, K.
Gaertner, K.
Gager, C.
Galloway, B.
Galston, A.
Galway, D.
Ganong, W.
Garden, A.
Gardner, G.
Gardner, N.
Garreau, L.
Gatlinger, A.
Geoffroy, C.
Gerard, J.
Gessner, J.
Ghini, L.
Gibson, A.
Giraud, H.
Glaser, J.
Gmelin, J.
Godwin, H.
Goebel, K.
Goeppert, H.
Goethe, J.
Goodale, G.
Goodding, L.
Gray, A.
Greene, E.
Gregory, P.
Greville, R.
Grew, N.
Griffith, R.
Griffith, W.
Grisbach, A.
Guignard, J.
Guilliermond, M.
Gwynne-Vaughan, D.

Haasis, F.
Haberlandt, G.
Hadac, E.
Haenke, T.
Hailstone, S.
Hales, S.
Hallier, E.
Hance, H.
Hansen, E.
Harper, R.A.
Harper, R.M.
Harrar, J.
Harriman, J.
Harris, J.
Harrison, J.
Harshberger, J.
Harvey, E.M.
Harvey, R.
Harvey, W.H.
Haworth, A.
Heald, F.
Hedwig, J.
Heer, O.
Hein, I.
Heller, A.
Henderson, J.
Henfrey, A.
Henrichs, J.
Henslow, J.
Hill, J.
Hillmann, F.
Hitchcock, A.S.
Hitchcock, R.
Hoagland, D.
Hobson, E.
Hofmeister, W.
Holm, H.
Holmgren, A.
Hooker, J.
Hooker, W.
Hornemann, J.
Horsfall, J.
Hosack, D.
Hough, F.
Howe, M.
Howe, W.
Howell, J.
Howell, T.
Huber, J.
Hudson, W.
Humphrey, H.
Humphrey, J.
Hutchinson, J.
Irvine, A.
Ivanov, L.
Ivanovsky, D.
Jacquin, N.
James, E.
James, T.
James, W.
Jameson, W.
Jefferson, T.
Jeffrey, E.
Jenner, E.
Jennings, O.
Jepson, W.
Johnson, D.S.

Johnson, M.
Johnson, T.
Jones, L.
Jordan, A.
Jussieu, A.
Jussieu, A.H.
Jussieu, A.L.
Jussieu, B.
Kaempfer, E.
Kauffman, C.
Kearney, T.
Keeble, F.
Kellerman, W.
Kellogg, A.
Kendrick, J.
Ker, J.
Keyserling, A.
King, G.
Kitaibel, P.
Klebs, G.
Knapp, J.
Knight, T.
Knuth, P.
Kolreuter, J.
Kraemer, H.
Kramer, P.
Krasnov, A.
Krausel, R.
Kuhn, A.
Kunkel, L.
Kunth, C.
Kuntze, C.
Kuprevich, V.
Kutzing, F.
Kylin, J.
LaBrosse, G.
Lamarck, J.
Lambert, A.
Lamson-Scribner, F.
Lang, W.H.
Lankester, E.
Laurenko, E.
Lawrence, G.
Lawson, G.
Lehenbauer, P.
Leighton, W.
Lemmon, J.
LeMonnier, L.
Lesquereux, L.
L'Heritier de Brutelle, C.
Lhwyd, E.
Lignier, E.
Linder, D.
Lindheimer, F.
Lindley, J.
Lindsay, W.
Linford, M.
Link, H.
Linnaeus, C.
Lister, A.
Livingston, B.
Livingston, J.
Lloyd, C.
Lloyd, F.
L'Obel, M.
Locke, J.
Lockhart, D.

Logan, J.
Longinos Martinez, J.
Lonicerus, A.
Lotsy, J.
Lovell, J.
Lundegardh, H.
Luxford, G.
Lyall, R.
Lyell, C.
MacBride, J.
MacBride, T.
MacDougal, D.
MacFarlane, J.
Machlis, L.
MacMillan, C.
Macoun, J.
Magnol, P.
Maguire, B.
Maheshwari, P.
Maige, A.
Mains, E.
Maire, R.
Maksimov, N.
Malesherbes, C.
Manardo, G.
Mangelsdorf, P.
Mangin, L.
Mann, A.
Marchant, N.
Marie Victorin
Markgraf, G.
Marshall, H.
Martius, K.
Martyn, T.
Marum, M.
Maskell, E.
Mason, H.
Mason, T.
Masson, F.
Mast, S.
Masters, M.
Matruchot, L.
Mattioli, P.
Matzke, E.
Mauri, E.
Maxon, W.
McBride, J.
McNab, W.
McNair, J.
Medicus, F.
Meehan, T.
Mell, P.
Merrill, E.
Mettenius, G.
Mexia, Y.
Meyen, F.
Meyer, F.
Michaux, F.
Micheli, P.
Miller, E.
Miller, J.
Miller, P.
Miller, W.
Millspaugh, C.
Miquel, F.
Mirbel, C.
Mocino, J.

Moench, C.
Mohr, C.T.
Moldenhawer, J.
Molliard, M.
Moore, G.T.
Moore, T.
Morison, R.
Mottier, D.
Mozino, J.
Muhlenberg, G.
Murray, G.R.
Mutis y Bossio, J.
Naegeli, C.
Naudin, C.
Nees von Esenbeck, C.
Nelson, A.
Nelson, R.
Newbould, W.
Newcombe, F.
Newell, M.
Newton, J.
Nicholas, G.
Nicholson, G.
Nicolaus
Nicot, J.
Nuttall, T.
Olney, S.
Osterhout, W.
Oudemans, C.
Overholts, L.
Overton, J.
Paine, J.
Pammel, L.
Parry, C.C.
Paulli, S.
Pavon y Jimenez, J.
Pearsall, W.
Peattie, D.
Peck, C.
Peirce, G.
Penhallow, D.
Perrine, H.
Persoon, C.
Petersen, N.
Petiver, J.
Petry, L.
Peysonnel, J.
Pfeffer, B.
Phillips, W.
Plumier, C.
Plunkenet, L.
Poivre, P.
Pontedera, G.
Porcher, F.
Porter, T.
Potzer, J.
Prain, D.
Pratt, A.
Presl, K.
Pringsheim, N.
Pritchard, F.
Pryanishnikov, D.
Pryor, A.
Pulteney, R.
Pursh, F.
Raber, O.
Ralfs, J.

Rames, J.
Ramond de Carbonnienes, L.
Rand, I.
Raper, J.
Raulin, J.
Rauwolf, L.
Ravenel, H.
Redoute, P.
Reed, H.
Reinking, O.
Relhan, R.
Rendle, A.
Renner, O.
Richards, F.
Richardson, R.
Riddell, J.
Ridley, H.
Robbins, W.
Robertson, J.
Robertson, R.
Robinson, B.
Robson, S.
Rolfnick, G.
Rose, J.
Rothrock, J.
Roxburgh, W.
Rudge, W.
Ruel, J.
Rufinus
Ruiz, H.
Rupert, J.
Rusby, H.
Rydberg, P.
Sachs, J.
Safford, W.
Salisbury, F.
Salisbury, R.
Sampson, H.
Sanio, K.
Sargent, C.
Sartwell, H.
Saussure, H.
Saussure, N.
Sauvageau, C.
Scaliger, J.
Scarth, G.
Schaffner, J.
Schimper, A.
Schimper, K.
Schimper, W.
Schishkin, B.
Schleiden, J.
Schneider, A.
Schweinitz, L.
Schwendener, S.
Scott, D.H.
Sesse y Lacasta, M.
Setchell, W.
Shamel, A.
Sharp, A.
Sharp, L.
Sharrock, R.
Shattuck, L.
Shear, C.
Shecut, J.
Sheldon, J.
Sherard, J.

Sherard, W.
Short, C.
Shreve, F.
Shull, G.
Shuttleworth, R.
Sibthorp, J.
Sims, J.
Sinnott, E.
Skottsberg, C.
Skutch, A.
Small, J.
Smith, E.
Smith, G.
Smith, J.E.
Smith, W.W.
Snow, G.
Sole, W.
Solms-Laubach, H.
Sotchava, V.
Spalding, V.
Spiegel, A.
Sprengel, C.
Spruce, R.
Stackhouse, J.
Stakman, E.
Stebbins, G.
Steckbeck, W.
Sternberg, K.
Steward, F.
Stiles, W.
Stopes, M.
Stout, G.
Strasburger, E.
Sturtevant, E.
Sukachyev, V.
Sullivant, W.
Suringar, W.
Swartz, O.
Tansley, A.
Taylor, W.R.
TenRhyne, W.
Teschemacher, J.
Thaxter, R.
Theophrastus
Thimann, K.
Thiselton-Dyer, W.
Thoday, D.
Thom, C.
Thomas, M.
Thomson, R.
Thouin, A.
Threlkeld, C.
Thunberg, C.
Thurber, G.
Thuret, G.
Thwaites, G.
Tidestrom, I.
Tieghem, P.
Tiffany, H.
Timiryazev, K.
Tournefort, J.
Tozzi, D.
Tracy, C.
Train, P.
Trelease, W.
Treub, M.
Treviranus, L.

Triana, J.
Trimen, H.
True, R.
Tschermak von Seysenegg, E.
Tsitsin, N.
Tsvett, M.
Tuckerman, E.
Tulasne, L.
Tumanov, I.
Turgot, E.
Turner, D.
Turpin, P.
Turrill, W.
Underwood, L.
Unger, F.
Vaillant, S.
Vasey, G.
Vaucher, J.
Vavilov, N.
Vavra, A.
Velley, T.
Vellozo, J.
Vesling, J.
Vilmorin, P.
Vines, S.
Voronin, M.
Wade, W.
Wahlenberg, G.
Walker, J.
Walker, J.C.
Wallich, N.
Watter, T.
Ward, C.
Ward, H.
Ward, N.
Wardlaw, C.
Warming, J.
Warner, R.
Watson, P.
Watson, S.
Watson, W.
Weatherby, C.
Webb, P.
Webber, H.
Wehmeyer, L.
Welwitsch, F.
Went, F.A.
Went, F.W.
Wetmore, R.
Wheeler, T.
Whetzel, H.
White, F.
White, G.
Wiegand, K.
Wieland, M.
Wiesner, J.
Wigand, A.
Wigg, L.
Wight, R.
Willdenow, K.
Williamson, W.
Willis, J.
Wilson, E.H.
Wilson, W.
Winch, N.
Withering, W.
Wolle, F.

Wood, A.
Wood, R.
Wood, W.
Woods, A.
Woods, J.
Woodville, W.
Worcester, D.
Wortman, S.
Wright, C.
Wylie, R.
Young, A.
Young, A.H.
Young, H.
Zaluzansky Ze Zaluzan, A.
Zimmerman, P.

CHEMICAL ENGINEERING

Adams, I.
Baker, E.
Baskerville, C.
Block, E.
Bird, R.
Boarts, R.
Boyer, M.
Breyer, F.
Brown, G.
Burgess, E.
Burrell, G.
Burt, W.
Canjar, L.
Chambers, A.
Chilton, T.
Costa, J.
Craig, D.
Curtis, H.
Danckwerts, P.
Davis, G.
Dean, E.
Denson, C.
Dodge, B.F.
Dorr, J.
Dow, H.
Eckerd, J.
Engelhard, C.
Esselen, G.
Freud, B.
Frolich, P.
Gardiner, W.
Gauger, A.
Gilchrist, P.
Gilliland, E.
Griffin, R.
Gregor, H.
Hachmuth, K.
Hampson, W.
Haslam, R.
Harreshoff, J.
Herstein, K.
Hirsh, L.
Hitchcock, L.
Horne, W.
Hottel, H.
Howard, H.
Howe, H.

Jacquet, P.
Jones, W.N.
Juve, A.
Katz, A.
Keith, P.
Kirkpatrick, S.
Knowles, C.
Landolt, P.
Lewis, W.
Lux, J.
Marsel, C.
Mason, D.
Mason, S.
McAdams, W.
McCabe, W.
McKenna, C.
Meade, R.
Miller, A.
Neri, A.
Norton, T.
Othmer, D.
Partridge, E.
Perry J.
Prutton, C.
Rahiya, M.
Ridgway, R.
Ritchey, H.
Robinson, C.
Rosengarten, G.
Sadtler, P.
Schnyder, W.
Sherwood, T.
Shreve, R.
Simmons, H.
Stein, E.
Stillman, T.
Stine, C.
Strahl, W.
Thorp, F.
Threfall, R.
Trice, V.
Tsao, G.
Walker, W.
Warner, R.
Watkins, G.
Weber, H.
Weisz, P.
Wetherill, S.
Whitaker, M.
White, A.
Whitman, W.
Wilhelm, R.
Wilson, R.
Withrow, J.
Work, L.
Young, J.
Zhavoronkov, N.
Zons, F.

CHEMISTRY

(See also
Biochemistry; Electrochemistry)

Abbott, R.
Abegg, R.

Abel, F.A.
Abelson, P.
Accum, F.
Achard, F.
Acheson, E.
Adam, N.
Adams, R.
Adamson, G.
Adet, P.
Adkins, H.
Aikin, A.
Aikin, C.
Akers, A.
Albright, A.
Alder, K.
Alekin, O.
Alexander, J.
Alimarin, I.
Allen, O.D.
Allen, P.
Allen, W.H.
Alsop, W.
Anders, E.
Anderson, A.
Anderson, J.
Anderson, T.
Andrews, T.
Andrianov, K.
Anschutz, R.
Appleton, J.
Aquinas, T.
Arbuckle, H.
Arbuzov, A.
Arfvedson, J.
Armstrong, E.F.
Armstrong, H.
Armstrong, J.T.
Arnett, E.
Arnold, C.
Arrhenius, S.
Aschan, O.
Aston, F.
Atkins, W.
Atwood, L.
Atwood, W.
Auer, K.
Austen, P.T.
Avogadro, A.
Ayers, J.
Babcock, J.F.
Babcock, S.M.
Babo, C.
Bache, F.
Bachmann, W.
Bachuone, A.
Baddiley, J.
Badger, R.
Badger, W.
Baekeland, L.
Baeyer, A.J.
Bagnall, K.
Bailar, J.
Bailey, E.H.
Bailey, J.W.
Baker, H.
Baker, J.
Baker, T.R.

Baker, W.
Balandin, A.
Balard, A.J.
Baldwin, H.B.
Balke, C.
Bamberger, E.
Bamford, C.
Bancroft, E.
Bancroft, W.
Barchusen, J.
Barger, G.
Barkenbus, C.
Barker, F.
Barnes, R.
Barnett, H.M.
Barrer, R.
Barreswill, C.
Barrett, J.
Bartell, F.
Bartlett, P.
Barton, D.
Bashkirov, A.
Basolo, F.
Bates, R.
Battersby, A.
Battley, R.
Baudrimont, A.
Bauer, E.
Bauer, N.
Baumann, E.
Baume, A.
Baumhauser, E.
Baumhauser, H.
Bawn, C.
Baxter, F.R.
Baxter, G.P.
Bayen, P.
Beal, G.
Bechamp, P.
Becher, J.
Beck, L.
Beckmann, E.
Beckwith, E.
Beddoes, T.
Bedford, C.
Beguin, C.
Behrend, A.
Belby, G.
Belcher, R.
Bell, J.
Bell, R.
Bellani, A.
Benedetti-Pichler, A.
Benedict, F.
Benedict, W.
Bennett, G.
Berard, J.
Bergel, F.
Bergius, F.
Bergman, T.
Bergmann, M.
Bergmann, W.
Berkeley, R.
Bernays, A.
Bernthsen, H.
Berry, E.R.
Berson, J.

Berthelot, C.
Berthollet, A.
Berzelius, J.
Bevan, E.
Bevilacqua, E.
Bhatnagar, S.
Bichkowsky, F.
Bigeleisen, J.
Bigelow, W.
Bingham, E.
Birch, A.
Bischof, C.G.
Bischoff, E.
Bishop, H.B.
Bishop, O.M.
Bjerrum, N.
Black, G.
Black, J.
Blagden, C.
Blair, A.
Blake, J.
Blake, R.
Blaker, E.
Blanck, F.
Blatherwick, N.
Bleininger, A.
Bloch, H.
Block, D.
Blodget, K.
Bloede, V.
Blomstrand, C.
Bodenstein, M.
Bodley, R.
Boerhaave, H.
Bogert, M.
Bohn, R.
Boisbaudran, P.E.
Bolshakov, K.
Bolton, E.
Bolton, H.
Bonvicino, C.B.
Booth, J.C.
Booth, H.S.
Borel, P.
Boreskov, G.
Borodin, A.P.
Borrichius, O.
Borrowman, G.
Bosch, C.
Bottger, R.C.
Boudart, M.
Bourne, E.
Bowden, F.
Bowdoin, J.
Bowen, E.
Bowen, G.
Bowen, H.
Bowman, J.E.
Bowman, J.R.
Boye, M.
Boyle, A.
Boyle, R.
Braconmot, H.
Bradbury, F.
Bradley, J.
Brady, S.E.
Brand, H.

Brande, W.
Brandt, G.
Brauman, J.
Brauner, B.
Bray, W.
Bredt, K.
Breithut, F.
Brewer, L.
Bridges, R.
Brierly, J.
Bright, H.
Bright, J.
Brill, H.
Brill, J.
Brill, R.
Brode, W.
Brodie, B.
Bronsted, J.
Brooker, L.
Brooks, B.
Broquist, H.
Brown, A.
Brown, H.
Brown, K.
Brown, M.
Brown, S.
Browne, A.
Browne, C.
Browning, P.
Brownrigg, W.
Brundage, P.
Brunner, J.
Bubriski, S.
Buchanan, J.
Bruchi, G.
Buchner, E.
Bucholz, C.
Buckingham, A.
Bucquet, J.
Budnikov, P.
Bulkeley, G.
Bullard, R.
Bullitt, J.
Bunsen, R.
Burg, A.
Burgeni, A.
Burnett, G.
Burton, W.
Burwell, R.
Busch, D.
Butenandt, A.
Butlerov, A.
Buys Ballot, C.
Byers, H.
Cabot, S.
Cadet de Gassicourt, L.
Cadet de Vaux, A.
Cadigan, J.
Cady, H.
Cady, W.
Cahours, A.
Caldwell, G.
Caldwell, M.
Callinicos of Heliopolis
Calloway, N.
Calvert, F.
Calvin, M.

Campbell, E.
Cannizzaro, S.
Caprio, A.
Carbutt, J.
Carhart, H.
Caro, H.
Carothers, W.
Carpenter, G.
Carr, E.P.
Carrington, A.
Carver, G.
Casamajor, P.
Case, T.
Caserio, M.
Caspersson, T.
Casselman, E.
Castner, H.
Cavanaugh, G.
Cavendish, H.
Caventou, J.
Cavett, J.
Centnerszwer, M.
Chamot, E.
Chance, A.
Chance, G.
Chandler, C.
Chandler, W.
Chaney, N.
Chapman, D.
Chamman, N.
Chaptal, J.
Charch, W.
Chardenon, J.
Chardennet, L.
Charpy, A.
Chase, M.
Chatt, J.
Chernyaev, I.
Cheronis, N.
Chesebrough, R.
Chevalier, J.
Chevreul, M.
Chichibabin, A.
Chirnside, R.
Chittlenden, R.
Chmutov, K.
Chufarov, G.
Ciamician, G.
Claisen, L.
Clark, C.
Clark, T.
Clark, V.
Clark, W.
Clarke, H.
Classen, A.
Claude, G.
Claus, A.
Claus, C.
Clement, N.
Clemo, G.
Clemson, T.
Cleve, P.
Clouet, J.
Clowes, G.
Coates, C.
Cochrane, A.
Coehn, A.

Coggeshall, G.
Cohen, E.
Cohn, E.
Cohn, L.
Cohoe, W.
Colbeth, I.
Coleman, D.
Collet-Descotils, H.
Collett, A.
Collie, J.
Collier, P.
Conant, J.
Cook, A.
Cook, G.
Cook, J.
Cook, M.
Cooke, J.
Cooke, L.
Cookson, R.
Coolidge, A.
Coolidge, W.
Cooper, T.
Copaux, H.
Cope, A.
Corey, E.
Cornette, C.
Cornforth, J.
Correns, E.
Coryell, C.
Cotting, J.
Cotton, D.
Cottrell, F.
Cottrell, T.
Couper, A.
Courtois, B.
Covert, L.
Cowan, G.
Cox, G.
Crafts, J.
Cram, D.
Cramer, J.
Crandall, W.
Crane, E.
Crawford, A.
Creighton, H.
Crell, L.
Cripps, R.
Cristol, S.
Cross, C.
Cross, L.
Cross, W.M.
Crossley, M.
Crum, W.
Cullen, W.
Cunningham, B.
Curie, M.
Curie, P.
Curme, G.
Curtis, F.
Curtius, T.
Curtman, L.
Cushing, J.
Cushman, A.
Cusick, J.
Cutbush, F.
Cutbush, J.
Cutts, H.

Czapek, E.
Dabney, C.
Dainton, F.
Dalton, J.
Dana, J.
Dana, S.
Danforth, S.
Daniell, J.
Daniels, F.
Danilov, S.
D'Arcet, J.
Daubney, C.
Davidson, N.
Davis, C.
Davis, T.
Davison, J.
Davison, W.
Davy, E.
Davy, H.
Davy, J.
Dawley, R.
Day, D.
Day, W.
Deacon, H.
Debierne, A.
Debray, H.
Debye, P.
Degering, E.
De la Rue, W.
Delaval, E.
Delepine, S.
Demarcay, E.
DeMilt, C.
Dennis, L.
Dent, C.
Derby, I.
Derosne, C.
Deryagin, B.
Desormes, C.
Dessaignes, V.
Deville, H.
Dewar, J.
Dewar, M.
Dewey, C.
Dexter, A.
Dickinson, R.
Diels, O.
Dinsmore, S.
Dittmar, W.
Dixon, H.
Djerassi, C.
Dobereiner, J.
Didge, F.
Dohme, A.
Dolgoplosk, B.
Donnan, F.
Doran, J.
Doremus, R.
Douglas, J.
Douglas, S.
Dow, W.
Downs, J.
Draper, H.
Draper, J.C.
Draper, J.W.
Drickamer, H.
Drown, T.

Dubbs, J.
Dubinin, M.
Ducatel, J.
Duchesne, J.
Dudley, C.
Duffield, S.
Duhamel, H.
Duhem, P.
Duisberg, C.
Dulong, P.
Demanski, A.
Dumas, J.
Dunbar, P.
Duncan, A.
Duncan, R.
Dundonald, A.
Dunnington, F.
Dunstan, W.
DuPont, E.
DuPont, F.G.
DuPont, F.I.
Dupre, A.
Durkee, F.
Dushman, S.
Dussauce, H.
Eaborn, C.
Easley, C.
Eastman, A.
Eaton, A.
Eaton, M.
Eavenson, A.
Eder, J.
Edman, P.
Egerton, A.
Egloff, G.
Eigen, M.
Eisenchiml, O.
Ekeberg, A.
Elder, A.
Elderhorst, W.
Eldridge, C.
Elhuyar, F.
Elhuyar, J.
Elion, E.
Eliot, C.
Ellet, W.
Ellis, C.
Ellms, J.
Emanuel, N.
Emeleus, H.
Emich, F.
Emmet, P.
Emmett, P.
Engelhardt, F.
Eppler, M.
Ercker, L.
Erdmann, O.
Erlenmeyer, P.
Erni, H.
Ernst, C.
Eschenmoser, A.
Esson, W.
Etard, A.
Eucken, A.
Evans, M.
Evans, W.
Evans, W.L.

Everett, D.
Ewell, E.
Ewing, D.
Ewins, A.
Eyring, H.
Fahlberg, C.
Fajans, K.
Falk, K.
Faraday, M.
Farber, E.
Farinacci, N.
Farkas, L.
Favorsky, A.
Favre, P.
Fehling, H.
Feige, F.
Ferguson, A.
Ferguson, W.
Ferry, J.
Field, F.
Field, G.
Fields, P.
Fieser, L.
Fife, H.
Finch, G.
Fischer, E.
Fischer, H.
Fischer, N.
Fischer, O.
Fisher, C.
Fisher, H.
Fiske, A.
Fittig, R.
Fitzgerald, W.
Fixman, M.
Fleck, A.
Flory, P.
Folkers, K.
Fordos, M.
Foreman, J.
Forster, M.
Fosdick, L.
Foster, L.
Foster, W.
Fourcroy, A.
Fourneau, E.
Fownes, G.
Fox, E.
Fox, T.
Francis, J.
Frankland, P.
Franklin, R.
Frary, F.
Frasch, H.
Frazer, J.C.
Frazer, J.F.
Frazer, P.
Frear, W.
Freas, T.
Frederick, W.
Freed, K.
Freer, P.
Freeth, F.
Freidlina, R.
Freind, J.
Freiser, H.
Fremy, E.

French, D.
Fresenius, C.
Freudenberg, K.
Freundlich, H.
Frey, H.
Friedel, C.
Friedlander, G.
Friedlander, P.
Friend, J.
Fritzsche, C.
Frumkin, A.
Fry, J.
Fuchs, J.
Fuchs, N.
Fullam, F.
Fuller, H.C.
Fuller, H.W.
Fuoss, R.
Furman, N.
Furukawa, J.
Fuson, R.
Gabriel, S.
Gadolin, J.
Gahn, J.
Ganble, J.
Garner, W.
Gatterman, L.
Gaudin, M.
Gaultier de Claubry, H.
Gautier, A.
Gay-Lussac, J.
Gee, G.
Geer, W.
Gehlen, A.
Gelmo, P.
Genth, F.
Geoffroy, C.
Geoffroy, E.
Gerhardt, C.
Gatman, F.
Geuther, A.
Ghering, L.
Giaque, W.
Gibbes, L.
Gibbs, O.
Giesel, F.
Gilbert, H.
Gilbert, J.
Gilman, H.
Giordani, F.
Girtanner. C.
Gist, L.
Gladding, T.
Gladstone, J.
Glaser, C.
Glauber, J.
Glockler, G.
Glueckauf, E.
Gobley, N.
Godfrey, A.
Godlove, I.
Goessmann, C.
Goldschmidt, J.
Goldschmidt, V.
Gomberg, M.
Goodyear, C.

Gordon, N.
Gorgey, A.
Gorham, J.
Gossage, W.
Graebe, K.
Graham, F.
Graham, T.
Grahame, D.
Grasselli, E.
Gray, H.
Gray, T.
Grebe, J.
Green, T.
Greene, W.
Greenaway, F.
Greenwood, N.
Gregory, W.
Gren, F.
Gries, P.
Griffin, J.
Grignard, F.
Grinard, F.
Grinberg, A.
Gross, I.
Grote, I.
Grotthuss, T.
Gruenwald, E.
Guggenheim, E.
Guibert, N.
Guldberg, C.
Gulland, J.
Gutbier, F.
Guthrie, S.
Gutowsky, H.
Guye, P.
Guyton de Morveau, L.
Haber, F.
Haensel, V.
Hahn, D.
Hahn, O.
Hale, W.
Hales, S.
Hall, C.
Hall, J.
Hall, L.A.
Hall, L.B.
Hall, R.A.
Hammett, L.
Hammick, D.
Hammond, G.
Hamor, W.
Hanford, W.
Hankel, W.
Hanks, H.
Hanmer, H.
Hanson, H.
Hantzch, A.
Harcourt, A.
Harcourt, W.
Hare, R.
Harkins, W.
Harned, H.
Harper, H.
Harries, C.
Harris, I.
Harris, J.
Harrison, J.

Hart, E.
Hartley, H.
Hartman, F.
Hartmann, J.
Harvey, E.
Hasche, R.
Haskins, C.
Hass, H.
Hassel, O.
Hassenfratz, J.
Haszeldine, R.
Hatchett, C.
Hauser, C.
Hauser, E.
Hautefeuille, P.
Hawkins, W.
Haworth, R.
Haworth, W.
Hayes, A.
Haynes, E.
Hazelhurst, T.
Hearst, W.
Heath, F.
Heilbron, I.
Heise, G.
Hellot, J.
Hellriegel, H.
Hempel, W.
Henbest, H.
Henckel, J.
Henderson, E.
Henderson, G.
Henderson, L.
Henderson, W.F.
Hendrey, W.
Hendrick, E.
Hendricks, S.
Hendrixson, W.
Henry, T.
Henry, W.
Herapath, W.
Hermbstaedt, S.
Herty, C.
Herty, C. Jr.
Hess, G.
Hevesy, G.
Hewitt, J.
Hiarne, U.
Hibbert, H.
Higgins, B.
Hildebrand, J.
Hildebrandt, G.
Hilditch, T.
Hill, A.
Hill, H.A.
Hill, H.B.
Hill, H.M.
Hill, W.L.
Hill, W.N.
Hillebrand, W.
Hills, F.
Hilton, R.
Hinds, J.
Hinshelwood, C.
Hirschfelder, J.
Hirst, E.
Hisinger, W.

Hitch, E.
Hitchcock, R.
Hittorf, J.
Hobbs, P.
Hodgkin, D.
Hoffmann, F.
Hoffmann, R.
Hofmann, A.
Hoke, C.
Holmes, H.
Holroyd, R.
Holton, E.
Homberg, W.
Honingschmid, O.
Hooker, E.
Hooker, S.
Hoover, S.
Hope, T.
Hopke, T.
Hopkins, B.S.
Hopkins, C.
Horn, D.
Hornig, D.
Horsford, E.
Horstmann, A.
Hoskins, W.
House, H.
Howard, C.
Howe, J.
Hudson, C.
Hughes, E.
Huisgen, R.
Huizenga, J.
Hulett, G.
Hume-Rothberg, W.
Hunt, M.
Hunter, A.S.
Hunter, H.
Huntress, E.
Hurter, F.
Iddles, H.
Iliff, N.
Ing, H.
Ingold, C.
Ipatieff, V.
Irinyi, J.
Irvine, J.
Irvine, W.
Irving, H.
Isermann, S.
Ittner, M.
Jack, K.
Jackson, C.L.
Jackson, C.T.
Jackson, F.
Jackson, H.
Jackson, J.
Jackson, R.
Jacobs, M.
Jacobs, W.S.
Jacquin, N.
Jaeger, A.
Jaeger, F.
Jahn, H.
James, C.
James, J.
Jarves, D.

Jayne, H.
Jenkins, E.
Jenkons, G.
Jewett, F.
Johnson, O.
Johnson, S.
Johnson, W
Johnston, J.
Johnston, J.F.
Jones, B.
Jones, E.
Jones, G.
Jones, H.
Jones, J.
Jones, J.K.
Jones, R.
Jones, T.
Jones, W.L.
Jordan, S.
Jorgensen, S.
Joy, C.
Julian, P.
Juncker, J.
Juve, W.
Kablukov, I.
Kahlenberg, L.
Kalbfleisch, M.
Kane, R.
Kapp, R.
Karas, S.
Karaveav, N.
Kargin, V.
Karle, I.
Karrer, P.
Kassner, J.
Kastle, J.
Katz, J.
Katzman, M.
Kaufman, J.
Kaufman, M.
Kaufmann, H.
Kawin, C.
Kazanskii, B.
Kazarnovskii, I.
Kebler, L.
Kedzie, R.
Keir, J.
Keith, W.
Kekule von Stradonitz, F.
Keller, H.
Kelley, L.
Kellner, D.
Kemp, K.
Kendall, J.
Kennaway, E.
Kennedy, A.
Kenner, G.
Kenner, J.
Kenny, F.
Kenyon, F.
Key, A.
Kharasch, M.
Khorana, H.
Khunrath, C.
Kidd, F.
Kienle, R.
Kiliani, H.

Killeffer, D.
Kimball, G.
King, F.
King, H.
Kinnicutt, L.
Kipping, F.
Kirchof, K.
Kirk, R.
Kirkwood, J.
Kirner, W.
Kirwan, R.
Kistiakowsky, G.
Kitaibel, P.
Kjeldahl, J.
Klaproth, M.
Klason, J.
Klemm, W.
Klyne, W.
Knight, C.
Knight, H.
Knox, W.
Knunyants, I.
Kochetkov, N.
Koenig, G.
Kohler, E.
Kohlrausch, F.
Kokatnur, V.
Kolbe, A.
Kolthoff, I.
Kondakov, I.
Kondratiev, V.
Koninck, L.
Konovalov, D.
Kopp, H.
Korotkov, A.
Korshak, V.
Kossel, A.
Kostanecki, S.
Koton, M.
Kovalskii, A.
Kraemer, E.
Kraus, C.
Kropa, E.
Kuckro, W.
Kuhlmann, C.
Kuhn, R.
Kuhne, W.
Kunckel, J.
Kurnakov, D.
Ladd, E.
Ladenberg, A.
LaForge, F.
Lamb, A.
LaMer, V.
Landee, F.
Landis, W.
Landolt, H.
Lange, N.
Langenbeck, K.
Langley, J.
Langmuir, I.
Lapworth, A.
LaRive, C.
Latham, G.
Latimer, W.
Lattimore, S.
Laudy, L.

Lauger, P.
Laurent, A.
Lavoisier, A.
Law, T.
Lea, M.
Leach, A.
Leake, C.
Leaming, T.
Lebedev, S.
Lebedinsky, V.
LeBel, J.
LeBlanc, M.
Leblanc, N.
LeChatelier, H.
Lee, R.
Leech, P.
Leeds, A.
Lefebure, N.
Leffmann, H.
Lemery, M.
Lennard-Jones, J.
Leonard, N.
Leonhardi, J.
Letheby, H.
Levich, V.
Levinstein, I.
Lewis, G.
Lewis, W.
Lewis, W.C.
Lewis, W.L.
Libby, W.
Liddie, L.
Liebig, J.
Lind, S.
Linderstrom-Lang, K.
Lingane, J.
Link, H.
Linnett, J.
Linstead, R.
Lipscomb, G.
Lipscomb, W.
Little, A.
Liveing, G.
Llewellyn, R.
Lloyd, J.
Loeb, M.
Lomonsov, M.
London, F.
Long, F.
Longuet-Higgins, H.
Looker, C.
Lorenz, C.
Loschmidt, J.
Lovelace, B.
Lovits, J.
Lowry, T.
Lubbock, R.
Lucas, H.
Luginin, V.
Lulek, R.
Lundell, G.
Lunge, G.
Luvalle, J.
Lynn, E.
Maass, O.
Mabery, C.
Macadam, J.

MacCulloch, J.
MacInnes, D.
Macintosh, C.
Mack, E.
Mack, P.
Maclean, J.
Macquer, P.
Macy, I.
Magellan, J.
Magnus, H.
Mallet, J.
Mallinckrodt, E.
Malouin, P.
Mandelkern, L.
Mann, F.
Mansfield, C.
Mapes, C.
Mapes, J.
Marchand, R.
Marcus, R.
Marggraf, A.
Marignac, J.
Marion, L.
Mark, H.
Markovnokov, V.
Marks, A.
Marsh, A.
Marshall, A.
Marshall, M.
Marti Franques, A.
Martin, A.
Martin, D.
Martinovics, I.
Marvel, C.
Mason, C.
Mason, R.
Massie, S.
Masson, D.
Masson, I.
Matheson, W.
Mathews, J.
Matthews, J.
Matthiessen, A.
Maxson, R.
Mayer, J.
Maynard, G.
Mayo, F.
Maywald, F.
McBain, J.
McBurney, J.
McClure, F.
McConnell, H.
McCoy, H.
McCreath, L.
McCulloch, R.
McCullough, C.
McElvain, S.
McGlashan, M.
McGrail, J.
McKenna, F.
McKenzie, A.
McMahon, H.
McMaster, L.
McMurtrie, W.
McNair, J.
McPherson, W.
McWeeny, R.

Medes, G.
Mees, G.
Mehl, R.
Melville, H.
Mendel, L.
Mendeleef, D.
Menghini, V.
Menshutkin, N.
Mercer, J.
Merck, G.
Merck, G.W.
Merrill, J.
Messel, R.
Metcalfe, S.
Metzger, H.
Meyer, J.F.
Meyer, J.L.
Meyer, K.
Meyer, V.
Michael, A.
Michaelis, L.
Middleton, P.
Midgley, T.
Mieli, A.
Miescher, J.
Miles, G.
Miller, E.
Miller, E.H.
Miller, S.
Miller, W.A.
Miller, W.L.
Milligan, C.
Millington, J.
Millon, A.
Mills, J.
Mills, W.
Miner, C.
Miner, H.
Minkowski, O.
Mislow, K.
Mitchell, J.K.
Mitchell, T.
Mitchill, S.
Mitscherlich, E.
Mittasch, A.
Moelwyn-Hughes, E.
Mohr, C.
Moisson, F.
Mond, L.
Mond, R.
Monnet, A.
Montenier, J.
Moody, H.
Moore, F.
Moore, G.E.
Moore, R.B.
Moore, R.J.
Moray, R.
Moreau, C.
Morehead, J.
Morey, G.
Morfit, C.
Morgan, A.
Morgan, C.E.
Morgan, G.
Morgan, J.
Morgan, P.

Morley, E.
Morris, K.
Morrison, H.
Morse, H.N.
Morse, H.W.
Morton, H.
Morton, H.A.
Mosander, C.
Moseley, H.
Moss, E.
Mott, H.
Moyes, H.
Muir, M.
Mulder, G.
Muller, P.
Mulliken, R.
Mulliken, S.
Mullin, C.
Munroe, C.
Murke, F.
Murphy, G.
Murphy, W.J.
Murray, A.
Murray, J.
Musgrave, W.
Muspratt, J.
Mysels, K.
Nair, J.
Nametkin, S.
Nason, H.
Natta, G.
Naumann, A.
Nef, J.
Nekrasov, B.
Nelson, E.
Nelson, J.
Nernst, W.
Nesbit, J.
Nesmeyanov, A.
Neumann, C.
Newberry, S.
Newitt, D.
Newlands, J.
Nichols, J.
Nichols, W.
Nicholson, H.
Nicholson, W.
Niemann, C.
Nieuwland, J.
Nikitin, N.
Nikolayev, A.
Nilson, L.
Nobel, A.
Noddack, I.
Normandy, A.
Norrish, R.
North, H.
Norton, J.
Norton, L.
Norton, S.
Noyes, A.
Noyes, W.A.
Nyholm, R.
Oberfell, G.
Oblad, A.
Odling, W.
Oenslager, G.

Olney, L.
Olszewski, K.
O'Neil, A.
Onsager, L.
Oparin, A.
Ordway, J.
Osborne, T.
Ostromislensky, I.
Ostwald, C.
Ott, E.
Overend, W.
Overstreet, R.
Pacsy, E.
Palmer, A.
Palmer, C.S.
Paneth, F.
Papadakis, P.
Parker, R.
Parkes, A.
Parkes, S.
Parmelee, H.
Parmentier, A.
Parr, S.
Parson, A.
Parsons, C.L.
Partington, J.
Pasteur, L.
Patterson, A.
Patterson, C.A.
Patterson, R.M.
Pauling, L.
Pauson, P.
Payen, A.
Pean de St. Gilles, L.
Pearson, G.
Pearson, H.
Pearson, R.
Pease, R.
Peat, S.
Peckham, S.
Pekelharing, C.
Peligot, E.
Pelletier, B.
Pelletier, P.
Pelouse, T.
Pemberton, H.
Pendelton, H.
Pennington, M.
Pennock, J.
Penny, F.
Perey, M.
Perkin, A.
Perkin, W.
Perkin, W.H.
Personne, J.
Persoz, J.
Peter, R.
Petrov, A.
Petrov, V.
Petryanov-Sokolov, I.
Pettenkofer, M.
Peyve, Y.
Pfannmuller, J.
Pfeiffer, P.
Pfizer, C.
Philips, P.
Phillips, F.

Phillips, R.
Pickard, R.
Pictet, A.
Piggot, A.
Pitzer, K.
Playfair, L.
Plummer, J.
Poggiale, A.
Polanyi, J.
Polanyi, M.
Pond, G.
Pope, W.
Popov, A.
Porrett, R.
Porter, G.
Porter, J.A.
Porter, J.J.
Pott, J.
Powell, F.
Power, F.
Powers, D.
Prausnitz, J.
Pregl, F.
Prelog, F.
Prescott, A.
Preston, W.
Price, C.
Priestley, J.
Progogine, I.
Prochazka, G.
Proust, J.
Prout, W.
Pryanishnikov, D.
Ptitsyn, B.
Pugh, E.
Puryear, B.
Pyke, M.
Queeny, E.
Queeny, J.
Raikes, H.
Rains, G.
Rammelsberg, K.
Ramsay, W.
Randall, M.
Randall, W.
Raney, M.
Raoult, F.
Raphael, R.
Revenel, St. J.
Ray, P.
Razuvaev, G.
Read, J.
Reade, J.
Rebinder, P.
Rector, T.
Redman, L.
Reed, T.
Reese, C.
Regnault, H.
Reichenbach, K.
Reichstein, T.
Reid, D.
Remsen, I.
Reutov, O.
Rey, J.
Reyerson, L.
Reynolds, J.

Rice, C.
Richards, E.
Richards, T.
Richter, J.
Rideal, E.
Ringwood, A.
Rising, W.
Rivett, A.
Robb, J.
Roberts, C.
Roberts, J.
Robertson, A.
Robertson, B.
Robertson, J.
Robertson, R.
Robey, A.
Robinson, R.
Robiquet, P.
Rodebush, W.
Roeber, E.
Roebuck, J.
Rogers, A.
Rogers, J.
Rogers, P.
Rogers, R.
Rogers, T.
Roginskii, S.
Rolfinck, G.
Ronalds, E.
Roozeboom, H.
Roscoe, H .
Rose, F.
Rose, H.
Rose, J.D.
Rosenheim, S.
Ross, B.
Rossini, F.
Roth, C.
Rouelle, H.
Rouelle, J.
Rowe, A.
Rowlinson, J.
Ruddiman, E.
Ruffin, E.
Runge, F.
Ruscelli, G.
Rush, B.
Russell, E.
Russell, W.
Rutherford, D.
Rutherford, E.
Rutzier, J.
Ruzicks, L.
Sabatier, P.
Sabin, A.
Sadtler, S.
Sage, B.
Ste-Claire Deville, H.
Sala, A.
Sanger, C.
Sanger, F.
Sarett, L.
Sargent, G.
Sarton, G.
Saugrain, A.
Saussure, N.
Scatchard, G.

Schaeffer, J.
Scheele, K.
Schieffelin, W.
Schiff, H.
Schlesinger, H.
Schmelkes, F.
Schmidt, G.
Schoenbein, C.
Schorlemmer, C.
Schott, O.
Schreiner, O.
Schrotter, A.
Schulze, F.
Schumb, W.
Schunck, H.
Schwartz, R.
Schwarzenbach, G.
Scott, D.
Scott, W.G.
Scott, W.W.
Scovell, J.
Scovell, M.
Seaborg, G.
Seabury, G.
Sechenov, I.
Sefstrom, N.
Seguin, A.
Seibert, H.
Seidell, A.
Seil, H.
Semenov, N.
Semon, W.
Senderens, J.
Serullas, G.
Seshadri, T.
Severgin, V.
Severinus, P.
Seybert, A.
Shank, J.
Shannon, H.
Sharp, D.
Shaw, L.
Shedlovsky, T.
Sheehan, J.
Shemyakin, M.
Sheppard, S.
Sherrill, M.
Sherts, J.
Shilov, N.
Shonle, H.
Shulkin, N.
Shuman, R.
Sidgwick, N.
Silliman, B.
Silliman, B. Jr.
Silverman, A.
Sim, G.
Simha, R.
Simmons, H.
Simon, W.
Simonsen, J.
Simpson, M.
Skraup, Z.
Slosson, E.
Small, L.
Smalley, P.
Smith, A.

Smith, A.W.
Smith, D.
Smith, E.
Smith, E.L.
Smith, J.
Smith, J.L.
Smith, L.H.
Smith, T.P.
Smith, W.A.
Smithels, A.
Smithson, J.
Smits, A.
Smyth, C.
Snell, F.
Snow, H.
Sobrero, A.
Soddy, F.
Solly, E.
Solvay, E.
Sorensen, S.
Sondheimer, F.
Sparks, W.
Sparre, F.
Spath, E.
Spedding, F.
Spence, P.
Spence, R.
Spencer, G.
Sperr, F.
Spielman, M.
Spitsyn, V.
Spoehr, H.
Spring, F.
Spring, W.
Springall, H.
Squibb, E.
Stacey, M.
Stahl, G.
Stanley, H.
Starkey, G.
Stas, J.
Staudinger, H.
Steacie, E.
Stead, J.
Stebbins, J.
Stein, R.
Steiner, L.
Stenhouse, J.
Stevens, T.
Stewart, A.
Stewart, D.
Stewart, T.D.
Stieglitz, J.
Stillman, J.
Stock, A.
Stoddard, J.T.
Stoll, A.
Stone, F.
Storer, F.
Stoughton, B.
Strassman, F.
Strohmeyer, F.
Strowd, W.
Stull, W.
Suchten, A.
Sugden, S.
Sullivan, E.

Sutherland, W.
Sutton, L.
Sveda, M.
Svedberg, T.
Swain, R.
Swan, R.
Swart, G.
Swarts, F.
Swenson, M.
Swift, E.
Sykes, K.
Synge, R.
Syrkin, Y.
Szebelledy, L.
Szily, P.
Szwarc, M.
Tachenius, O.
Taggart, W.
Takamine, J.
Talbot, H.
Talmud, D.
Tammann, G.
Tanenaev, I.
Tanberg, A.
Tarbell, D.
Tate, A.
Tatlow, J.
Tattersfield, F.
Taube, H.
Taylor, F.
Taylor, G.
Taylor, M.
Taylor, M.D.
Taylor, T.
Taylor, W.C.
Taylor, W.H.
Tedder, J.
Teeple, J.
Telkes, M.
Tennant, C.
Tennant, S.
Terenin, A.
Terentev, A.
Terry, E.
Textor, O.
Than, K.
Thenard, L.
Theophilus
Thiele, F.
Thiessen, G.
Thirsk, H.
Thode, H.
Thomas, C.A.
Thomas, J.
Thompson, H.
Thompson, K.
Thompson, S.
Thomsen, H.
Thomson, T.
Tiemann, J.
Tiffeneau, M.
Tilden, W.
Tilghman, R.
Tillet, M.
Tillotson, E.
Tishler, M.
Titus, R.

Tizard, H.
Todd, A.
Tolman, R.
Tompkins, F.
Topchiev, A.
Toropov, N.
Torrey, J.
Tower, O.
Traube, M.
Travers, M.
Trefouel, J.
Treneer, J.
Trevisan, B.
Trommsdorf, J.
Troost, L.
Troostwijk, A.
Trost, B.
Tucker, W.
Turner, E.
Turner, E.E.
Turner, R.
Turner, W.E.
Turquet de Mayerne, T.
Turrentine, J.
Turro, N.
Tyson, P.
Ubbelohde, A.
Underhill, F.
Unverdorben, O.
Urbain, G.
Ure, A.
Urey, H.
Ushakov, S.
Vagner, E.
Valko, E.
Van der Weyde, P.
Van Helmont, J.
Van Name, R.
Van Slyke, D.
Van Stone, N.
Van Straten, F.
Van Tamelen, E.
Van't Hoff, J.
Vaughan, E.
Vaughan, J.
Vaughan, V.
Vauquelin, L.
Vdovenko, V.
Veazey, W.
Venable, F.
Venel, G.
Vernon, A.
Vigani, J.
Vinograd, J.
Voevodskii, V.
Vogt, L.
Volfkovich, S.
Volhard, J.
Von Sochocky, S.
Vornees, E.
Vorozhtsov, N.
Waage, P.
Waddington, T.
Wagner, T.
Wain, R.
Wald, F.
Waldbauer, L.

Walden, P.
Walden, P.T.
Wall, L.
Wallach, R.
Walling, C.
Walls, H.
Walsh, A.
Walter, P.
Wanklyn, J.
Wansbrough-Jones, O.
Ward, J.
Warder, R.
Wardlaw, W.
Warington, R.
Warner, J.
Warner, L.
Warner, W.
Warren, C.
Washburn, E.R.
Washburn, E.W.
Washken, E.
Waters, W.
Waterston, J.
Watson, R.
Watt, G.
Watts, H.
Waugh, J.
Weber, H.A.
Webre, A.
Webster, J.
Wedel, G.
Wedgewood, J.
Weedon, B.
Weicker, T.
Weidlein, E.
Weigel, C.
Weightman, W.
Weisberg, M.
Weiss, J.
Weldon, W.
Wellman, V.
Wells, D.
Wendt, G.
Wenzel, C.
Werner, A.
West, C.
West, T.F.
West, T.S.
West, W.
Westheimer, F.
Wetherill, C.
Whiffen, D.
Whitby, G.
Whitcomb, W.
White, H.C.
White, H.J.
Whitesides, G.
Whiting, M.
Whitmore, F.
Whitney, J.
Whitney, W.
Whitney, W.R.
Whytlaw-Gray, R.
Wiberg, E.
Wiechmann, F.
Wiedemann, G.
Wiedemann, H.

Wiegleb, J.
Wieland, H.
Wigner, G.
Wiley, S.
Wilhelmy, L.
Wilkinson, G.
Willard, J.E.
Willard, J.L.
Williams, C.
Williams, J.W.
Williams, L.
Williams, R.L.
Williams, R.R.
Williams, T.
Williamson, A.
Willson, T.
Willstatter, R.
Wilson, C.
Wilson, E.
Wilson, G.
Wilson, J.A.
Windaus, A.
Winkler, L.
Winstein, S.
Wintersteimer, O.
Winthrop, J.
Winton, A.
Wislicenus, J.
Witt, O.
Witthaus, R.
Wittig, G.
Wohler, F.
Wolfgang, R.
Wolfrom, M.
Wollaston, W.
Wood, E.
Woodbridge, R.
Woodhouse, J.
Woodward, R.
Wormley, T.
Worrall, D.
Woulfe, P.
Wright, R.
Wright, S.
Wurtz, C.
Wurtz, H.
Wynkoop, F.
Wynkoop, G.
Wynne-Jones, W.
Yagoda, H.
Yanusov, S.
Young, A.
Yutzy, H.
Zambonini, F.
Zeisberg, F.
Zeise, W.
Zelinsky, N.
Zemplen, G.
Zerban, F.
Ziegler, K.
Zimmerli, W.
Zinin, N.
Zintl, E.
Zsiemondy, R.
Zwelfer, J.

CHRONOLOGY

Scaliger, J.

CLIMATOLOGY

Blodget, L.
Blumenstock, D.
Easton, C.
Hann, J.
Koppen, W.
Lamb, H.
Schouw, J.
Vouykov, A.
Williamson, H.

COMPUTERS

Amdahl, G.
Auerbach, I.
Babbage, C.
Backus, J.
Baker, C.
Comrie, L.
Dahl, O.
Davis, M.
Diebold, J.
Easley, A.
Gordon, G.
Griswold, R.
Hopper, G.
Iverson, K.
Jobs, S.
Kurtz, T.
Mauchly, J.
McCarthy, J.
Merwin, R.
Naur, P.
Nygaard, K.
Perlis, A.
Ross, D.
Sammet, J.
Schwartz, J.
Von Neumann, J.

CONCHOLOGY

Adams, A.
Anthony, J.
Binney, W.
Born, I.
Carpenter, P.
Gould, A.
Griffith, R.
Oldroyd, T.
Prime, T.
Ravenel, R.
Reeve, L.
Say, T.
Sowerby, G.
Tryon, G.
Turton, W.

CONSERVATION

Adams, A.
Albright, H.
Allen, D.
Austin, M.H.
Avery, C.
Aylward, D.
Baker, J.
Barnes, W.
Bartley, A.
Bear, F.
Bennett, H.
Bennett, L.
Benson, A.
Bingham, E.
Bradley, H.
Bradley, P.
Brandborg, S.
Brewer, G.
Bromfield, L.
Broome, H.
Brower, D.
Brown, C.
Browning, B.
Burnham, J.
Buyukmihci, H.
Cain, S.
Callison, C.
Caras, R.
Carhart, A.
Carr, W.
Chapline, W.
Chapman, J.
Clappel, L.
Clark, W.
Colby, W.
Commoner, B.
Condra, G.
Cottam, C.
Craig, J.
Darling, F.
Darling, J.
Dasmann, R.
Davis, D.
DeVoto, B.
Dilg, W.
Dodge, M.
Doremus, T.
Douglas, P.
Drury, N.
Duke, P.
Dutcher, W.
Edge, M.
Edminster, F.
Evans, C.
Evenden, F.
Fabian, H.
Farquhar, F.
Fell, G.
Fisher, J.
Fox, A.
Frank, B.
Fredine, C.
Frome, M.
Gabrielson, I.
Glick, P.
Goddard, M.

Gordon, S.
Gottschalk, J.
Graham, E.
Grant, K.
Griffith, G.
Gutermuth, C.
Hafenrichter, A.
Hallock, C.
Hartzog, G.
Heald, W.
Herbst, R.
Holbrook, S.
Holland, R.
Howe, S.
Hoyt, M.
Hubachek, F.
Huboda, M.
James, H.
Judd, B.
Kelley, C.
Kelly, J.
Kimball, T.
Kinney, A.
Lacey, J.
Langford, N.
Latham, R.
Leffler, R.
Leonard, R.
Leopold, A.
Linduska, J.
Lovejoy, P.
Lowdermil, W.
Marshall, G.
Marshall, R.
Mather, S.
Maxwell, G.
McCloskey, J.
McCrackin, J.
McGee, W.
McGregor, L.
Murie, O.
Nadel, M.
Oberholtzer, E.
Olmsted, F.
Olson, S.
Onthank, K.
Ordway, S.
Osborn, F.
Owings, M.
Palmer, E.
Partain, L.
Penfold, J.
Pettit, T.
Pinchot, G.
Poole, D.
Pough, R.
Powell, J.W.
Pratt, G.
Pritchard, H.
Regenstein, L.
Reid, K.
Richards, T.
Rockefeller, J.
Rockefeller, L.
Salyer, J.
Sawyer, R.
Schurz, C.
Sheldon, C.
Shields, G.

Shoemaker, C.
Simms, D.
Siri, W.
Smith, A.
Smith, G.A.
Stahr, E.
Stephens, E.
Storer, J.
Stroud, R.
Swift, L.
Tascher, W.
Taylor, W.P.
Train, R.
Trefethen, J.
Tunison, A.
Udall, S.
Vogt, W.
Walcott, F.
Waller, W.
Waring, P.
Watson, C.
Wayburn, E.
Weaver, R.
Westwood, R.
White, G.
Williams, D.
Wirth, C.
Zahniser, H.
Zimmerman, G.

COSMOLOGY

Bickerton, A.
Chamberlin, T.
Cortes de Albacar, M.
Danti, E.
Grisgono, F.
Hildegard of Bingen
Hubble, E.
Qazwini, Z.
Whiston, W.
Yativrsabha

CRYSTALLOGRAPHY

Astbury, W.
Barlow, W.
Belov, N.
Bokii, G.
Bradley, A.
Bravais, A.
Buerger, M.
Carangeot, A.
Dana, E.
Delafosse, G.
DesCloizeaux, A.
Dickinson, R.
Donnay, J.
Frankuchen, I.
Friedel, G.
Fyodorov, E.
Goldshmidt, V.
Groth, P.
Hauy, R.
Hermann, C.

Hessel, J.
Jaeger, F.
Karle, I.
Lonsdale, K.
Mauguin, C.
Miller, W.H.
Niggli, P.
Perutz, M.
Rome del'Isle, J.
Rose, G.
Schoenflies, A.
Senarmont, H.
Shubnikov, A.
Sohncke, L.
Tutton, A.
Weiss, C.
Wulff, G.
Wyckoff, R.

DAIRY SCIENCE

Gaines, W.
Kay, H.
Sommer, H.

DENTISTRY

Hayden, H.
Henry, J.L.
Sinkford, J.
Taylor, L.

ECOLOGY

Adams, C.A.
Albertson, F.W.
Buechner, H.
Chapman, R.
Clements, F.
Cowles, H.
Dorst, J.
Elton, C.
Gates, D.
Hardin, G.
Kuenen, D.
Macarthur, R.
May, R.
Milton, J.
Morozov, G.
Patrick, R.
Porter, E.
Sampson, A.
Sears, P.
Shelford, V.
Shimek, B.
Swank, W.
Watt, K.
Woodwell, G.
Zinn, D.

ELECTRICAL ENGINEERING

Adams, C.A.
Alekseev, A.
Amdahl, G.
Anderson, S.
Armstrong, E.H.
Ayrton, W.
Barkhausen, H.
Behrend, B.A.
Black, H.W.
Blackwell, O.B.
Brainerd, J.
Brown, G.
Bush, V.
Buss, R.
Carty, J.
Chesney, C.C.
Colpitts, E.H.
Cooke, W.
Crompton, R.
David, E.
Dawes, C.
DeForest, L.
Devyatkov, N.
Dyke, E.
Edgerton, H.
Edwards, M.A.
Espenschied, L.
Fano, R.
Ferranti, S.
Ferraris, G.
Forrester, J.
Gabor, D.
Gager, F.
Giorgi, G.
Gordon, J.
Haslett, C.
Henley, W.
Hounsfield, G.
Hubbard, P.G.
Hunter, P.
Jansky, K.
Jewett, F.
Jobs, S.
Jordan, E.
Karandeev, K.
Kennelly, A.
King, R.
Klopsteg, P.
Kobzarev, Y.
Kompfner, R.
Kostenko, M.
Kotelnikov, V.
Kouwenhoven, W.
Kovalenkov, V.
Kovalev, N.
Kulebakin, V.
Larionov, A.
Lear, W.
Lebedev, S.A.
Leclanche, G.
Lewis, W.
Little, W.
Marconi, G.
Mason, M.
McAdam, J.
McCoy, C.

McCune, F.
McMeen, S.G.
Merz, C.
Nyquist, H.
Oatley, C.
Oliver, B.
O'Neil, E.
Pearce, L.
Pistolkors, A.
Popkov, V.
Preece, W.
Rawcliffe, G.
Reber, G.
Rechtin, E.
Rice, E.
Rudenberg, R.
Ruska, E.
Ryan, H.
Schott, L.
Scott, C.
Seeley, W.
Silver, A.
Snell, J.
Sperti, G.
Squier, G.
Steinmetz, C.
Stillwell, L.
Stratton, J.
Swain, F.
Swinburn, J.
Swinton, A.
Tesla, N.
Timofeev, P.
Trapeznikov, V.
Twyman, F.
Van Depoele, C.
Varley, C.
Walker, C.
Wheeler, H.
Whittemore, L.
Wiesner, J.
Williams, F.
Zavalishni, D.

ELECTRICAL SCIENCE

Bennet, A.
Callan, N.
Children, G.
Crosse, A.
Davis, P.
DuMoncel, T.
Gassiot, J.
Gray, S.
Hausen, C.
Kinnersley, E.
Pacinotti, A.
Pixii, H.
Pohl, G.
Siemens, E.
Symmer, R.
Wilson, B.

ELECTROCHEMISTRY

Aall, C.
Becket, F.
Becquerel, A.C.
Carveth, H.
Case, W.
DeChalmot, G.
Eyde, S.
Fink, C.
Fitzgerald, F.
Gore, G.
Grove, W.
Heyrovsky, J.
Hunter, M.
Lowy, A.
Lukens, H.
Noad, H.
Petrie, W.
Watts, O.

EMBRYOLOGY

Aromatari, G.
Balfour, F.
Barry, M.
Brachet, A.
Chabry, L.
Coghill, G.
Dollinger, I.
Gage, S.
Hamburger, V.
Harrison, R.
Hoadley, L.
Hooker, D.
Hubrecht, A.
Huschke, E.
Ivanov, P.
Jankinson, J.
Kovalevski, A.
Lereboullet, D.
Levi, G.
Lillie, F.
MacBride, E.
Mall, F.
Mechnikov, I.
Meckel, J.
Pander, C.
Pensa, A.
Prevost, J.
Prochaska, G.
Rabl, C.
Rathke, M.
Reichert, K.
Roux, W.
Ruffini, A.
Serres, A.
Streeter, G.
Thomson, A.
Valentin, G.
Wiedersheim, R.
Zavarzin, A.

ENGINEERING

Abbot, H.
Aconcio, J.
Agricola, G.
Agrippa, M.
Aiken, H.
Alban, E.
Aleksandrov, B.
Alexander, A.A.
Alexander, J.H.
Alexanderson, E.
Amiraslanov, A.
Amman, O.
Apollodorus
Argyris, J.
Armstrong, W.
Artachaies
Artobolevskii, I.
Bailey, R.
Bairstow, L.
Baker, J.
Baldwin, L.
Barnard, D.
Barnard, J.
Barry, E.
Barthel, O.
Bauer, A.
Bazalgette, J.
Beath, J.
Becker, V.
Beckwith, E.
Bell, L.
Benedict, M.
Benz, K.
Berg, A.
Berkner, L.
Bertin, L.
Besson, J.
Betancourt y Moline, A.
Birkigt, M.
Bisat, W.
Bjornson, B.
Blondel, N.
Blumberg, R.
Bode, H.
Bodner, J.
Boyden, U.
Bradley, H.
Bramah, J.
Breckman, J.
Brindley, J.
Brisson, B.
Brown, S.
Brown, W.
Brunel, I.
Brunel, M.
Brunelleschi, F.
Brunton, W.
Buckingham, E.
Burr, T.
Bury, E.
Busignies, H.
Callendar, H.
Campbell, G.
Carre, E.
Casey, T.
Casey, W.

Castigliano, A.
Caus, S.
Cave, H.
Chadwick, W.
Chang Jung
Chang Ssu-Hsun
Chang Yongsil
Chen Teng
Chen Yao-Tso
Cheng Kuo
Cheng Tang Shih
Chersiphron
Chestnut, H.
Chia Jang
Chia Ku Shan Shou
Chuang Hsiung-Pi
Chubb, L.
Chukanov, Z.
Clapeyron, B.
Clark, J.
Clark, W.
Clark, W.T.
Clarke, E.
Clarkson, R.
Clement, J.
Clymer, G.
Cochrane, E.
Cockerell, C.
Cockerill, J.
Cohn, N.
Colding, L.
Collins, S.
Comstock, C.
Constant, H.
Cornelius, Y.
Cornell, E.
Cotton, W.
Craponne, A.
Crelle, A.
Crossfield, A.
Crosthwait, D.
Cugnot, N.
Culmann, K.
Curtis, C.
Dalen, N.
Dandelin, G.
Darby, A.
Darcy, H.
Davies, J.
Davis, H.
DeBrahm, W.
Debus, K.
DeLesseps, F.
Dent, F.
Deprez, M.
Dillon, J.
Dod, D.
Donnell, L.
Dorey, S.
Drake, E.
Drucker, D.
Dryden, H.
Dufour, G.
Duncan, W.
Dunn, G.
Durand, W.
Eads, J.
Eckert, J.
Edwards, G.

Edwards, W.
Ehricke, K.
Eiffel, A.
Ellet, C.
Ellsworth, L.
Emmet, W.
Emmons, H.
Emory, W.
Eupalinus
Eustis, H.
Ewbank, T.
Eyetelwein, J.
Fage, A.
Faget, M.
Fairbairn, P.
Fairbairn, W.
Fanning, J.
Farcot, M.
Farnsworth, P.
Farren, W.
Field, J.
Finley, J.
Fleming, J.A.
Flugge-Lotz, I.
Fontana, D.
Fopple, A.
Forfait, P.
Fourneyron, B.
Fowler, J.
Fox, C.
Francis, J.
Freeman, T.
Friedrich, H.
Froehlich, J.
Frontinus, S.
Froude, W.
Fubini, E.
Fuller, D.
Fuller, R.
Galin, L.
Galy-Cazalat, A.
Gardiner, J.
Gasche, F.
Gauthey, E.
Gautier, H.
Gherardi, B.
Giambelli, F.
Gibb, C.
Gibbs, G.
Gibbs, W.
Ginzton, E.
Girard, P.
Goethals, G.
Goldsmith, A.N.
Goldsmith, L.
Gough, H.
Graham, J.
Gregorius, J.
Griffith, A.
Guillemin, E.
Guy, H.
Han Kung-Lien
Han Tsen
Hancock, W.
Handyside, W.
Harbers, H.
Hathaway, J.
Hawthorne, W.
Heaviside, O.

Hedley, W.
Hefner-Alteneck, F.
Henderson, C.
Hero of Alexandria
Heron, S.
Hesketh, E.
Hess, F.
Hinton, C.
Hodgkinson, E.
Holaday, W.
Holmes, D.
Hooker, E.
Hoover, H.
Hornblower, J.
Houston, E.J.
Hovgaard, W.
Hsun Mao
Huber, M.
Hudson, W.
Humphreys, A.
Hund, A.
I Hsing
Imhotep
Inglis, C.
Jackson, W.
Jansky, C.
Jardine, J.
Jenkin, H.
Jessop, W.
Johnson, C.
Jones, B.
Jonsson, J.
Jouffroy D'Abbans, C.
Kalman, R.
Kao Hsuan
Katz, D.
Kavanagh, T.
Kellner, K.
Kennedy, A.
Kettering, C.
Khan, F.
Killian, J.R.
Kirkaldy, D.
Kleon
Knight, J.
Koenig, F.
Korolev, S.
Kraft, C.
Krylov, A.
Kuchemann, D.
Kungshu, P.
Kuo Shou-Ching
Kyeser, K.
Lamme, B.G.
Lanchester, F.
Langren, M.
Latrobe, B.
Lawrence, C.
Lecornu, L.
Lee, W.S.
Leeghwater, J.
Leupold, J.
Levy, M.
Leybenzon, L.
Li Chao-Te
Li Chieh
Li Chun
Li Fang-Hsien
Li Po

Li Shih-Chung
Liang Jui
Liang Ling-Tsan
Linde, K.
Lloyd, J.
Logan, H.
Loqsi
Lorenz, H.
Low, A.
Lu Tao-Lung
Ma Chun
Mahan, D.
Mandrokles
Martini, F.
Mason, W.
Mauchly, J.
Maudslay, H.
Maybach, W.
McAdam, J.
McCoy, E.
McNeely, E.
McNeil, J.
Medhurst, G.
Meigs, M.
Meikle, A.
Melentev, L.
Menabrea, L.
Metagenes
Metcalf, J.
Metius, A.
Michell, A.
Michie, P.
Mills, W.
Mints, A.
Modjeski, R.
Mohr, C.O.
Molard, F.
Moll, F.
Moody, P.
Moutard, T.
Muir, W.
Muller-Breslau, H.
Murphree, E.
Murray, M.
Myddleton, H.
Mylne, R.
Mylne, W.
Napier, R.
Nasmyth, J.
Navier, C.
Neilson, J.
Nelson, R.
Newall, R.
Newark, N.
Newcomen, T.
Newmark, N.
Newton, J.
Nicolle, E.
Oldham, J.
Olson, H.
Otto, N.
Paine, T.
Palladio, A.
Pambour, F.
Pan Chi-Hsun
Parsons, C.A.
Patel, C.
Paul, L.
Peabody, R.

Peck, R.
Perkins, A.
Perkins, J.
Perkins, L.
Perronet, J.
Petavel, J.
Peter of Colechurch
Petrov, N.P.
Pierce, J.R.
Pippard, A.
Pitot, H.
Popov, Y.
Porter, C.T.
Prager, W.
Pregel, B.
Prony, G.
Pye, D.
Rabinovich, I.
Ramelli, A.
Ramo, S.
Randolph, C.
Rankine, W.
Rateau, A.
Reech, F.
Reed, C.
Reichenbach, G.
Reissner, E.
Rennie, J.
Renwick, J.
Reuleaux, F.
Reynolds, O.
Ribacour, A.
Ribeiro Santos, C.
Ricordo, H.
Ricci, O.
Rickover, H.
Rillieux, N.
Riquet de Bonropos, P.
Roberts, G.
Roberts, N.
Robertson, A.
Robins, B.
Rogers, F.
Romans, B.
Rowledge, A.
Royce, F.
Runkle, J.
Sauvage, P.
Savage, J.
Savery, T.
Schairer, G.
Seguin, M.
Severud, F.
Sharp, C.
Shih Chi
Shih Lu
Shipley, T.
Shultz, J.
Simpson, J.
Sink, M.
Smeaton, J.
Soufflot, J.
Sporn, P.
Sprague, F.
Stanier, W.
Stanley, W.
Stanton, T.E.
Steinman, D.
Stephenson, G.

Stephenson, R.
Stevenson, T.
Stodola, A.
Streletskii, N.
Struminskii, V.
Styrikovich, M.
Suyya
Swain, G.
Swasey, A.
Symington, W.
Taccola, M.
Talcott, A.
Tao Hsun
Taylor, D.
Taylor, F.W.
Taylor, J.
Telford, T.
Tellier, C.
Terman, F.
Than Ston Rgyal Po
Thom, A.
Thompson, A.
Thomson, R.
Thurston, P.
Tilley, N.
Timoshenko, S.
Torres Quevedo, L.
Totten, J.
Town, I.
Trautwine, J.
Tredgold, T.
Tresaquet, P.
Trowbridge, W.
Twining, A.
Uni
Unwin, W.
Valturio, R.
Vannikov, B.
Vauban, S.
Venetz, I.
Verantius, F.
Vermuyden, C.
Vernier, P.
Vicat, L.
Vignoles, C.
Vyshnegradsky, I.
Walschaerts, E.
Wang Cheng
Wang Ching
Wankel, F.
Warren, G.
Watt, J.
Weatherbee, R.
Weber, E.
Wei Meng-Pien
Wertz, A.
Westinghouse, G.
Wheeler, G.
Whinnery, J.
Whipple, A.
Whipple, S.
White, C.
Whitehead, J.B.
Whitney, A.
Whittle, F.
Whitworth, J.
Willis, R.
Wilson, R.
Windhausen, F.

Wintringham, W.
Wolf, F.
Wolman, A.
Woolridge, D.
Woolf, A.
Wright, B.
Yarranton, A.
Yang Cheng Yen
Yevele, H.
Ying Shun-Chen
Young, C.
Zavenyagin, A.
Zeuner, G.
Zilker, C.
Zonca, V.
Zvonkov, V.

ENTOMOLOGY

Abbott, J.
Adams, C.F.
Ainslie, C.
Aldrich, J.
Annand, P.
Ashmead, W.
Back, E.A.
Baker, C.F.
Ball, E.
Banister, J.
Banks, N.
Barber, H.G.
Barber, H.S.
Barnes, W.
Beamer, R.H.
Bahr, H.
Bell, E.
Bellardi, L.
Benjamin, F.
Bethune, C.
Bilsing, S.
Bishopp, F.
Blackman, M.
Blaisdell, F.
Blatchley, W.
Bodenheimer, F.
Bolter, A.
Boving, A.
Britton, W.
Bromley, S.
Brues, C.
Bruner, C.
Buckler, W.
Buckton, G.
Burgess, A.
Burgess, E.
Burke, H.
Busck, A.
Buxton, P.
Calvert, P.
Carangot, A.
Casey, T.
Caudell, A.
Chittendon, F.
Clark, A.
Clerck, C.
Cleveland, L.

Cockerell, T.
Comstock, A.
Comstock, J.
Comstock, W.
Cook, A.
Cooley, R.
Coquillet, D.
Crampton, G.
Crawford, J.
Cresson, E.
Crosby, C.
Curtis, J.
Cushman, R.
Dampf, A.
Davidson, A.
Davis, J.
Davis, W.
Dean, G.
Denny, H.
Dietz, H.
Doten, S.
Doubleday, E.
Drake, C.
Drury, D.
Dury, C.
Dyar, H.
Edwards, H.
Edwards, W.
Elwes, H.
Emerton, J.
Engelhardt, G.
Essig, E.
Evans, W.H.
Ewing, H.
Fabre, J.
Fabricius, J.
Fall, H.
Felt, C.
Fernald, C.
Ferris, G.
Fitch, Λ.
Fletcher, J.
Flint, W.
Fluke, C.
Folsom, J.
Forbes, S.A.
Forbes, W.T.
Forel, A.
Franklin, H.
Friend, R.
Frison, T.
Fullaway, D.
Fuller, H.
Fulton, B.
Funkhouser, W.
Gahan, A.
Geer, C.
Gibbon, W.
Gillette, C.
Girault, A.
Glover, T.
Goedaert, J.
Grassi, G.
Grote, A.
Gyllenhaal, L.
Haddow, A.
Hagen, H.
Harris, T.

Hartig, T.
Hartzell, F.
Haseman, L.
Headlee, T.
Hebard, M.
Heidemann, O.
Heinrich, C.
Henshaw, S.
Hentz, N.
Herms, W.
Herrick, E.
Herrick, G.
Hessel, S.
Hewitt, C.
Hillman, F.
Hinds, W.
Hinton, H.
Hitchings, E.
Holland, W.
Holloway, J.
Hood, J.
Hope, F.
Hopkins, A.D.
Horn, G.
Howard, L.
Hubbard, H.
Hulst, G.
Hungerford, H.
Hunter, W.D.
Imms, A.
Jacques, H.
Johnson, C.W.
Jordan, K.
Kellogg, V.
Kennedy, C.
Kettlewell, H.
Kirby, W.
Klots, A.
Knab, F.
Knipling, E.
Koebele, A.
Komp, W.
LaRivers, I.
Latreille, P.
LeBaron, W.
Leconte, J.E.
LeConte, J.L.
Leng, C.
Light, S.
Lindsey, A.
Lintner, J.
Lovell, J.H.
Lubbock, J.
Lugger, O.
Lutz, F.
Lyonet, P.
MacGillvray, A.
MacLeay, A.
Malloch, J.
Mann, W.
Marlatt, C.
Marshall, G.
Marsham, T.
Marx, G.
Matheson, R.
McColloch, J.
McCook, H.
McDunnough, J.

McIndoo, N.
McLaine, L.
Melander, A.
Mellanby, K.
Melsheimer, F.
Messenger, P.
Metcalf, C.
Metcalf, Z.
Meyrick, E.
Mickel, C.
Moffett, T.
Morgan, H.A.
Morgan, J.H.
Morrill, A.
Morris, J.G.
Morris, M.
Morrison, H.
Morse, A.
Needham, J.
Newell, W.
Newport, G.
Ormerod, E.
Osborn, H.
Osten Sacker, C.
Packard, A.
Parker, J.
Parrott, P.
Parshley, H.
Pascoe, F.
Patch, E.
Pate, V.
Pauly, A.
Paykull, G.
Peairs, L.
Peckham, G.
Pergande, T.
Perkins, R.C.
Peterson, A.
Petrunkevitch, A.
Petiver, J.
Phillips, E.
Provancher, L.
Quaintence, A.
Quayle, H.
Rau, P.
Redi, F.
Rehn, J.
Riley, C.
Roark, R.
Rohwer, S.
Rye, E.
Sacken, C.
Sanders, J.
Sanderson, D.
Sanderson, E.
Sandhouse, G.
Sasscer, E.
Saunders, E.
Saunders, W.
Saunders, W.W.
Say, T.
Schaus, W.
Schronherr, C.
Schwardt, H.
Schwarz, E.
Schwarz, H.
Scott, H.
Scudder, S.

Shannon, R.
Skinner, H.
Slingerland, M.
Smith, H.D.
Smith, H.S.
Smith, J.B.
Snodgrass, R.
Snow, F.
Snyder, T.
Spender, G.J.
Stainton, H.
Stedman, J.
Stephens, J.
Streeker, F.
Stretch, R.
Strong, L.
Sullivan, W.N.
Swaine, J.
Swezey, O.
Tanquary, M.
Taylor, C.
Thomas, C.
Thomas, C.A.
Thompson, W.R.
Thwaites, G.
Torre-Bueno, J.
Townsend, C.
Tschopik, H.
Turner, C.
Uhler, P.
Ulke, H.
Uvarov, B.
Van Duzee, E.
Van Dyke, E.
Van Zwaluwenburg, R.
Viereck, H.
Volck, W.
Wade, J.
Wakeland, C.
Walsh, B.
Walton, W.
Webster, F.
Wehrle, L.
Wheeler, W.
White, F.
Wickham, H.
Wild, L.
Williams, C.B.
Williams, R.C.
Williamson, E.
Williston, S.
Wolcott, G.
Woodworth, C.

ETHOLOGY

Adamson, J.
Dawkins, R.
Fossey, D.
Galdikas, B.
Goodall, J.
Lorenz, K.
Malcolm, H.
McKeever, K.
Morris, D.

Pippard, L.
Pryor, K.

EVOLUTION

Darwin, C.R.
Goodrich, E.
Huxley, T.
Lamarck, J.
Lyell, C.
Romanes, G.
Severston, A.
Shull, A.
Smith, H.W.
Thomson, A.
Vries, H.
Watson, H.
Weldon, W.

EXPLORING

Amundsen, R.
Baffin, W.
Barrow, J.
Battuta
Bodega y Quadra, J.
Bruce, J.
Byrd, R.
Cook, J.
Czekanowski, A.
David, T.
Debenham, F.
Demidov, A.
Ellsworth, L.
Franklin, J.
Gould, L.
Harkness, R.
Henson, M.
Hillary, E.
Hubbard, B.
Lesson, R.
Malaspina, A.
Markham, A.
Niebuhr, C.
Peary, R.
Richardson, J.
Rodgers, J.
Ronne, F.
Ross, J.
Scott, R.
Sedov, G.
Thompson, E.
Verreaux, J.
Washburn, H.
Wellman, W.

FORENSIC SCIENCE

Bertillon, A.
Lombroso, C.
Noguchi, T.
Parsons, D.

Renshaw, A.
Spilsbury, B.
Willcox, W.

FORESTRY

(See also
Arboriculture; Tree Surgery)

Ahern, G.
Allen, E.
Allen, S.
Andrews, C.
Andrews, H.
Arnold, R.
Ashe, W.
Asplundh, C.
Baker, H.
Baxter, D.
Besley, F.
Bowers, E.
Boyce, J.
Bruce, D.
Butler, O.
Carlson, N.
Cary, A.
Chapman, H.
Clapp, E.
Clepper, H.
Cliff, E.
Coffman, J.
Collingwood, G.
Connaughton, C.
Cox, W.
Crafts, E.
Damtoft, W.
Dana, S.
Davis, K.
Dayton, W.
Drake, G.
Dunn, P.
Dutton, W.
Egleston, N.
Eldredge, I.
Fernow, B.
Forbes, R.
Fritz, E.
Garratt, G.
Gifford, J.
Gill, T.
Gillett, C.
Glascock, H.
Granger, C.
Graves, H.
Greeley, A.
Greeley, W.
Green, S.
Hagenstein, W.
Hall, W.
Hardtner, H.
Harper, V.
Hartig, T.
Hawes, A.
Hawley, R.
Heintzleman, B.

Hepting, G.
Herbert, P.
Herr, C.
Holmes, J.
Hornaday, F.
Hosmer, R.
Hough, F.
Howard, W.
Illick, J.
Jardine, J.
Jemison, G.
Kaufert, F.
Keen, F.
Kelley, E.
King, R.
Kneipp, L.
Leopold, A.
MacKaye, B.
Malsberger, H.
Martin, C.
Martineau, B.
Mason, D.
Maunder, E.
McArdle, R.
McClellan, J.
McGuire, J.
McNary, C.
Morton, L.
Mulford, W.
Nelson, D.
Nelson, J.
Olmsted, F.
Orell, B.
Pack, A.
Pack, C.
Pack, R.
Parker, L.
Pearson, G.
Peterson, R.
Pomeroy, K.
Potter, A.
Preston, J.
Price, O.
Rasmussen, B.
Reed, F.
Reynolds, H.
Robinson, R.
Roth, F.
Schenck, C.
Schlich, W.
Schmitz, H.
Shanklin, J.
Sherrard, T.
Shirley, H.
Silcox, F.
Smith, H.
Spurr, S.
Stuart, R.
Sudworth, G.
Toumey, J.
Towell, W.
Troup, R.
Vaux, H.
Vysotsky, G.
Warden, J.
Watts, L.
Wilmot, S.
Woodward, H.

Wyckoff, S.
Zivnuska, J.
Zon, R.

GENETICS

Ames, B.
Arber, W.
Auerbach, C.
Bateson, W.
Beadle, G.
Biffen, R.
Blakeslee, A.
Borlaug, N.
Bridges, C.
Brink, R.
Cavalli-Sforza, L.
Clausen, R.
Collins, G.
Correns, K.
Crew, F.
Danforth, C.
Davenport, C.
Demerec, M.
Dobzhansky, T.
Dunn, L.
East, E.
Emerson, R.
Ephrussi, B.
Fisher, R.
Ford, E.
Gates, R.
Haldane, J.
Iltis, H.
Jaynes, R.
Jones, D.
Kettlewell, H.
Kihara, H.
Kimura, M.
Koltzoff, N.
Lederberg, J.
Levine, P.
Lush, J.
Mather, K.
Mendel, G.
Michurin, I.
Morgan, T.
Neel, J.
Nilsson-Ehle, H.
Pearl, R.
Penrose, L.
Phillips, J.
Pontecorvo, G.
Punnett, R.
Russell, E.
Sager, R.
Sakharov, V.
Schultz, J.
Sears, E.
Sheppard, P.
Shull, G.
Smith, H.
Snell, G.
Sonneborn, T.
Sprague, G.
Stadler, L.

Stern, C.
Stevens, N.
Stone, W.
Sturtevant, A.
Tatum, E.
Tschermak von Seysenegg, E.
Vavilov, N.
Vries, H.
Weinberg, W.
White, M.
Wiebe, G.
Winge, O.
Wortman, S.
Wright, S.

GEOGRAPHY

Abert, J.
Abu Hamid, G.
Abul Fida, I.
Acosta, J.
Anuchin, D.
Anville, J.
Apian, P.
Arbos, P.
Atwood, W.
Baker, M.
Bakri, A.
Baranskii, N.
Behaim, M.
Berg, L.S.
Bering, V.
Blaeu, W.
Blanchard, R.
Blumenstock, D.
Bougainville, L.
Bowman, I.
Boyd, L.
Brunhes, J.
Buache, P.
Corenelli, V.
Dainelli, G.
Davidson, G.
Davis, W.
DeBentham, F.
Delisle, G.
Delisle, J.
Dokuchaev, V.
Everest, G.
Fleure, H.
Forster, G.
Gannett, H.
Gemma, F.
Germanus, H.
Gilbert, G.
Guyot, A.
Hakluyt, R.
Hamberg, A.
Hamdani, A.
Harper, R.M.
Hawqal, A.
Hercataeus
Hedin, S.
Heim, A.
Hoff, K.
Hutchins, T.
Ibanez, C.

Ibrahim ibn Yaqub
Idrisi, A.
Kaempfer, E.
Khurradadhbih, A.
Kimble, G.
Krasheninnikov, S.
Krasnov, A.
Kropotkin, P.
Leo the African
Lepekhin, I.
Litke, F.
Margerie, E.
Markham, C.
Marsh, G.
Martonne, E.
Masudi, A.
Mauro, F.
Mercator, G.
Morse, J.
Munster, S.
Mushketov, I.
Nordenskiold, N.
Ortelius, A.
Pallisher, J.
Petty, W.
Piri Rais, M.
Pomponius Mela
Potanin, G.
Przhevalsky, N.
Pytheas
Qazwini, Z.
Ratzel, F.
Reclus, E.
Rennell, J.
Ricci, M.
Romer, E.
Schoner, J.
Semyonov-Tyan-Shansky, P.
Shirakatsi, A.
Strabo
Tanfilev, G.
Tarde, J.
Tillo, A.
Toscanelli, P.
Varenius, B.
Voeykov, A.
Volney, C.
Waldseemuller, M.
Wolman, M.
Woolridge, S.
Yaqut al Hamawi al-Rumi, S.

GEOLOGY

Abich, O.
Adams, C.
Adams, F.
Adams, J.E.
Afanasyev, G.
Ainsworth, W.
Alberti, F.
Alexander, J.
Ameghino, F.
Anderson, C.A.
Anderson, E.M.
Andrusov, N.
Ansted, D.

Antisell, T.
Archiac, E.
Arduini, G.
Argand, E.
Arkell, W.
Ashburner, C.
Atwood, W.
Aubuisson de Voisins, J.
Babington, W.
Baier, J.
Bailey, L.
Bakewell, R.
Ball, M.
Barrell, J.
Barringer, D.
Barrois, C.
Barton, D.
Bascom, F.
Bassler, R.
Bauer, P.
Bauerman, H.
Bean, E.
Becker, G.
Beebe, B.
Beguyer de Chancourtois, A.
Bell, R.
Belousov, V.
Belt, T.
Benson, W.
Berkey, C.
Berner, R.
Beudant, F.
Beyer, C.
Beyer, S.
Bigsby, J.
Binney, E.
Bischof, C.
Black, J.
Blackwell, E.
Blanford, H.
Blanford, W.
Bleininger, A.
Boase, H.
Boll, J.
Bonney, T.G.
Boswell, P.G.
Boue, A.
Boule, M.
Boullanger, N.
Bourquet, L.
Boutwell, J.
Bowen, N.
Bowerbank, J.
Bowie, W.
Boye, M.
Bradley, F.
Bradley, J.
Brainerd, E.
Bramlette, M.
Breislak, S.
Brigham, W.
Bristow, H.
Brocchi, G.
Brochant de Villiers, A.
Brogger, W.
Broili, F.
Bromell, M.
Brongniart, A.
Brooks, A.

Brown, C.
Brown, H.
Bryan, F.
Bryan, K.
Bryce, J.
Buch, L.
Bucher, W.
Buckland, W.
Buckman, J.
Buddington, A.
Burnet, T.
Burress, W.
Butler, B.
Carll, J.
Carnall, R.
Carne, J.
Carr, E.S.
Cayeux, L.
Chamberlin, R.
Chamberlin, T.
Chambers, R.
Chernyshev, F.
Christy, D.
Chukhrov, F.
Cist, J.
Clark, W.
Clarke, E.
Clarke, F.
Clarke, W.
Claypole, E.
Cleve, P.
Cline, L.
Cloos, E.
Cloos, H.
Close, M.
Cloud, P.
Coan, T.
Cobb, W.
Cocchi, I.
Collett, J.
Conybeare, W.
Cook, G.
Cooke, C.
Cooper,T.
Cordier, P.
Cotta, C.
Cotting, J.
Cox, A.
Cox, L.
Credner, H.
Croll, J.
Cross, C.
Culver, H.
Cumming, J.
Cutting, H.
Czekanowski, A.
Czerski, J.
Dainelli, G.
Daintree, R.
Daly, R.
Dana, J.D.
Dana, J.F.
Dane, C.
Darwin, C.
Daubney, C.
David, T.
Davidson, D.
Davies, D.
Dawkins, W.

Dawson, J.
Deane, J.
Deiss, C.
De la Beche, H.
Delafield, J.
Deluc, J.
DeMargerie, E.
Dick, R.
Dietz, R.
Diller, J.
Dobbin, C.
Dolomiev, D.
Douglas, R.
Douglas, S.
Drake, N.
Drew, F.
Drygaiski, E.
Dufrenoy, O.
Dunbar, C.
Duncan, P.
Dunham, K.
DuToit, A.
Dutton, C.
Eaton, A.
Edson, D.
Eichwald, K.
Eights, J.
Elie de Beaumont, J.
Emerson, B.
Emiliani, C.
Emmons, S.
Englemann, H.
Ernst, W.
Escher Von Der Linth, H.
Escholt, M.
Eskola, P.
Eugster, H.
Evans, C.
Evans, G.
Ewing, W.
Farey, J.
Faujas de St-Fond, B.
Fearnsides, W.
Featherstonaugh, G.
Federov, S.
Fenneman, N.
Fermor, L.
Fersmen, A.
Field, R.
Fisher, E.
Fitton, W.
Fleming, J.
Flett, J.
Florensov, N.
Forbes, D.
Forbes, J.
Forchhammer, J.
Foshag, W.
Fouque, F.
Fowler Billings, K.
Fralich, C.
Frazer, P.
Frederick, F.
Freiesleben, J.
Fuchs, V.
Fuchsel, G.
Fyodorov, E.
Gabb, W.
Gagnebin, E.

Geer, G.
Geijer, P.
Geikie, A.
Geikie, J.
Gessner, J.
Gibbes, R.
Gilbert, G.
Gilluly, J.
Godwin-Austen, H.
Godwin-Austen, R.
Goethe, J.
Goguel, J.
Goldshmidt, V.
Goldsmith, J.
Gould, L.
Grabau, A.
Graton, C.
Grawe, O.
Green, A.
Greenough, G.
Gregory, J.
Gressly, A.
Griffith, R.
Groddeck, A.
Guettard, J.
Gunter, H.
Gustafson, J.
Haast, J.
Hager, A.
Hague, A.
Haidinger, W.
Hailstone, J.
Halbouty, M.
Hall, A.
Hall, J.
Hall, J. Jr.
Hamberg, A.
Hamilton, W.
Hanks, H.
Hanley, J.
Hardman, E.
Hares, C.
Harker, A.
Harris, G.
Harrison, J.
Harrison, T.
Hartt, C.
Haug, G.
Haughton, S.
Hawkes, L.
Hawkins, H.
Hawkins, T.
Hayden, F.
Hayden, H.
Hayes, J.
Hays, J.
Hector, J.
Hedberg, H.
Heezen, B.
Heilprin, A.
Heim, A.
Heim, A.A.
Heindi, L.
Helmersen, G.
Herold, S.
Hess, H.
Hewett, D.
Hickling, H.
Hicks, H.

Hind, H.
Hindes, E.
Hitchcock, E.
Hilgard, E.W.
Hoff, K.
Holland, T.
Hollick, C.
Holmes, A.
Holmes, W.
Holtedahl, O.
Hopkins, W.
Horner, L.
Huddleston, W.
Hutton, F.
Hutton, W.
Image, T.
Imbrie, J.
Jones, T.
Julien, A.
Karpinsky, A.
Kay, G.
Keith, A.
Kelly, W.A.
Kemp, J.
Kennedy, G.
Kennedy, W.
Kerr, W.
Keyserling, A.
Kinahan, G.
King, C.R.
King, W.
Kirman, R.
Knight, W.
Knopf, A.
Knopf, E.
Korzhinskii, D.
Kosygin, Y.
Koto, B.
Kuenen, P.
Kuno, H.
Kuznetsov, V.
Kuznetson, Y.
Lacroix, A.
Lang, W.B.
Lang, W.D.
Lapparent, A.
Lapworth, C.
Larsen, E.
Lartet, L.
Lawson, A.
LeConte, J.
Lees, G.
Leet, L.
Lehmann, J.
Leith, C.
Leonhard, K.
Leopold, L.
Lesley, J.
Leverett, F.
Levinson-Lessing, F.
Levorsen, A.
Lewis, T.
Lindgren, W.
Lister, M.
Locke, J.
Logan, W.
Lohest, M.
Longwell, C.

Lonsdale, W.
Lossen, K.
Lougee, R.
Lugeon, M.
Lyell, C.
Lyman, B.
Lyman, C.S.
Lyons, H.
Macbride, T.
MacCulloch, J.
Mackin, J.
Maclure, W.
MacNaughton, L.
Madison, J.
Maillet, B.
Mantell, G.
Marcou, J.
Marcy, O.
Margerie, E.
Marr, J.
Mather, K.
Mather, W.
Matthes, F.
Matthews, D.
Matuyama, M.
Mawson, D.
Maxson, D.
McCalley, H.
McCoy, F.
McDermott, E.
McGee, W.
McLaughlin, D.
McLintock, W.
McMahon, C.
McNair, A.
Mead, W.
Mease, J.
Medlicott, H.
Meek, F.
Mell, P.
Mendenhall, W.
Merrill, G.
Merwin, H.
Meyerhoff, H.
Michel-Levy, A.
Miklukho-Maklay, M.
Miller, H.
Miller, W.Z.
Mitchell, G.
Mitchell, J.A.
Miyashiro, A.
Mohr, C.
Mohs, F.
Moneymaker, B.
Moore, R.
Moro, A.
Morris, J.
Morse, W.
Morton, G.
Muir, J.
Murchison, R.
Mushetov, I.
Nalivkin, D.
Nathorst, A.
Naumann, K.
Necker, L.
Nelson, R.
Neumayr, M.

Newberry, J.
Newell, F.
Newell, N.
Newton, H.
Nicol, J.
Niggli, P.
Nikitin, S.
Nordenskiold, N.
Obruchev, S.
Obruchev, V.
Ochsenius, C.
Oldham, R.
Oldham, T.
Omalius-d'Halloy, J.
Ormerod, G.
Orton, E.
Owen, D.
Owen, G.
Ozersky, A.
Page, D.
Palissy, B.
Pardee, J.
Pavlov, A.
Peach, C.
Pearson, H.W.
Pecora, W.
Penck, A.
Penck, W.
Pengelly, W.
Percival, J.
Pettijohn, F.
Peyve, A.
Phillips, J.
Phillips, W.
Pirsson, L.
Platt, F.
Poldervaart, A.
Posepny, F.
Powell, J.
Prestwich, J.
Prevost, L.
Price, G.
Pritchett, H.
Proctor, J.
Pruvost, P.
Pugh, W.
Pumpelly, R.
Pustovalov, L.
Quenstedt, F.
Ramberg, H.
Rames, J.
Ramond de Carbonniers, L.
Ramsay, A.
Ransome, F.
Raspe, R.
Read, H.
Reade, T.
Reeside, J.
Renard, A.
Renevier, E.
Rengarten, V.
Reuss, F.
Reynolds, D.
Ribeiro Santos, C.
Rice, W.
Richardson, G.
Richey, J.
Richthofen, F.

Ridley, H.
Rio, A.
Roberts, G.
Roemer, F.
Rogers, H.
Rogers, W.B.
Rose, C.
Roth, J.
Rouelle, G.
Rovereto, G.
Roy, S.
Rozhkov, I.
Rubey, W.
Ruedemann, R.
Rulein, V.
Saks, V.
Salisbury, R.
Salter, J.
Sander, B.
Satpaev, K.
Saukov, A.
Saull, W.
Saussure, H.
Sayre, A.
Schardt, H.
Scheuchzer, J.
Schimper, K.
Schlotheim, E.
Schmitt, H.
Schneiderhohn, H.
Schoolcraft, H.
Schopf, J.
Schott, A.
Schultz, A.
Scilla, A.
Scrope, G.
Sederholm, J.
Sedgwick, A.
Selwyn, A.
Serres de Mesples, M.
Shakhov, F.
Shaler, N.
Sharp, R.
Sharp, S.
Sharpe, D.
Shcherbakov, D.
Shepard, F.
Shoemaker, E.
Shore, W.
Shumard, B.
Sibly, F.
Silliman, B. Jr.
Smirnov, V.I.
Smith, E.B.
Smith, E.P.
Smith, J.P.
Smith, W.
Smith, W.D.
Smyth, W.
Sobolev, V.
Sokolov, B.
Sokolov, D.
Soldani, A.
Sollas, W.
Sorby, H.
Soulavie, J.
Sowerby, J.
Speed, C.
Stanton, T.

Staszic, S.
Steno, N.
Stetson, H.
Stewart, F.
Stille, W.
Stockdale, P.
Strachey, J.
Strakhov, N.
Studer, B.
Stumm, E.
Suess, E.
Swallow, G.
Swedenborg, E.
Symonds, W.
Taylor, F.B.
Taylor, J.H.
Taylor, R.C.
Teall, J.
Teilhard de Chardin, P.
Termier, P.
Teschemacher, J.
Thomas, H.
Tilas, D.
Tilley, C.
Topley, W.
Toulmin, G.
Townsend, J.
Trask, J.
Trimmer, J.
Trofimuck, A.
Troost, G.
Troxell, E.
Tschermak, G.
Tuomey, M.
Tuttle, O.
Twenhofel, W.
Tylor, A.
Tyrrell, J.
Tyson, P.
Ure, D.
Van Hise, C.
Van Rensselaer, J.
Vanuxem, L.
Varentsov, M.
Vaughan, T.
Verneuil, P.
Vine, F.
Vinogradov, A.
Vlasov, K.
Vogt, J.
Vogt, T.
Voltz, P.
Von Engeln, O.
Wadia, D.
Wager, L.
Walcott, C.
Walker, J.
Ward, J.
Warren, G.
Washington, H.
Wasserburg, G.
Wasson, T.
Waters, A.
Webster, T.
Weeks, L.
Wells, D.
White, C.A.
White, C.D.
Whitehurst, J.

Whitfield, R.
Whitney, J.
Whittard, W.
Whittlesey, C.
Wilkinson, C.
Willard, B.
Williams, D.
Williams, H.
Williams, J.S.
Williams, N.
Williamson, J.
Williamson, W.
Willis, B.
Wilson, J.T.
Winchell, A.
Winchell, A.N.
Wisser, E.
Witchell, E.
Witham, H.
Wood, J.
Wood, S.
Woodring, W.
Woodruff, J.
Woods, J.
Woodward, J.
Woodward, S.
Worthen, A.
Wrather, W.
Wright, A.A.
Wright, T.
Yakovlev, N.
Yanshin, A.
Yeates, W.
Young, A.
Zejsner, L.
Zinn, J.
Zirkel, F.

GEOMORPHOLOGY

Davis, W.
Penck, A.
Russell, R.

GEOPHYSICS

Adams, L.
Allen, E.
Bache, A.
Bartels, J.
Bauer, L.
Bjerknes, V.
Birch, F.
Bullard, E.
Bullerwell, W.
Byerly, P.
DeGolyer, E.
Delambre, J.
Doell, R.
Elsasser, W.
Faye, G.
Federov, Y.
Ferrel, W.
Fleming, J.A.
Forbush, S.

Foster, H.
Fotiadi, E.
Frazer, J.
Halley, E.
Hassler, F.
Hayford, J.
Heiskanen, W.
Hilgard, J.
Holmes, A.
Hubbert, M.
Jaeger, J.C.
Jeffreys, H.
Joesting, H.
Johnson, D.W.
Johnson, W.D.
Joyce, J.
Juan y Santacilla, J.
Jukes, J.
Kater, H.
Kauraysky, V.
Knopoff, L.
Kochina, P.
Konkoly Thege, M.
Krasovsky, T.
Krayenhoff, C.
Lamb, G.
Lamb, H.
Lenox-Conyngham, G.
Leybenzon, L.
Love, A.
MacDonald, E.
Macelwane, J.
Miller, R.
Molodenskii, M.
Montanari, G.
Munk, W.
Murphy, L.
Obukhov, A.
Palmieri, L.
Press, F.
Reid, H.
Ricco, A.
Riznichenko, Y.
Roche, E.
Runcorn, S.
Saville, W.
Schmidt, C.A.
Schmidt, J.
Schott, C.
Schumacher, J.
Sharonov, V.
Shulaikin, V.
Slichter, L.
Soske, J.
Termier, P.
Tikhonov, A.
Tworbridge, W.
Van Orstrand, C.
Vening Meinesz, F.
Verhoogen, J.
Wallis, W.
Wegener, A.
Wiechert, E.
Wilkes, C.
Woodward, R.S.
Wright, F.
Yoder, H.

GLACIOLOGY

Avsyuk, G.
Charpentier, J.
Desor, P.
Forbes, J.
Guyot, A.
Venetz, I.

HERPETOLOGY

Hallowell, E.
Perkins, M.
Stewart, M.
Vaillant, L.

HORTICULTURE

Abercrombie, J.
Aiton, W.
Anderson, W.
Bailey, L.H.
Burbank, L.
Burpee, D.
Eisen, G.
Gerard, J.
Griffiths, D.
Hatton, R.
Knight, T.
Lindley, J.
Lippincott, J.
Meehan, T.
Miehurin, I.
Miller, P.
Naudin, C.
Nehrling, A.
Nehrling, H.
Riley, H.
Sessions, K.
Sweet, R.
Thompson, H.
Tubbs, F.
Veitch, H.
Wallace, T.
Warder, J.
Warner, J.
Wickson, E.

HYDROLOGY

Beaufort, F.
Fichot, L.
Horsburgh, J.
Huddart, J.
Lokhtin, V.
Meinzer, O.
Sarychev, G.

ICHTHYOLOGY

Ayres, W.
Bean, T.H.
Berg, L.S.
Clark, E.
Coates, C.
Davis, H.
Day, F.
Dean, B.
Eigenmann, B.
Embody, G.
Eschmeyer, R.
Evermann, B.
Fisk, M.
Gill, T.
Goode, G.
Gudger, E.
Jordan, D.
Kendall, W.
MacDonald, M.
Rondelet, G.
Schultz, L.
Seaman, E.
Storer, D.
Svetovidov, A.
Vaillant, L.
Van Oosten, J.

IMMUNOLOGY

Benacerraf, B.
Bordet, J.
Boyd, W.
Gorer, P.
Heidelberger, M.
Ishizaka, K.
Kabat, E.
Levine, P.
Medawar, P.
Ramon, G.
Salk, J.
Seaton, E.
Tarshis, M.

INSTRUMENTATION

Berthoud, F.
Bion, N.
Bourdon, E.
Brashear, J.
Breguet, L.
Cole, H.
Divini, E.
Fisher, C.
Fitz, H.
Fortin, N.
Gambey, H.
Gautier, P.

Graham, G.
Grassell, E.
Hadley, J.
Harrison, J.
Hartmann, G.
Hauksbee, F.
Holcombe, A.
Iwahashi, Z.
Jai Singh, S.
Kratzer, N.
Landriani, M.
Langlois, C.
Lemaire, J.
Martin, B.
Metius, A.
Negretti, E.
Nobert, F.
Powell, H.
Reichenbach, G.
Repsold, A.
Repsold, J.A.
Rittenhouse, D.
Ross, A.
Saugrain, A.
Saxton, J.
Soleil, J.
Stanley, W.
Thiout, A.
Tokugawa, Y.
Tompion, T.
Vernier, P.
Yi Chon

INVENTING

Adams, W.
Adler, C.
Ader, C.
Alger, C.
Allen, Z.
Anderson, J.
Appert, N.
Applegath, Λ.
Arkwright, R.
Aspdin, J.
Baird, J.
Ball, C.
Ballantine, A.
Barlow, E.
Bell, A.G.
Bell, H.
Bell, P.
Bendix, V.
Benton, L.
Berliner, E.
Bessemer, H.
Bickford, W.
Bickley, E.
Bigelow, E.
Blake, E.
Blanchard, T.
Boulton, M.
Boyden, S.
Boyden, V.
Boykin, O.

Braille, L.
Bramson, M.
Breckman, J.
Brower, E.
Brown, W.
Browne, R.
Browning, J.
Brush, C.
Burke, O.
Burr, T.
Burroughs, W.
Burt, W.
Bushnell, D.
Cadwallader, H.
Capstaff, J.
Carlson, C.
Carrier, W.
Cartwright, E.
Cave, H.
Chappe, C.
Chevrolet, L.
Claff, C.
Clanny, W.
Clark, T.
Clarkson, R.
Clegg, S.
Clymer, G.
Colt, S.
Cooper, P.
Corliss, G.
Cornelius, Y.
Cornell, E.
Cort, H.
Cowper, E.
Crompton, S.
Ctesibius
Curtiss, G.
Daguerre, L.
Daimler, G.
Dalen, N.
Dallery, T.
Danforth, R.
Davenport, T.
Davis, R.
Davy, E.
Deere, J.
DeLaval, C.
Derosne, C.
Diesel, R.
Donchian, P.
Donkin, B.
Drebbel, C.
Drummond, T.
Dudley, D.
Dunlap, M.
Dunlop, J.
Duryea, C.
Dyer, J.
Early, E.
Eastman, G.
Edgeworth, R.
Edison, T.
Elkington, G.
Elliott, E.
Ellis, F.
Ericsson, J.
Eve, J.

Fairchild, S.
Farmer, M.G.
Farnsworth, P.
Ferguson, T.
Fessenden, R.
Fitch, J.
Field, J.
Foregger, R.
Forsyth, A.
Fowler, J.
Foyn, S.
Freeman, B.
Friese-Greene, W.
Fuller, R.
Fulton, R.
Gabor, D.
Gally, M.
Gatling, R.
Geissler, H.
Goldmark, P.
Goodyear, C.
Gramme, Z.
Gray, E.
Greenwood, H.
Guinand, P.
Gurney, G.
Gutenberg, J.
Hall, C.
Hall, J.H.
Hammond, J.
Hancock, T.
Hans, E.
Hayden, G.
Heathcoat, J.
Henry, J.
Hewitt, P.
Hoe, R.
Holland, J.P.
House, R.
Howe, E.
Hubbard, P.
Huggins, L.
Huntsman, B.
Hussey, O.
Hyatt, J.
Jablochkoff, P.
Jacquard, J.
Jeffrey, M.
Jenkins, C.
Jones, F.M.
Kelly, W.
Kenyon, D.
Kettering, C.
King, E.
Knight, G.
Knight, M.
Konig, F.
Kroeger, W.
Krupp, A.
Lake, S.
Land, E.
Latimer, L.
Lebon, P.
Lenoir, J.
Leonardo da Vinci
Levison, W.
Levy, L.

Lister, S.
Loomis, M.
Lorin, R.
Lowell, F.
Lyon, G.
Lyon, H.
Macintosh, C.
Martin, P.
Martzeliger, J.
Mason, W.
Maxim, H.
McCormick, C.
McNaught, J.
McTammany, J.
Mege Mouries, H.
Mergenthaler, O.
Montgolfier, J.
Montgolfier, J.M.
Montgomery, J.
Moody, P.
Morey, S.
Morgan, G.
Morse, S.
Mudge, T.
Muench, C.
Muller, G.
Murdock, W.
Mushet, R.
Niepce, J.
Nipkow, P.
Norden, C.
Ohain, H.
Orr, H.
Otis, E.
Palmer, T.
Pattinson, H.
Pelton, L.
Pitman, I.
Polhem, C.
Poulsen, V.
Read, N.
Redfield, C.
Remington, E.
Rillieux, N.
Robert, N.
Roberts, R.
Roebling, J.
Ronalds, F.
Rumsey, J.
Schultz, C.
Selden, G.
Senefelder
Sholes, C.
Shrapnel, H.
Siemens, C.
Singer, I.
Slater, S.
Slayter, G.
Sperry, E.
Sprengel, H.
Stanhope, C.
Stanley, F.
Stanley, F.E.
Stevens, J.
Stevens, R.
Stokes, R.

Stirling, R.
Stott, R.
Strieby, M.
Strowger, A.
Stubblefield, N.
Su Sung
Swasey, A.
Talbot, W.
Tarlton, R.
Temple, L.
Thimonnier, B.
Tinnerman, A.
Treadwell, D.
Trevithick, R.
Tsai Lun
Tull, J.
Twining, A.
Varian, S.
Vaucanson, J.
Vreeland, F.
Walker, J.
Wallace, C.
Watson, T.
Watt, J.
Weaver, I.
Welsbach, C.
Wenner-Gren, A.
Westinghouse, G.
Whinfield, J.
Whitehead, R.
Whitney, E.
Wight, S.
Wilkinson, D.
Wilkinson, J.
Winzer, F.
Woods, G.
Wright, O.
Wright, W.
Zeppelin, F.

LIMNOLOGY

Birge, A.
Forel, F.
Welch, P.

MARINE BIOLOGY

Bidder, G.
Burkholder, P.
Hardy, A.
Hensen, V.
Herdman, W.
Hjort, J.
Jeffreys, J.
Knipovich, N.
Loven, S.
Marshall, S.
Mead, S.
Nutting, C.
Rathbun, M.
Ray, D.
Sars, M.

Schmidt, E.
Shaw, E.
Stimpson, W.
Vogt, C.

MATHEMATICS

Abel, N.
Abraham bar Hiyya
Abu Kamil, S.
Abul-Wafa al-Buzjani
Adams, D.
Adhemar, A.
Adrian, R.
Agardh, C.A.
Agnesi, M.
Aguilon, F.
Ahmad ibn Yusuf
Ahmose
Aida Yasuaki
Aiken, H.H.
Airy, G.
Aitken, A.C.
Ajima Naonobu
Albert of Saxony
Albert, A.A.
Alberti, L.
Alcuin
Alembert, J.
Alexanderoff, P.
Alexandrov, A.
Aley, R.
Allen, T.
Allman, G.
Ames, N.
Amili, B.
Ampere, A.M.
Anderson, A.
Anderson, R.
Ansler-Laffon, J.
Anatolius of Alexandria
Anaxagoras
Anaximander of Militos
Anderson, O.J.
Andoyer, H.
Andre, C.
Angeli, S.
Anthemius of Tralles
Antiphon
Apollonius
Appell, P.
Arbogast, L.
Archibald, R.
Archimedes
Archytas of Tarentum
Argand, J.
Aristaeus
Aristarchus of Samos
Arnauld, A.
Aronhold, S.
Arrow, K.
Artin, E.
Aryabhata I
Aryabhata II
Atiyah, M.

Atkinson, H.
Atwood, G.
Autolycus of Pitane
Auzout, A.
Ayres, W.
Azara, F.
Babbage, C.
Bachelier, L.
Bachet de Meziriac, C.
Bachman, P.
Backus, L.
Baghdadi, A.
Baines, J.
Baire, R.
Baker, A.
Baker, H.F.
Baker, T.
Balam, R.
Balbus
Balmer, J.J.
Banach, S.
Banna al-Marrakushi
Banneker, B.
Banu Musa, A.
Banu Musa, H.
Barbier, J.
Barnard, F.A.
Barocius, F.
Barrow, I.
Bartlett, W.
Batchelor, G.
Bateman, H.
Battani, A.
Bayes, T.
Baylis, E.
Bayma, J.
Beaugrand, J.
Bell, E.T.
Bellavitis, G.
Bellman, R.
Beltrami, E.
Benedetti, G.
Bernoulli, D.
Bernoulli, J.
Bernoulli, J.
Bernoulli, N.
Bernstein, B.A.
Bernstein, F.
Bernstein, S.N.
Bers, L.
Bertini, E.
Bertrand, J.L.
Berwick, W.E.
Besicavitch, A.
Besson, J.
Betti, E.
Bezout, E.
Bhaskara II
Bianchi, L.
Bienayme, I.
Billy, J.
Bird, J.
Birkhoff, G.
Biruni, A.
Bjerknes, C.
Blackwell, D.
Blaschke, W.J.

Blagrave, J.
Bland, M.
Blichfeldt, H.
Bliss, W.
Bobillier, E.
Bocher, M.
Bochner, S.
Bogolyubov, N.
Bohl, P.
Bohr, H.
Bolyai, J.
Bolza, O.
Bolzano, B.
Bombieri, E.
Bondi, H.
Bonnet, P.
Boole, G.
Borchardt, C.
Borda, J.
Borel, E.
Borthius, A.
Bortkiewicz, L.
Bortolotti, E.
Bossut, C.
Boulliau, I.
Bougainville, L.
Bouquet, J.
Bour, E.
Bourbaki, N.
Bourne, W.
Bouton, C.
Boutroux, P.
Bouvelles, C.
Bowditch, N.
Bower, G.
Bowker, A.
Bowser, E.
Bradwardine, T.
Brakenridge, W.
Bramer, B.
Brancker, T.
Brandreth, T.
Brashman, N.
Braunmuhl, A.
Braver, R.
Bredon, S.
Bremiker, C.
Bret, J.
Brianchon, C.
Briggs, H.
Brill, A.
Brillovin, M.
Bring, E.
Brinkley, J.
Brioschi, F.
Briot, C.
Brisson, B.
Brocard, P.
Brodetsky, S.
Bromwick, T.
Bronowski, J.
Brougham, H.
Brouncker, W.
Brouwer, L.
Brown, E.
Brown, M.
Brozek, J.

Bryson of Beracles
Bubb, F.
Budan de Boiblaurent
Bugaev, N.
Bullen, K.
Bunyakovsky, V.
Burali-Forti, C.
Burbury, S.
Burgi, J.
Burnside, W.
Burrau, C.
Burrow, R.
Buteo, J.
Byerly, W.
Byrhtferth
Cabeo, N.
Cain, W.
Cairns, W.
Cajori, F.
Calandrelli, I.
Caldwell, J.
Callipus
Campanus of Novara
Campbell, G.
Campbell, S.
Camus, C.
Cantor, G.
Caramuel y Lobkowitz, J.
Caratheodory, C.
Carcavi, P.
Cardano, G.
Carnot, L.
Cartan, E.
Casey, J.
Castel, L.
Castelnuovo, G.
Castillon, J.
Cataldi, P.
Cauchy, A.
Cavalieri, B.
Cavendish, C.
Cayley, A.
Cech, E.
Cell, J.
Cesaro, E.
Ceulen, L.
Ceva, G.
Chaplygin, S.
Chapman, S.
Chasles, M.
Chauvenet, W.
Chebotaryov, N.
Chebyshev, P.
Chern, S.
Cherry, T.
Cheyne, G.
Chin Chiu-Shao
Chou Kung
Christmann, J.
Christofel, E.
Chrystal, G.
Chu Shin-Chieh
Chuquet, N.
Ciruelo, P.
Clairaut, A.
Clark, C.
Clarke, H.

Clarke, S.
Clausen, T.
Clavius, C.
Clebsch, R.
Clifford, W.
Cocker, E.
Codazzi, D.
Coddington, H.
Coffin, J.
Coggeshall, H.
Cohen, A.
Cohen, P.
Colburn, Z.
Cole, F.
Coley, H.
Collingswood, E.
Collins, J.
Commandino, F.
Comte, I.
Condorcet, M.
Conon of Samos
Coolidge, J.
Cosserat, E.
Cotes, R.
Coulson, C.
Courant, R.
Cournot, A.
Courtenay, E.
Couturat, L.
Craig, J.
Craig, T.
Cramer, G.
Cramer, H.
Crathorne, A.
Crawley, E.
Crelle, A.
Cremona, A.
Cresswell, D.
Crousaz, J.
Cunha, J.
Cunningham, S.
Curtze, E.
Daboll, N.
Dalby, I.
Dandelin, G.
Danti, E.
Dantzig, G.
Darboux, J.
D'Arcy, P.
Darwin, G.
Dasypodius, C.
Davenport, H.
Davidov, A.
Davies, C.
Davies, T.
Davis, M.
Davis, W.
Dawson, J.
DeBeaune, F.
DeChales, C.
Dehn, M.
Delamin, R.
Deligne, P.
Delone, B.
Democritus
DeMorgan, A.
DeParcieux, A.

DesArgues, G.
Descartes, R.
Dickson, L.
Dickstein, S.
Dieudonne, J.
Digges, L.
Digges, T.
Dini, U.
Dinostratus
Diocles
Dionis du Sejour, A.
Dionysodorus
Diophantus
Dirac, P.
Dixon, A.
Dodgson, C.
Dominicus de Clavasio
Dominis of Larissa
Donn, B.
Doob, J.
Doodson, A.
Dositheus
Douglas, J.
Drach, J.
DuBois-Reymond, P.
DuChatelet, E.
Dudith, A.
Duhamel, J.
Dunbar, W.
Dunn, S.
Dupin, P.
Dupre, A.
Durer, A.
Dyck, W.
Eastman, J.
Eddy, H.
Egorov, D.
Eimbeck, W.
Eisenhart, L.
Eisenstein, F.
Ellicott, A.
Ellingson, H.
Elliott, E.
Ellis, A.
Emerson, W.
Engel, F.
Enriques, F.
Erdelyi, A.
Euclid
Eudoxus
Euler, L.
Eutocius of Ascalon
Evans, G.
Evans, L.
Evans, T.
Exley, T.
Ezra, A.
Fabri, H.
Faccio, N.
Faddeev, L.
Fagnano, G.
Fano, G.
Farrar, J.
Fatou, P.
Faulhaber, J.
Fefferman, C.
Feigl, G.

Feit, W.
Fejer, L.
Feller, W.
Fermat, P.
Ferrari, L.
Ferro, S.
Feurbach, K.
Fibonacci, L.
Fields, J.
Filon, L.
Fine, H.
Fine, O.
Fink, T.
Fischer, C.
Fisher, A.
Fisher, T.
Fletcher, A.
Folger, W.
Fontaine, A.
Ford, W.
Forsyth, A.
Foster, S.
Foster, W.
Fourier, J.
Fraenkel, A.
Francais, F.
Francais, J.
Francesca, P.
Franklin, F.
Frary, H.
Frazer, R.
Fredholm, I.
Frege, G.
Frenet, J.
Frenicle, B.
Friedmann, A.
Friedricks, K.
Fries, J.
Frisi, P.
Frobenius, G.
Frost, P.
Fry, J.
Fubini, G.
Fuchs, I.
Fueter, K.
Fuss, N.
Galerkin, B.
Galloway, T.
Galois, E.
Gauss, K.
Geiringer, H.
Geiser, K.
Gelfand, A.
Gellibrand, H.
Geminus
Gemma, F.
Gentzen, G.
Gerard of Brissels
Gerber d'Aurillac
Gergone, J.
Germain, S.
Ghetaldi, M.
Girard, A.
Glaisher, J.
Glenie, J.
Godel, K.
Godfrey, T.

Gold, J.
Goldbach, C.
Goldsbrough, G.
Goldstine, H.
Gompertz, B.
Gopel, A.
Gordan, P.
Gossett, W.
Goursat, E.
Grace, J.
Graffe, K.
Grandi, G.
Grassmann, H.
Graunt, J.
Grave, D.
Graves, J.
Gravesande, W.
Gray, J.
Green, G.
Green, G.M.
Greenwood, I.
Gregory, D.
Gregory, D.F.
Gregory, I.
Gregory, J.
Gregory, O.
Grew, T.
Grossman, M.
Guade Malves, J.
Guccia, G.
Guderman, J.
Guenther, A.
Guldin, P.
Gummere, J.
Gunter, E.
Haar, A.
Habash al Hasib, A.
Hachette, J.
Hadamard, J.
Hall, P.
Hall, W.
Halphen, G.
Halsted, G.
Hamilton, W.
Hammond, E.
Hankel, H.
Hann, J.
Harding, A.
Hardy, A.
Hardy, C.
Harriot, T.
Harrison, R.
Hartree, D.
Haselden, T.
Hassler, F.
Hausdorff, F.
Havelock T.
Hayes, C.
Hayward, R.
Heath, R.
Heath, T.
Hecht, D.
Hecke, E.
Hedrick, E.
Heilbronn, H.
Heine, H.
Hellinger, E.

Hemming, G.
Henrion, D.
Hensel, K.
Herbrand, J.
Herigone, P.
Hermann the Lame
Hermann, J.
Hermite, D.
Hero of Alexandria
Hesse, L.
Heuraet, H.
Heytesbury, W.
Hilbert, D.
Hill, G.
Hill, L.
Hill, T.
Hind, J.
Hindenburg, C.
Hippias of Elis
Hippocrates of Chios
Hironaka, H.
Hirst, T.
Hobbes, T.
Hodge, W.
Hodgkinson, E.
Hoene-Wrinski, J.
Hoffman, M.
Holder, O.
Holgate, T.
Holmboe, B.
Holwell, J.
Hood, T.
Hopf, H.
Hopkins, W.
Hopper, G.
Horner, W.
Hoskins, L.
Houel, G.
Howard, J.
Howes, E.
Hubbard, J.
Hudde, J.
Hugh of St. Victor
Humbert, P.
Humbert, M.
Huntington, E.
Hurwitz, A.
Hutchinson, J.J.
Hutton, C.
Hymers, J.
Hypatia
Hypsicles of Alexandria
Ibrahim ibn Sinan ibn Thabit
Ingham, A.
Ishlinskii, A.
Isidorus of Miletus
Ivory, J.
Jabir ibn Aflah al-Ishbili, A.
Jackman, A.
Jackson, D.
Jacobi, C.
Jacobson, N.
Jagannatha
Janiszewski, Z.
Jawhari, A.
Jayyani, A.
Jeffrey, G.

Jensen, J.L.
Jerrard, G.
Jevons, W.
Joachimsthal, F.
John of Gmunden
John of Ligneres
John of Murs
John, F.
Johnson, W.W.
Jones, H.
Jones, W.
Jonquieres de Nemore
Jordan, E.
Juel, S.
Jungius, J.
Kac, M.
Kaestner, A.
Kagan, B.
Kalman, R.
Kaluza, T.
Kamal al-Din
Kantrovich, L.
Kaplansky, I.
Karaji, A.
Karlin, S.
Karpinski, L.
Kashi, G.
Kasner, E.
Keckermann, B.
Keill, J.
Keldysh, M.
Kellogg, O.
Kelly, P.
Kemeny, J.
Kendall, E.
Kerekjarto, B.
Kersey, J.
Keynes, J.
Khalili, S.
Khayyami, G.
Khazin, A.
Khujandi, A.
Khwarizmi, M.
Kinchin, A.
King, L.
Kirkman, T.
Klein, C.
Kline, J.
Klugel, G.
Knesser, A.
Knopp, K.
Kobel, J.
Kochin, N.
Koenig, J.
Koenigs, G.
Kolmogorov, A.
Kolosov, G.
Konigsberger, L.
Kortweg, D.
Kotelnikov, A.
Kovalevsky, S.
Kraft, J.
Kronecker, L.
Krylov, A.
Krylov, N.
Kummer, E.
Kurschak, J.

LaCondamine, C.
Lacroix, S.
Ladd-Franklin, C.
LaFaille, C.
Lagny, T.
Laguerre, E.
Lahire, P.
Lalouvere, A.
Lamb, H.
Lamber, J.
Lame, G.
Lamy, B.
Lancret, M.
Landau, E.
Landen, J.
Landsberg, P.
Laplace, P.
LaRoche, E.
Laurent, P.
Launaha, J.
Lavrentev, M.
Lax, G.
Leavitt, D.
Lebesque, H.
Leeds, J.
Lefschetz, S.
Legendre, A.
Lehmer, D.
Leibniz, G.
Lemoine, E.
Leo the Mathematician
Leodamus of Thasos
Leonardo da Vinci
LePage, C.
LePoivre, J.
Lerch, M.
LeRoy, E.
Lesniewski, S.
LeTenneur, J.
Leurechon, J.
Levi ben Gerson
Levy, M.
Lewis, E.
Lexell, A.
Leybourn, W.
L'Hospital, G.
L'Huillier, S.
Li Chih
Liddel, D.
Lie, M.
Lilley, G.
Lin, C.
Lindelof, E.
Lindemann, C.
Linnik, Y.
Liouville, J.
Lipschitz, R.
Littlewood, J.
Liu Hui
Lobachevsky, N.
Loewner, C.
Loewy, A.
Loomis, E.
Loria, G.
Lotka, A.
Love, A.
Lovelace, A.

Lovering, J.
Lucas, F.
Ludlam, W.
Lueroth, J.
Lukasiewicz, J.
Luzin, N.
Lyapunov, A.
Lyusternik, L.
Macaulay, F.
MacDonald, H.
Macintyre, S.
MacKay, A.
Maclane, S.
Maclaurin, C.
MacMahon, P.
MacMillan, W.
Magini, G.
Magnitsky, L.
Mahalanobis, P.
Mahani, A.
Mahavira
Maior, J.
Malfatti, G.
Malthus, T.
Maltsev, A.
Mannheim, V.
Mansfield, J.
Mansion, P.
Mansur ibn Ali ibn Iraq
Markov, A.
Marrat, W.
Martin, A.
Mascheroni, L.
Maschke, H.
Maseres, F.
Mason, J.
Mathews, G.
Mathieu, E.
Maupertuis, P.
Maurolico, F.
Maxwell, J.
Mayer, C.
Mazurkiewicz, S.
McCartney, W.
McCay, C.
McClintock, E.
McColl, H.
McCullagh, J.
McShane, E.
Mello, F.
Menaechmus
Menelaus of Alexandria
Mengoli, P.
Meray, H.
Mercator, N.
Mercer, J.
Merrifield, C.
Mersenne, M.
Meshchersky, I.
Metius, J.
Meusnier de la Place, J.
Meyer, W.
Milankovich, M.
Milhaud, G.
Miller, G.
Millikan, C.
Milne, E.

Milner, I.
Minding, E.
Minkowski, H.
Minto, W.
Mises, R.
Mittag-Leffler, M.
Mobius, A.
Moerbeke, W.
Mohr, G.
Moivre, A.
Molin, F.
Mollweide, K.
Monge, G.
Monte, G.
Montgomery, D.
Montmore, P.
Montucla, J.
Moore, C.L.
Moore, E.
Moore, J.
Mordell, L.
Morgan, A.
Morganstern, O.
Morland, S.
Morley, F.
Morrey, C.
Morse, H.M.
Moseley, H.
Mouton, G.
Muhyil-Din al-Maghribi
Muller, J.
Mumford, D.
Munisvara Visvarupa
Murnaghan, F.
Murphy, R.
Muskhelishvili, N.
Mydorge, C.
Myers, T.
Mylon, C.
Nairne, E.
Napier, J.
Narayana
Nasawi, A.
Nayrizi, A.
Neander, M.
Neile, W.
Nekrasov, A.
Netto, E.
Neuberg, J.
Neumann, C.
Newell, H.
Newsom, C.
Newton, H.A.
Newton, J.
Neyman, J.
Nicholas of Cusa
Nicholson, P.
Nicollet, J.
Nicomachus of Gerasa
Nicomedes
Nielsen, N.
Nieuwentijt, B.
Nixon, H.
Noether, A.
Noether, M.
Norlund, N.
Norwood, R.

Nunez, P.
Nunez Salaciense, P.
O'Brien, M.
Ocagne, P.
Oenopides of Chios
Oliver, J.E.
Oresme, N.
Orr, W.
Ortega, J.
Osgood, W.
Ostrogradsky, M.
Oughtred, W.
Ozanam, J.
Pacioli, L.
Padoa, A.
Painleve, P.
Pappus
Parkinson, S.
Parkinson, T.
Parseval des Chenes, M.
Pascal, B.
Pasch, M.
Pasor, M.
Patrizi, F.
Patterson, R.
Peacock, G.
Peano, G.
Pearson, E.
Pearson, K.
Pecham, J.
Peck, W.
Peirce, B.
Peirce, B.O.
Peirce, J.
Pekeris, C.
Peletier, J.
Pell, J.
Pemberton, H.
Penrose, R.
Peres, J.
Perseus
Peter Philomena
Peterson, K.
Petrovsky, I.
Peurbach, G.
Pfaff, J.
Picard, C.
Pieri, M.
Pike, N.
Pincherle, S.
Pitiscus, B.
Plana, G.
Plato of Tivoli
Playfair, J.
Plucker, J.
Pogorelov, A.
Poincare, J.
Poinsot, L.
Poleni, G.
Poncelet, J.
Pontryagin, L.
Poretsky, P.
Porta, G.
Porter, M.
Post, E.
Potts, R.
Pratt, J.H.

Prevost, I.
Pringsheim, A.
Privalov, I.
Privat de Molieres, J.
Proudman, J.
Puerbach, G.
Puiseux, V.
Pythagoras
Qadi Zada al-Rumi
Quetelet, L.
Quhi, A.
Quillan, D.
Rademacher, H.
Rado, J.
Radon, J.
Ramanujan, S.
Ramee, P.
Ramsden, J.
Ramsey, F.
Razmadze, A.
Recorde, R.
Rees, M.
Reidemeister, K.
Reinhold, E.
Reissner, E.
Reye, T.
Rey Pastor, J.
Rheticus, G.
Ribaucour, A.
Riccati, J.
Riccati, V.
Ricci, M.
Ricci, M.
Ricci, O.
Ricci-Curbastro, G.
Richard of Wallingford
Richard, J.
Richard, L.
Richardson, A.
Richardson, R.
Riddle, E.
Riemann, G.
Ries, A.
Riesz, F.
Risner, F.
Ritt, J.
Roberts, M.
Robertson, A.
Robertson, J.
Roberval, G.
Robins, B.
Robinson, H.
Robinson, J.
Rogers, L.
Rogosinski, W.
Rohn, K.
Rolle, M.
Roomen, A.
Rosanes, J.
Rosenhain, J.
Routh, E.
Rowning, J.
Rudio, F.
Rudolff, C.
Ruffini, P.
Rumovsky, S.
Runge, C.

Runkle, J.
Russell, B.
Rutherford, W.
Rydberg, J.
Ryley, J.
Safford, T.
St. Venant, A.
St. Vincent, G.
Saks, S.
Salmon, G.
Samarqandi, S.
Samawal, Y.
Sault, R.
Saunderson, N.
Saurin, J.
Scheffers, G.
Schickard, W.
Schlafli, L.
Schmidt, E.
Schoenflires, A.
Schooten, F.
Schott, G.
Schoute, P.
Schouten, J.
Schroeder, F.
Schroeter, H.
Schubert, H.
Schur, I.
Schwarz, H.
Schweikart, F.
Scott, C.
Segre, C.
Seidell, P.
Seki, T.
Semple, H.
Serenus
Serre, J.
Serret, J.
Servois, F.
Sestini, B.
Severi, F.
Sezawa, K.
Shanks, W.
Shannon, C.
Sharp, A.
Shatunovsky, S.
Sherman, F.
Shirakatsi, A.
Shnirelman, L.
Shohat, J.
Siegel, C.
Sierpinski, W.
Siguenza y Gorgora, C.
Sijzi, A.
Simpson, N.
Simpson, T.
Simson, R.
Sinan ibn Thabit, A.
Skolem, A.
Slaught, H.
Sluse, R.
Slutsky, E.
Smale, S.
Smirnov, N.
Smirnov, V.I.
Smith, H.J.
Smith, J.

Smyth, W.
Snell, E.
Snell, W.
Sobolev, S.
Sokhotsky, Y.
Somerville, M.
Sommerville, D.
Somov, O.
Sonin, N.
Soule, G.
Spencer, D.
Spencer, W.
Spillman, W.
Sporus of Nicaea
Spottiswoode, W.
Sretenskii, L.
Sridhara
Sripati
Stackel, P.
Stampioen, J.
Staudt, K.
Steiner, J.
Steinitz, E.
Steklov, V.
Stepanov, V.
Stephanus of Alexandria
Stevin, S.
Stewart, M.
Stieltjes, T.
Stifel, M.
Stirling, J.
Stoddard, J.F.
Stoker, J.
Stokes, G.
Stolz, O.
Stone, M.
Stormer, F.
Story, W.
Stringham, W.
Strode, T.
Strong, T.
Study, E.
Sturm, F.
Suter, H.
Sylow, P.
Sylvester, J.
Szasz, O.
Tacquet, A.
Tait, P.
Tamarkin, J.
Tanner, J.
Tannery, J.
Tarski, A.
Tartaglia, N.
Tate, T.
Tauber, A.
Taurinus, F.
Taylor, B.
Taylor, G.
Taylor, H.
Thabit ibn Qurra, S.
Theaetetus
Theodorus of Cyrene
Theodosius of Bithynia
Theon of Alexandria
Theon of Smyrna
Theudius of Magnesia

Thiele, T.
Thomas, T.
Thomaz, A.
Thompson, J.
Thompson, Z.
Thomson, J.
Thomson, W.
Thue, A.
Thymaridas
Tikhonov, A.
Tilly, J.
Tinseau d'Amondans, C.
Titchmarch, E.
Todd, H.
Todhunter, I.
Toeplitz, O.
Torporley, N.
Townsend, R.
Tropfke, J.
Tschirnhaus, E.
Tsu Chung-Chih
Tunstall, C.
Turing, A.
Turnbull, H.
Turner, P.
Tusi, M.
Tusi, S.
Ulam, S.
Umawi, A.
Uqlidisi, A.
Uryson, P.
Valerio, L.
Vallee-Poussin, C.
Vance, S.
Vandermonde, A.
Van Vleck, E.
Varignon, P.
Vaughan, D.
Veblen, O.
Vekua, I.
Venable, C.
Venn, J.
Ver Eecke, P.
Verhulst, P.
Veronese, G.
Vessiot, E.
Viete, F.
Villalpando, J.
Vinogradov, I.
Vitali, G.
Viviani, V.
Vlack, A.
Volterra, V.
Von Neumann, J.
Voronoy, G.
Wald, A.
Wales, W.
Walker, F.
Walker, S.
Wallace, W.
Wallis, J.
Walsh, J.
Wangerin, A.
Waring, E.
Watson, G.
Watson, H.
Weber, H.

Wedderburn, J.
Weierstrass, K.
Weil, A.
Weingarten, J.
Wells, E.
Wells, W.
Werner, J.
Wessel, C.
Weyl, H.
Weyle, F.
Whately, R.
Wheeler, A.
Whiston, W.
White, H.S.
Whitehead, A.
Whitehead, J.
Whitney, H.
Whittaker, E.
Whyburn, G.
Widman, J.
Wieleitner, H.
Wiener, L.
Wilczynski, E.
Wilder, R.
Wilkins, J.
Wilks, S.S.
Wilson, E.
Wilson, J.
Wingate, E.
Winlock, J.
Wintner, A.
Witt, J.
Wittich, P.
Woepeke, F.
Wolstenholme, J.
Wood, J.
Wood, R.
Woodhouse, R.
Woodward, R.
Worthen, T.
Wren, C.
Wright, E.
Xenocrates of Chalcedon
Yang Hui
Yanney, B.
Yatisvrasabha
Yerushalmy, J.
Youden, W.
Young, G.
Young, J.
Young, W.
Yule, G.
Yunus, A.
Zanotti, E.
Zarankiewicz, K.
Zariski, O.
Zeno of Elia
Zeno of Sidon
Zenodorus
Zermelo, E.
Zeuthen, H.
Zhukavsky, N.
Zolotarev, E.
Zucchi, N.
Zygmund, A.

MEDICINE

(See also
Dentistry)

Abano, P.
Abbott, M.
Abernethy, J.
Abrams, A.
Abreu, A.
Acosta, C.
Adam of Bodenstein
Adams, R.
Addams, J.
Addison, T.
Aesculapius
Aetius of Amida
Agathinus, C.
Agnodice
Agricola, G.
Agrippa, H.
Alberti, S.
Albinus, B.
Albright, F.
Alcmaeon of Crotona
Alderotti, T.
Alexander of Trailles
Alibert, J.
Allbutt, T.
Alpini, P.
Alzheimer, A.
Anderson, E.
Andral, G.
Apathy, S.
Aranzio, G.
Arbuthnot, J.
Archigenes
Arderne, J.
Aretaeus the Cappadician
Armstrong, H.G.
Arnald of Villanova
Aschoff, L.
Asclepiades
Ashford, B.
Assalti, P.
Astruc, J.
Astwood, E.
Athenaeus of Attalia
Auenbrugger, J.
Avicenna
Ayerza, A.
Babinski, J.
Baccelli, G.
Baier, J.J.
Bailey, C.P.
Baillie, M.
Baillou, G.
Baker, W.M.
Bakulov, A.N.
Balavignus
Bang, B.
Banting, F.G.
Barany, R.
Bard, S.
Barnard, C.N.
Barringer, E.D.

Barry, D.
Bartolomeo de Varignana
Bartolotti, G.G.
Barton, W.P.
Bassini, E.
Bateman, T.
Bates, W.H.
Bayle, G.L.
Beck, L.C.
Beddoes, T.
Beevor, C.E.
Behring, E.A.
Belleval, P.R.
Bender, L.
Bennett, H.S.
Bennett, J.H.
Berard, J.F.
Berengario de Capri, G.
Berigard, C.G.
Beringer, J.B.
Berkman, B.
Berry, C.A.
Bichat, M.F.
Bigelow, H.J.
Bigelow, J.
Billings, J.S.
Bird, G.
Birnie, J.H.
Bizzozero, G.
Black, J.
Blackwell, E.
Blair, P.
Blake, F.G.
Blalock, A.
Blane, G.
Blumberg, B.S.
Blundell, J.
Bocage, A.
Bodington, G.
Boeck, C.P.
Boerhaave, H.
Bogdanov, A.
Bohn, J.
Bond, G.F.
Bonet, T.
Bonomo, G.
Bordeu, T.
Borel, P.
Borgognoni of Lucca
Bostock, J.
Botallo, L.
Bouillard, J.
Bourdelot, P.
Bourgeois, L.
Bovell, J.
Bowen, G.
Bowman, W.
Boyd, J.S.
Boylston, Z.
Bradford, J.
Braid, J.
Brain, W.
Bramson, M.
Breckinridge, M.
Bretonneau, P.
Brever, J.
Bright, R.

Broadbent, W.
Broca, P.
Brodie, B.C.
Broussais, F.
Brown, J.
Brunschwig, H.
Buchner, F.
Budd, W.
Buonamici, F.
Burdenko, N.
Burkitt, D.
Burnet, F.
Burwell, C.
Busk, G.
Butlan, A.
Cabanis, P.
Cadogan, W.
Cadwalader, T.
Caius, J.
Cardozo, W.
Carlisle, A.
Carpenter, W.
Carrel, A.
Carson, J.
Casal Julian, G.
Cawley, A.
Cazenave, A.
Chadwick, E.
Chagas, C.
Chalmers, L.
Chapman, N.
Charaka
Charcot, J.M.
Chardenon, J.
Charnley, J.
Chauliac, G.
Chayne, G.
Cheyne, J.
Christophers, S.
Churchill, E.
Clarke, C.
Clarke, N.
Coggeshall, L.
Cogrossi, C.
Cohen, J.
Colden, C.
Cole, R.
Colles, A.
Collie, J.
Colman, B.
Comfort, A.
Constantine the African
Cooley, D.
Coons, A.
Cooper, A.
Cooper, I.
Cooper, K.
Copland, J.
Cordus, E.
Cornely, P.
Corner, G.
Cornette, C.
Cornil, A.
Corrigan, D.
Corvisart, J.
Cotugno, D.
Cotzias, G.

Cournand, A.
Courrier, R.
Courvoisier, L.
Covina, S.
Crede, C.
Creighton, C.
Crollius, O.
Cruz, O.
Cullen, W.
Culpepper, N.
Curling, T.
Cushing, H.
DaCosta, J.
Dailey, V.
Dalechamps, J.
Dalldorf, G.
Danforth, S.
Darity, W.
Darwin, E.
Daubenton, L.
Davaine, C.
Davis, N.
Davison, W.
DeBakey, M.
DeChauliac, G.
Dedekind, J.
Dee, J.
DeForest, E.
Dejerine, J.
Delgado, J.
Demikhov, V.
DeMondeville, H.
Denis, J.
Dent, C.
Descourtilz, M.
Dioscorides, P.
Dix, D.
Djerassi, I.
Dmchowski, L.
Dobson, M.
Dochez, A.
Dock, L.
Dodoens, R.
Dombey, J.
Donaldson, H.
Dorn, G.
Douglass, W.
Dover, T.
Doyle, A.
Dragstedt, L.
Drake, D.
Drew, C.
Drowne, S.
Dubini, A.
DuBois, E.
DuChenne, G.
Duchesne, J.
DuCoudray, A.
Dudley, S.
Duffield, S.
Duke-Elder, W.
Dunham, E.
Eagle, H.
Eller von Brockhausen, J.
Elliott, T.
Ent, G.
Erasistratus

Erasmus, D.
Erb, W.
Escherich, T.
Eschscholtz, J.
Esmarch, J.
Fabricius, H.
Fabry, W.
Fairley, N.
Fallot, A.
Farber, S.
Farr, W.
Fauvel, S.
Fenger, C.
Fergusson, W.
Fernandez-Moran, H.
Fernel, J.
Ferrier, D.
Efirth, S.
Fibiger, J.
Fielding, G.
Fiessinger, N.
Finlay, C.
Finsen, N.
Fitz, R.
Flechsig, P.
Flickinger, D.
Flint, A.
Floyer, J.
Forel, A.
Forsmann, W.
Fothergill, J.
Fowler, L.
Fracastoro, G.
Francis, T.
Frank, J.
Frank, P.
Friend, J.
Freis, E.
Freke, J.
Frerichs, F.
Frohlich, A.
Galen of Pergamum
Gall, F.
Gamble, J.
Gant, J.
Garnett, T.
Garnot, P.
Garrod, A.
Garth, S.
Geminus, T.
Geoffroy, E.F.
Geoffroy, E.L.
Gerbezius, M.
Gershon-Cohen, J.
Ghisi, M.
Gibbon, J.
Gilbert, W.
Gilbertus
Gillain, M.
Girtanner, C.
Glisson, E.
Goldberger, J.
Golgi, C.
Gooch, R.
Good, R.
Gorer, P.
Gorgas, W.

Gorrie, J.
Gowans, J.
Gowers, W.
Graham, E.
Grant, D.
Grashchenkov, N.
Graves, R.
Grew, N.
Gross, S.
Gruber, M.
Gudden, J.
Guglielmo de Corvi
Guidi, G.
Guillemin, R.
Guinter, J.
Guion, C.
Gull, W.
Gullstrand, A.
Guthrie, G.
Guthrie, S.
Gyorgy, P.
Haddow, A.
Haden, R.
Hahnemann, C.
Hale-White, W.
Halford, H.
Hall, M.
Hallopeau, H.
Halsted, W.
Hamilton, A.
Hammond, W.
Harley, G.
Harpestraeng, H.
Harris, W.
Hartman, F.
Hartmann, J.
Harvey, W.
Havers, C.
Haygarth, J.
Head, H.
Heberdon, W.
Hebra, F.
Heister, L.
Helm, J.
Hench, P.
Henoch, E.
Henry of Mondeville
Henry, J.
Herapath, W.
Hering, H.
Herrick, C.L.
Hertz, R.
Heurne, J.
Hewson, W.
Hey, W.
Heymans, C.
Hiarne, U.
Hicks, J.
Hildegarte of Bingen
Hillary, W.
Hilleman, M.
Hippocrates of Cos
His, W.
His, W. Jr.
Highmore, N.
Hitchings, G.
Hoadley, B.

Hodges, N.
Hodgkin, T.
Hodgson, J.
Hoffmann, F.
Hogarth, W.
Holland, J.
Hollingsworth, D.
Holmes, G.
Holmes, O.
Home, E.
Home, F.
Hope, J.
Hopkins, L.
Horner, J.
Horsfall, F.
Horsley, V.
Hosack, D.
Howard, J.
Huebner, R.
Huggins, C.
Humphry, G.
Hunayn ibn Ighaq
Hunt, H.
Hunter, J.
Huntington, G.
Huntington, G.S.
Hutchinson, J.
Hutten, U.
Huxham, J.
Hyde, H.
Imhotep
Igenhousz, J.
Ingrassia, G.
Isaac Israeli
Isaacs, C.
Ishaq ibn Hunayn
Jackson, J.H.
Jacobi, M.
Jacobson, L.
Jadassohn, J.
Jaeger, G.
Jefferson, G.
Jenner, E.
Jenner, W.
Jex-Blake, S.
John of Goddesden
Jones, A.
Jones, J.
Jordan, S.
Juljul, S.
Kantrowitz, A.
Kaplan, H.
Kaposi, M.
Karim, S.
Karman, H.
Keates, J.
Keen, W.
Kellner, D.
Kelly, H.
Kelsey, F.
Khunrath, C.
Khunrath, H.
Kirkes, W.
Klebs, E.
Kleegman, S.
Klein, E.
Kline, N.

Koeher, T.
Kolff, W.
Koller, C.
Kolosov, N.
Konig, E.
Korsakov, S.
Kraepelin, E.
Krafft-Ebing, R.
Krasno, L.
Krehl, L.
Kretschmer, E.
Kunh, A.
Kumm, H.
Kussmaul, A.
LaBrosse, G.
Lachapelle, M.
Laennec, R.
Lambo, T.
LaMettrie, J.
Lamy, G.
Lancisi, G.
Landsteiner, K.
Lange, C.
Langenbeck, B.
Laragh, J.
Larghi, B.
Larrey, D.
Larson, L.
Laszlo, D.
Laveran, C.
Lawless, T.
Lawrence, W.
Laycock, T.
Lazear, J.
Leboyer, F.
LeCat, C.
LeClerc, D.
Lee, C.
Leonhardi, J.
Leoniceno, N.
L'Esperance, E.
Lettsom, J.
Levadit, C.
Lever, J.
Lewis, T.
Lewis, T.R.
Leyden, E.
Li, C.
Li, M.
Liceage, E.
Lieutaud, J.
Lillehei, C.
Linacre, T.
Lind, J.
Lister, J.
Lister, J.
Liston, R.
Loeb, L.
Loeb, R.
Logan, M.
Long, C.
Long, E.
Longcope, W.
Lorry, A.
Louis, P.
Lovejoy, E.
Lovelace, W.

Lovell, J.
Lowe, P.
Lower, R.
Lusitanus, A.
Lusk, G.
Macbride, D.
Macewen, W.
Mackenzie, J.
Mackenzie, M.
Macklin, M.
MacNider, W.
MacWilliam, J.
Magati, C.
Maggi, B.
Magnus, R.
Mahomed, F.
Maimon, M.
Majocchi, D.
Majusi, A.
Malgaigne, J.
Malpighi, M.
Manardo, G.
Mann, F.
Manson, P.
Marci of Kronland
Marcy, H.
Margai, M.
Marie, P.
Marliani, G.
Martin, H.
Marum, M.
Massa, N.
Masters, W.
Mather, C.
Mattioli, P.
Maugham, W.
Mauriceau, F.
Maxcy, K.
Mayerne, T.
Mayo, H.
Mazzini, L.
McBurney, C.
McCarty, M.
McClellan, G.
McDermott, W.
McDowell, E.
McGrigor, J.
McLean, J.
McMichael, J.
McQuarrie, I.
Mead, R.
Means, J.
Mease, J.
Meckel, J.
Mendel, B.
Mendenhall, D.
Menghini, V.
Meniere, P.
Menuret de Chambaud, J.
Mercati, M.
Mering, J.
Meriwether, W.
Merrem, D.
Mery, J.
Mesmer, F.
Mesnil, F.
Mettauer, J.

Meyer, H.
Mibelli, V.
Mikulicz, J.
Milkman, L.
Miller, C.
Miller, H.W.
Miller, J.F.
Millington, T.
Milroy, W.
Minkowski, O.
Minoka-Hill, L.
Minot, G.
Mitchell, S.W.
Moffett, T.
Moleschott, J.
Monakow, C.
Monardes, N.
Moniz, A.
Moore, N.
Morgan, J.
Morcichini, D.
Morin, J.
Morton, R.
Morton, W.
Moss, W.
Mott, V.
Mottram, J.
Moynihan, B.
Muralt, J.
Murchison, C.
Murphy, J.
Murphy, W.
Murray, G.
Murray, L.
Murrell, W.
Musgrave, W.
Nafis, A.
Naunyn, B.
Neander, M.
Neisser, A.
Nemesius
Nestor
Nettleship, E.
Nicolle, C.
Nifo, A.
Nightingale, F.
Nissl, F.
Noorden, C.
Nostradamus, M.
Nylander, F.
Ochsner, A.
Oddi, R.
Oribasius
Orta, G.
Osler, W.
Otto, J.
Oudemans, C.
Pacchioni, A.
Page, I.
Paget, J.
Palmer, C.E.
Palmer, W.
Pancoast, J.
Panum, P.
Paracelsus
Pare, A.
Parker, W.

Parkinson, J.
Parkman, P.
Parry, C.H.
Paul of Aegina
Paul, J.
Peacock, T.
Pearce, L.
Pekelharing, C.
Peletier, J.
Pendleton, E.
Penfield, W.
Percival, T.
Perkins, E.
Perrault, C.
Petit, J.
Petrov, N.
Pettenkofer, M.
Pettigrew, T.
Pezard, A.
Philinus of Cos
Philip, A.
Philolaus of Crotona
Physick, P.
Pinel, P.
Pirogoff, N.
Piso, W.
Pitcairn, A.
Pitts, R.
Platter, F.
Plencie, M.
Plummer, A.
Poggiale, A.
Poindexter, H.
Politzer, A.
Pollender, A.
Pollitzer, S.
Porta, L.
Portal, A.
Potain, P.
Pott, P.
Pourfour de Petit, F.
Powell, R.
Preston, A.
Priestley, J.G.
Pringle, J.
Prothro, J.
Pruner-Bey, F.
Putnam, J.
Quatrefages de Breau, J.
Queckenstedt, H.
Quff, A.
Quincke, H.
Qusta ibn Luqa
Rabb, M.
Rabelais, F.
Radcliffe, J.
Ramazzini, B.
Rammelkamp, C.
Ramsay, D.
Ranchin, F.
Ranson, S.
Raspail, F.
Rayer, P.
Raynaud, M.
Recklinghausen, F.
Redfern, P.
Redi, F.

Redman, J.
Reed, W.
Rehn, L.
Reil, J.
Reiter, H.
Remak, R.
Renault, J.
Rendu, H.
Rensselaer, J.
Retzius, A.
Retzius, M.
Rhazes
Richards, D.
Richardson, B.
Ricord, P.
Ridwan, A.
Riehl, G.
Rima, T.
Ringer, S.
Rio-Hortega, P.
Riolan, J.
Riva-Rocci, S.
Robertson, A.
Robertson, O.
Robitzek, E.
Rock, J.
Roger, H.
Rogers, L.
Roget, P.
Rokitansky, C.
Rollet, J.
Rollier, A.
Romberg, M.
Roomen, A.
Rose, M.
Rosen, N.
Rosen, S.
Rosenheim, M.
Ross, R.
Rosslin, E.
Rostan, L.
Rouget, C.
Ruel, J.
Ruffini, P.
Rufinus
Rufus of Ephesus
Rulan, M.
Ruscelli, G.
Rush, B.
Rushd, A.
Rusk, H.
Sabin, F.
Sabouraud, R.
Sacco, L.
Sala, A.
Salaman, R.
Salisbury, J.
Salviani, I.
Samawal, Y.
Samoylov, A.
Sanarelli, G.
Sanchez, F.
Sanctorius, S.
Santorini, G.
Sauerbruch, F.
Scaliger, J.
Scarpa, A.

Schally, A.
Scheer, A.
Schegk, J.
Schmiedeberg, O.
Schonlein, J.
Schrenck-Notzig, A.
Schroeder van der Kolk, J.
Sedgwick, W.
Selikoff, I.
Selye, H.
Semmelweiss, I.
Sennert, D.
Sergent, F.
Servetus, M.
Severino, M.
Severinus, P.
Sextus Empiricus
Shabanova, A.
Shannon, J.
Shattuck, L.
Shear, M.
Sherrington, C.
Shippen, W.
Shope, R.
Shumway, N.
Siebold, C.
Siegenmundin, J.
Simon, J.
Simpson, J.
Sims, J.
Sinnot, J.
Skoda, J.
Slavson, S.
Sloane, H.
Slye, M.
Smadel, J.
Smellie, W.
Smith, E.
Smith, N.
Smollet, T.
Snow, J.
Solandt, O.
Sones, F.
Soranus
Southam, C.
Speranskii, G.
Sperry, R.
Stamler, J.
Stapp, J.
Steel, G.
Steptoe, P.
Sternberg, G.
Stevens, E.
Still, G.
Stille, A.
Stokes, W.
Stone, C.
Strughold, H.
Strumpel, A.
Struss, J.
Stuart, M.
Suchten, A.
Sudhoff, K.
Susruta
Sutton, W.
Swieten, G.
Sydenham, T.
Sylvius, F.

Syme, J.
Tabari, A.
Tabari, A.
Tabor, J.
Tagliacozzi, G.
Tait, R.
Taussig, H.
Ten Rhyne, W.
Thacher, J.
Thayer, W.
Theiler, M.
Theodoric of Cervia
Thiersch, C.
Thomass, H.
Thorn, G.
Thornton, W.
Tibbon, M.
Tillett, W.
Tilmidh, A.
Tilton, J.
Tissot, S.
Todd, C.
Torre, M.
Tournefort, J.
Townsend, J.
Traube, L.
Travers, B.
Trendelenburg, A.
Troja, M.
Troshin, A.
Trousseau, A.
Trulli, G.
Tufayl, A.
Tulp, N.
Turck, L.
Turisanus
Turner, D.
Turner, W.
Turquet de Mayerne, T.
Tyson, E.
Ulstad, P.
Unna, P.
Unzer, J.
Urbach, E.
Vallisnieri, A.
Valverde, J.
Van Helmont, J.
Van Swieten, G.
Vaquez, L.
Varolio, C.
Vassale, C.
Velpeau, A.
Venel, G.
Vicq d'Azyr, F.
Vidal, E.
Vieussens, R.
Vigo, G.
Villemin, J.
Volkmann, R.
Von Graefe, A.
Waite, F.
Wakeman, A.
Wakley, T.
Walker, J.
Waller, A.D.
Waller, A.V.
Wallich, G.

Walsh, W.
Walshe, F.
Walter, W.
Wangensteen, O.
Warren, J.
Waterhouse, B.
Watson, M.
Watt, R.
Webb, W.
Webster, J.
Wedel, G.
Weigert, C.
Weld, J.
Wells, H.
Wepfer, J.
Werlhof, P.
Wernicke, C.
Wertheim, E.
Wharton, T.
Whistler, D.
Whitby, L.
White, C.
Whytt, R.
Wickersheimer, E.
Widal, F.
Wiener, A.
Wilbur, R.
Wilder, R.
Wilkins, R.
Wilks, S.
Willan, R.
Williams, D.
Willis, T.
Wilson, S.
Winterbottom, T.
Winthrop, J.
Wiseman, R.
Withering, W.
Wolff, J.
Wood, H.
Woodward, J.J.
Wotton, E.
Wright, E.
Wright, H.
Wright, I.
Wright, J.
Wright, L.
Wunderlich, C.
Yalow, R.
Yegorov, B.
Yerby, A.
Yersin, A.
Young, T.
Zahrawi, A.
Zaluzansky Ze Zaluzan, A.
Zambeccari, G.
Zuhr, A.

METALLURGY

Aall, C.
Ageev, N.
Allen, N.
Andrews, T.
Bain, E.

Barba, A.
Becket, F.
Beliaev, N.
Bell, I.
Belyayev, A.
Benedicks, C.A.
Biringuccio, V.
Bochvar, A.A.
Bragg, R.
Brinell, J.
Cancrin, F.
Carpenter, H.
Charpy, A.
Chernov, D.
Chevenard, P.
Chizhokov, D.
Clouet, J.
Cobb, R.
Cottrell, A.
Cowles, A.
D'Arcambal, A.
DeChalmot, G.
Desch, C.
Douglas, J.
Drown, T.
Edwards, C.
Elridge, C.
Elyutin, V.
Emelyanov, V.
Ercker, L.
Evans, U.
Frary, F.
Goodeve, C.
Guertlen, W.
Guillet, L.
Hadfield, R.
Haynes, E.
Heroult, P.
Heyn, E.
Hirsch, P.
Holloman, J.
Hume-Rothery, W.
Jars, A.
Jeffries, Z.
Karsten, K.
Kaufmann, A.
Kinzel, A.
Kirkaldy, D.
Kruesi, P.
Kurdyumov, G.
Kurosawa Motoshige
Mannesmann, R.
Martens, A.
Masamune
Mehl, R.
Merica, P.
Moray, R.
Mushet, D.
Oding, I.
Osmond, F.
Paton, B.
Pavlov, I.
Percy, J.
Pfeil, L.
Plattner, K.
Portevin, A.
Rinman, S.

Roberts-Austen, W.
Rosenhain, W.
Sage, B.
Sauveur, A.
Shimer, E.
Smirnov, V.I.
Smirnov, V.S.
Smith, C.
Snelus, G.
Stead, J.
Taub, J.
Theophilus
Thomas, S.
Udy, M.
Volskii, A.
Waring, W.
Zaymovskii, A.

METEOROLOGY

Abbe, C.
Aitken, J.
Babinet, J.
Bailey, S.
Beals, E.A.
Bentley, W.A.
Bergeron, T.
Bjerknes, J.
Blanford, H.
Blinova, E.
Bonaventura, F.
Brocard, P.
Brocklesby, J.
Brooks, C.
Broun, J.
Brunt, D.
Buys Ballot, C.
Byers, H.
Cabeo, N.
Capper, J.
Chalmers, L.
Charney, J.
Childrey, J.
Cline, I.
Coffin, J.
Cotte, L.
Craveri, F.
Daniell, J.
Dansgaard, W.
Dines, W.
Dorno, C.
Dorodnitsyn, A.
Dove, H.
Dunn, G.
Eliot, J.
Ellis, W.
Engelmann, G.
Erman, G.
Espy, J.
Ferrel, W.
Fitzroy, R.
Franklin, B.
Glaisher, J.
Gold, E.
Gregg, W.

Hann, J.
Hadley, G.
Harrington, M.
Hayden, E.
Hazen, H.
Hodgkinson, G.
Howell, W.
Howard, L.
Humphreys, W.
Jacobs, M.
Jeffries, J.
Johnson, N.
Joslin, B.
Kimball, J.
Kimble, G.
Klein, H.
Krick, I.
Lapham, I.
Leopold, L.
LeRoy, C.
Lining, J.
Lippincott, J.
Loomis, E.
Loveland, G.
Lowe, T.
MacKay, J.
MacKenzie, G.
Margules, M.
Marti Franques, A.
Martin, J.
Marvin, C.
Mason, B.
Masterman, S.
Maurer, J.
Maury, M.
McAdie, A.
Meldrum, C.
Mendenhall, T.
Mill, H.
Miller, B.
Mohn, R.
Mohorovicic, A.
Moyle, M.
Namias, J.
Nansen, F.
Odierna, G.
Oliver, A.
Orville, H.
Osler, A.
Palmen, E.
Palmieri, L.
Peek, C.
Piddington, H.
Plant, T.
Redfield, W.
Reichelderfer, F.
Richardson, L.
Riddell, C.
Robie, T.
Roche, E.
Ronalds, F.
Rossby, C.
Rotch, A.
Rowell, G.
Russell, H.
Schaefer, V.
Sekera, Z.

Seneca, L.
Shaw, W.
Sheppard, P.
Simpson, G.C.
Simpson, J.
Smallwood, C.
Smyth, C.
Spilhaus, A.
Sprung, A.
Starr, V.
Stevenson, T.
Swinden, J.
Symons, G.
Tacchini, P.
Teisserenc de Bort, L.
Vize, V.
Walker, G.
Wegener, A.
Welsh, J.
Wendelin, G.
Wexler, H.
White, R.
Wild, H.
Willett, H.
Wislizenus, F.
Young, C.

MICROBIOLOGY

Ames, L.
Beijerinkek, M.
Brown, R.
Bruce, D.
DeKruif, P.
Dubos, R.
Fitz-James, P.
Friend, C.
Gamaleya, N.
Gruby, D.
Hammon, W.
Hektoen, L.
Henrici, A.
Herelle, F.
Ierusalimskii, N.
Imschenetsky, A.
Ivanonsky, D.
Kelser, R.
Kendrick, P.
Krasilanov, N.
Kuznetsov, S.
Lochhead, A.
Loeffler, F.
Mayer, R.
McClendon, D.
Meisel, M.
Nathans, D.
Noguchi, H.
Pirie, N.
Prowazek, S.
Robbins, F.
Salk, J.
Schlessinger, D.
Schultze, F.
Shaposhnikov, V.
Smith, T.
Smith, W.

Steinhaus, E.
Tarshis, M.
Van Niel, C.
Vinogradsky, S.
Vishniac, R.
Wallace, J.
Weil, A.
Young, R.
Zinder, N.

MICROSCOPY

Amici, G.
Baker, H.
Barnard, J.
Bauer, F.
Beale, L.S.
Borries, B.
Brocklesby, J.
Chamot, E.
Gleichen-Russworm, W.
Harting, P.
Heldenhain, M.
Joblot, L.
Kohler, A.
Leeuwenhoek, A.
Power, H .
Pritchard, A.
Reade, J.
Riddell, J.
Salisbury, J.
Smith, H.L.
Stelluti, F.
Ward, R.

MINERALOGY

Alger, F.
Allan, T.
Babington, W.
Bauerman, H.
Baumhauer, H.
Baylak al-Qibjaqi
Becke, F.
Berthier, P.
Beudant, F.
Blomstrand, C.
Boodt, A.
Booth, S.
Born, I.
Bournon, J.
Breithaupt, J.
Brochant de Villiers, A.
Bruce, A.
Butschli, O.
Carpenter, G.
Chapman, E.
Chenevix, R.
Clarke, E.
Cleaveland, P.
Cordier, P.
Cronstedt, A.
Dana, E.
Davies, T.

De la Fosse, C.
D'Elhuyar, D.
Del Rio, A.
Doelter, C.
Donnay, J.
Dufrenoy, O.
Elhuyar, F.
Eskola, P.
Fersman, A.
Fouque, F.
Freiesleben, J.
Frenzel, F.
Fuchs, J.
Gahn, J.
Gaudin, A.
Genth, F.
Goldsmith, E.
Grammont, A.
Gregor, W.
Groddeck, A.
Groth, P.
Grubenmann, J.
Gua de Malves, J.
Haidinger, W.
Hartmann, C.
Hauy, R.
Henckel, J.
Henwood, W.
Hessel, J.
Hisinger, W.
Hjelm, P.
Hoke, C.
Hubbard, O.
Hudson, R.
Hutchinson, A.
Johannsen, A.
Jolly, J.
Joy, C.
Keating, W.
Koenig, G.
Lacroix, A.
Lametherie, J.
Leonhard, K.
Levy, S.
Ludlam, H.
MacKenzie, G.
Mallard, E.
Mauguin, C.
Mawe, J.
Meade, W.
Michel-Levy, A.
Miers, H.
Mitscherlich, E.
Mohs, F.
Monnet, A.
Muller, F.
Naumann, F.
Necker, L.
Neumann, F.
Nicholson, H.
Palache, C.
Penfield, S.
Reich, F.
Renard, A.
Reuss, F.
Richter, H.
Rio, A.
Rome de L'Isle, J.

Rose, G.
Scovell, J.
Severgin, V.
Seybert, H.
Shepard, C.
Silliman, B.
Smith, J.L.
Smyth, W.
Sobolev, V.
Spencer, L.
Tennant, J.
Tifashi, S.
Troost, G.
Valmont de Bomare, J.
Vernadsky, V.
Waage, P.
Wallerius, J.
Weiss, C.
Werner, A.
Widmannstatten, A.
Williams, G.
Yeates, W.
Zambonini, F.
Zirkel, F.

MINING

Agoshkov, M.
Babcock, E.
Bascom, W.
Beckmann, J.
Berthier, P.
Buddle, J.
Chinakal, N.
Combes, C.
Davies, D.
Day, D.
Dechen, H.
DesCloizeaux, A.
Emmons, S.
Hartmann, C.
Heynitz, F.
Irving, R.
Jars, A.
Justi, J.
Karsten, K.
Krylov, A.
Mallard, E.
Maynard, G.
Melnikov, N.
Newton, H.
Ozersky, A.
Ries, A.
Rulein, V.
Sato Nobuhiro
Shevyakov, L.
Tilas, D.
Trebra, F.
Tyrrell, J.
Voigt, J.
Winchell, H.

NATURAL HISTORY

Abano, P.
Abbott, C.
Abbott, W.
Acosta, C.
Adanson, M.
Agassiz, E.
Agassiz, L.
Akeley, C.
Alberti, L.
Aldrovandi, U.
Allen, A.
Alzate y Ramirez, J.
Anderson, C.
Anderson, J.
Anderson, W.
Andrews, R.
Andrews, W.
Arderon, W.
Argenville, A.
Arnold, J.
Atwater, C.
Audebert, J.
Azara, F.
Babcock, E.
Badham, C.
Baikie, W.
Bailey, A.
Baker, T.R.
Barham, H.
Barlow, F.
Barnard, W.S.
Barr, L.S.
Barraband, J.
Bates, H.W.
Beckmann, J.
Bell, J.G.
Beringer, J.B.
Bert, P.
Bewick, T.
Bickmore, A.S.
Bigelow, E.F.
Blake, J.
Bland, T.
Blomefield, L.
Bloxam, A.
Blumenbach, J.
Blyth, E.
Bohn, H.
Bol, H.
Boll, J.
Bollard, N.
Bolles, F.
Bonnet, C.
Bosc, L.
Botteri, M.
Bowles, W.
Bowman, J.
Boycott, A.
Brady, H.
Brehm, A.
Breislak, S.
Briggs, J.
Brightwen, E.
Brisson, M.

Brittain, T.
Browne, T.
Buchheister, C.
Buckland, F.
Buckley, S.
Bullock, W.
Buonanni, F.
Burchell, W.
Burden, W.
Busk, G.
Caras, R.
Carpenter, W.
Carter, T.
Carver, J.
Casal Julian, J.
Catesby, M.
Cestoni, G.
Cetti, F.
Charlevoix, P.
Cherrie, G.
Childrey, J.
Childs, G.
Chisholm, A.
Clark, J.
Cohen, D.
Collingwood, C.
Collinson, P.
Colman, B.
Commerson, P.
Comstock, F.
Conklin, W.
Coolidge, D.
Cooper, D.
Cooper, W.
Cornish, C.
Costa, E.
Couch, J.
Couch, R.
Couper, J.
Courten, W.
Cramer, P.
Craveri, F.
Cuming, H.
Cutting, C.
Dalibard, T.
Dall, W.
Dalyell, J.
Damiri, M.
Damon, W.
Dana, J.D.
Darwin, C.R.
Daubenton, L.
Delaroche, F.
Denton, S.
Denys, N.
Derham, W.
Descourtilz, J.
Dillwyn, L.
Donovan, E.
Doubleday, H.
Doubleday, N.
Douglas, D.
Douglas, J.
Douglass, W.
Drake, C.
Drake, D.
DuChaillu, P.

Dudley, P.
DuSimitiere, P.
Edmondston, L.
Edmondston, T.
Edwards, G.
Eights, J.
Eklund, C.
Ellis, J.
Eyton, T.
Fabre, J.
Farb, P.
Fischer, J.
Flagg, T.
Forester, J.
Forster, T.
Fraser, L.
Fuhlrott, J.
Gaimard, J.
Garden, A.
Garman, H.
Gesner, K.
Gibbes, L.
Gibson, W.
Gmelin, J.
Godman, J.
Gohory, J.
Good, A.
Gosse, P.
Grant, M.
Gray, J.
Gray, S.
Griffith, E.
Guettard, J.
Gunn, R.
Gunther, A.
Hagenbeck, C.
Hamilton, W.
Harris, M.
Heermann, A.
Heim, R.
Heller, E.
Henshall, J.
Herbert, W.
Hernandez, F.
Herre, A.
Hewitson, W.
Hildrith, S.
Hoeven, J.
Hogg, J.
Holder, C.
Holmes, F.
Hornung, J.
Horsfield, T.
Hough, R.
Hudson, C.
Hudson, W.
Ingersoll, E.
Jackson, F.
Jacob, E.
Jaeger, E.
Jahiz, A.
Jameson, J.
Jameson, R.
Jefferies, R.
Johnson, M.
Johnston, G.
Johnstone, J.

Josselyn, J.
Jussieu, J.
Kalm, P.
Kidd, W.
King, S.
Kingsley, C.
Kirk, J.
Kittel, C.
Konig, E.
Krutch, J.
Kunze, R.
Labat, J.
Lahontan, A.
Lamouroux, J.
Landsborough, D.
Lankester, E.
Lapham, I.
Lawson, J.
Leach, W.
Leconte, J.
Leclerc, G.
LeConte, J.
Ledermuller, M.
Lee, L.
Leigh, C.
LeMoyne, J.
Leperkhin, I.
Lesson, R.
Lewin, W.
L'Herminier, F.
Lincecum, G.
Linsley, J.
Lister, T.
Longinos, Martinez, J.
Lord, J.
Low, G.
Lucas, F.
MacGillivray, W.
Madison, H.
Marshall, A.
Marsili, L.
Martin, M.
Martin, W.
Matthiessen, P.
Maynard, C.
McCown, J.
McCoy, F.
Mearns, E.
Merrett, C.
Michener, E.
Miller, H.
Mills, E.
Mitchell, E.
Mitchell, J.
Mitchill, S.
Mivart, St. G.
Molina, J.
Montagu, G.
More, T.
Morris, F.
Morton, J.
Moseley, E.
Moseley, H.
Mottram, J.
Muir, J.
Mulaik, S.
Muller, F.

Murie, M.
Murphy, R.
Murray, A.
Needham, J.T.
Neill, P.
Nelson, E.W.
Newman, E.
Newport, G.
Nuttall, J.
Oken, L.
Orton, J.
Osborn, F.
Oviedo, G.
Palmer, E.
Palmer, E.L.
Parkinson, S.
Patterson, R.
Pavy, O.
Peach, C.
Peale, C.
Peale, T.
Peck, W.
Perkins, G.
Peron, F.
Perrault, P.
Pickering, C.
Pineda y Ramirez, A.
Pitcher, Z.
Pliny the Elder
Plot, R.
Plumier, C.
Plummer, J.
Pouchet, F.
Putnam, F.
Raffles, T.
Rafinesque, C.
Ray, J.
Rensselaer, J.
Rennie, J.
Ristoro d'Arezzo
Robinet, J.
Robinson, P.
Roddy, H.
Roesel von Rosenhof, A.
Romans, B.
Rondelet, P.
Roosevelt, T.
Rouelle, J.
Ruckdeschel, C.
Rudbeck, O.
Russell, A.
St. Hilaire, A.
Salvin, O.
Sanderson, I.
Sarett, L.
Scammon, C.
Schmidel, C.
Schopf, J.
Scouler, J.
Selby, P.
Seton, E.
Sharp, D.
Shaw, G.
Simpson, C.
Sinclair, A.
Solander, D.
Sonnerat, P.

Soper, J.
Southwell, T.
Sowerby, J.
Stejneger, L.
Steller, G.
Stillingfleet, B.
Stone, W.
Stratton-Porter, G.
Strickland, H.
Sykes, W.
Targioni Tozzetti, G.
Tate, G.
Teale, E.
Telfair, C.
Templeton, J.
Thomas of Cantimpre
Thompson, D.
Thompson, J.
Thompson, W.
Thompson, Z.
Thomson, T.
Tradescant, J.
Trevelyan, W.
Tristram, H.
Trouvelot, F.
Tuckerman, F.
Tunstall, M.
Turner, W.
Ulloa y de la Torre Giral, A.
Unanue, J.
Underwood, W.
Valmont de Bomare, J.
Vega, G.
Virey, J.
Von Hagen, V.
Vosmer, A.
Walcott, M.
Wailes, B.
Wallace, A.
Ward, H.
Waterhouse, G.
Waterton, C.
Weed, C.
Westwood, J.
Wied, M.
Wilkins, H.
Willisel, T.
Willughby, F.
Wilson, E.
Wislizenus, F.
Wolf, J.
Wollaston, A.
Wood, J.G.
Woods, J.
Woodward, S.
Worm, O.
Wotton, E.
Wright, A.A.
Wright, E.
Wright, M.

NATURAL PHILOSOPHY

Allen, H.S.
Alsted, J.
Ames, W.

Anaximenes
Aquinas, T.
Aristotle
Ashmole, E.
Bacon, R.
Basso, S.
Blasius of Parma
Borro, G.
Boskovic, R.
Burley, W.
Camparella, T.
Celaya, J.
Comenius, J.
Coronel, L.
Desaguliers, J.T.
Dietrich von Freiberg
Digby, K.
Empedocles
Epicurus
Grosseteste, R.
Harris, J.
Herodotus of Halicarnassus
John of Dumbleton
Knight, W.
Knott, G.
Leslie, J.
Magnenus, J.
Marsilius of Inghen
Neckham, A.
Paley, W.
Paul of Venice
Pomponazzi, P.
Sarpi, P.
Shizuki, T.
Soto, D.
Swinshead, R.
Telesio, B.
Tilloch, A.
Towneley, R.
Ulrich of Strassbourg
White, T.
Witelo
Wollaston, F.
Zabarella, J.

NAVIGATION

Dudley, R.
Duperrey, L.
Lisboa, J.
Majid, S.
Medina, P.
Norman, R.
Pereira, D.
Sumner, T.

OCEANOGRAPHY

(See also
Marine Biology)

Agassiz, A.
Albert I

Bascom, W.
Bauer, P.
Beebe, C.W.
Bellinsgauzen, F.
Bent, S.
Berner, R.
Blumberg, R.
Bogorov, V.
Bruce, W.
Buchanan, J.
Charcot, J.
Cousteau, J.
Davis, C.
Deacon, G.
Deryugin, K.
Ehman, V.
Evans, F.
Ewing, W.M.
Forchhammer, J.
Franklin, B.
Harris, R.
Harvey, H.
Hass, H.
Heezen, B.
Hill, M.
Iselin, C.
Kemp, S.
Lanzarev, M.
Lindenkohl, A.
Link, E.
Maillet, B.
Makarov, S.
Maury, M.
Mesyatsev, I.
Mohn, H.
Murrey, J.
Nansen, F.
Palmen, E.
Parr, A.
Pettersson, H.
Piccard, A.
Piccard, J.
Pillsbury, J.
Pourtales, L.
Proudman, J.
Revelle, R.
Rossby, C.
Shtokman, V.
Spilhaus, A.
Stewart, H.
Stommel, H.
Sverdrup, H.
Thompson, T.
Tizard, T.
Vaughan, T.
Vize, V.
Zenkevich, L.
Zubov, N.

OPHTHALMOLOGY

Cumming, W.
Dalrymple, J.

OPTICS

Amici, G.
Bacon, R.
Barnard, J.
Barrow, I.
Bird, J.
Blair, R.
Brade, D.
Castelli, B.
Cooke, T.
Cornu, M.
Dietrich von Frieberg
Dollond, J.
Fitz, H.
Fleischer, J.
Fraunhofer, J.
Fresnel, A.
Gasciogne, W.
Grosseteste, R.
Grubb, H.
Grubb, T.
Gullstrand, A.
Hamilton, W.
Haytham, A.
Henry, P.
Hobbes, T.
Jansen, Z.
Kamal al-Din Abul Hasan
Laurent, P.
Lippershey, H.
Lister, J.J.
Logan, J.
Lummer, O.
Marksutov, D.
Malys, E.
Mellor, L.
Molyneux, S.
Niceron, J.
Nicol, W.
Pecham, J.
Porro, I.
Qutb al-Din al-Shirazi
Risner, F.
Schmidt, B.
Short, J.
Taylor, E.
Witelo
Wollaston, W.
Zeiss, C.

ORNITHOLOGY

Abbott, J.
Abert, J.
Adams, E.
Albin, E.
Allen, A.
Allen, C.A.
Allen, R.
Altum, B.
Armstrong, E.
Audubon, J.
Bailey, F.A.

Baldwin, S.
Bannerman, D.
Bartram, W.
Bendire, C.
Bent, A.
Blakiston, T.
Bonaparte, C.
Brand, A.
Brandt, H.
Brewer, T.
Brewster, W.
Brown, L.
Buller, W.
Cabot, S.
Cassin, J.
Chapin, J.
Chapman, F.
Charleton, W.
Clayton, J.
Clement, R.
Coiter, V.
Cooper, W.
Cory, C.
Coves, E.
Daggett, F.
Delacour, J.
Eaton, E.
Eckelberry, D.
Eisenmann, E.
Finsch, C.
Fisher, A.
Forbush, E.
Forster, J.
Frederick II
Gambel, W.
Gilliard, E.
Gould, J.
Gray, R.
Griscom, L.
Hammond, W.
Hartert, E.
Heinroth, O.
Henshaw, H.
Hewitt, O.
Higginson, F.
Hochbaum, H.
Hoyt, W.
Illiger, C.
Kelly, J.
Kinnear, N.
Knowlton, F.
Lack, D.
Latham, J.
Lawrence, G.
L'Ecluse, C.
Levaillant, F.
Lewis, H.
Lincoln, F.
Meinertzhagen, R.
Nauman, J.
Naumberg, E.
Nehrling, H.
Newton, A.
Nice, M.
North, M.
Nuttall, T.
Nutting, C.

Ober, F.
Oberholser, H.
Olds, H.
Pallas, P.
Pearson, T.
Peters, J.
Peterson, R.
Pettingill, O.
Phillips, J.
Ray, R.
Richmond, C.
Ridgeway, R.
Roberts, T.
Rodd, E.
Rumpf, G.
Sage, J.
Samuels, E.
Saunders, H.
Saxby, H.
Schelgel, H.
Sclater, P.
Scott, P.
Seebohm, H.
Sennett, G.
Sharpe, R.
Skutch, A.
Sprunt, A.
Stoddard, H.
Strachey, W.
Sutton, G.
Swales, B.
Temminck, C.
Thayer, J.
Torrey, B.
Townsend, J.
Trumbull, G.
Vieillot, L.
Wayne, A.
Wetmore, A.
Whitehead, J.
Wilson, A.
Woodhouse, S.
Xantus, J.

PALEONTOLOGY

Abel, O.
Ameghino, F.
Andrusov, N.
Arber, E.
Arkell, W.
Arnold, C.
Barghoorn, E.
Barrande, J.
Barrois, C.
Bassani, F.
Bassler, R.
Bather, F.
Beecher, C.
Bellardi, L.
Berry, E.
Beyrich, H.
Billings, E.
Boucher, J.
Boule, M.

Broili, F.
Brongniart, A.
Bronn, H.
Broom, R.
Brown, B.
Brown, R.
Buckland, W.
Bulman, O.
Bunbury, C.
Carpenter, P.
Chaney, R.
Chernyshev, F.
Christol, J.
Clark, B.
Clarke, J.
Clift, W.
Coggeshall, A.
Colbert, E.
Conrad, T.
Cooke, C.
Cooper, G.
Cope, E.
Cox, L.
Cushman, J.
Cuvier, G.
Dall, W.
Davidson, T.
Davies, W.
Dawkins, W.
Dawson, C.
Dawson, G.
Decker, C.
Deperet, C.
DesHayes, G.
Desor, P.
Dollo, L.
Douglass, E.
DuBois, E.
Dubois, M.
Edinger, T.
Edwards, W.
Egerton, P.
Ehrenberg, C.
Eichwald, K.
Etheridge, R.
Foerste, A.
Forbes, E.
Fraipont, J.
Fuhlrott, J.
Gabb, W.
Gardner, J.
Gaudry, A.
Gibbes, R.
Gidley, J.
Gillmann, H.
Gilmore, C.
Goeppert, H.
Goldring, W.
Gordon, W.
Gorski, I.
Gosselet, J.
Gould, S.
Grabau, A.
Grandeury, C.
Granger, W.
Gregory, W.
Gressly, A.

Hall, J. Jr.
Halle, T.
Harris, G.D.
Hatcher, J.
Haug, G.
Hay, O.
Heer, O.
Heilprin, A.
Helbaek, H.
Hibbard, C.
Hollick, C.
Hyatt, A.
Jaccard, A.
Jackson, R.T.
Jaeger, G.
Jaekel, O.
Jones, T.
Kellogg, A.R.
Kidston, R.
Kirk, E.
Knorr, G.
Knowlton, F.
Koenigswald, G.
Konninck, L.
Kovalevsky, V.
Krausel, R.
Lang, K.
Lartet, E.
Leakey, L.
Leakey, R.
Leidy, J.
Lesquereux, L.
Lhwyd, E.
Lohest, M.
Loomis, F.
Lull, R.S.
Mantell, G.
Marcou, J.
Marsh, O.
Matthew, W.
Mayry, C.
Mayer-Eymar, K.
Meek, F.
Mercati, M.
Meyer, C.
Moore, R.C.
Munier-Chalmas, E.
Nalivkin, D.
Nehring, A.
Neumayr, M.
Newberry, J.
Newell, N.
Newton, E.
Nicol, W.
Noe, A.
Nopsca, F.
Obermeier, O.
Oliver, F.
Oppel, A.
Orbigny, A.
Orlov, Y.
Osborn, H.F.
Pander, C.
Peabody, G.
Phillips, J.
Piette, L.
Quenstedt, F.

Raymond, P.
Reck, H.
Redfield, W.
Renault, B.
Renevier, E.
Resser, C.
Reuss, A.
Roemer, F.
Roemer, F.A.
Romer, A.
Rouillier, K.
Ruedemann, R.
Ruffer, M.
Russell, L.
Rutimeyer, K.
Saporta, L.
Schlotheim, E.
Schlumberger, C.
Schmerling, P.
Schopf, J.
Schuchert, C.
Scott, D.
Scott, W.
Seeley, H.
Seward, A.
Shumard, B.
Simpson, G.G.
Smith, J.P.
Sokolov, B.
Sollas, W.
Solms-Laubach, H.
Spath, L.
Spencer, W.
Springer, F.
Stearns, R.
Sternberg, C.
Stock, C.
Teilhard de Chardin, P.
Thomas, H.H.
Troxell, E.
Trueman, A.
Ulrich, E.
Vallois, H.
Verneuil, P.
Wachsmuth, C.
Wagner, W.
Walch, J.
Walcott, C.
Ward, L.
Warren, J.C.
White, C.A.
Whitfield, R.
Wieland, G.
Williams, H.
Williston, S.
Witham, H.
Woodring, W.
Woods, H.
Woodward, A.
Woodward, J.
Yakovlev, N.
Yandell, L.
Zalessky, M.
Zeiller, R.
Zejsner, L.
Zittel, K.

PARAPSYCHOLOGY

Rhine, J.

PARASITOLOGY

Adler, S.
Brumpt, E.
Cameron, T.
Cobbold, T.
Grassi, G.
Hall, M.
Hallier, E.
Leiper, R.
Linton, E.
Perroncito, E.
Rothschild, M.
Siebold, K.
Taliaferro, W.
Ward, H.B.

PATHOLOGY

Anichkov, N.
Aitken, W.
Banti, G.
Burn, C.
Cameron, G.
Carswell, R.
Cohnheim, J.
Councilman, W.
Davie, T.
DeWitt, L.
Dick, G.
Drury, A.
Duncan, C.
Ewing, J.
Flexner, S.
Florey, H.
Frantz, V.
Goodpasture, E.
Hamilton, D.
Heltoen, L.
Henle, F.
Kellaway, C.
Kettle, E.
Lamb, D.
Leishman, W.
Lustig, A.
MacCallum, W.
Maizels, M.
Marchi, V.
Marchiafava, E.
Muir, R.
Negri, A.
Opie, E.
Rich, A.
Ricketts, H.
Turnbull, H.
Tyzzer, E.
Upton, A.
Virchow, R.

Warren, S.
Webster, L.
Weichselbaum, A.
Wells, H.G.
Whipple, G.
Wollstein, M.
Wright, A.E.
Zawadzki, E.

PHARMACOLOGY

Baytar al-Malaqi, D.
Booker, W.
Bovet, D.
Brodie, B.
Burn, J.
Cervantes, V.
Claus,C.
Cordus, V.
Coxe, J.
Cushny, A.
Dale, H.
Engelhardt, F.
Fischer, R.
Glaser, C.
Kosterlitz, H.
Leech, P.
Li Shih-Chen
Mellanby, E.
Meltzer, S.
Meneghetti, E.
Overton, C.
Pereira, J.
Pires, T.
Rice, T.
Richards, A.
Serturner, F.
Snyder, S.
Squibb, E.
Thompson, M.
Vane, J.
Verney, E.
Viehoever, A.
Vigani, J.
Wackenroder, H.
Wafid, A.
Wood, H.C.
Zwelfer, J.

PHILOLOGY

Hadley, J.
Trumbull, J.

PHILOSOPHY

Abailard, P.
Abul-Barakat, B.
Alain de Lile
Alexander of Aphrodisias
Andreae, J.

Apelt, E.
Augustine of Hippo (St)
Bachelard, G.
Bacon, F.
Bajja, A.
Bede
Bellarmine, R.
Bergson, H.
Bernard of Chartres
Bernard of LeTreille
Bernard of Silvestre
Bisterfeld, J.
Boehme, J.
Boethius, A.
Bogdanov, A.
Bolzano, B.
Bouvelles, C.
Braun, A.C.
Bruno, G.
Brunschvieg, L.
Buridan, J.
Cabanis, P.
Carnap, R.
Carr, H.
Cassirer, E.
Chwistek, L.
Comte, I.
Condillac, E.
Crescas, H.
Crousaz, J.
Cudworth, R.
Dewey, J.
Dingler, H.
Dullaert of Ghent
Duns Scotus, J.
Engels, F.
Erastus, T.
Eriugena, J.
Eudemus of Rhoses
Farbi, A.
Francis of Marchia
Francis of Meyronnes
Frank. S.
Gassendi, P.
Ghazzali, A.
Glanvill, J.
Haldane, R.
Hamilton, W.
Heraclitos
Herbert, J.
Hippias of Elis
Hoene-Wronski, J.
Hume, D.
Iamblichus
James of Venice
John Philoponus
Kant, I.
Leibniz, G.
Lenin, V.
Leucippus
Locke, J.
Lovejoy, A.
Lucretius
Malebranche, N.
Marinus
Mayerson, E.
Mill, J.

Montesquieu, C.
More, H.
Ockham, W.
Parmenides of Elea
Plato
Plotinus
Posidonius
Psellus, M.
Radl, E.
Rey, A.
Rohault, J.
Schelling, F.
Siger of Brabart
Simplicius
Speusippus
Tabari, A.
Thales
Themistus
Thierry of Chartres
Turgot, A.
Vanini, G.
Vives, J.
Weigel, V.
William of Auvergne
William of Sherwood
Wittgenstein, L.
Wolff, C.
Xenocrates of Chalcedon
Xenophanes
Zeno of Citium
Zeno of Elea
Zeno of Sidon

PHILOSOPHY OF SCIENCE

Berkeley, G.
Carus, P.
Cotten, M.
Holbach, P.
Reichenbach, H.
Schlick, M.
Stallo, J.
Wright, C.

PHOTOGRAPHY

Abney, W.
Adams, A.
Brooker, L.
Daguerre, L.
Harding, F.
Himes, C.
Land, E.
Laussedat, A.
Lumiere, A.
Lumiere, L.
Muybridge, E.
Porter, E.
Schumann, V.
Talbot, W.
Tuffle, F.
Wedgwood, T.

PHRENOLOGY

Fowler, L.
Fowler, O.
Grimes, J.
Watson, H.
Wells, C.
Wells, S.

PHYSICS

Abbe, E.
Abraham, M.
Abul-Barakat, B.
Adams, E.
Aepinus, F.
Aguilon, F.
Aigrain, P.
Aitken, J.
Albert of Saxony
Albright, J.
Alcock, N.
Aleksandrov, A.
Alekseevskii, N.
Alfven, H.
Alikhanov, A.
Alikhanyan, A.
Alpher, R.
Alter, D.
Alvarez, L.
Amagat, E.
Ames, J.S.
Amontons, G.
Ampere, A.
Anderson, E.E.
Anderson, P.W.
Andrade, E.
Andrew, N.N.
Andrews, T.
Andronov, A.
Angeli, S.
Angstrom, A.J.
Anthony, W.
Apker, L.
Appel, P.E.
Appleton, E.
Arago, D.
Archimedes
Aris Toxenus
Arkadiev, U.
Armstrong, J.
Arnold, H.
Arrhenius, S.
Arsonval, A.
Artsimovich, L.
Astin, A.
Aston, F.
Atwood, G.
Auger, P.
Austin, L.W.
Avogadro, A.
Ayrton, H.
Babinet, J.
Bacher, R.F.

Back, E.A.
Bagnold, R.
Baldi, B.
Baliani, G.
Balmer, J.
Bardeen, J.
Barkla, C.
Barlow, P.
Barnard, J.
Barnes, A.
Barschall, H.
Bartoli, D.
Barus, C.
Basov, N.
Bates, L.
Bauer, E.
Bayma, J.
Beams, J.
Beccaria, G.
Becquerel, A.
Bequerel, H.
Bedell, F.
Beeching, R.
Beeckman, I.
Beghin, H.
Bekesy, G.
Belidor, B.
Bell, L.
Bellani, A.
Benedetti, G.
Benoit, J.
Benzenberg, J.
Berg, E.
Bergman, T.O.
Berigard, C.
Berkner, L.
Bernal, J.
Bernoulli, D.
Bertholon, P.
Berti, G.
Betancourt y Molina, A.
Bethe, H.A.
Bhabha, H.
Bialobzeski, C.
Biot, G.
Biot, M.
Birge, R.
Birkeland, K.
Bjerknes, C.
Bjerrum, N.
Black, J.
Blackett, P.
Blair, W.
Blaker, E.
Bleaney, B.
Blizard, E.
Bloch, F.
Blodget, K.
Bloembergen, N.
Blokhintsev, D.
Blondel, A.
Blondlot, R.
Bohr, A.
Bohr, N.
Boltzmann, L.
Bonner, T.
Borda, J.

Born, M.
Borst, L.
Bose, G.
Bose, J.
Bose, S.
Bothe, W.
Bouguer, P.
Bourguet, L.
Boussinesq, J.
Bowdoin, J.
Boyle, R.
Boys, C.
Boys, S.
Bradbury, N.
Bragg, R.
Bragg, W.H.
Bragg, W.L.
Brandes, H.
Brans, C.
Brattain, W.
Braun, F.
Bravais, A.
Breit, G.
Brekhovskikh, L.
Brewster, D.
Bridgman, P.
Briggs, L.
Brillovin, M.
Brinsmade, J.
Briot, C.
Brisson, M.
Brode, R.
Broglie, L.
Broglie, M.
Brooke, J.
Brown, J.
Brueckner, K.
Brun, E.
Bucherer, A.
Buckingham, E.
Buckley, O.
Budker, G.
Bumstead, H.
Buono, P.
Buot, J.
Burch, C.
Burger, H.
Burgess, G.
Burhop, E.
Buridan, J.
Butler, S.
Cabrera, B.
Cagniard de la Tour, C.
Cailletet, L.
Callendar, H.
Campbell, N.
Canton, J.
Carnot, L.
Carnot, N.
Carrington, H.
Carter, E.
Case, T.
Casimir, H.
Cassegrain, N.
Castaing, R.
Castel, J.L.
Cavallo, T.
Cavendish, H.

Chadwick, J.
Chamberlain, C.
Chamberlain, O.
Chaplygin, S.
Chapman, J.
Chapman, S.
Charles, J.
Chazy, J.
Cherenkov, P.
Chew, G.
Chladni, E.
Christiansen, C.
Christie, S.
Christofilos, N.
Chrystal, G.
Clarke, S.
Clausius, R.
Clay, J.
Cochran, W.
Cockcroft, J.
Cohen, B.
Cohen, J.
Colding, L.
Coleman, E.
Coleman, J.
Compton, A.
Compton, K.
Comstock, D.
Condon, E.
Cooper, F.
Cooper, L.
Coriolis, G.
Cormack, A.
Cornelius, D.
Corti, B.
Coster, D.
Cottrell, A.
Coulomb, C.
Courtivon, G.
Cowan, C.
Crandall, I.
Crane, H.
Crawford, A.
Crew, H.
Crewe, A.
Crittenden, E.
Cronin, J.
Crookes, W.
Cumming, J.
Curl, G.
Curtis, W.C.
Curtis, W.E.
Dadourian, H.
Dalence, J.
Dalgarno, A.
Dalitz, R.
Darwin, C.
Davidov, A.
Davidson, W.
Davis, B.
Davisson, C.
Day, A.
Debye, P.
DeGroot, J.
Dehmelt, H.
Dellinger, J.
Deluc, J.

Democritus
Dempster, A.
Dennison, D.
Deslandres, H.
Deutsch, M.
Devaux, H.
Dewar, J.
Dicke, R.
Dillon, J.
Diocles
Dirac, P.
Ditchburn, R.
Dobson, G.
Dodge, H.
Dolbear, A.
Dominis, M.
Doppelmayr, J.
Doppler, C.
Doremus, R.
Dorn, F.
Douglas, A.E.
Dove, H.
Dresselhaus, M.
Drude, P.
Dryden, H.
Duane, W.
DuBridge, L.
DuBuat, P.
DuChatelet, E.
Duckworth, H.
DuFay, C.
Duhamel, J.
Duhem, P.
Dumond, J.
Dunning, J.
Dunoyer de Segonzac, L.
Dupre, A.
Dushman, S.
Dutton, C.
Dyson, F.
Dzhelepov, B.
Eccles, W.
Eckarsley, T.
Eddington, A.
Edlen, B.
Edlund, M.
Ehrenfest, P.
Eichenwald, A.
Einstein, A.
Eklund, A.
Ellicott, J.
Ellingson, H.
Ellis, C.
Ellwood, W.
Elster, J.
Enskog, D.
Eotvos, R.
Epstein, P.
Erikson, H.
Erman, G.
Esaki, L.
Esclangon, E.
Eshelby, J.
Essen, L.
Estermann, I.
Euler, L.
Euler, U.

Evans, R.
Evershed, J.
Ewing, J.A.
Fabbroni, G.
Fabry, C.
Farenheit, D.
Fairhall, L.
Faraday, M.
Farrar, J.
Fawcett, S.
Feather, N.
Fechner, G.
Fedderson, B.
Feld, B.
Fermi, E.
Ferraris, G.
Feshbach, H.
Fessenden, R.
Feynman, R.
Finkelnburg, W.
Fisk, J.
Fitch, V.
Fitzgerald, G.
Fizeau, A.
Fierov, G.
Fletcher, J.C.
Fletcher, H.
Flowers, B.
Fock, V.
Floey, A.
Foote, P.
Foppl, A.
Forbes, G.
Foster, J.S.
Foster, J.S. Jr.
Foucault, J.
Fourier, J.
Fowler, R.
Fowler, W.
Franck, J.
Frank, I.
Frank, P.
Franklin, B.
Franklin, W.
Fraunhofer, J.
Frazer, R.
Freeman, J.
Frenicle de Bessy, B.
Frenkel, Y.
Friedmann, A.
Fries, J.
Frisch, O.
Frish, S.
Frisi, P.
Fubini, S.
Fulcher, G.
Furry, W.
Gale, H.
Galerkin, B.
Galelei, G.
Galvani, L.
Gamow, G.
Gardner, I.
Gardner, W.
Gaydon, A.
Gay-Lussak, J.
Geiger, H.

Geitel, F.
Gell-Mann, M.
Ghiorso, A.
Giaever, I.
Gibbs, J.
Gilbert, W.
Giles of Rome
Ginzburg, V.
Glaser, D.
Glashow, S.
Glazebrook, R.
Goddard, R.
Godlove, I.
Goeppert-Mayer, M.
Goldberger, M.
Goldhaber, M.
Goldstein, E.
Goldstein, H .
Golitsyn, B.
Gomer, R.
Goodspeed, A.
Goodwin, H.
Gordan, W.
Gorter, C.
Gottlieb, M.
Goudsmit, S.
Gourdine, M.
Gouy, L.
Graham, T.
Gramont, A.
Grashof, F.
Graves, A.
Gravesande, W.
Gray, J.
Green, G.
Green, J.
Gren, F.
Griffiths, E.
Grinberg, G.
Gross, E.
Grotthuss, T.
Grove, W.
Guericke, A.
Guillaume, C.
Gunn, R.
Guthe, K.
Guye, C.
Haas, A.
Haas, W.
Haber, H.
Hachette, J.
Hafstad, L.
Hagen, J.
Hahn, E.
Hall, E.
Hallwachs, W.
Henkel, W.
Hansen, W.
Hansteen, C.
Hardy, A.
Harnwell, G.
Harriot, T.
Harris, C.
Harrison, G.
Hartree, D.
Hartsocker, N.
Harvey, F.

Hasenohrl, F.
Hasler, M.
Hastings, C.
Hauksbee, F.
Haworth, L.
Hay, D.
Heaviside, O.
Heisenberg, W.
Heitler, W.
Helmholtz, H.
Hennessy, H .
Henrichsen, S.
Henry of Hesse
Herapath, J.
Herb, R.
Hering, D.
Hermann, C.
Herring, W.
Herschel, J.
Hersey, M.
Hertz, H.
Herzberg, G.
Herzberger, M.
Herzfeld, K.
Hess, V.
Hibbs, A.
Higinbotham, W.
Hillier, J.
Hirn, G.
Hirschfelder, J.
Hittorf, J.
Hofstadter, R.
Holborn, L.
Hole, W.
Honds, K.
Hopfield, J.
Hopkinson, B.
Hopkinson, J.
Horton F.
Houghten, F.
Houston, W.
Hubbard, J.
Huckel, E.
Hughes, D.
Hugoniot, P.
Hull, A.
Humphreys, W.
Hund, A.
Hunt, E.
Hunt, F.L.
Hunt, F.V.
Hurwitz, H.
Huygens, C.
Hyer, R.
Hylleraas, E.
Infeld, L.
Ingenhousz, J.
Ioffe, A.
Ishiwara, J.
Ives, H.
Ives, J.
Jacobi, M.H.
Jacquinot, P.
James, R.
Jansen, P.
Jastrow, R.
Jazari, B.

Jeans, J.
Jensen, J.H.
Joblot, L.
Johnson, A.
Johnson, J.
Johnson, K.
Johnson, W.R.
Johnston, J.
Joliot, E.
Joliot-Curie, I.
Jolly, P.
Jones, J.
Jordan, E.
Jordanus de Nemore
Josephson, B.
Joslin, B.
Joule, J.
Judd, D.
Julius, W.
Kahn, H.
Kaluza, T.
Kamerlingh-Onnes, H.
Kantrowitz, A.
Kapitza, P.
Kaplan, J.
Kastler, A.
Kaufmann, W.
Kayser, H.
Keesom, W.
Keill, J.
Keldysh, M.
Kelly, M.
Kemble, E.
Kent, R.
Kepler, J.
Kerr, J.
Kershner, R.
Kerst, D.
Keys, D.
Khariton, Y.
Kharkevich, A.
Khitrin, L.
Kikoin, I.
King, L.
King, R.
Kingsbury, E.
Kirchoff, G.
Kirilin, V.
Kittel, C.
Kleist, E.
Klingenstierna, S.
Klugel, G.
Knudsen, M.
Knudsen, V.
Kochin, N.
Koenig, J.
Koenig, K.
Kohlrausch, F.
Kohlrausch, R.
Kohn, W.
Kolosov, G.
Kompfner, R.
Konig, A.
Konobeevskii, S.
Konstantinov, B.
Kossel, W.
Kouts, H.
Kraft, J.

Kramers, H.
Kramp, C.
Krasik, S.
Krishnan, K.
Kronberger, H.
Kronig, A.
Kruzhilin, G.
Kuenen, J.
Kundt, A.
Kurchatov, I.
Kurlbaum, F.
Kurti, N.
Kusch, P.
Kuznetsov, V.
Ladd-Franklin, C.
Ladenburg, R.
Lagrange, J.
Lamb, W.
Lambert, J.
Lamont, J.
Landau, L.
Landsberg, G.
Lane, J.
Langevin, P.
Langmuir, I.
Laporte, O.
Lapp, R.
LaRive, A.
Larmor, J.
Latour, C.
Lattes, C.
Laue, M.
Lauritsen, C.
Lauritsen, T.
Lawrence, E.
Lax, B.
Lazarev, P.
Lebedev, A.
Lebedev, P.
Lederman, L.
Lee, T.
Leedy, H.
Lehmann, O.
Leighton, R.
LeMonnier, L.
Lenard, P.
Lennard-Jones, J.
Lenz, H.
Leontovich, M.
LeRoy, C.
LeRoy, J.
Lesage, G.
LeTenneur, J.
Levi-Civita, T.
Levich, V.
Lewis, E.
Lewis, L.
Lewis, W.
Lichtenberg, G.
Liddel, U.
Lifshits, I.
Lighthill, M.
Lindemann, F.
Lindsay, R.
Linnik, V.
Lippmann, F.
Lissajous, J.

Livingston, M.
Lloyd, H.
Lodge, O.
Lomonosov, M.
London, F.
London, H.
Loomis, A.
Loomis, E.
Loomis, F.
Lorenz, E.
Lorenz, L.
Loschmidt, J.
Lovering, J.
Luekiesh, M.
Lyman, T.
MacCullagh, J.
Mac Donald, D.
Mac Donald, H.
Mach, E.
Mack, J.
Maclaurin, R.
Magellan, J.
Magiotti, R.
Magni, V.
Magnus, H.
Maignan, E.
Maiman, T.
Majorana, E.
Maltby, M.
Mandelshtam, L.
Mansfield, J.
Marci of Kronland
Margeneau, H.
Margules, M.
Mariotte, E.
Marliana, G.
Marsden, E.
Marshak, R.
Martyn, D.
Mascart, E.
Masius, M.
Mason, M.
Mason, W.
Masson, A.
Mathieu, E.
Matteucci, C.
Matthias, B.
Matuyama, M.
Mauchly, J.
Maxwell, J.
Mayer, A.
Mayer, J.R.
Mayer, M.
Mazer, J.
McCulloh, R.
McIlwain, C.
McLennan, J.
McMillan, E.
Mees, C.
Meggers, W.
Meitner, L.
Melloni, M.
Melvill, T.
Mendelssohn, K.
Mendenhall, C.
Merritt, E.
Mersenne, M.

Merton, T.
Mescheryakov, M.
Meschersky, I.
Meusnier de la Place, J.
Michelini, F.
Michels, W.
Michelson, A.
Michie, P.
Mie, G.
Migdal, A.
Miller, D.
Millikan, C.
Millikan, R.
Millionshchikov, M.
Mills, B.
Mills, M.
Milner, S.
Mitchell, J.W.
Mitra, S.
Mohler, J.
Moll, G.
Mollier, R.
Molyneux, W.
Morita, A.
Morley, E.
Morse, P.
Morton, H.
Moseley, H.
Mossbauer, R.
Mossotti, O.
Mott, N.
Mottelson, B.
Moyer, B.
Mueller, E.
Muller, G.
Muncke, G.
Muskhelishvili, N.
Musschenbroek, P.
Mydorge, C.
Nagaoka, H.
Nairne, E.
Natanson, W.
Neel, W.
Ne'eman, Y.
Nelson, H.
Neumann, C.
Neumann, F.
Newell, H.
Newton, I.
Nichols, E.F.
Nichols, E.L.
Nicholson, J.
Nielsen, H.
Nier, A.
Nipher, F.
Nobili, L.
Noble, A.
Noel, E.
Nollet, J.
Northrup, E.
Norton, W.
Novikov, I.
Nusselt, E.
Oberth, H.
Obreimov, I.
O'Brien, B.
Occhialini, G.

Oersted, H.
Ohm, G.
O'Keefe, J.
Okhotsimskii, D.
Oliphant, M.
Olszewski, K.
O'Neill, G.
Oppenheimer, J.
Ornstein, L.
Overhauser, A.
Page, C.
Page, L.
Page, R.
Panofsky, W.
Papin, D.
Pardies, I.
Parent, A.
Parker, H.
Paschen, L.
Patai, I.
Patel, C.
Pauli, W.
Pegram, G.
Peierls, R.
Peirce, B.
Peirce, C.
Peltier, J.
Pemberton, H.
Penney, W.
Penrose, R.
Penzias, A.
Pepys, W.
Perot, J.
Perrin, F.H.
Perrin, J.B.
Peter Peregrinus
Petavel, J.
Petit, A.
Petrov, G.
Pezenas, E.
Pfund, A.
Philo of Byzantium
Piccard, A.
Pickering, G.
Pickering, W.
Pictet, M.
Pierce, G.
Pippard, A.
Planck, M.
Plante, G.
Plateau, J.
Plaude, K.
Playfair, J.
Plucker, J.
Poggendorf, J.
Poiseuille, J.
Poisson, S.
Poleni, G.
Poli, G.
Poliniere, P.
Pollard, W.
Pomeranchuk, I.
Pontekorvo, B.
Popov, A.S.
Pouillet, C.
Pound, R.
Powell, B.

Powell, C.
Powell, W.
Power, H.
Poynting, J.
Prandtl, L.
Predvoditelev, A.
Prevost, I.
Prevost, P.
Prigogine, I.
Pringsheim, E.
Privat de Molieres, J.
Prokhorov, A.
Pulfrich, C.
Pupin, M.
Purcell, E.
Quincke, G.
Rabi, I.
Rabotnov, Y.
Rainwater, L.
Raman, C.
Ramsauer, C.
Ramsden, J.
Ramsey, R.
Randers, G.
Rankine, A.
Rasmussen, J.
Ratcliffe, J.
Rayton, W.
Read, T.
Reaumur, R.
Regener, E.
Regge, T.
Regnault, H.
Reines, F.
Relf, E.
Rentschler, H.
Renwick, J.
Reynolds, O.
Riabouchinsky, D.
Ricci-Curbastro, G.
Richardson, L.
Richardson, O.
Richmann, G.
Richter, B.
Richtmyer, E.
Riecke, E.
Righi, A.
Ringleb, F.
Ritchie, W.
Ritter, J.
Ritz, W.
Roberts, L.
Robertson, H.
Roberval, G.
Robinson, G.
Robinson, H.
Robinson, T.
Robison, J.
Roeser, W.
Rogers, W.A.
Rontgen, W.
Rood, O.
Rood, P.
Rosa, E.
Rose, M.
Rosen, L.
Rosenberger, J.

Rosenbluth, M.
Rosenfeld, A.
Rosenthal, A.
Ross, W.
Rossi, B.
Rothrock, A.
Rowland, H.
Rozhdestvensky, D.
Rubens, H.
Rumbaugh, L.
Runge, C.
Russell, H.
Rutherford, E.
Rydberg, J.
Ryde, J.
Sabine, E.
Sabine, P.
Sabine, W.
Saccheri, G.
Sadovskii, M.
Sadron, C.
Sagnac, G.
St. John, C.
Sakharov, A.
Salam, A.
Satcher, G.
Saunders, F.
Sauveur, J.
Savart, F.
Schiffer, J.
Schonland, B.
Schott, G.
Schrieffer, J.
Schrodinger, E.
Schulz, G.
Schulz, W.
Schuster, A.
Schweigger, J.
Schwinger, J.
Scott, E.
Scott, R.B.
Seamans, R.
Searle, G.
Sedov, L.
Seebeck, T.
Segner, J.
Segre, E.
Seguin, M.
Seitz, F.
Sekera, Z.
Seneca, L.
Shalnikov, A.
Sharpe, J.
Shaw, E.
Shchelkin, K.
Shenstone, A.
Shirane, G.
Shirkov, D.
Shockley, W.
Shoenberg, D.
Shull, C.
Siedentopf, H.
Siegbahn, K.
Sigaud de Lafond, J.
Sigorgne, P.
Simon, F.
Singer, S.

Sitterly, B.
Skinner, H.
Skobeltsyn, D.
Slack, C.
Slater, J.
Slichter, C.
Smekal, A.
Smith, F.
Smith, H.
Smith, L.
Smith, R.
Smith, T.
Smoluchowski, M.
Smyth, H.
Snell, E.
Snow, C.
Sobolev, S.
Sohncke, L.
Sommerfeld, A.
Southall, J.
Southworth, G.
Spottiswoode, W.
Spring, W.
Squire, H.
Stark, J.
Starr, C.
Stearns, J.
Stefan, J.
Steinheil, K.
Stepling, J.
Stern, O.
Stever, H.
Stewart, B.
Stewart, G.
Stokes, G.
Stoletov, A.
Stoner, E.
Stoney, G.
Strato of Lampsacus
Stratton, S.
Strelkov, P.
Strong, W.
Strutt, J.
Strutt, R.
Stuhlinger, E.
Sturgeon, W.
Sturm, C.
Sucksmith, W.
Suits, C.
Sutherland, G.
Sutherland, W.
Sutton, O.
Swaim, V.
Swan, J.
Swann, W.
Swinden, J.
Synesius of Cyrene
Szilard, L.
Tainter, C.
Tait, P.
Tamm, I.
Tate, J.
Taylor, A.
Taylor, L.
Taylor, T.
Teller, E.
Thaler, W.

Thekaekara, M.
Thollon, L.
Thomaz, A.
Thompson, B.
Thompson, L.
Thompson, S.
Thomson, G.
Thomson, J.
Thomson, J.J.
Thomson, W.
Thorne, K.
Thouless, D.
Ting, S.
Tinkham, M.
Titius, J.
Tolansky, S.
Tolman, R.
Tomonaga, S.
Torricelli, E.
Tousey, R.
Townes, C.
Townsend, J.
Townsend, O.
Treadwell, D.
Treland, L.
Troughton, E.
Trouton, F.
Trowbridge, A.
Trowbridge, C.
Trowbridge, J.
Tschirnhaus, E.
Tsiolkovsky, K.
Tuckerman, L.
Tudorovskii, A.
Turner, L.
Tuve, M.
Tyndall, A.
Tyndall, J.
Uhlenbeck, G.
Underwood, N.
Van Allen, J.
Van de Graaff, R.
Van der Waals, J.
Van Hove, L.
Van Vleck, J.
Varian, R.
Vavilov, S.
Vekshinskii, S.
Veksler, V.
Velikanov, M.
Venturi, G.
Verdet, M.
Vereschagin, L.
Vernov, S.
Vestine, E.
Villard, P.
Villari, E.
Violle, J.
Voigt, W.
Volkmann, P.
Volta, A.
Vonnegut, B.
Vonsovskii, S.
Vul, B.
Waidner, C.
Wallace, R.
Walton, E.
Warburg, E.

Warburton, F.
Waterman, A.
Waterston, J.
Watson, W.
Watson-Watt, R.
Weatherwax, J.
Webb, H.
Weber, W.
Webster, A.
Webster, D.
Wehnelt, A.
Weinberg, A.
Weisbach, J.
Weiss, P.
Weiss, R.
Weisskopf, V.
Wells, W.
Wente, E.
Wheatstone, C.
Wheeler, J.
Whiddington, R.
Whipple, G.
White, W.
Whiting, S.
Wick, F.
Wiechert, E.
Wiedemann, G.
Wien, W.
Wiener, L.
Wiener, O.
Wigner, E.
Wilcke, J.
Wilhelmy, L.
Wilkins, J.
Wilkins, T.
Wilkinson, D.
Williams, E.
Williams, J.H.
Wills, A.
Wilson, C.T.
Wilson, H.A.
Wilson, K.
Wilson, V.
Wilson, W.
Winthrop, J.
Wold, P.
Wolf, E.
Wolfe, H.
Woltman, R.
Wood, R.
Wooten, B.
Worthing, A.
Wright, A.W.
Wroblewski, Z.
Wu, C.
Wwedensky, B.
Yagoda, H.
Yang, C.
York, H.
Young, T.
Yukawa, H.
Zacharias, J.
Zavoiskii, E.
Zeeman, P.
Zeldovich, Y.
Zeleny, J.
Zernike, F.

Zernov, D.
Zeuner, G.
Zhukovsky, N.
Zhurkov, S.
Zinn, W.
Zwortkin, V.

PHYSIOLOGY

Adrian, E.
Anrep, G.
Asratyan, E.
Barbour, H.
Barcroft, J.
Bard, P.
Barthez, P.
Baudrimont, A.
Bayliss, L.
Bayliss, W.
Beaumont, W.
Bellini, L.
Berger, J.G.
Bernard, C.
Bernstein, J.
Bert, P.
Berthold, A.
Best, C.H.
Bezold, A.
Bidder, F.H.
Bischoff, T.L.
Blake, J.
Blundell, J.
Bohn, J.
Botazzi, F.
Bowditch, H.
Bradford, J.
Bremer, F.
Brever, J.
Brodie, B.C.
Bronk, D.
Brown, G.
Brown-Sequard, C.
Brucke, E.
Brunton, T.
Bunge, G.
Burdach, K.
Burdon-Sanderson, J.
Burton, A.
Carlson, A.
Cathcart, E.
Chabry, L.
Chauveau, J.
Combe, A.
Croone, W.
Czermak, J.
Dale, H.
Dalton, J.
Daly, I.
Davis, H.
Davy, J.
Dodart, D.
Dollinger, I.
Doners, F.
Douglas, C.
Dragstedt, L.

DuBois Reymond, E.
Dunglison, R.
Dutrochet, R.
Duval, M.
Eccles, J.
Edwards, W.
Einthoven, W.
Embden, G.
Engelmann, T.
Erlanger, J.
Evans, C.
Evans, H.
Fenn, W.
Fessard, A.
Fick, A.
Flemyng, M.
Flourens, M.
Folley, S.
Forbes, A.
Foster, M.
Franklin, K.
Fredericq, L.
Frey, M.
Fulton, J.
Gaddum, J.
Gamgee, A.
Gaskell, W.
Gasser, H.
Goltz, F.
Graham, C.
Graham-Brown, T.
Grainger, R.
Granit, R.
Grijns, G.
Gulliver, G.
Haldane, J.S.
Haller, A.
Halliburton, W.
Hansen, E.
Hardy, W.
Hartridge, H.
Harvey, E.
Hawthorne, E.
Hecht, S.
Heidenhain, R.
Helmholtz, H.
Henderson, Y.
Hensen, V.
Hering, K.
Hess, W.
Hill, A.V.
Hill, L.
Hitchcock, E.
Hollander, F.
Holmgren, F.
Houssay, B.
Howell, W.
Hubel, D.
Huggett, A.
Hughes, J.
Hunt, R.
Hutchinson, J.
Huxley, A.
Hyde, I.
Ingle, D.
Ivy, A.
Katz, B.

Keill, J.
Kety, S.
Keys, A.
Kielmeyer, C.
Kindi, A.
Kleitman, N.
Konorski, J.
Kreps, E.
Krogh, S.
Kronecker, H.
Kuffler, S.
Kuhne, W.
Landis, E.
Langley, J.
Lapicque, L.
Laurentiev, B.
Leake, C.
Leathes, J.
Legallois, J.
Lilly, J.
Lim, R.
Lining, J.
Loeb, J.
Loewi, O.
Lucas, K.
Luciani, L.
Ludwig, K.
MacLeod, J.
Magendie, F.
Marey, E.
Martin, H.
Matteucci, C.
Mayer, J.
Mayow, J.
Meissner, G.
Mellanby, J.
Meltzer, S.
Menuret de Chambaud, J.
Miescher, J.
Miller, F.
Mitchell, J.K.
Morat, J.
Moruzzi, G.
Mosso, A.
Muller, J.P.
Oliver, G.
Orbeli, L.
Ott, I.
Overton, C.
Pagano, G.
Pappenheimer, J.
Parsons, J.
Patt, H.
Pavlov, I.
Pfluger, E.
Piccolomini, A.
Pool, J.
Pratt, F.
Praxagoras of Cos
Prevost, J.
Preyer, T.
Priestley, J.G.
Prout, W.
Purkinje, J.
Ramey, E.
Ramon y Cajal, S.
Ranvier, L.

Reyna, F.
Reynolds, O.
Richet, C.
Rodahl, K.
Rolando, L.
Romanes, G.
Rosenblueth, A.
Roughton, F.
Rubner, M.
Rudolphi, K.
Rushton, W.
Samoylov, A.
Schiff, M.
Schmidt, N.
Schwann, T.
Sechenov, I.
Seguin, A.
Senac, J.
Senebier, J.
Sertoli, E.
Shannon, J.
Sharpey, W.
Sharpey-Schafer, E.
Shaw, T.
Shtern, L.
Sinkford, J.
Smith, H.W.
Smyth, D.
Stannius, H.
Starling, E.
Stevens, S.
Stewart, A.
Swedenborg, E.
Sutherland, E.
Thunberg, T.
Tiedemann, F.
Trevan, J.
Trotter, W.
Ukhtomsky, A.
Unzer, J.
Van Euler, U.
Van Slyke, D.
Verworm, M.
Visscher, M.
Voit, C.
Vvedensky, N.
Wagner, R.
Walker, A.
Weber, E.
Weber, H.
Weisel, T.
Wiggers, C.
Wilbrand, J.
Yeo, G.
Young, J.

POLYMATHY

Albertus Magnus
Kircher, A.
Lull, R.
Planudes, M.
Shen Kua
Varro, M.

PSYCHIATRY

Bender, L.
Berger, H.
Densen-Gerber, J.
Hitzig, E.
Kubler-Ross, E.
Larson, J.
Leuret, F.
Masserman, J.
Meerloo, J.
Niederland, W.
Rorschach, H.
Spurzheim, J.
Szasz, T.
Thurnam, J.
Wagner von Jauregg, J.

PSYCHOLOGY

Adler, A.
Angell, J.
Bain, A.
Bartlett, F.
Beach, F.
Bekhterev, V.
Bernheim, H.
Binet, A.
Boring, E.
Bronner, A.
Buhler, C.
Burt, C.
Carmichael, L.
Cattell, J.
Condillac, E.
Dodge, R.
Dunbar, H.
Ellis, H.
Erikson, E.
Estes, W.
Eysenck, H.
Fechner, G.
Frenkel-Brunswik, E.
Freud, A.
Freud, S.
Fromm-Reichmann, F.
Galambos, R.
Gantt, W.
Gesell, A.
Goodenough, F.
Guilford, J.
Hall, G.
Harlow, H.
Hebb, D.
Herbart, J.
Hering, K.
Hilgard, E.
Hollingworth, L.
Horney, K.
Hull, C.
Hunter, W.S.
Isaaca, S.
James, W.
Janov, A.

Johnson, V.
Jung, C.
Klein, M.
Kohler, W.
LaMettrie, J.
Lange, C.
Lashley, K.
McConnell, J.
Milgram, S.
Miller, G.A.
Miller, N.
Morgan, C.
Muller, G.
Murray, E.
Nissen, H.
Pfaffmann, C.
Piaget, J.
Pillsbury, W.
Pratt, J.
Rand, M.
Reik, T.
Richter, C.P.
Riggs, L.
Royce, J.
Rubin, T.
Rush, J.
Salk, L.
Schermann, R.
Seashore, C.
Skinner, B.F.
Spence, K.
Spencer, H.
Stekel, W.
Stratton, G.
Terman, L.
Thorndike, E.
Thurstone, L.
Tolman, E.
Troland, L.
Velikovsky, I.
Vives, J.
Washburn, M.
Watson, J.B.
Woodworth, R.
Wundt, W.
Yerkes, R.

ROCKETRY

Blagonravov, A.
Bossart, K.
Congreve, W.
Crocco, G.
Dixon, T.
Dornberger, W.
Draper, C.
Dunn, L.
Goddard, R.
Hale, W.
Hoffman, S.
Korolev, S.
Ley, W.
Malina, F.
Montgery, J.
Moore, W.

Oberth, H.
Parks, R.
Raborn, W.
Riedel, K.
Ritchey, H.
Sanger, E.
Schriever, B.
Shteinfeld, A.
Shultz, J.
Tikhonravov, M.
Toftoy, H.
Truax, R.
Von Braun, W.
Winkler, J.

SCIENCE EDUCATION

Cassiodorus Senator, F.
Cavendish, W.
Crocker, L.
Fontenelle, B.
Gerard of Cremona
Hartlib, S.
Isidore of Seville
Khuwarizmi, A.
Krause, E.
Magalotti, L.
Martianus Capella
Pluche, N.
Qutayba, A.
Valturio, R.

SCIENCE HISTORY

Bigourdan, C.
Boncompagni, B.
Buchner, F.
Gallois, J.
Koyre, A.
Sarton, G.
Sprat, T.
Tannery, P.
Voltaire, F.
Whewell, W.
Wolf, C.
Wolf, J.R.
Zubov, V.

SCIENCE ILLUSTRATION

Bosse, A.
Fuertes, L.
Lansdowne, J.
Wolfe, J.

SCIENCE WRITING

Asimov, I.
Barker, T.

Blakeslee, H.
Brayley, E.
Bronowski, J.
Burton, R.
Celsus, A.
Censorinus
Clerk, A.
Clerselier, C.
Clow, A.
Della Torre, G.
Dicaearchus
Diderot, D.
Edmonds, R.
Ewbank, T.
Forster, B.
Fox, C.
Fox, R.
Gamow, G.
Gough, J.
Hall, W.
Haynes, W.
Henshaw, T.
Hogben, L.
Hooker, W.
Hunt, R.
Jaffe, B.
Khaldun, A.
Kieran, J.
Killeffer, D.
Kirkpatrick, S.
Lametherie, J.
Lardner, D.
Michaud, H.
Morgan, G.
Oldenberg, H.
Osiander, A.
Phelps, A.
Potamian, M.
Sallo, D.
Steele, J.
Taylor, J.
Tomlinson, C.
Towson, J.
Velikovsky, I.
Vincent of Beauvais
Wahl, W.
Youmans, E.
Youmans, W.
Zim, H.

SEISMOLOGY

Benioff, V.
Golitsyn, B.
Gutenberg, B.
Heck, N.
Imamura, A.
Knott, C.
Koto, B.
Lehman, I.
Lynch, J.
Mallet, R.
Milne, J.
Mohorovicic, A.
Murphy, L.

Oldham, R.
Omori, F.
Orlov, A.
Richter, C.
Rockwood, C.
Sezawa, K.
Stoneley, R.
Tondorf, F.
Turner, H.

SOIL SCIENCE

Chepil, W.
Cosby, S.
Davis, W.
Dokuchaev, V.
Hester, J.
Hockensmith, R.
Kelley, W.
Kovda, V.
Tanfilev, G.
Thornton, H.
Vysotsky, G.

SPACE LAW

Haley, A.

SPACE SCIENCE

(See Astronautics)

SPECTROSCOPY

Brode, W.
Catalan, M.
Coblentz, W.
Meghnad, S.

SPELEOLOGY

Gurnee, J.

SURVEYING

Balbus
Churchman, J.
DeBrahm, W.
DeGraaf-Hunter, J.
Ellicott, A.
Fry, J.
Liesganig, J.
McArthur, W.
Mechain, P.
Mitchell, H.
Norwood, R.

Patterson, C.
Porro, I.
Wheeler, G.
Zach, F.

TEXTILES

Cockerill, W.
Hargreaves, J.
Hazard, R.
Jacquard, J.

TOXICOLOGY

Stevenson, T.

TRANSLATION OF SCIENCE
LITERATURE

Fryer, J.
Haak, T.
Hall, W.
John of Palermo
Michael Scot
Robert of Chester
Stephen of Antioch
Thevenot, M.

TREE SURGERY

Davey, J.

VETERINARY MEDICINE

Benchley, B.
Chauveau, J.
DuToit, P.
Fox, M.
Jensen, C.
Kelser, R.
Khrushchov, G.
Minett, F.
Ruffo, G.
Ruini, C.

VIROLOGY

Amos, H.
Andrewes, C.
Baltimore, D.
Cox, H.
Craigie, J.
Dulbecco, R.
Gajdusek, D.
Isaacs, A.

Koprowski, H.
Lensen, S.
Rous, F.
Sabin, A.
Smith, K.M.
Temin, H.
Theiler, M.
Weller, T.

VOLCANOLOGY

Fenner, C.
Jaggar, T.
Piyp, B.
Reck, H.

ZOOLOGY

Abercrombie, M.
Agassiz, A.
Agassiz, G.
Alder, J.
Allee, W.
Allen, G.
Alston, E.
Apathy, S.
Atkinson, G.
Audouin, J.
Ayres, W.
Bachman, J.
Baird, S.
Balfour, F.
Banta, A.
Barbour, T.
Barker, F.
Barton, B.
Bataillon, J.
Bates, M.
Beebe, C.W.
Belon, P.
Beneden, P.
Bennett, E.
Berkeley, M.
Bigelow, H.
Bilharz, T.
Binney, A.
Birge, E.A.
Blackwell, J.
Blainville, H.
Blanford, W.
Bodenheimer, F.
Bodine, J.
Bourne, G.
Brambell, F.
Brandt, J.
Bridge, T.
Brooks, W.
Broussonet, P.
Brown, H.
Bruner, H.
Buechner, H.
Bumpus, H.
Butler, A.

Butschli, O.
Bykhovskii, B.
Caldwell, P.
Calkins, G.
Calman, W.
Cannon, H.
Carlson, J.
Carpenter, F.
Carpenter, P.
Carter, T.
Carus, J.
Child, C.
Claff, C.
Clapp, C.
Clark, H.
Cole, F.
Cooke, C.
Coolidge, H.
Cooper, J.
Cowles, R.
Crampton, H.
Cuenot, L.
Cunningham, B.
Cuvier, F.
Czerski, J.
Davenport, C.
Dawson, A.
Dekay, J.
Deryugin, K.
Dimmock, G.
Ditmars, R.
Dixon, J.
Dobell, C.
Dobson, G.
Dogel, V.
Dohrn, F.
Dorst, J.
Draparnaud, J.
Duboscq, O.
Dujardin, F.
Dumeril, A.
Dunn, E.
Duplaix, N.
Eddy, S.
Edwards, E.
Elliot, D.
Emerson, A.
Errington, P.
Eschsholtz, J.
Field, H.
Finley, H.
Fleming, J.
Flower, W.
Forbes, S.
Forbes, W.
Forel, F.
Fox, H.
Fraipont, J.
Frandsen, P.
Fraser, F.
Friedmann, H.
Frisch, K.
Fritsch, G.
Garman, S.
Garnot, P.
Garrod, A.
Gatenby, J.

Geoffroy St. Hilaire, E.
Gilbert, C.
Girard, C.
Goethe, J.
Goette, A.
Goldschmidt, R.
Goodey, T.
Goodsir, J.
Gray, G.
Gray, J.
Griffin, L.
Grinnel, J.
Grzimek, B.
Gunther, R.
Guyer, M.
Haeckel, E.
Haldeman, S.
Hall, B.
Hall, M.
Hamilton, W.
Hancock, A.
Hanson, E.
Harlan, R.
Harris, J.
Harting, P.
Hass, H.
Hatschek, B.
Haughwout, F.
Heath, H.
Hegner, R.
Henking, H.
Hertwig, W.
Hickey, J.
Hill, J.P.
Hincks, T.
Hindle, E.
Hinton, M.
Hisaw, F.
Hoar, W.
Holbrook, J.
Holder, J.
Hollister, N.
Holtfreter, J.
Hornaday, W.
Harstadius, S.
Howes, T.
Hubrecht, A.
Hutchinson, G.
Huxley, T.
Hyatt, A.
Hyde, R.
Hyman, L.
Jayne, H.
Jenks, J.
Jennings, H.
Jones, T.
Juday, C.
Just, E.
Keeton, W.
Kellicott, D.
Kellogg, A.
Kellogg, V.
Kemp, S.
Kennicott, R.
Kerr, J.
Kinsey, A.
Kirby, H.

Kirtland, J.
Klein, J.
Kofoid, C.
Koltzoff, N.
Krogh, S.
Kuenen, D.
Kuyn, A.
Lacaze-Duthiers, F.
Lacepede, B.
Lagler, K.
Lamarck, J.
Lang, A.
Lankester, E.
Latreille, P.
Lea, I.
Lefevre, G.
Leger, U.
Leidy, J.
Leister, C.
Lereboullet, D.
Lesueur, C.
Leuckert, K.
Lichtenstein, M.
Lillie, F.
Lindauer, M.
Lister, M.
Locy, W.
Lyman, T.
MacCallum, G.
MacLeary, W.
Manton, S.
Marion, A.
Mark, E.
Markgraf, G.
Mattox, N.
Maupas, F.
Mayor, A.
McClung, C.
McIntosh, W.
Metcalf, M.
Metz, C.
Miles, M.
Miller, A.
Milne-Edwards, H.
Mitchell, P.
Mobius, K.
Montgomery, T.
Moore, C.
Morgan, A.
Morse, E.
Nehring, A.
Nelson, T.
Newell, M.
Nordenskiold, N.
Okkelberg, P.
Oliver, J.A.
Ord, G.
Osburn, R.
Osgood, W.
Ostwald, C.
Owen, R.
Painter, T.
Pantin, C.
Park, T.
Parker, G.
Patterson, J.
Pauly, A.

Pavlovsky, E.
Pearse, A.
Perkins, R.C.
Peron, F.
Perrault, C.
Perrier, E.
Peysonnel, J.
Pilsbry, H.
Plate, L.
Poulton, E.
Powers, E.
Prosser, C.
Provencal, J.
Pumphrey, R.
Quatrefages de Breau, J.
Quoy, J.
Rathburn, R.
Regan, C.
Ripley, S.
Ritter, W.
Roeder, K.
Rolleston, G.
Romanoff, A.
Romer, A.
Rosa, D.
Rothschild, M.
Russell, F.
Savage, T.
Schaudinn, F.
Schiff, M.
Schmalhausen, I.
Schmitt, W.

Schneider, F.
Schreibers, K.
Scott, J.
Scott, T.
Sedgwick, A.
Semon, R.
Serres de Mesples, M.
Sewell, R.
Shaw, T.
Shipley, A.
Shufeldt, R.
Siebold, C.
Siedlecki, M.
Smallwood, W.
Smith, F.
Smith, S.
Souleyet, L.
Spemann, H.
Spix, J.
Starks, E.
Stearns, R.
Stebbing, T.
Steenstrup, J.
Stephenson, T.
Stiles, K.
Struthers, P.
Swainson, W.
Swanson, G.
Tate, G.
Thomson, A.
Thomson, C.

Tinbergen, N.
Traill, T.
Trautman, M.
Trembley, A.
True, F.
Twitty, V.
Valenciennes, A.
Van Cleave, H.
Van Deusen, H.
Vejdovsky, F.
Verrill, A.
Vigors, N.
Vishniac, R.
Vogt, C.
Walker, E.
Wallich, G.
Walton, I.
Watson, D.
Weber, M.
Wegeforth, H.
Weismann, A.
White, C.
Wilder, H.
Wilson, J.
Wood, W.
Worcester, D.
Wynne-Edwards, V.
Yarrell, W.
Young, B.
Zeleny, C.
Zuckerman, S.